THE
VEGETABLE GARDEN.

ILLUSTRATIONS, DESCRIPTIONS, AND CULTURE

OF

THE GARDEN VEGETABLES

OF COLD AND TEMPERATE CLIMATES.

By MM. VILMORIN-ANDRIEUX,

OF PARIS.

ENGLISH EDITION,

PUBLISHED UNDER THE DIRECTION OF

W. ROBINSON, EDITOR OF "THE GARDEN."

Ten Speed Press

Ten Speed Press
P O Box 7123
Berkeley, California 94707

Reprinted through arrangement with the
Jeavons-Leler Press.

ISBN 0-89815-041-8

Copies of the hardbound edition are available from the
Jeavons-Leler Press
855 Clara Drive
Palo Alto, California 94303

10 9 8 7 6 5 4 3 2 1

PREFACE TO ENGLISH EDITION.

OUR best friends do not always get our best attention, and the very important subject of which this work treats has long been left without adequate study, so far as books show. Innumerable treatises on the cultivation of vegetables have been written, but "The Vegetable Garden" is the first work in any language in which are classified, described, and illustrated what are the most important of all plants to the human race. It is the production of men who in their work for many years past have had good opportunities of thoroughly studying the subject. No excuse is needed for "making English" such a book—for the benefit, not only of our own horticulture (increasing in interest and importance every year), but also for that of America, and of Australia and our other colonies, in which, happily, the plants herein described may be grown. It will be an aid in enabling us to realize the wonderful variety of light, pleasant, and excellent food now within our reach, and in making many a good vegetable more widely known. That it may widen our views in this respect will be acknowledged by every one who, with the usual limited ideas as to French Beans, for example, takes note of the many excellent kinds herein described.

The relation of the plants this book deals with to the movement towards diet reform and the greater use of the vegetable world for human food calls for a word at the present time. A generation ago this question was the theme of a very few writers; now the movement has taken shape in actual practice, and there are restaurants in London to-day where over a thousand dinners daily are served, wholly composed of cereals, vegetables, and fruits. Leaving out of view any exclusive tendency of this kind, all agree that the greater use of the best of these in our food would be a decided improvement. So far as I have yet seen, the restaurants devoted to this class of food show a limited knowledge of cookery and of the garden stores from which they might draw. It is a pity it is so, for the neglect or poor cookery of such things, both in private houses and hotels, is a serious loss.

The true reason why the more delicate and wholesome foods are neglected is because the cooks of Europe have served an apprenticeship of a thousand years on the carcases of ox, pig, sheep, deer, goose, hare, and other animals. We are meat-eaters because our fathers had little else to eat. The plains and green hills of the cold north were dotted with wild grazing animals, as an English park is now dotted with deer, or a Western prairie with antelope and bison. Men killed and cooked ; there was little else worth eating. A few generations only have passed since our now commonest vegetables came from the Continent. We are adding to their number every day, and by the aid of cultivation we are winning back our way to a simpler, healthier food, and one more like that which man enjoyed in the tropical or sub-tropical regions whence he originally came. But the education of the cook bars the way to progress. Even when he gives us French Beans, they swim in butter. The French cooks, supposed to be the best, systematically make the natural flavours of the many delicate vegetables of their markets secondary to that of butter—now, alas ! often mere grease or hardened oil. In our hotels the best fish and meat in the world are often procurable ; the vegetable kingdom is usually represented by a mass of ill-smelling Cabbage and a sodden Potato. We ought to grow more kinds of vegetables than we do, but we need still more a radical change in our modes of cookery, in the direction of cooking and serving for their own sakes (and in most cases without animal substance) the more delicate green vegetables and fruits that are and may be grown. Old or inferior vegetables require the coarser devices of the cook, and must be saturated with grease and spices to make them edible. The true cookery is to deal only with the best and tenderest of each kind, and jealously preserve its flavour ; this art is, in any general sense, as yet unpractised. In ten years more every district in London will have restaurants wholly supplied without the aid of the butcher. At the same time, those who share no such views as to food are equally desirous to improve and enlarge our garden supplies ; so it is clear that there will be a greatly increased demand for all such produce. This is a hopeful sign in the present day, when all seems so dark for our agriculture. Garden vegetables deteriorate enormously, even ours on their way to our own markets, so that clearly we cannot have rivals here from the Antipodes or across the Atlantic in them, unless, indeed, we grossly neglect our opportunities. And, apart from the important factor of distance, the climate of Britain has few equals for the growth of green vegetables.

In London the chaotic struggle and obstruction in Covent Garden tend much to deprive people of the good qualities of the garden produce grown so well in the suburban fields. One simple way to improvement would be the adoption of district markets for local supplies. To bring the vegetables grown at Chiswick to Covent Garden and cart them back to Hammersmith is a needless waste of force. For these markets it is by no means necessary that permanent structures should be built ; a wide road, or square, or river embankment would suffice. As wholesale dealings of this kind are usually done in the morning hours, it is easy to make good use of open spaces for this purpose. Some of the useful little district markets of Paris are held in public squares and on the boulevards, and an hour after they are over, tents, stands, refuse, and all other signs of the market are so completely removed that

one passing by does not suspect that the spot has served an
important use before the general public is abroad. Regular all-
day markets, where the householder could select, are also wanted.
Some of our English towns and Paris have admirable examples
of these. But while such must be waited for till public taste or
enterprise creates them, the wholesale district markets could be
established without cost or delay.

One point deserves the serious consideration of every owner
of a garden, and that is the " muddle" method of planting the
kitchen garden with fruit trees and bushes, and so cutting up
the surface with walks, edgings, etc., that the very aim of the
garden is missed. It is quite a mistake to grow fruit trees
over the kitchen-garden surface. We cannot grow vegetables
well under them, and in attempting to do so we destroy
the roots of the trees. This induces canker and other troubles,
and is the main cause of our poor garden-fruit culture. One-
fourth of the space entirely given to vegetables, divested of
walks, large hedges, old frame grounds, old walls, rubbish, and
other impediments, would give a far better supply. Such a
spot well cultivated would be a pleasure to see. It is not
merely the ugliness and the loss of the mixed garden which
we have to deplore, but the troubles of the unfortunate gardener
who has to look after such a garden in addition to other work.
How is he to succeed with the many things so hopelessly
mixed up? Here a decaying Plum, there on one side a ragged
patch of Black Currants, backed by a rank Privet hedge; and so
on through the sorry catalogue. In fact, if the whole cost of the
garden were doubled, and all expended on some of the kitchen
gardens of this sort that we see, it would still be impossible to
get a good result from this method. Put the fruit trees in one
part—the higher ground, if any—and the remaining part devote
to vegetables, cultivating the ground in the best way, and
having it always a fertile, green vegetable garden. The vegetables, too, would be more wholesome from continual good light
and air; for shade from ragged and profitless trees and bushes

and hedges is one of the evils of this hopeless kind of garden. The broken crops, too (for the most part sickly patches), are not such as one can be proud of. Separation of the two things, complete and final, is the true remedy. There should not be the root of a fruit tree in the way of the vegetable grower.

All who have to do with gardeners and seedsmen should fight against the deterioration of some of our best vegetables through their mania for size. Although the flavour of vegetables may be more subtle than that of fruit, it is none the less their essential quality. A change in size, by adding to the watery tissue and fibrous framework of the plant, may entirely destroy the quality we enjoy in it. A certain degree of openness to sun and air may govern the flavour ; this may be made impossible by doubling or trebling the size of the article itself, which has been done in the case of the Brussels Sprout. This is often no longer the true little rosette of green, but a coarse Cabbage sprout. This is a case of deliberate distortion of a favourite type. Less absurd, perhaps, but equally bad, is the raising of new varieties lacking in good flavour, and abolishing old kinds, from supposed deficiency in size. It generally means that the new ones are coarse ; it sometimes means that they are useless. There has been, for example, for the last few years a French Bean observable in our markets, very large and symmetrical, but without any of the good flavour of the smaller kinds. However, its huge mawkish pod has become popular with the market gardener. Here is a delicate vegetable, the value of which depends entirely upon its flavour, and whether we get quantity in the shape of six beans or one bean matters little to the consumer, if the object of growing the vegetable is lost sight of. So again in Peas. Where is the good in a new Pea if it has not a good flavour ? Mere size, or filling of a pod well, is a low quality from any point but that of the market grower, who wants his "stuff" to bulk up well. Sometimes a flavour may be made too rich ; many good cooks in London prefer the little long Turnip of the Paris market, which has a truer Turnip flavour than some of the

sweet kinds. We may lose much of what makes a garden worth
having by not efficiently controlling the thoughtless and harmful
mania for mere size, unless accompanied by other more desirable
qualities. The striving among gardeners to increase the size of
vegetables leads often to deterioration, and it is so common that
those who have influence with them should protest. Some of
the raisers of novelties have done a good deal to injure the
Tomato by sending out huge and coarse kinds, which, instead
of ripening in the natural way, burst into abscesses and "craters,"
and have a wretched flavour.

An important subject for all owners of gardens, big or little,
is the waste and loss through not gathering things in their best
state. The usual way of gathering when wanted should, I
think, be changed. In almost every garden, in summer and
autumn, one sees Kidney Beans and Peas in quantity in a
hard and uneatable state—useless themselves, while robbing
the plant of the power to give a succession of eatable
pods. All such crops should be *gathered at the right time,
whether wanted or not.* Those who want vegetables in the best
condition only would find it profitable to gather and give away
rather than pursue the usual way of growing only to waste. It is
a common practice with many market gardeners to allow things
to get old and hard before cutting, so as to ensure their filling
the baskets easily, instead of gathering them whilst tender,
These men must be the best judges of their own affairs, but
this practice is the cause of market vegetables being often useless
as compared with private garden produce. It is a common error
that those who grow their own fruits and vegetables necessarily
pay more for them than they would in the market. The
pleasure of having them quite fresh and of a proper age would,
however, be worth paying for if need be. The great advantage
which all who are happy enough to live in their gardens enjoy
might be much increased by growing only things delicate and
good in flavour, and gathering them at the right moment,
which is seldom done in the case of market produce.

Loss to all and much confusion arises from the practice now common among seed-merchants of naming almost every good vegetable after themselves. It has of late become a nuisance, and England has almost a monopoly of the evil practice, which is not carried out in France. Honourable houses may do it for self-protection with us, but it is nevertheless a great evil to the public, and scarcely less so to the trade. To be able to secure pure stocks of long-tried standard vegetables is not easy for the public while the seedsman affixes a new name and the name of his house to almost everything he sells. I cannot give any just idea of the waste and confusion resulting from this practice. A common cause of failure in the vegetable garden is too many kinds—too many experimental plantings, instead of the garden being devoted to the things we know and like. The liability to fall into this trap is increased tenfold by the chaotic state of the nomenclature of vegetables, and by every one who publishes a catalogue having his own set of names. Seedsmen and growers, at home, in our colonies, and in foreign countries, are compelled again and again to buy old things under new names, and to test them before embarking in their sale. If the practice were confined only to the new kinds raised or purchased by the houses who use these names, it would be less objectionable ; but by adopting it generally, even their own children cannot be recognized in the incongruous list. A common way of giving these new names is to secure a pure, well-selected stock of seed of some old, good kind, and re-christen it, say, some one's "Champion" or "Favourite." Changing the name of a good old kind in this way is an evil which the seed trade itself should associate to stop. Houses that practise it may no doubt get a large number of orders from both the public and the trade, but I think the loss is as certain to the trade in the end, as it certainly is to the gardening public. Of late years we have seen in London, Orchid, Pear, and other conferences, which, while leading to interesting meetings, have had really little more serious reason to be than the vanity or amuse-

ment of their promoters.   The disgraceful state of the nomenclature of our most valuable garden crops might well occupy the
attention of a body composed of representative seedsmen and
growers.   It would not be a very difficult task to seek out and
give their true names to all the older and finer types of our
vegetables, and to find some way to prevent confusion in the
future without interfering with any one's right to name a real
novelty in a fitting way.

The translation is wholly the work of Mr. W. Miller, author
of the *Dictionary of English Names of Plants:* it could not
be better done.   Messrs. Vilmorin contributed a very large
number of additions and corrections, which have all been
embodied in the book.   Mr. A. F. Barron, superintendent of the
Royal Horticultural Gardens at Chiswick, read the proofs
throughout; M. Henri Vilmorin did the same.   Of all men in
France and England these have probably the best knowledge
of cultivated vegetables.   I read the manuscript, and thought
it well to omit any but the most accepted foreign names and
the English names most generally used.   Also, as the culture
and constant supply of kinds is more important to the public
than any questions of nomenclature, it was thought well to give
the culture most generally practised in our gardens, both private
and for market.   This is printed in double columns throughout
the book.

As to the question of giving the weight of seed—a point
of minor interest to the public generally—it was thought best
to retain the French measures, it not being found possible to
express them in familiar English terms without the use of
fractions.   It may be stated here that the "litre" is equal to
$1\frac{4}{5}$ pint, English measure, and the "gramme" to $15\frac{2}{5}$ grains
Troy.

W. R.

November, 1885.

AUTHORS' PREFACE.

(Abstract.)

———•◦•———

WE have had some difficulty in fixing the limits within which we should confine ourselves in this work. It is not always easy to define exactly what a " vegetable " is, and to decide upon the plants to which the term is applicable and those to which it is not. In this respect, however, we thought it better to be a little over-indulgent rather than too strict, and, accordingly, we have admitted into the present work not only the plants which are generally grown for use in the green state, but also those which are merely employed for flavouring others, and even some which at the present day have, for the most part, disappeared from the kitchen garden, but which we find mentioned as table vegetables in old works on horticulture. We have, however, restricted our list to the plants of temperate and cold climates, omitting the vegetables which are exclusively tropical, with which we are not sufficiently familiar, and which, moreover, would interest only a limited class of readers.

We made it a point to determine the botanical identity of every plant mentioned in this volume by giving the scientific name of the species to which it belongs. Before commencing the description of any form of cultivated vegetable, we are careful to state, with strict exactness, the place in botanical classification occupied by the wild or primitive type from which that form is considered to have sprung. Accordingly, we commence every article devoted to one or more cultivated varieties, by giving a botanical name to all the subjects included in the article—a name which indicates the genus and species to which all these forms, more or less modified by cultivation, should be referred. For instance, all the varieties of garden Peas, numerous as they are, are referred to *Pisum sativum*, L. ; those of the Beet-roots to *Beta vulgaris*, L. ; and similarly in the case of other plants.

While on this subject, we may be permitted to remark that the constancy of a species is very remarkable and well deserves our admiration, if we merely take into view the period of time over which our investigations can extend with some degree of certainty. We see, in fact, species brought into cultivation before history began, exposed to all the modifying influences which attend seed-sowing incessantly repeated, removal from one country to another, the most important changes in the nature of the countries and climates through which they pass, and yet these species preserve their existence quite distinct.

Although continually producing new varieties, they never pass the boundaries which separate them from the species which come next to them.

Among the Gourds, for example, which are annual plants that have been in cultivation from times so remote that assuredly many thousand generations of them have succeeded one another under the conditions which are best calculated to bring about important modifications of character, we find, if we give ever so little attention to the subject, the three species from which all the varieties of cultivated edible Gourds have originated; and neither the influences of cultivation and climate, nor the crossings which may occur from time to time, have brought forth any permanent type or even a variety which does not speedily revert to one of the three primitive species. In each of these species the number of varieties is almost indefinite, but the limit of these varieties appears to be fixed. Does any plant exhibit more numerous or more diversified varieties of form than the cultivated Cabbage? Is any difference more marked than that which exists between a Round-headed and a Turnip-rooted Cabbage, between a Cauliflower and Brussels Sprouts, between a Kohl-Rabi and a Tree Cabbage? And yet these vast dissimilarities in certain parts of the plants have not affected the character of the essential parts of the plants, the organs of fructification, so as to conceal or even to obscure the evident specific identity of all these forms. While young, these Cabbages might be taken for plants of different species, but when in flower and in seed, they all show themselves to be forms of *Brassica oleracea,* L.

It seems to us that the long-continued cultivation of a very considerable number of kitchen-garden plants, while it demonstrates the exceedingly great variability of vegetable forms, confirms the belief in the permanence of those species that are contemporary with Man, and leads us to consider each species as a kind of system having a distinct centre (although this may not always be represented by a typical form), around which is a field of variation almost unlimited in extent, and yet having certain, though still undetermined, boundaries.

The idea of the species, in short, rests upon the fact that all the individuals of which it is composed are, to an indefinite extent, capable of being fertilized by one another, and only by one another. Now, as long as it has not been proved that a variety artificially produced by man has ceased to be capable of being fertilized when crossed with other individuals of the same species, while it continues fertile to an indefinite extent when impregnated by individuals of its own special form,—so long it cannot be said that a new species has been brought into existence, and, up to the present, no one, so far as we are aware, has ever asserted that such a case has occurred. Far from it, indeed, as this capability of being fertilized by its own members, and only by them, constitutes, so to say, the very essence of the species. It is this which alike insures its permanence, its pliability, and its power of adapting itself to the various conditions under which it may be compelled to exist.

Reverting, however, to the plan of our work,—after indicating the place which each of the plants described occupies in the botanical classification of species, we give, so far as we can, the different names by which the plant in question is known, both in the principal European countries and in America. We have taken care not to give any names that are not really in common use and well known, and have avoided mere translations. In publishing synonyms, we have been very cautious, taking especial care not to admit any that are not thoroughly well established, and, in most cases, verifying them by a comparative cultivation of those plants which we considered identical. Having accurately identified each plant under consideration by giving its botanical and various common names, we mention its native country, adding a brief history of the plant, when we possess any reliable data on this subject. After mentioning the native country and giving the history of the plant, we describe its mode of growth, whether annual, biennial, or perennial. Here it should be remarked that many plants are grown in the kitchen garden as annuals which are biennial or perennial as regards their fructification. For kitchen-garden purposes, it is enough that these plants attain in their first year a size sufficiently large for table use, and this is especially the case with most plants which are grown for their roots, such as Carrots, Beet-roots, Turnips, Radishes, etc.

The descriptions, properly so named, of the different kinds of kitchen-garden plants have been to us a subject of long-continued labour and much care. Some persons, perhaps, may consider them to be somewhat vague and elastic in their expression, and such a remark may apply to many of them; but, on the other hand, if they had been more hard and fast, and had been drawn up in more peremptory terms, they would not be so true. Account must be taken of the variable appearance of cultivated plants under the different conditions in which they are grown. A season more or less favourable, or sowing earlier or later the same season, is sufficient to produce a material alteration in the appearance of a plant, and a precise description of it as it then presents itself would obviously exclude other forms of it which should be included. Nothing is easier than to describe a single individual in the most exact terms, just as it is the easiest thing in the world to draw precise conclusions from a single experiment; but when a description is to be applicable to a great number of individuals of the same variety and the same race, the task is more difficult, in the same degree as it is when one endeavours to form a conclusion at the close of a series of experiments which give different and sometimes contrary results. Nearly all our descriptions, which, in the first instance, were drawn up with the growing plants before our eyes, have been, from time to time and season after season, read over again with new crops of the same plants before us. It is the variations which we have noted in the size and appearance of the same plants when grown under different conditions that has induced us to pen our descriptions with a broadness which enables them to include the different aspects which the same kind of plant assumes according to the different circumstances under which it is grown.

Whenever we have been able to seize upon any prominent and really permanent feature in the characteristics of a variety, whether that feature may be found in some important peculiarity or in a fixed uniformity in the size or shape of variable organs, we have been careful to bring it conspicuously into view, as the surest means of recognizing the variety in question. Most frequently, in fact, the experienced cultivator of kitchen-garden plants recognizes different varieties from one another by the general appearance of each, the peculiar aspect which the plant presents, and which more frequently depends on certain proportions in the position and relative size of the various organs than on any strictly structural characteristics. Such distinctive marks, although they never escape a practised eye, frequently baffle description and definition. Observation and practice alone can teach any one how to see and recognize them with certainty; therefore, we are fortunate, whenever a variety is distinguished by a constant perceptible feature, to be able to express its distinctness by a single word or a short phrase. Characteristic features of this kind are found in the presence of spines on the leaves of the Prickly Solid Cardoon (*Cardon de Tours*), in the reversed curve of the pods of the Sabre Pea, in the greenish colour of the flowers of the Dwarf Blue Imperial Pea (*Pois Nain Vert Impérial*), and similarly in many other cases.

A part of each description on which we have bestowed much attention is that which refers to the seed. In addition to noting the character of its external appearance, we have been careful to state, as precisely as we could, its actual size and relative weight; and, lastly, we mention the length of time during which the germinating power of the seed of each species continues active. It will be easily understood that this could only be expressed in figures representing an average. The duration of the germinating power really depends very much on whether the circumstances under which the seed has been harvested and kept have been more or less favourable. The figures given in this work represent the average taken from an exceedingly great number of trials most carefully carried out. The number of years tabulated is that during which the seeds under trial continued to germinate in a perfectly satisfactory manner. For our present purpose, we have considered seeds deficient in germinating power when they yield only half the percentage of plants which they did in the first year of trial which was made with seeds of the same year's growth. For example, if, in the first year, a certain quantity of seeds germinated to the extent of 90 per cent., we considered the same seeds to be deficient in germinating power as soon as they began to yield only less than 45 per cent. of plants. In a Table, which will be found at the end of the volume, we state, side by side with this average duration of the germinating power, the extreme periods of its duration which we have proved by sowing some of the same seeds season after season until at last they entirely ceased to germinate. In this way, we have reached some very high figures. Any seeds, of which the germinating power continues active for four or five years on an average, do not entirely lose it after the lapse of ten years or more. It is proper to add that our trials were all made with well-saved seeds. Nothing has a greater tendency to destroy the germinating power of seeds than the influence of dampness and heat. This is what makes carriage through tropical countries so often fatal to their good quality. Up to the present, no better method of keeping seeds has been discovered than that of putting them in linen bags and storing them in a dry, cool, well-ventilated place.

As often as we could, we have supplemented our descriptions with figures of the plants described. The size of the page did not generally allow of these figures being given in large dimensions, but we have endeavoured to exhibit at least their comparative sizes by figuring the different varieties of the same vegetable on a scale of uniform reduction, so far as this could be done. The reduction has been, necessarily, greater in the case of very large kinds of vegetables, such as Beet-roots, Cabbages, and Pumpkins, than that which applies to the small kinds; however, we hope that, thanks to the talent of the draughtsman, M. E. Godard, even the most reduced figures will still give a sufficiently correct idea of the plants which they represent. The Strawberries, the Peas in pod, and the Potatoes are almost the only subjects which it was possible to figure in their natural size. Under the figures we also give the scale of reduction in fractions of the actual diameter of the plant. For example, when a subject is described as reduced to $\frac{1}{6}$, that means that the plant, in its natural size, is six times taller and six times broader than the figure which the reader has before him. We have been careful not to select any subjects for our figures except plants that were thoroughly well marked and of average size. It may be that, in this respect, and also in our estimation of distinctive features, we have sometimes made mistakes. If so, we shall gladly acknowledge our errors and rectify them as soon as possible. Our only ambition, in preparing this work for the press, is to do so in good faith and without prejudice.

Our cultural directions are to be regarded as nothing more than a help to memory, and we do not in any way put them forward as intended to supply the place of the full cultural instructions which are given in standard horticultural works or in various excellent special treatises which the importance of many kinds of vegetable cultivation have given rise to in our own and other countries.

Finally, we conclude the article devoted to each plant with a few remarks on the uses to which it is applied, and on the parts of the plant which are so used. In many cases, such remarks may be looked upon as idle words, and yet it would sometimes have been useful to have had them when new plants were cultivated by us for the first time. For instance, the Giant Edible Burdock of Japan (*Lappa edulis*) was for a long time served up on our tables only as a wretchedly poor Spinach, because people would cook the leaves, whereas, in its native country, it is only cultivated for its tender fleshy roots.

There is one mistake against which professional cultivators, and also amateurs, especially those who have not had much experience, should be on their guard. This is the delusion of imagining that they have succeeded in raising a new variety when a form that seems to possess some merit makes its appearance amongst a number of seedlings. The plants raised from seed obtained by crossing should at first be regarded merely as units, which may have a certain value in the case of trees or plants that are long-lived and are propagated by division, but which, after all, are only units. Taken all together, they can only claim to be considered a variety when they have continued to reproduce themselves, for several generations, with a certain amount of fixity of character; and, almost always, the really difficult and meritorious part of the work is the establishment of the variety—a tedious and delicate operation, by which, when successful, the new variety is endowed with the constancy and uniformity of character without which it is not worth offering to the public.

Many varieties obtained in this way remain confined to their own localities, because they are not more widely known; some cannot reproduce themselves faithfully when sown under conditions different from those of their native place, from which fresh seed must be obtained, from time to time, if it is desired to keep the variety very pure; hence those local reputations which are one of the mainsprings of horticultural commerce. Generally most of the cultivated varieties, although they continue sufficiently distinct and true when they are grown with care, nevertheless are all the better for being raised from an importation of new seed from the place in which experience has shown that it is grown best and truest to name.

Paris, 4 Quai de la Mégisserie.

THE VEGETABLE GARDEN.

ALEXANDERS.

Smyrnium Olusatrum, L.   Natural Family, *Umbelliferæ*.
French, Maceron.

Native of Europe.—Biennial.—This plant was formerly used as a table vegetable, either in its natural state or blanched.   The leaf-stalks are fleshy, and have an aromatic flavour somewhat approaching that of Celery.   At present the cultivation of the plant is almost entirely neglected, as Celery has taken its place in nearly every garden.   Mr. Jones, now of the Royal Gardens, Frogmore, used to cultivate it when at Petworth some years ago.   He writes: "It was cultivated for its leaf-stalk, which, when blanched, was used for soups in spring, and it was also used as a pot-herb; in salads it has very pleasant flavour.   The seed, when sown, remains a long time in the ground, therefore it is better to sow towards the latter end of August.   If sown in spring, it will often not vegetate.   As soon as the plants are large enough they should be set out in rows, and in the beginning of the month of March they should be earthed up to blanch, which will make them very tender; in three weeks' time they will be fit for use; when they begin to shoot their stems for blooming, they are good for nothing."

ANGELICA.

Angelica Archangelica, L.; *Archangelica officinalis*, Hoffm. *Umbelliferæ*.

French, Angélique officinale, A. de Bohême, Archangélique. *German*, Angelica, Engel-wurtz. *Flemish*, Engelkruid. *Dutch*, Engelwortel. *Italian*, *Spanish*, and *Portuguese*, Angelica.

A native of the Alps.—Perennial.—This plant has a very thick, hollow, herbaceous stem, upwards of 4 ft. high; leaves very large, from 1 to 3 ft. long, reddish-violet at the base, long-stalked and termi-nating in three principal toothed divisions, which are subdivided into three similar smaller divisions.   Flowers small, numerous, pale yellow, in umbels which unite to form a roundish head.   Seed yellowish, oblong, flat on one side, convex on the other, with three prominent ribs, and membranous edges.   A gramme (15⅔ grains) contains 170 seeds, and the litre (1⅘ pint) weighs 150 grammes.   The germinating

B

power of the seed continues for a year, or at most two. Culture.—
Angelica requires a good, rich, slightly humid, and deep soil. The

seed is sown in spring or
summer in nursery beds,
and the plants are planted
out permanently in autumn,
and will commence to yield
in the following year (provided they are well grown),
when the leaves may be cut.
In the third year, at the
farthest, the plants run to
seed; in this year, both
stems and leaves are cut,
and the plantation is de-
stroyed. Uses.—The stems
and leaf-stalks are eaten
preserved with sugar. The
leaves are also used as a
vegetable in some parts of
Europe. The root, which
is spindle-shaped, is em-
ployed in medicine; it is
sometimes called "The Root
of the Holy Ghost." The
seeds enter into the com-
position of various liqueurs.

Angelica.

ANISE.

Pimpinella Anisum, L.   *Umbelliferæ.*

French, Anis. *German*, Anis, Grüner Anis. *Flemish* and *Dutch*, Anijs. *Italian*, Aniso,
Anacio. *Spanish*, Anis, Matalahuga or Matalahuva. *Portuguese*, Anis.

Native of Asia Minor, Greece, and Egypt.—Annual.—A plant of
from 14 to 16 inches high, with root-leaves, somewhat like those of

Celery, and extremely finely
divided stem-leaves, the divisions being almost thread-like,
like those of Fennel leaves.
The seed, which is small,
oblong, and grayish, is universally known for its delicate
flavour and perfume. A gramme
contains 200 seeds, and the
litre weighs 300 grammes. Its
germinating power lasts for
three years. Anise is sown,
where it is to remain, in April.
It prefers warm and well-
drained soil. It grows very
rapidly, and requires no care.

Anise.

The seed ripens in August. The plant is seldom seen in England, but we have grown it easily in the London district. Uses.—The seeds are frequently used as a condiment, or in the manufacture of liqueurs and comfits. In Italy, they are sometimes put into bread. It is of very ancient use in England, and was known to the ancients, being indeed among the oldest of medicines and spices. It is one of the spices which the Grocers' Company of London had the weighing and over-sight of from 1453. According to the wardrobe accounts of Edward IV., it appears the royal linen was perfumed by means of "lytill bagges of fustian stuffed with Ireos and *anneys.*"

ARACACHA.

Conium moschatum, H.B.　*Aracacha esculenta,* D.C.　*Umbelliferæ.*

Spanish American, Apio.

Native of South America.—Perennial.—Up to the present, the cultivation of this plant (which is highly esteemed and extensively grown in South America, especially in Columbia) has not succeeded very well in Europe. In its native country it produces bundled roots, something like those of Chervil, but much larger, as they attain the thickness of a man's arm. There are several varieties, distinguished in size, earliness, and the colour of the skin. The Aracacha may be propagated from seed, but the varieties do not come true by this method. Most commonly, after the roots are gathered, some of those which were last pulled up, are divided and replanted, and these, in about twelve months, yield a new crop. The roots are used as a vegetable in South America, somewhat in the same way as Potatoes.

ARTICHOKE (GLOBE).

Cynara Scolymus, L.　*Compositæ.*

French, Artichaut.　*German,* Artischoke.　*Flemish* and *Dutch,* Artisjok.　*Danish,* Artiskok.
Italian, Articiocca, Carciofo.　*Spanish,* Alcachofa.　*Portuguese,* Alcachofra.

A native of Barbary and South Europe.—Perennial (but cultivated plants will not yield profitably after two or three years).—Stem from 3 to 4 ft. high, straight, channelled; leaves large, about 3 ft. long, whitish-green above, and cottony underneath, decurrent on the stem, pinnatifid, with narrow lobes; terminal flowers very large, composed of an assemblage of blue florets, covered with membranous overlapping scales, which, in cultivated plants, are fleshy at the base. Seed oblong, slightly flattened, somewhat angular, gray, streaked or marbled with deep brown, numbering 25 to the gramme, with an average weight of 610 grammes to the litre. Its germinating power continues for six years. Culture.—The Artichoke may be propagated from seed, or by dividing the stools, or from suckers. The last method is that which is most usually employed, as it is the only one by which the different varieties can be reproduced true to their proper character. Old stools of Artichokes produce underground, around the neck, a certain number of suckers or shoots which are intended to replace the stems which flowered the year before. These shoots are generally too numerous on each stem to allow all to grow equally well, and it is the practice, in

spring, to uncover, down to below the part from which the shoots issue,
the old stools, which during the winter had been protected with a
covering of soil or leaves. The shoots are then all detached from the
stool, except two or three of the finest, which are allowed to remain to
contribute to the crop. The operation of detaching the shoots is one
which requires care and a practised hand, for it is important that along
with each shoot, a portion of the mother-plant (which is called the
"heel") should also be removed, without too severely wounding the
old stool, as this might cause it to rot away. The shoots, as soon as
they are detached, should be trimmed and dressed with a pruning-
knife, so as to remove from the "heel" any parts that are bruised or
torn, and to shorten the leaves a little. The shoots may then be
planted permanently; the best soil for a plantation of Artichokes
is that which has been well dug, and is rich, deep, almost humid, and
at the same time well-drained. Low-lying level ground and valley-
bottoms in which the soil is black and almost turfy are especially
suitable for the cultivation of the Artichoke. The shoots are planted
in rows, at a distance from each other of from about 2½ ft. to nearly
4 ft. (according to the richness of the soil and the variety grown),
and with the same distance between the rows. They are placed firmly
in the ground, but not too deep, and then well watered, after which it
is only necessary to keep the ground clean by frequent use of the hoe,
and to water plentifully when watering is necessary. If the plants are
sufficiently manured and watered, almost all of them will yield in the
autumn of the same year. Sometimes, instead of planting out the
shoots permanently immediately after they are detached, they are first
planted in nursery-beds, from which they are afterwards removed and
placed out permanently at the end of June or July. The success of
the plantation is, in this way, more certain, and the yield in autumn is,
at least, quite as abundant as that produced by following the other
mode of planting. When Artichokes are raised from seed, it should
be sown in February or March, in a spent hot-bed, and the plants should
be planted out permanently in May. Plants raised in this way may
yield in the autumn of the first year. A permanent sowing may also
be made at the end of April or in May, but the plants thus obtained
will not yield until the next year. At the commencement of winter,
Artichoke plants should be protected against frost, which often destroys
them in our climate. In order to do so, all the stems which have
flowered should be removed from the stools by cutting them off as
close to the root as possible. The longest leaves also should be
shortened, after which soil should be heaped on the stools to the height
of 8 or 10 inches above the neck of the root, care being taken not to
let any of it get into the heart of the plant. Should the frost be very
severe, it is advisable to give the stools an additional covering of dry
leaves or straw; but it is important that this covering should be
removed whenever the weather is mild, in order to prevent the danger
of its rotting the plants. At the end of March, or in the beginning of
April, when frost is no longer to be feared, the soil is stirred and
manured if necessary, the protecting heaps are removed from about the
stools, and the work of detaching the suckers or shoots is proceeded
with as described above. It is advisable to partially renew plantations

of Artichokes every year, and also not to allow any plantation to last more than four years.

Globe Artichokes are grown in every British garden, but rarely so well as they deserve to be, and the cook seldom uses them as much as she ought.

The culture of the Artichoke varies somewhat according to situation and climate. In the north and midlands, it is necessary to cover it in winter with litter or leaves, to protect it from frost; in the south it is sufficient to earth it up, but even this precaution is not taken everywhere. The plants are increased by seed and offsets. Varieties of it, however, do not always come true from seed, and they require, besides, more time than offsets before they produce heads; offsets, therefore, are most generally adopted. With good culture heads may be had for six months in succession. Commencing with established plants that have been protected through the winter, these will afford the first supply in May and June; and, for the next two months, good heads may be had from a planting of strong suckers made in March; for the end of summer and autumn, from a successional planting made in May. Another very good plan is to cut back, close to the earth's surface, a few old plants early in spring, and occasionally afterwards. These will produce a thicket of shoots, which should be early thinned by pulling and cutting the weakest, and allowing only a portion of the strongest suckers to remain. These will produce, in succession, nice young heads. If the heads be allowed to attain their full growth, or nearly so, they are not so fine in flavour, and have lost most of their tenderness, so that only a part of the base of each scale and the base of the head are fit to eat. The Artichoke will grow luxuriantly in rich moist land in summer, but it will not stand our winter in wet quarters. It will grow on any kind of soil, if well manured, trenched, and pulverized; but no soil suits it better than a good, open, sandy, rich loam, trenched and well manured. The plant is in its perfection at the second and third year after planting.

Years ago, it was the custom in most gardens at the approach of winter to cover the plants entirely, or nearly, with litter, and then to bank them up with earth, in which condition they remained through the winter. The Artichoke is, however, much hardier than was at that time supposed; and plants not protected seldom suffer injury. All the protection they require in the severest weather is a few dry leaves or a handful of Bracken placed over the crowns of each plant, to be removed when the weather changes. Plants are often allowed to remain too long in one spot, and where this occurs, the heads all come into use at one time. The best way to remedy this is to make a small plantation every year, which will come in after the old roots head.

Artichokes may be often seen starved under trees, where neither light nor sun can reach them. A clear, open piece of good soil, well manured and deeply trenched up into rough ridges, to get well pulverized and sweetened by atmospheric influences, free from trees and hedges, is the proper place to plant them—planting the first batch in March, and for succession another in May, afterwards keeping them thoroughly clean and maintaining an open free surface by often hoeing the ground about them. By such means a dozen stools will produce as many fine rich heads as double the quantity will do by the old-fashioned crowding, neglectful system. Make choice in early spring of good strong suckers, take off the stools carefully with a sharp, strong paddle-trowel or Asparagus knife, with some root or heel of the old stool to them, to hold them in the ground; plant them singly 2 ft. apart, in rows at least 4 ft.

apart, or in groups of three in triangles, at 4 ft. apart, at least, in the row. Protect them as soon as planted, against the sun and cutting winds, with Seakale pots which are out of use, or with evergreen boughs, or some other convenient protecting material. Those thus early planted will produce fine free crisp heads the same summer and autumn. If in cutting heads the *stems also* be cut close to the ground, new suckers will soon appear, and if duly thinned will produce a late crop; thus, in various ways, by a little trouble and attention a regular supply of good Artichokes may be had from May to October, which will be much more satisfactory than having a glut at midsummer and none afterwards.

Copious supplies of manure water may be advantageously given to Artichokes during dry weather, especially in the case of old stools that have been in the same soil for a length of time. Previous to watering, the soil between the rows should be slightly pricked over with a fork, to allow of the water soaking in more readily. Whenever watering is attempted, let it be done thoroughly, and if a good mulching of half-rotten manure can be afterwards applied between the rows, it will keep the roots in a moist state for a long time, and the effects of the watering will soon be seen. Where grown on poor or dry soils, the effect of covering the soil with light manure, lawn mowings, or any such material that can be spared is excellent. In rich, moist soils it is not wanted, except in very dry seasons.

USES.—The base of the scales of the flower, and also the receptacle or bottom of the Artichoke, are eaten either cooked or raw. The stems and leaves may also be used, when blanched, like those of the Cardoon, to which they are in no way inferior in quality. The culture of this good vegetable deserves more attention with us; it should be more used as a vegetable, and the good French varieties should be grown more extensively. It is a vegetable of the highest value and delicacy when gathered fresh and properly cooked, as it may be in various ways. The London market often has heaps of Artichokes shrivelled and " heated " on their long journey from the south of France, while our own valley soils are excellent for the plant.

VARIETIES.

Large Green Paris Artichoke (*Artichaut Gros Vert de Laon*).—A vigorous, comparatively hardy plant, of medium height; leaves silvery-gray, the ribs reddish, especially at the base, and without spines; stems stiff, erect, usually with two or three branchings. Heads large, broader than long, particularly remarkable for the breadth of the receptacle or bottom of the Artichoke. Scales very fleshy at the base, at first very closely pressed together, then broken, as it were, and in the two upper rows slightly bent backwards. They are of a pale-green colour throughout, except at the base, where they are slightly tinged with violet; they have few or no spines. The height of the stems does not exceed from 2½ to 3 ft., and a plant two years old will have three or four stems. This variety is the one which is most extensively cultivated in the neighbourhood of Paris. It is not a very early variety, but it is the best for yielding heads every year of its cultivation. No other variety has such a broad, thick, and fleshy receptacle or bottom ; it also reproduces itself fairly well from seed.

Green Provence Artichoke (*Artichaut Vert de Provence*).—A plant of medium height, with rather deep green leaves; heads green, somewhat more elongated than those of the preceding variety, but not so thick; scales of a uniform green, long, rather narrow and spiny, moderately fleshy at the base. This variety, which is extensively grown in the south of France, is particularly esteemed for eating raw with pepper sauce. The seeds of this variety, when sown, always produce a large proportion of spiny plants.

Purple Provence Artichoke (*Artichaut Violet de Provence*).—A rather low-growing plant, from 2 to about 2½ ft. high; leaves gray, much divided; heads swollen, short, and blunt, of a rather deep violet colour when young, and becoming green as they mature; scales emarginate, without spines, over-lapping each other rather closely. A very productive variety, but yielding abundantly only in spring, and somewhat impatient of cold.

Flat-headed Brittany Artichoke (*Artichaut Camus de Bretagne*).—A tall and vigorous-growing plant, 3¼ to 4¼ ft. high; leaves luxuriant; heads large, broad, and short, nearly globular in shape, flattened on the top; scales green, brownish or slightly tinged with violet on the edges, short and broad, rather fleshy at the base. This variety is very extensively cultivated in Anjou and Brittany, from

Large Green Paris Artichoke (⅓ natural size).

which provinces large quantities are sent in May to the Central Market in Paris.

As the number of varieties of the Artichoke is very great, we shall limit ourselves to mentioning only those which we consider the most worthy of notice next to the four which we have just described as being most generally cultivated.

Copper-coloured A. of Brittany (*Artichaut Cuivré de Bretagne*).—A rather low-growing plant; heads round, large, violet-coloured at first, but acquiring a reddish-coppery hue as they advance in growth; scales pointed.

Gray A. (*Artichaut Gris*).—A variety with elongated, rather thin and loose heads, widening out at the top. It is specially cultivated in the neighbourhood of Perpignan, is a very early kind, and flowers almost continuously. It is sent in large quantities to the Central Market in Paris during the winter and in the beginning of spring.

Black English A. (*Artichaut Noir d'Angleterre*).—A very distinct kind, with numerous heads of medium size, nearly round and quite flat-topped, of a handsome dark-violet colour.

Roscoff A. (*Artichaut de Roscoff*).—A very tall plant; heads egg-shaped, of a rather pale-green colour; scales spiny.

Oblong St. Laud A. (*Artichaut de Saint-Laud oblong*).—Heads large, elongated; scales loosely overlapping each other at the base, and much more closely set at the top, scarcely emarginate, with a small spine at the point.

Sweet A. of Gênes (*Artichaut Sucré de Gênes*).—A rather tender plant; heads pale green, elongated, spiny. The flesh of the receptacle is yellow, sweet, and very delicate in flavour.

Violet Quarantain A. of Camargue (*Artichaut Violet Quarantain de Camargue*).—Plant of medium height; heads rather small; scales round, erect, of a violet-tinged green colour. An early variety.

Violet St. Laud A. (*Artichaut Violet de Saint-Laud*).—Heads of medium size; scales green on the exposed parts, but violet on the parts covered by other scales, and also on the tips.

Florence A. (*Artichaut Violet de Toscane*).—Heads very numerous, elongated, pointed, of an intense violet colour. This variety is very much grown in the neighbourhood of Florence. The heads, gathered when young and tender, are generally boiled and eaten entire.

Artichoke, Jerusalem.—See **Jerusalem Artichoke.**

ASPARAGUS.

Asparagus officinalis, L.   *Liliaceæ.*

French, Asperge.   *German*, Spargel.   *Flemish* and *Dutch*, Aspersie.   *Danish*, Asparges.
Italian, Sparagio.   *Spanish*, Esparrago.   *Portuguese*, Espargo.

Native of Europe.—Perennial.—A plant with numerous simple swollen roots, disposed in the form of a claw, from which spring several stems over 4 ft. in length, straight, branching, very smooth, slightly glaucous, with very minute cylindrical fascicled leaves. Flowers pendent, small, greenish-yellow, succeeded by spherical berries about the size of a pea, which in autumn assume a very vivid vermilion colour. Seeds black, triangular, pretty large, numbering about 50 to the gramme, weighing 800 grammes to the litre, and preserving their germinating power for five years at least.

CULTURE.—Asparagus, which is one of our earliest spring vegetables, is also one of the most widely appreciated and extensively cultivated. In many districts, and notably in the neighbourhood of Paris, the culti-vation of Asparagus for market is a branch of industry of the highest importance; and although there are, undoubtedly, some soils and localities in which its cultivation is attended with special success, there is hardly any place in which a plantation of this vegetable may not be made, if only some pains are taken in establishing it and keeping it in order. A light and well-drained soil is the best for this purpose, but a plantation may be successfully made in any soil which is not either absolutely wet or impermeably stiff; stagnant moisture being, above all other things, fatal to this plant. In order to establish a plantation, the cultivator may either raise his own plants or purchase them ready for use. In the first case, the seed should be sown in March or April, in good, rich, mellow soil (in drills preferably), and lightly covered with soil, leaf-mould, or compost (a covering from $\frac{1}{2}$ to $\frac{3}{4}$ inch deep will be quite sufficient). After the seed is well up and the plants have begun to gain some strength, they should be thinned out, if necessary, so as to leave a space of about 2 inches from plant to plant in the drills. It is very important for the ulterior favourable development of the plants, and for the satisfactory appearance of the crop, that they should never suffer from the want of nourishment caused either by an insufficiency of manure or by the plants being placed too closely together. During the rest of the summer and autumn, water should be given copiously whenever there appears to be need of it, and the ground must be kept very clean by the use of the hoe, which should be carefully handled, so as not to injure the roots of the plants. Plants treated in this way will be ready to be planted out permanently the following spring; they will strike root sooner, and give better results than plants of two years' growth, while the crop which they yield will come in quite as soon.

Those who do not wish to take the trouble of raising plants themselves in this way, can easily procure them from nurserymen. Young Asparagus shoots may be kept for several days, and even weeks, out of the ground, without any detriment either to their striking root or to the appearance of the crop which they will yield. The raising of these plants for sale has become an important industry.

It has been already stated that, in order to establish a plantation of Asparagus, a light and well-drained soil should, if possible, be selected ; but if the cultivator has no other soil except one that is very stiff and damp, he should, by a thorough drainage, render it wholesome to the depth of at least 12 or 16 inches, and direct all his efforts to the improvement of the surface. The experience of the Asparagus growers at Argenteuil and other localities near Paris, who twenty years ago brought the culture of this plant to a degree of perfection unknown before, seems to prove that the best results are obtained by liberally manuring the upper portion only of the soil in which the plants are growing, as the roots have naturally no tendency to descend deeper, if they find sufficient nourishment near the surface. It is obvious that, in establishing a plantation of Asparagus, account must be taken of the nature of the soil in which it is to be made, and which, consequently, must be dug more or less deeply ; but it may be said generally that the chief point on which success mainly depends, is not to put the stools out of reach of the influence of heat, while, at the same time, placing them in a medium in which they will find an abundance of the nourishment which they require. The stools, then, should be planted at no great depth, and no great quantity of soil should be heaped over them, except at the time when the young shoots are growing, when it is absolutely necessary to do so, in order to obtain these of sufficient length. As to the disposition of the young plants, there is no fixed rule. They may be placed either in single rows, or in beds containing two or three rows each; but it is advisable, in all cases, to have a distance of at least 2 or 2½ ft. from plant to plant in all directions. This will be found advantageous from a double point of view, as insuring a crop of greater abundance and better quality.

Planting in beds being the most usual way, we shall briefly describe how it is done, first observing that the methods of establishing and cultivating the plants are almost exactly the same as those pursued with plants grown in single rows. In March or April, or even later, the ground for the plantation is carefully laid out, having been previously well dug and plentifully manured before winter. The surface of the beds is then slightly hollowed out to the depth of about 4 inches, the soil being transferred to the alleys. Well-rotted farm-yard manure, or some other active fertilizer, is then spread over the surface of the bed. (In the vicinity of Paris, night-soil or street-sweepings are much used for this purpose.) The positions for the stools are then marked out, in two or three rows according to the width of the beds, at the distances mentioned above. At each of these positions is deposited a small heap of well-manured soil or leaf-mould, about 2 inches high, on the top of which the young stool is placed, care being taken to spread out the roots all around and to press them gently into the soil. When all the stools are in position, they are covered with leaf-mould or soil mixed with rotted manure, and a sufficient quantity of soil is spread over all to restore the bed almost to its former level. In this way, the crowns of the stools will not be buried deeper than about 2 inches, and the ends of the roots not deeper than 4 inches. A good deal of soil which was replaced by the manure will remain in the alleys and between the rows, and this will be found useful afterwards for earthing-up the plants.

During the first year, the plantation requires no attention beyond the frequent use of the hoe and occasional waterings. At the commencement of winter, the stems are cut down to 8 or 10 inches from the ground, the portions so left serving to indicate the position of each stool. (It is a good plan also, at the time of planting, to stick a small rod into the ground beside each stool, to mark its position, as the manure can then be placed exactly over the roots, and there will be little danger of injuring them in the course of hoeing or in any other way.) A portion of the soil which covers the stool is then cautiously removed, leaving only enough to cover the stool to the depth of between 1 and 2 inches, and then the manure is applied. This is of various kinds. Those which, from experience, are considered the best, are well-rotted farmyard manure, street-sweepings or night-soil, to which a little sea-salt is sometimes added, and calcareous composts— plaster, marl, lime rubbish, quarry-dust, etc.,—if the soil is deficient in such ingredients. The manure is allowed to remain on the surface all through the winter, and at the end of March is dug into and well mixed with the soil. The surface is then neatly levelled down, and the plantation, during the remainder of the second year, is treated exactly in the same way as in the previous year. When the stools are uncovered in the autumn, care should be taken to cut away, close to the root, the withered remnants of the stems which were previously shortened in October. A fresh covering of manure is then applied, which, as before, is left to lie on the surface all through the winter and dug in at the commencement of spring.

In the third year, the plants are, for the first time, earthed-up. This operation consists in heaping up over each stool some of the soil taken from the alleys, so as to form a little hillock about a foot higher than the bed. If the plantation has been carefully attended to up to this time, some shoots may now be gathered for use, but not more than two or three from each stool : however, if it is desirable that the plantation should last for a considerable time, it is better to abstain from gathering any now, and to wait till the fourth year for the first gathering. In any case, it is very important to gather the shoots by breaking them off close to the neck of the stool, and not to cut them in the soil, as is often wrongly done, to the detriment, among other things, of the as yet undeveloped shoots. The best plan is to uncover the stools from which shoots are to be taken, by removing the soil of the hillock, and then neatly break off the shoots with the fingers or a special implement, replacing the soil of the hillock in its former position, as all the shoots are gathered from each stool. This is the invariable practice of careful cultivators in the neighbourhood of Paris. If, from any cause, portions of shoots are found attached to the stool in autumn, they should be altogether removed before winter sets in. In the open air, in the climate of Paris, Asparagus is gathered in the beginning of April, but it is well not to continue gathering after the 15th of June, if an abundant and early crop is expected the following year. About London it is ten to fourteen days later, and lasts so much longer.

In the fourth year, the treatment of a plantation of Asparagus is precisely the same as in the previous years, consisting simply of the necessary hoeing, watering, and manuring. It is not absolutely necessary to apply manure every year; nevertheless, as the Asparagus is a very greedy plant in the matter of manure, the crop will always be in proportion to the quantity of nourishment it receives in this way. A plantation properly made and carefully attended to will continue productive for ten years or more.

As by the common English way of growing Asparagus it is impossible to get a good result, we give here what are the

ESSENTIAL POINTS IN THE PRODUCTION OF GOOD ASPARAGUS.

Although the details of the system of growing good Asparagus require some little space to describe on paper, the essential differences between that and the system commonly employed in England are so very clear that they may be shortly stated. Each plant is treated as an individual—as a vigorous subject requiring much space in which to grow, if strong growth and strong shoots are desired. Long experience has taught cultivators that a smaller space than 4 ft. apart will not suffice to give the very best result. At first sight people in this country might suppose that this means a waste of ground, but it really is not so. At first, when the plantation is young, waste of ground is avoided by taking a light crop off between the lines—say one of Kidney Beans or of early Potatoes ; but after a good year's growth, and when the Asparagus gets strong, its roots really occupy the whole space, and the result is so much more satisfactory than in the common way that the ground affords a better and more satisfactory return. There are two principal ways of growing this crop near Paris—one, devoting a certain portion of ground to it, as usual with us ; the other, putting single plants between Vines or small fruits, or placing a plant wherever there is room for one. This last way is important, because it may be carried out in small gardens everywhere, and by its means we should become more readily convinced of the value of giving plenty of room to the roots. Single plants here and there in the open spaces, or in "blanks" between bushes, fruits, or dwarf pyramidal Apple or Pear trees, or single lines, wherever room can be found for them, would, from the superior result, soon convince all of the value of the system.

PLANTING. — Healthy yearling plants are always chosen, and they are planted about the time, or a little before the time, when growth commences in spring. They are invariably planted in a shallow trench somewhat like a Celery trench—not quite so deep and not manured as that is, supposing that the ground is in fair condition. In a trench about 8 inches deep the plants are placed on little low hillocks, and they are carefully attended to for the first year. The plants, be it noted, are 4 ft. apart in the line, and 4 ft. apart in the trench. It will be noticed that the second essential difference between the common way—that in use with us —and the way it is now desired to make known is, that in garden soil of fair quality no manure is used at the time of planting. There are soils in which drainage and preparation might be required; but assuming that the soil is as good as garden soil generally is, no preparation whatever is given beyond the opening of the trench and the planting of each root in a little fine surface soil; the great preliminary expense which has been supposed to be necessary in the culture of this plant is avoided. It is when the plants begin to get strong and well established that a little manure is applied. There is thus a great economy in two things—in plants and in manure, which under the usual system with us is used to the most wasteful extent; so much so, indeed, as to seriously limit production by causing alarm as to expense.

HOME CULTURE. — Our markets are full of Asparagus in spring, grown in other countries, sometimes hundreds of miles from London. It is a vegetable which, perhaps more than any other, loses quality every

day after it is cut. This is one reason why it should be grown in our own country. The soil and the climate of England, in almost every county, are admirably suited for the production of Asparagus. Nevertheless, not only do we not supply our own markets, but many possessing large gardens cannot get a really good sample. All this is wholly unnecessary, for every farmer's garden and every cottage garden might grow it well. In large places, where a few beds formed on a costly and wrong principle now furnish a very limited supply of very poor Asparagus, there ought to be an abundance of the best quality. Our markets ought to be supplied by our own people, the early supplies coming from the southern and the late ones from the northern counties.

BLANCHING. — The question of blanching it, more or less, is apart from the question of cultivation, and people may adopt the only true system of culture without blanching, if such be their taste. But a closer acquaintance with the subject will probably teach many that there *is* something in this despised system of blanching, which so many persons, lamentably ignorant on the subject beyond experiences of their own overcrowded and ill-grown beds, declare to be an absurd practice. All good judges and good growers know that it is necessary in the highest culture, and to secure the most delicate flavour, and also to prevent the rising shoots breaking in warm weather into scales or leaves before they are fairly developed. The best foreign Asparagus is blanched by piling little mounds of friable earth over the stools in spring.

FORCING ASPARAGUS.—Obtaining early supplies of Asparagus should be the aim of all who have gardens of any extent and with the usual appliances for forcing and heating. A peculiarity of this, the most delicate and most esteemed of all vegetables, is that it never retains its true and delicate flavour when "canned" or preserved. We have tried many samples, both from France and America, and never found one that did not taste unpleasantly of the tin. The true way is to prolong the season of the fresh Asparagus as long as we conveniently can.

Forcing may be commenced in November and continued till Asparagus is fit to gather in the open air. One of the best ways is to make a slight hot-bed with stable manure, leaves, and tan (these last materials, if easily obtained, will do well to mix with the manure), in a Melon pit, or under a common Cucumber frame about $2\frac{1}{2}$ ft. high; and on the surface of the bed should be placed a few inches of light soil, leaf-mould, or sifted potting refuse, on which to place the plants, because such material does not act so effectually in repressing the heat as ordinary garden soil. When the roots are taken up as completely and carefully as possible, and placed thickly on this, they should be covered with a few more inches of the same material. If the Asparagus be required of its natural colour, give the frame full light and air when fine. Water occasionally with tepid water. After one good watering in the early stage, a little will afterwards suffice, for the winter crops at all events, as the slow evaporation of the period and the moisture of the bed will preserve the soil in a sufficiently moist state. The heat of the bed must be preserved when it gets low by a lining, in the usual old-fashioned way, and by covering closely with mats or litter at night in cold weather—that is, if it be a common frame, but if in a brick pit this will not be necessary. The chief point is to be patient at first, to let it get a slow start, and not to be over-excited at any time, or it will start away and produce nothing but very weak, spindly shoots; whereas, by bringing it on gradually and regularly, a good cutting may be obtained.

An important way is by bringing the heat to the roots, and certainly by this plan a more permanent and stable kind of "grass" is obtained, because plant or root is not in the least disturbed. It is an expensive way, though simple. The beds are, in the first place, very well made of rich, deep soil, and the alleys of these beds are dug out to a depth of 3 ft. or so, and then bricked; or, in other words, the Asparagus beds are made between low brick walls, perforated with "pigeon-holes," to admit of the heat entering freely; and whenever forcing commences, the bricked trench on each side of a bed is filled with fermenting manure, covered over by a rough shutter, and the beds themselves with small wooden frames made to fit; these are, of course, only placed on during forcing, the beds being exposed in the summer season. The beds should not be more than 4 or 5 ft. wide, to admit of the ready percolation of heat. This method is, however, only suited for places where a good deal of expense is devoted to the garden. The modification or improvement of it, which consists in having hot-water pipes passing between each bed and the chamber covered with a slab of stone, is even a more expensive one. No matter what system is employed, a steady heat of from 60° to 65° will be found most suitable.

In the royal gardens at Frogmore the beds are about 75 ft. long and 7 ft. wide, their sides being built with brick, "pigeon-hole" style. The spaces between the beds are 4 ft. deep, the lower 2 ft. being filled with rich soil; and in the upper 2 ft. are flow and return hot-water pipes connected with a boiler that heats six such ranges. On the tops of the beds are frames. In special severe weather the sashes must be covered with mats or litter. The French mode of forcing Asparagus usually consists in digging deep trenches between beds planted for the purpose, covering the beds with the soil and with frames, filling in the trenches between the beds with stable manure, and protecting the frames with straw mats and litter to keep in the heat. A specialty is made of forcing the smaller-sized Asparagus. It is in the garden of M. Caucannier, Place de l'Église, at Clichy, and a number of iron houses are there devoted to the culture. There are frames within each house, just as in many propagating houses in England, and beneath them the Asparagus is forced for the markets, and in large quantities.

The houses are heated by hot water, and the culture in other respects resembles that which is practised in forcing gardens in England—that is, when the plants are taken up to be forced indoors or in pits. The disturbance weakens the roots a good deal, and the large table Asparagus is never forced by this method. M. Caucannier and other growers produce it specially in a small state for soups, etc., but it is impossible to obtain the large table Asparagus in this way.

USES.—The young shoots, blanched by being earthed-up, and gathered as soon as the points appear overground, are used boiled as a vegetable. In Italy and some other countries, they allow them to grow 4 or 6 inches overground, and to become quite green before they gather them. In France, blanched Asparagus with a reddish or purple coloured head is generally preferred. In Holland and Belgium, the shoots are completely blanched. Notwithstanding this, the Belgian and Dutch Asparagus has a delicate and excellent flavour. English people who only know good foreign Asparagus as specimens a week or more old, and gathered in Spain or France, make a great mistake in supposing that blanching destroys flavour. Fresh and properly cooked Asparagus is always delicate and good in flavour, whether blanched or not ; but growers, cooks, market men, and others who have much experience know that the blanched is the best, and laugh at the dictum of those who say that "only an inch of the blanched grass is fit to eat." Many who discuss the question do not even know how the large Asparagus is cooked, and have never tasted well-grown Asparagus freshly gathered and properly cooked. Another error is to suppose that only foreign produce is blanched, and our own green. The practice of the market gardeners of London has for many years been to blanch the shoots for most of their length. What they send to the London market is excellent in flavour, and has the advantage over the French of freshness. It may be useful to state here that French cooks boil the very fine Asparagus in bundles standing on end in the water, leaving an inch or so of the points above the water. This enables them to thoroughly cook the stem, without destroying the tops. These, if not enough cooked by the steam, are readily finished by laying the bundle on its side for a few minutes.—R.

VARIETIES OF ASPARAGUS

Are pretty numerous, or perhaps it would be better to say that every district in which its culture is successfully carried on has given its name to a kind more or less distinct. It is owing to this circumstance that we have such names as Asperge de Gand, A. de Marchiennes, A. de Vendôme, A. de Besançon, etc. We shall describe only those kinds which appear to possess some really distinctive characteristics.

Common Green Asparagus (*Asperge Verte*).—This variety appears to come nearest to the wild Asparagus; the shoots are more slender, more pointed, and turn green sooner than those of any other cultivated kind.

Giant Dutch Purple Asparagus (*Asperge de Hollande*).—The shoots of this variety are thicker and more rounded at the end than those of the preceding kind. They are only tinged at the points with rose-colour or violet-red as long as they are not exposed to the action of light. This is the variety which is most generally cultivated.

White German Asparagus (*Asperge Blanche d'Allemagne;* German, *Ulmer Spargel*).—Closely resembling the preceding variety, this is generally considered to be a little earlier and is somewhat more deeply coloured, but the difference is so trifling that the two varieties may be safely pronounced identical.

Early Giant Argenteuil Asparagus (*Asperge d'Argenteuil Hâtive*).—This very handsome variety, obtained by selection from seedlings of the Giant

Giant Dutch Asparagus (¼ natural size).

Dutch Purple Asparagus, forms the greater part of those fine bundles of Asparagus which are so much admired in the Paris markets in spring. The shoots are very notably thicker than those of the parent plant, the head is slightly pointed, and the scales with which it is covered are very closely set, overlapping each other. It is a little earlier than the parent variety.

Late Giant Argenteuil Asparagus (*Asperge d'Argenteuil Tardive*). —This variety is not inferior in appearance to the Early one, but it does not commence to yield quite so soon. It is called Late, not so much on account of this difference as because it continues to produce fine large shoots when those of the Early kind have become much thinner than they were at the beginning of the season, and shoots of the Late kind are used to set off the bundles. Experienced cultivators are able to distinguish this variety from the preceding one by the appearance of the point of the shoot, which in this kind has the scales parted from each other like those of the Artichoke, instead of being, as it were, glued down upon each other.

Intermediate Argenteuil Asparagus (*Asperge d'Argenteuil Intermédiaire*).—This kind, which is not so much grown as the two preceding ones, has no very distinct character. It appears to be a good seedling variety of the Giant Dutch Purple; like which, it has the heads or ends of the shoots blunt and rounded.

The **Lenormand Asparagus** (*A. Lenormand*) seems to be a good improved variety of the Giant Dutch Purple. The Argenteuil varieties have now almost entirely taken the place of this.

The Germans have a great number of varieties of Asparagus, under the names of Great Giant (*Grosse Géante*), Large Erfurt (*Grosse d'Erfurt*), Early Darmstadt (*Hâtive de Darmstadt*), Large Darmstadt (*Grosse de Darmstadt*), Large Early White (*Blanche Grosse Hâtive*), etc. All of these appear to us to come very close to the Giant Dutch Purple and the White German Asparagus (*A. d'Ulm*), both of which, as we have seen, are much about the same thing.

In England and America the variety named Conover's Colossal is very much extolled. From what we know of it, we do not think it superior to the Argenteuil varieties. [The difference in kinds is very often mere difference in cultivation. There is a difference between the Early Argenteuil and the Late Argenteuil, and the Early variety should be encouraged by English growers, who should try to supply their own markets as early as possible.—R.]

ASPARAGUS BEAN.

Dolichos sesquipedalis, L.   *Leguminosæ.*

French, Dolique Asperge, Pois ruban (à Cayenne), Haricot Asperge. *German*, Americanische Riesen-Spargel Bohne, Langschotige Spargel-Fasel. *Dutch*, Indianische boon. *Italian*, Fagiuolo Sparagio.

Native of South America.—Annual.—Stems climbing, 6 to over 9 ft. long; leaves deep green, rather large, elongated, pointed; flowers large,

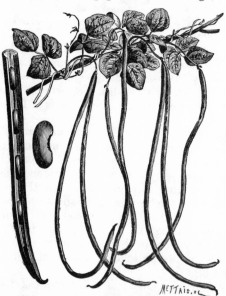

Cuban Asparagus Bean (¹⁄₁₀ natural size).

greenish yellow, with the standard bent backwards, remarkable for two small parallel auricles which compress the wings and the keel: they are borne either solitary or two together on the top of the flower-stalk. Pods pendent, cylindrical, of a light-green colour, very slender, and remarkably long; in fact, it is not unusual for them to exceed 1½ ft. in length. The seeds are few for the size of the pod, being generally from seven to ten in number; they are kidney-shaped, and of a reddish or pale wine-lees colour with a black circle round the white *hilum;* they are seldom more than about ½ inch long. A litre of them weighs 750 grammes, and 100 grammes contain 635 seeds. The plant is cultivated in the south of France, especially in Provence. The culture is similar to that which is employed in the case of late varieties of Tall Kidney Beans. A good position is desirable, the best being one against a wall. The green pods are used in the same way as Kidney Beans.

Cuban Asparagus Bean (*Dolique de Cuba*).—A vigorous climbing plant, attaining a height of from 10 to 13 ft.; leaves numerous; leaflets elongated, spear-shaped; flowers of medium size, greenish, mostly solitary, succeeded by pods of remarkable length, being often over 2½ ft. long when fully grown. They are then inflated by the swelling of the seed, and are about ½ inch broad. The seed, in form and colour, exactly resembles that of the preceding plant, of which this appears to be a variety, but a very distinct one, as it grows much taller and is a thorough climber. It is cultivated, however, in the same way, and the pods are similarly eaten when green, before they are fully grown. A litre of the seeds weighs 770 grammes, and 100 grammes contain 630 seeds.

BALM.

Melissa officinalis, L. *Labiatæ.*

French, Mélisse citronelle, Mélisse officinale. *German*, Citronen-Melisse. *Dutch*, Citroen-Melisse. *Danish*, Hjertensfryd. *Italian*, Melissa. *Spanish*, Toronjil, Citronella.

Native of South Europe.—Perennial.—A plant growing about 1½ ft. high, with numerous erect and spreading branches and leaves of

a pure green colour; flowers few, in small clusters; calyx covered with fine soft hairs; seeds brown, numbering about 2000 to the gramme, and weighing 550 grammes to the litre. Their germinating power lasts for four years. The leaves and all the green parts of the plant exhale a very agreeable and penetrating aromatic odour, especially when bruised. This plant is of very easy culture in England. It is increased by dividing the clumps in autumn, winter, or spring. Like most of the herbs that come from South Europe, it enjoys warm positions, but grows anywhere.

Balm (plant, 1/12; branch, 1/3 natural size).

USES.—The leaves are much used for seasoning, and especially in the manufacture of liqueurs and scents.

BASIL.

Ocymum Basilicum, L. *Labiatæ.*

French, Basilic grand, Herbe royale. *German*, Basilikum, Basilicum. *Flemish*, Basilic. *Danish*, Basilikum. *Italian*, Basilico. *Spanish*, Albaca. *Portuguese*, Manjericao.

A native of India.—Annual.—Stem about 1 ft. high, very branching; leaves green; flowers white, in whorled leafy clusters; seeds small,

C

black, covered with a mucilaginous substance, which swells in water like Flax-seed. A gramme contains 800 seeds, and the litre weighs 530 grammes. Their germinating power lasts for eight years.

Basil (⅛ natural size).

CULTURE.—As this plant is a native of warm countries, the best way is to sow the seed in a hot-bed in March or April. The seedlings are planted out in May, in the open air, on a warm border in sandy soil. All kinds of Basil are easily grown in pots. In England, Sweet Basil seeds should be sown about the middle of April, in a genial temperature, and when the seedlings are large enough to handle, they may be potted off singly, or they may be pricked into boxes or seed-pans, or into a frame on a slight bottom heat, from which they should be transferred to their positions in the open air about the beginning of June. Owing to the plant being very tender, this can seldom be done with safety at an earlier period. Sweet Basil succeeds best in a light, rich soil, in which the plants should grow at a distance of 6 or 8 inches apart, and should be well watered until they become established. As soon as they come into bloom they should be cut down to within a few inches of the ground, and the portion cut off should be tied up in small bunches and dried in the shade for winter use. As, however, green Basil is frequently required, the plants which have been cut down should have the soil surrounding them slightly stirred up, and the bed given a surface-dressing of fresh soil, when the plants will quickly form themselves into healthy little bushes, which will furnish a supply of green leaves until about the beginning of October. A portion of them should then be lifted and potted, or planted in boxes, and should be placed in a somewhat genial temperature, where they will continue to furnish a supply of green leaves when required throughout the winter.

USES.—The leaves are very aromatic and are used for seasoning. Formerly, and even still in some countries, Basil was considered to possess very active medicinal properties. Its agreeable perfume and flavour recommend it as a kitchen-garden plant.

Large Green Sweet Basil (*Basilic Grand Vert*).—This appears to be the type of the species. A low-growing plant, forming compact dense tufts about 10 inches or 1 ft. high, and about as much across. Leaves shining green, 1 to 1½ inch long ; flowers white, in long clusters.

Large Purple Sweet Basil (*Basilic Grand Violet*).—A plant of the same height and habit as the preceding, from which it differs in having the leaves and stems of a dark purplish-brown colour, and the flowers lilac.

Lettuce-leaved Basil (*Basilic à feuilles de Laitue*).—A variety with broad, crimped, undulating leaves, from 2 to 4 inches long, and of a low-growing thick-set habit, somewhat less branching than either of the two preceding kinds; but the plant is apparently derived from the same type. The flowers, which are closely set in clusters, make their appearance rather later in this variety. The leaves of this Basil, which are much larger than those of any other kind, are also much fewer in number.

Anise-scented Basil (*Basilic Anisé*).—This variety is distinguished from Sweet Basil by its more aromatic odour, which resembles that of Anise.

Green Bush Basil (⅛ natural size).

Lettuce-leaved Basil (⅕ natural size).

Curled-leaved Basil (*Basilic Frisé*).—A variety with green, jagged-edged, crisped or curled leaves ; very distinct.

Bush, or Dwarf, Basil (*Ocymum minimum*, L. *Basilic Fin*).—A much dwarfer, more compact, and more branching plant than the Common Basil ; the leaves also are smaller. Flowers white ; seeds like those of the Common Basil. Culture and uses, the same.

Green Bush Basil (*Basilic Fin Vert*).—This plant, which is of a pleasing green colour, is particularly suitable for growing in pots, and is very commonly cultivated in this way. It may be often seen in the windows of the poorest houses, especially in warm countries, being highly esteemed for the fresh, bright verdure of its foliage and its fine strong aromatic odour. It forms very compact tufts, covered, in the flowering season, with multitudes of small clusters of rosy-white flowers, which form an agreeable relief to the intense green of the foliage.

Compact Bush Basil (*Basilic Fin Vert Compact*).—The distinctive characteristic of this

Compact Bush Basil.

variety is the very great number of stems and leaves which it produces, causing each plant to present the appearance of a round mass or ball of verdure, close and compact. It is, consequently, far better suited for forming ornamental vases or pots of greenery than the Common Bush Basil. This variety was raised at Marseilles, and has deservedly received a large amount of favour wherever it has been introduced.

Purple Bush Basil (*Basilic Fin Violet*).—A plant of a deep-violet colour in all its parts, except the flowers, which are of a lilac-white. It forms a small, very compact, bushy, and leafy clump.

East Indian, or Tree, Basil (*Ocymum gratissimum*, L. *Basilic en arbre*).—The plant which is commonly found cultivated under the name of Tree Basil, or *Basilic en arbre*, does not appear to be the true *Ocymum gratissimum*, L., but rather *O. suave*, Willd. It is an annual, with an upright stem, branching from the base, and forming a pyramidal bush from 20 inches to 2 ft. high, and from 1 ft. to 16 inches in its greatest diameter. Leaves oblong, pointed, toothed; flowers lilac, in irregular spikes at the ends of the branches. The plant has an agreeable perfume, but it is late-growing and more suited for a warm climate. The seeds are very small; a gramme contains about 1500 of them, and the litre weighs 580 grammes.

THE COMMON OR BROAD BEAN.

Faba vulgaris, Mill.; *Vicia Faba*, L. *Leguminosæ.*

French, Fève, Gourgane. *German*, Garten-Bohnen. *Flemish*, Platte-boon. *Dutch*, Tuin boonen. *Danish*, Valske bonner. *Italian*, Fava. *Spanish*, Haba. *Portuguese*, Fava.

Native of the East.—Annual.—This plant has been cultivated, so far as we are able to learn, from the earliest ages, the large size and alimentary properties of its seeds having drawn attention to it and brought it into culture at some remote period of antiquity. As the size of the seeds varies very much in the different kinds, we shall always mention it in the description of each variety. In all the kinds, the germinating power continues for six years at least.

CULTURE.—Beans are usually sown, where they are to remain, about the end of February or the beginning of March. They like a rich, slightly humid, and well-manured soil, but they can be grown in almost any kind of ground. Many gardeners are in the habit of nipping off the tops of the plants when they are coming into flower, but, as far as we can judge, this practice is more effectual in preventing the plants from being attacked by *aphides*, than in inducing an earlier and more abundant crop. It is a good plan, whenever it can be done, to run the hoe a few times through the drills. There is seldom any occasion for watering, as the crop is generally gathered before this is required.

Beans may also be sown in a frame in January and planted out about a month afterwards. It is also not impossible, in the climate of Paris, to grow Beans after the winter mode of culture which is universally practised all through the south of Europe. According to this mode, a sowing is made at the end of October or the beginning of November, in a position with a south aspect and well-drained soil, and the young plants are sheltered during the winter by placing frames over them. Instead of frames, we have sometimes seen hoops of casks stuck into the ground across the beds, so as to form an arched support for straw mats, which were spread over them in very frosty weather. This mode of culture is particularly well suited for dwarf or half-dwarf varieties. The plants which have been pushed on in this way are in full bearing three weeks or a month earlier than those which were not sown until spring.

In English gardens, years ago, it was the practice to sow Broad Beans in October, November, and December for the earliest crops, but this is now seldom done; the plants are generally raised in pots, boxes, or frames, and afterwards transplanted to the open ground. This is undoubtedly the best plan, as the ground that would otherwise be occupied by the seed can be ridged or roughly dug, and exposed to the weather to get pulverized and freed from slugs, etc. By adopting the method of transplantation, fuller and more even rows can also be insured. The first sowing should be made early in January in a frame or pit from which frost is excluded, or a sowing may be made in heat in February and gradually hardened off after the plants are up. The plants should be grown stout and strong, and be in readiness for turning out early in March, provided the weather is favourable. A south border, under a wall or hedge, should be chosen for them if possible, and after planting, if planks or thin boards can be placed edgeways on each side of the rows, to protect them from cold winds, all the better. The rows should be planted from 2 to 2½ ft. apart, and the plants in the rows should be 4 or 5 inches apart. This will be found to be room enough for early crops if dwarf varieties be grown. If the weather be favourable throughout the spring, the crop will be fit for use by the middle of June, which is as early as Broad Beans are generally expected to be fit for use. Successional sowings may be made in the open ground in January and February, and the principal sowings should be in March

and April. If late crops be required, small sowings may be made as late as July; this is, however, seldom done. In order to obtain late crops, some growers, after gathering the produce from the main or summer crops, cut down the plants to within a few inches of the ground, then give them a good watering, and in a few days they throw out young shoots, which eventually furnish a fair crop of late beans, though, of course, not so fine as the previous crop. Others sacrifice part of the summer crops, and cut down the plants just as they are coming into bloom; the produce from these is, of course, finer than that from plants that have previously borne a crop. Either of these ways is, however, preferable to sowing for late crops, inasmuch as the plants are hardier, and, being well rooted, stand the dry weather late in the summer and the cold in the autumn. By this method beans of fair quality may be had up till late in November, unless the weather be unusually severe.

Sowings for successional and main crops may be made on open quarters, or between rows of Spinach or any other crop that will be cleared before the Beans get very high; the former, however, is best when ground can be spared. The seed should be sown in rows from 2½ to 3 ft. apart, the beans being placed about 4 or 5 inches apart, and they may either be put in with a blunt dibble, or drills may be drawn for them 2 or 3 inches deep. Previous to sowing main crops, the seed should be soaked in water for a few hours to accelerate vegetation. Earthing-up the young plants is advisable for early crops, for it affords a slight protection to the plants during cold, windy weather; for other crops it is not needed. When the plants show sufficient bloom to produce a good crop, their tops may be picked out in order to enhance the setting of the blooms and development of the pods. Where tall varieties are grown, some support should be given them to prevent their being broken by the wind. The best support is thick twine tied to strong stakes driven in the ground on each side of the rows. Long, slender sticks, tied to the stakes, lengthways along the rows, will answer, but the plants are apt to get bruised against them when swayed to and fro by the wind.

KINDS.—Although there have recently been many new and valuable additions made to our lists of Beans, there are some of the older kinds that still unflinchingly maintain their position. Dwarf kinds are sometimes preferred for the smallness of the beans rendering them more delicate-looking than some of the larger varieties. Of dwarf kinds, Beck's Green Gem and the Dwarf Fan are two of the best; the plants assume a neat, compact habit, are abundant croppers, and good in quality; in this respect, however, Beck's Gem is preferable, on account of its green colour. The taller kinds of Mazagan are not worth growing in comparison with the Long-pods and Windsors, but where small beans are preferred, they answer the purpose. Though recommended in every book on the subject, the Mazagan is for us the worst and most useless of its race. The Long-pods are earlier than the Windsors, and are therefore preferable to them for first and second early crops. Of these there is no variety better than Johnson's Wonderful; it grows from 4 to 5 ft. high, and is a fine cropper, producing green pods from 7 to 8 inches long, full of beans that are not excelled in quality. Mammoth Long-pod is likewise a very excellent variety. The Green Long-pod

is largely grown, the colour of the beans when fit for use being of a bright green. The Seville Long-pod is a variety of Broad Bean that has been for many years in cultivation on the Continent, especially in Spain, where it has done good service in supplying food during times of war. It well deserves the high commendations bestowed upon it, and ought to be in every good garden. It is a very early variety, with immensely long pods, the points of which reach the ground and seem to prop up the plant. It is rather tender. The variety named Agua-Dulce is said to be the true variety of this. It is a taller and somewhat stronger grower. The Windsor is most suitable for main or late crops.

SOIL, MULCHING, AND WATERING. —A deep, well-drained, strong loam is most suitable for Broad Beans, with the exception of early crops, when the soil may be of a lighter character. Where the soil is too light, it may be improved by treading it firmly whilst in a dry state, or planting without digging. If the ground in which Beans are to be grown has been manured for previous crops, it will be found sufficiently rich for them, as a very rich soil will produce too luxuriant a growth, which is inimical to the production of pods. During dry weather it is a good plan to give a good mulching of half-rotted manure between the rows of main crops of Beans to save watering, but it should be done before the plants are in bloom, in order to keep the roots in a moist condition whilst the blooms are setting, this being highly necessary to the production of large, full pods. Watering is seldom necessary for Broad Beans, if grown in a deep soil; where, however, the soil is shallow, it may sometimes be needed, in which case it should be thoroughly done, and afterwards the ground should be mulched.

In London market gardens, when these Beans are grown, dry and light soils in warm positions are chosen for early sowings, which consist of the Early Mazagan. Sowings of this kind are made in January, and again in February, in rows 2½ ft. apart, running across or obliquely in the borders or quarters. Large sowings of the Long-pod are made in the latter half of February and in March, in rows equally distant as for Mazagans, but with less particularity as regards the way in which they run, the position of the quarter, or the quality of the soil which they occupy. The Broad Windsor, which forms the principal crop, is generally sown in March.

The Green Broad Windsor is preferred by consumers; therefore market gardeners generally grow this sort for the main crop. Some cultivators grow Beans for seeding purposes, and in this case about one-half or two-thirds of the pods, consisting of the earliest formed, are picked off for marketing in a green or usable condition, the remainder being left to ripen. If all were left the seeds would not be so large, plump, or heavy as when the pods are thus thinned out.

USES.—The seeds, or beans, both in the green state and when dry, are eaten boiled. In the south of France the pods are sometimes boiled and eaten when young. Broad Beans are not thought so much of in private gardens as Kidney Beans, but by the poorer classes they are much grown. Generally they are not considered a remunerative crop, inasmuch as they do not continue long in bearing. The green-seeded varieties are usually preferred to the white ones, because they retain their green appearance when cooked, whilst the white ones become dark brown—a colour objectionable to many in England. The Bean suffers from the usual and bad practice of allowing the pods to become old and hard before they are used. It is an excellent vegetable when gathered at the right time and properly cooked, and as it is wholly distinct in flavour from any form of Kidney or Runner Bean, it deserves more attention both from the gardener and the good cook. Beans are often gathered for table before they have attained half their size; but this is not advisable, as they sometimes taste bitter when so small. The best-flavoured beans are those that are full grown but young. If any be required for soup, a row may remain until they become black-eyed. When gathering for exhibition, choose young, long, straight, and shapely pods, as nearly alike as possible, and the more beans they contain the better.

Large Common Field Bean (*Fève de Marais*).—Stem quadrangular, erect, about 2½ ft. high, and almost always tinged with red; leaves usually consisting of four or five oval leaflets of a grayish-green colour. At the base of each leaf, the stem is encircled, for about two-thirds of its circumference, by two broad, toothed, sheathing stipules marked with a blackish spot. Flowers, five to eight in number, in clusters, the first of which commences at the fifth or sixth leaf from the base of the stem; they are pretty large, white, marked on the standard with dark-brownish streaks, and with a spot of velvety black on each of the wings. Pods often two or three together, sometimes curved when fully grown, or becoming pendent from their weight, at other times remaining quite erect. They are something over 1 inch broad, and from 5 to 6 inches long, and contain from two to four very large seeds which are longer than broad. These seeds weigh 645 grammes to the litre, and 100 grammes contain about 55 seeds.

There are numerous sub-varieties of this Bean, which are generally earlier in proportion as they have been raised farther south.

French Long-pod Bean (*Fève à Longue Cosse*).—A somewhat stronger-growing plant than the preceding, with dark-coloured luxuriant foliage; stem quadrangular, frequently branching; pods in pairs, rarely three together, erect at first, afterwards slanting or horizontal, moderately flattened at the sides, and containing three or four white seeds, like those of the kind last described, longer than broad, thickish, and slightly depressed in the middle. A litre of these seeds weighs 650 grammes, and 100 grammes contain about 60 seeds. In the south of France, a variety is grown which comes very near this, but is distinguished from it by having more slender pods, of a deep green colour, cylindrical, erect until ripe, and sometimes growing three or four together. The seeds also are longer and narrower. These varieties are productive, and are some days later than the Large Common Field Bean.

Broad Windsor Bean.—Stem very stout, quadrangular, erect, of a reddish or bronzy tinge, which extends to the leaf-stalks, and is deeper

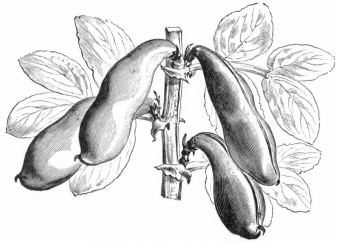

Broad Windsor Bean (⅓ natural size).

than the similar coloration of the stalks of the Large Common Field Bean. Leaves large, oval-roundish, of a rather deep glaucous green. Flowers of medium size, resembling those of the Large Common Field Bean, but not more than from four to six in a cluster, and having a reddish or violet-coloured calyx. In this variety the first cluster of flowers does not commence before the eighth or tenth leaf from the base of the stem. Pods solitary or in pairs, almost always curved, and usually very broad towards the end; they seldom contain more than two or three well-grown seeds. The seeds are very broad, with an almost regularly rounded outline; they weigh 625 grammes to the litre, and 100 grammes contain 40 seeds. A new variety of Broad Bean, named *John Harrison*, is described as being "very productive, hardy, and early; the pods containing six to eight large beans each, of excellent quality."

Green Windsor Bean.—This differs from the preceding kind only in the colour of its seeds, which, even when ripe, remain of a deep green colour. Windsor Beans are very strong-growing and productive varieties, but somewhat late, which is a serious drawback in dry climates, where Beans are exposed to the attacks of rust and aphides.

Seville Long-pod Bean (Spanish, *Haba de Sevilla o Tarragona*). Stem quadrangular, erect, 2 to 2½ ft. high, not very stout, sometimes quite green, and sometimes slightly tinged with red. The foliage is very clearly distinguished from that of other varieties by its lighter shade of green, and by the more elongated shape of the leaflets. The flowers in each cluster are not very numerous, usually from two to four, and sometimes there is even only one ; the standard is greenish white, longer than broad, and remains folded in the centre, even when the flower is fully blown. This peculiarity gives the flowers the appearance of being longer and narrower in this variety than in any other, and they have hardly any tinge of red or violet. The first cluster of flowers usually appears in the axil of the seventh leaf from the base of the

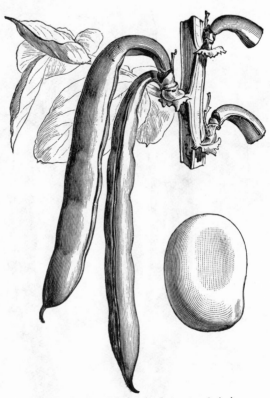

Seville Long-pod Bean (pods ⅓ natural size).

stem. Pods something over ½ inch broad, and from 8 inches to 1 ft. long, either solitary or in pairs, and soon becoming pendent with their weight. They contain from four to eight seeds each, resembling those of the Large Common Field Bean, but generally a little smaller ; they weigh 620 grammes to the litre, and 100 grammes contain 50 seeds. This is an early variety, but not so hardy as the preceding ones. It has longer pods than any other kind of Garden Beans.

Agua-Dulce Long-podded Bean.—This fine Bean, with its immense pods nearly 2 inches wide and 14 to 16 inches long, is not, properly speaking, a distinct variety, but is the real Seville Long-pod in the highest state of development. As usual, however, the number of the seeds is, in these plants, in inverse ratio to the increased size of the pods, and while the Large Common Field Bean or the Broad Windsor may have ten to fifteen pods on a stem, it is a rare occurrence to find a stem of the Agua-Dulce Bean bearing more than three or four well-grown pods.

Small July Bean (*Fève Julienne*).—The general appearance of this plant very much resembles that of the Large Common Field Bean. Stems quadrangular, very erect, reddish, and attain a height of about

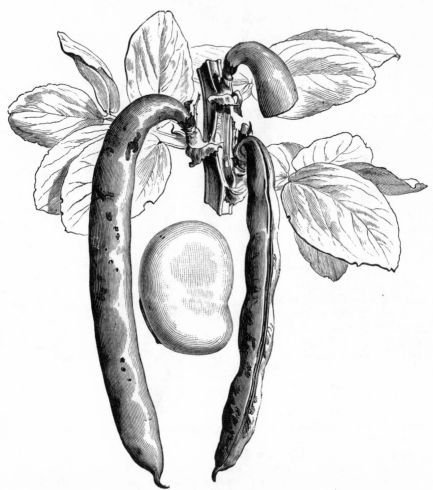

Extra Long-podded Agua-Dulce Bean (pods ⅓ natural size).

2½ ft.; leaves grayish, with oval-roundish leaflets; flowers reddish on the calyx and at the base of the standard, and with well-marked black spots on the wings, four to six in a cluster, the first cluster appearing in the axil of the fifth or sixth leaf; pods erect, often three or four together, nearly cylindrical, and not much thicker than one's finger. They usually contain three or four seeds each, which are elongated, thickish, and not flattened at the sides, like those of the preceding kinds. These seeds weigh, on an average, 720 grammes to the litre, and 100 grammes contain about 110 seeds. The July Bean is a hardy kind, and less affected by hot, dry weather than either the Windsor Bean or the Large Common Field Bean, and, notwithstanding the comparatively small size of its seeds, it yields almost as heavy a crop as either of those kinds; for, although its pods are shorter and narrower than those of the large-seeded varieties, they are produced in far greater numbers, and the seeds are, at the same time, very uniformly well grown and well filled.

Small Green July Bean (*Fève Julienne Verte*).—This variety exhibits the same characteristics as those of the preceding kind, except that its seeds are of a deep-green colour, and remain so even after they are ripe. The plant is also a little later, and the colour of its leaves is of a somewhat deeper green.

Purple Bean (*Fève Violette*).—We mention this variety, although it is now seldom grown, on account of the remarkable colour of the seeds, which, when ripe, assume a reddish or deep coppery hue. In all other respects it has a considerable resemblance to the July Bean. The seeds weigh 630 grammes to the litre; 100 grammes contain 72 seeds.

The Purple Sicilian Bean (*Fève Violette de Sicile*) is also a purple-seeded variety. Its habit of growth resembles that of the Large Common Field Bean, but it is a smaller and less-productive kind. The seeds are of a very pronounced violet colour, but they do not be-

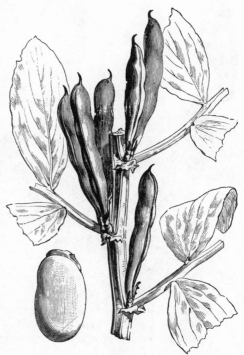

Small July Bean (pods ⅓ natural size).

gin to assume this hue until they are fully grown. Their peculiar colour is a drawback.

Early Mazagan Bean (*Fève de Mazagan*).— Under this name are cultivated several kinds, which are certainly distinct from one another, all of them small-seeded varieties, but varying in height and earliness. They usually produce numerous erect, very slightly flattened pods, each containing three or four seeds intermediate in size between that of the July Bean and a large Horse-Bean. A litre of these seeds weighs 750 grammes, and 100 grammes contain about 115 seeds.

Dwarf Fan, or Cluster, Bean (*Fève Naine Hâtive à Châssis*).—A plant growing 14 to 16 inches high, with a quadrangular stem tinged with brownish-red or copper-colour, and rather slender, but stiff and strong leaves, ashy-green, with rather small, oval-elongated, pointed leaflets. Flowers small, four to six in a cluster, with a slightly reddish calyx, and the standard more or less marked with purple at the base; the first flowers make their appearance in the axil of about the sixth leaf from the base of the stem. Pods erect, in twos or threes, each containing from two to four square-sided, thickish, bulging seeds, of the same colour as those of the Large Common Field Bean. These seeds weigh 675 grammes to the litre, and 100 grammes contain about 80 seeds.

Beck's Dwarf Green Gem Bean. — A very compact-growing variety, much dwarfer than the preceding kind, being only 1 ft. or 14 inches high. Stem stiff, green, or slightly tinged with red; leaves very closely set and arranged like a fan on each side of the stem; leaflets oval, rather pointed, of a glaucous or slightly metallic green colour; flowers smallish, with a purple tinge at the base of the standard; pods small but numerous, about the size of the little finger, each containing three or four dark-green, very full and rounded seeds, which are not much larger than a good-sized Horse-Bean. The seeds weigh 690 grammes to the litre, and 100 grammes contain about 110 seeds. Both the preceding kind and this one in particular are especially well suited for forcing

Dwarf Fan, or Cluster, Bean (pods ⅓ natural size).

in a frame. Although dwarf, they are great bearers, and even in the open air will yield a good crop without the drawback of throwing too much shade on other plants growing near them, which the taller-growing kinds of Beans sometimes do.

The **Very Dwarf Scarlet Bean** is a small and very early variety, but not very productive. It has erect, slender pods, about the size of the little finger, each generally containing two or three oblong seeds of a dark-brown colour.

Horse-Bean, or **Small Field Bean** (*Faba vulgaris* var. *equina. Féverole*).—For the feeding of cattle, several varieties of very small-seeded Beans are cultivated under the name of Horse-Beans, or Small Field Beans, which are utilized either by cutting the plants as green fodder, or allowing the seeds to ripen for winter use. They are stout, hardy plants, and are grown in the open fields. There is a variety which is sown in autumn, and which, on that account, is named the Winter Horse-Bean. The seeds are seldom used as a table vegetable, as they are very small and have a rather strong flavour.

The varieties most in cultivation are the following :—

Summer, or **Picardy, Horse-Bean** (*Féverole de Picardie*).—A plant with an erect, stiff stem, generally branching pretty evenly at the base, attaining a height of from 3 to about 3½ ft., and bearing pods from about 14 inches from the base of the plant. Leaves numerous, broadish, and of a dark-green colour. It is almost as early as the July Bean.

Small Summer, or Lorraine, Horse-Bean (*Féverole de Lorraine*).— A much taller growing and later kind than the preceding. Stems thick, stout, and stiff, from 3¼ to over 4 ft. high. The first pods commence about 2 ft. from the ground. The leaves are rather broader than those of the Picardy Horse-Bean, and also of a somewhat grayer colour.

Winter Horse-Bean (*Féverole d'Hiver*).—This variety, as has been mentioned, may be sown in autumn. In its manner of growth it bears some resemblance to the Lorraine Horse-Bean, which it nearly equals in height, but it is distinguished from that variety especially by having narrower and smaller leaves and considerably slenderer stems. It is chiefly remarkable for its hardiness, as it will endure the winter without any protection.

We occasionally find in cultivation a variety of Horse-Bean which has perfectly black seeds, and which, from its mode of growth, appears to be intermediate between the Picardy Horse-Bean and the July Bean. It does not, however, appear to possess any special merit.

KIDNEY BEAN, or FRENCH BEAN.

Phaseolus vulgaris, L. *Leguminosæ.*

French, Haricot, Phaséole, Pois. *German*, Bohne. *Flemish* and *Dutch*, Boon. *Danish*, Havebonnen. *Italian*, Faginolo. *Spanish*, Habichuela, Judia, Frijol. *Portuguese*, Feijao.

Native of South America.—Annual.—A plant of rapid growth, flowering and seeding soon after it is sown. Stem slender, twining, usually channelled or angular, rough to the touch, always twining in the direction of from right to left (but there are several dwarf varieties, with stiff stems, which do not require any support). Leaves large, composed of three triangular leaflets, which have the angles at the base rounded, are rough on the surface, and of various shapes and sizes. The flowers are produced in the axils of the leaves, in clusters containing from two to eight flowers each. They resemble other papilionaceous flowers, but are rather irregular in shape, the petals being often twisted in an unsymmetrical manner, and the keel especially being generally reduced to two small blades which are more or less convex and non-adherent to each other. Hence it results that the pistil is not so completely covered as it is in most other papilionaceous flowers, and consequently spontaneous crossing very frequently occurs amongst the varieties of this plant. The pods and seeds of the different kinds vary much in shape, colour, size, and substance.

We shall describe each variety separately, merely observing here that the difference in the texture of the pods has led to the division of the plants into two classes, viz. the Tough-podded (*Haricots à ecosser* or *Haricots à parchemin*), the pods of which become hard and leathery when ripe, and the Edible-podded (*Haricots mange-tout*, or *Haricots sans parchemin*), the pods of which never become stringy, even when dried. The germinating power of the seeds continues for three years.

The Kidney Bean does not appear to have been known to the ancients; for, although Columella and Virgil mention a plant under the name of *Phaseolus* or *Phaselus,* this could not have been our Kidney Bean, which, even in Italy, does not accommodate itself to being sown in autumn, like the *Phaseolus* of these authors. It is certain that the Kidney Bean is a native of a warm climate, and in the absence of positive documentary proofs of its original habitat and the time of its introduction into cultivation, there are good grounds for assenting to the opinion of Monsieur Alph. de Candolle, that it was originally a native of South America, and was introduced into Europe in the sixteenth century. The old French writers on kitchen-garden subjects do not mention it before that period, and give it but scant notice in comparison with that which they bestow on Peas and Garden Beans. Since their time, however, and chiefly owing to the power which the plant possesses of producing numerous varieties, its culture has acquired a considerable amount of importance. In France, every year, many millions of kilogrammes of the seeds are harvested (the kilogramme is equal to $2\frac{1}{5}$ lbs. avoirdupois); and, besides this, considerable quantities are imported, and form a large part of the national food. They contain more *azote* or nitrogen than almost any other vegetable, and their chemical composition in some degree approaches that of the flesh of animals.

CULTURE.—The Kidney Bean is very sensitive of cold, and will not grow well or vigorously in a temperature which is not over 50° Fahr. It is destroyed by one or two degrees of frost. It likes a rich, light, well-drained soil, with which manure has been thoroughly well mixed, and it may be observed that it does better in soil which has been well manured in the previous year than in newly manured ground. This remark applies to field cultivation, as well as to that of the kitchen garden.

We will now rapidly review the various modes of cultivation under which Kidney Beans are grown. As they delight in fresh air and light, they are seldom sown in hot-beds for a first crop before February (they are sometimes so sown in December or January, but it is not unusual to see plants which are raised at that time pine away or damp off). The seed is sown in a frame, placed on a bed of fresh manure, which is covered with good soil or leaf-mould to the depth of 5 or 6 inches. Air should be regularly given whenever the weather permits, taking care at the same time not to bring down the temperature to a degree that would be injurious. As the plants increase in size, all sickly or discoloured leaves should be removed, as well as any of the healthy ones which give too much shade or hinder the free circulation of the air.

The first crop may be gathered eight or ten weeks after sowing, and sometimes sooner when the weather is favourable. Sowings on hot-beds may be continued until March. The plants so raised in April are usually planted out in the open air; and, in fact, plants raised in hot-beds may be always advantageously pricked out. Some gardeners keep their forced Flageolet Beans growing, and after taking from them a crop of green pods, leave some to ripen, from which they obtain another crop of fresh ripe beans in May, when they command a high price. The varieties which are generally used for this purpose are the Dwarf Dutch Kidney Bean (*Haricot Nain de Hollande*), which is much the same as the White Flageolet; the Early Étampes Flageolet (*H. Flageolet Hâtif d'Étampes*), and the Scalloped-leaved Flageolet (*Flageolet à Feuille Gauffrée*). The Black Belgian Kidney Bean (*Haricot Noir de Belgique*) and the Yellow Chalindrey (*H. Jaune de Chalindrey*) are also well adapted for forcing.

The time for making a sowing, in the open air, of Kidney Beans which are intended to be gathered in the green state, commences as soon as all danger of frost is over, and the soil has become sufficiently warm. Successional sowings may be made from April to August. The seed may be sown either in holes made with the dibble, or in drills, according as the kinds sown vary in vigour of growth. This mode of culture requires hardly any attention except the use of the hoe and watering in hot weather. Some gardeners are in the habit of earthing-up the plants at the first hoeing, and this generally appears to be productive of good results ; the flowers come into bloom continuously, and the growth of the young pods is very rapid, so that gatherings may be made from the same drills every two or three days, and if the plants which were latest sown are protected from frost, green pods may be gathered in the open air up to the end of October. It is usually the tough-podded kinds which are grown for use in the green state, and the preference is given to those varieties in which the young pods are long, straight, very green, and rather cylindrical than flattish in shape. The kinds which are chiefly grown about Paris for this purpose are Swiss Kidney Beans, especially the Gray Swiss (*Suisse Gris* or *Bagnolet*), and the Black Flageolet (*Haricot Flageolet Noir*).

In gardens, hardly any kinds are grown for the seeds or beans except the White or Green Flageolets (*H. Flageolets Blancs ou Verts*), and they are cultivated just in the same way as the kinds of which the pods are used in the green state. The pods are gathered when they begin to grow yellow and are no longer brittle. Dry seeds are obtained by allowing them to ripen thoroughly, but some may be preserved tender for winter use by taking up the plants a short time before the pods are ripe, drying them in the shade, and then packing them closely together in a dry place, when the leaves will gradually fall off, while the pods continue attached, and the seeds will remain tender and possess nearly the same flavour as if they had been just newly gathered.

Tall-growing Kidney Beans, whether grown for the sake of the green pods or the seeds, are treated in exactly the same way as those already described, except that they require to be supplied with poles or branches to support their climbing stems. These supports, which are of different materials in different districts, vary in height from 5 to nearly 10 ft., according to the height of the variety grown. Those used about Paris consist chiefly of Chestnut loppings, with few branches or none, and when staked they are usually inclined inwards in the direction of the drills, so that every two rows of stakes meet at the top. The object of this arrangement is to make the rows firmer, and better able to resist high winds. Sometimes, for greater security, every two opposite stakes are tied together near the top, thus forming a series of gables, which are fastened to poles laid lengthways in the forks, and, in this way, although it may seem a little troublesome, a structure of great strength and stability is obtained.

Though we by no means make such good use of the Kidney Bean in its many and valuable dried forms as the French do, its culture in Britain is of the highest importance, and we look to its being much more so in the future, when the value of the many superior kinds described in this book is generally known.

SOWING AND CULTURE OUT - OF - DOORS.—An early sowing is generally made, in order to be able to pick Kidney Beans before it is possible to have those of the Scarlet Runner type in bearing; but as soon as these come in, French Beans too often are almost lost sight of. For small gardens the French Bean is invaluable as a summer vegetable, being easily grown, many kinds requiring no stakes, and being one of the most remunerative of vegetable crops. It may be had out-of-doors both earlier and later in the season than the taller-growing kinds, owing to its dwarf habit adapting itself to any situation—as, for instance, under hedges or walls, or other sheltered positions ; it also comes into bearing much more quickly than Runners.

Where French Beans are grown in the open air without protection, it is impossible to have them fit to gather before the latter end of June or the beginning of July, unless it be indeed an exceptionally favourable season. Where, however, they are sown in a warm, dry situation, and somewhat protected from cold winds and late frosts, they may be had fit for table during the second and third weeks in June. Where it is desirable to have Beans out-of-doors as early in the season as possible, it is a good plan to sow thickly under hand-lights in a warm corner, and then transplant when the plants have made the first pair of rough leaves. After preparing the ground in which they are to be planted, which should be the warmest, driest, and most sheltered available, they may be carefully lifted with as much soil adhering to the roots as possible, and planted in rows 1½ or 2 ft. apart, or in patches, whichever is most practicable ; in either case the plants should be about 6 inches apart. If the planting be done early in the day they may receive a gentle watering to settle the soil round the roots ; if otherwise, it will be better to leave them unwatered until the next morning. All possible protection should then be given them ; if hand-lights be plentiful they are the best, in which case planting in patches should be practised, as the lights can be more easily placed over them ; but small twigs of Laurel or Fir fixed neatly round them answer the purpose in the absence of anything better. Rough hay-bands stretched lengthways over the rows, about 6 or 8 inches from the ground, and firmly secured to stout stakes driven in the ground at each end of the rows, may be employed with advantage. A rough frame, made with sticks driven in the ground and others tied across them to admit of mats, straw hurdles, or any other protecting material being laid upon them at night, is also useful ; but whatever is used to protect them, care must be taken so to place it as to avoid draughts as much as possible. Sowings for this purpose may be made in the beginning of April. If the weather be favourable, the ground in which early Beans are to be grown should be deeply dug and left rather rough. The next day, when the sun is going down, the ground should be again turned over with a fork, in order to turn the warm soil underneath and expose the cold to the next day's sun. If this can be done two or three days consecutively a great advantage will be gained. The last time on which the soil is moved it should be made fine on the top, to prevent the under soil again becoming cold.

When the seed is sown where it is to remain, drills may be drawn with a hoe, 2 ft. apart and 2 inches deep, and sufficiently wide to admit of two rows of Beans being placed 3 or 4 inches apart. The distance from bean to bean in the rows should be 8 or 9 inches. Where, however, seed is no object, they may be sown much thicker, and thinned out to the required distances apart, after they are up, by removing the weakest plants. In any case, a few extra seeds should be thrown in at the ends of the rows to provide for filling up blanks, which often occur in early crops when the ground is cold and wet. The earliest sowing out-of-doors should be made the second or third week in April, if the weather be favourable, otherwise it is better to wait a little longer. It is not advisable to plant very largely for early crops, unless they are wanted in quantity; it will be found better to make two or three small sowings at intervals of a week or ten days during April; after that the principal or main sowings may be made until up to the middle of June, after which time make a few smaller sowings for autumn use. The last sowing should not be later than the end of July, unless protection can be afforded the plants in the autumn. For principal crops the plants should be thinned out to 9 inches or 1 ft. apart in the row, the rows being 2½ or 3 ft. asunder, according to the varieties grown. Earthing-up the row is a point that has been much disputed, some growers being of opinion that it is beneficial, while others think the reverse. For early crops we should, however, strongly recommend earthing-up, as it has a tendency to keep the soil around the roots in a drier, and consequently a warmer, state than it otherwise would be; for the main crops, however, we would recommend rather deeper planting, and heavy mulch-

ings in dry weather in preference to earthing-up. Stopping the points of the shoots is practised by some growers; it is, however, immaterial for general crops, but in the case of early Beans and those grown under glass it is advantageous.

SOIL.—French Beans like a light, rich, sweet soil; therefore if the ground do not already possess these qualities, good rotten manure or leaf-mould should be added. If worms abound, a good dressing of soot or lime should be given; and if this can be done in the winter, and the ground thrown into ridges or roughly dug, it will be all the better. For pots and beds under glass the soil should consist of three-quarters light turfy loam, and one-quarter decomposed manure or leaf-mould. Soil in which Cucumbers have recently been growing will generally answer well for Beans; in all cases a sprinkling of soot amongst it will be found beneficial. We have seen trimmings from the edgings of walks, chopped up and mixed with fresh horse-droppings, used for pot culture with the very best results.

MULCHING AND WATERING.—A good mulching of sea-weed or half-rotted manure from old linings, or litter from Vine borders, applied between the rows of all kinds of Kidney Beans that are grown out-of-doors, will be found beneficial in keeping the soil about the roots in a moist condition, and in promoting a free and luxuriant growth, which is highly necessary to the production of long supplies of fine, tender, and juicy Beans. Copious waterings will be necessary for all kinds of Beans, wherever they are grown, when they are coming into flower, if the weather be dry,—otherwise, instead of the blooms setting, they will fall off. Manure water may also be advantageously applied after they are set, but not before, as it promotes so much growth, which is inimical to bearing. Guano-water may be given to those grown in pots with advan-

D

tage ; but it is no better than good
manure water from the stable-yard,
or that made from cow manure.
Where, however, the latter is used,
a little lime should be previously
dissolved in it, otherwise it has a
tendency to make the soil sour and
breed worms. Water in all cases
should be applied in a tepid state ;
and avoid pouring it close to the
bases of the stems, as they may be
injured by so doing.

CULTURE IN PITS AND FRAMES.—
The method to be adopted for
growing Beans under glass must
necessarily depend upon the nature
of the structures in which they are
to be grown. Where only cold pits
and frames are employed Beans cannot, of course, be obtained during
the winter months, but by a little
attention and skill they may be had
very late in the autumn, and much
earlier in the spring than they can
be obtained in the open air. If
heating material, such as stable
litter and leaves, be plentiful, sowings may be made in pits or frames
early in March. If pits be used,
they should be filled up with
heating material to within 2 ft. of
the glass, firmly treading it down
as the work proceeds. This done,
a layer of rotten manure or leaf-
mould may be spread over the litter
to the thickness of 3 or 4 inches ;
6 or 8 inches of soil may then be
placed on the top, the lights put
on and allowed to remain until the
soil is found to have got warm,
when the beans may be put in
rather thickly, eventually thinning
out so as to leave the plants 6 inches
apart each way. If the soil be dry,
watering will be necessary, but too
much moisture must be avoided at
this season of the year. If a lining
of warm manure can be put round
the pit it will be beneficial to the
growth of the plants. A thick
covering will be necessary at night
to protect the plants from frost.
Where wooden frames or boxes are
used, a good bed of leaves and litter
should be made, and the box should
be placed upon it, building the

lining up round the box to the level
of the lights, as is done in the
case of Cucumbers and Melons. If
treated afterwards as recommended
for pits, the plants will grow rapidly
—*i.e.*, if the weather be at all genial.
When they have made two joints
beyond the seed-leaves, the plants
may be pricked out, in order to
keep them dwarf and sturdy, and
cause them to throw out stronger
side-shoots than they otherwise would
do. If a few small twigs be stuck
in the soil between the plants, they
will not be so liable to get broken.
Abundance of air will be necessary
when the plants are well established,
but it must be given with care, as
a rush of cold air suddenly admitted
would cause the tender foliage to
shrivel, and render the plants worthless. If it be found that too much
steam accumulates in the frame
during the night, it will be necessary
to leave a " crack " of air on. Beans
may be obtained in this way by the
end of May or beginning of June,
and, if properly treated, will yield
a fair supply until the early outdoor
crops come into use. If, however,
there be convenience, another sowing
may be made in the same way a
fortnight later, in order to insure
a supply in the event of any
disaster befalling the first outdoor
crop. Some growers prefer raising
the plants in pots or boxes and
transplanting them into frames, and
where time can be spared this plan
is not without advantages ; others
prefer growing them entirely in
pots, and plunging them in the pits
and frames. Thus managed, they
come into bearing rather sooner, but
they do not generally last so long,
neither is the produce so fine as
from those planted out. Where there
are pits heated by flues or hot-water
pipes, good Beans may be produced
throughout the winter by adopting
the same mode of culture as that
recommended in the case of cold
pits, with the exception that linings
will be unnecessary, neither will
bottom heat be needed ; but where
it is not used, growing in pots

placed upon boards near the glass is preferable to planting out, as the roots are not then surrounded by such a bulk of cold soil. In order to prolong the season, a sowing may be made in August in cold pits or frames; those lately cleared of Melons or Cucumbers will answer perfectly. It is, however, a good plan, previous to sowing, to choose a fine, sunny day, and give the soil a good soaking of water, and to wash well all the wood or brickwork with a syringe, after which close the lights and let the sun have full power on the glass; this will quickly put an end to insects. After sowing, the lights may be left off night and day, until the coldness of the weather necessitates their being put on. A good, warm covering should be afforded during cold nights. By this means a good supply of Beans may be had until late in November, unless the weather be very severe. For this crop stopping the shoots is unnecessary, inasmuch as the plants will continue longer in bearing if left undisturbed.

FORCING KIDNEY BEANS.—Forcing Kidney Beans in November, December, and January is not easy work, as, unless the house in which they are growing is light, airy, and well warmed, the crop can never be a profitable one. In badly heated, damp structures Kidney Beans may be induced to grow, and even bloom, but very few pods will be formed. Warm air alone suits them when in flower during the shortest days, and where this cannot be given freely forcing had better be deferred until February. When the days are lengthening and brightening forcing is easy. I have grown them in beds, in pits, in wooden frames, in boxes, and in pots, and for convenience I prefer and recommend the latter. The seeds may be sown in 3 or 4 inch pots. These should have a few leaves put into the bottom of each; then fill them half-way up with a mixture of sand, loam, and leaf-soil in the proportion of one part of the first and last to two of the loam. When all have been half filled and the soil made firm, six or eight seeds should be put into each; then cover them over with more soil.

As soon as sowing has been finished the whole should be placed in a house or pit, where the temperature ranges from 60° to 70°. Do not give any water until the growths are seen pushing through the soil; then never let them suffer from want of it. When the young plants have attained a height of 4 inches they should be put into their fruiting pots. These should be 8 or 9 inch ones, and, to begin with, they should be properly drained; over the drainage place a layer of leaves or rough pieces of soil. The mixture of soil this time should be substantial; no sand or leaf-soil need form part of it; loam and half-decayed manure should be the sole ingredients. Old Mushroom-bed manure answers well for this purpose, and we prefer it to any other.

The roots should not be disturbed when taken out of the small pots, and three or four of the small potfuls may be put together in one of a larger size. One hundred pots of seedlings may thus be reduced to thirty. Firm potting induces robust and fruitful growth. When potted, they should be again placed in a genial atmosphere, in which they will grow on rapidly and be in bloom from five to six weeks after sowing. Then it will take the pods about a fortnight to swell up, and the crop will be ready for the table in about eight weeks after sowing. As the pots fill with roots, large quantities of water must be given them, and frequent syringing as well, as having the atmosphere in which they are growing humid will prevent the attacks of insects. Red spider and thrips are very fond of indoor Kidney Beans, but both may be checked by water. When potted in good soil, manure water will not be required until the first pods have been formed; then it may be given them in quantity so long as they continue to bear. Sowings made every three weeks until the middle of April will keep up a constant supply of fine fresh pods until those sown outside come in.

Those who wish to keep up a contant supply of forced Beans should sow a quantity every fortnight, beginning in September. We have kept up a fair supply by sowing five dozen potfuls at a time, but this, of course, must be done according to the demand. At times we have placed only one of the small potfuls of young plants in the 8-inch one, but where space was limited we have put three small potfuls into this size. When this can be conveniently done, it is a profitable way of growing Beans, as a great many more are secured from the pots with the most plants than from the others, and the space required for both is about the same.

When in bloom the flowers should be kept as dry as possible, as the fruit forms with more certainty than when the blooms are damp. We never allow any of the growths to fall over the sides of the pots, as this checks them; but when any of them are so tall or weak as not to be able to stand without support, pieces of birch from old brooms are put in to hold them up. As soon as any of the pods become large enough to gather, they should be removed from the plants at once, as there is nothing so much against the production of a long succession of pods from the same plants as allowing some of the first-formed pods to become old. —J. M.

KIDNEY BEANS TO FORCE.—It was generally supposed that the best forcing Beans were Newington Wonder, Sir Joseph Paxton, Early Prolific, Osborn's New Early Forcing. Mr. R. Gilbert then took to forcing Canadian Wonder, and it is likely that a great many more kinds might be forced easily if any more were wanted.

CULTURE IN MARKET GARDENS.

When Peas and Broad Beans begin to get comparatively scarce, French Beans are always welcomed in the London markets. They always command a sale, provided they are good and fresh, and overstocking the market with them is almost a thing unknown; but when large quantities of them are introduced prices are of course affected. Under any conditions, however, and all through the summer, a good crop of Beans is a profitable one, and where soil and situation are at all suitable, market growers cultivate French Beans in large quantities. The principal kinds grown are the Newington Wonder and Long-podded Negro. which, although old varieties, are reckoned to be the best for the market. Their productive qualities are great, for when well attended to as regards timely picking of the pods, they continue fresh, vigorous, and fruitful for a long time, and their pods, as a rule, are less apt to turn tough and unusable with age than is the case with some varieties. The Black Belgian has also found its way into the market gardens; it is a good, dwarf, early sort, much like the Negro, of which it is considered to be a variety. It is very useful for late sowings and for early frame work. Some growers prefer the Newington Wonder to all other sorts; it is a very prolific, dwarf-growing kind. Other growers prefer the Negro, which they grow in frames, for their earliest, main, and latest crops; but most of them also grow the Newington Wonder. The Canadian Wonder or Red Flageolet is one which will doubtless be grown largely for market. It is a robust grower, a good cropper, and its pods are nearly as large as those of a Scarlet Runner and of good quality.

Early crops in market gardens are grown in frames, such as have been cleared of Cauliflower and Lettuce plants; the mould in the frames is pointed over with a spade, and the beans are sown in four rows under each light, and about 3 or 4 inches from seed to seed in the row, when the soil is dry. The middle of March is the common time for sowing in frames, and then the sashes are kept close till the seeds have germinated, when they are tilted up a little at the back in favourable weather; but care is always taken to keep them close in the case of cold winds, and to cover them over with mats or litter in the event of frost. As the plants advance they are treated more hardily, but judiciously, according to the weather. After the middle of May, when all fear of frost has passed, the sashes are entirely drawn off throughout the day, if fine, and replaced at night. Whilst growing, plenty of water is given them at the roots, and picking commences about the second or third week in June, or about three weeks sooner than the earliest border crops come into use. A few frames, too, are also frequently occupied by French Beans sown thickly, for the purpose of transplanting thence to the open ground, and to fill any blanks that may exist in the frames in which the sowings for fruiting therein have been made.

The first outdoor crop is usually transplanted from such frames, and the warmest possible position is selected for this purpose; the time for so doing entirely depends on the state of the weather and nature of the ground. If the weather be fine, the soil moderately dry and light, and the position warm and sheltered, the plants are commonly transplanted during the first fortnight of April, but if otherwise, they are delayed a little later. They are then lifted with as much earth adhering to their roots as possible, and are planted in little patches under hand-lights. The usual way is to draw lines 3 ft. apart across the border, others $2\frac{1}{2}$ ft. asunder lengthways, and upon the middle of every little square thus marked place an ordinary hand-light,

under which place six or eight plants. If there be not sufficient hand-lights for the whole space to be planted, half-bushel vegetable baskets are inverted over the plants; and, as they are so open to the wind, they are sometimes covered for a time with mats. As soon as the Beans have got a good hold of the soil and begun to grow, their protection is removed. Great care must be exercised with hand-light Beans, otherwise they are a deceptive crop, and sometimes die off altogether, especially when nursed too tenderly and changed too suddenly, if the ground be cold and wet, and their top covering insufficient. Those grown in frames, and which come into bearing early in June, last in good picking condition for six weeks; and those in warm borders begin to fruit in the last week of June or first week in July, and continue to yield a fair crop for nearly two months in a moderately moist season, if kept closely picked. The first main crop immediately follows the border ones, and, as a rule, lasts the longest. Drought makes them short-lived sometimes, but in rich soils, and warm, moist seasons, the yield is so heavy that it is scarcely possible to pick them as quickly as they grow. Drought, too, induces red spider, with which large fields are sometimes completely overrun; and although this pest is very prejudicial to the health and longevity of the crop, there is no remedy for it.

French Beans are gross feeders; they require manurial substances of such a character as can be speedily turned to account; therefore, land that was richly manured for the previous crop—such as for Celery— and which has afterwards again been liberally dressed with short manure, such as that from Mushroom beds or old Cucumber pits, suits them perfectly. The crop to succeed such as are grown under hand-lights is planted on a south border, in front of a wall or thick hedge if possible, which is dug over and lined off in cross-rows at 18 inches apart, drawing the lines in the form of seed-furrows with a hoe. Herein are planted beans 5 inches asunder in the row ; they are earthed-up in due time, and, if the weather be favourable, come into bearing three weeks after those grown in frames. Some growers erect barricades of mats in an upright position to stakes driven in the earth, and placed to the windward side of the borders; and they also surround frames containing them, but not covered with sashes, with the same protection to ward off cold and frosty winds.

Out - of - door sowing begins during the first fortnight in April, just as the state of the weather and soil permits, and the warmest available position is selected for the purpose. If the ground be free from all other crops at the time of sowing, there is more need for a sheltered place than if it were cropped. In sowing, the lines are drawn at 2, $2\frac{1}{2}$, and sometimes at 3 ft. apart, and the seeds planted about 4 or 5 inches asunder. The earliest crop is often sown in drills drawn between lines of Cauliflowers, Cabbages, or Lettuces. These crops, instead of being injurious to the French Beans when they appear above ground, are very beneficial to them, inasmuch as they protect them from cold winds until they have gained some strength and the weather becomes mild and warm, by which time the bulk of the Cauliflowers will have been removed for market. Even then, however, the Beans do not get all the space to themselves, for no sooner is the earth cleared of the other crop, than it is loosened a little between every alternate line, and those spaces replanted with Lettuces or similar crops. Thus one space contains another catch crop while the other is empty ; and by means of having this empty space to walk in, the women can pick two lines of Beans, one on either side of the empty alley, and never disturb the other crops in the alternate alleys. Should the French Beans have come up well, and be nearly ready for picking before the first occupants

of the soil are entirely removed, the alleys are not cropped again until they become exhausted. The drills for sowing are drawn in the morning of a fine day and left until the afternoon, when seeds are sown and some earth drawn over them.

The first main sowing is made in the open fields about the second or third week in April, under the same circumstances as that already mentioned, or the field may have been previously planted out with Cos Lettuces in lines 12, 15, or 18 inches apart ; between every two lines of these would be sown one of Beans. Along both sides of Asparagus ridges Beans also often find a place. Some growers sow late crops in rows 4 ft. apart, and plant two rows of Coleworts in every intervening alley. Before the seeds appear the soil immediately over the seeds is gone over and slightly loosened with an iron-toothed rake, so as to permit of an easy egress of the seedlings. When sown in bare fields, even though Lettuces be planted amongst them, a little ridge of soil is frequently drawn to the north or windward side of them as an additional protection from cold winds. Whilst the plants are growing they are rigidly attended to as regards keeping them clean and hoeing the soil, and when they reach 4 inches in height they are earthed up a little. The catch crops, too, are cleared away as soon as they are ready, in order to give the French Beans every opportunity of a healthy development. Successive sowings are made every fortnight or three weeks, until the end of June, by some, but most of the large growers sow about the 8th and 20th of April, the first and last week in May, and the first week in July. The last sowing consists of the Negro, and just yields a good crop of young and fine pods before being destroyed by frost ; whereas, were they sown a fortnight later, they would be apt to be nipped when coming into bloom.

Gathering is well attended to,

for if full-grown pods be allowed to remain too long on the plants they soon cease to bear. The Beans are gathered by women into baskets, which, when full, they carry on their heads to the ends of the rows, there to leave them to be carted home, where they are washed to remove the grit. They are then packed into round half-bushel vegetable baskets, which are covered with Rhubarb leaves fastened down with withies, and piled one above another on the waggons that convey them to market three times a week. Most market gardeners save their own seed, and a piece of the main sowing is generally selected for this purpose. The plants in the rows to be saved for seed are first subjected to two or three pickings for market; then they are left untouched until the beans are fully ripe, when the plants are pulled up by the roots, tied into little bunches, and slung in pairs across a fence or rail to dry. Sometimes, too, the haulm is spread over sashes to dry, and, in the event of wet weather, is strewed under some spare sashes, where it gets well dried without getting wet. They are then housed, and during wintry weather are threshed, cleaned, and stored in rough brown paper or canvas bags, or placed in drawers, or in the corner of a loft, until sowing time arrives.

USES.—The young and tender pods of many kinds are eaten boiled. Every one knows the use which is made in cookery of the seeds or beans, either when dried or when gathered before they are quite ripe, but when the pods can just be opened without difficulty. And lastly, the Edible-podded or *Mange-tout* varieties are used from the time the seeds begin to swell until they are quite ripe. We heartily wish that English housekeepers and gardeners would look into the qualities of many of the fine varieties described in this book. Apart from the greater variety of valuable kinds of the types they know so well, two very valuable series deserve attention—those of which the pods may be eaten when large and mature, and the Flageolet kinds, which are very little used with us.

TOUGH-PODDED KIDNEY BEANS.

French, Haricots à écosser. *Italian,* Fagiuoli da sgusciare.

I. TALL-GROWING VARIETIES.

Variétés à rames.

Soissons Large Runner Bean (*Haricot de Soissons à Rames*).—A plant with a slender green stem, growing 6½ ft. high or something more. Leaves pretty large, at wide intervals from each other; leaflets moderately crimped, rounded at the base, of a dark and slightly yellowish-green colour; lower leaves larger than the upper ones; flowers white, passing into yellow; pods green, but turning yellowish when ripe, broad, somewhat curved, and generally irregular in shape, owing to the unequal growth of the seeds, which are seldom more than four in number, and are white, kidney-shaped, and more or less humpy or round-backed; they are nearly 1 inch long, about ½ inch broad, and nearly ¼ inch thick. The litre-weighs about 720 grammes, and 100 grammes contain about 120 seeds. They are late in ripening. The dried seeds of this variety are highly esteemed for their delicate flavour and the thinness of the skin. The plant is found to succeed in the greatest perfection in its native district, where it most probably enjoys conditions of soil and climate which are specially favourable

to it; but, when grown under a warmer sky, it sometimes suffers from the heat—the skin of the seed becomes thickened, and the seed loses its fine quality, and also degenerates in size and colour.

Large White Liancourt Kidney Bean (*Haricot de Liancourt*). — Stem green, slender, tall, reaching a height of from 7 to nearly 10 ft.; leaves large, of a rather dark green, not quite so much crimped as those of the preceding kind, the upper ones much smaller than the lower ones; flowers white, turning yellow after impregnation; pods longer and narrower than those of the last-mentioned variety, slightly curved, each containing about five or six flat, slightly kidney-shaped seeds, rather irregular in form, like those of the Large White Runner (but of a dull or dead white, while the seeds of the latter variety glisten like porcelain), about $\frac{3}{4}$ inch long, a little over $\frac{1}{4}$ inch broad, and less than

Soissons Large Runner Bean ($\frac{1}{12}$ natural size).

$\frac{1}{4}$ inch thick. The litre weighs 750 grammes, and 100 grammes contain about 190 seeds. This is a rather hardy, strong-growing, productive, and half-late variety, and is chiefly grown for the ripe dried seeds.

Round White Rice Runner Kidney Bean (*Haricot Riz à Rames*). —A variety of moderate height, seldom exceeding about 5 ft., and sometimes not much over 4 ft. Stem very slender, of a light-green colour; leaves medium sized, elongated, pointed, not much crimped, and of a clear green colour; flowers white; pods green, narrow, very numerous, especially at the lower parts of the stems, where they often grow in clusters of fours or fives, while hardly any are produced near the tops of the stems; seeds five or six in each pod, nearly round, with a very smooth, thin, almost transparent skin, and not much over $\frac{1}{4}$ inch in diameter. The litre weighs 830 grammes, and 100 grammes contain about 700 seeds. This variety presents an appearance so peculiar and so different from that of most other kinds, that it might be readily supposed to be derived from a distinct botanical species, were it not that its flowers exactly resemble those of other Kidney Beans. It branches and spreads more than the majority of tall-growing varieties, forming a clump nearly 2 ft. wide, with weak, slender stems, which do not exhibit much of the climbing character. The seeds are so small and so peculiar in shape that it is difficult at first sight to imagine that they belong to a plant of the same species as the two last mentioned. However, as the pods are produced in very great numbers, the plant is productive enough. The dried seeds are of an exceedingly good and delicate quality, with a very thin skin, which seems to dissolve in cooking, on which account they are highly esteemed. The only defect which can be ascribed to the plant is that the pods are very liable to rot in wet seasons, when they trail to the ground before they are quite ripe.

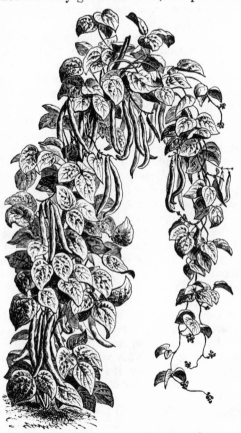

White Dutch, Scimitar, or Case-knife Bean
(1/12 natural size).

White Dutch, Scimitar, or Case-knife Bean (*Haricot Sabre à Rames*).—A very vigorous-growing kind, nearly 10 ft. in height. Stem thick and green; leaves very large, deep green, crimped; flowers large, white, fading to nankeen yellow, and forming long clusters; pods straight, sometimes undulating on the sides, 10 inches to 1 ft. long, containing eight or nine seeds each, numerous, produced in succession for a long time, especially when the first have been gathered green; seeds white, glistening, kidney-shaped, very like those of the Large White Runner, but more regular in shape and one-third less in size, seldom $\frac{3}{5}$ inch in length. The litre weighs 715 grammes, and 100 grammes contain about 245 seeds. They ripen rather late. The young pods may be used as green Haricots. The seed or bean, when used fresh from the pod, is one of the best; it is also very good when dried. This is certainly one of the best varieties; the only objection to it is that it requires very long stakes when growing. The Germans cultivate a great number of sub-varieties of it, characterized chiefly by having broader and straighter pods; but, notwithstanding numerous trials, we have never found any of them to surpass or even equal the variety here described; it is the most tender for use and also the most productive.

Dwarf White Long-pod Kidney Bean (*Haricot Blanc à Longue*

Cosse, à Demi-rames).—A plant 4 to 5 ft. high; leaves of medium size, smooth, of a clear green colour; flowers large, white; pods exceedingly numerous, very straight and long, and nearly cylindrical, of a fine green colour, passing into yellow when ripe; seed oblong, nearly as thick as broad, nearly ¾ inch long, ¼ inch broad, and nearly ¼ inch thick; skin exceedingly thin, almost transparent, in consequence of which the seed, instead of being pure white, is of a faint salmon colour. The litre weighs 790 grammes, and 100 grammes contain about 240 seeds. This variety, which requires only very short stakes, can be highly recommended for the production of green Haricots—perhaps there is no other kind which yields such fine young pods, and it has this advantage over dwarfer varieties, that the pods, growing higher on the stem, are not liable to trail on the ground and rot. The seeds are equally good when dried. They ripen tolerably early.

Chartres Red Kidney Bean (*Haricot Rouge de Chartres*).—This kind is very extensively used for field culture. It requires hardly any staking, as the plant is of compact growth and seldom more than between 3 and 4 ft. in height. Leaves of average size, of a fine green colour, and slightly crimped; flowers white or yellowish, pretty large; pods 4 or 5 inches long, slightly curved, each containing about five or six flat, short seeds, which are often square at one or both ends, of a deep wine-lees-red colour, and having an almost black circle around the *hilum;* their average length is about ½ inch, breadth a little over ¼ inch, and thickness less than ¼ inch. The litre weighs 765 grammes, and 100 grammes contain about 300 seeds. They ripen early. The seeds are almost entirely used in the dried state, and the variety is almost exclusively grown in the fields.

Partridge-Eye Kidney Bean (*Haricot Œil de Perdrix*).—A plant of medium height, with, lank, slender stems, and lilac flowers. Pods short and flat, each containing four or five seeds, which are flat, shortly oval, or almost square, and of a white colour finely streaked with greenish gray. This variety has been a long time in existence, but, being a poor bearer, it is very little grown.

There are many other Tall-growing varieties of Kidney Beans in cultivation, of which we shall only mention the following, as being very distinct and of special interest in various respects.

Harlequin Kidney Bean (*Haricot Arlequin*).—A tall-growing, rather late-ripening kind, with long, crimped leaves. Pods numerous, short, and curved; seeds very flat, oblong, scarcely kidney-shaped, coffee-coloured, and irregularly streaked and furrowed with black lines. It is a hardy and productive variety, and may be often seen in the Central Market at Paris.

Giant-podded Kidney Bean (*Haricot à Cosses Géantes*).—A very distinct kind, although evidently allied to the White Dutch or Case-knife Bean, from which it differs in having longer, narrower, and somewhat less stringy pods. It is also allied to the Edible Long-pod (*Haricot Mange-tout à Longues Cosses*), and thus forms a connecting link between the Tough-podded and the Edible-podded varieties.

Soissons Red Kidney Bean (*Haricot Rouge de Soissons*).—A tall, rather slender-stemmed variety, not overburdened with leaves. Pods long, slightly curved, and rather narrow; seeds nearly the same shape as those of the White Dutch or Case-knife Bean, and of a brilliant coral colour just before ripening, after which they assume a wine-lees red tint. This handsome kind is tolerably early, but only moderately productive.

Saint-Seurin Kidney Bean (*Haricot Saint-Seurin*).—A very vigorous and rapidly growing kind, with very large, broad, deep-green leaves, and lilac flowers. Pods very numerous, almost straight, marked when very young with violet-coloured streaks; seeds flat, kidney-shaped, salmon colour, marbled and spotted with black. It is a hardy, very productive, and early variety, and is particularly well adapted for rather warm climates.

II. DWARF VARIETIES OF TOUGH-PODDED KIDNEY BEANS.

Variétés naines (à écosser).

Dwarf White Flageolet, or White Canterbury (*Haricot Flageolet Blanc*).—This is the best known and most universally esteemed of the Tough-podded Kidney Beans. Not only has its name been extended to different varieties which approach it more or less closely, but it has been also applied to the seeds in the condition in which they are generally eaten, that is, when shelled just before they are ripe. It is a low-growing, thick-set variety, with a stout stem, not more than 1 ft. or 14 inches high; leaves smoothish or slightly pitted, of medium size, and of a deep-green colour; flowers white, with a faint tinge of nankeen yellow; pods numerous, rather flat and somewhat curved, and frequently irregular in breadth through the abortion of some of the seeds. These, usually four or five in a pod, are white, rather flat, and kidney-shaped, nearly ¾ inch long, over ¼ inch broad, and less than ¼ inch thick. A litre of them weighs 770 grammes, and 100 grammes contain about 350 seeds. In cases where only one variety of Kidney Bean can be cultivated, a better selection cannot be made than this one, for the young pods may be gathered and used as green Haricots, and the seeds can also be used either dried or fresh from the pod ; they are best, however, when fresh.

Dwarf White Long-pod Kidney Bean (*Haricot Flageolet Blanc à Longue Cosse*).—A remarkably vigorous variety, taller than the Common Flageolet, with thick, straight, erect stems. The pods are longer and straighter than those of the preceding variety, and, instead of being pendent, grow erect, which prevents them from trailing on the ground, as is usually the case with Dwarf Kidney Beans. While young, they are excellent as Haricots, and when ripe they yield a plentiful supply of beans for table use. This Bean is nearly as early as the Extra Early Dwarf Étampes Bean (*Haricot Flageolet très Hâtif d'Étampes*), and grows a little taller than that variety. It is a highly useful Kidney Bean.

Early Dwarf White Dutch Kidney Bean (*Haricot Nain Hâtif de Hollande, H. de Flandre*).—This is, properly speaking, merely a sub-variety of the White Flageolet, from which it is only distinguished by being a little dwarfer, by the leaves being a little more wrinkled, and by being a day or two earlier. These peculiarities cause it to be generally preferred for forcing under a frame ; but the differences are so trifling that the two kinds are often taken one for the other. A litre of the seeds weighs 775 grammes, and 100 grammes contain about 350 seeds.

Bonnemain Dwarf Kidney Bean (*Haricot Bonnemain*).—This is quite a new variety, recently raised from seed by M. Bonnemain, secretary of the Étampes Horticultural Society, and we class it among the Flageolets because it resembles them in dwarfness, earliness, and the white colour of the seeds; but it is totally distinct from all the other varieties, and this is seen at a glance. It forms very low-growing, thick-set clumps, with leaves of a pale grayish-green colour and white flowers; pods straight, almost cylindrical, comparatively short, and more slender than those of the Kidney Bean; seeds white, of an elongated egg-shape, thicker, and with less of the kidney outline than those of the White Flageolet. They are green until they ripen. The litre weighs 850 grammes, and 100 grammes contain about 480 seeds. The

Bonnemain Dwarf Kidney Bean (plant, ⅛; pods, ¼; and seed, full natural size).

great merit of this variety consists in its unequalled earliness, the seeds being ripe for shelling five or six days sooner than those of the Early Étampes Flageolet, which hitherto was considered the earliest kind of all. We have obtained very satisfactory results from growing the Bonnemain Kidney Bean in the open air, while its dwarfness and remarkable earliness render it a most suitable subject for frame culture. It is certain to become one of the most esteemed varieties for producing an early crop.

Extra Early Dwarf Étampes Kidney Bean (*Haricot Flageolet très Hâtif d'Étampes*). This new variety, which, like the preceding one, was raised by M. Bonnemain, is a decided improvement on

Extra Early Dwarf Étampes Kidney Bean (⅛ natural size).

the White Flageolet, and is distinguished from it in a marked degree by the appearance of its leaves, which are large, somewhat crimped,

and of a deep-green colour. The flowers, pods, and seeds do not perceptibly diffe from those of the White Flageolet, but the plant is earlier
by five or six days, and is a truly valuable variety, most probably
destined to gradually supersede the other in cultivation. The seeds
are white, even while the pods are green, and a litre of them weighs on
an average about 820 grammes, 100 grammes containing about 350
seeds.

Nettle - leaved Canterbury Kidney Bean (*Haricot Flageolet à
Feuille Gaufrée*). This variety is very distinct from the Common
White Flageolet, and is a dwarf,
hardy, early, and productive kind,
easily recognized by its leaves,
which are small, of a dark, almost
blackish, green colour, and finely
crimped on their entire surface.
A litre of the seeds weighs 800
grammes, and 100 grammes contain about 240 seeds. The dwarfness of this plant renders it very
suitable for frame culture, while
its hardiness causes it to be equally
well adapted for field cultivation,
the manner in which it is usually
grown about Paris. It ripens
nearly at the same time as the

Nettle-leaved Canterbury Kidney Bean
(⅓ natural size).

White Flageolet, and its chief merit consists in its capacity of
resisting disease and unfavourable weather, and in its being easily
distinguished by its foliage from all other varieties.

Long Green-seeded Flageolet Bean (*Haricot Flageolet à Grain
Vert*).—A sub-variety of the White Flageolet which has this peculiarity—that its seeds retain a green tinge even when ripe. Seeds
which possess this tinge always command a somewhat higher market
price than white ones, but the mode of gathering and drying has as
much to do with the preservation of the colour as the selection of the
variety grown for this purpose. A litre of the seeds weighs 770
grammes, and 100 grammes contain about 370 seeds. We may expect
to see this variety superseded by the following one.

Chevrier Dwarf Flageolet Bean (*Haricot Chevrier*).—This variety,
which is as yet little known, evidently belongs to the Flageolet group,
but it constitutes a very distinct and strikingly marked variety, from
the intense green colour which the plant presents in all its parts. Even
when ripe, the pods remain green exteriorly, the stems are of the same
colour, and, what is more important, the seeds have a very pronounced
green tinge. A litre of the seeds weighs 800 grammes, and 100
grammes contain about 380 seeds. In its habit of growth, this kind
differs but little from the White Flageolet, but the colour of its seeds
renders it a most interesting new variety. Every one knows how much
importance is attached to greenness of colour in the various preparations of Haricots, and especially in the preserved seeds. In this respect,
it is certain that the Chevrier Kidney Bean will be particularly valuable, for there is no doubt that its seeds remain very green when

cooked, the colouring matter not being confined to the surface merely, but extending all through the interior of the seed.

Wonder of France Dwarf Haricot Bean (*Haricot Merveille de France*).—A truly dwarf, but very vigorous-growing and branching

variety, remarkable for the size and robustness of its leaves. Flowers white, like those of the Flageolet Bean; pods very green, long, straight, and well filled; seeds or beans flat, slightly kidney-shaped, a little more so than those of the Chevrier Haricot. They become white if allowed to ripen and dry completely on the growing plant, but it is easy to harvest them entirely green by a little management. A remarkable peculiarity of this variety is that the plant loses all its leaves as soon as the pods are well filled and begin to wither. If the plants are then pulled up and placed in heaps or "stooks" in the shade, the beans will ripen without becoming white, but will continue to preserve a very decided green colour, which does not disappear even when they are cooked. This excellent variety was raised by M. Bonnemain, to whom we are indebted for several other good varieties of vegetables, the Extra Early Étampes Flageolet Bean being amongst the number.

Wonder of France Dwarf Haricot Bean.

Long Yellow, or **Pale Dun**, **Flageolet Bean** (*Haricot Flageolet Jaune*).—A vigorous-growing and very dwarf variety, about 18 inches high, with large broad leaves of a slightly grayish-green colour, somewhat plaited but not much crimped. Flowers white; pods large, long, straight, and broad, capable of being used as green Haricots, although they are of a rather pale colour; seeds oblong, very slightly kidney-shaped, about $\frac{3}{4}$ inch long, a little over $\frac{1}{4}$ inch broad, and about the same thickness, of a uniform chamois colour, with the exception of the *hilum*, which is white, surrounded by a circle of a rather dark-brown colour. A litre of the seeds weighs 775 grammes, and 100 grammes contain about 220 seeds. The seeds are most commonly eaten fresh, before they are fully grown, and they ripen somewhat earlier than those of the white-seeded kind. The plant is also much more productive.

Dwarf Canadian Wonder Kidney Bean (*Haricot Flageolet Rouge*. American, *Red, or Scarlet, Flageolet*).—A vigorous-growing kind, about the same height as the preceding one, but of a much darker green colour, with long, narrow, pointed leaves and rosy-white flowers. Pods long and straight, yielding very good green Haricots; seeds $\frac{3}{4}$ inch or more long, over $\frac{1}{4}$ inch broad, and about $\frac{1}{4}$ inch thick, straight, or slightly kidney-shaped, nearly cylindrical, and of a wine-lees red colour. A litre of them weighs 775 grammes, and 100 grammes contain about 155 seeds. This variety is one of the hardiest and most productive. It is chiefly grown for the sake of its seeds, which are of a remarkably good quality when dried. It also produces fine long straight pods, which make excellent green Haricots.

Negro Long-pod Kidney Bean (*Haricot Flageolet Noir*).—This is a very distinct variety, and one of the best for yielding green Haricots. Leaves large, not much crimped, of a deep-green colour, usually spreading horizontally and not pendent; flowers lilac; pods slender, very straight, and nearly cylindrical. The plant is particularly remarkable for the length of the young pods. The seeds are of moderate size, being between $\frac{1}{2}$ and $\frac{3}{4}$ inch long, and nearly $\frac{1}{4}$ inch broad and thick; they are entirely black, on which account they are not used in cookery, and the plant is only grown for the sake of the green pods. A litre of the seeds weighs 770 grammes, and 100 grammes contain about 280 seeds.

Dwarf Belgian Kidney Bean (*Haricot Noir Hâtif de Belgique*).— A very dwarf early kind, chiefly used for forcing under a frame. When

grown true to name, it seldom exceeds 10 inches or 1 ft. in height, and forms a small, close, compact tuft or clump. The leaves are of medium size, rather pointed, not much crimped, and of a pale wan green colour. Pods straight, very green while young, afterwards becoming slightly streaked with violet; seeds rather small, slightly kidney-shaped, and not much flattened, seldom over about $\frac{1}{2}$ inch long, of a fine black

Dwarf Belgian Kidney Bean
($\frac{1}{8}$ natural size).

colour, with a white *hilum*. A litre of them weighs 765 grammes, and 100 grammes contain about 430 seeds. Like the preceding variety, this, on account of the colour of its seeds, is only grown for the sake of the green pods.

Chocolate Dwarf Kidney Bean (*Haricot Chocolat*).—Another very dwarf and early kind, with small elongated leaves, not much crimped, and of a light-green colour. Flowers lilac; pods rather short, and curved to a remarkable degree, often to a semicircle; seeds flat, somewhat kidney-shaped, $\frac{1}{2}$ inch or more long, varying from a chamois colour to a deep slaty-gray, and often showing both colours together. A litre of them weighs 770 grammes, and 100 grammes contain about 330 seeds. This variety is chiefly remarkable for its earliness, and is well adapted for growing under a frame for an early crop of ripe seeds.

The Comte de Vougy Kidney Bean (*Haricot Comte de Vougy*), Mohawk (*A. Mohawk*), and the Dwarf Free-bearer (*H. Nain d'Abondance*), which are now seldom grown, are closely allied to the Chocolate Kidney Bean. They are, however, not so early, and, on that account, not so desirable.

Early Dwarf Chalindrey Kidney Bean (*Haricot Nain Jaune Hâtif de Chalindrey*).—An exceedingly dwarf and early variety, forming a compact clump seldom over 10 inches high. Leaves small, elongated, and of a lively green colour; flowers rose-coloured or pale lilac; pods slender, longish, and slightly curved; seeds small, almost cylindrical, with very little of the kidney shape, about ½ inch long, and of a light mahogany-brown colour. A litre of them weighs 810 grammes, and 100 grammes contain about 330 seeds. This kind is almost as early as the Étampes Flageolet, and is especially well adapted for forcing. Both green Haricots and fresh seeds may be obtained from it.

Royal Dwarf White Kidney Bean (*Haricot Suisse Blanc*).—Under the name of "Swiss Kidney Beans (*Haricots Suisses*) are grouped a certain number of varieties which are almost identical in habit of growth, and present hardly any difference except in the colour of the seed. In Italy these varieties are named *Fagiuoli cannellini*, and at Bordeaux they are known under the general name of *Haricot Capucine*. Almost all of them have a bad habit of sending out, above the leaves and flowers, a slender stem, of greater or less length, which never bears any pods, and never exhibits any tendency to twine itself round a support. The variety which we are now describing sometimes manifests this drawback, but, on the other hand, it possesses some very good qualities, especially great productiveness and hardiness, which render it very suitable for field culture. It has large and very rough leaves, of a dark-green colour, and sometimes finely crimped; flowers large and white;

pods long and numerous, each containing five or six seeds, which are white, straight, almost cylindrical, often flattened at one end (whence its French name of *Haricot Lingot*). They are usually about ¾ inch long, and something over ¼ inch in breadth and thickness. They can be eaten in the dried state, but the skin is rather thick. A litre of them weighs 800 grammes, and 100 grammes contain about 225 seeds.

A few years since, a variety was raised which is free from the objectionable habit of growth alluded to above, and

Black Speckled Kidney Bean (⅛ natural size).

which will, no doubt, in time, completely supersede the old one.

Black Speckled Kidney Bean (*Haricot Bagnolet*).—This kind is one of those which are most extensively grown about Paris, for the production of green Haricots. As a general rule, it does not exhibit the objectionable habit of growth alluded to in the description of the preceding variety, and, in this respect, it is superior to most of the Swiss Kidney Beans. It grows 14 to 16 inches high, and has large, deep-green leaves, not much crimped, and lilac flowers; pods straight, long, very green, and, when young, almost cylindrical; seeds straight, long, rounded at both ends, nearly as thick as broad, of a blackish-violet colour variegated with nankeen yellow streaks on about one-third of their surface, these markings being sometimes reduced to a few light-coloured spots on a nearly black ground. A litre of them weighs 755 grammes, and 100 grammes contain about 235 seeds. There is also a white-seeded variety, which is identical in all other respects.

Dwarf Red Speckled Kidney Bean (*Haricot Suisse Rouge*).—A vigorous-growing, branching variety, which does not usually produce the objectionable stem before mentioned. Leaves stiff, not very large or numerous, smooth, and of a slightly grayish-green colour; flowers lilac or rose coloured; seeds elongated, nearly straight, marbled with spots of a wine-lees-red colour, which are sometimes elongated and form longitudinal streaks on a pale-red ground. A litre of them weighs 780 grammes, and 100 grammes contain about 200 seeds. This is a very productive kind, and the dried seeds are much esteemed.

Dwarf Blood-speckled Kidney Bean (*Haricot Suisse Sang de Bœuf*).—This variety bears a most striking resemblance to the preceding one, both in habit and foliage. The flowers are of a pale-rose colour; seeds similar in shape to those of the Black Speckled Kidney Bean, but of a deep-red colour, dotted with white or salmon colour. A litre of them weighs 780 grammes, and 100 grammes contain about 180 seeds. For some years past, this variety has often been called "the Indian Kidney Bean" (*Haricot Indien*). Its dried seeds are sent in very considerable quantities to the Central Market at Paris.

Dwarf Light Dun-coloured Kidney Bean (*Haricot Suisse Ventre de Biche*).—A vigorous-growing variety, forming strong clumps, and not producing the objectionable stem of the Swiss Kidney Beans, but sometimes bearing clusters of pods above the foliage. The leaves are large, slightly crimped, and of a somewhat grayish-green colour; pods long, straight, nearly cylindrical, each containing five or six seeds, which are over $\frac{3}{4}$ inch long, about $\frac{1}{3}$ inch broad, and over $\frac{1}{4}$ inch thick, of a light chamois colour, becoming darker with age, and quite brown around the *hilum*, which is surrounded by a circle of still deeper brown, as in the Yellow Flageolet or Pale Dun Kidney Bean. A litre of them weighs 755 grammes, and 100 grammes contain about 220 seeds. This kind is much employed for field culture, and its dried seeds are of some value.

Besides the varieties of Swiss Kidney Beans which we have just described, the following also are in cultivation:—The Large Gray Swiss (*H. Suisse Gros Gris*), the seed of which is yellowish-white, streaked with black; the Bourvalais Swiss (*H. Suisse Bourvalais*), with white seed marbled with light violet; the Red Ingot (*H. Lingot Rouge*), the seed of which is paler than that of the Long Spotted French Bean and not marbled. Among the Swiss Kidney Beans may also be included the variety named the Giant Dwarf (*H. Nain Gigantesque*), which is remarkable for the width of its leaves and the length of its pods; but, in cultivation, it is now superseded by the improved variety of the Royal Dwarf White Kidney Bean (*H. Suisse Blanc*).

Sion House Dwarf Kidney Bean (*Haricot Turc*).—This is a variety for field culture, and is hardy, early, and productive. Leaves numerous, of medium size, slightly puckered, and of a rather deep-green colour; flowers rose-coloured or lilac; pods long and straight. The shape

E

of the seed resembles that of the Swiss Kidney Beans, but the colour is similar to that of the Cranberry Bean (*H. de Prague Marbré*), namely, flesh colour finely dotted with light red or lilac. A litre of them weighs 740 grammes, and 100 grammes contain about 245 seeds. Although true enough to its dwarf character, this kind forms less compact clumps than the Swiss Kidney Beans, and the stems are usually elongated and semi-trailing. It is not very particular about the quality of the soil in which it is grown, and requires very little attention, on which account it is one of the kinds which are most frequently sown in vineyards or amongst other crops.

Solitary Prolific Kidney Bean, or **Bush Haricot** (*Haricot Solitaire*).—A very branching plant, which forms a strong clump, does not produce the objectionable stem of the Swiss Kidney Beans, and attains a height of 16 to 20 inches. Leaves rather small, very numerous, long, pointed, and of a deep-green colour; flowers pale lilac. The seed somewhat resembles that of the Black Speckled Kidney Bean, but is much smaller, being seldom more than ½ inch long, or a little longer, and is of a more pronounced violet colour. A litre of them weighs 775 grammes, and 100 grammes contain about 315 seeds. The chief merit of this variety is that it forms a strong clump and branches very much, in consequence of which some cultivators sow each seed separately, instead of putting several into the same hole or pocket; hence its French name—*Haricot Solitaire.*

Russian Dwarf Kidney Bean (*Haricot Russe*).—A very good dwarf variety, equal to any other for producing green Haricots. The plant is a very vigorous grower, with exceedingly broad leaves, finely crimped, and of a dark and rather dull-green colour. Flowers lilac; pods very straight, and remarkably long and handsome. The seed, which in shape and colour has some resemblance to that of the Dwarf Light Dun-coloured Kidney Bean, exhibits a peculiarity by which it is easily distinguished from all other kinds, namely, the dull appearance of the skin, which is totally devoid of the glistening and varnished-like aspect presented by the seeds of all other varieties of Kidney Beans. A litre of them weighs 770 grammes, and 100 grammes contain about 200 seeds. There is a sub-variety of this plant which has small black seeds, and produces pods that are perhaps longer and more cylindrical than those of the ordinary kind. There are often six, or even seven, seeds in a pod, and as each seed is nearly ¾ inch long, and lies in the pod at some distance from the seed which is next to it, the length of the pods is easily accounted for.

Spread-Eagle, or **Dove, Kidney Bean** (*Haricot Saint-Esprit, H. à la Religieuse, H. à l'Aigle*).—Another dwarf tough-podded variety, which appears to belong to the section of the Swiss Kidney Beans, and grows to the height of 16 inches or more. Leaves of a clear green colour, broad, elongated, and finely crimped; flowers white, and rather large; pods straight and longish; seed very full, moderately kidney-shaped, and quite white, except near the *hilum*, where it is marked with a black or brown blotch, the outline of which has some resemblance to that of a bird with extended wings. Some have thought this most like an eagle, others a dove; hence its most common names of " Spread-Eagle " and " Dove " Kidney Beans.

Dwarf Soissons Kidney Bean (*Haricot de Soissons Nain*).—A variety which is true to its dwarf character, and also early, but only a moderate bearer. Plant low-growing and thick-set. Leaves rather broad, smooth, and of a dark glistening-green colour. It does not produce the objectionable stem of the Swiss Kidney Beans, but clusters of pods are sometimes borne above the foliage. Pods usually curved and of irregular width, owing to the unequal growth of the seeds, which are much smaller than those of the Large White Runner, and are more like those of the Liancourt Kidney Bean, being white, rather flat, and moderately kidney-shaped. A litre of them weighs 740 grammes, and 100 grammes contain about 260 seeds.

Dwarf Early White Scimitar Kidney Bean (*Haricot Sabre Nain Hâtif de Hollande*).—This very distinct and valuable variety differs completely from the old Dwarf Case-knife (*H. Sabre Nain*), which is now no longer culti-vated. It is a low-growing and very thick-set plant, with broad leaves, slightly crimped, and of a dark lustrous green colour. Flowers white; pods long, broad, straight, and well filled. The plant comes into flower almost about the same time as the White Flageolet, and its earliness, and also the fineness of its seeds, render it a valuable kind for forcing under a frame. The seeds are broad and well filled, nearly

Dwarf Early White Scimitar Kidney Bean
(⅓ natural size).

¾ inch long, over ⅓ inch broad, and ¼ inch thick, of a pure white colour, and with the skin sometimes slightly wrinkled. A litre of them weighs 750 grammes, and 100 grammes contain about 225 seeds.

Common Flat White Kidney Bean (*Haricot Blanc Plat Commun*). —An old variety, which is still employed in some districts for field culture, and might almost be classed among the Tall-growing kinds; for although the stems do not climb or twine very well, they grow to a considerable length, trailing along the ground. Leaves numerous, slightly crimped, rather small, and of a darkish green colour; flowers white; pods rather short, each containing four or five medium-sized seeds of nearly the same shape as those of the Liancourt Kidney Bean, and of a fine glistening white colour. A litre of them weighs 780 grammes, and 100 grammes contain about 250 seeds.

Dwarf White Rice Kidney Bean (*Haricot Comtesse de Chambord*). —A dwarf, but remarkably branching kind, forming clumps over 2½ ft. wide. Leaves very numerous, rather pointed, medium-sized or small, and of a clear green colour; pods short, but very numerous, each containing five or six seeds; seeds white, egg-shaped, nearly ¾ inch long, ¼ inch broad, and about the same thickness, with an exceedingly thin skin, and of remarkably good quality. They are, consequently, very much used in the dried state. A litre of them weighs 825 grammes, and 100 grammes contain about 650 seeds. Although the seeds of this variety are small, it is very productive, but it has the disadvantage of being somewhat late, in consequence of which the seeds are sometimes spotted and blemished when the autumn turns out cold and damp. There is a very small-seeded variety of this plant, which produces vast numbers of pods, and is known as the Dwarf Hungarian Kidney Bean (*Haricot Nain de Hongrie*), or the Hungarian Rice Kidney Bean.

Dwarf Yellow Hundredfold Kidney Bean (*Haricot Jaune Cent pour Un*).—A dwarf and very hardy variety, of compact growth, with medium-sized slightly puckered leaves, of a deep-green colour tinged with gray. Flowers white, passing into yellow; pods rather short, numerous, each containing four or five straight, almost cylindrical seeds, which are sometimes square at the ends, and are of a dark-yellow colour verging on brown. A litre of them weighs 815 grammes, and 100 grammes contain about 475 seeds. This is a very productive kind, and is mostly cultivated in the east of France, where it is often grown in the vineyards.

Round Yellow, or Six-Weeks, Dwarf Kidney Bean (*Haricot Jaune Hâtif de Six Semaines*).—A low-growing, thick-set kind, with slightly grayish and elongated leaves. Flowers pale lilac or rose-coloured; pods rather broad and short, each containing four or five egg-shaped seeds, about ½ inch long, and of a uniform deep-yellow colour, except about the *hilum*, where they are of a darker shade, closely approaching brown. A litre of them weighs 800 grammes, and 100 grammes contain about 340 seeds. A remarkably early and very productive variety.

Mexican Dwarf Kidney Bean (*Haricot Saumon du Mexique*).— One of the earliest of all the tough-podded Kidney Beans, of low and scantily branching growth, with medium-sized leaves, of a deep-green colour tinged with gray. Flowers very pale lilac; pods short and rather broad, each containing four or five egg-shaped, slightly flattened seeds, of a salmon-rose colour, with a brownish circle around the *hilum*. A litre of them weighs, on an average, 800 grammes, and 100 grammes contain about 225 seeds.

Dwarf Red Orleans Kidney Bean (*Haricot Nain Rouge d'Orléans*). —A variety which is usually true to its dwarf character, but occasionally runs at the top. Stems thick and short, forming a rather broad, compact clump; leaves stiff, medium sized, crimped, and of a glistening-green colour; flowers violet; pods rather numerous, short and slightly curved, each containing four or five rather small egg-shaped seeds, which are less than ½ inch long, of a deep, somewhat brownish, red colour, and with a black circle around the *hilum*. A litre of them weighs 800 grammes, and 100 grammes contain about 225 seeds. This variety is cultivated in the vineyards of Orléannais, just as the Yellow Hundredfold and the Turkish Kidney Bean are in the vineyards of Burgundy. It is sometimes erroneously confounded with the Chartres Red Kidney Bean, which is a tall-growing kind, with seeds of a flatter shape and more squared at the ends.

The following varieties of Dwarf Tough-podded Kidney Beans are still occasionally to be met with in cultivation :—

Dwarf White Bagnolet (*Bagnolet Blanc*).—A handsome, vigorous-growing, and hardy kind, which in its habit of growth is rather like the Black Speckled Kidney Bean, but differs from it entirely in the colour of its seed, which is white, rather flat, and kidney-shaped, and is good for use either when dried or in the green state.

Dwarf Barbès (*H. Barbès Nain*).—This kind very much resembles the Yellow Hundredfold, but is distinguished from it by its lighter-coloured seeds, which are also marked with a small brown circle around the *hilum*.

Haricot Impératrice (*H. Religieuse, H. Isabelle*).—In its general appearance and foliage this kind resembles the Swiss Kidney Beans, but it has broader and slightly curved pods. Seed large, full, kidney-shaped, and of a very remarkable colour, a large deep-red blotch encircling the *hilum*, and extending over about one-third of the surface of the seed, the remainder of which is of a pure white, thickly dotted with small red specks, which appear in bold relief on the white ground.

Neapolitan Kidney Bean (*H. de Naples*).—Under this name are grouped several varieties with white, egg-shaped seeds, like those which are imported in large quantities from the south of Italy and from Sicily; but it is more a commercial name than that of any special variety.

Haricot Plein de la Flèche.—A good variety, of vigorous, thick-set growth, and resembling both the Black Speckled (*H. Bagnolet*) and the Bush Kidney Bean (*H. Solitaire*); the former in its habit of growth, and the latter in its seed.

The following varieties are of English or American origin :—

Early Light Dun, and **Early Dark Dun.**—These two kinds bear some resemblance to the Yellow Flageolet (*H. Flageolet Jaune*), but their seed is of a uniform colour, without any circle around the *hilum*. The seeds of the two kinds are distinguished by those of the first being of a lighter brown or dun colour than those of the second.

Early Rachel.—A dwarf and productive kind, with dark-brown, elongated seeds, slightly spotted with pale brown or yellow. It has some resemblance to the Chocolate Kidney Bean.

MacMillan's American Prolific.—Somewhat resembles the Sion House Kidney Bean in its general appearance and in the colour of the seed, but is more compact in growth, forming denser clumps.

The Monster.—A dwarf and exceedingly vigorous-growing variety, with enormous leaves, resembling, in their amplitude, those of the most highly developed Swiss Kidney Beans. Pods of medium size, straight; seeds black, longer and more curved than those of the Belgian Negro Bean. A tolerably productive, half-early kind.

New Mammoth Negro.—The pods and seeds of this kind are rather like those of the Negro Long-pod (*H. Flageolet Noir*), but in its mode of growth and the colour of its leaves, it bears a greater resemblance to the Belgian Negro. It is not so good a kind for green Haricots as the Negro Long-pod.

Newington Wonder.—This dwarf variety can hardly be recommended for any other purpose than frame culture for the production of seeds, as its pods are too short for green Haricots. The seed is of a light-yellow colour and remarkably small.

Osborn's Early Forcing.—A good dwarf kind, of dense branching growth, producing large numbers of medium-sized pods, each containing four or five short, bulging seeds, of a deep-brown colour, with some spots of light yellow.

Refugee, or **Thousand to One.**—A rather compact-growing variety, with remarkably long, straight, smooth, dark-coloured leaves, and violet flowers. Pods straight and rounded; seed hardly kidney-shaped, almost cylindrical, of a light-yellow colour, variegated with wine-lees-red markings.

Sir Joseph Paxton.—A small-sized, very early, dwarf kind, with rather short pods. The seed is almost exactly like that of the Yellow Hundredfold (*H. Jaune Cent pour Un*), but is of a deeper, and nearly brown, colour.

Williams's New Early.—A very early and rather productive kind, the seeds and pods of which are marbled with violet colour. This colouring of the pods, added to their flat shape, diminishes their value for use as green Haricots.

Yellow Canterbury.—A dwarf variety, with small yellow, bulging, straight seeds, very much resembling the Yellow Hundredfold.

The variety known as the *Haricot Nain Panaché d'Inselbourg,* of German origin, is a kind of Swiss Kidney Bean of medium height, and yielding an abundance of long, straight, green pods. The seed very much resembles that of the *Haricot Plein de la Flèche.* It is a good half-late variety.

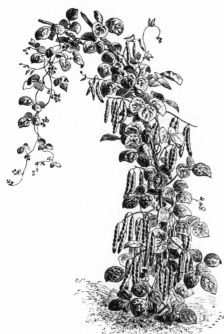

White Prédome Kidney Bean (½ natural size).

EDIBLE-PODDED KIDNEY BEANS.

French, Haricots sans parchemin. *German,* Zucker-, *oder* Brech-, Bohnen. *Danish,* Snitte-bonnen. *Italian,* Fagiuoli mangia tutto.

I. TALL-GROWING VARIETIES.

White Prédome Kidney Bean (*Haricot Prédome*).— Stem about 4 ft. high, green, thickish, and twisted; leaves of medium size, rounded at the base, crimped, and of a rather deep clear-green colour; flowers white, passing into yellow; pods very numerous, straight, fleshy, deeply indented on the sides by the bulging of the seeds, 3 or 4 inches long, each containing six or seven very white, nearly round seeds, which are often flattened at the ends, and are about ½ inch long, ¼ inch broad, and less than ¼ inch thick. A litre of them weighs 820 grammes, and 100 grammes contain about 470 seeds. The pods are very tender and brittle, and are perfectly free from membrane, in this respect surpassing all other varieties of Tall-growing Kidney Beans. The seeds, also, are of very good quality, so that the plant affords a supply of an excellent vegetable, not only while the pods are green and the seeds half-formed, but also when the seeds are fully grown and ripening. The pods, also, are without fibre, so that they can be cooked just as they are gathered, without any trimming. This is one of the best kinds of Edible-podded Kidney Beans, and is very extensively grown in France, particularly in Nor-mandy, where there are two or three forms of it which differ slightly from each other in the size of the pods and seeds. It is a half-late variety.

The *Haricot Friolet* and the *H. Petit Carré de Caen* are rather local forms of the Prédome Kidney Bean than distinct, well-marked

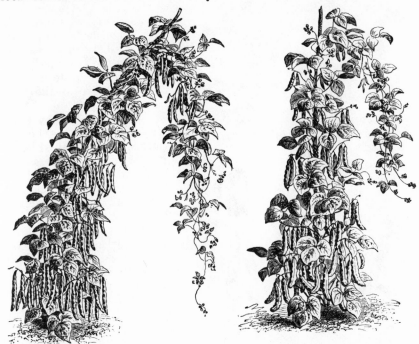

Princess Runner Kidney Bean ($\frac{1}{12}$ natural size).

Broad-pod Kidney Bean ($\frac{1}{12}$ natural size).

sub-varieties. The *Friolet* is usually considered to produce smaller seed, but this does not appear to be a universally constant cha-racteristic.

Princess Runner Kidney Bean (*Haricot Princesse à Rames*).—Stem green, thick, twisted, $6\frac{1}{2}$ ft. high or more; leaves roundish, of medium size, crimped, and of a deep-green colour; flowers white; pods very numerous (especially at the base of the stems, where they form regular bundles), straight, green, bulging greatly over the seeds, and turning yellow when quite ripe; they are from 4 to 6 inches long, and seldom contain more than eight seeds each. The seeds are white, slightly egg-shaped, and very like those of the preceding variety, except that they are never flattened at the ends. A litre of them weighs 840 grammes, and 100 grammes contain about 360 seeds. This is a very good, hardy, exceedingly productive, and pretty early variety. It is extensively grown in French Flanders, Belgium, and Holland. As has been already remarked, it certainly very much resembles the Prédome Kidney Bean; but it is sufficiently distinguished from that variety by the greater distance between the seeds in the pod, and also by growing fully one-third higher. When grown true to name, the seeds of the Princess Kidney Bean, which never touch each other in the pod, preserve their natural slightly elongated egg-shaped form, while those of the Prédome are pressed against each other, and, consequently, become flattened at the ends.

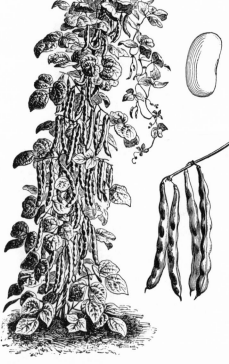

Geneva or Plainpalais White Butter Bean, or Wax Bean ($\frac{1}{12}$ natural size).

There is a sub-variety with longer pods and greater distances between the seeds, known as the Long-pod Princess, which is quite as early and productive as the ordinary variety.

Broad-pod Kidney-Bean (*Haricot Intestin*).—This variety, which was raised by M. Perrier de la Bathie, is one of the most singular and distinct varieties that has appeared for some years past. It is a vigorous-growing, latish, but productive kind, and remarkable amongst the Edible-podded varieties. Stem 4 to 6 ft. high, bearing pods abundantly near the base; leaves large, very green, slightly crimped; pods so thick and fleshy that the diameter from side to side is one-third greater than the distance between the front seam and the back. Notwithstanding this inflated appearance, there is no empty space inside the pod, the substance of which is so thick and fleshy that the seeds have hardly room to grow, and appear deformed by the pressure to which they are subjected. They are white, elongated egg-shaped, sometimes faintly kidney-shaped, about $\frac{1}{2}$ inch long, and $\frac{1}{4}$ inch broad and thick; they present the almost unparalleled peculiarity of being irregular in shape, being almost always flattened cross-wise, and the *hilum*, instead of occupying its usual position, is situated on one side of the line which would divide the seed into two equal parts. A litre of them weighs 800 grammes, and 100 grammes contain about 325 seeds. They vary very much in size, however, according to the season.

Geneva or **Plainpalais White Butter Bean**, or **Wax Bean** (*Haricot Blanc de Genève*).—This variety is highly esteemed by the Geneva market gardeners. It is a tall-growing kind, coming very near the preceding one, but differing from it in a few points. It is more decidedly a pole-bean, being a better climber than the other. The pods, which very much resemble those of the Broad-pod Kidney Bean, are not so fleshy, but they are produced in greater abundance, especially at the middle and towards the top of the stems; they also ripen more readily. The seeds, or beans, are white, and of an elongated and nearly cylindrical shape. It is, in fine, a good mid-season tall variety of Butter Bean.

White Coco Kidney Bean (*Haricot Coco Blanc*).—Stem green, about $6\frac{1}{2}$ ft. high; leaves of medium size, stiff, rather long and pointed, of a dark, rather dull-green colour, and slightly crimped; flowers white; pods of medium length, rather broad, green, each containing five or six white, egg-shaped seeds, about $\frac{1}{2}$ inch long, nearly $\frac{1}{2}$ inch broad, and over $\frac{1}{4}$ inch thick. A litre of them weighs 830 grammes, and 100 grammes contain about 250 seeds. This variety, although ranking amongst the Edible-podded kinds (especially when the pods are young), is more esteemed for its seeds, which are used in the dried state.

The **Sophie Kidney Bean** (*H. Sophie*) is considered to be only a sub-variety of the White Coco, from which it differs in having rather larger pods (which are sometimes tinged with red, like those of the Prague Kidney Beans) and somewhat larger leaves.

White Prague Kidney Bean (*Haricot de Prague*).—Although this variety resembles the preceding one in the colour and shape of the seed, it is clearly distinguished from it by several marked characteristics. In the first place, it is a later and longer-lasting kind; the leaves are more abundant and do not fall so soon; they are large, not much crimped, and of a rather dark-green colour, and those at the top of the stem are nearly the same size as the lower ones; flowers white; the pods, which are abundantly produced up to the tops of the stems, are longer and narrower than those of the White Coco; and, lastly, the seed is something flatter, and not so regularly egg-shaped. A litre of them weighs 780 grammes, and 100 grammes contain about 195 seeds. This can be recommended as a very productive variety, with the single drawback of being somewhat late in ripening, which would render it less valuable in localities where the autumn is cold and damp.

New Zealand Runner Kidney Bean (*Haricot de Prague Marbré*).— A variety of moderate height, seldom exceeding about 4 ft., with thick green stems. Lower leaves large, slightly crimped, the rest of medium size, narrow, and of a rather dark-green colour; flowers pale lilac or rosy-white; pods broad, about 5 inches long, green at first, afterwards becoming tinged with violet-red on a whitish ground, and sometimes entirely red when ripe, each containing five or six egg-shaped seeds, of a salmon-rose colour, spotted, dotted, and striped with deep red, and having a brownish-yellow circle around the *hilum*. A litre of them weighs 760 grammes, and 100 grammes contain about 210 seeds. This kind, which was introduced about the middle of the eighteenth century, is well known and extensively cultivated. It is more generally grown for the dried seeds than for the pods.

Red Prague Kidney Bean (*Haricot de Prague Rouge*).—This variety differs very little from the preceding one in its mode of growth, but is distinguished from it by having the seeds of a uniform dark brownish-red colour. A litre of them weighs 800 grammes, and 100 grammes contain about 225 seeds.

There is also a sub-variety, known as the *H. de Prague Bicolore*, the seeds of which are half red and white.

Among the Prague Kidney Beans should be included the variety named Imperial Austrian White Coco, or Bossin. This is a large, productive, and rather late kind, the seed of which is white and nearly round, with a black bird-shaped blotch around the *hilum*, something like that which characterizes the seed of the Spread Eagle, or Dove, Kidney Bean.

The **Two-coloured Italian Kidney Bean** (*H. Bicolore d'Italie*) should also be classed with the Prague Kidney Beans. It is a very productive, tall-growing kind, producing seeds of excellent quality for the table. There is a sub-variety of it, the pods of which, immediately before ripening, assume an exceeding lively uniform red colour, giving the plant quite an ornamental appearance. The seeds of both kinds are round, slightly egg-shaped, half white and half very pale chamois colour.

Black Algerian Butter Bean ($\frac{1}{12}$ natural size).

Black Algerian Butter Bean (*Haricot d'Alger Noir*).—A very distinct and well-known kind, probably the oldest of the varieties which are called Butter Beans from the colour of their pods. It is a plant of medium height, seldom exceeding about $6\frac{1}{2}$ ft., with rather thick stems of a pale or yellowish green colour, sometimes tinged with violet; leaves of average size, not much crimped, gradually decreasing in dimensions from the base to the top of the stem, and of a slightly ashy-gray colour. The pods, which are green at first, assume, when they are about 2 inches long, a pale-yellow, semi-transparent tinge, very much resembling that of butter or fine wax; they are usually somewhat curved, each containing from four to six seeds, which are blue at first, then violet, and when ripe quite black, of a slightly flattened egg-shape, and a trifle longer than those of the Prague Kidney Beans. A litre of them weighs 785 grammes, and 100 grammes contain about 175 seeds. This is a productive and moderately early kind, and one of the best Edible-podded varieties. The pods are entirely free from membrane, and have hardly any fibre, so that they are quite tender and fleshy when fully grown, and may be sent to table almost until they are perfectly ripe. The dried seeds are seldom eaten, on account of their very dark and unattractive colour.

The **Black Coco** (*H. Coco Noir*), a tall-growing and productive, but rather late kind, is distinguished from the Algerian Wax Bean by the greenish colour of its pods. As a variety, it does not possess much interest.

Tall White Algerian Butter Bean (*Haricot Beurre Blanc à Rames*).—A rather vigorous-growing kind, about 6½ ft. high, very remarkable for the light or yellowish tint of its leaves, which renders it conspicuous at a distance. Stems wax-yellow or white, as are also the leaf-stalks; flowers white; pods longer and more slender than those of the preceding kind, more or less curved, each containing, with some distance between them, five or six white, egg-shaped, somewhat elongated seeds over ½ inch long. A litre of them weighs 810 grammes, and 100 grammes contain about 250 seeds. As an Edible-podded variety, this is in no respect inferior to the preceding kind, and it has, besides, this advantage—that its dried seeds can be sent to table.

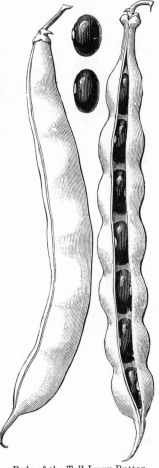

Pods of the Tall Ivory Butter Bean (natural size).

Mont d'Or Butter Bean (*Haricot Beurre de Mont d'Or*).—This handsome and good variety was raised near Lyons, whence it has been widely distributed throughout France. It is a very distinct kind, scarcely as tall as the Algerian Wax Bean, with pale green stems tinged with red, and smooth, uncrimped, light-green leaves, and blue flowers. Pods very numerous, straight, of a pale-yellow colour, like those of all the Butter Beans, nearly 6 inches long, very free from membrane, each containing five or six egg-shaped seeds of a violet colour, spotted and marbled with brown, and strikingly smaller than those of the Black and White Algerian Wax Beans. A litre of them weighs 720 grammes, and 100 grammes contain about 210 seeds. This variety, which is only grown for the pods, is particularly remarkable for its earliness and productiveness.

Tall Ivory Butter Bean (*Haricot Beurre Ivoire à Rames*).—A tall-growing kind, 6½ to over 8 ft. high. Stems whitish, slightly tinged with red on the side next the sun; leaves numerous, of medium size, and of a clear-green colour; flowers lilac; pods numerous, fleshy, straight, or slightly curved, entirely free from membrane, and especially remarkable for the white tint which they assume when they are two or three days old, and which becomes more pronounced as they advance to maturity. Each of them contains from five to eight egg-shaped seeds, of a reddish-violet colour, and of the same size as the seeds of the Red Prague Kidney Bean, from which they differ in colour only. A litre of them weighs 835 grammes, and 100 grammes contain about 210 seeds. This is a good Edible-podded variety, somewhat late, but an abundant and remarkably continuous bearer.

Edible-podded Black Scimitar Runner Bean (*Haricot Sabre Noir sans Parchemin*).—A very distinct kind, producing (like the two following varieties) flat kidney-shaped seeds, and pods entirely free from membrane. It is a tall-growing plant, being over 8 ft. high, with thick pale-green stems. Leaves large and broad, rather distant from each other, of a palish-green colour, and crimped; flowers lilac; pods long and broad, not curved, but frequently bulged or undulating on the edges, 6 to 8 inches long, of a violet colour at first, but losing this as they increase in growth, each containing six to eight seeds of the same size as those of the White Dutch Kidney Bean, but somewhat more humpy and irregular in shape, and with a very glistening, brilliant black skin. A litre of them weighs 700 grammes, and 100 grammes contain about 185 seeds. This variety is remarkable for the great size and beauty of its pods. It is very productive, but rather impatient of damp, and half-late in ripening.

Purple-podded Runner Kidney Bean (*Haricot à Cosse Violette*).—A very vigorous and tall-growing kind, sometimes attaining a height of 9½ ft. and upwards. The stems, which are stout and rather thick, are of a purple colour, as are also the leaf-stalks and the calyxes of the flowers; the leaves are rather distant from each other, very much crimped, and of a dull-green colour; flowers lilac; pods very numerous, straight, slender, and at first of a very deep purple colour, but, as they advance in growth, they become paler in hue, and more or less bulged and undulated, but always remain very solid and fleshy. They sometimes attain a length of 10 inches, preserving a relative degree of slenderness, and contain six to eight seeds each. The seeds are elongated and flattened in shape, and are something larger than those of the Flageolet Kidney Beans, while they are almost of the same shape, and are of a rosy colour, marbled with grayish lilac. A litre of them weighs 730 grammes, and 100 grammes contain about 250 seeds. A rather early and exceedingly productive kind, and one of the best edible-podded sorts. The pods of this variety are quite free from membrane; they lose their purple tinge in cooking, and become as green as those of any other kind.

Edible-podded Giant White Kidney Bean (*Haricot Blanc Géant sans Parchemin*).—This very fine new variety appears to be the offspring of the preceding one, of which it exhibits all the vigorous-growing and productive qualities; it has, moreover, the advantage of producing green pods and white seeds; that is to say, it is free from the only two blemishes that can be attributed to the Purple-podded Kidney Bean in the objectionable colour of its pods and seeds. It is a half-late but productive kind, with stout stems 6 to nearly 10 ft. high. Leaves very large, but not numerous; leaflets rounded and crimped. The flowers are white; pods very broad, and very numerous, 4 to 6 inches long, entirely free from membrane, thick and fleshy, each containing four to six flat white seeds, resembling those of the White Dutch or Case-knife Kidney Bean. A litre of them weighs 730 grammes, and 100 grammes contain about 250 seeds. When grown under favourable circumstances, this variety produces such an abundance of pods as to weigh down the stakes which support it.

From amongst the almost innumerable other varieties of Tall-growing Edible-podded Kidney Beans, we may also mention the following as possessing the greatest degree of merit :—

Giant Japan Butter Bean (*H. Beurre Géant du Japon*).—A tall kind, with long broad pods of a pale-yellow colour, somewhat resembling those of the Edible-podded Black Case-knife Kidney Bean, but with smaller seeds, which are of the colour of roasted coffee beans.

Saint-Joseph Butter Bean (*H. Beurre Saint-Joseph*).—This variety forms

Edible-podded Giant White Kidney Bean (plant, $\frac{1}{12}$; pods, $\frac{1}{4}$; seed, full natural size).

the connecting link between the Prague Kidney Beans and the Butter Beans properly so called. Its pods are straight or slightly curved, and are streaked with red on a ground of butter-coloured yellow. The seeds are indifferently marbled, either with violet on a rose-coloured ground or with rose-colour on a violet ground. The plant is not a tall-growing one, as it seldom exceeds about 4 ft. in height. It was raised about the year 1860, at the agricultural colony of Cîteaux, near Dijon.

Imperial Kidney Bean (*H. Impérial*).—This is distinguished from the Tall White Butter Bean only by the colour of its stems and pods, both of which are green instead of butter-yellow.

Climbing Yellow, or Dunes Yellow, Kidney Bean (*H. Jaune à Rames*).—Of medium height, productive, and tolerably early. Seeds yellow, nearly cylindrical, resembling those of the Yellow Hundred-fold. Pods straight, very fleshy and tender, and from 4 to 6 inches in length.

Lafayette Kidney Bean (*H. Lafayette*).—A tall variety, rather late, and with pods not altogether free from membrane. Flowers white ; pods pale green, becoming yellow when ripe, each containing six to eight chamois-coloured seeds marbled with light brown and shaded with reddish brown around the *hilum*.

Asparagus, or Yard Long, Kidney Bean (*H. Olive sans Parchemin,* or *H. Asperge*).—A very tall-growing kind, nearly 10 ft. high. Leaves very large and distantly placed ; flowers copper-coloured or lilac ; pods almost cylindrical, exceedingly long and slender, sometimes more than a foot in length ; seed very long, nearly cylindrical, but narrowed at both ends, of a more or less coppery chamois colour. A late kind, requiring a warm climate.

Rose-coloured Prédome Butter Bean (*H. Prédome Rose à Rames,* or *H. Mange-tout*).—A plant of medium height, seldom exceeding 4 ft., but branching and clumpy. Flowers rose-coloured ; pods exceedingly numerous, growing in profusion from the base to the top of the stem, but seldom exceeding 2 or 3 inches in length, and each containing four to six small, nearly round seeds of a salmon rose-colour.

Val d'Isère Kidney Bean (*H. de la Val d'Isère*).—This is a very vigorous-growing, leafy, late kind, laden, in the end of autumn, with green, fleshy, well-filled pods, which are very much curved. Seed black, egg-shaped.

Villetaneuse Kidney Bean (*H. de Villetaneuse*).—This variety, which was formerly very much grown about Paris, is now almost entirely superseded by the Tall-growing Butter Beans. It is a productive, somewhat late kind, bearing rather long, tender, and thick pods, each containing five or six flattened, almost square, coffee-coloured seeds marbled and streaked with brown.

Gray Zebra Runner Kidney Bean (*H. Zébré Gris à Rames*).—A late and very vigorous-growing kind, nearly 10 ft. high, with large, spreading leaves and lilac flowers. Pods thick, fleshy, curved, streaked with violet on a green ground ; seeds egg-shaped, of a dark-gray colour, dotted with lighter gray, and striped with black. Raised by M. Perrier de la Bathie.

The American variety, Giant Red Wax Pale Bean, is a Tall-growing Edible-podded Kidney Bean, 6½ ft. high, with large flat white or yellow pods, resembling those of the Edible-podded Black Case-knife Kidney Bean, and red seeds. It is a rather late kind.

II. DWARF EDIBLE-PODDED VARIETIES.

Prédome Dwarf Kidney Bean (*Haricot Prédome Nain*).—The pods and seeds of this variety are exactly like those of the tall-growing Prédome Kidney Bean, but less abundantly produced, and this deficiency is not redeemed by any other particular merit. A litre of the seeds weighs 830 grammes, and 100 grammes contain about 560 seeds. The ordinary Prédome Kidney Bean does not require very tall stakes, so that it is not one of those kinds in which the raising of a dwarf variety is any very great improvement.

Princess Dwarf Kidney Bean (*Haricot Princesse Nain*).—This is not a very vigorous-growing kind, and its crimped and rounded leaves are very liable to disease, arising either from the attacks of insects or from minute fungus growths. It is also rather late. The pods are short and curved, free from membrane, and of a deep-green colour. A litre of them weighs 850 grammes, and 100 grammes contain about 400 seeds. The remark made upon the Dwarf Prédome is also applicable to this variety; however, as the ordinary variety of the Princess attains a tolerable height, it may sometimes be advantageous to have a dwarf form of it.

There is a variety grown in Holland, under the name of the Large-seeded Princess (*H. Princesse à Gros Grain*), which is quite distinct from the Dwarf Princess. It has curved, green, and rather fleshy pods, and comparatively large egg-shaped seeds, which resemble those of the White Coco Kidney Bean.

Prédome Dwarf Flesh-coloured Kidney Bean (*Haricot Prédome Nain Rose*).—A small variety, distinguished by the colour of its seeds, which is unlike that of any other kind. Stem short, very branching; flowers white; pods short, straight, rather bulging over the seeds, tolerably fleshy, and very free from membrane; seeds nearly round, or egg-shaped, of the same size as those of the Prédome Kidney Bean, but of a uniform salmon-rose colour, except the *hilum*, which is white, surrounded by a brown circle. A litre of them weighs 815

Early Yellow Canadian Dwarf Kidney Bean
(⅓ natural size).

grammes, and 100 grammes contain about 400 seeds.

Pink-marbled Dwarf Prague Kidney Bean (*Haricot de Prague Marbré Nain*).—A very dwarf, compact-growing, moderately productive kind, with rather abundant grayish-green leaves and lilac flowers. Pods green, straight, or very slightly curved, plentifully striped with red, each containing four or five seeds resembling those of the common Cranberry Bean, but somewhat smaller. A litre of them weighs 810 grammes, and 100 grammes contain about 230 seeds.

Early Yellow Canadian Dwarf Kidney Bean (*Haricot Jaune du*

Canada).—A very good variety, hardy and productive, but somewhat late, well adapted for market-garden or field culture. Stems rather vigorous, branching, 16 to 20 inches high, thickly covered with medium-sized uncrimped leaves of a clear green colour. Flowers lilac; pods very numerous, green at first, changing to yellow, each usually containing five egg-shaped seeds a little smaller than those of the Prague Kidney Beans, and of a deep-yellow colour, merging into brown about the *hilum.* A litre of them weighs 815 grammes, and 100 grammes contain about 260 seeds. The dried seeds of this variety are much esteemed. The pods, to have them tender, should be gathered before they are fully grown. Although closely resembling the Yellow China Kidney Bean, this variety is distinguished from it by the deeper colour of its seeds, and by its leaves being larger, less crowded together, moderately crimped, and of a darker green colour.

Oval Yellow China, or Robin's Egg, Kidney Bean
(⅛ natural size).

Oval Yellow China, or **Robin's-Egg, Kidney Bean** (*Haricot Jaune de la Chine*). —A rather branching kind, with stems about 16 inches high, forming an airy-looking clump. Leaves medium-sized, and of a lively green colour, those at the top of the stem being small and long-stalked; flowers white; pods green, turning yellow when ripe, each containing five or six egg-shaped seeds of a sulphur-yellow colour, with a more or less marked bluish circle around the *hilum.* A litre of them weighs 825 grammes, and 100 grammes contain about 300 seeds. This variety is one of the most widely cultivated in different parts of the world, and is to be met with almost everywhere in the colonies and America, under the same name and exhibiting the same characteristics.

Dwarf Algerian Black-seeded Butter Bean (⅛ natural size).

Dwarf Algerian Black-seeded Butter Bean (*Haricot d'Alger Noir Nain*).—An established dwarf variety of the Algerian Wax or Butter Bean, with rather large yellowish-stalked leaves, the colour of which varies, on the same plant, from dark to light green. Flowers lilac; pods very fleshy and of a butter-yellow colour; seeds black, egg-shaped, a little smaller than those of the tall-growing variety. A litre of them weighs 730 grammes, and 100 grammes contain about 250 seeds. This is an early kind, very productive, and of excellent quality, and is one of the most extensively grown varieties of Kidney Beans.

Long-podded Dwarf Algerian Butter Bean (*Haricot d'Alger Noir Nain à Longue Cosse*).—This appears to be a sub-variety of the preceding kind, but it is very clearly distinguished from it by its longer pods, and also by the shape of its seeds, which, instead of being egg-shaped, are almost cylindrical, and are nearly $\frac{3}{4}$ inch long and over $\frac{1}{4}$ inch broad and thick. The pods are very free from membrane, and are more slender and less fleshy than those of the preceding kind. A litre of the seeds weighs 800 grammes, and 100 grammes contain about 240 seeds. This variety has come into very

Long-podded Dwarf Algerian Butter Bean ($\frac{1}{8}$ natural size).

general cultivation about Paris, where it is grown in the fields for the city markets.

Dwarf White Algerian Butter Bean (*Haricot Beurre Blanc Nain*). —A very good, but somewhat tender variety, forming low, broadish clumps which sometimes sprawl on the ground. The leaves become smaller and paler in colour as they approach the top of the stems. Flowers white; pods almost transparent, of a waxy-white colour, and about 4 inches long, each containing five or six short, egg-shaped, creamy-white seeds, which are sometimes slightly wrinkled. The dried seeds are of excellent quality for the table. A litre of them weighs 740 grammes, and 100 grammes contain about 250 seeds.

Mont d'Or Dwarf Butter Bean ($\frac{1}{8}$ natural size).

Mont d'Or Dwarf Butter Bean (*Haricot Beurre Nain du Mont d'Or*).—A very productive and very early variety of Dwarf Butter Bean. Stems 1 ft. to 16 inches high, branching; leaves large, rough, but not crimped, of a deep-green colour, and remarkable for the very variable shape of the terminal leaflet, which is sometimes long and pointed, and sometimes nearly round and quite blunt at the end;

F

pods very numerous, 4 or 5 inches long, well filled, and of a pale-yellow colour; seeds small and round, of a very dark red, deepening into black. A litre of them weighs 700 grammes, and 100 grammes contain about 210 seeds.

Flageolet Butter Bean (*Haricot Flageolet Beurre*).—A vigorous-growing, yet persistently dwarf variety, 16 to 18 inches high. Leaves very large, uncrimped, and of a light or yellowish green colour; flowers lilac; pods long, broad, straight or slightly curved, quite yellow (like those of the Algerian Kidney Beans), but rather flattened and pointed (like those of the Tough-podded Kidney Beans); seeds almost exactly like those of the Canadian Wonder in shape and colour. A litre of them weighs 750 grammes, and 100 grammes contain about 150 seeds. This is a very fine and distinct kind, but, unfortunately, its pods are not entirely free from membrane, at least, when they come near ripening; but, if gathered before the seeds are too much grown, they are a very tender, fleshy, and excellent variety of Edible-podded Kidney Beans.

Émile Dwarf Kidney Bean (*Haricot Émile*).—An exceedingly

Flageolet Butter Bean (⅓ natural size).

dwarf and remarkably early variety, seldom more than 8 or 10 inches high. Leaves medium sized, of a rather dark green, and slightly crimped; flowers white or very pale lilac; pods somewhat curved, 4 or 5 inches long, very fleshy, green before ripening and never turning white or yellow, each containing from five to seven oblong seeds of a violet colour marbled with light gray, about ½ inch long, and ⅓ inch broad and thick. A litre of them weighs 790 grammes, and 100 grammes contain about 235 seeds. This variety, which was recently raised by M. Perrier de la Bathie, seems to us to be both the dwarfest and the earliest of all the Edible-podded Kidney Beans, and is specially suitable for forcing.

Early Dwarf White Edible-podded Kidney Bean (*Haricot Nain Blanc Hâtif sans Parchemin*).—Stem tallish and branching, attaining a height of 20 inches; leaves medium sized, numerous, rather crimped; flowers white; pods 6 inches long, flat, very thick and fleshy, almost always curved or twisted, each containing five or six white, flattened, moderately kidney-shaped seeds, which are sometimes slightly squared at the ends, varying from ½ to nearly ¾ inch in length, about ¼ inch broad, and about ⅙ inch thick. A litre of them weighs 810 grammes, and 100 grammes contain about 165 seeds. This variety is a tolerably good one for field culture. It is a good bearer and pretty early, but the seeds are easily spoiled by cold or damp autumn weather.

Unique Dwarf White Kidney Bean (*Haricot Nain Blanc Unique*).—Stem tallish, vigorous-growing, and tolerably branching; leaves rather deep green, large, rounded, and crimped; flowers large, white; pods numerous, straight, 5 or 6 inches long, each containing five or six seeds, which are white, long, very bulging, straight or curved, and almost as thick as they are broad. A litre of them weighs 820 grammes, and 100 grammes contain about 200 seeds. This is one of the best Dwarf Edible-podded Kidney Beans. Its dried seeds also are of excellent quality, and perfectly white— a great recommendation, as Kidney Beans of this colour are generally preferred for table use.

Quarantain Dwarf White Kidney Bean (*Haricot Nain Blanc Quarantain*).—A plant of medium height, with branching stems, forming a rather compact clump. Leaves of average size, stiff, almost tri-angular, elongated and pointed, of a dark lustrous-green colour; flowers white; pods flat and broad, and from 4 to 6 inches long. A litre of the seeds weighs 830 grammes, and 100 grammes contain about 270 seeds. A hardy, early, and tolerably productive variety, with this drawback—that it cannot be relied upon for al-ways maintaining a strictly dwarf habit of growth.

Besides those already de-scribed, there are many other varieties of Dwarf Edible-podded Kidney Beans in cul-tivation, of which we shall only mention the following :—

Variegated White-podded Butter Bean (*H. Beurre Pa-naché à Cosse Blanche*). It is the seed of this variety that is variegated; it is straight and almost cylindrical in shape, of

Pods of the Émile Kidney Bean (natural size).

a creamy-white colour, with spots and marblings of a wine-lees-red or reddish-violet colour. The variety is dwarf and rather tender. The American variety *Early Valentine* may be considered identical with it.

Two-coloured China Kidney Bean (*H. de China Bicolore*).—This variety does not seem to be very extensively grown, and yet it is known almost everywhere. It is a rather tall and very branching kind, with white flowers. Pods of medium size, pretty free from membrane, turning white when ripe, and each containing five or six straight, cylindrical seeds, which are often square at the ends, and are deeply striped with red around the *hilum* to the extent of half the surface of the seed, while the other half is entirely white. A rather productive and very early kind.

Unique Dwarf White Kidney Bean (⅓ natural size).

Dwarf White Malmaison Kidney Bean (*H. Nain Blanc de la Malmaison*).—A productive and moderately early variety, with fine fleshy, bulging pods, which are usually straight. Seed rather long, oval, and white.

Dwarf Aix Kidney Bean (*H. Nain d'Aix*).— A variety with small round seeds, of a rosy-white colour. Pods yellow, and rather short, but very free from membrane.

The new English varieties, *Long Sword* and *Ne Plus Ultra*, are described as being remarkably productive; the former bearing from thirty to forty pods on a plant. The last-named is a very dwarf kind (about 1 ft. high), early and compact in growth.

The three following kinds are of American origin :—

Crystal Wax White Bean.—Dwarf, but usually running at the top. Pods short and white, almost transparent; seeds white and oblong.

Iron-pod Wax Bean.—Not a reliably dwarf kind nor very productive. Pods free from membrane, white, tinged or slightly striped with violet; seeds white.

New Golden Wax Bean.—A fine, productive, and early kind. Pods free from membrane, and of a pale-yellow colour; seeds white, partly marbled with deep red, almost like those of the Two-coloured China Kidney Bean. This is a good variety.

SCARLET RUNNER BEANS.

Phaseolus multiflorus, Willd.

French, Haricots d'Espagne.   *German*, Arabische Bohne.   *Dutch*, Tursche boon.   *Italian*, Fagiuolo di Spagna.

Native of South America.—Naturally a perennial, but cultivated as an annual.—These plants, while extremely valuable as vegetables, are esteemed as ornamental climbers, on account of their rapid growth and the abundance of their flowers.

The Scarlet Runner, which our French friends do not appreciate as we do, is the most valuable, and frequently the most beautiful, plant in English cottage gardens. It is grown in thousands of gardens, even in London and our large cities and towns, hiding with its quick-running and vigorous shoots many ugly surfaces in summer, and affording a quantity of wholesome food. The pods are often, like those of other vegetables, allowed to get too old and hard before being gathered.

Scarlet Runners are generally raised from seed, but the roots may, if desired, be taken up in autumn and preserved through the winter in dry sand or in soil in any shed or cellar from which frost is excluded. If roots thus wintered be brought out and planted about the latter end of May, they come into bearing a fortnight or three weeks earlier than those raised from seed sown at the same time. They are also sometimes left in the ground all the winter, and protected from frost by a good thick layer of coal ashes placed over the rows. Thus treated, they start early in May, if the weather be favourable; and when they have attained the height of 3 or 4 ft., if stopped, will produce beans much earlier than by any other method; but if a profitable crop be desired, this plan is not to be recommended, as the plants do not continue in bearing so long as those that are raised from seed. Among positions chosen for Scarlet Runners may be named small patches of ground at the corners of walks, planting five or six seeds in a patch, 5 or 6 inches apart. Three stout poles or sticks, as used for Peas, are then placed round them in the form of a triangle, bent so as to meet at the top, where they are tied. In small gardens they are often trained over wire or woodwork, so as to form summer-houses or coverings for walks.

CULTURE.—In large gardens the general practice is to sow in open quarters, and where beans are required as long in the season as they can be obtained, and in large quantities, this is undoubtedly the best plan. They should be allowed a distance of at least 6 ft. between the rows, and if more can be afforded them, all the better. For early crops, a few rows may be made close under a south wall or fence, keeping the points regularly pinched out, in order to keep them dwarf and encourage the earlier development of the pods. In this case they will, of course, need no support, but be allowed to lie in a thick row along the ground. Beans may be produced in this way several weeks earlier than in open quarters, but they do not continue so long in bearing, nor do they produce such abundant crops. Where, however, earliness is an object, this plan may be followed with advantage. Seeds for this purpose may either be sown in heat and transplanted, or sown in the open ground where the plants are to remain. The former is the more troublesome, but it is the best where covering is at hand to protect them from cold winds and frosts after they have been planted. If sown in heat, the seeds should be put in about the second week in May, either in boxes or pots, the former being the best; they should be shallow—say, not more than 4 or 5 inches deep—their size in other respects being of no great importance; they should have holes at the bottom for drainage, and should be half filled with half-rotted leaf-mould pressed down rather firmly with the hand; slightly cover with fine soil, and upon this sow in rows 2 inches apart, and cover with about ½ inch of finely sifted leaf-mould, giving the whole a good watering. If placed in a Cucumber or Melon frame at "work," they will soon be up, and should be kept as near the glass as possible, in order to prevent them from becoming drawn.

After they have made two single leaves, they should be taken to a cold frame or pit, gradually inuring them to the open air, so as to make them as hardy as possible previous to planting out, which may be done the first week in June. Before planting them out, they should have a good watering, and be taken out of the boxes with as much earth adhering to them as possible. Plant either in double or single rows, 4 or 5 inches apart, as close to the wall or fence as may be convenient. If they be then well watered and shaded from the sun for a day or two, and protected from cold at night, they will soon make a good start.

SOWING IN OPEN GROUND.—The first sowing in the open ground for a general crop should be made not earlier than the first week in May, for if they are up before the end of that month they are liable to be cut off with frost, unless protection can be afforded them—a rather troublesome matter where large quantities are grown. Some draw drills in which to sow the seeds, but the best way is to plant them in with a dibble about 1 inch deep, and then draw the rake over the ground to fill in the holes. Double rows are to be preferred to single ones, as they produce more beans. Each seed should be at least 6 inches apart. Managed in this way they grow strongly, and if stopped when they have attained the height of 5 or 6 ft., they will produce fine large trusses of bloom from top to bottom. Where successions are desired, several sowings must be made. The general rule is to sow one good crop and let that serve all purposes; but if a sowing be made the first week in May, a second a few weeks afterwards, and another not later than the 1st of July, a continuous supply of young and tender beans will be the result; the last sowing, however, should be only a small one. Sowing in trenches has lately been much practised, and in some cases no doubt with advantage; but when sown in deeply dug ground, trenches are unnecessary.

They are generally made with the view of affording an effectual means of watering the plants; but they necessitate the water being applied close to their bases, which is hurtful rather than beneficial to Runner Beans. Where, however, the earliest crop of Scarlet Runners has to be sown in open quarters, the best way is to take out a trench, say, 3 or 4 inches deep, laying the soil on each side of it in ridges. Pea-wires or bent Hazel sticks may then be placed on the rows after the seed has been sown and covered; these will afford good supports for mat or canvas protections until the plants will do without covering; after which time the soil may be put back in the trench, and no further earthing-up will be necessary.

STICKING SCARLET RUNNERS.— Where procurable, common Peasticks are best adapted for Runner Beans, but they require to be rather larger and stronger than for Peas; for unless firmly sticked, they are apt to suffer during rough, windy weather. Where, however, such sticks are not obtainable, stout poles, 7 or 8 ft. long, may be used, placing them firmly in the ground at intervals of 12 or 14 ft. apart along each side the row. Slender sticks cut the same length as the distance the poles are apart may then be tied lengthways along the poles, 1 or $1\frac{1}{2}$ ft. apart; the plants will twine firmly round these, and thus support themselves.

With respect to soil, a light rich loam is best adapted to growth of the Scarlet Runner, and it should be deep, to allow of the roots descending in time of drought. Previously to planting, the ground should be deeply trenched and enriched by means of a liberal supply of good rotten manure. Where, however, time cannot be spared for this, trenches may be taken out, 2 ft. wide and from 2 to 3 ft. deep, according to the depth of the soil. The soil thus taken out should then have plenty of good manure mixed with it, and be replaced in the trench. If this be done in autumn it will be all the better.

MARKET GARDEN CULTURE.—Scarlet Runners, on account of their taking up more room, are not so much grown in London market gardens as the dwarf French Beans. Their yield is not so great in proportion to the ground occupied, and they are also, unless supported by stakes, more difficult to gather. Around Wandsworth, and in some parts of Kent, within twenty miles of London, however, large fields are devoted to their culture. In some places stakes are used, but, as a rule, the points of the shoots are kept stopped, and the haulm is allowed to rest on the ground. In some respects this latter practice is best, for the rows can be placed close together, and, moreover, the haulm shades the ground and keeps the soil moist, a condition essential to the growth of Scarlet Runners. A rich, light soil and an open situation is that usually chosen for them. Some plant a few rows in warm, sheltered places for early use, the seeds of which are sown in a temporary frame in April, and are transplanted from thence to the open ground as soon as the weather is warm enough to admit of it, but, as a rule, the seed is sown in drills in an open field about the first week in May. Ground previously occupied by Celery suits these Beans perfectly, the soil being deep, well worked, and rich. The seeds are sown in broad drills from 4 to 8 ft. apart, according to whether the plants are to be staked or not. Two rows occupy each drill, and the plants when up are left from 4 to 6 inches apart each way, the thinnings being used to fill up gaps, should such occur. When the plants are fairly up, a ridge of earth is drawn to each side of them, to protect them in some measure from cutting winds and late frosts. When in full flower, the points of the shoots are pinched off, which causes the stem to branch and keep dwarf. Early in July Scarlet Runners appear in Covent Garden, and when that happens French Beans are not in so much demand as hitherto, the majority of vegetable consumers preferring Runners to French Beans. Some market gardeners sow successional crops for autumn use, but the bulk of the produce is brought to market in the end of July and throughout August.

There are several varieties, differing in the colour of their flowers and seeds; the principal are :—

1. The **Scarlet Runner** (*H. d'Espagne Rouge*).—The seeds of this variety are of a light wine-colour, blotched with black.

2. The **Black-seeded Runner** (*H. d'Espagne à Grain Noir*).—The flowers of both this and the preceding variety are of a uniform scarlet colour.

3. **Painted Lady, Bicolor**, or **York and Lancaster Runner** (*H. d'Espagne Bicolore*).—The seed of this variety hardly differs from that of the Scarlet Runner, but the flowers are half red and half white, the keel and wings being white, and the standard scarlet-red.

4. **Hybrid Scarlet Runner** (*H. d'Espagne Hybride*).—The seeds of this kind are very distinct, being of a grayish yellow blotched with brown; the flowers are variegated like those of the Painted Lady.

5. The **White Runner** (*H. d'Espagne Blanc*).—This is the only kind that is sometimes grown in France as a vegetable.

The two following new English varieties are highly recommended:—

Champion Scarlet Runner.—A variety with very long, thick, fleshy pods.

Girtford Giant Scarlet Runner.—The pods of this variety are borne in clusters, and surpass all others in length, breadth, thickness, and fine flavour, and may be cooked either in the usual way, or stringed and served up whole, like the Butter Beans.

White Runner Bean ($\frac{1}{12}$ natural size).

White Runner Bean (*Haricot d'Espagne Blanc*).—Stems very vigorous-growing, climbing, attaining a height of nearly 10 ft. in a few weeks; flowers white, in numerous long-stalked clusters; pods broad, very flat, seldom containing more than three or four seeds each; seeds white, full, very large, kidney-shaped, sometimes 1 inch long, $\frac{3}{5}$ inch broad, and $\frac{2}{5}$ inch thick. A litre of them weighs 735 grammes; 100 grammes contain about 75 seeds. The seeds of Runner Kidney Beans do not usually ripen well in the climate of Paris. In the south of France, however, this species, which is very hardy and very productive, is grown, to a moderate extent, as a vegetable, and in some other countries it is very highly esteemed. In the north of France, the seeds are found to have the skin too thick, and to be deficient in delicacy of flavour. They certainly contain a great deal of *farina*, but are inferior, especially in the dried state, to any of the good French varieties of Kidney Beans. In England the pods are most generally used in the young green state, many preferring the flavour of these when quite young to that of the Kidney Beans in a similar stage.

LARGE LIMA KIDNEY BEAN.

Phaseolus lunatus, L.

French, Haricots de Lima.   *German*, Breitshottige Lima Bohne.   *Italian*, Fagiuolo di Lima.   *Spanish*, Judia de Lima.

Native of South America.—Annual.—Stem climbing to the height of nearly 10 ft.; leaves composed of three triangular leaflets, longer and narrower than those of ordinary Kidney Beans; flowers small, greenish-white, in numerous stiff elongated clusters; pods short, very flat and very broad, rough on the outside, like those of the Runner Kidney Beans; seeds flat and short, slightly kidney-shaped, with one half nearly always larger than the other, and usually marked with wrinkles or flutings from the *hilum* outwards. The varieties of this Kidney Bean are grown in the same manner as the ordinary Tall-growing Kidney Beans, but they are later, and seldom ripen seed in the climate of Paris. The seeds are sent to table either fresh or in the dried state. They contain a great deal of *farina*, and are highly esteemed in the United States and in some warm countries. The bean is distinct and very good in quality.

Common Lima Kidney Bean (*Haricot de Lima*).— Rather late-growing, never ripening more than a portion of its pods in the climate of Paris, and never ripening there at all in cold damp seasons. Stems thickish, and of a pale-green colour; leaves medium sized, smooth, and of a grayish green; seed broad and flat, white, slightly tinged with yellow, over $\frac{3}{4}$ inch long, about $\frac{3}{5}$ inch broad, and nearly $\frac{1}{4}$ inch thick. A litre of them weighs 725 grammes, and 100 grammes contain about 90 seeds. There is a green-seeded variety, and another which has white seed, like that of the type, but marked with a small brown or blackish blotch close to the *hilum*.

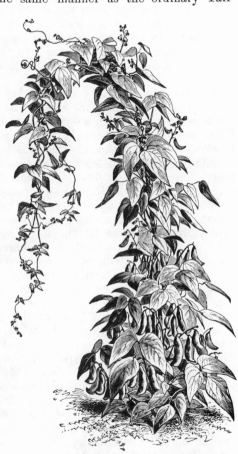

Large Lima Kidney Bean ($\frac{1}{12}$ natural size).

Mottled Lima, or **Marbled Cape, Kidney Bean** (*Haricot du Cap Marbré*).—This is distinguished from the preceding kind only by the very peculiar variegation of the seed, in which a large patch of red, more or less deep, surrounds the *hilum*, from which it extends to one end of the seed, which it entirely covers for about one-third of its length; the remainder of the surface being finely dotted with the same red colour on a white ground. A litre of the seed weighs 675 grammes, and 100 grammes contain about 100 seeds. This variety is almost as late as the preceding one.

Small Lima, or **Sieva, Kidney Bean** (*Haricot de Sieva*).—Stems slender and green; leaves smaller and darker in colour than those of the Common Lima Kidney Bean.   This variety of *Phaseolus lunatus* is distinguished from the preceding ones by the much smaller size of its seeds, which in other respects resemble those of the Common Lima Kidney Bean, but are seldom over $\frac{2}{3}$ inch in length, about $\frac{1}{3}$ inch broad, and $\frac{1}{6}$ inch thick.   A litre of them weighs 780 grammes, and 100 grammes contain about 220 seeds.   The Small Lima Kidney Bean is also earlier than the other varieties of *Phaseolus lunatus*, and its first pods ripen regularly in the climate of Paris; but it is very far from being as productive there as it is in warm climates, where it often continues bearing for three months.   In the United States a variety is grown which has the seed streaked with red.

Several species of the genus *Dolichos* also are cultivated as kitchen-garden plants, especially in warm countries.   Of these, we shall only mention the kinds which are capable of being grown in the climate of Paris, and which are the only ones that are successfully cultivated in France, even in Provence and the south-western districts.

Black-eyed Bird's-Foot Bean (*Dolichos unguiculatus*, L. *Leguminosæ.   Dolique Mongette*).—An annual plant, usually growing from 20 inches to 2 feet high, with leaves composed of three triangular, elongated leaflets, which are rounded at the base, very smooth, and of a dark-green colour.   Flowers large, changing from white to rose-colour and lilac, with a deeper-coloured blotch at the base of the petals, and growing in twos or threes on a thick stout flower-stalk; pods of a pale-green colour, straight, or curved as they become heavy, varying in length from 6 to 10 inches, nearly cylindrical, and slightly bulged over the seeds, which usually lie at some distance from each other; seeds rather variable in size and colour, usually white, of a short kidney shape, blunt or square at both ends, slightly wrinkled, and marked with a very pronounced black blotch around the *hilum*.   A litre of them weighs 760 grammes, and 100 grammes contain about 530 seeds.   In those countries where, as in Italy, it is extensively cultivated, a great number of varieties are grown, which differ from one another principally in the size of the seeds.   The climate of Britain is too cold for these plants, but many parts of the colonies are suited for their culture.   They bear a degree of heat which injures the Beans that thrive with us.   CULTURE is the same as that of the Dwarf varieties of Kidney Beans.   This plant, however, is not much affected by hot, dry weather, nor very particular as to the soil in which it is grown.   The young pods are cooked in the same way as green Haricots.

A few years ago, M. Durieu de Maisonneuve, director of the Botanic Garden at Bordeaux, introduced a very singular variety of this plant, the pods of which, instead of being straight, are curved round and round, from which peculiarity it received the name of Ram's-Horn Bean (*Dolique Corne de Bélier*).   Its culture and uses are the same as those of the ordinary variety. (See also **Asparagus Bean** and **Lab-lab**.)

BEET-ROOT.

Beta vulgaris, L.   *Chenopodiaceæ.*

French, Betterave, Bette, Racine d'abondance.   *German*, Runkel-Rübe.   *Dutch* and *Flemish*, Betwortel.   *Danish*, Rodbede.   *Italian*, Barbabietola.   *Spanish*, Remolacha. *Portuguese*, Betarava.

Native of Europe.—Biennial.—A plant which, in the first year of its growth, forms a more or less long, thick, and fleshy root, and runs to seed in the second year.   The fruiting stem is about 4 ft. high, and as the calyx of the flower continues to grow after the flower has faded, and completely covers the seed, it becomes corky in substance and appearance, and forms what is commonly called Beet-seed, but which is really a fruit, nearly as large as a pea, and almost always containing several seeds.   A gramme contains about 50 of these fruits or so-called seeds, and a litre of them weighs 250 grammes.   The true seeds are very small, kidney-shaped, of a brown colour, and with an exceedingly thin skin.   They retain their germinating power for six years or more.

It is not exactly known when the Beet-root was first introduced into cultivation.   The ancients were acquainted with the plant, but we have no account from which we can be certain that they cultivated it. Olivier de Serres mentions it as having been introduced into France from Italy not long before the time at which he wrote.

CULTURE.—Beet is sown, where the crop is to grow, in the open air, as soon as the spring frosts are over, and best in drills, for greater convenience in hoeing; and the young plants are thinned out, with a greater or less space between them according to the size of the variety grown.   They prefer a deep, rich, well-manured, and well-tilled soil. It is a good plan to dig in the manure in the autumn, as fresh strawy manure is apt to cause the roots to become forked.   A few waterings in dry weather will be the only additional attention required by the growing plants, the roots of which come to maturity from July to the end of autumn, according to the time at which sowings were made.

A deep sandy loam, trenched to a depth of at least 30 inches, suits it better than any other kind of soil, and if poor, it should have been well manured for the previous vegetable crop.   In such soil, the evenest and cleanest roots are produced; but Beet will also succeed on calcareous soils, if of sufficient depth.   Heavy or stiff loams intended for its growth should be thrown up into ridges before winter sets in, so as to get well pulverized, and, if very heavy, a light dressing of coal ashes worked into them would prove advantageous, and materially assist in producing " clean " roots.   Stable manure should not be added to the soil unless it is trenched deeply, when it may be placed quite at the bottom of the trench; if otherwise, as soon as the roots reach it they become forked, instead of making straight and well-shaped roots; therefore, if the soil be so poor as to require manure, a sprinkling of guano or superphosphate, applied to it between the rows as soon as the plants are fairly established, will be found the best stimulant.

SOWING, ETC.—Beet must have an open situation; it never grows or looks satisfactorily when grown under the shade of fruit trees—a position to which it is often relegated; but this should not be, for most varieties of Beet are ornamental as well as useful, and one would, therefore, suppose that a conspicuous place would be selected for them. The time for sowing varies from the beginning of April to the middle of May. In the majority of soils, about the 20th of April will be found to be the best time; if sown too early, especially if the soil be rich, it is liable to run to seed, or the roots to grow too large—medium-sized roots being always most highly valued, more particularly for salading. The seed should be sown in drills 15 inches asunder, and 1½ inch deep; and it should be covered in by hand, —a rake should not be employed for this purpose, as by its use half the seed is often drawn out of the drills, and the plants come up irregularly. Thin out the seedlings, as soon as they are large enough to handle, to 9 inches apart in the row, and if dark, bronzy-leaved kinds be grown, see that the greenest-looking plants are drawn out. After thinning has been completed, by means of the hoe frequently loosen the soil between the rows—an operation which will aid the growth of the Beet, and at the same time keep down the weeds. If blanks, through failures, occur in the rows, they should be filled up with young plants in showery weather, though roots obtained in this way rarely prove satisfactory, being small and irregular in growth; still it is worth doing, if only for the sake of appearance.

VARIETIES.—As a rule, the colour of the roots is the first consideration; but flavour should in our opinion have precedence, rather than colour. Where both are combined, however, as is the case in Dell's Crimson, which has many synonyms, such a variety must be the best to grow; moreover, this variety has the additional attraction of deep crimson-coloured foliage, and is of no small importance as an ornamental plant. Other good varieties are—Henderson's Pine-apple, Dirhmick's Nonpareil, Nutting's Dwarf Red, and Egyptian Turnip-rooted, the last

being more especially valuable for early summer supply, as it comes into use nearly a fortnight earlier than any of the long-rooted sorts. It is also suited for growth on shallow soils, and, although pale in colour, is of excellent quality.

STORING BEET-ROOT. — Frost is most injurious to Beet-roots, which should, therefore, be dug up by the end of October, or provision should be made for protecting them in the ground, in the event of severe weather setting in. Stable litter, hay-bands, or Bracken (*Pteris aquilina*) will effectually protect Beet; but, where neatness is studied rather than utility, this manner of protection should not be thought of. In that case, the roots should be dug up at the time mentioned above, and " clamped " in the same way as Potatoes; or they may be layered in dry soil or sand, in a cool shed,—but it must be really cool, or they will start into growth, and the flavour will go.

For market-garden culture, a good crop of Beet-root is very remunerative, and when there is a ready sale for it in the market it pays better than any other root crop. The main sowing is made to succeed Wallflowers, Radishes, Spinach, or Cabbages, and it is also often grown on Asparagus ridges, between rows of fruit bushes, and between lines of Vegetable Marrows; and even when growing in the open field, it is often intercropped. An early sowing is usually made, in lines about 15 inches apart, in the first week of May, between rows of Cabbages or Lettuces, recently planted; after the seeds germinate and the plants are well above ground, they are thinned out into patches with short hoes, and when they have formed a few rough leaves they are thinned out to single plants by hand. Some make a sowing even as early as in March, in a sheltered piece of ground, for yielding an early supply. In harvesting a crop of Beet-root which has to be kept through the winter, the roots are carefully dug up, preserving them their whole length intact, and keeping 2 inches of the stalks attached after the leaves have been twisted off by hand. They are then built in pyramidal-shaped clumps, and covered with straw, over which a coating of soil is put to exclude frost. Leaving the roots in the ground is the best plan, as their proper flavour is thereby preserved better than when lifted and stored; but they are liable to be injured by frosts in January, or to be locked in the soil when it might be convenient to send them to market. Some of the darkest and finest-shaped roots are kept for seed-bearing plants, and are planted in some out-of-the-way nook by themselves. Transplanting Beet is only resorted to to fill up vacancies in the rows, as in the operation the main roots are often broken, or otherwise so damaged as to render it almost impossible for them to produce good roots. Dark crimson-coloured Beets are those which are most esteemed by market gardeners, most of whom grow their seeds saved from selected plants. Carters' St. Osyth is a favourite kind with many growers, but none are liked so well as the selected Dark Crimson.

The different varieties of Beet-root are not all, properly speaking, kitchen-garden plants. However, as it is difficult to determine exactly the kinds which are grown as garden vegetables and those which are cultivated rather for agricultural or economic purposes, we shall here mention all the principal known varieties, noting especially those which are more particularly grown as kitchen-garden plants.

Uses.—A great number of varieties are grown for table use, the roots being either plainly boiled or baked, or pickled, or mixed in salads. Other varieties are used for feeding cattle, or for the manufacture of sugar—for purely agricultural purposes, in fact. When lifted, the tops should not be cut, but screwed off, and the roots should not be injured more than can be helped, as injury to them induces decay. Before cooking, the roots should be well washed, but not peeled or scraped, or in any way bruised; for, if such be the case, much of the saccharine matter escapes during the boiling. Boiling doubtless renders Beet most agreeable to the generality of consumers; though some prefer to bake it, by which mode a deeper colour and a firmer texture of flesh are insured.

GARDEN BEET.

Betteraves potagères.

I. Red-fleshed Varieties.

Rough-skinned, or Red, Beet-root (*Betterave Crapaudine, B. Écorce*).—This is one of the oldest varieties, and is very easily distinguished from all the others by the peculiar appearance of the skin, which is black and broken by small cracks or crevices, like the bark of a young tree, or perhaps still more resembling the skin of a Black Winter Radish. Root rather long, almost entirely buried in the soil, and frequently somewhat irregular in shape; flesh very red, sugary, and firm; leaves numerous, slightly twisted, spreading rather than

erect, almost entirely green, and with red stalks. This variety affords
a striking instance of the absence of any necessary correspondence
of the colour of the flesh of a Beet-root to the colour of its leaves.
No other kind has deeper-coloured flesh than this, and yet many
have the leaves much more deeply tinged with red.

The varieties known as the Little Negress of Rennes (*Petite
Négresse de Rennes*) and the Red Beet-Root of Diorières (*B. Rouge des
Diorières*) do not appear to differ from the ordinary variety.

Small Deep Blood-red Castelnaudary Beet (*Betterave Rouge de
Castelnaudary*).—Root smallish, nearly buried in the soil, rather
slender, straight, sometimes with a tap-root of some length; skin
blackish red; flesh very dark red, compact, solid, and very sugary;
leaves dark red, with long stalks. This variety does not yield a heavy
crop, but its quality is excellent. The English varieties Long Deep-
red and Very Dark-red are very similar to this.

The Covent Garden Red Beet (*Betterave Rouge de Covent Garden*)

Rough-skinned, or Red,
Beet-root (⅕ natural size).

Small Blood-red Castelnaudary
Beet (⅕ natural size).

is a very handsome kitchen-garden
variety, with a long, slender root,
quite sunk in the soil, and smoother
and cleaner skinned than that of the Castlenaudary; leaves spreading,
not very large, slightly crimped, and of a nearly black-red colour;
flesh deep red, compact, and sugary.

Dwarf Red Beet (*Betterave Rouge Naine*).—A very handsome
variety. Root very symmetrical in shape, small, slender, longish, deeply
sunk in the soil; leaves deep red, half erect, uncrimped, slightly
undulated, and much longer than broad. This variety, like the preceding one, produces small roots, but to make some amends for this,

they can be grown very close together.   Both varieties are moderately early.

Dell's Dark Crimson Dwarf Beet (*Betterave Rouge Naine de Dell à Feuille Noire*).—This variety is distinguished by the dark-red colour of its leaves, which are broadly crimped and have an almost glazy lustre. Like those of the preceding variety, they grow curving towards the ground. .This variety is doubly valuable for the delicate flavour of the root and the ornamental character of the foliage.

Many other English varieties resemble the Dwarf Red and Dell's Crimson, without being exactly like either of these kinds.   Of these we will only mention Bailey's Fine Red, Sang's Dwarf Crimson, and the Saint Osyth Beet.   The two following varieties are to be com-

Dwarf Red Beet
($\frac{1}{3}$ natural size).

Dell's Crimson Beet
($\frac{1}{3}$ natural size).

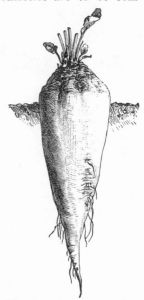

Whyte's Black Beet ($\frac{1}{3}$ natural size).

mended :—*Omega Dwarf-topped*, a medium-sized, handsomely shaped Beet, with delicately sweet, rich crimson flesh; and *Nonpareil Dwarf Green-top*, a very dwarf kind, with small, well-formed, scarlet-fleshed roots.

Whyte's Black Beet. Synonyms: Osborn's Improved Blood-red, Barratt's Crimson, Oldacre's Blood-red, Perkins's Black (*Betterave Rouge Foncé de Whyte*).—A handsome medium-sized kind.   Root long, thickish under the neck, sometimes a little angular instead of being regularly rounded; skin smooth, of a very deep slate colour; flesh blackish red, firm, and of good quality; leaves rather stout, slightly crimped and undulated, of a brownish-red colour, more or less tinged and mixed with green; leaf-stalks red. This is one of the best varieties; the flesh is very deeply coloured, and the root can be easily distinguished from all others by the grayish or leaden hue of the skin. It is tolerably productive, and keeps well.

Large Blood-red Beet (*Betterave Rouge Grosse*).—This is the kind which is most extensively grown in France, being intermediate between the garden and the field varieties.   It is very productive, very hardy, and of good quality for table use. It is also the kind which is most frequently brought ready boiled to the market-places. Root almost cylindrical, as thick as a man's arm, and 1 ft. to 14 inches long, growing with nearly one-third of its length overground, sometimes becoming tap-rooted and forked at the extremity. The colour of the skin of the part covered by the soil is of a uniform deep red, while the part overground is more or less reddish and wrinkled. Flesh a deep-red colour; leaves large and stout, green marbled, and veined with red; leaf-stalks very red. The large size of the roots of this variety and the heavy crop which it yields recommend it as the best of the kitchen-garden varieties for field culture. For some time past, very red-fleshed and red-juiced kinds of Beet have been much sought after for various economic or manufacturing purposes, and the variety now described is eminently adapted for such uses.

Large Blood-red Beet (⅕ natural size).

The **Gardanne Beet** (*B. de Gardanne*), which is in high repute in the south of France, comes very near this variety, differing from it only by being a little thicker under the neck, and growing with less of the root overground.

American Long Smooth Blood-red, Radish, or **Long Smooth Rochester Beet** (*Betterave Rouge Longue Lisse;* German, *Lange Dunkelrothe Glatte Amerikanische Salat-Rübe*).—Root very long, almost cylindrical, attaining a length of 14 inches, with a diameter of hardly 2 inches, and almost entirely underground; skin smooth and uniform, of a dark-red colour; flesh blackish red. A handsome variety, of good quality, and keeping well. To grow well, it requires a deep, well-dug, and well-manured soil.

Strasbourg Pear-shaped, Non Plus Ultra, or Intermediate Dark Beet (⅕ natural size).

Strasbourg Pear-shaped, Non Plus Ultra, or **Intermediate Dark Beet** (*Betterave Piriforme de Strasbourg*).—An intermediate variety, very deeply sunk in the soil. Skin and flesh of an extremely deep-red colour, as are also the leaves and leaf-stalks, both of which are almost black. This is the deepest coloured of all the kitchen-garden varieties. It must be observed, however, that it is not a very productive kind, and that the leaves and leaf-stalks are rather largely developed in proportion to the size of the root, which, unlike that of the Dwarf Red variety, when pulled, belies the promise given by the foliage.

Early Blood-red Turnip-rooted Beet (*Betterave Rouge Ronde Précoce*).—An early variety, with a round and half-flattened root, scarcely half of which is buried in the soil; skin dark violet-red; flesh of a fine red; leaves rather large, green, broadly marbled and veined with brownish red. To this variety may be referred, as almost identical with it, the kinds named Flat Blackish-red (*B. Rouge Noir Plate*), Black-leaved Round Red (*B. Rouge Ronde à Feuilles Noires*), and the English variety Early Blood-red.

Early Blood-red Turnip-rooted Beet (⅕ natural size).

Eclipse Turnip Beet.—This variety comes pretty near the Turnip-rooted Red Beet, from which it is chiefly distinguished by its somewhat slighter foliage, and the form of the root, which is more top-shaped, often resembling that of the Early Round Parsnip. This, indeed, was the shape of the Turnip-rooted Beet itself at first, and it was only by means of successive improvements in its cultivation that it has now come to have only a very small and slender tap-root.

Bastian's Turnip Beet.—Like the preceding variety, this closely resembles the Turnip-rooted Red Beet, of which it may be regarded as a sub-variety. It is of good quality and well coloured, both in the leaves and the flesh, but for earliness and regularity of shape the Eclipse Turnip Beet appears to us to be preferable.

Dewing's Early Blood-red Beet.—A handsome small variety, rather distinct, and tolerably regular in shape. It might be said to be intermediate between the Egyptian Dark-red Turnip Beet and the Trévise Red Beet mentioned on p. 82. The plant is of small size and rather early, and the root is thicker, more deeply buried in the soil, and not so flat as that of the Egyptian Turnip Beet. The leaves are of no great size, and are of a deep blackish red, almost exactly resembling those of the Dwarf Red Beet. The flesh is of a very deep red, firm, and of good quality.

Egyptian Dark-red Turnip-rooted Beet (*Betterave Rouge Noir Plate d'Egypte*).—An exceedingly early variety, and certainly the best of the early kitchen-garden kinds. Root rounded and flattened, especially underneath, almost entirely overground, and resting on the surface (to which it is held down by a rather slender tap-root), very symmetrical in shape until it has grown larger than the fist, when it frequently becomes irregular or sinuated in form as it increases in size. Skin very smooth, of a violet or slaty red colour; flesh of a dark blood colour; leaves slight, brownish red, more or less mixed with green; leaf-stalks long and slender, and of a lively red colour. When sown in the open air under favourable conditions, the roots of this variety may be pulled for table use in June, when they are about as big as a small orange, their quality being then at its best.

Egyptian Dark-red Turnip-rooted Beet (⅕ natural size).

If sown on a hot-bed, they may be pulled still earlier. Like the Dwarf Red variety, the roots of this kind also may be grown very close together.

Early Flat Bassano Beet (*Betterave Rouge de Bassano*).—A stout-

G

growing, broad, flat variety, with numerous but rather slender green leaves; leaf-stalks tinged with red; skin of the root grayish red, especially the part over-ground; flesh in bands or zones of white and rose-colour, firm, sugary, delicate, and highly esteemed in some countries. This is a moderately early and very productive kind.

Early Flat Bassano Beet
(⅕ natural size).

The following varieties deserve to be mentioned as very distinct:—

Trévise Early Salad Beet, or **Turin Red Spring Beet** (*B. Rouge à Salade de Trévise,* or *B. Rouge printanière de Turin*). —A very dwarf variety, with a flattened, deeply buried root, the skin of which is almost black, and the flesh blood-coloured; leaves dark red, and as small as those of the Dwarf Red variety. This variety, which is almost as early as the Egyptian Dark-red Turnip-rooted Beet, may to a certain degree supply the place of the latter. Intermediate between them is the American variety named Dewing, or Dewing's Extra Early Turnip Beet, which, while having the root somewhat more deeply sunk in the ground than the latter variety, has the small, fine, very highly coloured leaves, and the very dark-coloured flesh of the former.

Short's Pine-apple Beet, Pine-apple Dwarf Red, or **Henderson's Pine-apple Beet.**—A compact-growing kind, with a rather short root, which is tap-rooted, and about 2 or 3 inches in diameter; flesh very dark coloured; leaves stiff and spreading, red, with orange-coloured stalks.

Victoria Beet.—A variety of German origin, with an intermediate root of a deep-red colour, less remarkable for its value as a vegetable than for the singular metallic appearance of its leaves, and quite as much grown for ornamental as it is for kitchen-garden purposes.

Long Blood-red Beet.—An American variety, with a long, deeply buried root, which is rather prone to forking, apart from which drawback it is a good, productive, and well-coloured kind.

Long Yellow, or Orange, Beet
(⅕ natural size).

II.　Yellow-fleshed Varieties.

Long Yellow, or **Orange, Beet** (*Betterave Jaune Grosse*).—This variety is almost as much grown in the fields as in the kitchen garden, and is the kind which is principally cultivated by the cow-keepers of Paris and its vicinity, on account of its highly reputed nutritious and milk-producing qualities. Root long, almost cylindrical, about half of it overground; leaves erect, stout, green, with yellow stalks; skin of the root orange yellow; flesh golden yellow, marked with zones more or less pale, and sometimes nearly white. It is the most productive and one of the best Yellow-fleshed kinds.

Yellow Castelnaudary, or **Small Yellow, Beet** (*Betterave Jaune de Castelnaudary*).—A small variety, with a rather slender root, which is completely buried in the soil, and is sometimes forked; flesh deep yellow, exceedingly sugary, firm, and solid; leaves usually spreading, numerous, crimped; leaf-stalks and ribs of the leaves deep yellow.

Yellow, or **Orange, Turnip Beet** (*Betterave Jaune Ronde Sucrée*).—Root slightly top-shaped, with a stout tap-root; skin orange yellow; flesh bright yellow, zoned with pale yellow or white; leaves rather short and broad, crimped, undulated, with yellow ribs and stalks. A very sugary and fine-flavoured variety, the root, when well boiled, becoming tinged with orange. It is one of the best additions which of late years has been made to the list of kitchen-garden plants.

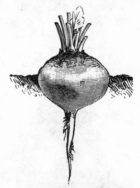

Yellow, or Orange, Turnip Beet (⅓ natural size).

CATTLE-FEEDING VARIETIES.

French, Betteraves fourragères. *German*, Mangel-Wurzel, Futter-Rübe, Futter-Runkelrübe. *Flemish* and *Dutch*, Mangel-Wortel. *Spanish*, Remolacha de gran cultivo, Betabel campestre.

Thick Red Mangold-Wurzel (*Betterave Disette Camuse*).—This was perhaps the earliest-cultivated form of the Mangold-Wurzel. Root spindle-shaped, almost entirely buried in the soil; skin wine-red; flesh white or zoned with rose-colour; leaves stout, erect, broad, sometimes tinged with brownish red. This variety, being only moderately productive, and the roots not easily pulled out of the ground, is now very little grown. The following kinds are generally preferred, and justly so :—

Thick Red Mangold-Wurzel (⅓ natural size).

Long Red Mangold (*Betterave Disette d'Allemagne*).—Root long, almost cylindrical, not uncommonly as much as 20 inches in length, with a diameter of 5 or 6 inches; skin bright or violet-tinted red on the portion underground, and more or less grayish or bronzy on the exposed upper part; leaves like those of the preceding variety. The upper portion of the root, which bears the scars of the leaves which have grown and fallen from it one after another through the entire period of the development of the plant, is of a conical shape, more or less elongated. It is no great blemish in these Cattle-feeding Mangolds that this part of the root should be of

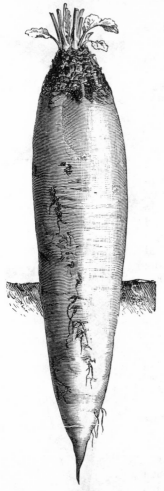

Long Red Mangold
(⅕ natural size).

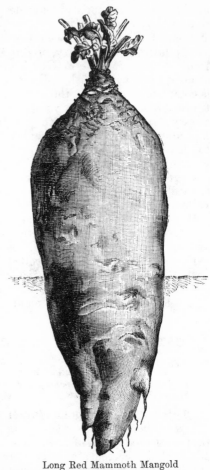

Long Red Mammoth Mangold
(⅕ natural size).

some considerable size, since it is very nearly as nutritious as the rest of the root; nevertheless, a clean-skinned and well-formed neck is always one of the marks of the most refined or improved varieties.

The English variety Elvetham Long Red Mangold seems to be exactly intermediate between this and the following variety.

Long Red Mammoth Mangold (*Betterave Disette Mammoth*).—This is a short, thick variety of the preceding kind, from which it differs principally in its fuller, more thick-set, and less cylindrical shape, the diameter of the root being nearly equal to half its length. Skin pale red or rose-colour; neck shortly conical; leaves rather large, green, or slightly bronzed, usually somewhat crimped; leaf-stalks more or less tinged with red. In very good soils, this variety will yield as heavy a crop as the preceding kind, or even heavier, and that without any distortion or warping of the roots sideways. The roots are also comparatively easy to pull out of the ground.

Long Red Ox-horn Mangold (*Betterave Disette Corne de Bœuf*).—A very long and slender variety of the Long Red Mangold, which almost always becomes more or less distorted, during its growth, into the shape

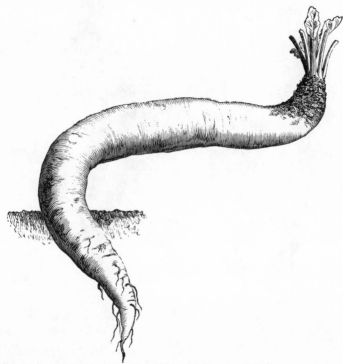

Long Red Ox-horn Mangold (⅕ natural size).

from which it takes its name. In certain districts of France it is esteemed above all other kinds, although the peculiar shape of the roots would appear likely to give a good deal of trouble in carrying and storing them. The leaves are more frequently tinged with reddish brown in this variety than in the ordinary Long Red.

Large Black, or **Long Negro Red-fleshed, Mangold-Wurzel** (*Betterave Disette Négresse*).—A somewhat new variety, of late years often highly spoken of from many districts in France. It may be described as being almost intermediate between the Long Red and Large Blood-red varieties. It is shorter and grows more out of the ground than the Long Red, but it is of a very decided red colour in all its parts, even the flesh being either entirely red or deeply zoned with blood-red; the leaves also are very highly coloured. Although the root is shorter than that of the Long Red, it is nevertheless a very productive kind, as the roots are generally thick and somewhat bulging at the sides. Its nutritive qualities are considered equal to those of the Yellow-fleshed varieties.

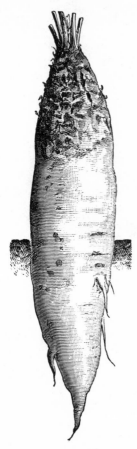

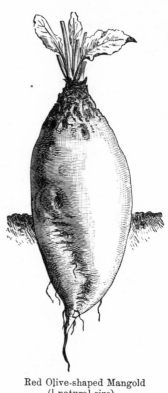

Red Olive-shaped Mangold
($\frac{1}{5}$ natural size).

Long White Green-top Mangold
($\frac{1}{5}$ natural size).

Long White Green-top Mangold (*Betterave Disette Blanche à Collet Vert*).—A very vigorous kind, which continues to grow for a long time, and is consequently late, but at the same time extremely productive. Root about 20 inches long, with a diameter of 5 or 6 inches, often slightly squared or angular, and growing one-half, or sometimes two-thirds, overground ; skin of the part underground very white, that of the exposed upper part greenish ; neck of a long conical shape ; leaves numerous, erect, very stout, entirely green, as are also the leaf-stalks. This is one of the most productive varieties, but it is best suited for stiff, clayey, moist soils, which do not suffer from very dry weather nor from early frosts.

Long White Red-top Mangold (*Betterave Disette Blanche d'Argent*). —A rather new and very productive kind, somewhat resembling the preceding variety, but with cleaner roots, the underground portion of which has the skin tinged with rose-colour, which is also very marked on the neck of the root and on the leaf-stalks. It appears to be somewhat earlier than the Long White Green-top, and is in every way worthy of cultivation. The root presents a striking likeness to that of the Gray-top Sugar Beet, but is considerably longer and larger, and the leaves are stouter and more numerous. Both kinds are precisely alike in colour. The neck of the root of the Long White Red-top Mangold is usually fine and well-shaped.

Red Olive-shaped, Red Ovoid, Red Giant, or Red Intermediate Mangold (*Betterave Rouge Ovoide*).—This variety does not usually attain the large dimensions which its French name of *Disette Géante* would lead one to expect. It is more remarkable for the regular shape of the root and for its earliness. The root is seldom more than from 12 to 14 inches long, and 6 or 7 inches broad, egg-shaped, narrowing a good deal towards the neck and towards the root. In colour it resembles the Long Red Mangold. Leaves not very numerous, narrow, erect, on longish stalks, and almost always of a deep-reddish colour; flesh white. Although the Red Olive-shaped Mangold has been a long time in cultivation, it has never exhibited the same constancy of character which many newer varieties are found to maintain.

Red Globe Mangold (*Betterave Rouge Globe*).—This kind presents nearly the same characteristics as the preceding one, with the exception of its shape, which is quite spherical. Leaves slight, brownish red, like those of the Red Olive-shaped, which this variety also resembles in its earliness. The two kinds are generally considered less productive than most of the other sorts of Mangold, but then they could perhaps be grown closer together, which would, in some degree at least, lessen the disparity in the yield which arises from the smaller size of the individual roots, and which is partly compensated by the greater earliness of the crop.

Red Globe Mangold ($\frac{1}{5}$ natural size).

Long Yellow White-fleshed Mangold (*Betterave Jaune d'Allemagne*).—Root almost cylindrical, buried in the soil for one-third or two-fifths of its length, the skin of the underground part being of an ochre or slightly orange-yellow colour, while that of the part above ground is of a greenish or grayish yellow; the portion of the root immediately under the neck is often slightly bulged or swollen. Leaves green, large, hardly or not at all crimped; leaf-stalks stout, half erect, of a pale-green colour, without any tinge of yellow when the plants are true to name; flesh of the root perfectly white, firm, very solid, and tolerably sugary. This variety is somewhat smaller and less productive than the Long Red or the Long White Red-top kinds, but it is considered by most cultivators to make amends for these deficiencies by its greater earliness and superior nutritive qualities, and especially by its capability of being successfully cultivated in dry or calcareous soils, in which the white or rosy-skinned kinds do very badly. From this kind have, very probably, been derived the Yellow Globe and Yellow Des Barres Mangolds, which, on account of their shape, are now generally cultivated in preference to it. There is also another

Yellow Olive-shaped Mangold (⅕ natural size).

Long Yellow White-fleshed Mangold (⅕ natural size).

form of it, which has an exceedingly slender root, very often curved like the Ox-horn Mangold. This is pretty extensively grown in some districts of France, although it does not appear to be preferred on account of any intrinsic merit that it possesses. There is, besides, another variety with a long, large, thick root, bearing nearly the same relation to the Long Yellow which the Long Red Mammoth does to the ordinary Long Red. These two varieties do not appear to have proper names, and are merely variations of the ordinary forms, possessing no special merit. The Ox-horn kinds, indeed, have this very serious drawback—that their roots, even before they are half grown, twist and turn themselves across the spaces between the rows, so as to render it impossible to use any machines or implements drawn by horses in keeping the ground clean.

Yellow Olive-shaped, Yellow Intermediate, or **Yellow Ovoid Barres Mangold** (*Betterave Jaune Ovoide des Barres*).—A handsome variety, similar in shape to the Red Olive-shaped, but more rounded at the extremities, and of perceptibly greater size. It has all the good qualities of the Yellow Globe Mangold, and, moreover, yields a heavier crop. It is a very suitable kind for calcareous soils. Repeated trials prove that it is entitled to a place in the first rank of Mangolds for productiveness and general good quality. It is hardy, very productive, and as a great part of the root grows overground, the labour of pulling the crop is not very heavy. The leaves are of a very light green, with pale green ribs and stalks. The flesh of the root is firm, very nutritious, and white, like the flesh of the Yellow Globe Mangold, but the skin is of a more orange yellow. The root of this Mangold contains so much sugar that it is sometimes used in rural distilleries for the manufacture of alcohol; in fact, from the same area, and under similar conditions of growth, it produces nearly twice as heavy a crop of roots as the ordinary kinds of Sugar Beet, from which the relative yield of alcohol is not double the quantity obtained from the same weight of the roots of this Mangold. Besides, the crop is more easily pulled than the Sugar Beets, and keeps remarkably well. This variety was raised and established forty years since by M. Vilmorin, senior, on his estate of Barres (Loiret), by means of a continued selection of choice roots of the Long Yellow Mangold. From its combination of good qualities, it soon became one of the most generally cultivated varieties in other countries as well as in France. In England it is one of the kinds most extensively cultivated, and all the varieties known by the names of Yellow Oval, Yellow Mammoth Intermediate, and Giant Long Yellow Intermediate Mangold are, in fact, to be referred to it.

Yellow Globe Mangold (*Betterave Jaune Globe*).—This is one of the most extensively grown of all the varieties of Mangolds, being hardy, productive, easily pulled, and a good keeper. It is nearly spherical in shape, and of a slightly orange-yellow colour, the part overground somewhat grayish. Leaves numerous, erect, with green stalks. The flesh of the root is white, firm, and sugary. Cattle are particularly fond of it, and it may also be grown for distillery uses. In England, where this kind is very much grown, a great number of sub-varieties exist, which are named either after the person who raised them or from the district in which they are more especially grown. Such are the kinds known as Berkshire Prize, Champion Yellow Globe, Improved Orange Globe,

Yellow Globe Mangold (⅙ natural size).

Normanton Globe, Warden Orange Globe, Wroxton Golden Globe, etc. All these sorts are generally noticeable for their clean-skinned and finely necked roots.

White Globe Mangold (*Betterave Blanche Globe*).—This very distinct kind, which was raised twenty-five or thirty years ago by M. Gareau, appears to have now almost entirely disappeared from cultivation, having been superseded by the Yellow Globe, which is more productive and keeps better.

Flattened Globe Mangolds (*Betteraves Globe Aplaties*).—These
sub-varieties, which appear to have been entirely neglected by French
cultivators, are still preserved in Germany, where they are known as
Oberndorf Mangolds. They differ from the ordinary Globe varieties by
having the root quite flat underneath, and growing entirely on the
surface of the soil. There are three forms of them, viz., the White, the
Yellow, and the Red.

Golden Melon, or Dobito's Improved, Mangold.—A variety of the
Yellow Globe, which has the flesh and also the leaf-stalks more or less
tinged with yellow. It is reputed to possess more nutritive properties
than the ordinary Yellow Globe, but, so
far as we have seen of it, it seems very
much inclined to degenerate, and is no
great cropper.

Yellow Tankard Mangold (*Betterave
Jaune Tankard*).—This variety is to the
Des Barres Yellow Olive-shaped what the
Golden Melon is to the Yellow Globe.

Orange Globe Mangold.

Yellow Tankard Mangold
(⅓ natural size).

The root is not so distinctly egg-shaped
as that of the Barres variety, but is
rather almost cylindrical, narrowing abruptly at both ends. The skin is of a
rather deep orange red, the leaf-stalks are tinged with yellow, and the
flesh of the root is zoned with yellow and white.

All the yellow-skinned varieties are considered to be more especially
adapted for calcareous soils than any other variety of Mangold. At
any rate, it is certain that they are perfectly hardy, withstand drought,
and contain a greater amount of nutritive matter, weight for weight,
than the red or white-skinned kinds; but they are, for the most part,
inferior to the red kinds in the weight of the crop. The latter,
although not quite so well shaped, and producing a larger proportion
of foliage, yield a heavier crop to the acre—a very important quality
in a cattle-feeding plant.

Orange Globe Mangold (*Betterave Orange Globe*).—This handsome variety exhibits the good points of which we have just spoken ; that is, it produces exceedingly clean roots, of an almost regularly spherical shape, having only very small rootlets on the lower part, and with few and slight leaves, which, when they fall, leave hardly any scars on the neck of the root, so that when it is pulled it is smooth and even up to the small tuft of leaves which remains. The Orange Globe Beet differs, however, from all the varieties already mentioned in the much darker colour of the skin, which is of a true orange colour. The flesh, nevertheless, is white, and the leaf-stalks quite green. This variety should not be confounded with the Golden Melon Beet, which is described above, and which has yellowish bronzy leaf-stalks, and the flesh zoned with yellow.

SUGAR BEET.

French, Betteraves à sucre. *German*, Zucker-Rübe. *Flemish* and *Dutch*, Suiker-wortel.
Spanish, Remolacha de azucar. *Portuguese*, Betarava branca d'assucar.

White Silesian Sugar Beet (*Betterave Blanche de Silésie*).—This name, which marks the variety from which all the kinds of Sugar Beet

White Silesian Sugar Beet
(⅓ natural size).

White Imperial Sugar Beet (⅓ natural size).

have sprung, is now no longer applied to any particular sort, but is used to denote all the varieties in general, and especially those which exhibit the greatest analogy in shape and size to the original or parent form of the Sugar Beets, to which, as more or less modified varieties, the following kinds must be referred :—

White Silesian Small-rooted Sugar Beet (*Betterave Blanche à Sucre Allemande*).—Root almost entirely underground, not very long, rather broad under the neck ; leaves numerous, usually spreading. Under average conditions, this variety will yield 40,000 kilogrammes of roots to the hectare (*i.e.* about 16 tons to the English acre), containing sugar to the amount of 12 or 13 per cent.

The *Breslau* White Sugar Beet (*B. Blanche à Sucre de Breslau*) is a sub-variety of this, with clean-skinned but very short roots. On the other hand, the *Magdeburg* and *Klein Wanzleben* varieties have small slender roots, very rich in sugar, and growing deeply sunk in the ground.

White Imperial Sugar Beet (*Betterave Blanche à Sucre Impériale*).— A rather long, slender variety, rich in sugar. Leaves spreading horizontally. Raised from selections by M. Knauer.

Electoral White Sugar Beet (*Betterave Blanche à Sucre Electorale*). —Not quite so rich in sugar as the preceding kind, but with more bulky roots, yielding a heavier crop.

Vilmorin's Improved White Sugar Beet (*Betterave Blanche à Sucre Améliorée Vilmorin*).—A small variety, exceed-

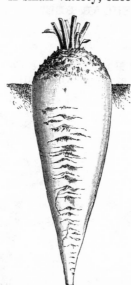

Vilmorin's Improved
White Sugar Beet
(⅓ natural size).

French White Green-top
Sugar Beet (⅓ natural size).

Brabant White Green-top
Sugar Beet (⅓ natural size).

ingly rich in sugar, often producing rootlets, always leafy; neck of the root wide, and skin rather wrinkled; flesh very compact. Under average conditions, it yields about 14 tons of roots to the acre, containing 16 to 18 per cent. of sugar.

French White Green-top Sugar Beet (*Betterave Blanche à Sucre à Collet Vert, race Française*).—A more vigorous-growing kind than the Small-rooted White Silesian, and with longer and thicker roots, which usually grow one-fourth or one-fifth of their length overground, the exposed part being more or less tinged with green. Leaves generally erect, numerous, stout, entirely green, as are also the leaf-stalks. This is a more productive variety than the Small-rooted White Silesian, but not so rich in sugar. Under average conditions, it will yield a crop of nearly 20 tons to the acre, containing 11 or 12 per cent. of sugar.

Brabant White Green-top Sugar Beet (*Betterave Blanche à Sucre à Collet Vert, race Brabant*).—This is a very good variety of the preceding kind. The roots are long, straight, well sunk in the ground, and usually somewhat richer in sugar than those of the ordinary variety.

French White Red-top Sugar Beet (*Betterave Blanche à Sucre à Collet Rose, race Française*).—This is a good, productive, hardy, and generally well-shaped variety, and is the kind which is most commonly grown in France. Leaves numerous, stout, erect, the stalks being more or less tinged with rose-colour; root slender, of a very elongated egg-shape, or like a half-long Carrot, almost entirely rose-coloured, except in the lower part, where, for one-third of its length, it is generally all white. Under average conditions, this variety will yield a crop of nearly 20 tons to the acre, containing 12 per cent. of sugar.

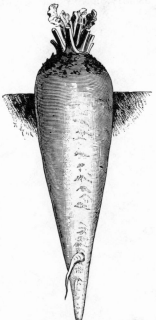

French White Red-top Sugar Beet (⅕ natural size).

Early Red-skinned Sugar Beet (*Betterave à Sucre Rose Hâtive*).—A very distinct variety, well marked by its entirely red roots, which are of medium size, with a flat and rather broad neck, and taper gradually downwards, emitting fibres and rootlets pretty plentifully, and also by its numerous, small, and very horizontally spread leaves, the stalks of which are rose coloured. This variety, which is still new, seems to be especially suitable for light calcareous soils, and yields a remarkably early crop. Under average conditions, it produces about 20 tons of roots to the acre, containing 13 to 14 per cent. of sugar.

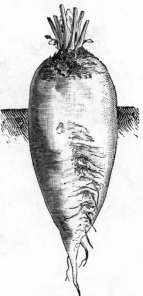

White Gray-top, or **Small-top, Sugar Beet** (*Betterave à Sucre à Collet Gris*). — A very productive

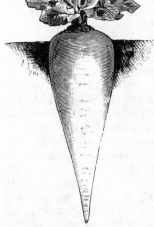

Early Red-skinned Sugar Beet (⅕ natural size).

White Gray-top Sugar Beet (⅕ natural size).

kind. Root egg-shaped, two-thirds or three-fourths of it underground;

skin of the buried part rose-coloured, neck gray or bronzy; leaves erect, usually narrow and slight. Rather weak in percentage of sugar, but a good cropper, and roots easily pulled. Under average conditions, this variety will produce up to nearly 22 tons of roots to the acre, containing 11 to 12 per cent. of sugar.

Yellow Sugar Beet (*Betterave Jaune à Sucre*).—Under this name is grown a variety which, up to the present, does not appear to be well established. Its roots are rather elongated in shape, with a yellow skin, and the flesh is zoned with yellow and white. Its best quality is that its colour prevents it from being mistaken for any other kind.

Black-skinned White-fleshed Sugar Beet (*Betterave Noire à Sucre à Chair Blanche*). —The only merit possessed by this variety is that it is easily recognized at once by its black wrinkled skin—a distinguishing mark useful to sugar-makers. It is of average rich quality, containing about 10 per cent. of sugar. The juice, being without colour, does not affect that of the other Beets with which it may be mixed in the process of manufacture.

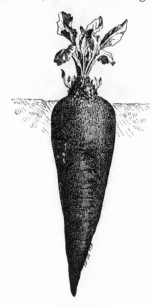

Black skinned Sugar Beet.

BORAGE.

Borage (⅛ natural size).

Borago officinalis, L. *Boraginaceæ.*

French, Bourrache officinale. *German,* Borretsch. *Flemish,* Bernagie. *Italian,* Boragine. *Spanish,* Borraja. *Portuguese,* Borrajem.

Native of Europe and North Africa.—Annual.—Stems 12 to 18 inches high, hollow, bristly, with pointed hairs; leaves oval, rough and sharp-haired like the stems; flowers in a scorpioid cyme, about 1 inch broad, of a fine blue colour in the common variety, sometimes violet-red or white; seed rather large, grayish-brown, oblong, slightly curved, streaked and marked with a projecting midrib or ridge. A gramme contains about 65 seeds, and a litre of them weighs, on an average, 480 grammes. Their germinating power continues for eight years. CULTURE AND USE.—This plant can be grown without trouble, by sowing the seed in any corner of the garden at any time from spring to the end of autumn. It will come into flower in a few months. In the London market-gardens it is grown in temporary frames out-of-doors for supply during late autumn and winter; for spring use seedlings are raised in heat and transplanted into glass-covered frames, which can be easily removed when the weather is sufficiently mild to admit of the plants being exposed without injury. Throughout the summer and autumn it is as easily grown out-of-doors as any common annual or weed, yet in remote country districts we have seen people much puzzled to find a sample when they required it! It is so vigorous and hardy that there need be no difficulty in country places in naturalizing it on any half-waste place, chalk bank, steep slope, or copse; a handful might be found in such a place in case its culture had been forgotten in the garden. It is one of the pretty true blue flowers, and almost worth growing in certain places for its beauty. It is naturalized in various counties in England, but is not a true native plant, belonging naturally to the shores of the Mediterranean, where so many of our old garden plants are native. It is sold chiefly to hotel-keepers for making claret-cup. The flowers are used for garnishing salads, but the plant is grown for the manufacture of cordials.

BROCCOLI.

Brassica oleracea Botrytis, D.C.

French, Choux Brocolis, Chou-fleur d'hiver. *German,* Broccoli, Brockoli, Spargelkohl.
    Flemish, Brokelie. *Danish,* Broccoli, Asparges kaal. *Italian,* Cavol broccolo.
    Spanish, Broculi.

The Broccoli, like the Cauliflower, is a cultivated variety of the Wild Cabbage, and is grown for the sake of the head, which is produced in the same way and has the same qualities. The growth of the Broccoli, however, is much more prolonged, and instead of producing the head the same year in which the plants are sown, it usually does not do so until early in the following spring. The two plants also differ somewhat in appearance, the Broccoli usually having more numerous, broader, stiffer, and narrower leaves than the Cauliflower, and generally bare leaf-stalks; the veinings of its leaves are also stouter and whiter. Its heads, although handsome, firm, and compact, are seldom as large, in this climate, as those of good varieties of Cauliflower. The seed of both plants is identical in appearance.

The cultivation of the Broccoli dates back to a more remote period than that of the Cauliflower, as the name, at least, would lead us to infer. In Italy, the name *broccoli* is applied to the tender shoots which, at the close of the winter, are emitted by various kinds of Cabbages and Turnips preparing to flower. These green and tender young shoots have, from time immemorial, been highly esteemed as a vegetable by the Italians, who, consequently, became careful to select and cultivate only those kinds which produced the most tender shoots in the greatest abundance. The Sprouting, or Asparagus, Broccoli represents the first form exhibited by the new vegetable when it ceased to be the earliest Cabbage, and was grown with an especial view to its shoots: after this, by continued selection and successive improvements, varieties were obtained which produced a compact white head, and some of these varieties were still further improved into kinds which are sufficiently early to commence and complete their entire growth in the course of the same year: these last-named kinds are now known by the name of Cauliflowers.

CULTURE.—The seed is sown in a nursery-bed from the beginning of April to the end of May, according to the earliness of the variety; the seedlings are usually pricked out in a bed, and in June or July are finally transplanted. Like all plants of the Cabbage family, they are benefitted by frequent hoeings and waterings. At the beginning of winter, a mulching of manure is applied, and the plants are earthed up to the lowest leaves, or they may be taken up altogether and laid in in a sloping trench, with the heads turned to the north. The ground in which they are to pass the winter should be sweet and well-drained, and the plants should, if possible, be protected in severe frosty weather. In March the heads begin to form, and may be cut until June, if successive sowings have been made.

As a rule, in private gardens Broccoli is cut when about a third or half its full size; the aim of growers should be, not the production of gigantic heads, but a constant succession of firm, compact Broccoli of medium size. Some growers choose a few good kinds and make successional sowings, whilst others select a number of varieties that will naturally succeed each other, although they be all sown and planted out at the same time.

This is doubtless the best plan when the ground intended to be occupied with Broccoli can be all spared and got ready at one time; but it frequently happens, where the demand for vegetables is great, that part crops must be planted as the ground becomes vacant. Many people plant Broccoli between rows of Potatoes, and where the ground is limited and the kind of Potatoes grown are dwarf and planted a good distance apart, it is doubtless a good system. Where this system is adopted the hardest pieces of land should be selected; the firmer the land, the better the plants stand the severity of the winter. They also come into use more regularly in rotation in their several seasons, and form larger and closer hearts than if planted in less compact soil. Plenty of room to grow must be allowed

them. Supposing two rows of early or second early Potatoes are planted from 20 inches to 2 ft. apart, there should be two rows of Potatoes between every two rows of Broccoli, which will place the rows of Broccoli about 3 ft. 6 in. or 4 ft. apart; and this distance is not too much, as it gives both crops plenty of room to develop themselves. The Potato haulm should be turned from the Broccoli to the unoccupied space between each two rows of Potatoes. It is now a common practice to plant Broccoli with a crowbar; the holes are filled in with fine soil, and afterwards thoroughly soaked with water.

SOWING AND PLANTING.—Though June is the month in which most plantations of Broccoli are made, yet it is frequently July before the work is done. Plants put out in August will make nice heads, but the sooner the planting is done after the middle of June the better. Though planting early insures the finest plants and largest heads, the time of sowing or planting does not materially affect the plants as regards the time they come into use. The time for sowing Broccoli seed varies from February till April, according to different localities; as a rule, from the end of March to the middle of April is the best time if the weather be genial.

The best manner of sowing is in shallow drills, 6 inches apart, and, if the seed be good, it should be sown thinly. The whole sowing may be made at the same time, and planted at the same time, for convenience' sake; and by planting many varieties a regular supply throughout winter and spring may be insured when the winters are mild—for it is certain that no practice as to time of sowing or planting will insure the heads forming at a certain time, if during winter we have protracted periods of frost or cold, during which all growth is at a standstill. Plants from sowings made early in April will, under favourable circumstances, be large enough for pricking out by the middle of May; they should have a moderately rich, open border, where they can have the benefit of the sun to keep them strong and sturdy. They should be pricked out 7 or 8 inches apart from plant to plant, and by the beginning of June the ground should be prepared and the plants finally planted out,—choosing a showery time, if possible. Many people never transplant their Broccoli previous to final planting; but where time can be spared it is much the best, as the plants get stronger and better able to resist the attacks of slugs, snails, etc., than small plants put out direct from the seed-bed.

If practicable, the ground should be trenched two or three spades deep, or at least double-digged. When there is not time for doing either of these, then the ground must be dug over a spade deep only, taking care to break the soil up thoroughly, as deeply as a good spade will do it, and working in some well-decayed manure at the same time, the soil being broken up well in the trench, and the surface a little rough. Plant as soon as the digging is finished. If the planting be done in June or July, from 2½ to 3 ft. must be allowed between the plants; if deferred till August, they need not be allowed so much room. If the weather be dry, the seed-bed

or that from which the plants are taken should be watered well the night before, to soften the soil. The holes to receive the plants should always be made sufficiently large to admit of their being easily put in without breaking their roots. "Buttoned" and stunted plants are in many cases caused by bad planting. They are put in with broken and mutilated roots; and those that have a tap-root often have it bent double in getting it into the hole, and instead of the point being at the bottom of the hole, it will be sticking up above the surface. No one should wait a very long time for wet weather in which to plant Broccoli: it is better to get the planting done and water well once or twice, and the plants will then do till rain comes. When the plants are fairly established, and have grown a little, they must be earthed up with the hoe, which will prevent the wind from twisting them about and disturbing their young roots.

SOIL AND MANURE. — Broccoli thrives best in a deep loamy soil, well drained; but it is not very particular in this respect, and will produce fine heads in any well-enriched soil of which the staple is loam. In old garden soils in which humus has accumulated, it is often attacked with the grub or maggot, which causes "clubbing." In such cases lime may be applied with advantage, or burnt clay and fresh loam. The ground should be trenched two or three spades deep previous to planting, and the manure, if rotted, well incorporated with the soil, or, if rank, buried in the bottom of the trench. If trenching cannot be done, then Broccoli should follow some other crop, such as Potatoes or Onions, or any crop not belonging to the Cruciferæ or tap-rooted section, such as Carrots, Turnips, or Beet, and the ground should be dug as deeply as a good spade will go, and well manured. Where the soil in which Broccoli is to be planted is naturally of a light character, if moderately rich, it should not be

H

dug, but made as firm as possible round the plants. The best kind of manure for Broccoli is undoubtedly well-rotted stable manure, with a sprinkling of soot added to destroy worms. Watering is seldom necessary after plants get well established.

HEELING-IN BROCCOLI.—As regards the heeling-in or layering of Broccoli, many growers think it a great advantage, whilst others think it at least unnecessary. As a rule, private growers are in favour of the practice of layering; their objects being, firstly, to check growth, as they believe that disturbing the roots has the effect of hardening the whole plant, and of enabling it better to withstand severe weather; secondly, to place the plants in such a position that the sun, during alternate frost and thaw, will not get to the hearts, as these suffer more after being thawed by the sun in the day than when continuously frozen. For this reason the heads are laid so as to face the north or west. To accomplish this, if the rows run east and west, they commence on the north side of the first row, and take out a spit of soil just the width of the spade, so as to form a trench within 2 or 3 inches of the stems of the plants, laying the soil, as the work proceeds, on the side away from the row. This necessarily removes the soil from the roots, no more of which is broken off than can be avoided. All the plants in the row are then regularly bent over, until their heads rest on the ridge of soil taken out of the trench. When this is done, commence with the next row, taking the soil out so as to form a similar trench, and laying it in a ridge upon the stems of the row of plants bent over, so as to cover them right up to their bottom leaves; and, in this way, proceed until the whole is completed. If the rows stand north and south, the work is begun on the west side. By this process, as will be seen, all the roots on one side of each row, and a portion of those on the other, are disturbed. This causes

the leaves to flag a good deal for a week or two, and checks growth. The larger and more vigorous the plants, the greater the need for thus preparing them for winter. In light soils, where they can be got up without much mutilation of the roots, should it be desirable to prepare the ground for some other crop before the Broccoli is off in spring, they may be taken up altogether and laid in some more convenient place, lifting them, as far as possible, with all their roots intact. Where time can be spared, we believe this to be a good system, as we have noticed that where Broccoli is managed in this way, it is only during exceptionally severe winters that it gets destroyed. The length of time during which this vegetable affords a succession, at a period of the year when there does not exist much variety, makes it worth while to do all we can to prolong its season. Fortunately, however, severe injury to the Broccoli crop is the exception rather than the rule, and is quite as likely to be the consequence of imperfectly ripened stems as of hard weather.

PROTECTING. — When Broccoli comes into use in too large quantities at a time, and a blank in the supply is likely to occur, some of the plants may be taken up and placed in an open shed in which there is a fair amount of light and air. Some ordinary soil may be put into it, and the plants, the heads of which shall have attained a usable size, may be placed in the soil,—but not too thickly, or the leaves will turn yellow and injure the heads. If this be done in succession as the plants form heads, there will always be on hand a supply of Broccoli. Frames or pits are better than a shed in which to keep them, but these are generally required for other purposes. The practice of taking up Broccoli in autumn when nearly fit for use, and hanging them head downwards in a shed or other building, is not good; for, although they will keep for a time in that way, they get tough and inferior compared with those that have had their roots in moist soil.

GROWING FOR EXHIBITION.—When Broccoli is required for exhibition, small plantations should be made in different situations, in order to make sure of having them in at the required time. For this purpose large compact heads are indispensable, though it is better to have them somewhat small and close than large and open. Trenches are sometimes dug for the plants, and it is a good system where time can be spared. The trenches should be dug 2 ft. wide and two spits deep; the top spit being taken out and laid on each side, then a good thick coat of fresh horse-droppings, or rotten manure, thrown in the trench, to be turned in and well incorporated with the second spit. The plants may then be put in, and as they grow the soil that was taken out of the trench may be put back round the stems of the plants and trodden in firmly. Good soakings of manure water may be given when the soil is dry, but after the heads are once formed it must be discontinued, or it will cause the flower to open. In cutting, the whitest and firmest heads should be selected, and the more they resemble each other in size and appearance the better; they should never be trimmed until they are going to be put on the exhibition table, and then not so severely as is often done. If it be necessary to cut the heads some time previous to their being shown, the best way is to divide them with 5 or 6 inches of stem and place them in shallow pans filled with cold water standing in a cool spot. The leaves should be tied over the flower, and, if an occasional sprinkling overhead be given them, it will help to keep them fresh. This will be found better than pulling up the roots and hanging them up in sheds and similar places.

CULTURE FOR MARKET.—This crop is grown by market gardeners near London chiefly under the shade of fruit trees, but in the valley of the Thames there are acres of Broccoli in the open fields. The early supplies of Broccoli brought to the market are produced in the west of England, where the climate is mild, and the heads produced there are superior in size and quality to those grown near London. In mild seasons Broccoli is so good and plentiful as to be of little profit to the grower. In the winter of 1878 many never brought their produce to market at all, but made use of it at home, so low were the prices offered for it in the market. In the market gardens about London, the Purple Sprouting, the Walcheren, Snow's Winter White, and Veitch's Autumn Giant are the kinds chiefly grown. The first sowing is usually made during the month of April on beds of rich soil. Sometimes, however, the time of year when ground will be vacant to receive the plants influences the time of sowing, for it is an important matter to have the young plants healthy and stocky at planting time. If sown so early as to have to be kept long in the seed-bed, they become "drawn," and consequently do not yield such good results. Another sowing is generally made in the middle of May; indeed, from this sowing the principal winter crop is obtained, and more plants are raised than are required, so that all clubbed and weakly ones can be discarded at planting time.

A sowing of Sprouting Broccoli is made in the end of May or early in June, from which is obtained a supply of sprouts during the following winter and early spring, a time when they are in great demand. When the young Broccoli plants appear aboveground they are first hand-weeded, and afterwards thinned by means of narrow hoes. As soon as they are strong enough for transplanting they are planted in rows under fruit trees, or in any convenient situation. When planted between rows of fruit bushes, two lines of plants are inserted in the intervals between every two rows of trees; if two drills of Potatoes occupy the space between the trees, then only one line of

Broccoli is planted, and that between the two drills of Potatoes. Should the whole space under an orchard be planted with Potatoes, as soon as these are earthed-up, Broccoli is planted between the rows *without the soil being loosened or dug.* The Potatoes ripen before the Broccoli can injure them much, and when the Potatoes are removed the Broccoli has the whole space to itself. The trees lose their leaves in October; then the Broccoli, having the benefit of increased light, becomes invigorated, and some of the plants then begin to afford a good supply of sprouts, which are not all gathered at once, even from the same plant, but at intervals as they become fit for use. The immense breadths of Broccoli grown in some of the market gardens render it almost impossible to have all heeled in as we often see them in private gardens; yet it is seldom they are injured by frost, and the fine white, firm heads that may be seen by thousands in Covent Garden Market during the autumn are seldom surpassed, if even equalled, in private gardens. In the neighbourhood of Shepperton, in the Thames valley, may be seen breadths of Broccoli from twenty to thirty acres in extent, and from this place alone it is calculated that in the height of the season as many as 30,000 heads per week are sent to market. In some parts of Kent Broccoli is grown to a large extent, one grower yearly planting over 200,000 plants.

USES.—Exactly the same as those of the Cauliflower. The value of the vegetable to the many who depend on the markets for their supplies is greatly lessened by the deterioration it suffers from being cut long before being used. Early crops being grown in perfection in Cornwall, and at considerable distances from London, the heads are often stale before being used, even when they do not seem so. We have frequently noticed an intensely bitter flavour in the Broccoli sent to market, even when cooked in the most careful manner. Every one who can should grow their own, and cut it an hour before dinner!

Large White French Broccoli (*Brocoli Blanc Ordinaire, B. Blanc de Saint-Brieuc*).—A vigor-

Adam's Early White Broccoli (1/10 natural size).

ous-growing plant, with rather numerous long, stiff leaves, of a glaucous-green colour, and deeply undulated on the edges; the interior leaves which cover the head are very much twisted and almost curled; head white, very compact and hard, continuing firm for a long time. A hardy and easily grown variety.

Adam's Early White Broccoli (*Brocoli Blanc Hâtif*).—This variety differs but little in its general character from the preceding one, from which it is particularly distinguished by being ten or twelve days earlier. It produces a great number of leaves, which are undulated at the edges to a remarkable degree.

Roscoff White Broccoli (*Brocoli Blanc de Roscoff*).—This very excellent kind, which is most extensively cultivated in the department of Finisterre, is very like the preceding one, of which it may be considered a very constant and very early local form. This is the variety of which such large quantities are brought to Paris, every year, at the end of the winter.

Large White Mammoth Broccoli (*Brocoli Blanc Mammoth*).—A thick-set variety, lower in growth than the preceding kinds, and with shorter and broader leaves of a dark-green colour, very numerous, surrounding and protecting the head well; the inner or heart leaves are often twisted; head very large and white, and of remarkably good quality. This is one of the latest varieties which continue to bear for the longest time.

Easter Broccoli ($\frac{1}{10}$ natural size).

Easter Broccoli (*Brocoli de Pâques*).—This is a very handsome, early, and distinct variety. Its leaves are not so numerous as those of most other kinds of Broccoli, and have a very peculiar appearance, being rather short, broad at the base, and pointed at the end, so that they are nearly triangular in shape; they are stiff, not much undulated, and are finely toothed on the edges; their grayish colour is equally characteristic. This variety, which in the south of France is also called the Easter Cauliflower (*Chou-fleur de Pâques*), is very early, requires less attention than many other kinds, and even the weakest plants of it form very regular heads. It is one of the best kinds, though tender.

Purple Sprouting, or Asparagus, Broccoli ($\frac{1}{8}$ natural size; detached portion, $\frac{1}{4}$ natural size).

Purple Sicilian Broccoli (*Brocoli Violet*).—An exceedingly hardy kind, totally distinct from all other varieties; leaves rather deeply lobed, numerous, longish, spreading, of a pale grayish-green colour, with purple-tinged veins; head purplish, rather firm, of medium size, and latish in forming.

Purple Sprouting, or **Asparagus, Broccoli** (*Brocoli Branchu, B. à Jets, B. Asperge*).—Under this name different varieties have been cultivated; that which is now most commonly grown has both the stems and leaves of a purplish colour, resembling a curled Red Cabbage up to a certain point, and producing not only in the heart but also in the axils of the leaves rather thick and fleshy purplish shoots, the flower-buds of which do not become abortive, as in the case of those varieties which form a true head. These shoots are produced in succession for a long time, and they are gathered as they lengthen and before the flowers open, and are used like green Asparagus, from which circumstance the plant has received the name of Asparagus Broccoli.

Under the name of *Sprouting Broccoli*, a variety with green shoots is most commonly grown in England, the flowers of which are partially abortive and form at the end of every shoot a small bulging mass or lump, of a greenish-yellow colour. The *Marte* Cauliflower, of Bordeaux, is a true Sprouting Broccoli, which produces a great number of small, compact, purplish heads of very good quality. This variety, unfortunately, does not endure severe winters at Paris.

The number of kinds of Broccoli is extremely large, as it is one of those vegetables of which it is difficult to establish the varieties. In England, more than forty different forms of it are grown. Of these we mention here the kinds with coloured heads :—

Green Cape.—A greenish-headed variety, which comes in in October and November.

Late Green, or Late Danish.—The head of this is of the same colour as the preceding kind, but comes in in April and May.

Late Dwarf Purple, or Cock's-comb Broccoli.—A very hardy, purplish-headed kind, coming in only in April and May.

Among the white-headed kinds, the most esteemed are :—

Backhouse's Winter White.—Distinct from Snow's and Osborn's, with the good qualities of both.

Osborn's Winter White.—A fine mid-winter variety, with heads as white as a Cauliflower.

Improved White Sprouting.—A variety very productive of sprouts.

Early Penzance (Cornish).—Turns in very early ; fine, compact, pure white head.

Knight's Protecting.—A very useful protecting variety.

Sulphur.—Very useful, extremely hardy, and produces fine heads.

Champion (Barr).—A very distinct, hardy, early Broccoli. The flower is well protected, and, with good culture, if allowed to attain its full size, produces very large heads.

Criterion (Barr).—The best of all the late Broccoli, coming into use after the middle of May, and giving a succession till the Cauliflowers are ready to cut.

Chappel's Cream.—A fine variety, with large creamy-white, compact heads.

Lauder's Protecting Late White Goshen.—A fine, hardy, late variety.

Leamington (Perkins).—A well-protected, first-rate late Broccoli.

Ledsham's Latest of All.—Certificated by the Royal Horticultural Society as one of the finest and latest varieties known ; head " white as snow."

Cattell's Eclipse.—A handsome late form of the Mammoth Broccoli.

Grange's Early Cauliflower Broccoli, or Bath White.—An extremely early kind, which begins to come in in October.

Cooling's Matchless.—A rather leafy kind, but producing a fine white head, like the White Roscoff.

Snow's Superb White Winter.—A compact, short-stemmed variety, which may be grown to come in either at the end of autumn or in spring.

Veitch's Protecting.—A good hardy kind, the fine white heads of which are naturally protected by the peculiar growth of the leaves.

Wilcove's.—A good late variety, which withstands the winter well.

The Italians cultivate a great many varieties of Broccoli, and we know that Italy is the country in which this vegetable originated, but as Cauliflowers of every kind pass the winter there without injury, they give the name of Cauliflower to all the varieties which produce white heads, the name Broccoli being restricted to the sprouting coloured varieties. The Giant Cauliflower of Naples is called a Broccoli in its native country. On all the coasts of the Mediterranean there are varieties of Cauliflower which come in all through the winter, in uninterrupted succession to the autumn kinds. There are also, among the purplish-coloured Broccolis, particular kinds for every month of the winter; those which come in in November are named *San-Martinari*, in December *Nataleschi*, and the rest *Gennajuoli*, *Febbrajuoli*, *Marzuoli*, and *Apriloti*, according as they come in in January, February, March, and April.

BRUSSELS SPROUTS.—See Cabbage.

BUCK'S-HORN or HART'S-HORN PLANTAIN, or STAR OF THE EARTH.

Plantago Coronopus, L. *Plantagineæ.*

French, Corne-de-cerf, Pied-de-corbeau. *German*, Hirschhorn Salat. *Flemish*, Veversblad, Hertshoorn. *Italian*, Corno di cervo, Coronopo, Erba stella. *Spanish*, Estrellamar, Cuerno de ciervo.

Native of Europe.—Annual.—Leaves numerous, long, narrow, deeply lobed, bearing a few long hairs and forming a very regular rosette close to the ground; stems each surmounted by a spike of minute yellowish flowers,

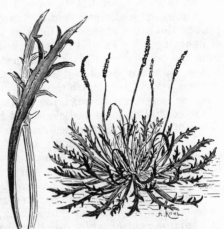

Buck's-horn or Hart's-horn Plantain, or Star of the Earth (⅛ natural size; separate leaves, ½ natural size).

which are succeeded by small membranous capsules filled with very small, egg-shaped seeds, of a light-brown colour. A gramme contains 4000 seeds, and a litre of them weighs 740 grammes. Their germinating power continues for four years. CULTURE.—The seed is sown, where the crop is to grow, either in spring or autumn; in either case, the ground is cleared off at the end of summer. The plants require no attention, except whatever weeding is needed to keep the ground clean, in addition to plentiful waterings, without which the leaves soon become hard and leathery. As the plant yields abundantly, the sowings are usually made on a limited scale. USES.—The young leaves are used for mixing in salads. Very rarely cultivated in England. It is a widely distributed and common native plant in sandy and stony places, especially near the sea.

CABBAGE.

Brassica oleracea, L.   *Cruciferæ.*

French, Chou cultivé.   *German,* Kohl, Kraut.   *Flemish* and *Dutch,* Kool.   *Danish,* Kaal.
Italian, Cavolo.   *Spanish,* Col.   *Portuguese,* Couve.

Cabbage, a plant which is indigenous to Europe and Western Asia, is one of the vegetables which have been cultivated from the earliest times. The ancients were well acquainted with it, and certainly possessed several varieties of the head-forming kinds. The great antiquity of its culture may be inferred from the immense numbers of varieties which are now in existence, and from the very important modifications which have been produced in the characteristics of the original or parent plant.

The Wild Cabbage, such as it still exists on the coasts of England and France, is a perennial plant with broad, lobed, undulated, thick, smooth leaves, covered with a glaucous bloom. The stem attains a height of from nearly 2½ to over 3 ft., and bears at the top a spike of yellow, or sometimes white, flowers. All the cultivated varieties present the same characters in their inflorescence, but, up to the time of flowering, they exhibit most marked differences from each other and from the original wild plant. In most of the Cabbages, it is chiefly the leaves that are developed by cultivation; these, for the most part, become imbricated or overlap one another closely, so as to form a more or less compact head, the heart or interior of which is composed of the central undeveloped shoot and the younger leaves next it. The shape of the head is spherical, sometimes flattened, sometimes conical. All the varieties which form heads in this way are known by the general name of Cabbages (*Choux pommés*), while other kinds with large branching leaves, which never form heads, are distinguished by the name of Borecole or Kale (*Choux verts*).

In some kinds, the flower-stems have been so modified by culture as to become transformed into a thick, fleshy, tender mass, the growth and enlargement of which are produced at the expense of the flowers, which are absorbed and rendered abortive. Such are the Broccolis and Cauliflowers. In other kinds, the leaves retain their ordinary dimensions, while the stem, or the principal root, has been brought by cultivation to assume the shape of a large ball or Turnip; as in the case of the plants known as Kohl-Rabi (*Choux-raves*) and Turnip-rooted Cabbage or Swedish Turnip (*Choux-navets*). And, lastly, there are varieties in which cultivation and selection have produced modifications in the ribs of the leaves (as in the Couve Tronchuda), or in the axillary shoots (as in Brussels Sprouts), or in several organs together (as in the Marrow Kales and the Neapolitan Curled Kale). We make no mention here of the Colza, another variety, grown exclusively for the sake of its seeds, from which an oil is obtained, and which, therefore, is to be classed amongst the plants which are grown for economic or manufacturing purposes.

CULTURE.—The different kinds of Cabbages vary so much in constitution and treatment that it is impossible to lay down precise general rules for the cultivation even of each entire class or section. We shall, therefore, when describing each variety, give instructions as to the proper times for sowing and planting it, merely mentioning here a few particulars which are applicable to the cultivation of almost all kinds of Cabbages. A cool moist climate seems to be the most suitable of all for the culture of Cabbages, which generally grow to greater perfection in districts near the sea-coast than they do in either low-lying or elevated inland parts of the country. Heat and drought are injurious to them, while they grow admirably well in moist, foggy weather, even when it is somewhat cold. They like a clayey, rather stiff soil, rich in manure and decayed organic matter; they do not seem to mind a little sourness in the soil, and grow well in ground that has been newly broken up. In the kitchen garden, Cabbages should occupy the coolest and moistest positions, except the early spring kinds, which require a warm and sheltered aspect; the ground should be deeply dug and plentifully manured, and should be always kept clean and free from weeds. The plants should be watered from time to time during the summer, and care should be taken to prevent them from being overrun by the caterpillars of the white Cabbage butterfly, which, if not attended to, will damage them severely.

SOWING AND PLANTING.—The most important sowings of Cabbage are those which are required to form a supply through the spring and early summer months. These sowings should consist of several varieties that succeed each other in coming into use. However, very early kinds should not be sown too early in the summer, as there is a possibility of their running to seed in dry weather. From the middle of July to the middle of August is the time usually chosen for sowing; but much will depend upon the season, soil, and locality. The beginning of August will in most places be found to be the best. Plants from seed sown at that time are generally ready to plant out by the end of September or beginning of October, and they have then ample time to get established before the winter sets in. For autumn supply a sowing should be made from the middle of March to the beginning of April, and planted out in June and July,—they then come into use in August and September; and if a second and rather larger sowing be made in the last week in April, and planted out in July and August, they will come into use from October to December; and a small sowing of a dwarf kind that hearts quickly, sown in May, will form nice little heads for use in January, which, with the Greens produced from the stumps of those that have been cut, will last until the spring Cabbage comes in. Cabbage plants intended to stand the winter are best planted with a crowbar in firm undug ground, such as has recently carried a crop of Onions, or other surface-rooting plants that have not impoverished the ground too much. The ground must, of course, have been well manured for the crop previous to Cabbage, or good results cannot be expected. A firm, stiff, rich soil is best for Cabbages; for if grown in loose, light soil, they do not "heart" so well, neither is the quality so good. Cabbage seed should at all times be sown on light rich land, and the plants should not be allowed to overcrowd each other before they are put out, but as soon as large enough to handle be pricked out 6 or 8 inches apart, or be thinned out, and the remainder transferred to their final positions as soon as they are sufficiently large. The distance to plant them apart depends upon the variety grown; but 2 ft. between the rows, and from 15 to 18 inches from plant to plant in the rows, will generally be found sufficient space if the ground be in good heart.

CUTTING.—A little more attention might be advantageously paid to this than is generally the case; for although Cauliflowers and Brussels Sprouts cannot always be had just when wanted, tender Cabbage may be had with very little management. Supposing we plant Cabbages in autumn, they will come into use tender towards the beginning of summer; but if the household be generally not able to use them as fast as they grow, the heads are allowed to swell until they burst, or go to seed or rot, and eventually become quite useless for cooking purposes. In gardens from which large houses have to be supplied, Cabbages are generally wanted as soon as they are ready, and a number of heads are cut daily; but the experienced gardener does not cut the head off at the surface of the soil, but just at the neck, leaving

a few of the bottom leaves. Consequently, before the quarter has been cut over the first-cut plants have made another break and become furnished with a whole cluster of young succulent heads, which heart immediately, and are fit to cut before the first heads are quite finished. The plants will even break and heart a third time, and in this way a plot of Cabbage may be made to afford a supply nearly all the year round. The vigour, free growth, and tenderness of the heads will be greatly promoted by frequent stirrings of the soil between the rows, and mulching with any loose material, such as short Grass or leaves, at command. Cut your Cabbages, therefore, if you have to give them away to your neighbours, before the heads get over-ripe and useless, and you will have a continuance of young and tender heads, which are greatly to be preferred to those which are large, white, and hard.

The Cabbage is one of the most important of green vegetables for market-garden culture, and although not considered by many so profitable on account of its gross-feeding character, it comes into use when there is little else to send to market, and often realizes high prices. In spring large areas of Cabbages may be seen about Wandsworth, Fulham, Gunnersbury, and, in fact, all round the suburbs of London. The Cabbages sent to market in April, May, and June are the produce of seed sown in July, and the plants are put out in September or early in October. Succession crops are sown in spring as soon as the weather is favourable. If sown too soon, as is sometimes done, the young leaves get injured by frosts, especially if these occur immediately after a period of mild weather.

The Enfield Market Cabbage is that which is principally used in the market gardens about London. It is one of the oldest in cultivation, and one of the best, and for this reason the growers generally save their own seed, and take great care that their plants of it are not crossed with other sorts. The sowing for the principal crop of this Cabbage is generally made about the end of July and up to the middle of August, on poor ground if possible, as in that case the plants come up stocky and hardy, and stand the winter well; whereas, if made on rich ground, a soft rank growth is produced, which is much more easily injured. This sowing is, as a rule, made in 4 ft. wide beds—a width found to be convenient for weeding and hoeing amongst the plants. When sufficiently strong to be transplanted, they are planted on ground cleared of Onions or Potatoes, and a second batch is planted on land cleared of Celery, French Beans, or Vegetable Marrows. Every empty space, under fruit trees or elsewhere, is, indeed, planted with Cabbages. In planting, the ground is lined off into rows 30 inches apart, and in these the plants are put 15 inches asunder. Between every two rows first planted another is then put in with less care, thus making the plants stand 15 inches apart each way. Early in spring the alternate lines of plants, and also every other plant in the lines or rows left, are lifted and sold as Coleworts. This allows the permanent crop plenty of room to come to maturity. With a view to subsequent plantations, which are made all through the winter wherever ground is vacant, the young plants in seed-beds are removed and pricked out into others a little further apart, in order to keep them in good condition for planting out as long as possible. In this way, indeed, many of the plants are kept till spring, when they are transplanted to suc-

ceed those planted out in autumn, and to come in before the produce of the spring sowings, made late in February or early in March, to furnish Cabbages from June to August. The plants from this sowing are put out in rows 2 or 2½ ft. apart, and in the intervening spaces are put lines of Lettuces, a plant of which is also set between every Cabbage in the row. In May men may be often noticed busily engaged in tying up early Cabbages in the market gardens at Fulham and elsewhere. The operation is simple—just, in fact, that adopted in the case of Cos Lettuces. The succulent outer leaves are folded carefully around the heart or centre of the plant, and the whole is bound firmly with a withy or a piece of bast. There are several good reasons for this practice. The centre being protected from the weather, the Cabbages heart sooner than they otherwise would do, and they are more easily handled in gathering and packing for market. Early Cabbages, the leaves of which are so brittle, would lose half their value if some precaution of this kind were not taken to keep them from being broken by loading and unloading them. Red Cabbages are sown in March, but the produce of the July sowing is generally considered better than that of spring. The plants are put out in rows from 3½ to 4 ft. apart, and the plants stand about 3 ft. asunder in the rows. As this crop stands until the heads are large and solid, a piece of rich land is devoted to it, and intercropped with Potatoes, ordinary Cabbages, Lettuces, French Beans, or other vegetables of that kind.

The different sections of Cabbages differ perceptibly from one another in the size of the seed, the Borecoles and Kohl-Rabi producing the largest seed; next to these, the ordinary round-headed varieties, and the Turnip-rooted Cabbage or Swedish Turnip; and, lastly, the Cauliflowers and Broccolis, which have the smallest seed of all. However, the seeds of all these kinds weigh almost uniformly about 700 grammes to the litre, and their germinating power continues for five years.

USES.—The leaves of the common headed varieties and of the Borecoles are cooked in various ways, or used in salads, as in America, or fermented so as to form what is termed Sauer-kraut; the heads of the Cauliflowers and Broccolis, the stems of the Kohl-Rabi, the roots of the Turnip-rooted and the Swedish Turnip, and the small heads which grow along the stems of the Brussels Sprouts are most usually eaten boiled, although they are also well treated in other ways by foreign cooks. The very commonness and cheapness of Cabbages leads to a regrettable ignoring of their existence on the part of many superior persons! It is a great mistake, however, as they are by far the most precious vegetables we have, eaten young, in the right season, and well cooked! Though forms of the same wild plant, the variety of flavours is remarkable. It is not more remarkable, however, than the way the common cook usually spoils this vegetable. In the hotels and restaurants it is usually a disgusting mess, heavily charged with soda. The best cookery of Cabbages may frequently be observed among cottagers and servants brought up in country cottages. We have known a duke, with one of the finest gardens in England, bring from London a specimen of some Cabbage that he had relished, thinking the attraction was in the variety. There was, however, plenty of the same in his own garden, but the cook had spoiled it—or, we should say, the "vegetable maid," for the great cooks seldom condescend to vegetables! One result of the neglect of Cabbage on the part of the affluent is that they miss some of the most delicate and wholesome vegetables we have, in various little known forms of this family, which will be described further on in this book. This vegetable in its wondrous variety is better fitted for our country than for any other, and comes to greatest perfection in it. To despise and neglect it is a mistake and a loss. Those possessing good gardens would do well to grow and use the more delicately flavoured forms and those best suited to their localities, and thus lead the poor to a fuller knowledge of things so easy for all to grow, and which yield so abundantly. It is only fair to add, however, that the cookery of Cabbages is frequently so detestable that it is not surprising that some have been led to neglect them. But, under the best conditions, not a few of them are as good as any vegetable that is grown, and, if rare, they would be sought as delicacies.

THE COMMMON CABBAGE.

Brassica oleracea capitata, D.C.

French, Chou cabus, C. pommé. *German*, Kopfkohl, Kraut. *Flemish*, Kabuiscool. *Dutch*, Slutkool. *Danish*, Hoved kaal. *Italian*, Cavolo cappuccio. *Spanish*, Col repollo. *Portuguese*, Couve repolho.

This section is usually divided into two classes, viz. the Smooth-leaved, and the Curled-leaved or Milan (Savoy) kinds. In describing the varieties of both classes, we shall do so, as far as possible, in the order of their respective degrees of earliness, at the same time duly noting the affinities of the different kinds. It may be observed that the seeds

of the varieties of Common or Round-headed Cabbage average in
number 320 to the gramme.

Early Dwarf York C. (*Chou d'York Petit Hâtif*).—We commence
our descriptions of Cabbages with this variety, because, although it is
not the earliest of all, it is one of the best known and most generally
cultivated of early kinds, and it will be easier to characterize the
analogous varieties by comparing them with it. The head is of an oval
or reversed-cone shape, oblong, nearly twice as long as broad, small, and
tolerably compact. Leaves of a dark-green colour, with a slight bluish,
glaucous, or grayish tinge on the under side, the outer ones of those

Early Dwarf York Cabbage
($\frac{1}{12}$ natural size).

Superfine Early Cabbage.

which form the head covering the others like a hood ; those on the
very outside, which do not help to form the head, are few in number,
and bent back in the contrary direction, often having the edges turned
towards the midrib on the back, and very smooth ; veins rather broad, of
a greenish white ; stem slender and about the same length as the head.

The Superfine Early (*Chou Superfin Hâtif*) is a sub-variety of
the Early Dwarf York, from which it hardly differs in appearance, with
the exception of being a trifle dwarfer, but it is about a week earlier.

Large York C. (*Chou d'York Gros*).—Larger in all its parts than the
preceding kind, this variety has
the head thicker and stouter in
proportion to its length, the
transverse diameter being about
two-thirds of the length. The
outer leaves are stiffer, firmer,
and broader, and usually not so
bluish in tint ; the stem also is
shorter in proportion. This is
an excellent early kind, very
productive, and of good quality.
The only fault, perhaps, which
it has, is that it takes up rather

Large York Cabbage ($\frac{1}{12}$ natural size).

too much ground for the size of the head, in consequence of the large
outside leaves spreading so much in the horizontal direction.

Sugar-loaf C. (*Chou Pain de Sucre*).—Head very long, like a
reversed sugar-loaf in shape, regularly oblong, and at least twice as long
as broad, very like a Cos Lettuce in form, whence its French name of
Chou Chicon ; leaves of a pale or light green on the upper surface and
whitish green underneath, of an elongated spoon-shape, and covering
each other in a remarkable manner with their hood-shaped tops so as to

form the head; outer leaves erect, like those of a Cos Lettuce; stem com-

paratively short, being not more than a third or half the length of the head. This variety is very distinct and productive, and is almost as early as the preceding kind. Like the two foregoing kinds, it answers as well for sowing in autumn as in spring, and, growing tall and slender, it does not occupy much ground relatively to the size of its head. It is also slow in running to seed—a good quality for which it deserves to be specially men-

Sugar-loaf Cabbage (¹⁄₁₂ natural size).

tioned. It is somewhat singular that, although a very old variety and well known in every country in Europe, it does not appear to be extensively grown anywhere.

Early Ox-heart C. (*Chou Cœur de Bœuf Petit*).—The shape of the head of this variety is well expressed by its name, and is that of a

short, thick-set, blunt-pointed cone, the length of which does not exceed the breadth by more than one-fourth or one-fifth. The outer leaves are broad and nearly round, and are of a less glaucous green than those of the York Cabbages; those which form the head are rather wrapped round each other than hood-shaped. The stem is rather short, being shorter than the head, which begins to form very early, and is fit to cut about the same time as the Early York. The Ox-heart Cabbage may be con-

Early Ox-heart Cabbage (¹⁄₁₂ natural size).

sidered the type of a rather numerous class, to which the following varieties belong:—

Early Étampes C. (*Chou Très Hâtif d'Étampes*).—From several comparative trials which we have made, this variety seems to be the earliest of all the headed Cabbages. In most points it resembles the Early Ox-heart, but it has a longer and more conical head, and is also

a somewhat bulkier plant. It was raised by M. Bonnemain, Secretary of the Étampes Horticultural Society, and is well adapted for spring culture. The *Chou Préfin de Boulogne* is a sub-variety of the Ox-heart, remarkable for its earliness, and easily distinguished by its light colour and the broadness of the ribs of its leaves, which spread like a fan over the whole width of the leaf. The Early Louviers Cabbage, another sub-variety of the Ox-heart, very much resembles the Étampes Cabbage, but it is not so early, and has a somewhat shorter

Early Étampes Cabbage (¹⁄₁₂ natural size).

head. The *Chou Prompt de Saint-Malo*, which is a little larger, and has broader leaves and a rather shorter and broader head than the foregoing kinds, has, like them, been advantageously superseded by the Very Early Étampes variety.

Very Early Paris Market C. (*Chou Cœur de Bœuf Moyen de la Halle*).—This variety is intermediate in height between the Large and the Small Ox-heart Cabbage, resembling the latter more closely in its broad, low shape, in the large number of its outer leaves, and in the shortness of its stalk. The two kinds differ but little in point of earliness, both being two or three weeks earlier than the Large Ox-heart variety. If sown in March, the intermediate variety is fit to cut in the end of June, only a few days later than the Étampes Cabbage, and well-grown heads of it weigh from four to over six pounds each.

Very Early Paris Market Cabbage
($\frac{1}{12}$ natural size).

Prince's Nonpareil, or Barne's Early Dwarf C. (*Chou Nonpareil*). —Intermediate between the Ox-heart and the Tourlaville varieties comes one which is very extensively grown in England under the name of " Nonpareil." This is an early kind, with a rather elongated but blunt conical head, and with leaves which are of a dark-green colour on the upper surface, and very coarsely crimped. It differs from the Tourlaville variety in not having the leaf-stalk naked at the base, nor the leaves so much twisted in shape. It is a good early variety, requiring about the same time to come to perfection as the Large York.

The variety named *Enfield Market*, of which the Nonpareil appears to be a good sub-variety, is not quite so early, and may be ranked between the Tourlaville and the Ox-heart varieties.

Tourlaville Early C. (*Chou de Tourlaville*).—The head of this variety is rather long and pointed, and is formed by the leaves being wrapped upon each other in such a manner that some of them contribute only their lower part to its formation, while they stand clear of it in the upper part. Leaves large and broad, of a very dark green, and with ribs very thick and round near the stem, curving abruptly so as to press the leaves close to the head. This is a very distinct, early, and vigorous-growing variety, and is sent to Paris in large quantities at the close of the winter from the neighbourhood of Cherbourg, where it is extensively grown. When cultivated outside of

Tourlaville Early Cabbage
($\frac{1}{12}$ natural size).

its native district, it does not appear to possess any marked superiority over the ordinary Ox-heart kinds, and, besides, it is rather variable in its leaves, which are sometimes smooth and sometimes crimped.

French Ox-heart C. (*Chou Cœur de Bœuf Gros*).—A vigorous and productive kind, heading very soon, coming in a fortnight or three weeks later than the Early Ox-heart, but growing three or four times the size of that variety. Outer leaves large, rounded, rather thick, and of a darker colour on the upper surface than underneath; head large, very obtusely conical in shape, and of a somewhat grayish-green colour; stem rather short, seldom more than two-thirds of the length of the head. This is a good variety for market-garden culture on a large scale—approaching field culture. It is hardy enough to require but

little attention when growing, and when the heads are formed, they maintain their compactness longer than the Early varieties without bursting or losing shape too speedily.

Jersey Wakefield C.—This variety is well distinguished from the other forms of Ox-heart Cabbages by the yellowish tint and very stiff texture of its leaves, and it has a longer stalk than any

French Ox-heart Cabbage ($\frac{1}{12}$ natural size).

of the Ox-heart Cabbages properly so called. The outer leaves, which are of a pale glaucous-green colour, are rounded in shape, very faintly undulated at the edges, and remarkably firm and stiff; those which immediately surround the head are often hollowed like a spoon. The head itself, which is of a very pale-green colour, is of a short, bluntish, conical shape, and often tinged with red on the side exposed to the sun. This is an early and productive variety, and the head keeps firm for a considerable length of time—an important advantage when it is grown as a field crop.

Lingreville C. (*Chou de Lingreville*).—Stem rather short; leaves large, of a pale, almost light, green colour, moderately undulated and

crimped, soon forming a head of an oblong and almost pointed shape, by twisting themselves over one another rather than taking the ordinary hood or cap form. In appearance and size, this variety is almost intermediate between the Tourlaville and the Early Bacalan varieties, and, as in those two kinds, the formation of the head is commenced by leaves which are at some distance from each other on the stem. In the axils of

Early Bacalan Cabbage ($\frac{1}{12}$ natural size).

these lower leaves, shoots sometimes grow which form small heads themselves about as large as an apple or an orange. The variety which produces these secondary heads is known in Normandy by the name of *Chou Grappé* or *Chou Grappu*.

Early Bacalan C. (*Chou Bacalan Hâtif*).—Head oblong, conical, thick, and rather compact, resembling that of the Ox-heart variety, but perceptibly longer; leaves large, very slightly crimped, and undulated on the edges; stem longish. Although larger than the Ox-heart variety, this is equally early, but it is especially adapted for the mild seaside climate of the west of France. It appears to have been raised at Saint-Brieuc, whence it was brought to Bordeaux, and is very largely grown and highly esteemed in both these localities, especially for autumn sowing.

Large Bacalan C. (*Chou Bacalan Gros*).—When this variety comes true to name, it is distinguished from the preceding one by its somewhat larger size and by its more compact and rather more pointed head. There are all kinds of intermediate forms between these two varieties, which were themselves very certainly identical in origin. The Large Bacalan heads almost as soon as the preceding kind and keeps its shape better.

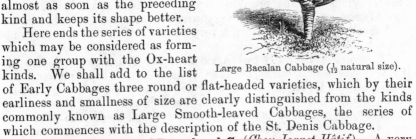

Large Bacalan Cabbage ($\frac{1}{12}$ natural size).

Here ends the series of varieties which may be considered as forming one group with the Ox-heart kinds. We shall add to the list of Early Cabbages three round or flat-headed varieties, which by their earliness and smallness of size are clearly distinguished from the kinds commonly known as Large Smooth-leaved Cabbages, the series of which commences with the description of the St. Denis Cabbage.

St. John's Day Dwarf Drumhead C. (*Chou Joanet Hâtif*).—A very distinct variety, with an extremely short stem. Head very hard and compact, rather broader than long, and somewhat bulging in the upper part; outer leaves not very numerous, of a deep-green colour, and very smooth; those forming the head of a paler green. This variety is very extensively grown in Anjou and Lower Brittany. In the neighbourhood of Paris it does not easily withstand a very cold and damp winter. In its native district it is chiefly sown in autumn for a spring crop; grown in this way, the heads are not so flat as they turn out when the sowing is made in spring.

St. John's Day Dwarf Drumhead Cabbage ($\frac{1}{12}$ natural size).

Small Early Erfurt C. (*Chou Petit Hâtif d'Erfurt*).—A very handsome little variety, an almost exact miniature of the Hundredweight Drumhead Cabbage. Stem short; head flattened; outer leaves not very numerous, spreading, slightly toothed, and marked with a great number of white veins, just like the Hundredweight variety. The stem is so short

Small Early Erfurt Cabbage ($\frac{1}{12}$ natural size).

I

that the head almost seems to rest on the ground. As the head is small and the outer leaves few, the plants may be grown very close together. This variety possesses the good quality, rare amongst Early Cabbages, of keeping the head compact and in good form for a considerable time. It does best when · sown in spring, as autumn-sown plants are apt to run to seed without heading.

Henderson's Early Summer C.—This variety, which is of American origin and rather esteemed in the United States, cannot be more properly placed than next after the preceding kind, which it much resembles in size and appearance. It has, however, a longer stalk, a thicker head, and leaves of a more grayish tint. In earliness, it comes immediately after the Jersey Wakefield Cabbage, and before all the other large-headed Cabbages.

To the foregoing may be added—*Ellam's Dwarf C.*, a very early variety, with small compact heads, of delicate flavour, a continuous supply of which may be had throughout the year by making successional sowings. *Carter's Heartwell C.*, a valuable medium-sized Cabbage, and one of the earliest, remarkable also for its compact uniform growth. This and the preceding are two of the best kinds in cultivation. *Cocoa-nut* (Wheeler), a very distinct, compact, valuable small Cabbage. *Imperial* (Wheeler), a very fine selection, the variety being one of the best for general use.

CULTURE.—The Early Cabbages, among which may be classed all the varieties which have just been enumerated (except, perhaps, the Large Bacalan Cabbage), are usually sown about Paris during the last ten days of August or the first ten days of September. In October, the seedlings are either planted out permanently, or else pricked out into a bed, where they are allowed to remain until they are planted out permanently in spring. In well-drained, warm, light soils, they may be generally planted out permanently at the end of autumn ; but in damp soils, or in localities which are exposed to severe frosts and snow or excessive rains, it is better not to plant out permanently until after winter is over. The earliest York Cabbages should be planted in warm and sheltered positions in a bed with a south aspect. In February, it

is a good plan to make a sowing of early kinds on a hot-bed, pricking out the seedlings on a hot-bed also, and using the plants thus obtained to fill up vacancies caused by any of the autumn-sown plants having either perished from the severity of the winter or run to seed prematurely under the influence of unusually mild weather. Early Cabbages may also be sown in spring, from March to May, and planted out as soon as the seedlings are big enough, if

St. Denis Drumhead Cabbage
(½ natural size).

there is ground ready to receive them. This is the simplest and easiest way of growing them, but it is not so much practised as sowing in autumn, as these early varieties are mostly grown for spring crops.

Saint-Denis Drumhead C. (*Chou de Saint-Denis*).—This variety, which is one of the most extensively grown about Paris, and also one of the oldest, may very aptly be placed first on the list in the enumeration of the different varieties of Smooth-leaved Cabbages, as its well-known characteristics will serve as points of comparison to which we shall refer other varieties of foreign origin or more recent introduction. It has a longish stem, quite as long, at least, as the head, which is round, depressed, and almost flat when fully grown, and of a wine-lees-red colour on the top.   Outer leaves large, rather stiff, with the lower part closely pressed against the head, and the upper part turned backwards, of a rather deep and slightly glaucous-green colour, and regularly rounded in outline, entire, not toothed nor undulated; veins rather large, of a pale-green colour.   In the neighbourhood of Paris, where, as we have said, this variety is very much grown, it is usually sown from March to May, and the heads are cut in the autumn up to the commencement of winter.

A sub-variety of the Saint-Denis, which is a little earlier, was for a long time grown under the name of *Chou de Bonneuil,* but it has now either gone out of cultivation or become mixed up with the ordinary variety.   And yet, if we refer to the descriptions of the two

Late St. John's Day Cabbage
(¹⁄₁₂ natural size).

Early Dutch Drumhead Cabbage
(¹⁄₁₂ natural size).

kinds which were published in the latter half of the last century, it would appear as if it was really the old Saint-Denis variety which has gradually disappeared and been superseded by the *Chou de Bonneuil.* The characteristics of the latter, as described in the eighteenth century, were, in fact, the same as those which we recognize at the present day in the Saint-Denis Cabbage, while the variety which was then named Saint-Denis had a fuller and less-flattened head and a longer stem, and resembled the Late Flat Dutch Cabbage up to a certain point.   The *Almanach du Bon Jardinier,* in its earliest editions, mentions these two kinds as distinct, and it is only since the year 1818 that it gives the two names as synonymous.

Late St. John's Day C. (*Chou Joanet Gros*).—Stem shorter than that of the preceding kind ; head rounder and not so broad ; outer leaves smaller, rounder, and of a deeper green.   The plant does not take up so much ground as the Saint-Denis, and comes in some days earlier, but it does not appear to bear frost so well.   The stem is so short that the head seems almost to rest on the ground.

Early Dutch Drumhead C. (*Chou de Hollande à Pied Court*).—A handsome variety, very distinct, and comparatively early.   Stem short and thick ; outer leaves rounded in shape and standing up around the heart, which is spherical in shape and of a pale-grayish or ashy-green colour, as are also the outer leaves. It is one of the best Early Round-headed Cabbages, and, with the exception of its very peculiar colour, is not unlike the preceding variety in its appearance.

Large Late Drumhead C. (*Chou de Brunswick à Pied Court*).—An

excellent kind, very distinct, and highly deserving recommendation. Leaves and head of a fine clear-green colour, far less glaucous than those of the Saint-Denis, and with less of the grayish tinge than those of the Hundredweight Drumhead; head thick and broad, very much depressed, and quite flattened on the top; outer leaves growing closely against the under part and sides of the

Large Late Drumhead Cabbage
(½ natural size).

head, which, from the shortness of the stem, appears to be almost resting on the ground.   The plant is almost as early as the Saint-Denis Cabbage.

The Large Late Flat Brunswick C. (*Chou de Brunswick Ordinaire*), which has a longer stem and a less-flattened head, has not been much grown since the present kind, which is superior to it in every respect, became more generally known.

Schweinfurt, or Quintal, Drumhead C. (*Chou de Schweinfurt*).—

This is the largest, if not the most productive, of all the Cabbages, and is, at the same time, a very early kind. When sown in April, it may be cut at the end of August or in September. The head is remarkably broad, frequently attaining a diameter of 20 inches and more; it is, like the outer leaves, of a pale light green, crossed with white veins, and often tinged with brownish or violet red; the leaves which compose it do not press very closely upon one

Schweinfurt, or Quintal, Drumhead Cabbage
(½ natural size).

another, in consequence of which the head is rather soft and deficient in compactness, so that its weight is not at all proportioned to its great size.   Nevertheless it is a good kind for the kitchen gardens of farms or large establishments, on account of its productiveness and earliness.

Fumel C. (*Chou de Fumel*).—This kind, and also the two following varieties, might be considered as intermediate between the Smooth-leaved Cabbages and the Savoy Cabbages, as the leaves are coarsely crimped and almost curled. We shall, however, follow the usual custom in classing them with the Smooth-leaved kinds, and they cannot be more properly placed than next to the Schweinfurt Cabbage, which they resemble in their earliness and in the softness of the head. The Fumel Cabbage appears to have originated in the south of France ; at least, it is very much grown there, and also in Algeria. It has a very short stem, and not many outside leaves, which spread horizontally close to the ground, are of a dark-green colour, and broadly crimped. The head, on the other hand, is of a very light colour, loose in texture, broad, and very much flattened; it is almost as large as that of the Saint-Denis Cabbage, but not nearly so heavy, and goes out of shape very soon. This is one of the earliest of all the Cabbages, but it does not appear to answer the climate of northern districts, where it rots too easily.

Fumel Cabbage.

Early Drumhead Cabbage ($\frac{1}{12}$ natural size).

Early Drumhead C. (*Chou de Habas*).—A variety grown in all the south-western districts of France, where it is sometimes confounded with the following kind. It is a pretty early Cabbage, with a short stem, and numerous crimped leaves, rather light in colour, the lower ones almost spreading on the ground; the inner leaves form a rather loose head of a yellowish-green colour.

Dax Drumhead C. (*Chou de Dax*).—Stem pretty long; leaves very numerous, coarsely crimped, of a darker and more glaucous green than those of the preceding kind, and resembling those of the Large Drumhead Savoy to some extent; head round, seldom well formed, at least in the climate of Paris, and always rather small in comparison with the luxuriance of the leaves. A half-late variety, which appears to be of little account outside of its native locality.

Dax Drumhead Cabbage ($\frac{1}{12}$ natural size).

Late Flat Dutch Drumhead Cabbage ($\frac{1}{12}$ natural size).

Late Flat Dutch Drumhead C. (*Chou de Hollande Tardif*).—Head rather large, round, somewhat depressed in shape, very full and firm; outer leaves pretty numerous, large, and clasping, broadly crimped to some extent. This variety has a longer stem and is more glaucous and later than the Saint-Denis Cabbage. Its principal merit is that of being exceedingly hardy and capable of enduring the most severe frost. The Ecury C. (*Chou d'Écury*), which is well known and highly esteemed in Champagne, resembles it very much.

Hundredweight, Quintal, or **Mason's Drumhead C.** (*Chou Quintal, C. de Strasbourg;* German, *Centner Kraut*).—One of the oldest and best Late Cabbages. Head broad, very large, very much flattened, and very

Hundredweight, or Mason's Drumhead, Cabbage   Early Winnigstadt Cabbage
($\frac{1}{12}$ natural size).   ($\frac{1}{12}$ natural size).

firm; leaves of a pale glaucous or ashy-green colour, with very numerous white veins, and the edges often cut or toothed; outer leaves rather numerous, but not growing to a very great size, turned back at the tops and showing the head well. This is a late, very hardy, and very productive kind, and is one of the sorts which are most used for making *Sauer-kraut*. Probably no other variety of Cabbage is so extensively employed for field culture. The *Melsbach* Cabbage (*Chou de Melsbach*) appears to be a somewhat earlier sub-variety of this.

Early Winnigstadt C. (*Chou Pointu de Winnigstadt;* German, *Winnigstädter Weisser Spitzer Kopfkohl*). — In its pointed shape, this variety somewhat resembles the Ox-heart Cabbages, but differs from them very strikingly in the close and compact manner in which the leaves forming the head are wrapped round each other, and the consequent greater hardness and firmness of the head. Stem short; outer leaves largish, of a glaucous-green colour, and moderately undulated at the edges; the inner

Filder, or Pomeranian, Cabbage ($\frac{1}{12}$ natural size).

ones are folded almost in the shape of a twisted or conical paper bag, and form an exceedingly solid and firm head, almost spherical in shape, but pointed at the top, and weighing heavy for its size. Although only a middling early kind, it is an exceedingly productive one, and cannot be too highly spoken of. It is also one of the best for field culture.

Filder, or Pomeranian, C. (*Chou Conique de Poméranie;* German, *Pomer'sches Spitziges Kraut, Filderkraut*).—Stem long, usually swollen under the head; outer leaves rather numerous and large, of a clear-green colour; head of a very elongated cone-shape, very solid and compact, and very white at the heart, ending at the top in a point formed by a leaf rolled in the shape of an inverted paper bag. This is a rather late variety, succeeding better when sown in spring than when sown in autumn, and keeping well for some time in winter. It is pretty generally grown in the north of Germany, where there are a great number of local varieties, differing more

Green Glazed American Cabbage ($\frac{1}{12}$ natural size).

or less from one another in the length of the stem and head, and the colour of the leaves. The variety which we have just described appears to us to be the most deserving of notice, as it is productive without being excessively late.

Green Glazed American C. (*Chou Vert Glacé d'Amérique*).—An exceedingly distinct variety. Stem of medium length; leaves rounded in shape, very firm and stiff, of a dark-green colour, and appearing as if glazed or varnished all over. This kind does not head very well, but in some degree resembles the Borecoles, from which, however, it differs in the amplitude of its leaves and the shortness of its stem. It is most suitable for spring culture, and is often sent to table shredded in vinegar like Red Cabbage.

Vaugirard C. (*Chou de Vaugirard*).—Stem rather short; outer leaves numerous, stiff, of a rather dark grayish-green colour, often hollowed or spoon-shaped, and always undulated and cut at the edges; veins numerous and distinctly marked; head of roundish form, depressed, rather flat, firm and hard, of a violet-red colour on the upper part, as are also the edges of the outer leaves. This is one of the hardiest kinds, and is very much grown in the neighbourhood of Paris for winter use;

Vaugirard Cabbage ($\frac{1}{12}$ natural size).

it bears frost, however, better when the head is not fully formed before severe weather comes on, in consequence of which the Parisian cultivators are careful not to sow it too early, seldom doing so before June, if it is intended to pass the winter in the open ground.

Early Dark-red Erfurt C. (*Chou Rouge Foncé Hâtif d'Erfurt ;* German, *Erfurter Bluthrothes Frühes Salat Kraut*).—A very handsome,

small, dwarf kind, with a spherical head not much larger than a big orange. Leaves rounded in shape, not very numerous, of an extremely dark-red colour, almost black. The heart of the head, however, is not of so dark a colour as its outer tinge would lead one to suspect ; it is, nevertheless, a very handsome little variety for the kitchen garden, taking up little space, and coming in early. The stem is short but well defined, as the outer leaves stand up well around the head, as in

Early Dark-red Erfurt Cabbage ($\frac{1}{12}$ natural size).

the Late St. John's Day Cabbage. This variety does not do well, unless when sown in spring—at least, in the neighbourhood of Paris.

Utrecht Red C. (*Chou Rouge Petit*).—Stem rather long; head round, compact, and of a dark-red colour ; outer leaves rather numerous, of medium size, rounded in shape, and rather stiff; the heart of the head is not very deeply coloured. A half-late variety, coming in soon after the Saint-Denis Cabbage.

Large Red Dutch Pickling C. (*Chou Rouge Gros*).—Stem rather long ; outer leaves very large, broadly undulated at the edges, of a

violet-red colour, sometimes slightly mixed with green, and covered very abundantly with bloom, which gives them a slightly bluish tinge ; head rather large, rounded in shape, slightly depressed, not so deeply coloured on the outside as that of the two other Red varieties, but much more deeply coloured at the heart. This variety is more productive than the preceding one, and is only a few days later. It is the best kind for field culture. All the kinds

Large Red Dutch Pickling Cabbage ($\frac{1}{12}$ natural size).

of Red Cabbage are used in the same ways as the other kinds, but they can also be eaten raw, as salad; when shredded fine and pickled with vinegar, they turn a brilliant red colour.

Marbled Burgundy Drumhead C. (*Chou Marbré de Bourgogne*). —Stem longish ; leaves numerous, stiff, rounded in shape, narrowly undulated at the edges, of a pale grayish-green colour, with red ribs and veins ; head rather small, very compact, flattened on the top, formed of shortish leaves, which often do not completely cover one another, and leave a pit-like depression or cavity in the centre of the top. In addition to the principal head, other small heads, about the size of a hen's egg, and very hard and compact, are often produced in the axils of the lower outside leaves. It is chiefly from the marbled appearance which the heart of the head presents when cut that this variety derives its name. It is considered a very hardy kind, and is very extensively grown in the eastern districts of France and in Switzerland.

Culture.—The Smooth-leaved Cabbages, the series of which terminates here, are most usually sown in spring, from March to June, according to the varieties grown, and the time it is desired the crop should come in. The sowings are made in the open ground, and the seedlings are pricked out as soon as possible into a bed, from which, as soon as the stems have grown as thick as the lower part of a goose-quill, they are planted out permanently in well-tilled and richly manured ground. Plentiful waterings should be given, at first to insure the rooting of the young plants and afterwards to counteract the great evaporation which takes place in the long hot days of summer. Over a great part of Britain this is not needed. The kinds which are cut in autumn do not require any special treatment. In countries visited by severe frosts, those which are for winter use should not be allowed to remain where they were

Marbled Burgundy Drumhead Cabbage
($\frac{1}{12}$ natural size).

planted, except in localities where the winter climate is mild; everywhere else, they should be taken up and trimmed of all decaying and superfluous leaves, and then replanted closely in rows, in an inclined position, with the top of the head, if possible, turned towards the north. In some countries the following curious, but very effectual, method is adopted : a sort of a wall is constructed of soil, in which the stems and roots of the Cabbages are placed horizontally, the heads remaining outside. In this way, they will keep very far into the winter.

Besides the Smooth-leaved varieties already described, we may mention the following kinds, which were formerly more or less esteemed, and the names of which are still to be met with in horticultural works, although the plants themselves are now not so often seen in cultivation ; also a few local varieties, which at present are hardly distributed beyond their native districts.

Alsace Autumn C. (*Chou d'Alsace*).—Stem long; head large, compact, flattened in shape, and sometimes slightly tinged with brown on the upper part; outer leaves short, stiff, and rounded in form. This variety resembles the Saint-Denis Cabbage, but it has a longer stem, and comes in somewhat earlier.

Large La Trappe, or **Mortagne, C.**—This handsome kind is hardly grown beyond the neighbourhood of Mortagne, in the department of l'Orne. It is somewhat like the Saint-Denis Cabbage, but is later, uch larger, and of a deeper green colour.

Death's-head C. (*Chou Tête de Mort*).—A very thick-set, dwarf variety. Head of average size, very compact and regular in shape, of a light colour, and almost perfectly spherical; outer leaves roundish, not very large. A very distinct variety, but now almost universally superseded by the Late St. John's Day Cabbage.

We shall now enumerate the principal local varieties grown in England, other parts of Europe, and the United States, observing that it is rather remarkable that, while a great number of the varieties of other vegetables are almost exactly the same in France and England, most of the varieties of Garden Cabbages are quite different in the two countries. This is probably owing to the difference of climate, as the Cabbage is a plant which is most highly susceptible of the effects of a dry or a moist climate. We shall only mention those English varieties which are most generally grown, noting, as far as possible, the French varieties which they most closely resemble.

Atkin's Matchless C.—This variety is very like the Very Early Étampes Cabbage, but it is not so early, and its leaves are more undulated.

Battersea, Enfield Market, Vanack, or Fulham C.—This kind is one of the most extensively grown for the London markets. As we have already observed, it resembles the French Large Ox-heart Cabbage, with a tendency in the direction of the Tourlaville or the Bacalan variety.

Cocoa-nut, Carter's Heartwell, and Little Pixie, or Tom Thumb, are good varieties with very smooth, rounded, entire leaves, and an oval obtuse-shaped head.

Cornish Paington, or Early Cornish, C.—This presents some resemblance to the Bacalan Cabbage, but the head is less compact, and is of an extremely light colour, like that of the Fumel Cabbage. It is not a very hardy kind.

Of the varieties grown in the north of Europe, the following are the most noteworthy :—

Amager C. (*Chou Amager*).—A very hardy Danish variety, somewhat like the Saint-Denis C., but with a longer stem and coming in later.

Kaper-kohl C. (*Chou Câpre*).—Another very hardy kind, with a rounded, slightly flattened head, deeply tinged with violet or brown on the upper part, as are also the rather undulated edges of the numerous outer leaves. It is something like the Vaugirard Cabbage.

Lubeck C.—A variety of medium size, with a compact, flattened head. The leaves are rather glaucous, resembling those of the Saint-Denis Cabbage in hue. A late and very hardy kind.

Giant Flat Gratscheff C.—A very leafy and large-sized variety, the chief merit of which, perhaps, is its capacity for enduring severe frosty weather without injury.

The varieties which have originated in the south of Europe are not very many. We shall only mention the following :—

Pisa Round C. (Italian, *Cavolo Rotondo di Pisa*).—This Cabbage is very extensively grown and highly esteemed in Italy and Algeria. In size and general appearance it is rather like the Late St. John's Day Cabbage; the head is almost round, but terminating at the top in a blunt cone; stem rather long; outer leaves not many, rounded, and almost spoon-shaped. There are several sub-varieties, differing from one another in size and earliness; the earliest of them heads almost as quickly as the York Cabbages.

Murcian C. (Portuguese, *Couve Murciana*).—An exceedingly distinct variety, of which the leaves are almost round, thick, of a dark green on the upper surface and nearly gray underneath, and overlap one another like the leaves of a Cabbage Lettuce. It is a very early variety, but the head is singularly loose in texture and almost quite hollow throughout, keeping its shape only for a few days. In the climate of Paris, it is of no account.

In the United States of America, many English, French, and German varieties of Cabbages are grown, but there are also some native varieties which are very highly thought of there, the best known of which are:—

Bloomsdale Early Drumhead C.—A late summer or autumn variety, with a large and not very flat head, and a longish stem, resembling the Common Brunswick Cabbage.

Bloomsdale Early Market C.—This has a conical head, and appears to be intermediate between an Early Bacalan and a pale-green, half-early Winnigstadt Cabbage.

Marble-head Mammoth, Silver-leaf Drumhead, and **Bergen C.**— These are all large and rather late kinds, resembling the Hundredweight Drumhead Cabbage.

SAVOY CABBAGES.

Brassica oleracea bullata, D.C.

French, Chou de Milan. *German*, Wirsing, Savoyerkohl, Börskohl. *Flemish* and *Dutch*, Savooikool. *Danish*, Savoy-kaal. *Italian*, Cavolo de Milano. *Spanish*, Col de Milan, C. risada. *Portuguese*, Saboia.

Under this name are grouped all the varieties of Cabbage which, instead of having the leaves smooth, have them crimped, or, as they are sometimes incorrectly termed, "curled" all over. This appearance, according to De Candolle, is owing to the circumstance that, in these varieties, the parenchyma, or spongy substance, of the leaf is developed more rapidly than the nerves or veins, and consequently becomes raised above their level, not finding room enough to grow flat in the space between them. The area of the surface of the leaves is increased by these numerous crimped divisions, and the head, being formed of all the leaves while they are still young, is, in consequence, more tender than it is generally found in any of the Smooth-leaved kinds. The flavour also of the Savoy Cabbage is considered milder and less musky. The mode of growing them does not differ from that which has been already described for the ordinary kinds.

St. John's Savoy Cabbage (1/12 natural size.)

St. John's Savoy C. (*Chou de Milan de la St. Jean*).—This handsome variety might almost be described as the Ox-heart Savoy, as it forms a head much in the same manner as the Ox-heart Cabbage, and almost as promptly. The stem is extremely short, and the leaves are of a somewhat pale and wan green colour, and considerably but not finely crimped. The head forms very quickly, more so than in any other variety of Savoy. It does not, however, keep its shape long, but bursts and grows out of form, if it is not cut in time—a remark which also applies to nearly all the very early Cabbages.

Ulm, or Early Green Curled, Savoy C. (*Chou Milan Petit Hâtif*).—

Ulm, or Early Green Curled, Savoy Cabbage ($\frac{1}{2}$ natural size.

Stem longish ; head small and round; leaves not numerous, of a deep-green colour, rather coarsely and deeply crimped. This is the smallest and one of the earliest of all the Savoy Cabbages. The New Dwarf Ulm (Little Pixie) Savoy, a fine dwarf variety, the Vienna Early Dwarf (Tom Thumb, or King Coffee) Savoy, the dwarfest of all varieties, and the Dwarf Green Curled Savoy, a fine medium-sized variety, are three kinds highly deserving recommendation. The first two kinds should be planted 1 ft. apart.

The Vienna Savoy (*Chou Milan de Vienne*) is a sub-variety of this, with leaves not so much crimped and a slightly oblong head. It is a very small and very early kind.

Very Early Paris Savoy C. (*Chou de Milan Très Hâtif de Paris*).—

Very Early Paris Savoy Cabbage ($\frac{1}{2}$ natural size).

This variety is closely allied to the preceding one, but, nevertheless, very distinct from it. Head rounded and firm, of a clear-green colour, and surrounded by a few spreading leaves, which are not of very large dimensions, and are of a rather dark-green colour and somewhat more broadly crimped than those of the foregoing variety. The Very Early Paris Savoy is remarkable for its symmetrical and regular shape, its dwarf stature, and its earliness, which surpasses that of all the other Savoy Cabbages by a week or ten days. It heads almost as quickly as the York Cabbages or the earliest Ox-heart varieties.

Small Early Joulin Savoy C. (*Chou Pancalier Petit Hâtif de Joulin*).—Still earlier than the Early Ulm Savoy, this variety is distinguished

Small Early Joulin Savoy Cabbage ($\frac{1}{2}$ natural size).

from it by its short stem and its largish leaves, the outer ones of which spread to the ground, while all are very coarsely and broadly crimped. The head is of a rather deep-green colour, and the outer leaves, which have an almost black tint, are of a very fleshy texture, their parenchyma, or spongy substance, being very abundant and very thick, so that they are as good for table use as the head itself, especially after they have been made tender by frosty weather.

Dwarf Early Green Curled Savoy C. (*Chou Milan Court Hâtif*).—
An excellent variety, very distinct, and of first-rate quality. Stem
very short; leaves large and broad, of a rather deep clear green, finely
crimped, and spreading on the ground in a broad rosette before the
head is formed; head firm, moderately flattened in shape. This
variety is extensively grown about Paris for the winter markets. It
is sown all through the summer, planted out permanently just as
winter commences, and supplies the markets all through the winter.
Generally the head is only beginning to form when the plants are cut,

Dwarf Early Green Curled Savoy Cabbage　　Early Flat Green Curled Savoy Cabbage
(1/12 natural size).　　　　　　　　　　(1/12 natural size).

but the numerous outer leaves, which closely surround the head, form
an excellent vegetable after they have been softened and made tender
by frosty weather.

Early Flat Green Curled Savoy C. (*Chou Milan Ordinaire*).—Stem
rather long; leaves of a somewhat glaucous-green colour, largish and
pliant, and not so finely crimped as
those of the preceding kind. This
Cabbage somewhat resembles the
Large Drumhead Savoy, but has a
much smaller head. It is one of the
most extensively cultivated kinds,
and is chiefly worthy of note as being
hardy, and not particular as to the
soil in which it is grown.

Tours Savoy Cabbage (1/12 natural size).

Tours Savoy C. (*Chou Pancalier de Touraine*).—Stem short; leaves
very large and numerous, of a very dark-green colour, and coarsely and
broadly crimped, the outer ones
almost entirely spreading on the
ground: head round, rather small in
proportion to the size of the plant,
not very compact, and often imperfectly formed. As in the case of
the Dwarf Green Curled Savoy,
the outer leaves form as important
a part of the crop as the head.

This variety resembles the
Early Joulin Savoy C., but the
latter is an earlier and smaller
kind.

Victoria Savoy Cabbage (1/12 natural size).

Victoria Savoy C. (*Chou Milan Victoria*).—Stem of average length;
leaves rather numerous, of a clear-green colour, and very finely crimped,

in which respect they are distinguished from those of all other Savoys except the following kind; head round, compact, largish, and of a light-green colour. This is an excellent variety, of very good quality, and keeping its head well for winter use. Its leaves are remarkably tender and delicate in flavour, and yet they withstand frost and damp equally well. No other variety has the fleshy substance of the leaves so abundantly developed in proportion to the size of the veins or nerves.

Cape, or **Large Late Green, Savoy C.** (*Chou Milan du Cap*).— Stem longish; leaves finely crimped, pretty large, and of a glaucous-green colour; head medium-sized, round, and very compact. This variety would bear no bad resemblance to the Victoria Savoy, only for the much deeper bluish tint of its leaves.

Limay Savoy C. (*Chou Milan Petit Très Frisé de Limay*).—Stem long; outer leaves large, spreading horizontally, and coarsely and densely crimped; head small, rounded in shape, and not very

Limay Savoy Cabbage ($\frac{1}{12}$ natural size).

compact. This variety is extremely hardy, and resists the severest frosts. Like the Dark Green Curled Savoy, it forms a large rosette of leaves rather than a head, properly so called, and it is considered not inferior to that variety in the markets.

Yellow Curled, or **Golden, Savoy C.** (*Chou Milan Doré*).—Stem short; outer leaves largish, of a rather deep clear-green colour, broadly crimped, and almost turned backwards; head of a slightly elongated egg-shape, medium-sized, not very compact, in winter turning to a very light, almost yellow colour. This Cabbage is very tender to eat, especially after frosty weather. There are several forms or sub-varieties of it which exhibit various degrees of difference in size and earliness, while retaining all the main charac-

Yellow Curled, or Golden, Savoy ($\frac{1}{12}$ natural size).

teristics of the variety just described. One of the most highly esteemed of these is the *Blumenthal*, a rather large and late kind.

Long-headed Savoy C. (*Chou de Milan à Tête Longue*).—Stem of medium length, about one-half or two-thirds the length of the head, which is oblong in shape, almost like that of the Sugar-loaf Cabbage, of a light-green colour, and not very compact; outer leaves rather narrow, elongated, erect, rather broadly crimped, and of a somewhat glaucous-green colour. A moderately early variety, of good quality, and yielding a fair crop, notwithstanding the smallish size of the plants.

Long-headed Savoy Cabbage
($\frac{1}{12}$ natural size).

Large Drumhead Savoy Cabbage
($\frac{1}{12}$ natural size).

It possesses the good property of heading well in the latter end of autumn, so that it can be sown to advantage rather late in the season.

Large Drumhead Savoy C. (*Chou Milan des Vertus*).—Stem 6 to 8 inches high, stout, bearing a broad, thick, compact head, which is flattened on the top, sometimes slightly tinged with a wine-lees-red colour, and almost perfectly smooth, being only partially crimped at the edges of the leaves; outer leaves rather numerous, large, broad, stiff, well spread out, of a rather dark and slightly glaucous-green colour, and not so finely or abundantly crimped

Large Hardy Winter Drumhead Savoy Cabbage
($\frac{1}{12}$ natural size).

as those of most other Savoy Cabbages. This variety is grown on a large scale around Paris, and especially in the Plain of Aubervilliers, where they commence to cut it for market at the end of autumn and in the early part of winter. When it is grown true to name, the heads are only completely formed at that time, and they bear the early frosts pretty well. It might be truly said that mountains of this Cabbage are sent to the Central Market at Paris during a considerable part of the winter.

Large Hardy Winter Drumhead Savoy C. (*Chou Milan de Pontoise*).—Stem longish; leaves numerous, large, stiff, coarsely crimped, and of a rather deep and glaucous-green colour; head round, forming rather late, very full, compact, and hard. This is a good winter variety, coming in after the preceding one. Some people consider it to be the original form of the Large Drumhead Savoy, and that the latter is an accidental improvement of the market gardeners on the primitive variety, which is not so early, and does not produce so fine a head.

Norwegian Savoy C. (*Chou Milan de Norvége*).—This kind has the

Norwegian Savoy Cabbage (1/12 natural size).

leaves so little crimped, that it might almost be taken for an ordinary Smooth-leaved Cabbage. The stem is longish, and the leaves numerous, stiff, and standing well up about the head, which is round, comparatively small, and very late in forming. All the leaves, in winter, become of a reddish or violet colour. This Cabbage is distinguishable in appearance from the Vaugirard Cabbage only by its longer stem and somewhat more numerous leaves. It is the latest of the Savoys, and will bear the hardest frosts.

In Belgium, there is a coarsely crimped variety of Savoy grown under the name of *Chou de Mai*, the head of which is formed by the leaves being twisted, instead of folded or wrapped over one another in the ordinary way. It is sown in August, and planted out either before, during, or after winter, coming in in the following May. After the head is cut, the plant produces two or three small secondary heads in the axils of the lower leaves.

In the London market gardens Savoys are not so much esteemed as Cabbage, but they are largely cultivated by some growers. The seed is sown in March, and the plants are put out under fruit-trees, or in similar positions in the same way as Cabbages. The varieties mostly grown are the Dwarf Green Curled, Early Ulm, and Drumhead. Sometimes they are used as Coleworts when half-grown, in which case they are planted thickly among other crops in any vacant places in the same way as Cabbage Coleworts. During winter, when greens are scarce, Savoys are most in demand. They are very hardy, and are all the better for being subjected to frost, and for this reason they are a good winter crop. The refuse of the seed-beds are sometimes planted out in August to supply Coleworts in winter and spring.

Braganza, Portugal, or Sea-Kale C. (*Chou à Grosses Côtes*; Portuguese, *Couve Tronchuda*).—Stem

Braganza, Portugal, or Sea-Kale Cabbage (1/12 natural size).

shortish; leaves closely set, with thick, white, fleshy ribs, undulated and slightly cut on the edges, and usually hollowed or spoon-shaped, all forming at the latter end of autumn a small loose kind of head. For a long time a distinction was made of two varieties of this plant, one with green and the other with light-coloured leaves, but the difference is so unimportant that at the present day the two kinds are considered identical. The outer leaves and the head of the Couve Tronchuda are very tender to eat. It withstands frost very well, and

even requires it to bring out its full quality.   Under the name of Dwarf
Portugal Cabbage, a more com-
pact and better-headed variety is
sometimes grown in England.

Curled Couve Tronchuda C.
(*Chou à Grosses Côtes Frangé*).—
The ribs of this variety are not
so much developed as those of
the ordinary kind, but the blade
of the leaf is much more curled
and undulated.   It forms an im-
perfect head, but bears frost very
well, like the preceding kind, like
which also it can be cut all
through the winter, when autumn

Curled Couve Tronchuda Cabbage
(½ natural size).

Cabbages have become scarce and the spring crops have not yet
come in.

Curled Winter Borecole C. (*Chou Bricoli*).—For some years past,
towards the end of winter, one might see in the Central Market, at
Paris, a variety of Cab-
bage which does not
form a head, and which
the market gardeners
call *Bricoli* Cabbage.
This seems to be an
intermediate kind be-
tween the Green Curled
Kale and the Curled
Couve Tronchuda.   As
far as we have seen, it
possesses no special
merit beyond its great
degree of hardiness.

The Thick-leaved
Coutances C. (*Chou de
Coutances*) exhibits a

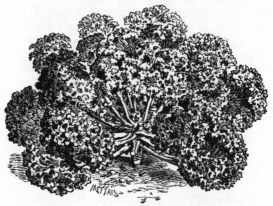

Curled Winter Borecole Cabbage (¹⁄₁₂ natural size).

great resemblance to the Couve Tronchuda.   The midrib of its leaf
is not so large, but, on the other hand, it forms a much better head,
which in the course of the autumn becomes very compact, white, and
exceedingly firm at the heart.

BRUSSELS SPROUTS.

French, Chou de Bruxelles.   *German*, Brüsseler Sprossen-Wirsing.   *Flemish* and *Dutch*,
Spruitkool.   *Danish*, Rosenkaal.   *Italian*, Cavolo a germoglio.

This variety of Cabbage bears some analogy to the Savoys in its
dark-green and somewhat crimped leaves ; but, on the other hand, it
has a longer stem than any of the other head-forming Cabbages, and
its leaves, although very numerous, do not form a true head.   It is
grown for the sake of the sprouts, which are produced in the axils of
the leaves all along the stem, and of which the small spoon-shaped

K

leaves are very closely and compactly wrapped round one another so as to form small heads, which are round in shape and produced in great abundance. They make their appearance first at the bottom of the stem, and, as these are cut away, fresh "sprouts" are developed in succession almost up to the top of the stem. This long-continued production of sprouts, which is maintained in the severest frosty weather, and also the very fine quality of the vegetable, have caused the Brussels Sprouts to be one of the most highly esteemed and most generally grown kitchen-garden plants. There is something singular, from a physiological point of view, in the circumstance that the principal rosette of leaves of this plant does not form a head, while the secondary shoots or sprouts regularly form very perfect heads. The very reverse of this is mostly found to occur in other Cabbages and in Lettuces, in which the principal leaves of the head enwrap one another closely, while the leaves of the sprouts which they produce stand apart at greater or less distances from one another on the shoots which bear them. Be that as it may, we are indebted to this anomaly for an excellent vegetable.

CULTURE.—The Brussels Sprout is a plant of rather slow growth, and in order to have a crop from the end of October to March, sowings should be commenced in March or April, and continued in succession until June, if a successional crop is desired. When the seedlings are strong enough, they are planted out permanently, leaving a space of 20 inches in all directions from plant to plant of the ordinary variety, and of 16 inches for plants of the dwarf kind. The sprouts will be fit to cut in October, and the plants will continue to bear them all through the winter. They like good, rich, well-drained soil, which, however, should not be too highly manured, otherwise the growth would become too rank, to the detriment of the sprouts, which, under such circumstances, do not head well. In Paris, the "sprouts" which are grown in the fields and on a large scale for market are the most highly esteemed. These are sown at the end of February, and planted out in May and June.

As a rule, in England, Brussels Sprouts are only cultivated in large and market gardens, although they are well deserving of a place in every garden, however small. With a little skill and forethought, they may in warm districts be got to supply the table from September till April. The common rule is to sow one good batch in March or April, and let that serve all purposes. Where, however, a long supply is desired, this is decidedly a mistake, inasmuch as Brussels Sprouts ought to be made use of as soon as they are ready, otherwise they burst or rot, and are useless. Successional sowings should be made to keep up a constant supply.

For early crops the best plan is to sow a pinch of seed in a shallow box, well drained, early in January, and place it in a pit or frame where the temperature is from 40° to 45°. The plants will soon be up, and should be kept close up to the glass until they are large enough to handle, when they should be pricked off into other boxes, or out into a bed in a frame. Plenty of air must be admitted to them after they have again commenced to grow, and if the weather be favourable in the middle of March, they may be planted out-of-doors on the warmest border that can be spared for them. If the plants be taken out with a good ball of earth and planted during showery weather, they will grow away without a check, and a crop of fine large sprouts in September will be the result.

The first sowing out-of-doors should be made in February or March, the main sowing early in April; and if later supplies be required, a small sowing may be made in May or June. When the plants are large enough to be conveniently handled, they should be pricked out in rows into narrow beds or borders, 5 or 6 inches apart, or more if practicable. The distance apart of the plants for the final planting must in some measure be governed by the space at disposal, but in any case there is nothing gained by overcrowding. Plants for the main crop should be allowed at least 2 ft. apart each way, but if 3 ft. can be allowed between the rows it will be all the better. If extra fine sprouts are desired, 3 ft. from plant to plant each way must be allowed. For early and late plantations it is not necessary to allow quite so much space as for the main crop.

SOIL.—Brussels Sprouts will succeed in almost any kind of soil, provided it is well and deeply cultivated and fairly manured. Poor sandy soil will require a heavy dressing of good manure, whilst lime and burnt clay may be beneficially applied to cold clayey land in preference to rank manure just previous to planting, which would have a tendency to produce gross open sprouts instead of the close medium-sized buttons so much liked in the kitchen. Frequent stirrings of the soil, clean culture, and removing decaying leaves add to their growth and cleanly appearance, and ought to be insisted on. As regards earthing-up the stems, there has been much dispute as to its merits and demerits, but we have seen them grown both with and without that assistance, with much about the same result. In windy places earthing-up is certainly to be recommended, in order to enable them to resist the power of the wind; but as Brussels

Sprouts, unlike Cabbage or Broccoli, bear all up the stems, it is not desirable to bury them to any great depth, beyond giving them necessary support. The Cabbage-like heart from the centre of the plant should not be cut off until the crop is fit for gathering. The Brussels Sprout in its proper state is a small, compact one; and very rich culture, while giving large rosettes, does not improve the quality.

Manure water given to Brussels Sprouts during dry weather will help to keep them in a vigorous and healthy growing state; but it is well to remember that overfeeding will spoil this vegetable, which in its best state is neat and compact. By making it coarse and large we make it useless to the good cook, who knows what it ought to be.

GATHERING.—In gathering, Brussels Sprouts are frequently broken from the stems of the plants, and sometimes with a portion of the stem adhering to them. This is wrong, inasmuch as it destroys the second crop of young sprouts. A sharp knife should always be used to cut off the sprouts, leaving as much spur as possible. The largest and hardest should always be gathered first.

Brussels Sprouts are chiefly grown in the London market gardens as catch crops, under orchard trees, or between other vegetables. The seed is sown in April, and the plants, when large enough, are put out wherever a vacant piece of ground occurs. Market gardeners prefer Brussels Sprouts with medium-sized stems to those of rank growth, as from the former they get harder and better sprouts, which realize the most money in the market. In gathering Brussels Sprouts most market gardeners pull up the plants and cart them to the packing shed, where women divest the stalks of the Sprouts and pack them in half-bushel or bushel baskets, the largest and plumpest being always put on the top. The Cabbage-like tops are packed separately in large baskets.

Some growers, however, pick the sprouts from the plants as they grow, and leave them to supply a second crop. Brussels Sprouts when in the seed-bed are often attacked by small white-winged flies, which congregate on the under side of the leaves and greatly injure the plants. In order to get rid of these, an old sack is nailed to two poles, about 6 inches being allowed to hang over one of the poles to act as a flapper. The sack, but not the flapper, is then tarred all over, and two men, one each side the seed-bed, walk quickly along with the sack directly over the plants. The flapper drags over the plants and disturbs the flies, which fly upwards and get stuck to the tar. This several times repeated gets rid of the majority of the insects.

USES.—In Belgium, preference is given to small-sized sprouts, which grow very thickly and close together on the stems; but in France the largest-sized sprouts, as big as a good-sized walnut, are most in favour —an illustration of the numerous instances in which the fine appearance of a vegetable or a fruit is not always an index of its quality, for the smallest and hardest Brussels Sprouts are certainly the most delicate in flavour.

Dwarf Brussels Sprouts ($\frac{1}{10}$ natural size).

Tall Brussels Sprouts ($\frac{1}{10}$ natural size; sprout, $\frac{1}{2}$ natural size).

Tall Brussels Sprouts (*Chou de Bruxelles Ordinaire*).—Stem $2\frac{1}{2}$ to over 3 ft. high, comparatively slender, bearing numerous leaves which do not grow very close to one another, and have the stalk bare for a great part of its length, and the blade roundish, slightly hollowed or spoon-shaped, and very faintly crimped. Sprouts of medium size, very firm, rather pear-shaped than spherical, and never growing so closely together as to touch one another, even when they have attained their full size. This is the kind which is the most extensively grown in the fields around Paris; it is hardy, and continues to bear for several months, producing the smallest, most delicate, and best "sprouts."

Dwarf Brussels Sprouts (*Chou de Bruxelles Nain*).—Stem stout
and stiff, usually not exceeding 20 inches in height; leaves growing
more closely together than those of the preceding kind, and nearly
similar in appearance, but more crimped. Sprouts generally larger
and rounder in shape; being of greater size, and growing closer
together, they are usually crowded upon one another in this variety,
while in the Tall variety there is always more or less space between
them. This variety is generally somewhat earlier than the Tall one,
but it does not continue to bear so long in winter.

A number of so-called Brussels Sprouts—usually much larger than
the true form—have been raised in England, but they are of little
value. Instead of being improvements on this well-known plant, they
are mere distortions, so to say, from the original type. The seed of the
true Brussels Sprouts—Tall or Dwarf, as may be desired—should be asked
for. Its rosettes are what the good cook wants—he would be puzzled
to know what to do with the large hybrid forms of late years, devoid
for the most part of any characteristic of the Brussels Sprouts.

Before going on to describe the Borecoles, we must notice two very
distinct kinds of Cabbages, which constitute the connecting-link, so to
say, between the varieties which form heads and those which do not.
These are the Rosette Colewort (*Chou Rosette*) and the Russian Kale
(*Chou de Russie*).

Green Rosette Colewort.—Under the name of Rosette Colewort
or Collard, a very distinct variety is cultivated in England, which,
although capable of forming a head, is generally cut for use as a
Borecole while the leaves are in the rosette form and still young and
tender. It is very dwarf, the stem seldom exceeding 8 or 10 inches in
height, and bearing numerous closely set leaves, which are slightly
crimped, rounded, and deeply hollowed or spoon-shaped. If sown early
in spring, it comes in in August, and, if left in the ground longer,
forms a small, round, very compact head. But as Cabbages of all
kinds are plentiful in autumn, there is no advantage in sowing this
kind so early ; whereas, if sown in early summer, it comes in at a time
when tender greens are scarcest and most in demand.

Russian Kale (*Chou de Russie*).—A singular plant, which, at first
sight, one would be inclined to take for anything else but a Cabbage.
Stem rather large and thickish, 16 to 20 inches high ; leaves of a
grayish-green colour, the outer ones of a darkish hue and half-spreading, the central ones erect and paler in colour, all of them cut nearly
down to the midrib into rather narrow divisions, which are entire, or
sometimes lobed, and are coarsely crimped on the upper surface. At
the latter end of autumn, this Cabbage forms a sort of a head, which
is small, pretty white, and very compact. Its chief merit is that of
bearing frosty weather very well. Apart from its singular appearance,
it is not easy to say what this plant has to recommend it. It is
certainly no advantage to have its leaves cut as they are; that is, to
have the veins merely fringed with a narrow border of parenchyma, or
spongy substance, instead of being connected by an unbroken tissue, as
they are in other Cabbages. Having been grown for some time chiefly
in botanical collections, the Russian Kale appeared to have become
almost forgotten, when, within the last few years, it was, with a great

deal of fuss, introduced as a novelty into England; but it is doubtful whether the present craze for it will last for any considerable time.

CULTURE.—The culture of Coleworts is very extensive and important in London market gardens. These are Cabbages pulled for market when about half grown, and for supplying such, every spare corner in market gardens is planted. As soon as fruit bushes have been cleared of their crops rows of Coleworts are planted between them; they are also planted under fruit-trees, no matter how large the trees may be, and also between rows of Moss Roses. The space between Celery ridges is likewise generally planted with Coleworts, as is also that between Asparagus ridges, the edges of which, too, are often cropped with Coleworts. Between the rows of French and Runner Beans and Late Savoys, the Colewort is also planted; and, in fact, like Lettuces, it is planted in every empty space where there is a probability of its growing. Whole fields, too, are sometimes cropped with it, and are cleared in good time for winter Radishes. Cock's Hardy Green Colewort more resembles an ordinary Cabbage than the Rosette, which is grown largely for market, and, being hardier, is sown a month or six weeks later, so as to form a succession to that sort. A sowing of the Rosette is usually made in May in beds in an open piece of ground; and, when up, the young plants are thinned with small hoes. The strongest plants are first selected for transplanting, and are put in chiefly as catch crops between other vegetables. For spring Coleworts, only the thinnings of the Fulham Cabbage are used. The Rosette is, perhaps, the greatest favourite in the market, its beautiful white heads, when bunched, having an attractive appearance; but, as regards quality, nobody would eat the Rosette who could get Cock's Hardy Green—*i.e.*, if they were acquainted with the respective flavours of the two varieties. A kind called Blue Colewort is largely grown for a November crop, as earlier in the year it is apt to "bolt." Coleworts are tied in bunches, packed in waggons, and sold in this way in market.

Scotch Kale, Tall German, or Winter Greens (½ natural size).

BORECOLE or KALE.

Brassica oleracea acephala, D.C.

French, Choux verts. *German,* Winterkohl. *Flemish,* Bladerkool. *Dutch,* Boerenkool. *Italian,* Cavolo verde. *Spanish,* Coles sin cogollo, Breton, Berza.

To this section belong a number of very hardy and excellent vegetables, as we think, often more delicate in flavour than the hearting Cabbages. The sprouts of the Scotch and Cottager's Kales, gathered in spring from the stems cut in winter, are excellent in flavour. The number of seeds contained in a gramme is, on an average, 300.

Tall Green Curled, or **Scotch, Kale; Tall German,** or **Winter Greens** (*Chou Frisé Vert Grand*).—Stem stout and straight, 3 to 5 ft. high, bearing a plume of rather narrow, lobed, deeply cut leaves, which are very much curled at the edges, and often turned backwards at the end, of a fine, clear-green colour, and from 16 to 20 inches in length. This is a useful variety, and its leaves are very tender and good after they have been exposed to the action of frosty weather; besides, the whole plant is highly ornamental, and especially deserving of recommendation for very cold climates. In the open ground, even in the severest winters, it yields a supply of fresh vegetables of excellent quality.

Mosbach Winter Kale (*Chou Frisé de Mosbach*).—One might suppose that this variety is a cross between the Tall Green Curled Kale and the Couve Tronchuda Cabbage, so much does it resemble the latter in its leaves, which are, to a great extent, entire in the blade, and have very stout stalks, midribs, and veins. Only the margin of the leaves is curled and very finely puckered, almost in the same way as the leaves of the Curled Kales. The stem is of medium height, rarely exceeding 2 or 2⅓ ft., and the leaves are disposed along it in tiers, are bent upwards, instead of downwards,

Mosbach Winter Kale.

from the middle, and are distinguished by their pale, almost yellowish-green colour. This plant is not only useful as a table vegetable, but also possesses some degree of merit as an ornamental plant. It is not very hardy.

Intermediate Moss-curled Kale (*Chou Extra-frisé Demi-nain Vert*). —This variety is intermediate in height between the Dwarf Curled Kale, the leaves of which spread upon the ground, and the Tall Green Curled Kale, which sometimes grows 6 ft. or more high. The present variety rarely exceeds about 32 inches in height, and is characterized by having the leaves curled to an extreme degree, comparatively short, but very broad, and with the margin curiously puckered and twisted. It is perfectly hardy, and in this respect differs widely from the preceding variety, which is rather sensitive to cold. It may be usefully employed for the winter furnishing of small circular raised beds of medium height, or else

Intermediate Moss-curled Kale.

to form a gradation between the Tall and the Dwarf varieties of ornamental Kales in large groups.

Dwarf Curled Kale, German Greens, Dwarf Curlies, Canada or **Labrador Kale** (*Chou Frisé Vert à Pied Court*).—This is a dwarf variety of the preceding kind, which it resembles in the characteristics of its

leaves; but its stem does not grow more than from 16 to 20 inches high, so that the ends of the leaves often rest upon the ground. Besides its value as a vegetable, it is also a very ornamental plant, either for small circular raised flower-beds in winter or for garnishing dishes on the table.

Dwarf Curled Kale, German Greens, Dwarf Curlies, Canada or Labrador Kale (¹⁄₁₂ natural size).

Jerusalem Green Curled Kale, or Asparagus Kale.—A variety of dwarf but sturdy growth, which has the margin of the leaves very much crisped or curled, and the partially undeveloped centre leaves tinged on the tips with purple, with veins of a subdued crimson colour. In spring this plant throws out numerous

long, stout, succulent shoots, which may be cooked either green or blanched. The Imperial Hearting Scotch Kale is also very productive of sprouts in spring.

Tall Purple Borecole, Tall Purple Kale, or **Purple Winter Greens** (*Chou Frisé Rouge Grand*). —This plant resembles the Tall Green Curled Kale in every respect except the colour of its leaves, which are of a very deep violet-red hue.

Dwarf Purple Curled Borecole (*Chou Frisé Rouge à Pied Court*).—A sub-variety of the preceding kind, growing only from 16 to 20 inches high. When it is grown true to name, the colour of its leaves is almost black, and contrasts very strikingly

Variegated Varieties of Borecole or Kale.

with that of the Green Curled Kale, which it equals in hardiness.

Variegated Borecole, or **Garnishing Kale** (*Choux Frisés Panachés*). —Stem from 20 inches to 2½ ft. high; leaves divided, slashed, curled, and undulated, like those of the preceding varieties, but, instead of being of a uniform colour, they are variegated, especially after frost, in different ways, either with green, red, or lilac on a white ground, or with red on a green ground. Several of these forms can be raised individually from seed, especially the Red Variegated and the White Variegated Kale. Perhaps one of the best varieties is Melville's Improved Variegated Curled Kale, in which the variegation of colours ranges from white and green to purple-crimson, rose, and crimson. All these kinds are very ornamental, and in winter very pretty beds can be made with them in the open ground, while the leaves may also be found useful for garnishing the dinner-table. They will bear very severe frosty weather, if they have not previously suffered from an excess of moisture. In growing them, when the plants are sufficiently large, transplant them into poor soil in an open situation. In autumn, select the most beautiful, and, breaking off the large under-leaves, plant sufficiently deep to bring the head close to the surface of the soil.

Georgia Collard's.—The Cabbage, as we remarked at the beginning of the general article on this vegetable, is a plant which properly belongs to cold and temperate climates, and accordingly, amongst cultivated varieties, we find but very few which can endure the summer heat of warm latitudes. The present variety is one of these, and is very highly esteemed in the Southern United States. It is a Cabbage which, properly speaking, does not form a head ; but the leaves, which are large, undulated, and slightly curled at the edges, are somewhat folded at the heart or centre, so as to form a sort of bunch, being also variegated with white on the ribs, and presenting somewhat of the appearance of the central leaves of the Cauliflower when the head is just about to form. These leaves are very tender and delicate when cooked, and, in fact, form an excellent table vegetable. The plant grows from 2 to 3 ft. high, according to the nature of the soil in which it is grown and the liberal amount of culture bestowed upon it.

Proliferous Borecole (*Chou Frisé Prolifère*).—This rather singular variety is remarkable for producing on the midrib, and sometimes on the smaller veins of the leaf, certain leaf-like appendages, which are curled and cut in the same manner as the leaf itself is at the margin. The plants are also usually, at the same time, variegated with white or red. They are chiefly noticeable as ornamental plants.

Neapolitan Curled Borecole (*Chou Frisé*, or *Chou Rave de Naples ;* Italian, *Cavolo Pavonazza*).—This variety is intermediate between the Borecoles and the Kohl-Rabi. Its stem, like that of the Kohl-Rabi, is swollen, but, instead of being so immediately above the neck of the root, it commences to swell 2 or 3 inches above the surface of the ground. This swelling, which is usually oval in shape, produces a great number of leaves at the top, while along the sides and at the bottom it sends out shoots or prominences which terminate in clusters of leaves. The leaves are 10 to 12 inches long, with a long slender stalk, and are very deeply cut into narrow fringed, curled strips or segments, producing a very ornamental effect with their elegant form and glaucous-green colour relieved by the white veins. The swollen part of the stem is fleshy, and can be eaten like the Kohl-Rabi ; but the plant is more grown for ornament than for table use.

Palm-tree C. or **Borecole** (*Chou Palmier*).—Stem straight, or slightly curved, attaining a height of 6½ ft. or more, and bearing at the top a cluster of leaves, which are entire, from 2 to over 2½ ft. long and 3 or 4 inches broad, with the edges turned and rolled underneath, of a dark, almost blackish, green colour, and finely crimped, like those of the Savoy Cabbages. They grow straight and stiff at first, but afterwards become curved outwards at the ends, giving the plant a very elegant appearance. The Palm-tree Cabbage does not often flower before the third year of its growth, at which time it attains its greatest height. In France it is almost exclusively grown as an ornamental plant. In Italy, a variety is grown for table use under the name of *Cavolo Nero*, which seems to us to be identical with this.

Tree C., or **Jersey Kale** (*Chou Cavalier*).—A very large and vigorous-growing plant, presenting, when fully grown, the appearance, one would almost say, of a young tree. Its French name of *Chou Cavalier* is

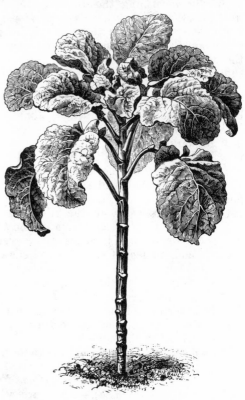

Palm-tree Cabbage or Borecole (young, 1/20 natural size).

Tree Cabbage, or Jersey Kale (1/12 natural size of plant one year old).

said to have been given to it because its height is sometimes equal to that of a man on horseback. The stem is straight, stiff, and strong, but comparatively slender, as it seldom attains a diameter of 1¾ inch. In the first year of its growth it does not usually exceed 3 or 4 ft. in height. The plant produces a great number of leaves, which are green, large, cut at the base, but oval-rounded at the end, slightly crimped or puffed on the upper surface, and often over 2½ ft. long. They grow at some distance from one another, and after they have fallen or have been plucked, a scar is left where the stalk was parted from the stem. The variety is a hardy one, and will bear the cold of ordinary winters at Paris. It does not always run to flower in the spring of its second year, but often continues producing leaves and growing taller, in which case it does not flower until the spring of its third year (including the year in which it was sown), when it reaches its greatest height. The leaves are usually pulled to feed cattle, the stems being allowed to remain in the ground until the next spring, when the tops which are about to run to flower are cut off and applied to the same uses as the leaves. The stems, having become hard and woody, cannot be utilized in this way; but they are sometimes dried and made into walking-sticks.

Large-leaved Jersey Kale or **Sarthe Cow C.** (*Chou Fourrager de la Sarthe*).— This variety, which comes very near the preceding kind, but is usually not so tall, is especially remarkable for the enormous size of its leaves, which often grow more than 3 ft. long and from 12 to 14 inches broad. The blade of the leaf is of an elongated-oval shape, with entire uncut margin, and tolerably crimped surface. It is a very productive cattle-feeding Cabbage, succeeding best in rich soil in a temperate climate, as it is not perfectly hardy.

Flanders Purple Borecole, or **Flanders Kale** (*Chou Caulet de Flandre*).—A cattle-feeding plant of large size, but somewhat smaller than the Tree Cabbage, from which it is also distinguished by the violet-red colour of its leaves and stem. It bears frost extremely well, even better than the Tree Cabbage, on which account it is

Flanders Purple Borecole, or Flanders Kale ($\frac{1}{12}$ natural size).

Thousand-headed Cabbage, or Branching Borecole ($\frac{1}{12}$ natural size).

preferred to any kind for field culture in

the north of France.   The plant is sometimes branched, in which respect it differs from the Tree Cabbage, the stem of which is most usually unbranched.   The leaves of the Flanders Kale also are smaller and narrower in proportion to their length. They are often undulated and, as it were, puckered at the edges, giving them some slight resemblance to the leaves of the Borecoles.

Thousand-headed C., or **Branching Borecole** (*Chou Branchu du Poitou*).—Another very large kind, distinguished from the Tree Cabbage by its stem being usually divided into a number of branches, each of which bears large leaves almost like those of the Tree Cabbage. Although it does not grow so tall as that variety, it is generally considered more productive, but it is not so hardy, and often suffers from the winters of the middle and north of France.   It originated in some part of the west of France, and is more suitable for the climate of that region.

French Thousand-headed Cabbage ($\frac{1}{12}$ natural size).

French Thousand-headed C. (*Chou Mille Têtes*).—A very distinct variety, raised in La Vendée, and, unfortunately, rather sensitive to cold.   It branches still more than the preceding kind, and forms a sort of large tuft or small bush, 3 to 4 ft. high, and exceedingly dense and leafy.   The leaves are entire, rather long, broader at the base than at the end, and of a very peculiar light or yellowish tint. This plant is not to be confounded with the English Thousand-headed Cabbage, which is described in the preceding article.   It is rather tender for the winter climate of the greater part of England.

Marrow Kale ($\frac{1}{12}$ natural size).

Marrow Kale (*Chou Moellier Blanc*).—A large variety of Cattle-feeding Cabbage, with a very stout and thick unbranched stem, which is swollen chiefly in the upper two-thirds of its length and filled with a sort of marrow or tender flesh, which forms excellent food for cattle. The leaves are very long and broad, and constitute a considerable part of the crop. The stem grows 5 ft. or more high, with a diameter of 3 to 4 inches in the thickest part. The Marrow Kale, like the Thousand-headed Cabbage, has the disadvantage of being sensitive to cold, and the crop must be gathered before severe frost sets in. At the end of summer, and all through the autumn, the leaves are cut and given to cattle. At the commencement of hard weather, when the leaves are all cut, the stems are taken up and stored in an outhouse or shed, where they will be safe from frost, and in this way they will keep all through the winter.

This plant forms, as it were, the connecting-link between the common Cattle-feeding Cabbages and the Kohl-Rabi, and, in a more general way, between the Cabbages which are grown for their leaves and those which are grown for their swollen stems. The Kohl-Rabi is only a Marrow Kale with the stem shortened into the form of a ball, the marrow or substance of the swollen part being of the same nature, consistence, and taste in both plants.

The stem of the Marrow Kale, if cut while young, when the swollen part does not measure more than 20 inches or 2 ft. in length and 2 or 3 inches in diameter, would, in our opinion, form a very palatable vegetable.

Red Marrow Kale (*Chou Moellier Rouge*).—This differs from the preceding kind only in the red or purplish colour of its stem. It has the same good qualities and the same deficiencies.

Lannilis Borecole (*Chou de Lannilis*).—The stem of this variety, like that of the Marrow Kale, is strikingly thick ; it seldom exceeds about 5 ft. in height, and bears a great abundance of leaves, which are usually entire, elongated, rather thick, more or less undulated, and especially remarkable for their light-green colour, which resembles that of the Thousand-headed Cabbage.

A variety is sometimes met with in cultivation which bears the name of Butter Kale (*Chou à Beurre*). This is a branching kind, with roundish, slightly crimped leaves, and very light-coloured and almost yellow at the heart. It is a rather tender variety.

Buda Kale (*Chou à Faucher*).—Stem very short, almost wanting ; leaves 1 ft. to 16 inches long, deeply lobed or lyrate, intensely green, with whitish stalks, the whole plant forming a fodder-like tuft, which can be mown several times in succession. The leaves may be used as a table vegetable ; but for this purpose, and also for cattle-feeding, this variety is now almost entirely superseded by newer and better kinds. In Germany, there is a variety which has violet-tinted leaves, and is known by the name of *Brauner Schnittkohl*.

Allied to the Buda Kale is the Perennial Daubenton Kale, a kind of Colza with an almost woody and branching stem, which continues to grow for 4 or 5 years, some only of the branches flowering every year, while the rest go on growing and producing leaves. Of all the cultivated Cabbages, this one comes nearest to the Wild Cabbage of the sea-coasts of Western Europe, one of the distinctive characteristics of which is that it produces flowers only at the extremities of some of the branches, the rest of the plant continuing to increase in size, while other branches are preparing to come into flower in the following year.

In England, a great number of kinds of Borecole or Kale are grown, the leaves of which are either entire or divided, and smooth or faintly crimped, and some of them are as useful in the garden as the much-curled sorts. The principal sorts are :—

Cottager's Kale.—A rather variable kind, with green or violet-coloured, and more or less curled leaves. Its chief merit is its extreme hardiness.

Egyptian Kale.—A very dwarf variety, which in spring produces great numbers of fleshy shoots, covered with small tender leaves.

Jerusalem, or **Delaware, Kale.**—The leaves of this are curled at the edges and of a violet tint. The plant produces shoots in spring, like the preceding kind.

Milan Kale.—This is a Borecole, and should not be confounded with the French *Chou de Milan* Savoy. Except that they both belong to the same genus, there is no resemblance whatever between the Milan Kale and the Savoy. The Milan Kale produces a stem from 18 inches to 2 ft. high, clothed with plain, bluntly toothed leaves, and terminated by a close rosette of leaves forming a small head. In spring it throws out a quantity of succulent shoots, which, when cooked, form one of the most delicious dishes of the winter-green class; hence the plant has been called Asparagus Kale.

Ragged Jack.—A hardy and productive variety, with long, irregularly cut or slashed leaves, and a short, often branching, stem.

The Gallega Cabbage, of Portugal (*Couve Gallega*), is a variety with very large green leaves, which are very much crimped and puffed on the upper surface. It is a good cropper, but sensitive to cold.

Culture.—The culture of the Cattle-feeding varieties of Cabbage does not come within the scope of this work. We shall only say, with respect to such of the Kales or Borecoles as are grown for ornament or table use, that they require the same treatment as late ordinary Cabbages and Brussels Sprouts. They are sown in spring in a nursery-bed, the seedlings are pricked out in May, and afterwards finally transplanted in the course of the summer. The crop comes in through the autumn and winter, and is sometimes prolonged through the whole of the following year. The plants do not run to seed until the spring of the second year after that in which they were sown.

KOHL-RABI.

Brassica Caulo-rapa, D.C.

French, Choux-raves. *German,* Knollkohl. *Flemish,* Raapkool. *Italian,* Cavolo rapa.

The useful part of this plant consists in its swollen, fleshy, and pulpy stem. Some Cattle-feeding varieties of Cabbages, and also the Neapolitan Borecole, afford examples of enlargements of this kind, but in none of them is the stem so completely swollen or so much altered in appearance. In the Kohl-Rabi, the swelling of the stem, which commences close to the surface of the ground, takes the shape of an almost regular ball, the size of which in some varieties does not exceed that of an average-sized orange, while in others it nearly equals that of a man's head. The seeds, like those of the other Cabbages, number about 300 to the gramme. The Kohl - Rabi is not sufficiently known or valued in France or England, for it forms an excellent vegetable, especially when used before it is fully grown, in which state it is generally eaten in Germany, while in Italy the swollen stem is often eaten before it has grown as large as a hen's egg.

Common White Kohl-Rabi (⅓ natural size).

Culture.—The kitchen-garden varieties are sown in a nursery-bed from March to the end of June. When the seedlings are from a month to six weeks old, they are permanently planted out, and the plants may commence to be cut for use about two months after. In planting them out, a space of from 14 to 16 inches should be left from plant to plant, according to the variety grown. Some varieties also are grown for cattle-feeding, and for this purpose the largest and latest kinds are employed. They are sown in April, planted out in May and June, and cut for use only in autumn.

Uses.—The swollen part of the stem is eaten before it is quite fully grown, when it is tender and has the combined flavours of a Cabbage and a Turnip.

Common White Kohl-Rabi (*Chou-rave Blanc*).—Leaves rather stout, 1 ft. to 16 inches long, with white stalks as thick as the little finger; ball, or swollen stem, of a very pale green, almost white, and 6 to 8 inches in diameter. This variety takes a long time to form the ball, requiring about four months before it is large enough to be eaten and six or seven months before it is fully grown. The ball is not always quite spherical; sometimes it is more or less flattened, and at other times elongated and almost oblong in shape. The leaves, after falling, leave behind them broad whitish scars.

Vienna Kohl-Rabi (⅓ natural size).

Purple Kohl-Rabi (*Chou-rave Violet*).— This differs from the Common White Kohl-Rabi only in the colour of the ball, the leaf-stalks, and the veins of the leaves.

Vienna Kohl-Rabi (*Chou-rave Blanc Hâtif de Vienne*).—A handsome, very delicately formed, and early variety, which is at once distinguished from the Common White kind by the fewness and smallness of its leaves, which are seldom more than 8 or 10 inches in length, with stalks no thicker than a goose-quill. The ball also forms more speedily in this variety, and is large enough to be eaten in two months and a half or three months from the time of sowing.

Early Purple Vienna Kohl-Rabi (*Chou-rave Violet Hâtif de Vienne*). —This variety, the ball of which is purplish, presents in most other respects the same appearance as the preceding kind, but it has not the same degree of delicacy of form or of earliness. They are the two best kinds for kitchen-garden culture, especially for forcing or late sowings.

The Artichoke-leaved Kohl-Rabi (*Chou-rave à Feuilles d'Artichaut*) is a rather late and moderately productive variety, only remarkable for the peculiarity of its leaves, which are divided into segments, and at some distance look like the leaves of an Artichoke.

The Neapolitan Kohl-Rabi (*Chou-rave de Naples*), with curled leaves, has already been described under the name of Neapolitan Borecole. It is, in fact, of more account as a Borecole than as a Kohl-Rabi, as the swelling of the stem is often limited to very small dimensions.

TURNIP-ROOTED CABBAGE (SWEDISH TURNIP).

French, Choux-navets.　*German,* Kohl-rübe.　*Dutch,* Koolraapen onder den grond.
Italian, Cavolo navone.

White Swedish Turnip, or White Swede
(⅕ natural size).

The varieties of Turnip-rooted Cabbages differ from the Kohl-Rabi in this respect, that, instead of having the stem swollen over-ground, they produce, partially buried in the soil, a thick root which is nearly as long as it is broad, resembling a huge Turnip, and of which the flesh is yellow in the Rutabagas or Swedish Turnips, and white in the other kinds. The characters of the leaves and flowers of these plants indicate plainly that they are true Cabbages. The seeds number about 375 to the gramme.

CULTURE.—All the varieties like a stiff and moist soil, and grow best in climates that are a little moist. They suffer from very hot weather, but are not at all affected by frost, one of their chief recommendations being their extreme hardiness. They are best sown, where the crop is to be grown, in May and June, and the plants are thinned out so as to leave a space of 14 to 16 inches from plant to plant in every direction, after which no other attention is necessary, except the occasional use of the hoe, and watering when needed.

Uses.—The roots are eaten boiled, and have almost the same flavour as the Kohl-Rabi. They are in the best condition for table use if lifted before they have reached their full growth. The Swedish or Turnip-rooted Cabbage is an excellent vegetable, deserving to be more used than it is.

White Swedish Turnip, or **White Swede** (*Chou-navet Blanc*).— Root short and broad, somewhat top-shaped, and often irregular in form; skin white, sometimes slightly tinged with green around the neck; leaves 14 to 20 inches long, cut at the edges, and resembling those of the Kohl-Rabi. Flesh of the root white.

White Purple-top Swedish Turnip (*Chou-navet Blanc à Collet Rouge*).—A sub-variety of the preceding kind, from which it differs

Smooth White Swedish Turnip
(¼ natural size).

Green-top Swedish Turnip (⅕ natural size).

only in the red or purplish tinge of the neck of the root; the leaf-stalks and the veins of the leaves also are often of the same colour. Flesh of the root white.

Smooth White Swedish Turnip (*Chou-navet Blanc Lisse à Courte Feuille*).—A very distinct variety, with a flattish root, which is broader than long, and more clean-skinned and generally more regular in shape than the two preceding kinds. The leaves are shorter, more entire, and of a somewhat deeper green colour. This is especially a kitchen-garden variety, and is considerably earlier than any of the preceding kinds, so that it can be sown up to July. The flesh of the root is white.

Green-top Swedish Turnip (*Rutabaga à Collet Vert*).—Root round, almost spherical, with a yellowish skin, deeply tinged with green on the part overground, and especially around the neck. Flesh yellow.

Under the name of Finland Water-Radish (*Rave d'Eau de Finlande*), a plant used to be cultivated, which did not appreciably differ from this, or, at the most, was only a form of it in which the root was slightly flattened.

L

A variety which is almost the same as the Green-top Swede is found in the United States under the name of American Green-top Yellow Rutabaga. It only differs from the other in having its leaves slightly twisted and almost curled.

Yellow Purple-top Swedish Turnip (*Rutabaga à Collet Violet*).—This variety only differs from the preceding one in having all the overground portion of the root of a purplish-red colour. In Great Britain, where Swedish Turnips are grown on a very large scale, and take almost the same place in field culture which the varieties of Mangold-Wurtzel occupy in France, the Purple-top Swede is most in favour. Of this there are a great many forms, the most noteworthy of which are the Skirving, the Fettercairn, and Sutton's Champion, all of which are to be recommended for the great size and very regular form of their almost perfectly spherical roots; also Laing's variety, which has an equally large and well-shaped root, and is especially distinguished by having the leaves entire. It is altogether owing to the climate that Swedes are not so much grown in France as they are in England. Hot, dry summer weather is unfavourable to this plant, which does best in a climate that is rather moist, and bears frost well. In Brittany, where the climate is nearly the same as that of England, Swedes are very extensively grown and do well. Laing's Swede is a very well-flavoured sort for those who care for these as vegetables.

Yellow Purple-top Swedish Turnip (⅓ natural size).

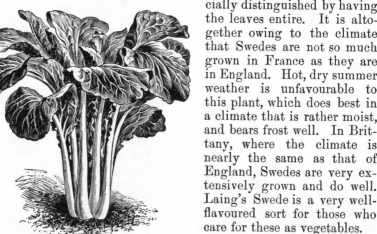

Chinese Cabbage (1/10 natural size).

Early Flat Yellow Swedish Turnip (*Rutabaga Jaune Plat Hâtif*).—This is more a kitchen-garden than a field variety, with a flat, smooth, and clean-skinned root, which is faintly tinged with green on the upper part; leaves rather few, short, and closely set. The root of this variety swells more speedily than that of any other kind, and it is the best for kitchen-garden culture.

Other and true Turnips will be found in their place further on in this book.

Chinese Cabbage (*Brassica sinensis,* L., *var. Chou de Chine;* Chinese, *Pak-choi*).—Native of China.—Annual.—Although this plant is undoubtedly a Cabbage, it is more like a Leaf-Beet or Chard. The leaves are oblong or oval, of a dark shining-green colour, and narrowed to a long, very white, swollen and fleshy stalk. It soon runs to seed, and the flower-stems resemble those of a Cabbage; the seed-vessels, however, are shorter and thicker than those of the European Cabbages. The seed is round, small, and of a brownish or blackish red colour. A gramme contains, on an average, 300 seeds, and a litre of them weighs 700 grammes. Their germinating power lasts for five years. CULTURE.— The Pak-choi grows rapidly, and may be sown almost all through the year; if sown in spring, however, or in summer, there is the disadvantage of the plants running to seed soon. Accordingly it is usually grown in the same way as Turnips; that is, it is sown about the end of July, or in August, for an autumn or early winter crop. The seed is sown in drills, with a space of 16 to 20 inches between them, and the seedlings are thinned out two or three times. When they are fully grown, the leaves are often 20 inches long, including the stalk. The leaves are eaten boiled, like Borecole, and the ribs are sometimes sent to table like Asparagus, Broccoli, or Chard Beet.

Chinese Cabbage, or Pe-tsai (*Brassica sinensis,* L., *var. Chou de Shangton;* Chinese, *Pe-tsai*).—Native of China.—Annual.—The Pe-tsai, like the Pak-choi, differs entirely in appearance from the Cabbages of Europe, being rather like a Cos Lettuce in aspect. Like it, it sometimes forms an elongated, rather full and compact head, and sometimes grows in a plain cluster of half-erect leaves, disposed in the form of a funnel. The ribs are not of such a pure white colour as those of the Pak-choi; they are pretty thick and fleshy, and the blade of the leaf, although narrower at the base, is continued down the whole length of the stalk. The leaves are slightly crimped, undulated at the edges, and of a pale or light-green colour. The seed very much resembles that of the Pak-choi. A gramme contains 300 seeds, and a litre of them weighs 700 grammes. Their germinating power lasts for five years. The floral parts of the plant are similar to those of the Pak-choi, and both plants are cultivated and used in precisely the same manner. Within the last few years, there has also been imported from China a form of *Brassica sinensis* with perfectly round leaves of a dark-green colour, and narrowed at the base into the stalk, forming extremely dense tufts or rosettes; the flower-stems also are much shorter than those of the Pe-tsai or the Pak-choi. This plant does not appear to be of much account as a table vegetable. Botanically, it exhibits in excess the characteristics which distinguish *Brassica sinensis* from *Brassica oleracea.*

CAPER-BUSH.

Capparis spinosa, L. *Capparidaceæ.*

Caprier.

A native of the south of Europe.—Perennial.—A shrub growing 3 to 5 ft. high, with numerous branches, bearing a pair of hooked spines at

the base of each leaf-stalk.   Leaves alternate, roundish in shape, thick,
and glistening; flowers about 2 inches in diameter, white, with numerous
violet-coloured stamens, which produce a very pleasing effect; seed
largish, kidney-shaped, of a
grayish-brown colour, numbering about 160 to the gramme,
and weighing 460 grammes
to the litre.   There is also a
variety without spines, from
which the crop is more easily
gathered and without any
danger of wounding the hands.
It is to be recommended in
preference to the spined one,
and can be reproduced from
seed.   Culture.—The Caper-
bush can only be cultivated
profitably in the climate of
the Olive tree, where it is
almost always planted in dry
stony places, on embankments,
declivities, and other positions
which are difficult to utilize
in any other way.   It differs

Caper-bush ($\frac{1}{10}$ natural size; detached branch,
$\frac{1}{3}$ natural size).

from most of the plants described in this work in being really a wiry
bush, but as the buds are so much used in cookery, it is included here.
In some of our colonies it could be easily grown; in England, or cold
countries, it only lives when protected, and then with difficulty.   We
have, however, grown and flowered it in brick rubbish in a large pot.
The flower is very beautiful and distinct, especially to those not familiar
with it in countries where it grows freely.   Uses.—Under the name
of "Capers," the flower-buds, gathered when they are as large as Peas,
are pickled in vinegar.   They are valued in proportion to the smallness
of their size.

CAPSICUM, or CHILI PEPPER.

Capsicum annuum, L.

French, Piment.   *German*, Pfeffer.   *Flemish* and *Dutch*, Spaansche peper.   *Italian*,
Peperone.   *Spanish*, Pimiento.   *Portuguese*, Pimento.

Native of South America.—Under cultivation, this plant is an
annual, although several species may be perennial in warm countries.—
All of them have erect, branching stems, which become almost woody.
The leaves are spear-shaped or more or less widened, terminating in a
point, and narrowed at the base into a more or less elongated stalk;
flowers white, star-shaped, solitary in the axils of the leaves, and
succeeded by seed-vessels very diversified in shape, with a somewhat
fleshy skin, at first of a dark-green colour, and turning red, yellow,
or dark violet when ripe, always hollow, and containing white, flat,
kidney-shaped seeds, which are from $\frac{1}{8}$ inch to nearly $\frac{1}{4}$ inch long, and
attached in great numbers to a sort of fleshy cord.   These seeds, and

also the interior tissue of the seed-vessel of most of the varieties, contain an acrid juice which is very hot or burning to the taste. A gramme of them contains about 150 seeds, and a litre of them weighs 450 grammes. Their germinating power lasts for four years.

CULTURE.—The Capsicum is grown in the same manner as the Egg-plant (see Egg-plant). In the climate of Paris, all the varieties require to be sown in a hot-bed, and even in the south of France this practice is followed, at least in the case of the large-fruited kinds. In Spain, where they are very extensively grown, they are almost always forwarded by sowing in February under a frame, the seedlings being planted out in the open air towards the end of April.

Capsicums may in some warm parts of England be successfully grown in the open air, but where large supplies are needed it is advisable to have some under glass also, in case of failure of the out-door crop. The seeds should be sown early in April, on a gentle hot-bed, or in pots or pans, well drained and filled with sandy loam and leaf-mould in equal parts; and if plunged in a gentle bottom-heat they will germinate more quickly, and the plants will be much stronger, than when only placed on plain shelves, etc. As soon as the plants are large enough they should either be potted off singly into 4-inch pots, or three plants placed triangularly in 6 or 8 inch ones. In the latter case, it will be found best to only fill the pots three-parts full at first, with a view to earthing them up when the soil becomes full of roots. In order to have dwarf and healthy plants, it is necessary to place them as close to the glass as possible, in a temperature of 65° to 70°, giving them plenty of water and admitting air freely. Plants that are potted into 4-inch pots should not be allowed to become pot-bound, but be shifted into 6 or 8 inch ones.

Those plants that are to be turned out-of-doors should be gradually hardened off towards the latter end of May, and in June they may be planted out into a warm border under a south wall. They should be planted 10 or 12 inches apart, well watered when necessary, and in the event of cold weather setting in should have some slight protection

afforded them; and if the season be favourable, they will ripen their fruit from the end of August to the middle of September. It is only in the warm southern counties that we have seen a good result with Capsicums in the open air.

Where there are pits or frames available for growing Capsicums, they are the best places in which to grow them. Frames recently cleared of Early Potatoes answer the purpose capitally. The plants should be put in 1 ft. apart, kept well watered at the roots, and be frequently syringed overhead on sunny afternoons, and shut up with plenty of sun-heat. When in flower, abundance of air must be given them, to assist them to set their fruit, after which time liberal supplies of manure water may be given them with advantage. By adopting this method it is astonishing the quantities of fine large fruit that can be gathered from a three-light frame.

A light, rich soil, composed of turfy loam, rotted leaf-mould, and cow-manure in equal parts, with a little silver sand added, is best suited to them; but when grown and fruited in pots, a more solid soil will be found best.

Well-ripened pods of Capsicums will keep good for several years if placed on a dry shelf, and the seed will germinate at six or seven years old if kept in the pods until it is sown.

INSECTS, ETC.—The principal enemies of the Capsicum are green fly and red spider: the fly may be easily kept in subjection by fumigation, and the spider by a free use of the syringe on the foliage, and maintaining a warm, humid atmosphere. Those planted out-of-doors are generally most affected by red spider. The best way in this case is to give the plants frequent waterings overhead and at the roots, and promote a free growth. Curl in the leaf and fruit may often occur in outdoor plants in the autumn; this is, however, more or less occasioned by the cold nights, following days of extreme heat. The remedy is to shade slightly during the day, and afford a warm covering at night. In the many districts where the culture of Capsicums may not be possible in the open air, the pits, frames, and houses, often little used during the summer months, offer good places in which to grow them.

In the London market gardens, Capsicums are grown in Cucumber houses or similar places where a brisk heat and plenty of moisture are maintained. The seeds are sown in pots in April, and when large enough the young plants are potted six or eight together in an 8-inch pot in good rich soil and put on stages in a well-lighted position. Plenty of water is given them whilst growing. Some plant them out in frames, and in this way obtain abundance of fruit, but the most profitable way is pot-culture or frame-culture.

Uses.—The seed-pods, green or ripe, are very much used as seasoning, especially in hot countries; they are also pickled in vinegar. When dried and ground, they form cayenne or red pepper. The pods of some of the large kinds, which are very fleshy and not hot to the taste, are used as vegetables. A good instance of the slowness with which the use of vegetables is made known is afforded by the large green mild variety of Capsicum, which is so much eaten over a great part of Spain and some of the adjoining French departments. It was carried by the Spaniards into Naples during their dominion there in the sixteenth and seventeenth centuries, and has ever since remained in common use there, without spreading farther. It makes an excellent salad, having all the flavour of the Capsicum without pungency, and enters into various light and pleasant dishes of the Italian and Spanish cooks.

Long Red Capsicum, or Guinea Pepper (⅓ natural size).

Common Capsicum (*Piment*).—A great many, if not all, of the cultivated varieties of Capsicum appear to have been derived from this species, which is successfully cultivated in the climate of Paris as an annual, with the assistance of a little artificial heat at the commencement of its growth. It grows pretty tall, has leaves longer than broad, white and rather small flowers, and usually long seed-pods. It appears that the acrid or burning principle in the seed-pods of this plant is in inverse proportion to their size. The large kinds are usually mild in flavour, the medium-sized sometimes mild and sometimes the reverse, while the small kinds are invariably very pungently hot to the taste.

Long Red Capsicum, or Guinea Pepper (*Piment Rouge Long*).—This variety, which is the most extensively grown of all, presents all the characteristics of growth which have just been described. The seed-vessels are pendent, slender, of an elongated conical shape, often curved and twisted, sometimes 4 to 5 inches in length, and about 1 inch in diameter at the base. When ripe, they are of a very fine brilliant red colour, and usually rather hot to the taste, but in this respect great differences occur between one plant and another, without any external indication to mark which are very hot and which are mild in flavour.

Long Cayenne Pepper (*Piment de Cayenne*).—Under the occasional name of Long Cayenne Pepper (*Piment de Cayenne*), a sub-variety of the preceding kind is grown, which has the seed-vessels narrower, slightly curved at the end, pendent, seldom more than $\frac{2}{5}$ inch in diameter and about 3 inches in length, and always very hot to the taste. This plant, however, should not be confounded with the true

Long Cayenne Pepper
($\frac{1}{3}$ natural size).

Cayenne Pepper, which is a perennial and belongs to a different botanical species, that is too tender for the climate of France.

Long Yellow Capsicum (*Piment Jaune Long*).—This variety only differs from the Spanish or Guinea Pepper in the colour of the seed-vessels, which are of a bright glistening yellow, and usually very hot in flavour, seldom more than 4 inches long, slender in shape, and often slightly curved.

Purple Capsicum (*Piment Violet*).—A vigorous-growing kind, often upwards of $3\frac{1}{4}$ feet high, with the stems usually purplish-coloured, especially at the base of the branches and of the leaf-stalks, and somewhat more branched and spreading than those of the Spanish or Guinea Pepper. Leaves small, short, and narrow, with long stalks; flowers white, often tinged with purple on the tips of the divisions

Long Yellow Capsicum
($\frac{1}{3}$ natural size).

of the corolla; flower-stalks very long; seed-vessels pendent, horizontal, or erect, very variable in shape, sometimes shortly conical, but most frequently three or four times as long as they are broad, 2 or 3 inches in length, at first of a deep-green colour plentifully tinged with blackish violet, and becoming of a deep purplish red when quite ripe. They are extremely hot to the taste.

Chili Pepper, or Chillies ($\frac{1}{3}$ natural size).

Chili Pepper, or **Chillies** (*Piment du Chili*).—The appearance of this

variety is very distinct from that of the other kinds, as it has a very branching, rather low-growing stem, the spreading branches of which form a dwarf broadish bush, seldom more than 16 to 20 inches high. Leaves small, narrow, and numerous; flowers small and white, succeeded by slender and long-pointed seed-vessels about 2 inches long and scarcely $\frac{2}{5}$ inch in diameter, very often growing erect, of a very bright scarlet colour when ripe, and very hot to the taste; they are produced in the greatest abundance, sometimes appearing to equal the leaves in number. This is one of the earliest and most productive kinds, and is the most suitable variety for gardens in the north of France. In addition to its value as a kitchen-garden plant, it is also highly ornamental, from the fine effect produced by the numerous brilliant-coloured seed-vessels relieved against the green of the foliage.

Seed-vessels of Chili Pepper (⅓ natural size).

Cherry Pepper (*Piment Cerise*).—Some botanists make this a different species under the name of *Capsicum cerasiforme*. In its habit of growth, however, it comes very close to the varieties of *Capsicum annuum*, and is distinguished from the Spanish or Guinea Pepper by the shape of its seed-vessels, which are almost spherical, with a diameter of nearly 1 inch in all directions. They are extremely hot to the taste, and somewhat late in ripening. In support of the opinion that this Pepper is simply a variety of *Capsicum annuum*, is the circumstance that it is often found bearing seed-vessels of a more or less elongated shape, and apparently reverting to the common Spanish or Guinea variety. There is a sub-variety of it with yellow seed-vessels, which is very seldom met with in cultivation, and which, except in the colour of its seed-vessels, exactly resembles the ordinary Cherry Pepper.

Cherry Pepper (branch, $\frac{1}{10}$; fruit, ½ natural size).

Large Bell Pepper or **Capsicum** (*Piment Gros Carré Doux, P. Cloche*).—A plant of rather thick-set growth, with largish leaves of a clear-green colour; branches short

Large Bell Pepper or Capsicum (⅓ natural size).

and stiff; flowers large, and often irregular in form; seed-vessels blunt and truncate, or, as it were, squared at the ends, and with four deep furrows and four corresponding prominent ridges along the sides; flesh rather thick; seeds comparatively few. This Pepper is entirely free from the acrid or burning pungency which characterizes some other kinds, its seed-vessels and their contents being of the mildest flavour. The variety of it which is most commonly grown produces seed-vessels about 2 inches in length and the same in diameter. This is a form that may be eaten as a vegetable, and a very pleasant addition it is, as the Italians cook it.

In the south of France and in Spain, a form is cultivated which has the seed-vessels much larger and somewhat rounder in shape, but with the furrows very deeply marked, especially towards the end of the seed-vessel. It is not unusual, in this variety, to see seed-vessels measuring from 3 to 4 inches across every way. It is a very late kind, and does not keep well.

Improved Bull-nose Capsicum, or Sweet Mountain Pepper (*Piment Gros Carré d'Amérique*).—A variety evidently derived from the preceding one, but distinguished by its greater earliness and the larger size and more regular shape of the pods. The plant does not grow so tall or so branching as the Common Bell Pepper, and the pods, which number from twelve to fifteen on each plant, ripen almost all at the same time and a fortnight earlier than those of the Common kind.

Monstrous Capsicum (*Piment Monstreux*).—The seed-vessels of this variety are, up to a certain point, intermediate between those of the Guinea Pepper and those of the Bell Pepper, but they surpass both in size. They are of an irregular ovoid or conical shape, swollen in the part next the stalk, and narrowed at the other end, usually more abruptly on one side than on the other, so that one side is generally quite convex, while the other is more or less concave. The appearance of the seed-vessel is well indicated by the name of Sheep's-head Pepper, which is sometimes given to it. When it is well grown, it measures about 6 inches in length, with a

Monstrous Capsicum (⅓ natural size).

diameter of about 3 inches in the thickest part; and, when ripe, it is of a fine deep-red colour, is perfectly mild in flavour, and therefore one of the kinds that have a distinct value for use in the green state.

Spanish Mammoth Capsicum (*Piment Doux d'Espagne*).—The seed-vessels of this variety resemble those of the preceding one in size, but their shape is that of a cone, or rather a prism, with rounded angles and truncated at the end. They are 6 or 7 inches in length,

with a diameter of between 2 and 3 inches at the base, and rather more than 1 inch at the extremity. They are very handsome in appearance and very mild in flavour.

Of this variety there are two forms, one of which has bright red, and the other fine yellow seed-vessels. It requires a very warm climate for the seed-vessels to attain their full development. Very fair specimens of it, which have come from Valencia or Algeria, may be seen in Paris, in the shops where the produce of the south of Europe is sold; but it is almost impossible to grow anything like these in the climate of Paris.

Red Tomato Capsicum, or American Bonnet Pepper (*Piment Tomate*).— This Pepper has some resemblance to the Bell Pepper, but the seed-vessels are much shorter, and are marked with numerous ribs and furrows, like some kinds of Tomato. When ripe, they are

Spanish Mammoth Capsicum (⅓ natural size).

of a fine bright-red colour, and measure about 2 inches across and about 1 inch in depth. This is not a very productive kind, and is chiefly

interesting on account of the singular shape of the seed-vessels, which are usually mild in flavour and only hot in exceptional cases; the flesh is always rather dry and thin. There is a sub-variety with yellow seed-vessels.

The names of Bird's-beak Pepper (*Piment Bec d'Oiseau*) and Mad Pepper (*Piment Enragé*) are sometimes given to the seed-vessels of the smallest varieties of *Capsicum annuum*, which are remarkably hot to the taste; but, properly speaking, these names should be applied to the seed-vessels of *Capsicum frutescens*, which only grows well in tropical climates.

Red Tomato Capsicum, or American Bonnet Pepper (⅓ natural size).

CARAWAY.

Carum Carui, L.   *Umbelliferæ.*

French, Carvi, Cumin des prés.   *German,* Feld-Kümmel.   *Dutch,* Karvij.   *Italian,* Carvi.

Native of Europe.—Annual or biennial.—Root as thick as the thumb, long, yellowish, with white compact flesh, which has a slight

Carroty flavour; leaves chiefly radical, numerous, composed of opposite whorled leaflets; leaf-stalk channelled, hollow, and undulated; stem straight, 1 to 2 ft. high, branching, angular, glossy, and smooth; flowers small, white, in umbels; seeds oblong, rather curved, marked with five furrows, aromatic, and of a light-brown colour. A gramme of them contains about 350 seeds, and the litre weighs 420 grammes. Their germinating power lasts for three years. CULTURE.—The seeds are often gathered in the meadows, where the plant grows spontaneously. When the plant is cultivated, the seed is sown in drills, in May or June. As soon as the seedlings are pretty strong, they are thinned out, and nothing further is required, except to keep the ground free from weeds, until the crop is gathered in the July of the year after that in which the seed was sown. By sowing some of the seed as soon as it is ripe, plants may be raised which will run to seed in the summer of the following year, and a month or two may thus be saved in the cultivation of the crop, as compared with the ordinary mode of sowing. USES.—The leaves and young shoots are sometimes eaten. The seeds are used for flavouring bread in Germany and other countries, and certain kinds of cheese in Holland. They are of very ancient use, and are now very extensively used as a spice in bread, pastry, cheese, sweets, and sauces.

CARDOON.

Cynara Cardunculus, L.   *Compositæ.*

French, Cardon.   *German,* Kardon.   *Flemish,* Kardoen.   *Italian, Spanish,* and *Portuguese,* Cardo.

Native of Southern Europe.—Perennial.—Notwithstanding the different botanical names which have been given to them, the Artichoke and the Cardoon appear to belong to the same species, cultivation having, in the case of the latter, developed the leaf-stalks, and, in the former, the receptacle of the flower. The Cardoon is a larger plant than the Artichoke, and of a more vigorous habit of growth, but the botanical characteristics and the general appearance of both present the greatest analogy to each other. In the Cardoon, the stem, which attains a height of from 4 to $6\frac{1}{2}$ ft., is channelled and of a whitish hue; the leaves are very large, pinnatifid, of a slightly grayish-green colour on the upper surface, and almost white underneath, and armed, in several varieties, at the angle of each division with very finely pointed yellow or brown spines from about $\frac{1}{4}$ inch to over $\frac{1}{2}$ inch long. The very fleshy leaf-stalks or ribs are the edible part of the plant. The flowers, which have usually pointed scales, resemble those of the Artichoke, but are smaller. The seed is thick, oblong, slightly flattened, and angular, gray in colour, striped or streaked with dark brown. A gramme contains about 25 seeds, and a litre of them weighs 630 grammes. Their germinating power lasts for seven years.

CULTURE.—Unlike the Artichoke, which is almost always propagated by means of offsets, the Cardoon is always raised from seed, which is usually sown in May, in holes or "pockets" filled with compost, and made at a distance of about a yard from one another in every direction. It might be sown earlier in pans on a hot-bed, but this practice has few advantages, as the Cardoon has ample time to develop itself during the summer and autumn, and is not a vegetable that is sought after before its natural season. The ground must be kept very clean, and the plants should be plentifully watered through the summer. As they will not have grown large enough to touch one another before September, the ground between the rows may be utilized in the meantime by sowing some other crop there. Before Cardoons are sent to table, the stalks or ribs are blanched by tying them together and wrapping them round with straw, which is also tied up with cord, bast, etc. The plants are then earthed up, and left so for about three weeks, when the stalks or ribs will be in proper condition for use ; but if left longer than this, they will be in danger of rotting. The Cardoon does not bear frost ; therefore, before severe weather comes on, the plants should be taken up and placed in a vegetable-house for winter use.

The Cardoon, if treated in the same manner as Celery, will generally be found to succeed ; the only difference there is exists in the mode of blanching, which requires more care than blanching Celery. Thorough blanching is essential, in order to bring out the delicacy of flavour possessed by the Cardoon, without which it is worthless. It is better to have small heads well blanched and crisp than to have large rank ones half-blanched, and consequently tough and strong. In order to have good tender heads, it is necessary to grow the plants from the beginning to the time of blanching without a check, and this can only be done by planting them in deep, rich soil, and keeping them well supplied with water at the roots during dry weather.

Where Cardoons are in demand early in winter, it is necessary to sow seeds of them in heat early in March, and to transplant in either May or June, according to the weather. For this purpose seed may either be sown in small pots and placed in a warm house, or sown in drills 4 or 5 inches apart, in a gentle hot-bed. The former plan is, however, considered to be the best, inasmuch as the plants can be more easily removed when required to be hardened off, and they are not so liable to a check when transplanted as when lifted out of a bed. The best-sized pots for the purpose are 4-inch ones, in each of which should

be sown four or five seeds, thinning out the plants as they advance in growth, and finally leaving only the strongest one. They should be placed close to the glass, where they will get plenty of light and air to keep them strong and stubby, gradually hardening them off early in May ; and towards the end of the month they may be transferred to the trenches in which they are to grow, if the weather be favourable, planting them from $2\frac{1}{2}$ to 3 ft. apart in the row. It is a bad practice to sow too early, as the plants become pot-bound before they can be planted out, and consequently checked in growth. A second sowing may be made in May in open trenches, and the main sowing early in June. The trenches should measure at least 4 ft. from centre to centre, and be dug 2 ft. wide and 18 inches deep. Into the bottom of these should be placed 2 or 3 inches of good rotten manure, which should be dug in with a fork, and well incorporated with the soil in the bottom of the trench. The seeds should then be sown in patches from $2\frac{1}{2}$ to 3 ft. apart, and slightly covered with fine soil well watered, and flower-pots should be placed over them until the plants are up, when they may be removed and the weakest plants thinned out, eventually allowing only the strongest to remain. The subsequent treatment consists in keeping them well supplied with water at the roots until the end of

September, when they will have nearly completed their growth, and when they will require moulding up. Those planted earlier will, however, be ready before that time, and should be earthed up as early as possible —the aim in this case generally being earliness rather than large heads.

Tying and Earthing up.—Choose a fine day, when the foliage of the plants and the soil are dry. The leaves should be carefully brought to an upright position, and then placed neatly together and tied with broad pieces of matting. A good armful of dry hay or straw should then be placed round the base of each plant, and secured by strong haybands being wound round it, gradually narrowing to the top, leaving only the tips of the leaves bare. This done, the soil between the trenches should be turned over and well broken with the spade, and afterwards placed equally and firmly round the plants,

forming an even ridge by beating the sides with the back of the spade. The plants will be well blanched and fit for use four or five weeks after earthing. Blanching may also be done by placing a drainpipe over the plants, after tying the leaves closely together, the apertures between the plants and pipes being filled with sand. This plan, though a good one, is generally considered too expensive where many plants are grown. Many lift their Cardoons on the appearance of severe weather, and place them in dry cellars or sheds from which frost is excluded. This is, however, really unnecessary so far as the plants are concerned, as they can be effectively protected by placing litter, etc., along the ridges; but there is one advantage in lifting them, and that is, they may be got at easily in hard weather, whereas those left out-of-doors sometimes cannot be dug out without much labour.

Uses.—The blanched stalks or ribs of the inner leaves are chiefly used as a winter vegetable, as well as the main root, which is thick, fleshy, tender, and of an agreeable flavour. Cooked in a delicate way, it is excellent, but with the ordinary cook this, like many another good vegetable, is often spoiled. The degree of tenderness to which it is boiled should be studied, and the sauce should not be rank with salt and spice after the vulgar fashion.

Prickly Tours Cardoon (*Cardon de Tours*).—This is one of the smaller varieties, and has very thick and solid stalks or ribs. On the other hand, it is the most spiny kind of all, which, however, does not prevent it from holding the first place in the estimation of the market gardeners of Tours and Paris.

Prickly Tours Cardoon ($\frac{1}{15}$ natural size).

Smooth Solid Cardoon ($\frac{1}{13}$ natural size).

Smooth Solid Cardoon (*Cardon Plein Inerme*).—This variety, which is almost entirely free from spines, is something larger than the preceding kind, has longer leaves and ribs, and grows from about 4 to $4\frac{1}{4}$ ft. high. The ribs are always broader than those of the Prickly Tours Cardoon, but not so thick, yet they become hollow sooner, if the plant is allowed to suffer ever so little from drought or want of nourishment. The leaves are neither quite so much cut, nor quite so whitish in hue, as those of the Prickly Tours variety.

Long Spanish Cardoon (*Cardon d'Espagne;* Spanish, *Cardo Comun*).—A large variety, which is chiefly grown in the south of Europe, with large, broad-ribbed leaves. It is not spiny, but the ribs are not so solid as those of the preceding varieties.

Artichoke-leaved Cardoon (*Cardon Puvis*).—A very distinct variety, which is entirely free from spines. Leaves very broad and large, not much cut, and of a rather dark-green colour. It is a plant of vigorous growth, with broad ribs, which are usually half-solid, and is chiefly grown in the vicinity of Lyons, where it attains about the same height as the Smooth Solid Cardoon, but is broader in all its parts.

Red-stemmed Cardoon (*Cardon à Côtes Rouges*).—A variety closely allied to the Long Spanish Cardoon, differing from it mainly in the reddish tinge of its stalks or ribs, which are usually only half-solid.

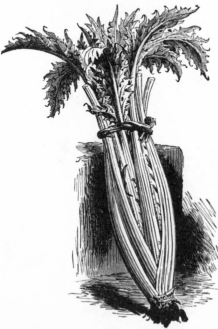

Artichoke-leaved Cardoon ($\frac{1}{13}$ natural size).

CARROT.

Daucus Carota, L.   *Umbelliferæ.*

French, Carotte.   *German,* Möhre, Gelbrübe.   *Dutch,* Wortel.   *Italian,* Carota.   *Spanish,*
Zanahoria.   *Portuguese,* Cenoura.

Native of Europe.—Biennial.—The root of this plant, when artificially developed by cultivation, exhibits the widest differences in
shape, size, and colour. The leaves are very much divided, and twice
or thrice pinnate, the divisions being deeply cut and pointed. The
flowers, produced in umbels, are small, white, crowded together, and
with long linear bracts, and are borne on the top of a stem from 2 to
5 ft. high, and do not appear until the year after the seed is sown. The
seed is small, of a greenish or grayish-brown colour, slightly convex on
one side, and flat on the other, channelled, and set with recurved points
or bristles on two of the ridges; they have a very strong, peculiar,
aromatic odour. Including the bristles, they weigh 240 grammes to
the litre, and a gramme of them contains 700 seeds. Without the
bristles they weigh 360 grammes to the litre, and a gramme contains
from 900 to 1000 seeds. Their germinating power lasts for five years.

CULTURE.—The cultivation of the Carrot is most simple. The seed
is sown in the open ground, where the crop is to be grown, from
February to autumn. The soil should be well prepared by being
manured, if possible, six months at least beforehand, and deeply dug
for the long-rooted varieties. As soon as the plants appear, hoeing
should commence, and be continued as long as the crop remains in the
ground. This operation will be found all the easier if the plants are
sown in drills. The seedlings are thinned out two or three times,
leaving them more or less far apart according to the size of the kind
grown. The short and very early varieties are most usually sown
broadcast, either in the open ground, or under a frame. A first thinning out is made while the plants are young, and afterwards the
removal of such as have grown large enough for eating gradually
makes room for the slower-growing ones that are left. By making
successional sowings, crops of Carrots may be obtained from April to
June, on hot-beds, and from July to November, in the open ground. In
November, the plants should be pulled up and stored for winter use in
a dry, sheltered place. Sometimes they are left in the ground,
covered with straw, leaves, or earth, and dug up as they are required
for the table. Plants sown late in the open ground, and protected in
severe weather by a covering of some kind, will sometimes get through
the winter, and yield an early crop in the ensuing spring.

Carrots require a good, light, warm
soil, well trenched, and which has
been previously well manured. Sowing must be done in dry weather; for,
should a shower happen soon after
the seed is in the ground, the crop
will, in most cases, be a failure, if
not sown again immediately. Drills
ought to be preferred to broadcast
sowing. On account of its numerous
bristles, Carrot seed is somewhat
difficult to sow with regularity;
therefore it is mixed with sand or
dry soil. This difficulty is obviated
now by buying cleaned seed from
seedsmen. Laying the seed in wet
sand or wet loam a few days before
sowing, in order to stimulate ger-

mination, was once much practised; but this method is now seldom employed. It may, however, do under some circumstances; for instance, in forcing and sowing in the open ground, where drought is feared.

FORCING.—The French Forcing and the Scarlet Horn Carrots are best for this purpose, but the former is to be preferred. Prepare mild hot-beds 2½ ft. high in November or December and 1½ or 2 ft. in January or February; put on the frames, cover the bed with 5 or 6 inches of rich soil or mould, and, as soon as the whole is sufficiently heated, sow the seed broadcast, cover with ½ inch of mould, smooth the surface, and cover the glass with mats until the seed comes up. Should the interior get dry, give a slight watering, but be careful of damp. When the plants have four or five leaves, thin them ½ inch apart; admit air as often as the temperature will allow it, which will give strength to the seedlings. Take care the heat does not exceed 60° during the day and 50° at night, which may be easily regulated by tilting the glass. In the case of sharp frost, covering with mats is preferable to artificial heat. Shading, if needed, must not be omitted. Sowing in November, if carried on practically, will produce fine young Carrots at the end of February, which will last through March and April. Subsequent sowings—in December for March to April, in January for April to May, and lastly, in February for April to June—must be attended to as required by market gardeners; but, in private gardens, the first bed should be made in November and the second in January; these will afford an ample supply until new open-ground Carrots are fit for use. Where frames are not available, prepare, at the beginning of February, in some warm corner, a bed of hot manure mixed with leaves, covered with 4 or 5 inches of mould; sow the seed and protect with mats supported by sticks or other apparatus. As soon as the seed comes up, remove the covering every day as frequently as the weather will permit, and the crop will be ready from the end of April to the end of May.

EARLY AND MAIN CROPS.—For the first outdoor crop the seed should be sown in February, on a warm, dry border, in 5-inch drills; cover the seed with ½ inch of fine mould; when the young plants have formed a few leaves, thin them to 1 or 2 inches apart, hoeing and watering as required. The crop should be ready by the end of May, and will last until the general crop comes in. The best variety for this purpose is the Scarlet Horn. In June sow the same kind of Carrot again, if small roots be preferred. Intermediate Scarlet and Intermediate Nantes are the best varieties for general crops. Sow from March to May (the latter month for winter Carrots), in well-prepared soil, in 9 to 12 inch drills, ½ inch deep. As the Carrots make their appearance, hoeing, weeding, watering, and thinning them to ½ inch apart, should be duly attended to. As soon as the plants attain the size of a lead pencil, thin them to 3 or 4 inches apart without hesitation. Thinning generally receives too little attention in every country; and the Carrots, crowded when young, are left to be taken up for use when they have attained sufficient size. In most cases the ground gets dry and hard, and thus prevents the lifting of the roots, which are then left until the autumn, when only small, useless Carrots are the result.

AUTUMN SOWING.—In August and September, select a warm border. Sow French Forcing or Scarlet Horn Carrot, as for the early crop. The roots must remain in the ground the whole winter; but, if well protected and the bed covered with 1 inch of mould, healthy little Carrots will be ready from February until May.

STORING.—In October, before the frosts occur, and on a fine day, take up the crop, cut the leaves ½ inch from the top, clear the roots from soil, and store them at once in a cold shed or cellar; there arrange them in tiers, spreading between each a layer of sand or dry soil, up to the height of 3 ft., the length being determined by the quantity of roots; two boards will secure the ends of the pile. By this means the roots can be easily and often examined, and those that are decayed removed. On the first symptoms of vegetation appearing, pull down the pile and build it again, and this method will enable the Carrots to be kept in a good state as late as possible. *Another method.*—In open ground, in a dry place, remove the soil to the depth of 1 ft., trench the bottom, adding some sand if possible; plant the roots vertically close to each other, and protect from frost and from wet. The objection to this plan is, that decay cannot be attentively watched, and vegetation is much more liable to be excited, to prevent which the roots must be lifted and again buried. Heaps should be avoided in the case of garden varieties.

Diseases and Insects.—The Carrot is a prey to many enemies. Perhaps the worst to be feared is the rust, and this occurs generally from the roots being grown in wet soil, or having suffered from dryness in summer. Too much fresh manure will also provoke it. There is no effective remedy for it, but salt and quicklime applied to the ground before sowing is an excellent preventive as well as a fertilizer. At spring-time, in hot-beds or borders, the young plants of the first sowings are sometimes entirely destroyed by a small spider. Gardeners watching young Carrots are surprised the next day to see that every plant has disappeared. Soot spread over the drills, or the entire bed, will effectu-

ally prevent such a disaster. Snails and slugs are very fond of young Carrots, one of them being able to destroy a small bed in a single night. Quicklime spread over the young plants (which it does not injure), and around the beds, will secure the crop; for one application effectually destroys these marauders.—D. G.

The Carrot-louse attacks the young plants almost as soon as they appear, often doing much damage, like the Turnip-fly, if growth be retarded at the beginning. Then the Carrot-grub is even more destructive, boring into the roots, and often ruining a crop. Wireworm, millepeds, and several other enemies sometimes do much mischief.

Early Carrots are largely supplied for the London market from France; they are tender and delicious, and often far better than those obtained from the London market gardens. Seed of early varieties is sown from February to March, after which the main crop is put in, and the plants are not thinned out quite so much as other root-crops. The Early Horn is the kind used for early sowings; and, when in good condition, they sell well in the market. In our market gardens the Long Surrey and Long Orange are the chief kinds grown for main crops, and roots of these are furnished by hundreds of tons all through the winter months. Some market growers force the Early Horn on hot-beds and in frames, in order to have them ready for use in March or April, and these realize good returns. Some also sow beds in a warm position in August and September for winter use. If the weather is mild, fine little roots are obtained, and they sell readily at good prices.

Uses.—The roots are well known and extensively used, both as a table vegetable and as forming excellent food for cattle. The seed is employed in the manufacture of some kinds of liqueurs, and the juice of the Red varieties is used for colouring butter. The delicate and tender little Carrots which the London cook prefers usually come from Paris, where they are excellently grown in the market gardens.

M

French Horn, or Early Short Horn, Carrot (*Carotte Rouge Très Courte à Châssis*).—Root almost globular, or slightly top-shaped, of a half-transparent orange-red colour, paler towards the point; neck very fine and very short; leaves very few. This variety, which is generally pulled when it has only four or five leaves, is used in open-air culture for very early or very late sowings, but it is especially suitable for forcing under a frame, both on account of its earliness and the shortness of its root. The market gardeners of Paris grow a very glossy-skinned form of it, rather pale in colour, and broader than long, which is exclusively adapted for growing in vegetable mould.

French Horn, or Early Short Horn, Carrot (⅓ natural size).

The forcing of the Carrot demands no particular care, except that of pressing the soil down well after sowing the seed, and giving the plants as much air as possible while they are growing.

Early Scarlet Dutch Horn Carrot (*Carotte Rouge Courte Hâtive*).—Root nearly twice as long as broad, perceptibly thicker at the neck than at the point, which is generally blunt; neck fine; leaves very few, yet not so few as those of the preceding kind. This is an excellent Carrot for open-air culture, and, in certain cases, may be found suitable for forcing. Both it and the preceding kind are most usually pulled for table use while they are young, and before they have attained their full size—a practice which might well be carried out with regard to all Carrots for the table.

Early Scarlet Dutch Horn Carrot (⅓ natural size).

Blunt-rooted Guérande Carrot (*Carotte Rouge Demi-courte de Guérande*).—This variety, which is very suitable for market-garden culture, is grown in the neighbourhood of Nantes. It is a thick Carrot, 5 or 6 inches long, very blunt at the lower extremity. It grows very rapidly, and the root very frequently attains a weight of more than a pound. It succeeds best in light, rich, alluvial soil. The neck of the root is comparatively fine, and the leaves are not very large nor numerous. The colour of the root is orange red on the outside and yellow at the centre. It is not

Blunt-rooted Guérande Carrot.

coreless, like the Early Nantes Carrot, but still is a tender and well-flavoured variety, which may be classed among the Half-long kinds.

English Horn, or Early Half-long Scarlet, Carrot (*Carotte Rouge Demi-longue Pointue*).—Root spindle-shaped, two and a half or three times as long as broad; neck often tinged with green or brown, level with the surface of the soil, and slightly hollowed out around the base of the leaf-stalk; leaves somewhat stouter than those of the preceding kind. A good, productive, and pretty early variety, grown on a large scale in many localities for market supply.

EnglishHorn,or Early Half-long Scarlet, Carrot (⅓ natural size)

James's Intermediate Carrot.—This variety is evidently an improved form of the Half-long Red Carrot, but as it has now been a good while in very general cultivation, it has undergone a considerable amount of modification, in consequence of which it exhibits at the present day numerous diversities of character in different districts. In a general way it may be described as a handsome Half-long Carrot, with a long, pointed, well-coloured root, of vigorous and rapid growth, and having a stoutish neck, as might be expected from a variety which is as much grown in fields as in gardens. The variety is, in fact, a very vigorous-growing and productive one, and consequently much in request for field culture. There is a sub-variety of it which has the neck of a pretty well-pronounced green colour, the true James's Intermediate having the root entirely red. Up to the present this is the most extensively cultivated Half-long Carrot in England, both in fields and gardens, but in many cases some of the Continental kinds might, perhaps, be advantageously grown instead of it.

Half-long Blunt Scarlet Carrot (*Carotte Rouge Demi-longue Obtuse*). —This may be considered as a variety of the pointed kind. The root is not so slender, and ends in a blunt cone, but there is no apparent difference in the leaves or in any other respect. The Blunt-pointed variety is to be preferred for kitchen-garden culture. It may be regarded as the form from which have been derived in succession the Early Scarlet Horn and the French Forcing (or French Horn) Carrot, both of which, like the present variety, are characterized by the blunt, rounded end of the root, the fineness of the neck, and the paucity of leaves. There seems to be a sort of reciprocal dependence and an intimate correlation between the blunt form of the end of the root and the fineness of the neck in the Carrot tribe. Those varieties which have few leaves and a very short and very fine neck have almost invariably a blunt-pointed root, and *vice versâ*. Great earliness also is generally found to accompany these physical characteristics.

Half-long Blunt Scarlet Carrot (⅓ natural size).

Early Carentan Carrot (*Carotte Demi-longue de Carentan sans Cœur*).

—A very distinct, slender, almost cylindrical variety, with a very fine neck and very small and few leaves; skin glossy smooth; flesh

red, without any heart or core. This variety can be sown very thick, and is consequently very well adapted for frame culture. It does best when grown in very rich soil or compost. Being a fancy kind, it is not suitable for cultivation on a large scale, but it is one of the most exquisite varieties known for perfection of shape and fineness of quality.

Early Nantes Carrot (*Carotte Demi-longue Nantaise*).—Root almost perfectly cylindrical, not much widened at the neck, and with a blunt, rounded point; skin very smooth; neck fine, hollowed out around the base of the leaf-stalks;

Early Carentan Carrot (⅕ natural size).

leaves not very large; flesh of the root entirely red, very sweet and mild in flavour, and almost wholly devoid of the broad yellow heart or core which is seen in most of the other kinds of Red Carrots. Although this variety only began to be distributed a few years ago, it has already become one of the most generally cultivated of all the kitchen-garden varieties of Carrots. Indeed, by a remarkable combination of good qualities, it justifies the preference which is given

to it. It excels all the other kinds of Half-long Carrots in earliness, without being inferior to them in productiveness. Its roots, which are very clean-skinned and even in shape, are easily pulled, and keep well; and, lastly, its somewhat deeper colour and freedom from heart or core cause it to be preferred to all the other kinds for table use. For all these reasons the Early Nantes Carrot deserves to be very generally grown; but it requires a certain amount of care, for, like all improved and early varieties, it suffers more than the ordinary coarser kinds from want of nourishment and watering. It only attains its full quality in a mellow, deep soil which has been previously well incorporated with vegetable

Early Nantes Carrot (⅕ natural size).

mould, compost, or manure, and which is sufficiently substantial and kept moist by frequent waterings. The roots are more regular in shape and smoother in skin in proportion as the soil is soft and free from stones and gravel. Any attention given to the cultivation of this Carrot will be amply repaid by a more abundant crop, and especially by the finer appearance and improved quality of the roots.

In the neighbourhood of Nantes another Half-long variety of Carrot is grown, which has a very blunt-pointed root, sometimes broader at the end than at the neck, like the Jersey Navet Turnip. This variety is larger than the Nantes Carrot which we have just described, and also differs from it in having a very large yellow heart or core.

Luc Half-long Carrot (*Carotte Demi-longue de Luc*).—Root rather broad at the neck and a little longer than that of the preceding kinds; the lower end is usually more blunt than pointed, although the whole root narrows gradually from the neck to the lower extremity. This is an early and productive variety, and is suitable for spring culture in the open ground. It is not entirely free from heart or core, although the difference between the central and the exterior layers of the flesh are not so clearly defined in it as they are in many other varieties.

Long Surrey, or Long Red, Carrot (*Carotte Rouge Longue*).—Root long, narrowing gradually to the lower extremity, five or six times as long as broad, not unusually 1 ft. to 14 inches in length ; neck broadish, flat, or slightly hollowed out around the base of the leaf-stalks ; leaves stout and numerous. This variety, which often attains a considerable weight, is very much used, both for field and market-garden culture. It requires a rather deep soil, but in return yields a very remunerative crop. By protecting the plants with a covering of straw or leaves, they

Luc Half-long Carrot (⅕ natural size).

Long Surrey, or Long Red,
Carrot (⅕ natural size).

may be left in the ground for a long time in winter, and taken up as they are wanted for table use.

Long Horn, or Long Red Dutch, Carrot (*Carotte Longue Rouge de Brunswick*).—A sub-variety of the preceding kind, somewhat narrower at the neck, very smooth, regularly narrowed from neck to point, and with flesh a little redder interiorly than that of the Red Surrey Carrot, which it is said to excel in keeping qualities. It is a kind to be recommended.

Coreless Long Red Carrot (*Carotte Rouge Longue Obtuse sans Cœur*).—This Carrot rather resembles the Early Nantes variety, but is very strikingly longer, and consequently more productive. It is almost cylindrical in shape, blunt at the lower extremity, and has extremely red, very melting, sweet, and fine-flavoured flesh. This is especially an early small-leaved kitchen-garden variety.

Altringham Carrot (*Carotte Rouge Longue d'Altringham*).—This variety, which is of English origin, has been for a long time known and valued in France. It is a very long, slender kind, with the flesh entirely red (like that of the Coreless varieties) and of excellent quality. The neck, instead of being flattened, or even hollowed, like that of many other kinds, is raised in the form of an obtuse cone. The root is usually of a bronzy or violet colour on the over-ground portion, which is

Orange Belgian, or Long Orange Green-top, Carrot (⅕ natural size).

Coreless Long Red Carrot (⅕ natural size).

Altringham Carrot (⅕ natural size).

from 1 to 2 inches in length. The length of the whole root is often 20 inches or more, and its diameter is relatively small, the length being equal to eight or ten times the diameter. Its surface exhibits a series of alternate ridges and depressions, having the appearance of being tightly bound around with a thin cord. This Carrot requires a rich and deeply dug soil, and, from its peculiar shape, it is liable to be broken when pulled. For these two reasons it is not so generally cultivated as it deserves to be on account of its good quality and great productiveness.

Orange Belgian, or **Long Orange Green-top, Carrot** (*Carotte Rouge Longue à Collet Vert*).—This very hardy and productive kind is more generally grown in the fields than in the kitchen-garden. The root is, at least, six times as long as broad, of a rather pale orange colour on the underground portion, and quite green on the part overground, which is about one-fourth of its entire length ; hence it is indifferently termed the Green-top Red, or Green-top Yellow, Carrot. It keeps well, and is considered to be very nutritious.

St. Valery Carrot ½ natural size).

St. Valery Carrot (*Carotte Longue Rouge de Saint-Valery*).—A large handsome variety, which may be regarded as the connecting-link between the Half-long and Long varieties of Red Carrot. The root, which is very straight, very smooth, and of a bright-red colour, is very broad at the neck, where it is frequently 2 to 3 inches in diameter, so that the entire length, which may be 10 to 12 inches, is only about four times the diameter, which would almost bring it into the category of the Half-long varieties. It is suitable for

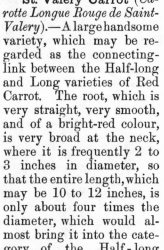

Flanders, or Sandwich Carrot (⅛ natural size).

field-culture, but does best in light, rich, well-dug soil. The leaves are remarkably slight for the size of the root. This fine variety was for a long time grown only in its native locality. Since it became more generally known it has come more and more into favour ; for, along with a handsome appearance and good quality, it combines the distinguishing properties of both good kitchen-garden and good field Carrots—that is, great productiveness, and at the same time a fine, regular shape, and thick, sweet, tender flesh.

Flanders, or **Sandwich, Carrot** (*Carotte Rouge Pâle de Flandre*).—A kind of Half-long Red Carrot, much used in field culture on account of its great productiveness. Leaves abundant; neck flat and broad; root almost entirely sunk in the soil, of a rather bright orange-red colour, and regularly narrowed from neck to point. It is only about three times as long as broad, the entire length being about 8 inches, with a diameter of between 2 and 2½ inches at the neck. The chief merit of this variety is that it is large, productive, early in forming, and keeps well. Formerly quantities of it were sent to the Paris market from Flanders in waggons at the close of winter, when the Scarlet Horn and the Long Red Carrots were beginning to grow scarce. It is now less frequently seen there since

Long Lemon Carrot (⅛ natural size).

the Parisian cultivators discovered that by late successional sowings fresh Carrots can be raised at all seasons.

Long Lemon Carrot (*Carotte Jaune Longue*).—Root rather slender, four or five times as long as broad, almost entirely sunk in the ground, and of a bright-yellow colour, except at the neck, where it is slightly tinged with green. It is extensively grown in the fields in the north-west of France, but is not without merit as a kitchen-garden plant, especially when young, as when it has advanced in growth it sometimes becomes hard and almost woody at the heart. The flesh is yellow. When it is desired to be used in winter without becoming hard, it should be sown rather late—about the end of May or the first days in June. This is one of the oldest French varieties of Carrot.

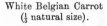

We find it described in old horticultural works before there was any mention made in them of the Red or Orange varieties. In the present day these are most generally preferred; and the place which the Lemon Carrot formerly occupied in cultivation for market supply is now filled by the Common Long Red Carrot, which, in its turn, is being largely superseded by the St. Valery Long Red variety.

Short Lemon Carrot (*Carotte Jaune Courte*).— Root scarcely twice or thrice as long as broad, conical in shape, and sunk in the ground; neck flat and wide, of a rather pale-yellow colour, which extends through the entire substance of the flesh of the root.

White Belgian Carrot (*Carotte Blanche à Collet Vert*).—Root thick and long, sunk in the ground for two-thirds or three-fourths of its length, white on the underground portion, and green or bronze purple on the part overground; leaves erect, stout, and numerous; flesh of the root white, with a marked tendency towards a more or less decided yellow tinge. This is the field Carrot *par excellence.* There is hardly any farm on which it is not grown to some extent for feeding cattle, and especially horses. It yields a heavy crop, and in this respect rivals the Beet-root. This variety appears to have sprung from the old Long White Carrot, which was formerly grown in kitchen-gardens, but has now almost entirely gone out of cultivation. Numerous attempts have been made to render it more hardy, so as to have the crop come in at the latter end of

White Belgian Carrot autumn without running the risk of having it injured
(⅓ natural size). by frost. These attempts have not been successful. The leaves of the plant will bear four or five degrees of frost, but this is sufficient to produce a change in the tissue of the roots, even in the overground part, which has been inured to variations of temperature. The underground portion of the root is very sensitive to cold, and becomes disorganized by the slightest frost. It is therefore necessary, when these Carrots happen to be pulled in frosty weather, to protect them at once from the action of the atmosphere, by covering them

with straw or earth, or with their own leaves cut and heaped over them.

Orthe Carrot (*Carotte Blanche à Collet Vert d'Orthe*).—A sub-variety of the preceding kind, from which it only differs in having a somewhat shorter and broader root, about 1 inch of which is over-ground, and which is usually about four times as long as broad. As it is also narrowed from neck to point more abruptly than the preceding kind, it is less liable to be broken when pulled. It yields as heavy a crop as the other, as the roots are thicker, so that they regain in that way what they lose in length. We owe this excellent variety to the late M. J. Roussel, iron-master, of Orthe (Mayenne), who raised it from seed of selected plants of the Common White Belgian Carrot.

Vosges White Carrot (*Carotte Blanche des Vosges*).—Root very broad at the neck, en-

tirely sunk in the ground, narrowed abruptly to the point, nearly twice as long as broad, the entire length being about 8 inches, with a diameter of from 4 to 5 inches; leaves pretty numerous; neck of the root flat or slightly hollowed out. This is a field variety, and especially suitable for soils that are not very deep; it is productive, easily pulled, and keeps well. The colour of the skin often inclines to a yellowish tint.

Vosges White Carrot
(⅕ natural size).

Orthe Carrot (⅕ natural size). The flesh is rather soft and watery, of a dull-white colour in the outer part, but clearer in the central portion which corresponds to the heart or core, and which is so largely developed that it occupies two-thirds of the transverse diameter of the root. The flavour is strong, rather unpleasant, and deficient in sweetness, so that it cannot be recommended for table use. A variety which comes very close to this is sometimes grown in Germany under the name of Palatinate White Carrot (*Carotte Blanche du Palatinat*).

Breteuil White Carrot (*Carotte Blanche de Breteuil*).—This variety differs very little from the preceding one in appearance and character; however, the root is more slender, somewhat less regularly rounded, and sometimes angular. It does not keep so well, but, on the other hand, the flesh is firmer and of far better quality, which may be sufficient to recommend it for kitchen-garden culture, while the White Belgian and the Vosges White varieties are more properly cattle-feeding kinds. The leaves, which are somewhat finer than those of the Vosges White, frequently assume a purplish tinge in autumn.

From all appearances, it is to this variety that we should refer a kind mentioned by old French writers under the name of Round White Carrot (*Carotte Blanche Ronde*), which had a short top-shaped root, and was grown as a kitchen-garden Carrot, chiefly in stiff or not very deep soils.

Transparent White Carrot (*Carotte Blanche Transparente*).—Root elongated spindle-shaped, entirely sunk in the ground, quite white, and nearly four times as long as broad. This variety, which appears to have the same origin as the White Belgian, continues to be grown chiefly as a kitchen-garden Carrot. It is principally distinguished by its very white, fine, and, as it were, transparent flesh.

Purple or **Blood-red Carrot** (*Carotte Violette*).—Root entirely sunk in the ground, slender, spindle-shaped, five or six times as long as broad ; leaves erect, very stout; skin of the root smooth, with a purplish tinge, which penetrates the flesh to a variable depth, seldom reaching the heart, which is almost always yellow. This is not a thoroughly constant variety, and appears to be rather a curious than a really useful one, yet it is pretty largely grown in certain parts of some warm countries, in the climate of which it may possibly exhibit good qualities which the climate of France fails to develop.

Improved Wild Carrots.—About the year 1830, M. Vilmorin, sen., commenced several cultural experiments with the view of obtaining from the Wild Carrot enlarged and edible roots similar to those of the cultivated varieties. In the course of a few years, his sowings yielded him a certain proportion of plants with fleshy roots of various colours. Some of these forms remained constant for several years, reproducing themselves from seed with great regularity. The most remarkable of them were the Improved White Wild Carrot, which was rather like the Breteuil White Carrot, and had a fine flavour and odour, but was deficient in sweetness ; and the Improved Red Verrières Wild Carrot, which was not productive, but was very regular in shape, with a very fine neck and remarkably slight leaves. These varieties, however, after having been grown for some time as a scientific curiosity, did not come into general cultivation, and were eventually discarded.

Amongst the varieties which do not come under any of those which have just been described, we may mention the following :—**Bardowick Carrot.**—A fine variety of Long Red Carrot, almost free from core, and somewhat resembling the Altringham Carrot. The Dutch variety named *De Duwick* is a rather shorter kind than the Half-long Red varieties, yet bears no analogy to the Early Scarlet Horn. It is a pretty good kind for field culture, but the Blunt-pointed Half-long varieties are much better. The **Long Orange Carrot** is a variety grown in the United States of America, of a lighter colour, greater length, and with a broader neck than the Common Long Red Carrot.

COMMON CATERPILLAR.

Scorpiurus vermiculatus, L.   *Leguminosæ.*

French, Chenille grosse.   *German*, Grosser Raupenklee.   *Italian*, Erba bruca.

Native of Southern Europe.—Annual.—A plant with a prostrate, almost creeping, stem. Leaves oblong, with narrow stalks; flowers small, yellow; pod rather large, rolled lengthways upon itself, and marked with longitudinal furrows which are almost entirely hidden by the rows of stalked tubercles between them, the thick swollen heads of which almost meet from one row to another; seed large, oblong, yellowish, flattened at the ends. A gramme is about equal to the weight of three pods, and a litre of them weighs about 200 grammes. The germinating power of the seed lasts for six years.

PRICKLY, or SMALL, CATERPILLAR.

Scorpiurus muricatus, L.

French, Chenille petite.   *German*, Kleiner Raupenklee.   *Flemish* and *Dutch*, Schorpioen-kruid.   *Spanish*, Escorpioides.

Native of Southern Europe.—Annual.—Pod narrow, twisted like a caterpillar rolled upon itself, marked with longitudinal furrows, which are separated on the outer part of the curve by brownish crests bristling with sharp, crooked points bearing a considerable resemblance to the rough hairs with which some caterpillars are covered. Seed largish, curved, wrinkled, and of a yellowish colour.

| Common Caterpillar (natural size). | Striped Caterpillar (natural size). | Hairy Caterpillar (natural size). |

STRIPED CATERPILLAR.

Scorpiurus sulcatus, L.

French, Chenille rayèe.   *German*, Gestreifter Raupenklee.

Native of Southern Europe.—Annual.—Pod rolled upon itself, making about two complete turns, swollen over the seeds, deeply marked on the outer part with six smooth grayish furrows, separated by projecting toothed crests or ridges of a brownish-violet colour, the two central crests being more deeply toothed than the others. Seed very like that of the preceding kind, but rather larger.

HAIRY CATERPILLAR.

Scorpiurus subvillosus, L.

French, Chenille velue.

Native of Southern Europe.— Annual.—Pod very like that of the Prickly Caterpillar, but rather longer and more twisted, making as many as three or four turns upon itself. The four dorsal crests or ridges bear stiff, sharp, crooked points, and are more or less tinged with a violet-brown colour. Seed rather larger than that of the Prickly Caterpillar. The pods of the last three kinds weigh about 180 grammes to the litre; a gramme is equal in weight to about six of them. The germinating power of the seeds continues for six years.

CULTURE and USES.—The cultivation of the species of Caterpillars is of the most simple kind. They are sown, where they are to be grown, in April or May, and commence to bear in two or three months' time without requiring any attention whatever. They are seldom grown, however, except as curiosities, from the singular appearance of the young pods, which resemble various kinds of caterpillars in a very striking manner. They are sometimes, as a harmless practical joke, put into salads, for the purpose of startling those who are unacquainted with them, but, as a vegetable, their flavour is very indifferent.

CAT-MINT.

Nepeta Cataria, L.   *Labiatæ.*

French, Menthe de chat.

Native of Europe.—Perennial.—A tall plant, with erect branching stems about $3\frac{1}{4}$ feet high. Leaves stalked, oval or heart-shaped, notched at the edges, and whitish on the under surface ; flowers white, in terminal clusters composed of small heads which are wide apart at the bottom, but become more crowded towards the top ; seed brown, smooth, ovoid, with three well-defined angles. A gramme contains about 1200 seeds, and a litre of them weighs about 680 grammes. Their germinating power lasts for five years. It is easily raised from seed sown in spring or autumn in lines, which should be 20 inches apart, as the plants attain a considerable size. They require no attention, and will last for several years, if the ground is kept free from weeds. The leaves and young shoots are used for seasoning.

CAULIFLOWER.

Brassica oleracea Botrytis, D.C.

French, Chou-fleur.   *German*, Blumenkohl.   *Flemish* and *Dutch*, Bloemkool.   *Italian*, Cavol-fiore.   *Spanish*, Coliflor.   *Portuguese*, Couve-flor.

In the different varieties of Cabbage known as Cauliflowers, it is the floral organs, or, more properly speaking, the flower-stems, which have been artificially modified in size and appearance in the course of cultivation. The flowers themselves have, for the most part, been rendered abortive, and the branchlets along which they grow, gaining in thickness what they lose in length, form a sort of regular corymb with a white fleece-like surface, which is rarely broken by a few small leaves growing through it. These floral branchlets, having become large, white, thick, and very tender, produce nothing but a homogeneous mass, so to say, and the rudiments of the flowers are only represented by the minute and almost imperceptible prominences which are found on the upper surface of what is termed the " head " of the Cauliflower. The seeds number about 375 to the gramme.

CULTURE.—It may be said that the cultivation of the Cauliflower is one of the most simple processes, and, at the same time, one of the most difficult to carry out well. In fact, with the exception of the spring Cauliflowers, which are sown in autumn and wintered under frames, it is grown as an annual, which is sown in the spring in the open ground, and yields a crop in the course of the same year, without requiring any attention whatever except frequent waterings. But, on the other hand, it is certain that, in order to obtain a fine crop, the cultivation of the Cauliflower requires a certain amount of skill and tact which no mere cultural directions can supply. The " head " will not be regularly formed unless the growth of the plant proceeds rapidly and without any check from beginning to end, and the greatest watchfulness and most assiduous care sometimes fail to insure this.

At Paris, there are three principal seasons or successional periods for growing Cauliflowers. In the first, the seed is sown in autumn, and the crop comes in in spring. In the second, the seed is sown late in autumn or in winter, the crop, in this case, not coming in until the following summer. In the third, the seed is sown at the end of winter or in spring, and the crop is gathered in the autumn of the same year. Those which are sown in autumn, for the spring crop, are sown either in the open ground, or (most usually) on a hot-bed, in September. In the course of the autumn, the seedlings are pricked out under a cold frame, or in the open ground in a border with a warm aspect, where they are protected with *cloches* or bell-glasses. In January or February, they are transplanted to a hot-bed, six plants to each light. The heads obtained in this way are the first that appear in the market in May. Almost at the same time that the plants are removed to the hot-bed, other plants are placed in cold frames ; the crop from these is naturally later, and comes in in succession to that which was obtained from the hot-bed.

The Cauliflowers of the second season are sown in the beginning of January, in a hot-bed ; the plants are pricked out into another hot-bed, and are not transferred to the open ground until they are pretty strong, about the end of March or the beginning of April, at which time they have no further need of artificial heat ; the crop from these comes in about the end of June or the beginning of July. Successional sowings are made in February and March, and the seedlings, reared under frames or bell-glasses, are planted out a little later than those which were sown in hot-beds. This second season, in which the plants are pushed forward by special treatment and artificial heat, produces by far the largest quantities of Cauliflowers that are sent to the Central Market at Paris.

Lastly, in the third season, the entire growth of the plant is effected, without the help of artificial heat, in the open ground. The seed is sown in May or June in a sheltered or shaded border, and the seedlings are planted out permanently in July, without having been previously pricked out. This method, which at first sight appears the simplest of all, does not always produce the best results, owing to the difficulty of protecting the plants from excessive heat and drought in the early stages of their growth, and, later on, from early frosts, which often mar the formation of the heads.

In England this is a summer and autumn vegetable, and at that season fills the position occupied by the Broccoli in winter and spring. The most valuable crops are the early ones in spring and the late in autumn. In summer they are frequently unsatisfactory during hot weather, and when Peas and French Beans are plentiful they are not so much in demand.

The first sowing is in a general way made about the 25th of August, the time being varied according to latitude, as experience may direct. In some places the first week in September may be early enough. Select an open situation where the land is in good condition from a previous manuring. If the weather is hot and the land very dry, stir the surface for a foot or so in depth with the fork, and give water enough to moisten it. Draw drills 9 inches apart, and sow the seeds (which should have been obtained from a good source) thinly. Cover with nets to keep off birds; and if the weather continue hot, shade a little by laying a few branches with the leaves attached over the net. As soon as the plants are up and are large enough to move safely (which will be early in November), prepare one or more frames by placing a layer of coal-ashes in the bottom, and on the ashes, which should be beaten down firmly with the back of the spade, place 5 inches of light rich soil. Into the bed so formed dibble the plants 3 inches apart, and give water to settle the soil round them. During the winter the frames should be fully ventilated when the weather is mild, keeping out cold rains. In times of severe frost scatter a little dry litter or Fern over the lights. Sometimes Cauliflower plants pass through the winter safely pricked out at the foot of a south wall, or on the south side of a thick hedge, and sheltered in severe weather by placing evergreen branches among them. Another way of raising early plants, and an excellent one, is to sow in heat

about the 1st of January, and treat the plants as we should treat tender annuals. The seeds are sown in pans covered lightly with sandy soil, and placed on a shelf in a house where the temperature is about 60° at night. When the young plants appear they will occupy a position in the full light near the glass, and when large enough will be pricked off into 60-sized pots, one plant in each pot. The soil and the pots will be taken into the house to warm a little before the potting takes place. The plants will be grown on in the same temperature till March, when they will be well established; they should then be hardened off, and early in April planted out. This plan will not give more trouble than is taken every spring with the same number of bedding plants, and they do not bolt, as sometimes happens with the plants raised in August. Still another way of raising the first early Cauliflower plants may be described as intermediate between the cool treatment first mentioned and the warm plan last described. About the middle of October sow the seeds in boxes and place in a frame which rests on, say, an exhausted Melon or Cucumber bed, and which still retains a little of the summer's warmth. Keep close till the seeds germinate, then give air freely, and when the plants are large enough pot off singly in small pots. Winter on a shelf in the lightest part of the greenhouse.

PLANTING UNDER HAND-LIGHTS.— These are old-fashioned but excellent contrivances. About March, acting as all must according to the character of the weather, arrange the lights for the early crop in a warm, sunny, sheltered position, where the soil is deep and rich, 3 ft. apart each way, and plant four plants under each light. As the season advances, ventilation will be required, either by placing the lights on bricks, or, if the lights have movable tops, by altering their position. A few early Cauliflowers may generally be obtained by planting in front of a south wall, almost close to it, to take advantage of the sun's warmth, which accumulates there both on the soil and in the air. Such plants may be further assisted by a ridge of soil in front, and when the weather gets warm, later in the season, this ridge of soil will help to confine the soakings of liquid manure which good cultivators will obtain by hook or by crook for their early Cauliflowers.

SUCCESSIONAL SOWINGS should be made in March in heat. A few seeds may be sown among any other young crops, such as Early Horn Carrots, as the Cauliflowers will be transplanted before any harm can be done. If it is not convenient to do this, sow the seed in a box, and place it where there is some artificial warmth, harden off, and plant out as seems necessary. The Autumn Giant should be sown at this time for late summer and autumn use. This is a very valuable Cauliflower for hot seasons. It is very difficult with any other sort to secure close, firm hearts in August and September, but the cross of the Broccoli, that is so apparent, and which gives this kind its hardiness, almost makes it heat and drought proof—hence its great value, not only in the late autumn, but also through the season from August up till Christmas. Sow the Walcheren in April, and again in May and June for autumn. This, with the Autumn Giant, will furnish a supply till the winter Broccoli turn in. In some situations Cauliflowers are very uncertain; they must have plenty of rich manure. In such, to get them good, I have opened a trench 4 ft. wide all across a quarter, worked in plenty of manure, then drawn three drills at equal distances apart in the trench, and sown seeds of the Walcheren thinly. If it is necessary to sow in trenches, this is a better plan than having single rows, as the better soil and manure being in bulk will retain the moisture longer, and the plants will do better. When the seedlings are strong enough to transplant,

single them out, leaving the strongest, and for this crop they may with advantage be left much thicker than we should plant them generally. Small, white, close hearts are in the hot weather more useful than large ones, which nearly always develop a tendency to open. Some of the plants thinned out may be useful if planted under a north wall in rather deep drills. This is acting on the principle of never throwing a chance away. The crop in the trench had better be started about the first or second week in June, and if well attended to, and grown without a severe check, they will be sure to produce nice useful hearts at a very small expense. And it is worth something to feel that, under all circumstances, we may rely upon any particular crop turning out right.

WATERING AND MULCHING.—Mulching with manure in hot summers is to this crop invaluable, and, except in extreme cases, will obviate the necessity for much watering, though, of course, a good soaking of liquid manure in a dry season will never come amiss. The three sowings in the open air in April, May, and June, with the previous sowings under glass, will, if planted out in the usual order when the plants are large enough, furnish a supply from June till Christmas, if need be; indeed, I have had both the Walcheren and the Autumn Giant till after Christmas in good condition in a cold pit. The distances between the rows, as well as the distance between the plants in the rows, will vary according to the situations and seasons, but 2 ft. between the rows and 18 inches separating the plants from each other in the rows, may be taken as a good average distance.— E. H.

CULTURE IN MARKET GARDENS.— In London, it is hardly possible to overstock the market with this vegetable. It has the advantage over Broccoli in this particular, viz. that pickle merchants are always ready to buy up any quantity of

Cauliflowers in summer, whilst for this purpose scarcely any Broccoli is used. In May, before Peas and Beans can be had at reasonable prices, good Cauliflowers realize good profits to the grower. Early Cauliflowers are usually grown under hand-lights, or are protected by old baskets or small boughs of evergreen trees. To provide plants for this purpose, a sowing is made on a well-sheltered piece of ground or a warm open quarter, in beds, in the second or third week of September. The young plants are allowed to remain in the seed-bed until the end of October, or even the middle of November. Should frosty weather set in whilst the plants are in the seed-beds, they are protected by mats supported on short stakes 18 inches above the ground. Sometimes a stout plank is set on edge along the centres of the beds, and two rows of short stakes are put one on either side to support it, and over this are placed mats. When the weather becomes too severe for them to be thus protected, and when they require to be transplanted, they are taken up and planted in frames or under hand-lights. The frames are placed in a sheltered spot sloping to the south, and are filled to within 8 or 9 inches of the top with ordinary soil firmly trampled down with the feet; over this better soil is sifted to a thickness of 3 or 4 inches, and in this the Cauliflowers are planted 3 inches or so apart. In this position they remain until the February following or early part of March without any further care beyond that of closing the sashes to exclude frosts, cold winds, hail, or rain, and tilting them up at front and back during favourable weather, and on very fine days drawing them off entirely. Cold rains are very injurious to Cauliflowers, but a warm shower in February benefits them. Sometimes the plants grow so strongly that their leaves touch or press against the sashes; when that happens, the sashes are tilted up at front and back, night and day, with pieces of wood or brick, otherwise frost would injure such leaves as touch the glass. Dry sand, kept in a shed for the purpose, is scattered amongst the plants two or three times while they are in frames, in order to guard against damp, and such plants as show signs of " buttoning " are immediately pulled out to give the others more room. Where room is limited and the weather appears mild, young Cauliflowers are often wintered in the beds where they are sown, or they are pricked off into raised beds of light soil not likely to be soaked with wet in winter. Here they are sometimes left unprotected, and at other times they are covered with hoops and mats. Continued dampness of soil and atmosphere is their worst enemy, as it induces growth so soft that it cannot withstand frost so well as that produced on high and dry ground. Where hand-lights are employed, an open field or quarter is lined off into squares measuring about 6 ft. each way. At every intersection nine Cauliflowers are planted in a sufficiently small space to be conveniently covered with *cloches* or hand-lights, which are immediately placed over them, and a little earth is drawn around the base of the lights so as to shut up all apertures. The empty spaces between the rows of hand-lights are planted with Coleworts. In spring these Coleworts are either thinned out or entirely removed for market, and a crop of Cos Lettuces is planted in their place. As soon as the Cauliflowers have become established they are allowed abundance of air, and otherwise treated the same as those grown in frames. When the plants become too thick, they are all lifted from under the hand-lights and planted in open quarters or under other hand-lights.

Market gardeners generally begin to cut from Cauliflower plants raised in this way some time in the month of May, according to the mildness or otherwise of the season. The best growers seldom make many sowings of Cauliflowers; one or two in autumn and one or two in spring being the usual number. The first autumn sowing, as before stated, is made out-of-doors some time between the last week in August and the third week in September; and the second one, in frames, in the last week of September or first week in October. From these two sowings Cauliflowers are obtained from the last week in April to the end of June. The first spring sowing, if the autumn one is a failure, is made in a frame in the last week of February or first week of March, or it may be made in the open border any time during the first fortnight of March; from this sowing a crop is obtained from the middle of June till August or September. The third sowing is commonly made in beds, in some open quarter, between the middle of April and the first week in May, in order to furnish an autumn supply. Different market gardeners have different times for sowing Cauliflowers, but it is well understood that strong, grossly grown plants do not stand the winter so well as medium-sized ones, and they are also more liable to "button." Moderate-sized plants are decidedly the best for mild winters, but in the event of very severe winters occurring, strong plants are the best. Cauliflowers which have been wintered in frames or under hand-lights are often planted on ground cropped with Radishes before the latter crop is marketable, and by the time it is so and has been cleared off, the Cauliflowers will have gained good strength, when the ground will be intercropped with Lettuces. In other instances, fields are marked off into beds 5 ft. wide, with 1-ft. alleys between them, and these beds are sown with Round-leaved Spinach. As soon as this is done, three rows of Cauliflowers are planted along the beds. The Cauli-

flowers outgrow the Spinach, which, by continual picking for market, is kept in check until it is eventually exhausted, leaving the Cauliflowers masters of the field. The autumn crops obtained from spring sowings are thinned out a little in the seed-beds, and, when large enough for handling, are planted where they are to remain permanently. Should the weather be dry at planting time, a pint of water, or a little more, is given to each plant, and the sodden soil is soon afterwards freshened up by the hoe, thus, in some measure, preventing evaporation. Late Cauliflowers are nearly always inter-cropped with some other vegetable, such as Lettuces, French Beans, Celery, Seakale, etc. Some large growers, however, depart from this rule, and save much labour; for, if intercropping be practised, people must be employed to keep down weeds by means of the hoe; but when Cauliflowers alone occupy the ground, horse-hoes can be freely worked among the rows. The Early London is the variety used for the first crops by most market gardeners, but some use the Walcheren for that purpose. The Walcheren is the kind almost entirely grown for use after June, because it suffers less from drought than any other sort, and is not liable to "button." Snow's Winter White, an excellent sort, is, as a rule, regarded as a Broccoli; nevertheless, it has fine white, solid heads, and is largely grown to succeed the Walcheren, being hardier than that sort. Snow's White, if sown together with the Walcheren in April or May, makes a fine succession to it, and comes in usefully till January. Early Cauliflowers are always sent to market, but those produced in summer and autumn are disposed of to a large extent to pickle merchants.—S.

USES.—The head, boiled or pickled, is the only part of this plant which is usually eaten, and it is one of the best appreciated of all vegetables, though it is seldom had in the freshest and best condition by the numerous people in cities who could appreciate and afford it.

N

Early Dwarf Erfurt Cauliflower (*Chou-fleur Nain Hâtif d'Erfurt*).
—A very early, very distinct, and really valuable variety, but difficult
to keep true to name. It is somewhat
under middle height, and has a rather
short stem. Leaves oblong, entire,
of rounded outline, scarcely undulated, and of a peculiar light grayish-
green tint, which, added to their
shape and rather erect position, gives
the plant some resemblance to the
Sugar-loaf Cabbage. The head, which
is white, compact, and fine-grained,
forms quickly and keeps firm for a
long time. When exposed to the
sun, it soon acquires a violet tint.

Early Dwarf Erfurt Cauliflower
($\frac{1}{10}$ natural size).

Imperial Cauliflower (*Chou-
fleur Impérial*). — This handsome
variety very much resembles the
Dwarf Erfurt, but it is of a darker
green colour and larger in all its parts. It is an early kind, with a fine,
white, broad, firm head, and remarkable for the regularity of its growth
and productiveness. When grown true to name, it is certainly one of
the best early varieties of Cauliflower.

Earliest Paris Forcing Cauliflower (*Chou-fleur Tendre de Paris*).—
A variety with a slender and rather long stem. Leaves comparatively
narrow, almost straight, not
much turned back at the ends
nor much folded at the edges;
head of medium size, forming
soon, but not continuing firm
very long. This kind is especially suitable for sowing in
summer; if sown in April or
May, the head forms in August
or September.

Alleaume Dwarf Cauliflower.

**Alleaume Dwarf Cauli-
flower** (*Chou-fleur Alleaume
Nain Très Hâtif*).— An exceedingly dwarf and very early
variety of the preceding kind.
The stem is so short that the
head appears almost to rest
on the ground, like that of
the Early Dwarf Erfurt Cauli-
flower. From this variety, however, it differs entirely in the appearance of the leaves, which are broad, undulated at the margin, and
generally twisted. The head forms very quickly, but soon grows out
of shape, if it is not cut in time.

Lenormand's Cauliflower (*Chou-fleur Lenormand*).—It is twenty
years since attention was first drawn to this variety, chiefly on account
of its great hardiness and its handsome head. Externally it does not

exhibit any great difference from the Earliest Paris Forcing Cauliflower, only the leaves are a little larger. It certainly does not require so much care, when growing, as most other kinds, but its chief merit is that of having given rise to the following variety, which is now one of the most highly esteemed.

Lenormand's Short-stalked Cauliflower (*Chou-fleur Lenormand*

Lenormand's Cauliflower ($\frac{1}{10}$ natural size).

à Pied Court).—The appearance of this variety is very characteristic, and distinguishes it at once from all other kinds when it comes true to name. The stem, which is extremely short, stout, and thick-set, is furnished almost to the ground with short, broad, roundish leaves, which are not much undulated except at the edges, and are very firm and stiff, rather spreading than erect, and of a deep and almost glaucous green colour. The head is very large and firm, of a splendid white colour, and keeps firm for a long time. The plant is early, hardy, and productive, and takes up comparatively little ground, so that it is not surprising

Lenormand's Short-stalked Cauliflower ($\frac{1}{10}$ natural size).

that its cultivation has been very much extended in the course of a few years.

Large White French Cauliflower (*Chou-fleur Demi-dur de Saint-Brieuc*).—A large, stout plant, with elongated, undulated, deep-green leaves. Stem long; head firm, compact, and keeping pretty well. This variety, which is very much grown in the neighbourhood of Saint-Brieuc, whence the heads are sent to Paris, and even to England, is very hardy and highly suitable for culture in the open ground.

Late Paris Cauliflower (*Chou-fleur Dur de Paris*).—This is the latest of the varieties grown by the market gardeners about Paris. It differs from the preceding variety chiefly in being somewhat later, and the head has the advantage of remaining hard and firm for a longer time. It also differs in the appearance of its leaves, which are very numerous, elongated, very much undulated, and of an intense green colour. It is the least extensively grown of the three kinds which are most commonly cultivated about Paris, the market gardeners there only using it for summer sowings to bring in a crop in the latter end of autumn.

Early London, or **Early Dutch, Cauliflower** (*Chou-fleur Dur de Hollande*).—A large and hardy variety, suitable for field culture. Stem long and rather slender; leaves elongated, not very broad, of a grayish-

green colour, and tolerably undulated. This is one of the kinds of Cauliflower which have the midrib of the leaf bare at the base for the greater part of its length. The head is hard and firm, but not very large. It is a half-late variety, and, in its native country, succeeds better than the French kinds. It is grown on a large scale about Leyden, whence great quantities of it are exported to England, to compete in the London markets with the Cauliflowers sent from the French coasts, especially from Brittany. The name of *Dwarf*

Early London, or Early Dutch, Cauliflower
($\frac{1}{10}$ natural size).

Dutch Cauliflower given to it by the Germans is only in comparison with other Dutch varieties, for it is a tall kind compared with the French varieties.

Late Asiatic Cauliflower (*Chou-fleur Dur d'Angleterre*).—A vigorous-growing kind, with numerous, large, undulated leaves, of a rather dark green colour and with a shorter stem than that of the preceding variety, like which it is hardy and rather late. It is suitable for growing in the open ground, and should not be sown later than May, to bring in a crop in the autumn. This is a large and very highly esteemed late variety.

Stadtholder Cauliflower (*Chou-fleur de Stadthold*).—Very nearly allied to the Early Dutch Cauliflower, this variety exhibits almost the same characteristics of growth, and its difference is that it is a few days later. In this respect, it is intermediate between the Early Dutch and the Walcheren Cauliflower. The stem is shorter than that of the other Dutch kinds and the leaves are more undulated at the edges.

Another most valuable late kind is the variety named *Knickerbocker*, which possesses the fine qualities of Stadtholder, but has a shorter stem and shorter leaves, and produces large, compact, snow-white heads.

Walcheren Cauliflower, or Walcheren Broccoli (*Chou-fleur de Walcheren*).—This is the latest of all Cauliflowers, and, at the same time, one of the hardiest, so that it may be regarded as intermediate between the Cauliflowers, properly so-called, and the Broccolis, among which it is not unusual to find it classed. It has a long, stout stem, and numerous elongated leaves, which are tolerably stiff and erect, and of a slightly grayish-green colour. The head forms very slowly ; it is handsome, large, very white, and of a fine close grain. The seed should be sown in April to insure the head being well grown before the approach of frosty weather. When sown late, it often withstands the winter and heads early in spring.

Veitch's Autumn Giant Cauliflower ($\frac{1}{10}$ natural size).

Veitch's Autumn Giant Cauliflower (*Chou-fleur Géant de Naples Hâtif*).—A large and vigorous-growing variety, with a longish stem and large, tolerably undulated leaves of a dark-green colour. Head very large, firm, very white, and well covered by the inner leaves. It is a late kind, coming in about the same time as the preceding variety, but it is not so hardy. In the north of France it can only be grown for a late autumn crop in the open ground. It should be sown in April or May.

Giant Italian Self-protecting Cauliflower (*Chou-fleur Géant de Naples Tardif*).—Before the head forms, it is not easy to distinguish this variety from the preceding one, like which it has long and broad leaves, and the leaf-stalks copiously tinged with purple on the part next the stem ; the ends of the leaves, however, are somewhat narrower and more pointed. When the head is about to form, the central leaves turn and fold themselves over it so as to cover it completely until it has attained nearly its full size, when it comes into view for the first time. Although this variety is very distinct, it is not invariably constant, and, in the best samples of seed which are imported from Italy, the two forms of this Cauliflower are usually found mixed.

Intermediate Paris Cauliflower (*Chou-fleur Demi-dur de Paris*).— A plant of medium size, with largish leaves of a deep and somewhat glaucous green colour, surrounding the head well, and having the ends turned towards the ground, the edges being undulated and coarsely toothed. Stem rather short and stout; head large, very white, and keeping firm for a long time. This variety was formerly more extensively grown than any other by the Parisian market gardeners, but at the present day it is rivalled by the Short-stalked Lenormand and several other new varieties.

The **Half-early Lemaitre Cauliflower** (*Chou-fleur Lemaitre*) is a good Paris variety. The stalk is short, and the head is handsome, large, very compact, and very white.

Algerian Cauliflower (*Chou-fleur d'Alger*).—An extremely vigorous-growing variety, larger and stouter than the preceding kind. Leaves very large, undulated, almost crimped, of a very dark-green colour with glaucous reflections; stem thick, stout, and longish; head handsome, white, and remarkably large. In its habit of growth it resembles the preceding kind, but the crop comes in at the same time as that of the Dutch and the English Cauliflowers. It is especially suitable for cultivation in the open ground in warm countries.

Purple Cape Broccoli (*Chou-fleur Noir de Sicile*).—In its appear-

ance and habit of growth, this variety has some resemblance to the preceding kind. It has a longish stem, and very large dark-green leaves, which are rather wavy, almost crimped, short, and broad for their length. It differs from all other kinds of Cauliflower in the colour of the head, which is of a purplish colour and coarser grained than that of any other variety, although it is very compact, firm, and large.

Purple Cape Broccoli (⅒ natural size).

This is not a very late variety. It is always grown in the open ground, and the crop begins to come in early in September.

The varieties of Cauliflower grown in Germany under the names of *Cyprischer*, *Asiatischer*, etc., have always appeared to us to come very close to the Dutch varieties.

CELERY.

Apium graveolens, L.   *Umbelliferæ.*

French, Céleri.   *German,* Sellerie.   *Flemish,* Selderij.   *Danish,* Selleri.   *Italian,* Sedano, Apio.   *Spanish,* Apio.

Native of Europe.—Biennial.—A plant with a fibrous root which is naturally rather fleshy. Leaves divided, pinnatifid, smooth, with almost triangular toothed leaflets, of a dark-green colour ; leaf-stalks rather broad, furrowed, concave on the inside ; stem, which does not appear until the second year, about 2 feet high, furrowed, and branching ; flowers very small, yellowish or greenish, in umbels ; seed small, triangular, five-ribbed, and having a very aromatic odour. A gramme contains about 2500 seeds, and a litre of them weighs about 480 grammes. Their germinating power lasts for eight years.

CULTURE. — In England Celery may be had in use from the beginning of September till late in April. The ground on which it is to be grown must be well drained to the depth of 3 or 4 ft., and trenched 2 ft. deep, enriching it at the same time with good stable-yard manure and rotten leaves. The best way is to trench and ridge the ground at the same time, burying the manure deeply, so as to encourage deep rooting, an advantage during dry weather. Some time before the ground is required, level down the ridges; if the soil is heavy, fork it over several times, in order to bring it into good condition before forming the trenches. The latter, for tall-growing varieties, should be 6 ft. apart, and for dwarfer sorts 4 ft. apart. Make them 18 inches deep and 15 inches wide. If possible, they ought to run north and south, in order that the plants may have the benefit of the midday sun. Tread the bottom of them quite firm, and place in them from 6 to 9 inches of perfectly rotten manure, always preferring rich, well-decayed material from the stable-yard. On this must be placed some soot, when the trenches will be ready to receive the plants. By placing the manure deep the roots reach it just when the centre leaves that are blanched are coming up, and if the plants are well fed at that time they form large hearts, crisp, and white as ivory.

FOR VERY EARLY CELERY, prepare some rich soil and fill a seed-pan or box with the compost, firming it well; sow the seeds thinly, cover them over lightly with some finely sifted soil, and water through a fine-rosed watering-pot, placing the pans or boxes upon a shelf in the stove or in a vinery at work. The seeds will soon germinate, and when the young plants have made two or three leaves, prick them off into boxes in rich loamy soil with plenty of manure, a portion of leaf-mould, and a sprinkling of silver sand to keep the compost open. Seeds for the early crop ought to be sown in February, and the seedlings will be ready to plant out as soon as all danger from frost is over. Sometimes early Celery plants are grown in 4-inch pots where pits or houses are at command, and thus treated when planted out they sustain no check when planted in the trenches and well watered.

A second sowing may be made about the middle of March, either in boxes in a warm house or pit, or a slight hot-bed on which are put 6 inches of fine, rich soil made pretty firm, covering lightly with some finely sifted soil. Prepare a piece of ground by treading it firmly and placing on it 6 inches of rotten horse manure and leaf-mould in equal portions, tread firmly, and cover with 2 inches of fine, rich soil. When the plants have made two or three leaves, prick them out in rows 4 inches apart upon the bed thus prepared, firming them well in as the planting proceeds, and watering them with a fine-rosed pot, so as to settle the soil round them. If at hand, a frame might be placed over the bed for a short time until the young plants have got established, giving plenty of air during the daytime, or the plants can be covered with mats at night. If properly cared for, they will be fit to be transplanted into the trenches in two months from the time the seed was sown.

For late plants a sowing may be made in April the same as in March, only the plants will need no protection when pricked out.

TRENCHES for Celery are often made between rows of early Peas, which shade the Celery plants when newly planted in hot weather, and when the Pea crop is harvested the Celery has the full benefit of sun and air. The trenches being ready for the reception of the plants, water them the day previous to transplanting; lift them carefully with a trowel, preserving every fibre, replant 1 ft. apart, press the soil firmly round the roots, water well, and shade for a few days if the weather be dry and warm. The summer treatment consists in keeping the ground free from weeds by frequent hoeings, watering twice a week if the weather is very dry, and once if dull. When the plants are from 6 to 9 inches high, weak manure water may be given them once a week. This is prepared by soaking either cow or horse manure in a large tub or tank, applying a portion of soot with the manure water, or a handful of soot may be scattered occasionally around the plants before watering them. This destroys slugs and feeds the plants, giving them a fine green colour. In exposed situations it is often necessary to tie the leaves up when 1 ft. or so high, to save them from being broken by high winds, using for the purpose strands of fine matting, but be careful that the ties do not cut the

leaves when growing. It is best not to earth the plants up much until they have nearly completed their growth. Merely scatter a little soil over the roots once a fortnight to serve as a mulching and induce the roots to come to the surface.

BLANCHING requires from five to seven weeks after the final earthing. Before commencing to earth up, all small leaves and any suckers, or secondary shoots, which may have grown from the base of the plants should be removed; tie the leaves carefully with some pieces of thin bast, which will give way as the plants swell. Some use tubes for blanching, such as drain-pipes, placed round the plants; others paper collars, and some employ clean paper, which keeps the soil from getting into the hearts of the plants when earthing is being performed, raising the collars as the earthing proceeds, or the collars may be left upon the plants. If tubes are not used, the soil must be banked up in the usual way at several times, being careful to keep the leaves close together, so that the heads may be straight and compact after being blanched. Choose dry weather for earthing, for if damp the hearts are sure to rot. Before earthing, scatter a little lime round each plant, which destroys all slugs, which are often destructive to Celery during the winter in damp soil. A sprinkling may also be used when proceeding with the earthing.

Celery may be grown in single rows or as many as may be thought fit, making the trenches wide enough to receive the number of rows intended. One row is the most convenient in private gardens, and even market growers adopt single rows more than double ones. When the earthing is finished, and before severe frost sets in, cover the tops of the ridges with dry straw, or better, if at hand, some dry bracken, which prevents the frost from injuring the tops of the leaves and keeps the hearts of the plants dry. Perfect specimens of Celery must have the following good points, viz. the leaf, or stalk, must be broad, thick, crisp, free from ridges and stringiness, and the heads good in form and weight.—W. C.

MARKET GARDEN CULTURE.—The valley of the Thames is well adapted for Celery culture, and many acres of land in the Fulham fields and elsewhere are occupied by it. The sowing for the first crop of Celery is generally made early in February; a large main sowing is made in March, and for the latest crop sowing takes place in the middle or end of April. The early and main sowings are usually made in frames on hot-beds, but for a late crop the seed is sometimes sown in the open air on manure beds or in similar positions. The seed is sown at all times rather thickly, in moist, light soil, and is but lightly covered. When up, the seedlings, if too thick, are thinned out to 1 inch or so apart. Some dig out trenches and fill them with fermenting material, on which they place a few inches thick of light rich soil, and after sowing the seed cover the bed with mats or rough litter until the seed has germinated, when the coverings are removed during the daytime and replaced at night should the weather be unfavourable.

In all cases the beds on which Celery seed is sown are made firm either by treading or rolling, and a little light soil is sifted through a fine sieve over the seed after it has been sown. The seedlings in all cases are freely exposed to light and air in order to render them stout and stocky. Those from the first sowing, when large enough, are pricked out in frames on a bed of rotted manure, and those from the main and later sowings are pricked out in May and June on beds similarly prepared on a sheltered border out-of-doors. In these positions they receive abundance of water in order to keep them growing, for a check at any period in the growth of Celery plants is very detrimental. The plants are usually pricked out in rows from 6 to 8 inches apart, about half that distance being allowed between the plants in the rows. When planting time has arrived a spade is run between the rows and a good soaking of water is given, after which nothing more is done for a few days. A spade is then pushed under the plants, which are thus carefully raised, separated, and taken on hand-barrows or in boxes direct to the trenches. When planted, a good watering is given them, and thus they sustain a very slight check through removal; but market gardeners seldom plant Celery in double rows, as is done in private gardens, one row in each trench being considered the most profitable way. The strongest plants are in all cases selected and placed in trenches by themselves, and the weaker ones by themselves. In that way a succession is formed, uniformity in the size of the heads is secured, and thus a whole row of plants becomes marketable at one time. They need no sorting, and the ground being cleared is made available for other crops.

The ground on which it is intended to plant Celery is, if possible, prepared in autumn by being heavily manured and trenched, the surface being either thrown up in ridges or left in as rough a state as possible until spring, when it is levelled down to be sown with Radishes. In that case the land is marked out into a series of beds from 5 to 6 ft. wide, leaving good wide alleys between them. In these alleys is placed an extra supply of manure, and in them are planted the earliest Celery plants. By the time these require earthing up the Radishes will have been marketed and the ground cleared of weeds, etc. Sometimes however, whole fields are marked off in beds and the trenches dug out in winter in readiness to receive the Celery, the beds being planted with Lettuces or early Cauliflowers. Market gardeners never plant Celery in deep trenches; on the contrary, they contrive to allow the roots, after the crop is fully earthed up, to be considerably above the bottom of the ridges. Especially is this the case as regards late crops, which in damp, badly drained soils are very precarious. During the growing season Celery is abundantly supplied with water, as are also the crops of salad plants, or French Beans, which are invariably grown between the lines.

Earthing up is performed for the first time when the plants have become fairly established and are 6 inches high; the sides of the trenches are chopped down on the morning of some fine day, well broken up, and allowed to dry for an hour or two, when two men, one on each side of the row, push the soil with the back of a wooden rake to within a few inches of the plants, so as to leave a ridge for the reception of water. At the next earthing the soil is pressed tightly round the bases of the plants, and more of it is chopped down from the ridges; and at the third, which is the final earthing, the ridges are made firm and smooth in such a way as to effectually throw off the rain. The Red and White varieties of Celery are the principal kinds grown, and under the treatment just recorded they become very crisp and solid. Sometimes a crop of Celery is grown for culinary purposes early in spring, and in that case the seeds are sown in June, and the young plants are pricked out rather closely together; they are never earthed up more than once, the object being to secure plants with flavour rather than crispness and good quality.

KEEPING CELERY.—In severer climates than ours it is often necessary to resort to other and better methods of preserving Celery than are generally practised in this country. In America, where the winters are much harder than they are here, various methods are practised, but the following, described by Mr. Peter Henderson, of New York, we consider the neatest and best, and it would be as well, in cases of a severer season than usual, that it should be known in this country. Indeed, it would be better to adopt it always, as by so doing this vegetable, which all enjoy, may be kept better. Much disagreeable labour may also be avoided in digging in all sorts of weathers, apart from the injury to the plant from exposure to greatly varying temperatures and conditions of weather, as it is at present. "Get a box 4 or 5 ft. long, 12 inches wide, and 20 or 24 inches deep. In the bottom place 2 or 3 inches of sand or soil—it makes little difference what, provided it is something that will hold moisture. Into this box at the time when Celery is dug up (which in this district ranges from October 25 to November 25) have the Celery stalks packed perpendicularly with the roots resting on the sand. All that is necessary is to see that it is packed moderately tight, for if not packed tight the air would get around the stalks and prevent blanching. The box may be then set in any cool cellar, and will keep from the time it is put away until March if necessary. A box of the size named will hold about from seventy-five to one hundred roots, according to size. It is quite common for many families to purchase their Celery from the market gardeners, place it away in a box in this manner in their cellars during the winter, where it can be conveniently got at, and it costs also in this way less than half what it does when purchased tied up from the benches in the market in the usual way. We have for many years used this method for what we want for our own private use, finding it much more convenient to get it out of the boxes in the cellar than to go to the trenches in the open ground for it in all weathers."

USES.—The leaf-stalks of some kinds and the roots of others are eaten either raw or boiled. In England the seeds (or an extract from them) are used for flavouring soups. Popular as Celery is in England as a cooked vegetable, we have still much to learn about it. The Turnip-rooted, the best of all winter roots, is hardly ever seen out of a few foreign houses, and these have to depend on imported supplies—often stale!

Cultivation, in developing the leaves and the root of the Celery, has produced two very distinct varieties of the same plant, which are differently employed and require a different mode of culture. These are known as the Common, or Stalked, Celery, and the Celeriac, or Turnip-rooted Celery.

Common Celery (French, *Céleri a Côtes ;* German, *Bleich-Sellerie ;* Danish, *Blad-Selleri*).—This is undoubtedly the most anciently known and the most commonly cultivated kind. It requires a good, rich, soft, well-manured soil, rather moist than dry, and is not usually sown where the crop is to be grown. The earliest sowings are made on a hot-bed in January, February, or March, and the seedlings, while still small, are pricked out into another hot-bed, and not planted out permanently until the end of April or the beginning of May. Subsequent sowings, which may be continued till June, are made in the open ground, so as to have a successional supply of fresh, tender stalks all the year round. The seedlings of these later sowings are not pricked out, but simply thinned and allowed to remain where they were sown, until they are finally planted out. When this takes place, the plants are set in rows, with a distance of 10 to 12 inches from plant to plant in all directions, and the only attention they require is that of hoeing, and frequent and plentiful waterings, in which they delight.

Before the stalks are sent to table, they are blanched by excluding the light from them. This is done in many ways, most usually by tying up the outer leaves around the inner ones, and then earthing up the stalks as far as the lowest leaves.

Solid White Celery (⅙ natural size).

This is not generally done all at once, but at first the stalks are earthed up for about one-third of their height, and, eight or ten days afterwards, up to two-thirds, the remaining third being completed at the end of eight or ten days more.

Sometimes the plants are taken up with balls and planted side by side in a trench, which is then filled with soil ; and sometimes they are planted in spring in trenches, where they are blanched when the time comes, without being transplanted, by filling in the trench with the soil which was taken out in opening it.

Solid White Celery (*Céleri Plein Blanc*).—A vigorous-growing

Curled Solid White Celery
(⅙ natural size).

kind, 16 to 20 inches high, with fleshy, solid, and tender stalks, which, in blanching, become of a yellowish-white colour. Leaves erect.

Mammoth White Celery (*Céleri Turc*).—A sub-variety of the preceding kind, of extremely vigorous growth, attaining a height of from 20 inches to 2 ft. Stalks very solid, thick, and long, but relatively not so broad as those of the last-mentioned variety. This form seems to be disappearing.

Curled Solid White Celery (*Céleri Plein Blanc Frisé*).—A very distinct variety, with numerous large leaves. Leaflets crisped and undulated, and of a lighter green colour than those of any other variety. The stalks are thickish and perfectly solid, and the leaves, instead of being bitter, like those of other kinds, have a mild flavour and can be used in salads. This new variety was raised in the neighbourhood of Niort (Vendée), and began to be distributed about the year 1870. It is, perhaps, somewhat more sensitive to cold than the plain-leaved kinds.

Dwarf Solid White, Sandringham, or Incomparable Celery (*Céleri Plein Blanc Court Hâtif*).— A more thickish kind than the common Solid White Celery. Stalks broad and very solid; leaves short. This variety is easily blanched, on account of the great number of its leaves, which cover one another closely, so that very white stalks may be obtained from it by merely earthing them up, without the trouble of tying up the leaves. In the United States a variety is grown, under the name of Boston Market Dwarf Celery,

Golden Yellow Celery.

which comes very close to the present kind, differing from it only in being somewhat taller. Unfortunately, very frequently it has the defect of sending out underground shoots or suckers.

Golden Yellow Celery (*Céleri Plein Blanc Doré, Céleri Chemin*).— A variety of the Dwarf Solid White Celery, remarkable for the yellow or golden hue which suffuses the leaves and stalks, a peculiarity of coloration which does not appear in any way to affect the vigour of the plant. It grows rapidly and to as large a size as the Dwarf Solid White variety. The leaves exhibit the golden tint more especially towards their extremities, and render the variety easy to be recognized among all other kinds. The stalks are naturally of an ivory-white colour, so that they do not require to be artificially blanched to improve their appearance ; *nevertheless, they are more tender and better for table use when earthed-up in the usual way.* This variety was raised by M. Chemin in his market gardens near Paris.

White Plume Celery.—For some time past a great deal has been said in America about a new variety of Celery, to which the above name has been given, and which has even been asserted by some to be identical with the Golden Celery described in the preceding article. Several comparative trials, however, which we have made, have convinced us that the two varieties are entirely distinct. The White Plume variety has evidently sprung from the ordinary Solid White Celery, and not from the Dwarf Solid White kind. It grows much taller, and has more slender and narrower stalks than the yellow-tinted variety, from which it also completely differs in being of a silvery green colour, in striking contrast to the warm golden hue of the French variety. It is a very good kind.

Dwarf Solid White Celery (*Céleri Plein Blanc Court à Grosses Côtes*).—This variety, allied to the preceding kind, affords the same facility for blanching, and it has the additional advantage that it does not produce suckers. The stalks are extremely broad, solid, and erect, so that the plants may be grown very close together, thereby obtaining from an equal area as heavy a crop as that produced by the larger varieties. The stalks are more largely developed in proportion to the dimensions of the leaves in this variety than in any other.

Amongst good English varieties of White Celery the following are worthy of note :—*Danesbury Celery*, or *Veitch's Solid White Celery*,

Dwarf Solid White Celery (⅙ natural size).

and *Dickson's Mammoth White Celery.*—These are compact varieties, with very solid stalks, something like those of the Dwarf Solid White Celery. *Seymour's White, Goodwin's White,* or *Northumberland White*

Celery.—A very tall kind, somewhat resembling the Mammoth White Celery.

London Market Red, or **Ivery's None-such Celery** (*Céleri Violet de Tours*).—A vigorous-growing kind, with very broad stalks of a purplish-tinged green colour, and very solid, tender, and brittle. Leaves half-spreading, broad, and of a dark-green colour. It is a very hardy variety, and of excellent quality.

Soup Celery (⅙ natural size).

In England a great number of varieties of Red-stalked Celery are grown, of which, in addition to the present one, we may mention :— *Carter's Incomparable Crimson,* or *Hood's Dwarf Red, Celery.*—This is dwarfer than any other Red variety, but very solid and crops well. *Major Clarke's Solid Red, Wilcox's Dunham Red, Ramsey's Solid Red,* or *Turner's Red Celery.* — A vigorous-growing variety, almost as tall as the Mammoth White, but with more branching leaves, which are also of a deeper green colour. *Manchester Red, Laing's Mammoth, Sulham Prize Pink,* or *Giant Red, Celery.*—An extremely vigorous-growing kind, attaining a height of over 3 ft.

Soup Celery (*Céleri à Couper*).—A variety that has been very little improved by cultivation, and is probably a reversion towards the wild state. It is hardy, and produces an abundance of erect-growing leaves. Stalks hollow, rather thin, tender, and brittle. The plant sends up great numbers of suckers, and is grown for its leaves, which are cut, like Parsley, and used in soups and for seasoning. After being cut it produces new leaves.

CELERIAC, or TURNIP-ROOTED CELERY.

French, Céleri-rave. *German,* Knoll-Sellerie. *Flemish* and *Dutch,* Knoll-Selderij. *Danish,* Knold-Selleri. *Italian,* Sedano-rapa. *Spanish,* Apio-nabo.

In this kind of Celery it is the root which has been developed by cultivation, and not the leaf-stalks, which remain hollow and of moderate size, while the flavour is so bitter that they are unfit for table use. On the other hand, the root (which, even in the wild plant, forms an enlargement of some size before it divides into numerous rootlets) has been brought by cultivation to easily attain the size of the fist, and often even double that size. The Turnip-rooted Celery is an excellent vegetable, but, as its introduction into cultivation is of comparatively recent date, it is not, as yet, very commonly grown. It keeps well, and forms a valuable contribution to the winter supply.

CULTURE.—It is grown nearly in the same way as the Common Celery, and, like it, requires good, rich, moist, mellow, and well-manured soil. It is generally sown in a nursery-bed in March, and planted out in May. The plants require no further attention than frequent waterings, and to have the ground kept free from weeds. The market gardeners of Paris are in the habit, while the plants are growing, of chopping off with the spade the rootlets which grow around the main root, under the (perhaps erroneous) impression that by doing so they cause the main root to attain a greater size.

Common Celeriac, or **Turnip-rooted Celery** (*Céleri-rave Ordinaire*).—Leaves smaller than those of the Common or Stalk Celery; stalk always hollow, bitter-tasted, and tinged with a red or bronzy hue; root forming a sort of ball, which is roundish or conical in the upper part, and divided underneath into a great number of rootlets or ramifications, which are more or less fleshy and tangled together. The weight of this, when trimmed of the leaves and rootlets, ranges from 7 to over 10 oz. in the Common variety, but roots of

Common Celeriac, or Turnip-rooted Celery (⅙ natural size).   Apple-shaped Celeriac (⅙ natural size).

much larger size have been obtained from other varieties, of which the following is one.

Smooth Paris Celeriac (*Céleri-rave Gros Lisse de Paris*).—Root generally broader than long, and somewhat irregular in shape; leaves rather numerous, more spreading than erect.

Early Erfurt Celeriac (*Céleri-rave d'Erfurt*).—A smaller kind than the preceding one, but also earlier. Root very clean-skinned, regularly rounded in shape, and with a fine neck.

Prague Celeriac (*Céleri-rave Géant de Prague*).—This may be described as a highly-developed form of the preceding variety, the roots of which are almost spherical, evenly shaped, and without rootlets, except on the under part. They are usually double the size of those of the Erfurt variety, and the leaf-stalks are somewhat stouter and whiter.

Apple-shaped Celeriac (*Céleri-rave Pomme à Petite Feuille*).—A sub-variety of the Early Erfurt kind, with slight, half-erect leaves, and long purplish leaf-stalks. Root very regularly rounded in shape, and entirely free from rootlets on the upper part.

There is an extraordinarily small kind of Turnip-rooted Celery, the leaves of which are only 4 or 5 inches long, while the root is seldom larger than a walnut. It is more curious than useful, and is known as the Tom Thumb Erfurt Turnip-rooted Celery (*Céleri-rave d'Erfurt Tom Thumb*).

CHERVIL.

Scandix Cerefolium, L.; *Anthriscus Cerefolium*, Hoffm. *Umbelliferæ.*

French, Cerfeuil. *German*, Kerbel. *Flemish* and *Dutch*, Kervel. *Danish*, Have-kjorvel. *Italian*, Cerfoglio. *Spanish*, Perifollo. *Portuguese*, Cerefolio.

Native of Southern Europe.—Annual.—Leaves very much divided, with oval, incised, pinnatifid leaflets; stem 16 to 20 inches high, smooth and few-leaved; flowers small, white, in umbels; seed black, long, pointed, marked with a longitudinal furrow. A gramme contains about 450 seeds, and a litre of them weighs about 380 grammes. Their germinating power lasts for two or three years. The seed may be sown all through the year in the open ground, where the crop is to grow, but in very hot weather it is better to sow in a shady position with a northern aspect. According to the season, the leaves may be cut in from six weeks to two months after sowing. The leaves are aromatic, and are used for seasoning and in salads. It is in much demand in English gardens.

Common, or Plain-leaved, Chervil (*Cerfeuil Commun*).—Leaves slight, very much divided, and of a light-green colour; stems slender, slightly swollen below the joints, channelled, and smooth; flowers in thin umbels produced in tiers on all the upper half of the stem. This is one of the most widely distributed and best known of all kitchen-garden plants. It is seldom used by itself, but, from its fine, strong, aromatic flavour, forms an almost indispensable accompaniment to a great number of dishes. It constitutes the basis of the mixture known by the French name of *fines herbes*. It can be grown in almost any climate, but, where the heat is great, it should have a shaded position.

Curled Chervil (*Cerfeuil Frisé*).—A variety of the preceding kind,

Curled Chervil (¼ natural size).

with crisped or curled leaves. It has exactly the same perfume and flavour as the Common, or Plain-leaved, Chervil, and is better for garnishing dishes. It should always be grown in preference to the Common kind, as it has all the following advantages, viz. it is easily cultivated, early, of vigorous growth, productive, and, as we have just mentioned, it is handsomer and more ornamental. Its chief merit, however, is that it cannot be confounded with any other plant; for although the least-practised eye may be able to distinguish the Chervil from other umbelliferous plants, there is a double security in cultivating a form of it for which no wild plant whatever can possibly be mistaken.

TURNIP-ROOTED CHERVIL.

Chærophyllum bulbosum, L.   *Umbelliferæ.*

Cerfeuil tubéreux.

Native of Southern Europe.—Biennial.—Plant hairy, with leaves very much divided, spreading on the ground, and with violet-coloured leaf-stalks. Root very much swollen, almost like a short Carrot, but generally smaller, with a very fine skin of a dark-gray colour, and yellowish-white flesh; stem very stout and tall, 3 ft. or more in height, swollen below the joints, of a violet tint, and covered on the lower part with long whitish hairs; seed long, pointed, slightly concave, of a light-brown colour on one side, and whitish on the other, and marked with three longitudinal furrows of no great depth.

Turnip-rooted Chervil (½ natural size).

A gramme contains about 450 seeds, and a litre of them weighs about 540 grammes. Their germinating power lasts for only one year.

CULTURE.—The seed should be sown in autumn, in well-prepared, mellow, well-drained soil, care being taken to cover it very slightly. It is generally quite sufficient to press the soil down well after sowing. The seed-bed should be kept very free from weeds, as the seeds will not germinate before spring. The seed may also be sown in spring, if the precaution is taken of keeping it in the meantime between layers of sand in a box, basin, or other vessel, in which it should be placed as soon as it is ripe. If this is done, it will germinate immediately after it is sown, but if kept in any other way, it will not germinate until the spring of the following year. While growing, the plants require no attention at any time, except frequent waterings. About July, the leaves begin to lose colour and to dry up, which indicates that the roots are nearly matured. When the leaves are quite withered, the roots may be taken up, if the ground is required for other purposes, but it is better not to commence using them too soon, as they improve very much in quality by being allowed to remain in the ground some weeks or even months, provided they are in well-drained ground and safe from frost.

USES.—The roots are eaten boiled. The flesh is floury and sweet, with a peculiar aromatic flavour. They keep well all through autumn and winter.

Attempts have been made of late years to introduce into kitchen gardens the culture of the Prescott Chervil (*Cerfeuil de Prescott*), a

o

native of Siberia, which produces large edible roots like those of the variety just described, and is grown much in the same way. Its roots are longer and larger than those of the Common Tuberous-rooted Chervil, but their flavour is coarser and more like that of the Parsnip. There is no doubt that several other biennial umbelliferous plants, which have naturally fleshy roots, might be converted by cultivation into useful vegetables.

CHICKLING VETCH.

Lathyrus sativus, L.　*Leguminosæ.*

French, Gesse cultivée, Lentille d'Espagne, Pois carré.　*German*, Essbare Platterbse, Weisse Platterbse, Deutsche Kicher.　*Flemish*, Platte erwt.　*Spanish*, Arveja. *Spanish-American*, Muelas.

Native of Europe.—Annual.—Stem winged, 16 to 20 inches high, maintaining an erect position with difficulty without some support; leaves compound, pinnate, without an odd one, the place of which is supplied by a prehensile tendril; leaflets four in number, long and narrow; flower-stalks slender, axillary, one-flowered, commencing to appear at the fifth or sixth joint of the stem. Flowers smaller than those of the Pea, but of the same shape, white, tinged with blue on the standard; pods broad and short, very flat, thick, and winged; seed white, somewhat variable in shape, triangular or square, broader and thicker at the side of the *hilum* than at the other side. A gramme contains four seeds, and a litre of them weighs about 750 grammes. Their germinating power lasts for five years. The seed is sown in spring, like Peas, in the place where the crop is to grow, and the growing plants require no special attention. The unripe seeds are eaten like green Peas; when ripe and dried, they may be used to make pea-soup. The use of this Vetch is very little understood in England, but we have heard that Spanish cooks make a nice dish of it.

CHICK-PEA.

Cicer arietinum, L.　*Leguminosæ.*

French, Pois chiche.　*German*, Kicher-Erbse.　*Italian*, Cece.　*Spanish*, Garbanzos. *Portuguese*, Chicāro.

Native of Southern Europe.—Annual.—A rough-stemmed plant, almost always branching near the ground, and from 20 inches to 2 ft. in height. Stem hairy, as are also the leaves, which are compound, pinnate with an odd one, and with small, roundish, toothed leaflets; flowers axillary, small, solitary, white in the ordinary variety, and reddish in the kinds which have coloured seeds; pods short, very much swollen, hairy, like the rest of the plant, with a hard membranous lining, and each containing two seeds, one of which is often abortive. Seed roundish, but compressed and flattened at the sides, and with a kind of beak formed by the projection of the radicle; its appearance resembles that of a ram's head and horns, whence the specific name of the plant. A litre of the seeds weighs about 780 grammes, and 10 grammes contain about 30 seeds. Their germinating power lasts, like that of all other Peas, for at least three years.

Culture.—The seed is sown in spring, as soon as the ground is warm enough, preferably in drills 16 to 20 inches apart, and so that the plants will be 8 to 10 inches from one another in the drill. They are treated much in the same way as Dwarf Kidney Beans, and require no attention except the occasional use of the hoe. They bear dry weather better than almost any other kind of leguminous plant. In the south of France the seed may be sown in February.

USES.—The ripe seeds are eaten either boiled entire or made into pea-soup. They are sometimes roasted and used as a substitute for coffee.

White Chick-pea (*Pois Chiche Blanc*).—This is the most generally cultivated variety, and, indeed, is the only one that deserves to be considered a table vegetable. There are a great many forms of it, differing slightly from one another in earliness and the size of the seed. In Spain some kinds of remarkable size and beauty are grown.

There are two varieties of the Chick-Pea grown in the East, one of which has red and the other black seeds. The former is very extensively cultivated in the East Indies, both as a table vegetable and for feeding cattle, and is one of the kinds known as Horse Gram, as it is very much used for feeding horses. The Black-seeded variety is more curious than useful.

CHICORY, or SUCCORY.

Cichorium Intybus, L.   *Compositæ.*

French, Chicorée sauvage, C. Barbe-de-capucin. *German*, Wilde *oder* bittere Cichorie.
Danish, Sichorie. *Italian*, Cicoria selvatica, Radicchio, Radicia. *Spanish*, Achicoria
amarga, o agreste. *Portuguese*, Chicoria.

Native of Europe.—Perennial.—Radical leaves of a deep-green colour, sinuated, with pointed, toothed, or cut lobes, and hairy, often reddish, stalks; stems from 5 to over 6 ft. high, cylindrical, downy, green or reddish, and with spreading branches; flowers large, blue, axillary, almost sessile; seed generally smaller, browner, and more glistening than that of the Endive. A gramme contains about 700 seeds, and a litre of them weighs about 400 grammes. Their germinating property lasts for eight years.

The Common Chicory, which is found in almost all parts of Europe in the wild

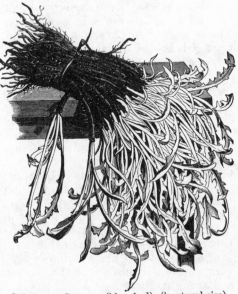

Chicory, or Succory (blanched), (⅙ natural size).

state, has been used from time immemorial for salads, and also as a medicinal plant. When cultivated, its produce is increased in quantity and improved in quality, the leaves losing much of their natural bitterness. Forced in darkness, in winter, it forms the highly esteemed blanched vegetable known as *Barbe-de-capucin.* The large-rooted variety of it, treated in the same way, produces the vegetable known in Belgium by the name of *Witloof.*

CULTURE.—The Common Chicory is an exceedingly easy plant to grow. The seed is sown in spring, in the place where the crop is to stand, in drills, or, more commonly, along the sides of alleys, and is generally sown very thick, in order that the leaves of the plants may be closely crowded together. The leaves are gathered as they are wanted by cutting them near the ground with a sickle or a knife. They may be cut several times in the same year. It is a good plan to make a fresh sowing every year, clearing out the old plants which have fallen off in produce and are about to run to seed. In order to produce the *Barbe-de-capucin,* plants are employed which have been sown rather thinly in the open ground about the end of June. At the beginning of winter, these are taken up, and the leaves are trimmed off about ½ inch above the neck of the root; then, in a dark cellar, or other place, the temperature of which is not too cold, sloping heaps are made, composed of alternate layers of sand or of soil taken from well-drained ground, and of Chicory roots placed horizontally and with the necks of the roots pointing outwards, clear of the sand or soil, so that the leaves may grow freely. If the soil used is too dry, a slight watering will be necessary, after which the plants are left to themselves, and in about three weeks' time, if the temperature is not too low, leaves 8 to 10 inches long may be gathered.

A few years ago, in the neighbourhood of Paris, they began to use for this purpose the Large-rooted Chicory, the roots of which are allowed to attain the thickness of the finger before they are forced. These roots, being very straight and regular in shape, are easily arranged in the forcing heaps, and the leaves are generally much larger and stouter than those of the Common Chicory.

USES.—The leaves are used as salad, either in their natural state or blanched, as described above. Cut into thin shreds, and mixed with oil and vinegar, they are very largely used in some countries as a seasoning for boiled beef.

Red Italian Chicory (*Chicorée Sauvage à Feuille Rouge*).—In the Common Chicory the leaves are sometimes marked with red, but generally only on the midrib; in this variety the coloration extends to the blade of the leaf, where it appears in the form of irregular spots or blotches, which are of a brown colour on leaves that are green, and of a fine bright red on leaves which have been blanched in a dark place. This variegation has a very pretty effect, and constitutes the chief merit of the variety, which, either by itself or mixed with the Common Barbe-de-capucin, makes a very nice salad.

Large-rooted Chicory (*Chicorée Sauvage à Grosse Racine*).—This variety is distinguished by the large size of the root, which is thick and straight, attaining a length of 12 to 14 inches, with a diameter of about 2 inches below the neck. It is the kind which is employed for the manufacture of " Coffee Chicory." This is obtained by cutting the roots into thin slices, which are then roasted and ground. The plant is grown for this purpose chiefly in Germany, Belgium, and the north of France. There are two very distinct varieties of it, named the *Brunswick* and the *Magdeburg* Large-rooted Chicory.

The *Brunswick* variety has very deeply cut leaves, divided like those of the Dandelion, and more or less spreading horizontally, while the leaves of the *Magdeburg* variety are undivided and stand quite

Brunswick Chicory (⅓ natural size).   Magdeburg Chicory (⅓ natural size).

erect. The latter is considered the more productive of the two. Its roots are longer and thicker, although not quite so regular in shape. It is not unusual to find single roots of it which weigh from 14 to 17 oz., and which look very like dwarf White Sugar Beets, such as the German kinds, when they are grown very close together. As already mentioned, the Large-rooted Chicory is often employed to form the *Barbe-de-capucin*.

Witloof, or Large Brussels Chicory (*Chicorée à Grosse Racine de Bruxelles* ; Flemish, *Verbeterde Hofsui-kerij*).—This plant may be considered as a sub-variety of the Magdeburg Large-rooted Chicory. Its principal merit consists in the width of its leaves and the great size of their ribs or stalks. When blanched in the way described further on, it forms the vegetable which the Belgians call *Witloof,* as already mentioned. As shown in the illustration, this very much resembles a blanched head of Cos Lettuce in appearance.

Witloof, or Large Brussels Chicory (⅓ natural size).

CULTURE.—In order to obtain good specimens of *Witloof,* well-grown roots of the plant should be used; and to obtain these, the seed should be sown in the open ground, in June, in drills 10 or 12 inches apart, selecting good, deep, rich soil for the purpose. The plants are allowed to grow on till the beginning of winter, without any attention except keeping the ground free from weeds, and watering when necessary. In the beginning of November, the roots (which by that time should have attained a diameter of from 1¼ to nearly 2 inches) are taken up, those which have divided or too narrow leaves being thrown aside, if any such are met with, as well as any which bear several heads. The leaves of all the selected roots are then trimmed off about 1½ inch from the neck, and any secondary shoots that may appear on the sides of the roots are pinched out, the lower end of the roots being also shortened so as to bring them all to a uniform length of 8 to 10 inches. They are then ready for planting, for which a trench 16 to 18 inches deep is opened, and the roots are placed upright in it, about 1½ inch from one another ; the necks of the roots will thus be about 8 inches below the level of the ground. The trench is then filled up completely with good, light, well-drained soil. If a speedy growth is desired, the surface of the trench, or of whatever portion of it is to be forced, should be covered with a layer of manure varying in depth according to the quality of the manure and the prevailing temperature, but never less than 16 inches, nor more than a little over 3 ft. In about a month's time, the leaves will have attained their proper size. The manure is then taken off, the roots are dug up, and the blanched head is cut off with a portion of the neck of the root attached. Attempts have been made, with some amount of success, to force the same roots a second time. In this case, a number of fresh shoots are emitted around the cut at the neck, each consisting of a number of leaves which produce a crop intermediate in appearance between the *Witloof* and the common *Barbe-de-capucin*. The *Witloof* is eaten raw as a salad, and also boiled, like the Curled Endives.

Broad-leaved Chicory (*Chicorée Sauvage Améliorée*).—This is a very different-looking plant from the Common Chicory, of which it is a

variety obtained by successive sowings of seeds from selected plants. The leaves are broad, very large, undulated and sometimes crimped, always more or less covered with short hairs, and often resembling those of the Green Broad-leaved Winter Endive in their form and arrangement. When the plant runs to seed the flowering stems are exactly like those of the Common

Broad-leaved Chicory (⅛ natural size).

Chicory, so that it is very certain that this plant is a variety of it, and not a hybrid between the Common Chicory and the Endive, as some persons are inclined to think. We should be much more disposed to assign this hybrid origin to the Curled-leaved Chicory, described further on.

Improved Variegated Chicory (*Chicorée Sauvage Améliorée Panachée*).—A form of the preceding variety, which has the leaves blotched and striped with red, or, in the case of plants grown in the open air with brown, which, however, changes to red if the plants are placed in darkness. This variegation, which is very bright in colour, causes plants which have been artificially blanched to form a very pretty salad.

Curled-leaved Chicory (*Chicorée Sauvage Améliorée Frisée*).—This variety, curious from the appearance of its leaves, which are very finely cut, slashed, and curled, appears to take after the Endive to a certain extent. There is the more reason for supposing it to be a cross between the two species as it is extremely variable, the leaves being often nearly quite smooth, and it does not appear to be quite as hardy as the other garden varieties of Chicory.

M. Jacquin, sen., who assiduously and successfully occupied himself in improving the Common Chicory, formerly effected the complete establishment of a certain number of varieties. None of them, however, we believe, are now in cultivation.

CHINESE AMARANTH.

Amarantus spec.   Amarantaceæ.

Amarante de Chine.

Native of China.—Annual.—Several species or varieties of Amaranth are often grown as table vegetables in the warm parts of Asia, and chiefly in China and the East Indies. Seeds of these have, on several occasions, been brought to Europe, where, however, the plants do not appear to have ever come into general cultivation, notwithstanding their undeniable value; for their quality as a table vegetable is quite equal to that of Spinach, their produce is very considerable, and their cultivation extremely easy. These remarks are especially applicable to the Chinese Amaranth, which was imported in the year 1839 by Captain Geoffroy. This is a branching plant, very like the *Amarantus tricolor* when it degenerates and becomes of a green or brownish-red colour. Its chief defect is that it is a late plant, and ripens its seeds with difficulty in the climate of Paris. The seed is sown in the open ground, in the place where the crop is to be grown, in May, and the plants should be plentifully watered during the summer. By sowing earlier, in a hot-bed, so as to have plants ready to plant out at the end of May, they may be had fit for use several weeks sooner. The leaves are used in the same way as Spinach.

Two other kitchen-garden varieties of Amaranth have been introduced into Europe, and have been equally neglected, notwithstanding their suitability for hot, dry localities. These are *Amarantus Mirza*, a native of the East Indies, and *Amarantus Hantsi-Shangaï*, which was brought under the notice of the Royal Horticultural Society of London by Mr. Robert Fortune.

CHIVES.

Allium Schœnoprasum, L.   Liliaceæ.

French, Ciboulette, Civette.   *German,* Schnittlauch.   *Flemish* and *Dutch,* Bieslook.
Italian, Cipollina.   *Spanish,* Cebollino.

Native of Europe.—Perennial.—A plant growing in thick tufts. Bulbs oval, small, scarcely as large as a hazel-nut, forming a compact mass by the intertangling of the fibrous roots; leaves very numerous, slender, and of a deep-green colour, resembling those of a grass, but

hollow, like those of the Onion; flower-stems very little taller than the leaves, bearing small terminal clusters of violet-red flowers, which are usually barren. Chives are always propagated by division of the tufts. The best time for dividing them is in March or April. The plants are usually grown as an edging, and appear to do better that way than when grown in a bed. It is a good plan to take them up and replant them every two or three years, as this has the effect of freshening up the tufts. The leaves, when wanted for table use,

Chives (⅛ natural size; separate stem, ¼ natural size).

are cut with a knife, and seem to grow more vigorously the oftener they are cut. They are used for seasoning, and are still much asked for and much grown in British gardens, more especially in the north.

CLARY.

Salvia Sclarea, L. *Labiatæ.*

Sauge Sclarée.

Native of South Europe.—Perennial, but cultivated as an annual or a biennial.—An herbaceous plant, with the radical leaves very broad,

oval-obtuse, broadly sinuated or toothed, woolly haired, of a grayish-green colour, and crimped like the leaves of Savoy Cabbage. Stem very tall, quadrangular, branching in the upper part and bearing long spikes of white or lilac flowers in clusters of two or three; seed brown or marbled, smooth, and shining. A gramme contains about 200 seeds, and a litre of them weighs about 650 grammes. Their germinating power lasts for three years. The plants do not run to seed until the second year from the time of sowing. After they flower, it is better to pull them up and replace them by young

Clary (1/12 natural size; detached sprig, ¼ natural size).

plants. The seed is sown in April, in drills 16 to 20 inches apart, or in a seed-bed, from which the seedlings are pricked out in May at the same distance from one another. During the summer hoeing and watering must not be neglected. In August, the first leaves may be gathered, and the plants will continue to yield up to June or July in the following year. The leaves are used for seasoning.

COCK'S-COMB SAINTFOIN.

Onobrychis Crista-galli, Lamk. *Leguminosæ.*

Hérisson.

Native of Southern France.—Annual.—Under the name of *Hérisson* (Hedgehog) a variety of Saintfoin is sometimes grown in France, which is remarkable for the singular form of its pods or seed-vessels. It is a small plant with slender leaves, the lower part of the stem almost trailing along the ground, and the remaining portion erect and bearing small spikes of rose-coloured flowers, which are succeeded by short, almost kidney-shaped pods, which have on the outer margin a toothed ridge or crest bearing some resemblance to the comb of a cock; the remainder of the pod being covered with short sharp-pointed projections. A litre of these pods weighs about 110 grammes, and a gramme contains about 9 of them. Each pod contains two seeds, the germinating power of which lasts for five years. The culture is of the simplest description. The seed is sown in spring, and the plants come into flower the same year. The plant is only grown as a curiosity, on account of the singular shape of the pods.

Cock's-comb Saintfoin (⅕ natural size; detached seed-vessels, ½ natural size).

CORIANDER.

Coriandrum sativum, L. *Umbelliferæ.*

French, Coriandre. German, Coriander. Flemish and Dutch, Koriander. Italian, Coriandorlo. Spanish, Culantro.

Native of Southern Europe.—Annual.—Stem branching, 2 to over 2½ ft. high; radical leaves not much divided, with incised-toothed leaflets of a roundish shape; stem leaves very much divided, with linear segments; flowers small, whitish, in umbels. Seed generally united in pairs, presenting the appearance of a small seed-vessel of the Flax-plant. Each seed is hemispherical, slightly concave on the side which joins the other seed, and of a lighter colour than the outer and convex side, which is of a brownish yellow and marked with deepish

longitudinal furrows.   A gramme contains about 90 seeds, and a litre
of them weighs about 320 grammes.   Their germinating power lasts for
six years.   The Coriander likes a warm and rather light soil.   The seed
is sown in autumn or spring, and the crop comes in in summer.   Uses.—
The seeds form an important article of commerce.   They are used in
the manufacture of liqueurs, and in a great number of culinary preparations.   Some writers say the leaves are used for seasoning, but this
statement seems odd, as all the green parts of the plant exhale a very
strong odour of the wood-bug, whence the Greek name of the plant.

CORN-SALAD.

Mâche.

A great number of kinds of Corn-salad, before running to seed, form
rosettes of tender edible leaves.   The genus Valerianella, to which
they all belong, is very rich in species, and these are not always easily
distinguished from one another.   They are, for the most part, small
plants of rapid growth, flowering but once, their entire period of
cultivation embracing the latter part of one year and the early part of
the next.   They generally run to seed in April or May, and the seed,
falling to the ground as soon as it is ripe, seldom germinates before
August.   Amongst the most commonly grown kinds are *Valerianella
olitoria* and *V. eriocarpa.*

COMMON CORN-SALAD, or LAMB'S-LETTUCE.

Valerianella olitoria, Mœnch.   *Valerianaceæ.*

French, Mâche commune.   *German,* Ackersalat.   *Flemish* and *Dutch,* Koornsalad.
Italian, Valeriana.   *Spanish,* Canonigos.   *Portuguese,* Herva benta.

Native of Europe.—An annual autumnal plant, that is, germinating
from seed in autumn and flowering and seeding in the ensuing spring.
—Radical leaves sessile, of an elongated spoon-shape, and of a slightly
grayish-green colour, with rather strongly marked veins, and growing
in pairs, placed cross-wise over one another, and forming a rather dense
rosette; stem angular, entirely herbaceous, forking several times, and
bearing very small flowers of a slightly bluish-white colour, in terminal
clusters at the extremities of the branches; seed almost globular,
slightly compressed, and grayish in colour.   A gramme contains about
1000 seeds, and a litre of them weighs about 280 grammes.   Their
germinating power lasts for five years.   This is one of the commonest
native plants, especially in cultivated ground, and, in some countries,
large quantities of it are gathered amongst the growing crops of winter
and spring wheat.   The wild form, however, is now seldom used for
kitchen-garden culture, and is only gathered where it is found growing
naturally, having been superseded in cultivation by the improved kinds
which we are about to describe.

Culture.—The seed is sown at the end of summer, or in autumn,
in any kind of soil, and the plant produces leaves from October to spring,
without requiring any attention or protection.   Generally, small thick-
set plants are preferred to those of coarser growth, the leaves of which

become too large and long. Contrary to what is experienced in the case of most other cultivated plants, seeds of the Corn-salad sown the same year in which they ripened do not germinate so soon or so well as those which are kept for a year before they are sown.

This plant is grown to some extent by the London market gardeners. The seed is sown for succession crops from August to October, the result being a supply from October till spring. There are two kinds grown —the Round and the Régence; the former is considered the best for winter use, but it runs to seed earlier in spring than the latter kind, therefore the Régence is sown in October for a supply after the Round kind has run to seed. The land on which the seed is sown is of a rich character, and in many cases it is sown broadcast among winter Onions or some similar crop for which the land has been liberally manured and otherwise well prepared. No more preparation is needed beyond raking the surface before and after the seed is sown. In gathering, the plants are pulled up by their roots, washed, and sold in small punnets. Most growers save their own seed. For this pur-pose a bed is specially prepared, levelled, and made fine on the surface, after which it is rolled or otherwise pressed down firmly. Good plants from the general sowing are then selected and planted thickly, and the bed is afterwards kept free from weeds. In summer the seed which ripens is allowed to fall on the bed, after which the old plants are pulled up and the seed is carefully swept off the hard surface and placed in water to separate it from the soil, which sinks to the bottom. The seed is then dried gradually in the sun and put in bags in a dry place, and under such conditions it will retain its vitality perfectly for several years. Corn-salad is not considered of itself a paying crop, but when sown amongst other crops it takes up but little room, and therefore in such cases may be considered to be fairly remunerative.

Uses.—The whole of the plant is used as a salad, and an excellent and distinct salad it is, far too little used in England. This forms with the outer stalks of Celery, one of the few really good mixed salads.

Round-leaved Corn-salad (*Mâche Ronde*).—A very distinct variety, differing from the Common kind in having much shorter leaves, which are narrowish at the base and widen upwards into an oval, almost rounded, blade. They also stand half-erect, instead of spreading on the ground, like those of the Common kind, and are of a clearer green colour, with the veins much less marked. The plant is productive and of rapid growth, and is the kind which is almost exclusively grown by the market gardeners around Paris. When sown in good soil in August, and

Round-leaved Corn-salad (⅓ natural size).

kept carefully free from weeds, it is wonderfully productive.

Large-seeded Corn-salad (*Mâche Ronde à Grosse Graine*).—A strong-growing kind, differing from the Common Corn-salad in the greater size of the plant, and also of the seed, which is nearly double as large as that of the other kind, a gramme containing only from 600 to 700 seeds. The leaves, like those of the Common kind, are comparatively narrow for their length, and are of a slightly grayish-green colour, and marked with numerous secondary veins. This variety is very much grown in Holland and Germany.

Étampes Corn-salad (*Mâche Verte d'Étampes*).—This variety is especially characterized by the ex-

tremely dark colour of its leaves, which, like those of the Common kind, are rather narrow and marked very perceptibly with veins; they are also often undulated or folded back at the edges. The whole plant forms a rosette somewhat more compact and stiff than that of the Common kind, and the leaves are rather thicker and more fleshy than those of the other varieties. They bear cold weather remarkably well, and they have the

Étampes Corn-salad (⅓ natural size). advantage of losing their freshness less than those of any other kind while they are being brought to market—a valuable quality in plants which have sometimes to be sent to markets at a considerable distance.

Cabbaging Corn-salad (*Mâche Verte à Cœur Plein*).— A very distinct variety, with short, roundish, smooth, half-erect, stiff, and intensely green leaves, the veins of which are hardly visible. It forms a compact rosette, the heart of which is full and firm. It is, to all appearance, a less-productive kind than the Round-leaved variety, but firmer, more compact, and much more agreeable to the taste in a salad. Like the preceding variety, it bears carriage well.

Cabbaging Corn-salad.

A very compact variety, with smooth green leaves, was grown for some years, under the name of the Chevreuse Smooth-leaved Green Corn-salad (*Mâche Verte de Chevreuse*). The Cabbaging Corn-salad is very probably derived from this variety, which it has superseded in cultivation.

ITALIAN CORN-SALAD.

Valerianella eriocarpa, Desv.

Mâche d'Italie, Régence.

Native of Southern Europe.— Annual.— This species is easily distinguished from the Common Corn-salad and its varieties, by the much lighter colour and greater length of its leaves, which are slightly hairy, and somewhat toothed on the edges towards the base. Seed of a more or less pale brown-colour, flattened, convex on one side and hollowed out on the other into a deepish channel, and surmounted by a sort of collar shaped like a twisted paper bag. A gramme contains about 1000 seeds, and a litre of them weighs about 280 grammes. Their germinating power lasts for four years. This variety is thought very highly of in

Italian Corn-salad (⅓ natural size).

the south of Europe, where it does not run to seed so soon as the Common kind, but in the neighbourhood of Paris it has the drawback of being somewhat sensitive to cold. Its culture and uses are exactly the same as those of the Common variety.

Lettuce-leaved Italian Corn-salad (*Mâche d'Italie à Feuille de Laitue*).—Leaves spreading on the ground, broad, roundish spoon-shaped, and of a very peculiar golden tint. The plant is larger and stouter than the ordinary Italian Corn-salad, and more suitable for southern than for northern climates.

Varieties of Corn-salad with variegated leaves have often been highly spoken of, but none of them have ever appeared to us to be as good as the good varieties of the green-leaved kinds. Variegation, as a rule, does not add to the value of a table vegetable, and it is almost always a sign of weakness of growth. Of these variegated kinds, one has leaves marbled with white, and another has the heart and the base of the central leaves of a bright yellow colour. These variegations, becoming more intense in hue after the first touch of frosty weather, have rather a pretty effect.

COSTMARY, or ALECOST.

Balsamita vulgaris, Willd. *Compositæ.*

Baume-coq, Herbe de Sainte-Marie.

Native of Southern Europe.— Perennial.— A very long-lived plant, growing in broad tufts or clumps. Leaves oval, obtuse at both ends, more or less toothed or notched, the radical ones stalked, the stem leaves sessile and sheathing; stem unbranched, erect; flower-heads small, in a terminal corymb. The plant does not always flower in the north of France. All its parts have a rather bitter taste and a pungent aromatic odour. It is easily propagated by division of the tufts or clumps, in autumn or spring. In the climate of Paris it is advisable to plant it in a warm position. The leaves are often used for seasoning. In England they were formerly used for flavouring ale.

CRESS, or GARDEN CRESS.

Lepidium sativum, L. *Cruciferæ.*

French, Cresson alénois. *German,* Garten-Kresse. *Flemish,* Hofkers. *Dutch,* Tuinkers. *Danish,* Havekarse. *Italian,* Agretto. *Spanish,* Mastuerzo. *Portuguese,* Mastrugo.

Native of Persia.—An annual plant of very rapid growth. The pungent flavour of its leaves has caused it to be used as a condiment from time immemorial, and its culture is so easy that it finds a place in the humblest kitchen garden. The radical leaves are very much divided and very numerous, forming a straggling rosette, from the centre of which soon rises a smooth branching stem furnished with a few almost linear leaves. The flowers are white, small, and four-petalled, and are succeeded by roundish pods, which are very much flattened and slightly concave. The seeds are comparatively large, furrowed, oblong, and of a brick-red colour; they have a biting taste and a garlicky flavour. A gramme contains about 450 seeds, and a litre of them weighs about 730 grammes. Their germinating power lasts for five years.

CULTURE.—There is no plant more easy to grow than this. It may be sown at any time and in any kind of soil, with the certainty of having leaves fit to cut in a few weeks; only, during very hot weather, it is best to sow in a moist and shaded position, in order to obtain more tender and more abundant leaves. In summer, it is a good plan to make successional sowings, as the plants run very quickly to seed. The seed germinates with very great rapidity. In a temperature of 10° to 15° Centigrade (or 49° to 59° Fahrenheit) it usually germinates in less than twenty-four hours. This rapid growth is sometimes utilized for the purpose of furnishing rooms with verdant foliage in winter, and to do this, it is sufficient to sprinkle Cress-seed plentifully on wet moss or sand, or on a vase or anything else covered with wet moss or moist clay, and in a few days a mass of verdure will be produced, which has a very pleasing effect.

In the London market-gardens, Cress is grown to a large extent, along with Mustard, in beds made on the floors of vineries, a portion being sown and a portion cut every other day. During February and March the floors of such Vineries remind one of a verdant pasture, so green and so healthy do the crops of Cress and Mustard in various stages of growth appear. After sowing, a good watering is given, and the beds are covered with mats until the seeds have germinated, when they are immediately removed. The Mustard and Cress are cut when they attain a height of 1½ to 2 inches, a long-bladed knife with a crooked handle being used for the purpose. With this implement in one hand the operator cuts as much at a time as he can hold with the other, which is about as much as will fill a punnet; he then deftly takes the cut material up with both hands and places it in an upright position in the punnet. So precisely do practised hands perform this work, that one would almost imagine the Mustard and Cress had been sown in the punnets. During January, February, and March, Mustard and Cress fetch from 2s. to 4s. per dozen punnets, but later on they become much cheaper. Rape is often sold for Mustard. It is mild in flavour and, perhaps, equally wholesome; it is also stiffer, and keeps longer in good condition in a cut state than Mustard. On hot-beds out-of-doors, in temporary frames, and in warm moist borders, Mustard and Cress are grown in enormous quantities, some using as much as 500 bushels of seed in one season!—C. W. S.

USES.—The radical leaves are much used as a condiment, and for garnishing dishes, especially of roast meat. They are also used for side-dishes and in salads.

Common Garden Cress (*Cresson Alénois Commun*).—This form, which is most commonly grown, is a decided improvement on the wild plant. The leaves are larger, of a deeper green colour, and more abundantly produced.

Curled, or **Normandy, Garden Cress** (*Cresson Alénois Frisé*).—In this variety the divisions of the leaves are finer and more numerous than in the Common kind; they are also curled and more or less twisted on themselves, which gives the foliage a very pleasing appearance.

Curled, or Normandy, Garden Cress (⅓ natural size).

Broad-leaved Garden Cress (*Cresson Alénois à Large Feuille*).—This variety, which in appearance is just the reverse of the preceding one, differs from the type in having the blade of the leaf entire, without any divisions, and merely notched here and there on the edges. The leaves are oval in shape, about 2 inches long, and about 1 inch broad. They have slender stalks and a somewhat irregular outline.

Extra-curled Dwarf Garden Cress (*Cresson Alénois Nain Tres-frisé*).—The Common Curled Garden Cress has

Broad-leaved Garden Cress (⅓ natural size).

the leaves deeply cut, and the divisions folded and twisted in such a manner as to give the plant a very peculiar appearance. In the present variety the blade of the leaf is divided into a few lobes, which are almost entire, the edges only being cut into a kind of fringe. The divisions, however, are very fine, numerous, and curled in such a

manner as to cover nearly the whole surface of the blade of the leaf, causing the plant to resemble a tuft of green moss. The leaf-stalks are comparatively short, in consequence of which the plant presents a dense and compact appearance.

Golden, or Australian, Garden Cress (*Cresson Alénois Doré*).—This might be taken for a sub-variety of the Large-leaved Garden Cress, as the leaves are similar in shape and only differ in their colour, which is a pale yellowish green, and always so marked that it strikes even the most unpractised eye at once. These two varieties differ so much in the appearance of their leaves from

Extra-curled Dwarf Garden Cress.

the Common Garden Cress, that any one seeing them growing side by side before flowering would be strongly inclined to think they were plants of quite different species.

WATER-CRESS.

Nasturtium officinale, R. Br. *Cruciferæ.*

French, Cresson de fontaine, C. de ruisseau, Santé du corps. *German*, Brunnenkresse. *Flemish* and *Dutch*, Waterkers. *Danish*, Brondkarsen. *Italian*, Nasturzio aquatico, Crescione di fontana. *Spanish*, Berro. *Portuguese*, Agroião.

Native of Europe.—Perennial.—An aquatic plant, with long stems, which readily take root, and which even send out into the water white rootlets serving to supply the plant with nutriment. Leaves compound, with roundish divisions, slightly sinuated, and of a dark-green colour; flowers small, white, in terminal spikes; seeds usually few, very fine, in slightly curved siliques or pods. A gramme contains about 4000 seeds, and a litre of them weighs about 580 grammes. Their germinating power lasts for five years.

Water-cress (⅓ natural size).

Culture.—The pleasant and peculiar flavour of the Water-cress, and also its well-known hygienic properties, have from time immemorial caused it to be highly esteemed for table use. The preference which the plant exhibits for moist positions and even running streams renders the cultivation of it rather difficult, so that most people are content to gather it where it grows naturally in brooks, ditches, or springs. In the neighbourhood of some large towns, however, it is cultivated systematically, and usually very profitably. For this purpose, a portion of a meadow or pasture field is selected which has a clear stream or rivulet running by or through it, and across this portion, from one side to the other, a number of large trenches are excavated. These are from about 16 to 20 ft. wide, and about 13 ft. distant from one another, and are so arranged that the water may run from one to another. This is managed by having a slight difference in the level of the trenches, so that the water may run out of each of them at the end opposite to that at which it flowed in. Thus the water does not finally leave the trenches until it has made a long serpentine course through all of them. After the soil at the bottom of the trenches has been properly prepared, the finest and strongest stems that can be selected are pricked in with a dibble. The water is then let into the trenches, and the plants are not interfered with until they have grown strong enough to allow the leaves to be gathered without injury. After the plants are well established, and growing vigorously, the leaves may be gathered all through the year, except in very frosty weather, when the trenches should be flooded and entirely submerged for the protection of the plants. Plantations of the same kind, on a smaller scale, might be made anywhere where there is a sufficient supply of pure fresh water. It is not even absolutely necessary that it should be running water, if it can be renewed often enough to keep it clear and pure. Water-cress has also been grown almost without water, by planting it in tubs half-filled with good soil and kept in a moist shaded position, under which circumstances occasional waterings will suffice for the growth of the plants. This mode of culture, however, has its drawbacks, and all who attempt it are not equally successful.

Water-cress is said to have grown in a wild state on the banks of the Thames and other places near London for many years before its culture for market was attempted on anything like an extensive scale, and there being then little demand for it, the supplies from these quarters were sufficient; but as it gained popularity in France, Prussia, and elsewhere, so the demand for it in London also increased, and beds for its culture were formed at Springhead and Northfleet, near Gravesend, as far back as the beginning of the present century. Springhead Cress is still noted for its superior quality.

Large supplies are now obtained from Waltham, Cheshunt, Uxbridge, and other low-lying places near the Great Eastern Railway, and the annual amount realized by growers for London alone is very great. The space at Springhead allotted to Water-cress culture is about three acres in extent, and consists of a winding ditch varying in width from 6 to 20 feet. The supply of water is furnished by numberless springs of fresh clear water, which bubble out near the banks of the stream in various places. The water contains a good deal of iron, and on the sides of the Cress-beds, where

P

it is somewhat stagnant, the Cress assumes a less healthy colour than that in the middle of the stream. The Cress-beds at Springhead lie in a warm sheltered valley; the sloping banks on both sides of the stream, which appear to be exceedingly fertile, are covered with fruit trees, such as Apples, Plums, etc. The Water-cress is replanted yearly, generally in August and September, and sometimes in spring. Tufts of the roots are taken up and pulled apart, and planted in rows about 1 ft. apart, after which they are trodden or rolled down, with a view to induce the roots to take quickly. The water is just deep enough to cover the roots, and when fully grown the young shoots in summer form a miniature meadow of Water-cress. Cutting is done three times a week, as much being cut at a time as the markets require.

USES.—The Water-cress is such a well-known plant that a description of its uses is almost superfluous. At Paris, where the market is always very abundantly supplied with it, it is used for garnishing, in salads, and sometimes also boiled and minced, like Spinach. The practice of serving fresh good Cress in liberal quantities with broiled meat or roast fowl should be more in vogue in England— at least, when the Cress is good, which is not always the case in our markets.

AMERICAN, or BELLE-ISLE, CRESS.

Barbarea præcox, R. Br.   *Cruciferæ.*

French, Cresson de terre.   *German,* Amerikanische perennirende Winterkresse.
Flemish, Wilde kers.   *Danish,* Winterkarse.

Native of Europe.—Biennial.—The leaves of this plant have some resemblance to those of the Water-cress, but the plant itself always grows on the dry land. If sown in spring, it forms during the summer a tolerably full rosette of compound leaves of a dark and very glistening green colour. In the following spring, the flower-stems

American, or Belle-Isle, Cress (⅓ natural size).

make their appearance, and bear rather elongated spikes of bright yellow flowers, which are succeeded by slender siliques or pods, containing small, gray, rough-skinned seeds, which are slightly flattened on one side and roundish on the other. A gramme contains about 950 seeds, and a litre of them weighs about 540 grammes. Their germinating power lasts for three years. CULTURE.—This is extremely simple and easy. The seed may be sown during the whole of the spring, summer, and autumn, in any kind of garden soil, and successional sowings are unnecessary, as there is no fear of the plants running to seed too soon. On the other hand, if the plant is easily grown, its produce is not so valuable as that of the Water-cress or the Common Garden Cress, as the leaves are always hardish, and their pungent flavour is accompanied with a certain amount of acridity. The radical leaves are used for seasoning and garnishing.

The Winter Cress of English gardens is *Barbarea vulgaris.* Its culture and uses are precisely the same as those of the American Cress.

LADY'S SMOCK, CUCKOO FLOWER, or MEADOW CRESS.

Cardamine pratensis, L.   *Cruciferæ.*

French, Cresson des prés, Cressonnette.   *German,* Wiesenkresse.   *Spanish,* Berros de prado.

Native of Europe.—Perennial.—A wild plant, common in moist meadows and on the banks of rivers, etc. Leaves pinnate, somewhat like those of the Water-cress, but far less fleshy and often tinged with violet-brown; stem erect, furnished with a few leaves which are cut into linear divisions; flowers largish, rose-coloured or pale lilac, opening very early in spring; seed small, oblong, somewhat irregular in shape, and of a brown colour. A gramme contains about 1500 seeds, and a litre of them weighs about 580 grammes. Their germinating power lasts for four years. This plant is not of very much account as a table vegetable. There is, however, a double-flowered variety of it, which, with its clusters of pale-lilac blossoms, has a pretty effect in gardens, when winter has just ended. The leaves, which have a biting and pungent taste, are eaten like those of other Cresses, but in England in modern days we have never heard of it being used in this way—nor is there any need for it, considering the good and easily grown salad plants we have.

PARÁ CRESS.

Spilanthes oleracea, L.   *Com-positæ.*

French, Cresson de Pará.   *German,* Para kresse.   *Flemish,* ABC kruid.

Native of the Antilles.— Annual.—An almost creeping plant, with entire oval leaves, which are truncate at the base. Flowers in conical heads, without petals, and of a yellow colour, borne on the top of the stem; seed very small, oval, flat, grayish, and covered with small round pro-minences. A gramme contains about 3400 seeds, and a full

Brazil Cress (⅓ natural size).

litre of them weighs only about 200 grammes. Their germinating power lasts for at least five years. The seed is sown, in the place where the crop is to grow, in March or April. The plants commence to flower in about two months afterwards, and continue to bloom all through the summer. In hot weather they require to be watered plentifully. USES.—The leaves, when mixed with salads, impart to them a pungent flavour, and have the effect of stimulating the action of the salivary glands. This use of them, however, is not common, and the plant may be regarded as belonging to the province of pharmacy rather than to that of the kitchen garden.

Brazil Cress (*Cresson de Brésil*).—This plant appears to differ from the Pará Cress only in the brownish tint of its stems and leaves, which also extends to the upper part of the flower-heads. The culture and uses of the two plants are exactly the same.

CUCUMBER.

Cucumis sativus, L.   Cucurbitaceæ.

French, Concombre. *German,* Gurke. *Flemish* and *Dutch,* Komkommer. *Danish,* Agurken. *Italian,* Cetriolo. *Spanish,* Cohombro. *Portuguese,* Pepino.

Native of the East Indies.—Annual.—A creeping plant, with herbaceous stems, which are flexible, angular from the commencement of their growth, rough to the touch, and furnished with tendrils. Leaves alternate, placed opposite the tendrils, angular heart-shaped, bluntly toothed, rough like the stem, of a dark-green colour on the upper surface and grayish underneath. Flowers axillary, on short stalks, of a more or less greenish-yellow colour, some male, others female, the latter placed on the top of the ovary, which becomes the fruit, and which is of some size before the flower opens on it. The plant continues to produce flowers in succession for a long time, and the intervention of insects or of man seems to be necessary to fertilize them. The fruit is oblong and more or less cylindrical in shape, smooth, or bearing protuberances which end in a hard spine; flesh abundant and very watery. Seed of a yellowish-white colour, very flat, elongated oval, enclosed at the centre of the fruit in three longitudinal compartments, which are filled with a pulpy substance, and are nearly as long as the fruit itself. A gramme contains about 35 seeds, and a litre of them weighs about 500 grammes. Their germinating power seldom declines before the tenth year.

CULTURE. — The Cucumber is grown extensively in almost all parts of the world, and in warm countries is brought to perfection without the aid of artificial heat. In Great Britain, however, the case is different; and in order to secure a good supply of Cucumbers, even during the warmest seasons of the year, artificial heat is indispensable. Cucumbers are grown in a variety of ways—as in houses, pits, frames, etc., and occasionally out-of-doors. The best mode of culture is that of growing them in houses, which, if properly constructed, will yield a supply at all seasons of the year. Propagation is effected by seeds and cuttings. The best kind of house is that with a span roof, a pathway running through the centre, and a bed on each side. The size of the house must depend upon the demand. Small houses are, however, best for Cucumber-growing; and if two can be used for them and Melons alternately, it will be found much more convenient than having one large house. A house entirely devoted to Cucumber - growing all the year round must necessarily be larger than when it is only used for winter or spring crops—inasmuch as, having to keep up a continuous succession, fresh plantations must be constantly made; therefore the best kind of house is that with a bed on each side, as before mentioned, planting the beds alternately as each set of plants becomes exhausted. A span-roofed house, from 15 to 20 ft. long and 10 or 12 ft. wide, will, if properly managed, afford a sufficient supply for most private establishments, unless they are very extensive. Houses with comparatively low-pitched roofs generally yield the best results, with least trouble from scorching or red spider. They should be built high enough to allow of head-room, but not higher than is really necessary, as low, close houses are most suitable. Heat produced by hot-water pipes is decidedly the best for giving warmth, as it is of a more humid nature than that produced by flues. There should always be sufficient piping to keep up the required temperature without being obliged to make the pipes intensely hot—the latter being productive of many evil results, such as scalding, red spider, etc. Evaporating pans, placed over the pipes, are of great assistance in keeping the atmosphere of the house in a moist state. Cucumbers may be successfully grown in low lean-to houses, with no other glass than that of the roof—the heat being supplied by means of a brick flue running round the house, and a stage consisting of rough wooden slabs or planks, supported upon brick piers or wooden posts, erected over the flue along the front of the house. The stage should be 3½ ft. from the glass, which will allow for 18 inches of soil, and 12 inches for the plants to grow before reaching the trellis, supposing the trellis to be 12 inches from the glass. If the front of the stage be boarded up, a good bottom-heat may be secured.

Bottom-heat is considered by many to be indispensable in Cucumber - growing; this, however, has been proved to be a mistake, and we have often seen the best Cucumbers grown without it. That plants are benefited to a great extent by the use of bottom - heat judiciously applied, we do not for a moment dispute; but still it is not absolutely necessary, except in the case of early Cucumbers grown in pits and frames. Where, however, it is applied, it must be done with judgment, for there are often crops of Cucumbers ruined by an excessive bottom-heat. Stable manure is frequently used to supply bottom-heat to Cucumbers; and where it can be properly regulated it is the best. As the heat gradually declines, the roots descend into the decaying manure and draw therefrom a vast amount of nourishment to support the heavy crops of fruit they carry. A considerable amount of labour in root-watering is also saved. In private gardens hot water is much cleaner and perhaps gives less trouble, and where the pipes are laid in a tank, and the tank at intervals supplied with liquid manure, good results can be obtained.

WINTER AND SPRING CUCUMBERS.— For this crop many cultivators obtain plants by means of cuttings, with the view of getting fruit quicker than from those raised from seed. There can be no doubt that if cuttings be put in at the same time as seeds, the cuttings will make plants capable of bearing fruit earlier; but they will not continue in a bearing condition so long, nor produce such good fruit, as healthy seedling plants. Where any particular kind is grown, and it is desirable to keep it true, propagation by cuttings is the only sure way of attaining that object; but as a rule seedling plants are the best. Where, however, cuttings are preferred, they should be put in about ten or twelve days before they are required to be planted out. The best way is to stop the plants from which the cuttings are to be taken a week or two previously ; they will then send out side-shoots, which should be taken off with a joint of the older wood attached to them, and inserted singly in small pots well drained and filled with a compost of leaf-mould, loam, and sand, in equal parts. If inserted close to the side of the pot they will strike sooner than if placed in the centre. The pots should then be plunged in a bottom-heat of 70°, have a hand-light or bell-glass placed over them, and be shaded from the sun ; and if kept well watered and sprinkled overhead, they will be sufficiently rooted in a few days to allow of the hand-lights being taken off; thus the plants will be gradually inured to the light and sun, which treatment will effectually prevent them from becoming drawn. If the plants be likely to become pot-bound before the bed is ready to receive them, they should be shifted into larger pots, otherwise they will be materially injured. In order to obtain a good supply of Cucumbers during the winter and spring, it is necessary to sow sufficiently early to allow of the plants becoming strong and in a fruit-bearing condition before the short dark days arrive; strong plants should therefore be in readiness for putting out not later than the end of September. If plants be obtained from cuttings, they will require to be put in the second or third week in that month ; if from seed, a week or ten days earlier.

Many cultivators soak their Cucumber seeds in water for a few hours previously to sowing ; and in the case of old or very dry seeds it is an excellent plan, inasmuch as it softens the seeds and causes them to germinate quicker than they otherwise would. There are various methods of sowing : some growers sow single seeds in small pots, and thence turn them out into the beds ; others sow a quantity of seed thickly in pans or large pots, and transplant them. We have found it a very excellent plan to put two or three seeds into 48-sized pots half filled with light leaf-mould and sand, just covering the seeds, and when they are up select the strongest of the plants to remain, and pinch the others out. By the time the remaining plants have made a pair of rough leaves, roots will frequently be seen pushing from the bases of the stems. The pots should then be filled up with soil to within half an inch of the rim, into which their roots will quickly penetrate, and thereby strengthen the plants, and afford them more room to grow without disturbing the roots, as would be the case in re-potting or transplanting. In whatever way they may be sown, they should, if possible, be placed in a gentle bottom-heat, and kept moderately moist until they are up, when they must be placed near the glass, or where they can obtain plenty of light and sun, in order to keep them dwarf and stocky. Whilst the plants are becoming established the bed should be prepared for planting, bottom-heat being provided by means of hot-water pipes or fermenting material. A layer of good thick turves should be laid on the bottom of the bed, grassy side downwards ; upon this lay the soil in a ridge along the centre of the bed, and when it is sufficiently warm the plants may be turned out into it 2 ft. apart, planting them 1 or 2 inches deeper than they were in the pots, and afterwards watering them copiously with tepid water. A good brisk heat should be kept up until the plants get well established in the beds— say 65° by night and 70° by day, allowing the glass to rise 10° higher by sun-heat, with a bottom-heat of 65° to 70°. After the plants begin to root freely into the soil in the bed, air should be admitted in the morning on every favourable opportunity, closing early in the afternoon in order to secure all the sun-heat possible. No more fire-heat than is absolutely necessary to keep up the required temperature should be used, inasmuch as all plants thrive much better under the influence of solar than of artificial heat. The subsequent treatment consists of training the leaders of the plants up the wires and stopping them when they reach the top. This will cause them to send out side-shoots all the way up the stem, which shoots should also be stopped at the second or third joint; these shoots always show fruit, but only one or two should be left on each plant at first, and more as the plants get older and stronger. The stopping of the shoots must be continued at every second or third joint from the last pinch, and also thinned out when needful. Crowding of the wood and foliage should always be avoided. The object of planting 2 ft. apart at first is only to secure a good crop of Cucumbers early by taking one or two fruits off each plant as soon as possible; but this space is too little ultimately for each plant, and when it becomes necessary, every alternate plant may be removed to give the others more room. Watering must be attended to regularly. The bed should be kept moist, and when water is given it should be a thorough soaking till it runs out at the bottom of the bed, and should always be of the same temperature as that of the soil. Syringing in the morning and afternoon must also be attended to, and more or less air should be admitted according to the state of the weather. The roots should be top-dressed every two or three weeks with a little fresh soil. If these simple directions be carried out, a supply of Cucumbers during the winter and spring will not be found a difficult matter. The Cucumber is an easy plant to grow; unlike the Melon, the fruit is not wanted ripe, but only when half swelled; and the way to obtain it is to keep the plants in a healthy growing state.

CUCUMBERS IN PITS AND FRAMES.—Where hot-water pits are employed for growing winter Cucumbers, it is a good plan to apply a thick lining of fermenting material round the pit; also a covering of mats or other warm material over the glass during the night: by these means less fire-heat

will be required, and the plants consequently kept in a healthier condition. To train Cucumbers, pieces of wire trellis-work should be fitted in each light about 1 ft. from the glass, the bed containing the plants being about 8 or 9 inches below this, which will afford greater facility for applying top-dressing; whereas if the ordinary mode of pegging down be adopted, top-dressing cannot be given without injury to the foliage. The greatest objection to pits for winter Cucumbers is the inconvenience of attending to the plants in severe weather; and plants are frequently allowed to run wild and get dry at the roots, in consequence of not being able to take off the lights when there is a continuance of frosty weather. Where there is no other convenience for growing Cucumbers in winter, a few plants may be put into large pots and placed in corners of a warm house, such as a Pine or plant stove. The pots should be well drained, and filled three parts full of compost, adding a little at a time, as the plants require it, until the pots are full. Plenty of water must be given them, without causing the soil to become sodden, and when they are in bearing occasional soakings of manure water will be beneficial in keeping them in a healthy state.

SUMMER AND AUTUMN CUCUMBERS.—Plants put out in September will, if properly treated, continue in bearing until May or June; therefore, to have plants ready to succeed them, a sowing should be made early in April, and grown either in houses, pits, or hot-beds, whichever is at hand; these will generally continue in bearing until August, by which time plants that have been put out in cold frames, such as those in which Potatoes have been grown, will be in bearing, and these, if liberally treated, will give a supply far into the autumn. They will, however, require to have linings applied, and be covered up at night when the cold nights set in. If thus treated they will last until late in October, by which time those planted for winter will be progressing towards fruit-bearing. Where a hot-water pit can be spared, a few plants may be put out in July or August, to give supplies during the early part of the winter.

GROWING CUCUMBERS ON HOT-BEDS. —Though hot-beds have been superseded to a great extent by hot-water pipes, they still occupy a place in gardens, especially in those of moderate extent, and are often very serviceable as Cucumber and propagating frames combined. A moderate and steady temperature is what is required, and this can be secured in a well-made hot-bed for six months. The materials required for a lasting hot-bed are stable litter and leaves in equal quantities: in the absence of leaves, use half-decayed hot-bed manure, refuse turf-choppings, or any other materials likely to moderate the fermentation of the stable litter—a material to be had in most establishments.

The first consideration is the selection of a site for the bed, which should always be in a dry and sheltered situation. Nothing extracts heat so rapidly as cold winds; indeed, where a hot-bed is made up annually, it is better to have it sunk two-thirds in the ground. It would be preferable, in fact, to have it wholly in the ground, but as the bed will settle down at least one-third of its height during the summer, the frame would get below the ground-line, which would be inconvenient. For a frame 9 by 5 ft. the pit would require to be 14 ft. long and 10 ft. wide; and if the bed were intended to last eight or nine months it should be quite 4 ft. deep—which, allowing one-third of the bed to be above ground, would give a total breadth of 6 ft. of fermenting material. If the pit be double-boarded with strong rough deal, so as to form a 2-inch cavity all round between the earth and the sides of the bed, the heat will last a considerable time longer, as the cavity prevents the bed from being robbed of its heat by the cold

earth. Another advantage of having a pit for the bed is that the latter is made with greater facility, for it requires a skilled hand to build up a compact and permanent hot-bed on the surface of the ground. Whatever kind of site is prepared, the next step is to have the materials placed conveniently near. These may be thrown roughly together the first time, sprinkling plenty of water upon them if they be at all dry. In a week or ten days the heap will usually be found to be heating violently, when it should be turned over again, taking care to mix the litter thoroughly, adding more water if required. A week or so later it will want another turning, which as a rule ought to be sufficient to bring it into a fit condition for making up into a bed, even though it be heating strongly, for the temperature will subside a good deal after the materials are well trodden down. Where the hot-bed is the only accommodation, the seed, of course, cannot be sown till the bed is ready; but where there is a hothouse or pit, it is by far the best to sow the seed about the time the first preparations are made for making the bed; and when the bed is ready the plants will be strong and fit for planting. The seed may be sown in small pots, well drained, and the seeds covered with about $\frac{1}{4}$ inch of fine soil plunged in a bottom-heat of 75° or 80°, with a moist atmospheric heat of from 65° to 70° at night, and 75° to 80° by day. The seeds should not be watered for a day or two after planting, when they should be well soaked; and from this time forward the soil about the roots of the plants should never be allowed to get dry, nor wet enough to become sour. When the plants are up they should be placed near the glass, to keep them strong and stocky, and should be planted out before they become pot-bound.

In preparing the bed for planting, the bottom of the frame should be covered with turves, grassy side downwards; on the top of these lay a ridge of soil the whole length of the frame. This should afterwards be levelled up, as the plants root out in both directions. Frequent soilings are an evil in hot-bed culture, for such operations cannot be performed without disarranging the foliage and injuring the plants. The bed being prepared, and presuming the bottom-heat to have subsided to about 75° or 80°, the plants should be planted, one in the centre of each light. If not done before, they should at the same time have their tops pinched off above the second or third leaf. After planting, with the assistance of linings, in the shape of stable litter and a careful economization of sun-heat, the bottom-heat may be kept at 70° at least, and the top-heat at 70° at night, and 80° or 85° with sun. In very bright weather a shading of thin canvas should be rolled over the frame during the hottest part of the day, but shading should not be resorted to more than can be helped. Air must be admitted at all times, and even in severe weather the sashes should be raised the thickness of a label to let the steam escape. The bed should be kept moist, but not sodden, and the plants should be sprinkled every afternoon in bright weather with soft, clean, tepid water. Under this treatment they will soon start into growth by sending out two strong leaders below where they were pinched. One should be trained towards the back of the frame and the other towards the front, and when they have come within about 1 ft. of the sides of the frame they should be pinched again, which will cause them to throw out laterals, showing fruit in all probability, which, with the exception of three or four on each limb, should be picked off, and the laterals stopped one joint beyond the fruit. If the foliage be large and vigorous, it will perhaps be found advantageous to cut out some of the laterals altogether. It is much better to thin out the foliage and wood frequently than to let the plants get over-crowded, and then cut out a great quantity of wood at one time. After this the training of the plants consists in laying the shoots out, so as to cover the bed, stopping them regularly, and disposing of them generally so as to secure the greatest amount of light and air possible to every leaf. The plants should not be allowed to bear too heavily, if expected to keep up the supply for any length of time. When cropped moderately, and the fruit cut as fast as it is ready, the plants bear continuously from April to November.

Soil and Manure.—A great depth of soil is unnecessary for Cucumbers; indeed, it is to be avoided, for they will succeed far better if they be planted in a little soil at first, and receive frequent top-dressings afterwards. For planting, 8 or 10 inches of soil is quite deep enough, if the bed receive slight dressings of stable manure mixed with soil to keep the plants in a vigorous state of health. Good turfy loam mixed with rotten manure is the best material in which to plant them, but the dressing should be of a richer nature. Many people use a quantity of peat mixed with the loam for winter Cucumbers; others use leaf-mould, but it is too light; the plants thrive well in it, but do not last so long nor fruit so freely as when grown in more holding soil. Cocoa-nut fibre refuse is highly recommended by some as a good dressing for Cucumber beds; but stable manure is by far the best kind of surfacing, and may be applied fresh from the stable, and if a little old mortar or brick rubbish be mixed therewith it will be better still. Weak guano water is the best kind of stimulant to apply to Cucumbers; other kinds of manure water are said to affect the flavour of the fruit. Abundance of water is at all times necessary to Cucumber plants growing under advantageous circumstances.

In Market Gardens. — During summer the long ranges of pits and frames in market gardens devoted in winter to the protection of tender culinary plants are applied to Cucumber culture, and from these are cut thousands of fruits weekly. Indeed, few frame crops pay better than Cucumbers where they succeed well, and therefore every frame that can possibly be spared is planted with them. One grower at Fulham has a field of frame-ground, containing many ranges of frames with from 800 to 1000 ordinary sashes, in summer entirely devoted to Cucumbers. From this field are sent to market weekly during the summer from 200 to 220 dozen fruits. Two or three men are usually kept at work in these frame-grounds, and on three days of the week (Monday, Wednesday, and Friday) they are employed in cutting fruits for market, and on the other three week-days they are busy stopping and regulating the shoots of the Cucumbers, watering, etc. Should any young fruits exhibit a tendency to become crooked, they put them into cylindrical glasses open at both ends. These glasses are about 12 or 15 inches long, and 1½ or 2 inches in diameter, and several thousands of them are employed in one large frame - ground, as one good and straight Cucumber is worth nearly a dozen small and deformed ones. The crooked ones are disposed of for pickling. Should any "nosed" fruits, as they are termed, or such as have swelled at the point, be found, which occurs late in the season, a piece of string is tied round them, and they are left to ripen, as such fruits are certain to contain good seed. When the seed-fruits become yellow and are cut, they are placed under sashes or on boards exposed to the sun, so as to get thoroughly ripe and hard before being separated from the pulp.

The first sowing to supply plants for growing in frames is made in little punnets or flower-pots, early in the year, which are placed in hot manure frames. When the seeds germinate and are fit for potting off, two plants are potted into a 6-inch pot, and the whole replaced in the frames, keeping them near the glass. As soon as the frames to be planted can be spared, they are moved aside, and trenches cast out 5 ft. wide and 2 ft. deep, and firmly filled with stable litter. Over this some soil is placed, and the frames set on again. Another sowing is generally made to succeed the first one; but, as a rule, there are seldom more than two sowings made, and the second is only sown because all the frames are not empty at one time to be filled by the first sowing. When the heat is at a proper temperature for planting, a little more soil is introduced into the frames, and one potful (containing two plants) is planted under each sash, and one of the plants is trained towards the front of the frame and the other towards the back. The sashes are then put on and all is kept close for a few days, and, if need be, a little shading is also given by strewing some litter over the glass. Afterwards, until the plants have fairly begun to grow, no more ventilation is given than is necessary to prevent scorching in the case of bright sunshine. For several weeks after having been planted they are covered up at night with litter, removing it next morning; indeed, this covering is not discontinued until the month of June. When the plants have grown sufficiently to come into bloom, they are most attentively looked after in the way of regulating the growths, pegging them down, and stopping the lateral shoots at the joint beyond the embryo fruit, and preventing an accumulation of superfluous growths. Throughout the day they are allowed to have plenty of air during the summer, but it is all taken off at night; in the morning the sashes are tilted up a little, and as the heat of the day increases they are still further opened.

Water is given in the morning abundantly to those requiring it, whilst those that are not dry have simply a sprinkling overhead. It is cold water from the tap that is entirely used, and doubtless this is the greatest drawback to Cucumber growing with which the market gardener has to contend, as where one or several acres are covered with frames, it would be almost an impossibility to make tepid all the water that would be required. Large hogsheads, however, are sunk here and there about the frame-ground, and brick or cement tanks are frequently used for containing water, with which they are filled for the next day's use. Guano water is sometimes given during the summertime, being applied through a fine rose overhead. This application is not only useful as a stimulant, but when given overhead has been found to be of material benefit in destroying or preventing red spider, as well as invigorating old plants. In reference to woodlice, toads are put in the frames to destroy them. Cucumbers require sunny weather to set well, and in dull wet seasons they do not thrive well, especially in the earlier part of the year. Should the summer be hot and bright, the sashes are shaded a little, and this is done by strewing some rank litter over the glass; but many market gardeners, by way of economy of labour, paint the sashes with whiting. By August the plants are getting exhausted; therefore careful attention is paid to thinning out old and bare vines, and encouraging young wood by means of stimulants, in the way of manure water and coverings from cold; and in this way they last till September. No fruits are saved for seed until August, for if left sooner they would materially weaken the crop of marketable fruit. Until August, Cucumbers are liable to red spider, thrips, green fly, mildew, canker, and various other diseases; the only remedy being that of keeping the plants in as vigorous growth as possible. When mildew attacks the Cucumber it is generally the result of insufficient ventilation and too low a temperature. When it does appear, dusting thinly but evenly with flour of sulphur through a piece of muslin cloth is the only cure. Thrips are

the most terrible of the insect enemies which attack the Cucumber; for these, and also for green fly, which is sometimes troublesome on the young growths, fumigating with Tobacco is usually resorted to; but the foliage of the Cucumber is so tender, especially when forced, that fumigation, unless done very carefully, is a cure which is often worse than the disease, and should never be attempted by the inexperienced.

CUCUMBERS IN THE OPEN AIR.— Market gardeners in the neighbourhood of London grow but few Cucumbers in the open air. Many have attempted it, but most of them have now abandoned it, the result not having proved very satisfactory. Where, however, it is carried on, they are grown under glass and hardened off and planted out 6 ft. asunder and 10 ft. row from row, and hand-glasses are put over them. When they begin to grow, the ground is well mulched with straw, to keep the earth moist and the fruit clean. Due attention is paid to their after-culture in the way of stopping, thinning, etc., and in some cases fairly good results are obtained. In one or two counties, the soil and climate of which seem unusually well adapted to their growth, large quantities are grown in the open air for the London markets; from such sources there are said to be sent to London not less than 600 tons a week during what is termed the Cucumber season. Of these upwards of 100 tons have been known to be sent to Covent Garden in a single day. In good Cucumber-growing localities the seed is sown about the beginning of May, where the plants are intended to grow, in rows some 4 ft. apart, and the plants stand nearly 2 ft. asunder in the row. In favourable seasons they soon push into active growth and cover the ground with vines, which, during the latter end of May, the whole of June, and beginning of July, spread in all directions and come into bearing. During their growth, weeding and thinning their superfluous shoots are well attended to, and if the plants should not entirely cover the ground, or wherever blanks occur, Mangold-Wurzel is planted in the vacant spaces. About 4 yards apart are also rows of Onions, set early in the spring, which, being allowed to run to seed, serve in some measure both for shade and shelter. Where Onions are not used for this purpose, Rye, sown in the autumn, 4 or 5 yards apart, and cut as soon as the vines cover the ground, is employed instead : Peas are also sometimes used for the same purpose. In this way the ground is made to produce two or three kinds of crops at the same time, and if one should happen to fail, one or more of the others, as the case may be, take its place. By the middle of July or earlier, according to the season, the crop is ready for a first gathering, and from that time to the end of September fruit varying in length from 10 to 12 inches, green and solid, though sometimes unshapely, is continually being cut.

GHERKINS.—These are extensively cultivated in London market gardens, some growers frequently gathering from 18,000 to 20,000 fruit in one day. The seed is sown in May in rows, where the plants are to remain, in well-manured land. The rows are usually about 9 ft. apart, and the plants, which are thinned out when sufficiently advanced to admit of the strongest being discerned and left,

allowed to stand 6 ft. apart in the rows. The after-treatment is exactly the same as that practised in the case of outdoor Cucumbers, except that the shoots of the Gherkins are allowed to grow unpinched. The fruit is gathered when about the size of a man's finger, placed in bushel baskets, and sent direct to the pickle manufacturers. A good place for Gherkins, and one often devoted to them, is the alleys between the rows of spring-sown Cabbages or Radish beds. The alleys are dug over, the drills for the seeds opened in the morning, and the seeds are sown in the afternoon when the ground is warm. When the Radishes or other crops are cleared off the intervening beds, the latter are dug, and a line of Cauliflowers or French Beans is planted along the centre of them, or sometimes two or three lines of Lettuces are put in. Some sow the Gherkins on an open quarter in patches of three or four seeds together, in rows about 5 or 6 ft. apart, and 3 or 4 ft. asunder in the row. Hand-glasses are then placed over the seeds, and when the young plants have come above ground, abundant ventilation is given until they show flower, when they are fully exposed. In most cases, however, they are raised in frames and transferred to the open ground in June, and in this way they fruit earlier and usually give less trouble and better results.

USES.—Cucumbers are eaten raw, boiled, or pickled. They are very good as a vegetable in the hands of a good cook, but are not used enough in this way in England.

The varieties of Cucumbers are extremely numerous, and the designed or accidental crossings of different varieties are still producing new ones. We shall confine ourselves to the description of the kinds which are most distinct and most valuable for cultivation.

Early Russian Gherkin (*Concombre de Russie*).—A truly miniature Cucumber, with a slender stem 20 inches to 2 ft. long, and small, bright-green leaves. It is perfectly well adapted for frame culture, each plant producing from six to eight fruit, which are short, egg-shaped, yellow, smooth, and a little larger than a hen's egg. This variety, which is the earliest of all, ripens fully in less than three months, and does not require any pinching or stopping. The flesh of the fruit is not very thick, and is slightly bitter, but its remarkable earliness makes some amends for these trifling defects. In Russia there are many varieties of it, the earliest of which, generally producing but one fruit to each plant, is said to complete its entire growth in ten or eleven weeks.

Brown Netted, or **Khiva, Cucumber** (*Concombre Brodé de Russie*).— As the very early small-fruited Cucumbers grow better in Russia than any other kind, a great many distinct forms of them are cultivated in that country. They are not all so well known in France. We shall, however, notice, next to the preceding variety, which is remarkable for its extreme earliness, another kind, which, although coming very near it in some respects, is strikingly distinct from it in the colour and appearance of the skin of the fruit. When ripening, the fruit of this variety does not take on the yellow tint common to a great number of other varieties of Cucumbers, but its skin turns brown, intersected

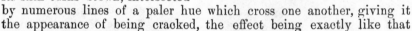

Early Russian Gherkin (⅛ natural size; detached fruit, ½ natural size).

by numerous lines of a paler hue which cross one another, giving it the appearance of being cracked, the effect being exactly like that of an oil painting the varnish of which has become chippy, or of cracked delft or china-ware. The fruit is something larger, and the plant stronger than in the preceding variety, but not quite so early.

Early White Cucumber (*Concombre Blanc Hâtif*).—A variety with quite elongated, almost cylindrical fruit, nearly three times as long as broad, at first pale green, but turning, as they ripen, to a porcelain white. The fruit ripens early, but considerably later than that of the Early Russian Gherkin.

Brown Netted, or Khiva, Cucumber (¼ natural size).

Long White Cucumber (*Concombre Blanc Long*).—This kind, which comes very near the preceding one in shape and colour, is distinguished from it chiefly by being something larger and later. It is very suitable for growing in the open ground.

Bonneuil Large White Cucumber (*Concombre Blanc Très Gros de Bonneuil*).—This Cucumber, which is almost always grown in the open ground, is quite distinct from all other varieties. The fruit, instead of being almost regularly cylindrical, is ovoid in shape, swollen about the middle, and, moreover, very perceptibly flattened from end to end in three or four places, producing the same number of more or less rounded angles. It is very large, not unfrequently attaining the weight of four pounds and a half. Like the fruit of the Early White variety, it is at first of a pale-green colour, and gradually becomes white as it increases in size. This is the Cucumber which is most generally grown about Paris for the perfumers, who use large quantities of it in their manufactures.

Early Yellow Dutch Cucumber (*Concombre Jaune Hâtif de Hollande;* Dutch, *Lange Gele Komkommer*).—Plant usually branching, with rather slender stems.

Leaves of a clear green colour, and with well-marked angles; fruit longer and later than that of the Early Russian variety, but still well adapted for forcing. It is at first of a yellowish-green colour, but becomes of a slightly orange yellow when quite ripe. There are usually only two or three fruit on each plant.

Large Yellow Cucumber (*Concombre Jaune Gros*). —Fruit at first pale yellow, turning to bright yellow when ripe, somewhat narrowed towards the stalk, rather

Bonneuil Large White Cucumber (⅓ natural size).

more than twice as long as broad, and attaining a weight of about three pounds and a half, moderately early, ripening about the same time as the Long White variety. The skin of the fruit is slightly warted and spined.

Common Long Green Cucumber (*Concombre Vert Long Ordinaire*).

—A rather large and vigorous-growing plant. Fruit slender and narrowed like that of the Early Yellow Dutch variety, but still longer and more pointed at both ends, and covered with very numerous and prominent spiny excrescences. It remains of a dark-green colour until it is just ripe, when it turns to a brownish yellow. The flesh of this variety is thick, firm, and crisp, on which account it is highly valued for use in

Early Yellow Dutch Cucumber (⅓ natural size).

salads before it is ripe, generally when only half or three-quarters grown.

Long Prickly Cucumber (*Concombre Vert Long Anglais*).—In England the Cucumber is very extensively cultivated, most usually in houses specially constructed for the purpose, and with very great care and attention. Under these circumstances, the various kinds could not fail to become greatly improved in the size and appearance of the fruit, earliness and hardiness being considered only secondary qualities. This is precisely the result, and there are now in England many varieties of the Long Prickly Cucumber which have long, almost cylindrical fruit, and but few spines, with very solid flesh, and producing remarkably few seeds. We shall only mention the most noteworthy of these numerous varieties.

Rollisson's Telegraph.—Plant rather compact, branching, with stout but short stems. Leaves large and bright coloured. Fruit 14 to 16 inches long, of a clear-green colour, perfectly smooth and shining for one-third of its length next the stalk, a portion of which is also more or less curved, while the remaining portion bears a few black spines; flesh solid and of excellent quality. A very free-bearing variety and very extensively grown. It is reputed to have been raised from Syon House, a variety having the fruits quite smooth, which, in its turn, was raised from the White Cucumber.

Blue Gown.—Fruit very long, frequently over 2 ft., cylindrical, covered with a glaucous bloom. Spines few, white, with black points. A very handsome variety.

Tender and True.—This variety resembles Rollisson's Telegraph, of which it may be said to be a very fine selection.

Duke of Edinburgh.—Fruit very large, 24 to 30 inches long, and thick, of a dull-green colour, almost smooth, or with but few spines, which are singularly small.

Marquis of Lorne. — Fruit very large, often exceeding 30 inches in length, solid, and of good quality, but, like the Duke of Edinburgh, a somewhat shy bearer.

Of other good kinds may be mentioned : — **Pearson's Long Gun.**—A very long and favourite sort.—**Cardiff Castle.**—A short, prolific variety, excellent for winter forcing.

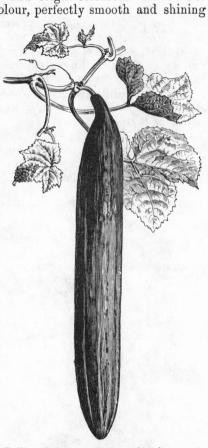

Rollisson's Telegraph Cucumber (⅓ natural size).

Ridge Cucumbers.—The following varieties, on the other hand, although growing better in artificial heat, can be grown without it in the open ground, whence they have received the general name of *Ridge Cucumbers.*

Bedfordshire Ridge Cucumber.—A handsome, productive, and early kind, resembling *Pike's Defiance*, but with rather shorter fruit.

Gladiator.—Fruit about 1 ft. long, nearly cylindrical, straight, gradually narrowed at the stalk end and more abruptly so at the other. Flesh white, firm, and solid.

Pike's Defiance.—The fruit of this variety only differs from that of the preceding kind in being somewhat lighter in colour, but the plant is rather earlier, hardier, and remarkably productive. It is one of the best kinds for growing in the open ground.

Of the open-air varieties which are not of English origin, we may mention the following:—

Quedlinbourg Giant (*Concombre Très Long Géant de Quedlimbourg*).—A very productive and rather early kind, with few-spined, pale-green fruit, which turns yellow when ripe.

Goliath Green (*Concombre Vert Goliath*).—This seems to be only a variety of the preceding kind, from which it differs in being a little later and having the fruit a trifle longer.

Tuscan Solid Green (*Concombre Vert Plein de Toscane*).—Fruit handsome and long, smooth, nearly cylindrical, becoming of a bronzy colour as it ripens.

Long White-spine. — An American variety, with long, green, white-spined fruit, rather like the Long Green Chinese Cucumber.

Greek, or Athenian, Cucumber (*Concombre Long Vert d'Athènes*).— A vigorous-growing plant, but of low thick-set habit, rather than very tall.

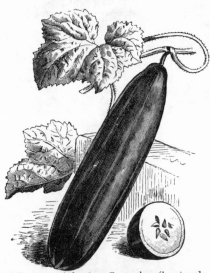

Greek, or Athenian, Cucumber (⅓ natural size).

Stems stout, and not more than 4½ to a little over 5 ft. long, with the joints pretty close to one another. Leaves dark green, large, entire, or with three faintly marked lobes, toothed at the edges, decreasing rapidly in size from the base to the end of the stem. Fruit always solitary in the axil of a leaf, three or four to a strong plant, nearly cylindrical, 10 to 12 inches long, sometimes narrowed near the stalk; skin smooth, and entirely devoid of spines, of a uniform green colour until nearly ripe, when it turns to a bronzy yellow; flesh white, firm, thick, completely filling the interior of the fruit, with the exception of a small portion of the centre occupied by the seeds. When gathered a short time before ripening, the fruit of this variety keeps fresh and firm for several days. The Greek Cucumber is an excellent, productive, and moderately early kind. It is also hardy and well adapted for growing in the open ground.

Long Green Chinese Cucumber (*Concombre Vert Très Long de*

Chine).—Leaves most usually entire, but sometimes with three to five well-marked lobes. Fruit slightly flattened on three sides, 10 to 14 inches long, of a rather pale-green colour, marked longitudinally with whitish lines and bearing a few spines, which are entirely white, short, and easily detached from the skin. The colour of the fruit becomes paler as it ripens, until it is finally of a yellowish white with scarcely a shade of green. The flesh is very white, tender, and almost as thick as that of the Long White or of the Early White Cucumber. The plant is very productive, bearing for a long time in succession. It is a half-late variety.

Long Green Chinese Cucumber (⅓ natural size).

Gherkin, or Pickling, Cucumber (*Concombre à Cornichons*). — A vigorous-growing, free-flowering, and productive plant, with stems from 5 to over 6 ft. long. Fruit oblong in shape, and intermediate between the Early Russian and the Early Yellow Dutch varieties. They are almost always gathered soon after the plant flowers, when they are about as thick as the finger, and they are used almost exclusively for pickling, for which purpose they are very extensively grown. There are two distinct kinds of Gherkin, viz. the *Southern* variety (*Cornichon Court du Midi*), which is more properly a small yellow Cucumber, very productive, and of rapid growth, and the Small Green *Paris* variety (*de Paris*)—a more thick-set and more productive plant, with smaller fruit.

Gherkin, or Pickling, Cucumber (natural size of young fruit).

The American variety, known as the *Boston Pickling Cucumber*, has very short fruit scarcely differing from that of the Early Russian Gherkin.

SNAKE CUCUMBER.

Cucumis Melo, L. *var. ; Cucumis flexuosus*, L.   *Cucurbitaceæ.*

French, Concombre serpent.   *German*, Grüne lange gekrummte Sohlangen-Gurke.
Italian, Anguria.

Native of the East Indies.—Annual.—Stem creeping, slender, round
or bluntly angled, and covered with short hairs ; leaves roundish, almost
kidney-shaped, or with five obtuse angles ; flowers monœcious, pale
yellow, small, with five roundish divisions, exactly resembling the flowers
of a Melon and quite unlike those of a Cucumber ; fruit very long
and slender, almost always bent and twisted, of a dark-green colour,
marked with paler longitudinal furrows, and thickest at the end
farthest from the stalk.   They are about 3 ft. and sometimes more in
length, and change to a yellowish colour when ripe, at which time they
also exhale a strong odour of Melons.   The seed is like that of the
Melon.   A gramme contains about 40 seeds, and a litre of them
weighs about 450 grammes.   Their germinating power lasts for seven
or eight years.   This species, notwith-
standing its common name, is a true
Melon.   Individual plants of it are
found bearing at the same time fruit,
some of which are long and snake-like,
while others are broad and oval in shape.

Snake Cucumber ($\frac{1}{15}$ natural size).   Prickly, or West Indian, Gherkin ($\frac{1}{12}$ natural
size ; detached fruit, $\frac{1}{3}$ natural size).

Sometimes even the same fruit will be thin and snake-like near the
stalk, and swollen at the other end into the semblance of a Melon.
The culture is almost exactly like that of the Melon.   The plant does
not grow well in the open air in the climate of Paris.   The Snake
Cucumber is chiefly grown as a curiosity, but it may be used for
pickling, like the Gherkin.

PRICKLY, or WEST INDIAN, GHERKIN.

Cucumis Anguria, L.   *Cucurbitaceæ.*

Concombre des Antilles.

Native of Jamaica.—Annual.—A creeping and very branching
plant.   Stem slender, covered with rough hairs, from 6 to nearly 10 ft.
long, and furnished with simple tendrils.   Leaf-stalks as long as the

blade of the leaf, which is divided into five or seven roundish, slightly toothed lobes. Male flowers yellow, very small, less than ½ inch in diameter, numerous, on short slender stalks; female flowers long-stalked. Fruit oval, green, with whitish longitudinal streaks, turning pale yellow when ripe, covered all over with fleshy protuberances, which are pointed or curved like true spines or prickles. When ripe, it is about two inches long, and over an inch in diameter. The stalk is nearly twice as long as the fruit. The interior of the fruit is almost entirely filled with the seeds. The flesh is very scanty, but white, firm, and of a very agreeable Cucumber flavour, without the slightest bitterness. Seed small, oval, and rather swollen. A gramme contains about 130 seeds, and a litre of them weighs about 550 grammes. Their germinating power lasts for at least six years. In the colonies the fruit is eaten boiled or pickled.

GLOBE CUCUMBER.

Cucumis prophetarum, L. *Cucurbitaceæ.*

Concombre des prophètes.

Native of Northern and Central Africa.—Probably perennial, but annual in France.—A plant with a rather short creeping or climbing stem, which seldom exceeds from about 3 to 5 ft. in length, and is very rough and of a grayish colour. Leaves also grayish, oval, and divided into five roundish lobes. Fruit oblong in shape, about 2 inches long and about 1¾ inch in diameter, marked with alternate bands of yellow and dark green, and covered all over with stout and almost spiny hairs; the flesh is scanty, and too bitter to be edible. Seed small, flat, oval, but terminating in a point at each end, and with a smooth, almost white skin. A gramme contains about 100 seeds, and a litre of them weighs about 500 grammes. Their germinating power lasts for over six years.

With this species is sometimes confounded the Gooseberry Cucumber (*Cucumis myriocarpus*, Ndn.)—a plant with long stems and very green leaves, which produces an abundance of very small fruit covered with stout greenish hairs, and exactly resembling Gooseberries in shape and size.

CUMIN or CUMMIN.

Cuminum Cyminum, L. *Umbelliferæ.*

French, Cumin de Malte. *German*, Römischer Kümmel. *Dutch*, Komijn. *Italian*, Comino di Malta. *Spanish*, Comino.

Native of Upper Egypt.—Annual.—A very low-growing plant, seldom more than 4 to 6 inches high, and branching from the base. Leaves reduced to mere linear blades; flowers small, lilac, borne in terminal umbels of from ten to twenty flowers on the extremities of very divergent branches; seed largish, elongated, concave on one side and convex on the other, with six rather prominent ribs on the convex side, and bearing pretty long hairs, which fold up when the seed is ripe. The seeds have a hot taste and a strong aromatic flavour. A gramme of them contains about 250 seeds, and a litre of them weighs about 350 grammes. Their germinating power lasts tolerably well for three years, but declines visibly after the second year. CULTURE.— The seed is sown in the open ground as soon as it has become warm enough, that is, in the beginning or middle of May. The plants grow rapidly, and the seed commences to ripen at the end of July. No attention is necessary, except the occasional use of the hoe. The seeds are used for flavouring soups and pastry, and also in the manufacture of some kinds of liqueurs.

DANDELION.

Leontodon Taraxacum, L.　*Compositæ.*

French, Pissenlit, Dent-de-lion.　*German,* Löwenzahn.　*Flemish,* Molsalaad.　*Italian,* Dente di leone.

Native of Europe.—Perennial.—Leaves all radical, spreading into a rosette, smooth, oblong, runcinate, with triangular-lanceolate lobes, and entire towards the extremity ; youngest leaves often brownish at the commencement of their growth. Flower-stalks hollow, one-flowered ; flower-heads large, with florets of a golden-yellow colour. Seed compressed, oblong, rough or scaly, and prickly at the top. A gramme contains from 1200 to 1500 seeds, and a litre of them weighs, on an average, 270 grammes. Their germinating power lasts for two years.

Formerly, people contented themselves with gathering Dandelion

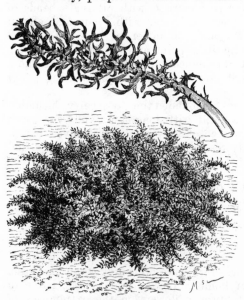

Moss-leaved Dandelion.

in the meadows or fields where it grew naturally, but, as it became an important article of commerce in the Central Market of Paris, the idea was started, about fifteen years ago, that it could be cultivated and improved by the selection of seed from choice plants. The result is that the plant has been improved to a remarkable degree, as any one may easily see by comparing the produce of seeds gathered from the wild plant with that of seeds obtained from the cultivated plants.

CULTURE.—The seed may be sown in March or April, either where the plants are to stand, or in a seed-bed, from which the seedlings are to be pricked out, in May or June, in rows, which should be 14 to 16 inches apart. The plants are extremely hardy, and require no attention beyond occasional hoeings and waterings. In autumn they commence to yield, and will continue to do so all through the winter, if they are looked after. The quality of the Dandelion is much improved by blanching, which may be effected either by covering the bed with a layer of sand, or by placing an inverted flower-pot over each plant, having previously gathered the leaves up together. The pot should be large enough to cover the plant without pressing the leaves too closely against one another. In winter the plants lose most of their leaves, but an abundant new growth takes place in spring, and any plants which have not yielded much the first year do so plentifully in the spring of the second. Uses.—The whole of the plant is used for salad; if blanched, so much the better.

Moss-leaved Dandelion (*Pissenlit Mousse*).—A distinct variety of Curled-leaved Dandelion which forms a much denser and more compact tuft of leaves than the Common kind, very recently raised from seed by Messrs. Vilmorin-Andrieux and Co., of Paris, and apparently permanent in its characteristics. The blade of the leaf is divided and, as it were, slashed into narrow strips. The plant can be easily blanched, and in that condition affords a salad not unlike Curled Endive, but coming in early in spring, when it is very difficult to have any Endive fit for table use.

Thick-leaved, or Cabbaging, Dandelion (⅕ natural size).

Thick - leaved, or **Cabbaging, Dandelion** (*Pissenlit Amélioré à Cœur Plein*).—A very distinct variety, obtained by cultivation, and surpassing the wild plant not so much in the size as in the very great number of its leaves, which form a regular tuft or clump, instead of a plain rosette. It yields a very abundant crop without taking up much ground, and blanches very easily and, indeed, almost naturally. It appears to us to be the best variety that has been obtained up to the present.

There is a sub-variety

Very Early Dandelion (⅕ natural size).

which forms the tuft or clump somewhat earlier, and also comes into leaf sooner after winter. This is known as the Improved Early Dandelion (*Pissenlit Amélioré Très Hâtif*).

Very Early Dandelion.—Another variety, obtained from seed, and also called the Broad-leaved Dandelion. The plant forms a simple rosette of very large and broad leaves, which in summer are nearly entire. The rosette is sometimes 20 inches across. The produce of this variety, however, is not in proportion to the amount of space which it occupies, and the Full-hearted kind is preferable to it in every respect. The Curled-leaved Dandelion, on the other hand, forms very compact tufts, which do not occupy much space. Its leaves are twisted and intertangled, the blade of the leaf being almost entirely cut up into divisions, which are also somewhat turned and twisted. It is a pretty good small kind, but not very productive.

DILL.

Anethum graveolens, L. *Umbelliferæ.*

French, Aneth. *German,* Dill. *Flemish,* Dille. *Danish,* Dild. *Italian,* Aneto.
Spanish, Eneldo.

Native of Southern Europe.—Annual.—A plant 2 to over $2\frac{1}{2}$ ft. high. Leaves very much cut into thread-like segments; stem glaucous green, hollow, very smooth, and branching; flowers yellowish, with very small petals which are rolled inwards and very fugacious, borne in compound umbels without bracts; seed very flat, and having a strong and bitter flavour. A gramme contains about 900 seeds, and a litre of them weighs about 300 grammes. Their germinating power lasts for three years. The plant, in its general appearance, very much resembles the Common Fennel, and all its green parts have a flavour like that of Fennel and Mint combined. Sown in April, where the plants are to stand, it succeeds well in the open air, in any kind of well-drained soil, especially in a warm position. The seeds are used as a condiment, or for pickling along with Gherkins. In the north of France, they are often employed for flavouring winter preserves.

EGG-PLANT.

Solanum Melongena, L. *Solanaceæ.*

French, Aubergine. *German,* Eierpflanze. *Flemish,* Eierplant. *Italian,* Petonciano.
Spanish, Berengena. *Portuguese,* Bringela.

Native of South America. — Annual. — Stem erect, branching; leaves entire, oblong, of a grayish-green colour, more or less powdery, and often spiny on the veins. Flowers solitary in the axils of the branches, shortly stalked; corolla monopetalous, and of a dull violet colour; calyx often spiny, increasing in size with the fruit. Seed small, flattish, kidney-shaped, and yellow. A gramme contains about 250 seeds, and a litre of them weighs about 500 grammes. Their germinating power lasts for six or seven years.

Culture.—In the climate of Paris, the Egg-plant can seldom be grown without the aid of artificial heat. The seed is usually sown on a hot-bed in February or March, and the seedlings are pricked out into another hot-bed six weeks or two months later. Early varieties raised in hot-beds may also be planted out in the open air about the end of May, when the ground has become well warmed. The plants require a warm and sheltered position, and plentiful waterings. In order to obtain handsome, well-grown fruit, a certain number only should be allowed to remain on each plant, proportioned to its strength. It is a good plan also to pinch the extremities of the branches towards the end of summer. In England we have never seen this plant well grown even under glass. In the Eastern States of North America we were surprised at the fine health it attained in the fields, and the great size of the fruit— as large as well-grown Melons.

USES.—The fruit is sometimes eaten raw, but most usually cooked. The different varieties are highly esteemed for table use in the countries of the south of Europe and South America.

Long Purple Egg-plant (*Aubergine Violette Longue*).—Stem greenish, or faintly tinged with brown. Leaves oval, entire, slightly sinuate-lobed, and bearing a few purplish-coloured spines on the veins of the upper surface; youngest leaves purplish-coloured at the base, the others entirely green. Flowers lilac, large, axillary, with a brown calyx, which increases very much in size after the flower fades, so that it is three or four times larger when the fruit is ripe than it was when the flower opened. Fruit oblong-oval, slightly club-shaped, thickest at the end farthest from the stalk, very smooth and glistening, and of an almost black-purple colour; flesh pretty firm and compact, containing few seeds, and best in quality before the fruit is fully grown. When quite ripe, the fruit is from 6 to 8 inches long, and 2 to 3 inches in diameter. A well-grown plant may carry from eight to ten fruit. This is the best variety for table use in all countries where

Long Purple Egg-plant (⅓ natural size).

the summer is long and warm, as it requires five or six months' growth to ripen the fruit. It is therefore especially suitable for the countries of the south of Europe, but for the climate of Paris the following kind is to be preferred.

Early Long Purple Egg-plant (*Aubergine Violette Longue Hâtive*).— A sub-variety of the preceding kind, in comparison with which it is not quite so strong growing nor so large, being of more slender habit. Stem almost black; leaves oval, entire, with hardly any spines, and with the stalk and veins very deeply tinged with purple on the upper surface. The general tint of the leaves is grayer than that of the leaves of the preceding kind, and the fruit is smaller and more slender. This variety, on account of its earliness, is the most suitable for culture in the climate of Paris.

Round Purple Egg-plant (*Aubergine Violette Ronde*). — Stem brownish, as are also the leaf-stalks and the veins of the leaves. Leaves rather large, very green, broad, and almost always sinuated at the edges ; veins purplish-coloured on the upper surface, and bearing a few spines ; stalks very spiny. Fruit very large, and of a paler and duller purple colour than the fruit of the preceding varieties. It is not quite round, but more like a short Pear. The variety is later than the two preceding kinds, and is especially suitable for southern climates. A plant of it should not carry more than three or four fruit.

Round Purple Egg-plant (¼ natural size).

New York Purple Egg-plant (*Aubergine de New York*).—Stem stout, not very tall, usually branching, and of a grayish green, slightly, or not at all, tinged with purple. Leaves entire, undulated at the edges, or faintly lobed, and bearing short spines on the ribs on both sides. Flowers pale lilac, rather large. Fruit very large, of a very short Pear-shape, and slightly flattened at both ends ; it is somewhat paler in colour than that of the Round Purple Egg-plant, but is larger and fuller and entirely devoid of ribs or longitudinal furrows. The fruit-stalk, and also the persistent calyx, usually remain green up to the time of ripening. This variety is distinguished from those already enumerated by its lower stature, its more compact and thick-set habit, and especially by the quality of the flesh, which almost entirely fills the interior of the fruit, leaving but very little space for the seeds. A plant seldom carries more than two fruit. The Common Giant Egg-plant is to be referred to this variety, which is steadily superseding it in cultivation.

Early Dwarf Purple Egg-plant (¹⁄₁₀ natural size).

Early Dwarf Purple Egg-plant (*Aubergine Violette Naine Très Hâtive*).—A very early variety, and therefore very valuable for our climate. Plant low-growing and branching, with a black stem and dark violet-coloured flowers. Leaves of a slightly grayish-green colour, elongated, and faintly waved at the edges ; veins black on the upper surface ; leaf-stalk dark violet, as are also the divisions of the calyx. Fruit ovoid, 3 or 4 inches long and about 2 inches in diameter at the thick end, numerous, of a rather deep but dull purple colour, and not glistening like those of the Long Purple variety. They are fit to gather at least a month earlier than those of any other kind, and each plant may be allowed to carry a dozen or so. The dwarf habit of this plant renders it very suitable for frame culture in early spring. This variety should be looked after, as one of the most likely to suit our English climate, in which the Egg-plant has not yet been successfully cultivated.

Striped, or **Guadaloupe, Egg-plant** (*Aubergine Panachée de la Guadaloupe*).—This variety resembles the Round Purple Egg-plant, but is of much lower growth and less deeply coloured in all its parts. Fruit ovoid, almost twice as long as broad, and smaller than that of the Long Purple variety. The chief distinction of this plant is the peculiar variegation of the fruit, which is striped, lengthways, with pale purple on a white ground.

Chinese Brinjal, or **White China Egg-plant** (*Aubergine Blanche Longue de Chine*).—A very distinct variety, with long slender white fruit, which are almost always curved. A late kind.

New York Improved Egg-plant (*Aubergine Violette Améliorée de New York*).—The fruit of this variety is exactly like that of the Round Purple kind, but the plant itself is dwarfer and of a grayer colour. The flesh of the fruit is very firm, and contains few seeds. This variety is, unfortunately, rather late for the climate of Paris, and still more so for ours.

Black Pekin Egg-plant (*Aubergine Ronde de Chine*).—A strong-growing plant, almost entirely of a blackish-purple colour. Fruit nearly quite spherical, 5 or 6 inches in diameter, of a blackish-purple colour, glistening, and exhibiting this peculiarity—that those parts of it which are protected from the action of the sun by being covered with the divisions of the calyx remain quite green. This variety is not of much account for the climate of Paris, as it is late, and the fruit has a very decided acridity in its flavour.

There are a great many other varieties of Egg-plant, which are more or less closely allied to those just described. The most note-worthy of these we shall briefly mention, as follows :—

Catalonian Egg-plant (*A. de Catalogne*).—A late, spiny kind, resembling the Round Purple variety.

Murcian Egg-plant (*A. de Murcie*).—Fruit purple, round, marked with a few ribs; stem and leaves spiny; the leaves are more lobed and the veins are more deeply coloured than those of the Round Purple variety.

Antilles Giant Egg-plant.—This is a strong-growing late kind, without spines, and bearing fruit resembling that of the Round Purple variety.

Green Egg-plant (*A. Verte*).—This does not appear to be a distinct and fixed variety, as, amongst the White Egg-plants, fruit are frequently met with which are more or less greenish or variegated with green.

Thibet Egg-plant (*A. du Thibet*).—A late variety, with elongated fruit of a greenish-white colour. It was introduced about twenty years ago, and seems to have gone almost out of cultivation.

WHITE EGG-PLANT.

Solanum ovigerum, Dun.

French, Aubergine blanche. *German,* Weisse Eirpflanze.

A rather low-growing, branching plant. Stem and leaf-stalks green, or very faintly tinged with purple, and bearing a few white

spines; leaves wavy at the edges; flowers lilac; fruit white, exactly resembling a hen's egg, but turning yellow when ripe. This variety is more ornamental than useful. The fruit is even (but probably erroneously) considered by some to be unwholesome. There is a form of it which has larger fruit, and another of dwarfer growth and with much smaller fruit, which is known as the Dwarf White Egg-plant.

All the forms are cultivated in the same way as the common kinds. The fruit is not eaten, but may be used as ornaments in baskets of mixed fruits at desserts, etc.

White Egg-plant (⅓ natural size).

EDIBLE BURDOCK, or GOBO.

Lappa edulis, Hort. *Compositæ.*

French, Bardane géante. *Japanese,* Gobo.

Native of Japan.—Biennial.—Radical leaves very large, heart-shaped, somewhat resembling those of the Patience Dock, but not so much elongated; stem reddish, very branching; flowers violet red, in heads bearing hooked scales like those of the Common Burdock; roots of the kind known as tap-roots, cylindrical, rather fleshy and tender when they are young; seed oblong, grayish, with a hard covering, resembling that of the Artichoke. A gramme contains about 80 seeds, and a litre of them weighs about 630 grammes. Their germinating power lasts for five years.

It is doubtful whether this plant is specifically distinct from the Common Burdock (*Arctium Lappa*), a very common weed in all parts of Europe. It is certainly larger in all its parts, but this might be the result of cultivation, as it has long been grown in Japan in exactly the same manner as Salsafy and Scorzonera are with us.

Uses.—The roots, which grow from 1 ft. to 16 inches long, are boiled and served up in various ways. The plant was introduced into Europe from Japan by the traveller Von Siebold, who says that it succeeded well in his garden at Leyden. In order to have the root tender and agreeable to the taste, it should be used when it is two and a half or three months grown. If it is left until it is fully grown, it

branches and becomes hard and almost woody, so that it is not surprising that when sent to table in that state, it has often been pronounced
detestably bad, whereas if eaten when young, as it is by the Japanese,
although it cannot be termed delicious, it is certainly not a bad
vegetable.

Almost all hardy biennial plants with fleshy roots should be experimented on with the view of converting them into kitchen-garden
vegetables, and many, perhaps, might
be available for this purpose under
the conditions of their roots being not
too fibrous, nor possessing any disagreeable flavour which cooking would
not remove. The Wild Carrot and
the Wild Beet are not superior in
quality to the Burdock, and the second
of these plants certainly has a more
disagreeable flavour, and yet continued
cultivation and persevering selection
have converted these two plants into
excellent vegetables, producing roots
which are large, tender, and well
tasted, at least when they are cooked,
and quite different from what they
are in the wild state. There is no
reason, then, why the Burdock should
not be converted into a good table
vegetable, if the plant appears to be
worth the trouble. It is hardy, vigorous, and of rapid growth ; its roots

Edible Burdock, or Gobo (⅛ natural
size).

are long and naturally fleshy, and consequently can be increased in
size and made tender by judicious cultivation. At the present moment,
in the condition in which we now have the plant, a bed of it will yield
as heavy a crop as a bed of Salsafy, and in half or one-third of the
time. As a vegetable it is, therefore, deserving of serious consideration.

ELECAMPANE.

Inula Helenium, L.　*Compositæ.*

French, Aulnée.　*German,* Alant.

Native of Europe.—Perennial.—A tall Composite plant, with broad,
long, oval-lanceolate leaves, narrowed for a considerable length towards
the leaf-stalk ; stem-leaves sessile, sheathing. Stem erect, branching
at the top, 3 ft. or more high, bearing on the ends of the branches
broad solitary flower-heads of a fine bright-yellow colour.

We mention this plant merely to give some account of it, as its
cultivation in the kitchen garden is now almost entirely abandoned.
Formerly its thick fleshy roots were used in the same way as the roots
of Salsafy and Scorzonera are at present, but nowadays they are only
used for medicinal purposes.

ENDIVE.

Cichorium Endivia, L. *Compositæ.*

French, Chicorée Endive. *German,* Endivien. *Flemish* and *Dutch,* Andijvie. *Danish,*
Endivien. *Italian,* Indivia. *Spanish,* Endivia.

Native of the East Indies.—Annual and biennial.—A plant with
numerous radical leaves, smooth, lobed, more or less deeply cut, and
spreading into a rosette. Stem hollow, from 20 inches to over 3 ft.
high, channelled, and branching; flowers blue, axillary, sessile; seed
small, angular, elongated, grayish, ending in a point on one side, and
having a sort of membranous collar on the other. A gramme contains
about 600 seeds, and a litre of them weighs about 340 grammes. Their
germinating power lasts for ten years. All the varieties which have
sprung from *Cichorium Endivia* are distinguished by having the leaves
entirely smooth, both on the blade and on the stalk, and by being of a
more tender constitution and more sensitive to cold than the cultivated
varieties of *Cichorium Intybus*.

CULTURE.—As Endive is a plant of rapid growth, and one of the
most highly esteemed for table use, it is grown all the year round.
The gardeners about Paris commence sowing it in the open ground in
April, and make successional sowings up to the end of August. In
September and October they sow under cloches (or bell-glasses), and
from December to April in hot-beds. (As far as possible, no plants are
grown in the open ground except those which have been sown there, as,
if planted out from hot-beds, they are liable to run to seed the same
year.) The seedlings are pricked out as soon as they are strong enough
and have seven or eight leaves, at a distance of from 10 to 16 inches
from plant to plant, according to the variety, and, from the time they
strike root until they are fully grown, should be frequently and plentifully watered. Endive grown in the open ground may be gathered for use
from August, and the plants will continue to yield, if properly looked
after, either where they stand, or removed to a vegetable-house, up to
the end of winter. During the remainder of the year, the plants which
are sent to table are raised under bell-glasses or in hot-beds. Before
they are gathered, the plants are usually blanched. For this purpose
they are left until nearly full grown, when the leaves are all tied up
together, so as to protect the heart of the plant effectually from the
action of sunlight. The plants are allowed to stand where they
grow, and are watered when necessary, care being taken not to let any
water get into the hearts, or they will be liable to rot. Endive treated
in this way will be fit for use in about twenty days. Any plants which
are standing when frosty weather comes on will continue to grow if
protected by a covering of leaves or straw mats, which should be
removed when the weather becomes mild. In this way the yield of
the different varieties, and especially of the Batavian Endive, may be
prolonged for several weeks. Late-grown plants may be taken up with
balls and removed to a vegetable-house, where they can be blanched.
For particulars of the ways in which Endive is forced, we must refer to
special treatises on market gardening and early spring crops.

CULTURE IN BRITAIN.—Endive requires much less heat than Lettuce, and is more particularly valuable as an autumn and winter salad vegetable. In many gardens, if sown before August, it is almost certain to run to seed prematurely, and consequently it is unwise to depend upon one, or even two sowings.

SOWING.—Our plan is to make a small sowing of the Moss-curled and Green Curled about the middle of July, another of the same varieties and Improved Broad-leaved Batavian about the first week in August, and a final sowing of Green Curled and Batavian at the middle of August. The Moss-curled is close-growing and blanches quickly, but is the least hardy, and is not at all suitable for late work. This variety requires less room than the others, and may be sown in drills 6 inches apart, and the plants should eventually be thinned out to the same distance asunder. The other two are strong growers, and the rows may well be 12 inches apart and the plants 10 inches asunder in the rows. Our first sowing is made on a small border previously used for pricking out Cauliflowers and Brussels Sprouts, and but few of the seedlings are transplanted unless it be to make up blanks. A long border previously well enriched for early Cauliflowers is devoted to the second sowing, this being prepared by simply having the surface lightly coated over with lime and heavily hoed. The drills are drawn and watered, the seed sown thinly and lightly covered. For the final sowing a warmer or rather better drained border is preferred—one previously cropped with early Potatoes. Digging being unnecessary in the former case, it is still less so when planting or sowing ground after Potatoes, but if the ground be at all poor I would certainly fork in, but not bury deeply, a dressing of short manure. We usually experience a great difficulty in preserving the young plants from slugs, and not unfrequently it is necessary to sow seeds in a frame so as to have sufficient plants to make up the large blanks caused by these pests. In some gardens where the soil is light, and the drainage good, it is a good plan to plant the Endive in shallow drills, say, about 6 inches wide and 3 inches deep. In such positions they can be easily watered, and an occasional supply of liquid manure poured between them will cause them to grow to a great size. These drills also render blanching a simple matter, all that is necessary being to cover a few plants a few days before they are wanted with either boards or slates. In order to have Endive in good condition over as long a period as possible, extra pains must be taken with the

BLANCHING AND PROTECTING.—Unless properly blanched, Endives are not appreciated, and unless some measures are taken to insure protection, they are liable to be much injured, if not actually killed, by frosts. All that is necessary in the case of the early crops is to either tie up a certain number at weekly intervals, much as we would Brown Cos Lettuces, or cover with boards, or with rough litter or hay, and the same methods of blanching may be adopted with those protected. Of the three styles of blanching I prefer the hay, as under this the Endive blanches perfectly, without being soiled or injured in any way. Only a given number, according to the demand, however, should be covered at a time, as they will not keep long after being blanched. Where portable garden frames are abundant, any number of plants may be covered with these, the lights being put on and further protection in the shape of mats and litter given when necessary. It is when frames are scarce that the grower has to adopt various contrivances in order to meet the demand for salading. In some districts Endive does not keep well if lifted and stored, but in less moist neighbourhoods I have kept great numbers closely packed in frames. In this case the plants were lifted before severe frosts were anticipated, as if only slightly injured an early decay is certain to follow. A dry day was selected, the plants carefully tied up, lifted up with a trowel so as to secure a good ball of earth to the roots, and they were then carried in hand-barrows to the frame ground. Frames previously used for Melon, Cucumber, and Tomato culture were filled rather closely with the Endive, and into the good soil they soon pushed fresh roots. The whole of the plants were untied, and were blanched with hay according as required, the last to be covered being the Batavian, this being the best keeping sort. We do not care to leave any quantity of Endive in the open from want of frame room, and have frequently stored some in a Mushroom house for early use, and many more in a dry shed, these proving serviceable in lengthening the period before those better stored under the frames, or covered where grown, are cut. Whatever plan of storing is adopted, care should always be taken to lift before the plants are injured and when as dry as possible. The small or half-grown plants of the hardiest sort sometimes stand out uninjured during the winter, especially if planted on a dry or raised border, and these sometimes prove of service in maintaining the supply of salading till such times as the frame Lettuces are fit for use.—W. I.

Endive is largely grown in nearly all market gardens round London, and especially in those situated in moist districts. The first sowing is usually made early in May, either in frames or on prepared beds in the open air. In either case, good rich soil is used in which to sow the seed, and the surface after sowing is made firm by being beaten with the back of the spade. The chief point in reference to early sown Endive is to keep the plants continually growing, as if they experience the least check they run to seed or "bolt," as it is termed. On this account early Endive, as a rule, is not grown in very large quantities. The principal sowing is made early in June, and is succeeded by smaller ones to the end of July. In most cases the outdoor sowings are made on the ground on which they are to grow, as on Celery ridges or between the rows of any crops where there is room, and for which the ground was well manured. Sometimes, however, the seed is sown on beds, and the seedlings thinned out if too thick, and transplanted when sufficiently large to handle. In any case the distance apart of permanent plants is from 12 to 15 inches. Endive and Lettuces are frequently planted on land alternately, large fields being often devoted to them; sometimes whole fields of Endive alone occur. Blanching is effected by tying up the leaves like those of Lettuces with withies or pieces of bast. In from twelve to fifteen days after being tied up Endive is ready for market. The most forward piece is then cleared by pulling the plants up by their roots, and in this state they are packed in hampers and conveyed to market. The Dwarf Green Curled and the Batavian are the kinds chiefly grown, but the former sort is that which is grown in the greatest quantity. The produce from the earliest sowings is ready for market early in August and onwards until Christmas, and even later. A few growers house plants for winter and spring supply, but now, when they have to compete in the market with the French, the prices obtained scarcely remunerate them for their trouble and house-room.

Uses.—The leaves are eaten boiled or in salad. In England we make no such good use of Endive as a boiled vegetable as the French do. Many vegetables as we have, the distinct flavour of certain varieties of Endive when boiled should make them as well liked as table vegetables as they are abroad.

Small Green Curled Summer Endive (*Chicorée Fine d'Été*).—
Under this name, two very distinct varieties are very extensively
cultivated, namely, the *Paris*
and the *Anjou.* The *Paris,* or
Italian, variety is the older
of the two kinds. It has its
leaves arranged in a dense rosette, full even at the centre,
and from 12 to 14 inches in
diameter. The leaves are very
much divided in the upper half
into slender segments, which
are not much curled. The lower
half of the leaf is reduced to a
rib or stalk over 1 inch wide,
and of a faint rosy colour, especially at the base.

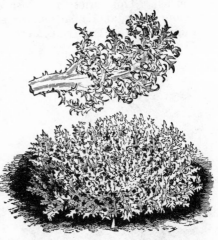

The *Anjou* variety began to
be very generally cultivated
about ten years ago, and is
superseding the other variety,
to which it is very much supe-

Small Green Curled Summer Endive (Anjou
variety) (⅛ natural size).

rior. It forms a rosette nearly as broad as that of the Paris variety,
but much denser and more convex in shape. The leaves are very
numerous, and closely crowded together ; the leaf-stalk or rib is
entirely white at the base, ½ inch or more broad, and edged on the
lower half with white thread-like leafy segments. In the upper
half of the leaf the midrib widens perceptibly, is often more or less
contorted, takes a green tint, and is furnished with very finely cut leafy
appendages, which are only slightly curled, and are of a clear-green
colour, changing to a butter yellow in the heart of the plant. The
extremities of the leaves become intertangled to such an extent that
one leaf cannot be distinguished from another, and the whole plant
almost resembles a great tuft of Moss. These two kinds are cultivated
in the same way. They are both suitable for forcing and for open-air
culture, especially in summer and early autumn, but later on they are
very liable to rot.

Small Green Fine-curled Winter Endive (*Chicorée Frisée de
Meaux*).—This variety forms
a broader rosette than the
preceding kind, but not so
full. It is usually from 16
to 18 inches across. The
leaves are longer, and their
divisions are more curled and
crisped than in the summer
variety. The midrib, which
is tinged with rose-colour on
the lower part, is often ½ inch
or more broad, the middle
part being furnished with very

Small Green Fine-curled Winter Endive
(⅛ natural size).

much divided, crisped and curled, leafy segments. The terminal portion of the leaf is entire and almost flat, with the margin notched and curled. This variety is not so early as the preceding kinds, but it is more hardy, and is particularly suitable for an autumn crop.

Picpus Curled Endive (*Chicorée Frisée de Picpus*).—This kind is nearly the same size as the preceding one, the diameter of the rosette being from 14 to 16 inches, but the leaves are far more finely cut, and the heart of the rosette is fuller and firmer. The two varieties differ remarkably in the formation of the terminal part of the leaf. In the *Picpus* variety, this is very narrow and almost reduced to a midrib; while in the other kind it has some degree of width. The midrib or stalk of the *Picpus* also is much narrower, is destitute of the rosy tinge, and only furnished here and there with leafy appendages, which gives it a very peculiar appearance. The *Picpus* is a very good and hardy kind of Endive, and is well adapted for open-air culture.

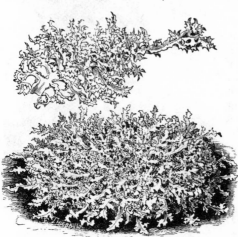

Picpus Curled Endive (⅓ natural size).

Rouen, or Stag's-horn, Endive (*Chicorée Fine de Rouen*).—A handsome and very distinct variety, forming a very full rosette, 14 to 16 inches in diameter. The leaves are not so finely divided, nor are the divisions so much curled, as in the preceding varieties; they are also of a duller and grayer colour. The midrib is deep, but very narrow, and entirely white. This is one of the kinds which are most extensively cultivated at Paris, and through all the north of France. It is particularly well adapted for open-air culture, and, being hardy, yields a crop until late in autumn.

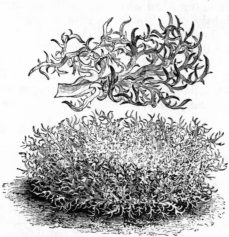

Rouen, or Stag's Horn, Endive (⅓ natural size).

Louviers Endive (*Chicorée de Louviers*).—This variety, which seems to be derived from the preceding kind, is very distinct and good. The plant forms a rosette, which is not so broad as the Stag's-horn variety, but is fuller, more compact, and more convex. The leaves are paler in colour, but the divisions are more regular and narrower. The heart of the rosette is remarkably dense, so that plants of this variety, although occupying less space than those of the preceding kind, yield quite as heavy a crop. In con-sequence of the almost hemi-spherical form of the rosette, it contains a greater number of blanched leaves, in proportion to its size, than any other variety; so that, bulk for bulk, it yields a larger amount of useful produce.

Louviers Endive (⅕ natural size).

Moss-curled Endive (*Chicorée Mousse*).—Rosette rather small, seldom exceeding 10 or 12 inches in diameter, and not often very compact. Leaves clear dark green, very much cut, curled, and crisped, so that it is difficult to distinguish one leaf from another, and the whole plant resembles a tuft of Moss. The midribs of the leaves are narrow and very white. This is not a very productive variety, but it is sometimes in request on account of its peculiar appearance. As it occupies but little space, it is very suitable for growing under bell-glasses. Another equally dense thick-set variety is sometimes met with under the name of the Short Bell - glass Endive (*Chicorée Courte à Cloche*). This appears to be intermediate be-tween the Moss-curled and the Small Green Curled Summer Endive, coming nearer, how-ever, to the latter.

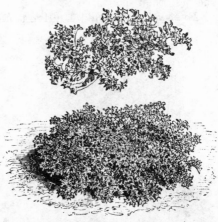

Moss-curled Endive (⅛ natural size).

Ruffec Green Curled En-dive (*Chicorée Frisée de Ruffec*). —Rosette very large, often 16 to 18 inches in diameter, at first sight slightly resembling that of the Moss-curled variety, but more tufty, and fuller in the centre. The midrib of the leaf is very white and thick, very tender and fleshy, nearly an inch broad, but looking much broader on account of the blanching of a large portion of the blade of the leaf, the remainder of which is cut and curled almost like the Moss-curled variety. The *Ruffec* is cer-tainly one of the best kinds for open-air culture, and is equally suitable for summer and autumn. We do not know any other variety which bears cold weather so well, and we have seen it in the open ground, simply covered with leaves, surviving winters in which all other kinds perished.

R

Imperial Curled Endive (*Chicorée Frisée Impériale*).—A handsome Curled variety, forming a broad, tall, and well-furnished rosette, and

Ruffec Green Curled Endive (⅛ natural size).

resembling the preceding kind more than any other variety. It differs from it, however, in the lighter colour of the leaves, which are also less finely cut, but have the segments very much curled and folded. This variety is especially noticeable for the circumstance that its leaves do not exhibit a bare midrib at the bottom, like those of other varieties, but run down to the very ground, where they are from ⅘ inch to nearly 1¾ inch broad. They are also perfectly white for at least one-half their length.

Ever-White Curled Endive (*Chicorée Toujours Blanche*).—Rosette not very dense nor well furnished, 14 to 16 inches in diameter; midrib of the leaf yellow, and tinged with rose colour; leaves very pale in hue, having the appearance of being artificially blanched. This peculiar colour is the chief distinction of the plant, as it is neither very productive nor of particularly good quality; yet it is always welcomed in the markets, on account of its blanched appearance.

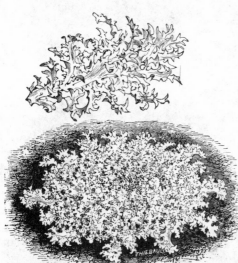

Ever-White Curled Endive (⅛ natural size).

A variety of White Curled Endive, in which the leaves are wavy and curled rather than much divided, was formerly in cultivation, but it has been superseded by the present very finely cut variety.

Large Green Curled Endive (*Chicorée Verte d'Hiver*).—It is only in the warmest parts of France, or in districts by the seaside, that

Endive can be safely left exposed to the open air during winter. The present variety, which has often been recommended as quite hardy in the climate of Paris, is in reality almost as sensitive to cold as the other varieties, and quite as much so as the Ruffec Curled Endive, which is one of the hardiest. It forms a rosette, 20 inches broad at the most, and not very full at the heart, composed of long straight leaves, which are very much divided, somewhat curled, and of a darker green than those of any other kind of Endive. It is, in fact, a variety which has been very little improved, and hardly differs from the half-wild variety which is grown in Provence under the name of *Chicorée Verte* (Green, or Curled, Endive), and is elsewhere known as *Chicorée du Midi* (Southern Endive).

Green Curled Upright Endive (*Chicorée Frisée Grosse Pancalière*). —Under this name a variety of Curled Endive is sometimes met with in Normandy, which, in its general appearance and the divisions of the leaves, very much resembles the Small Green Curled Winter Endive, from which it is distinguished, however, by the abundance of its leaves, which completely fill up the centre of the rosette, so that the central leaves stand quite erect and the plant is blanched naturally, without requiring to be tied up.

Intermediate Bordeaux Endive (*Chicorée Bâtarde de Bordeaux*).— This kind, which is very little known outside of its native district, forms the connecting link between the Curled-leaved and the Broad-leaved, or Batavian, varieties. It is a vigorous-growing plant, with long broad leaves, which are rather lobed than truly cut, and would form a rosette 20 inches at least in diameter, if they had not a greater tendency to turn upwards than to spread on the ground. The heart is not very full, but by tying up the leaves the interior of the tuft is readily blanched, and affords an abundant and pretty tender salad. In the south-west of France this variety grows in the open air all through the winter, and at Paris it bears the early frosts well.

Broad-leaved, or **Batavian, Endive** (French, *Chicorée-Scarole Ronde;* German, *Grüne Vollherzige Breitblättrige Escariol;* Dutch, *Escarol, Kropandijvie;* Italian, *Endivia Scariola;* Spanish, *Escarolo de Hojas Anchas*).— Rosette broad, often 16 inches in diameter; leaves entire, toothed at the edges and more or less twisted or waved, with broad, thick, white midribs. The central leaves, being partially turned inwards, serve to cover and protect the heart of the plant, thus forming a sort

Broad-leaved, or Batavian, Endive (⅓ natural size).

of a very decided dwarf head. When the plant is in this condition, the French gardeners say that it is "*bouclée*," or "curled." When well grown and artificially blanched in the manner described at the commencement of this article, this plant forms one of the best winter salads. The blanched inner leaves are particularly tender and crisp, and have a fine and very agreeable flavour. This variety is far more extensively cultivated than any other kind.

Broad-leaved Limay Endive (*Scarole Grosse de Limay*).—Leaves very large, arranged like the rose-work in architecture, of a palish-green colour, puckered, entire, the inner ones cut into rather deep but not very numerous lobes, very much puckered, and forming a stoutish kind of head. This is a larger variety than the Common Broad-leaved kind, to which it is preferred in some localities near Paris, without any very apparent reason.

White Batavian Endive (*Scarole Blonde*).—Rosette somewhat broader than that of the Common Broad-leaved kind, but not so full, and especially remarkable for the very pale colour of the leaves. This variety heads to a much less extent than any other kind, and is usually cut when young, before it is fully grown. It is also less hardy than the Common Broad-leaved kind, and more liable to be spoiled by dampness, but, on account of its light colour, it is in much request for salad. It is chiefly grown for summer and autumn use, and by making successional sowings it can always be had tender.

White Batavian Endive (⅛ natural size).

Broad-leaved Winter Endive (*Scarole en Cornet*).—This variety differs very much in appearance from the other kinds of Endive, and even from the other Broad-leaved kinds. Its leaves are fewer, but much larger, being almost as broad as long, and cut at the edges into numerous long teeth. The midrib appears to branch from the base of the leaf, over which it diverges in all directions. The leaf, which is at first folded up in the centre of the plant, opens out as it grows, like a twisted paper bag unfolding itself; frequently it forms a kind of hood, which continues to envelop the younger leaves for a considerable time, thus producing a genuine head. If the plant were improved in this direction, it would afford an excellent winter salad, as it is comparatively hardy and withstands ordinary winters in the climate of Paris, when protected with a covering of leaves or

Broad-leaved Winter Endive (⅛ natural size).

straw mats. It is especially suitable for the west and south of France. It is possible that, by attention and perseverance, a sub-variety may be raised from this plant with a perfect head like that of a Lettuce or a Cabbage, but it is to be feared that it is not quite hardy enough for the northern and central districts of France.

EVENING PRIMROSE.

Œnothera biennis, L.   *Onagraceæ.*

French, Énothère bisannuelle.   *German,* Rapuntica.   *Flemish,* Ezelskruid.
Italian, Rapontica.

Native of Peru.—Biennial.—A plant with a rather thick, long tap-root, the flesh of which is white and firm. Radical leaves growing in a rosette, stalked, obovate or elliptic in shape, sinuate-toothed at the base; stems erect, branching, over 3 ft. in height, bearing lanceolate leaves which are more or less narrowed into the leaf-stalk; flowers yellow, large, in leafy terminal clusters; seed-vessels long, furrowed, narrowed at both ends ; seed small, brown, with five or six flat facets. A gramme contains about 600 seeds, and a litre of them weighs about 375 grammes. Their germinating power lasts for three years. The culture and uses of this plant are almost the same as those of the Salsafy. It is more, however, as a curiosity that we mention it, although its rather tender and fleshy root is sometimes used as a table vegetable. It should be employed for this purpose at the end of the first year of its growth, when the plant has put forth only one rosette of leaves.

Evening Primrose (⅓ natural size).

FENNEL.

Umbelliferæ.

French, Fenouil.   *German,* Fenchel.   *Flemish* and *Dutch,* Venkel.   *Danish,* Fennikel.
Italian, Finocchio.   *Spanish,* Hinojo.

Native of Southern Europe.—Perennial.—The following three plants of the genus *Fœniculum* are in cultivation, and most authors are agreed in thinking that each of them should be referred to a different botanical species.

Common Wild, or Bitter, Fennel (*Fœniculum vulgare,* Gartn. *Fenouil Amer*).—Perennial.—Rather common in France, in the wild state. Leaves very much divided into thread-like segments; leaf-stalks broad, almost membranous, clasping the stem, which is smooth, hollow, and about 5 feet high; flowers greenish, in broad, terminal umbels; seed long, rounded at both ends, and retaining the remains of the withered stigma, of a dark-gray colour, with five ribs, three of which are on the back of the seed, and one at each side. A gramme contains about 310 seeds, and a litre of them weighs about 450 grammes. Their germinating power lasts for four years. This plant requires no attention. It is perennial and hardy to such a degree that it is often found growing on old walls, rubbish-heaps, etc. Sometimes, but rarely, the leaves are used for seasoning. The plant is chiefly grown for its seeds, which are often used in the manufacture of liqueurs.

Common Garden, or **Long Sweet, Fennel** (*Fœniculum officinale,* All.; *Anethum Fœniculum,* L. *Fenouil Doux*).—Native of Southern Europe.—Biennial, or annual in cultivation.—Although this plant bears some resemblance to the Wild Fennel, it differs from it in having much stouter stems, and the leaves much less divided, the segments being also of larger size, and of a more glaucous-green colour. It also differs in the remarkable size of the leaf-stalk, the sides of which spread and are curved in such a manner as to sheath part of the stem and even the base of the leaf above it. Flowers greenish, in broader umbels than those of the Wild Fennel, and with stouter and stiffer rays; seed at least twice as long as that of the wild kind, flat on one side and convex

Finocchio, or Florence Fennel
(⅕ natural size).

on the other, traversed by five thick yellowish ribs, which occupy almost the entire surface of the skin. A gramme contains about 125 seeds, and a litre of them weighs about 235 grammes. Their germinating power lasts for four years. CULTURE. —The seed is sown in drills, chiefly in autumn, in order to have the crop come in during the following spring. It is sometimes used raw as a side dish; the seeds are also used in the manufacture of liqueurs.

The famous "*Carosella,*" so extensively used in Naples, and scarcely known in any other place, is referred by authors to *Fœniculum piperitum,* D.C.; a species very closely related to *F. officinale.* The plant is used while in the act of running to bloom; the stems, fresh and tender, are broken and served up raw, still enclosed in the expanded leaf-stalks. They are esteemed a great delicacy and are obtained only from the end of March till June.

Finocchio, or **Florence Fennel** (*Fœniculum dulce,* D.C. *Fenouil de Florence;* Italian, *Finocchio Dolce*).—Native of Italy.—Annual.—A very distinct, low-growing, and thick-set plant, with a very short stem, which has the joints very close together towards the base. Leaves large, very finely cut, and of a light-green colour; leaf-stalks very broad, of a whitish-green hue, overlapping one another at the base of the stem, the whole forming a kind of head or enlargement varying in size from that of a hen's egg to that of the fist, firm, white, and sweet inside. The greatest height of the plant, even when run to seed, does not exceed from 2 to about 2½ feet. The flower umbels are large, with thickish rays, which have a mild, sweet flavour. Seed oblong, very broad in proportion to its length, flat on one side and convex on the other, with five prominent ribs, in the intervals between which the gray colour of the seed is well shown. A gramme contains about 200 seeds, and a litre of them weighs about 300 grammes. Their germinating power lasts for four years.

CULTURE AND USES.—The seed is usually sown in spring for a summer crop, and towards the end of summer for a late autumn crop, in warm countries. It is sown in rows 16 to 20 inches apart. All the attention required is to thin out the seedlings so as to have them 5 or 6 inches apart, and to water the plants as often and as plentifully as possible. When the head or enlargement of the leaf-stalks at the base of the stem has attained about the size of a hen's egg, it may be slightly earthed-up so as to cover half of it, and in about ten days afterwards cutting for use may be commenced with the most forward plants, and continued as each plant advances in growth. The plant is usually eaten boiled. In flavour it somewhat resembles Celery, but with a sweet taste and a more delicate odour. Up to the present time, it is not much used in France, but it deserves to be more extensively cultivated. We have not seen it used in England.

FENNEL FLOWER.

Nigella sativa, L. *Ranunculaceæ.*

French, Nigelle aromatique. *German,* Schwartz-Kummel. *Flemish* and *Dutch,* Narduszaad. *Spanish,* Nigela aromatica.

Native of the East.—Annual.—An erect-growing plant, with a stiff, somewhat hairy, and branching stem. Leaves very deeply cut into linear segments, and of a grayish-green colour; flowers terminal, pale or grayish blue, succeeded by toothed seed-vessels filled with almost triangular seeds, which are rough-skinned, black, and have a rather strong aromatic flavour. A gramme contains about 220 seeds, and a litre of them weighs about 550 grammes. Their germinating power lasts for three years. There is a variety with yellow seeds, but resembling the type in every other respect. The seed is sown in April or May, and preferably in light warm soil. The plants require no attention while growing, and the seed ripens towards August. The ripe seeds are used for seasoning in various culinary preparations. In

Fennel Flower (flower and seed-vessel) (½ natural size).

Germany the name of Schwartz-Kummel is also applied to the seeds of the single-flowered *Nigella damascena.*

COMMON GARLIC.

Allium sativum, L. *Liliaceæ.*

French, Ail ordinaire. *German,* Gewöhnlicher Knoblauch. *Flemish,* Look. *Dutch,* Knof-look. *Danish,* Hvidlog. *Italian,* Aglio. *Spanish,* Ajo vulgar. *Portuguese,* Alho.

Native of Southern Europe.—Perennial.—A bulbous plant, all the parts of which, and especially the underground portion, have a very strong and well-known burning taste. The bulbs or heads are composed of about ten cloves, enveloped by a very thin white or rose-coloured membranous skin. The plant hardly ever flowers, in the climate of Paris at least, and is propagated exclusively by means of the cloves, for which purpose those on the outside of the head should be selected, in preference to the inner ones, which are not so well developed. CULTURE.—At Paris the cloves are most usually planted as soon as winter is over. Sometimes, especially in the south of France, they are planted in October for an early summer crop. The plant likes rich, deep, well-drained soil. In damp soils, or when watered too much, it often rots. When the stem is fully grown, gardeners are in the habit of twisting it into a knot, in order to increase the size of the bulbs. After the stems have withered, the bulbs are taken up, and will keep well from one year to another. The Common Garlic is the kind which is most extensively grown. The membranous skin or covering of the bulbs is of a silvery-white colour.

Common Garlic (¼ natural size).

Plant the cloves (*i.e.* the separated portions of the bulbs) in shallow drills about 1 ft. asunder, and 6 inches apart in the row, covering them with soil to the depth of 1 or 2 inches; or plant whole bulbs 1 ft. apart each way, and never deep, as wet is apt to get down among the cloves, causing canker and mildew. Merely stretch a line or measure; take the bulbs by the neck and press them half or, say, two-thirds into the soil; then drop a pinch of fine sifted cinder-ashes over them, to prevent worms from drawing them out of the ground. February is about the best season to plant them. A small quantity may be planted in autumn, if it be desired to have a stock early the following season. From this autumnal or, to speak more precisely, October planting, bulbs may be taken up for use early in the succeeding summer. Any time after the leaves turn yellow the crop may be taken up and dried, hanging it up in bunches by the stalks in any airy room.

USES.—In southern countries Garlic is very much used in cookery, but it is not so highly esteemed in the countries of the North. It is only just to say, however, that, when grown in cold climates, it has a stronger and more biting or burning flavour than it has in warm countries.

Early Pink Garlic (*Ail Rose Hâtif*).—This is an earlier variety than the Common Garlic, and is also distinguished from it by the pink or rosy colour of the skin which covers the head. About Paris, this variety is almost always planted in autumn, as it is said not to succeed well if planted in spring. About fifteen years ago, a variety came into notice, under the name of *Ail Rond du Limousin*. This did not appear to us to differ appreciably from the Common Garlic, from which round heads or bulbs can always be obtained by planting late in the season ; and, if these heads are replanted entire in the following year, they will produce heads of enormous size.

Great-headed Garlic (*Allium Ampeloprasum*, L. *Ail d'Orient*).—Native of Southern Europe.—Perennial.—This plant produces a very large head or bulb, composed of cloves, in the same way as that of the Common Garlic, but of milder flavour. The stem, leaves, and flowers are so like those of the Leek, that there is every reason to think that both plants have originated from the same type, and have been differently modified by cultivation, the bulb in the one case and the stem in the other having been the subject of improvement. When Leeks produce cloves, which occurs pretty often, these cloves are exactly like those of the Great-headed Garlic. The flowers, which grow in a large round head, yield fertile seeds, but the plant is most usually propagated by means of the cloves, this being a speedier method. The culture and uses are the same as those of the preceding kinds.

GOLDEN THISTLE.

Scolymus hispanicus, L. *Compositæ.*

French, Scolyme d'Espagne. *Dutch*, Varkens distel. *Italian*, Barba gentile. *Spanish*, Escolimo.

Native of Southern Europe. — Biennial. — A plant with a white and rather fleshy tap-root. Radical leaves oblong, usually variegated with pale green on a dark-green ground, very spiny, and narrowed at the base into the leaf-stalk; stem very branching, from 2 to 2½ ft. high, furnished with sessile, decurrent, and very spiny leaves; flowers of a bright yellow colour, in sessile heads of two or three flowers each ; seed flat, yellowish, surrounded by a white scarious appendage. A gramme contains about 200 seeds, and a litre of them

Golden Thistle (1/12 natural size; root, ⅓ natural size).

weighs about 125 grammes. Their germinating power lasts for three years. The seed is sown in March or April, in well-dug soil, in the same manner as Salsafy, and the plants are afterwards treated in exactly the same way as Salsafy plants. The roots may commence to be taken up for use in September or October, and will continue to yield a supply during the winter. The roots are eaten, like Salsafy. They are often 10 to 12 inches long, and nearly 1 inch thick.

GOOD KING HENRY.

Chenopodium Bonus-Henricus, L.   *Chenopodiaceæ.*

French, Ansérine Bon-Henri.   *German,* Gemeiner Gänsefuss.   *Flemish* and *Dutch,* Ganzevoet.   *Italian,* Bono Enrico.

Native of Europe.—Perennial.—Stem about 2½ ft. high, smooth, slightly channelled; leaves alternate, long-stalked, arrow-shaped, undulated, and smooth, of a dark-green colour, frosted or mealy on the under surface, rather thick and fleshy; flowers small, greenish, in close, compact clusters; seed black, small, kidney-shaped. A gramme contains about 430 seeds, and a litre of them weighs about 625 grammes. Their germinating power lasts for five years.

CULTURE AND USES.—This plant, being perennial and extremely hardy, will grow and yield abundantly for several years, without any attention except the occasional use of the hoe. It is easily raised from seed, which is best sown in spring, either where the plants are to stand or, preferably, in a seed bed. In the latter case, the seedlings are pricked out once before they are permanently planted out 16 inches apart every way. The leaves are eaten, like Spinach, and it has been suggested to use the shoots, like Asparagus, as a very early vegetable, blanched by simply earthing them up.

We think it an excellent vegetable for England, and deserving to be more generally planted. It is extensively grown by the Lincolnshire farmers, almost every garden having its bed, which, if placed in a warm corner and well manured, yields an abundant supply of delicious shoots a fortnight before Asparagus come in, and for some weeks afterwards. From a south border cutting generally commences early in April, and continues until the end of June. Some say they like it better than Asparagus. When properly grown, the young shoots should be almost as thick as the little finger, and in gathering, it should be cut under the ground something the same as Asparagus. In preparing it for use, if the outer skin or bark have become tough, strip it off from the bottom upwards, and then wash and tie it up in bunches like Asparagus. It is best boiled in plenty of water. When tender, strain and serve simply, or upon toast. Some have melted butter with it, others eat it simply with the gravy and meat. In cultivation, the Mercury will grow anywhere; but, to have it in the best form, good cultivation is necessary. To this end you cannot have the ground too deep nor too rich. Hence we should say, trench the ground 2 ft. deep, mixing in an abundance of rich manure, and plant as early in the spring as possible. As the plant is a perennial, it is necessary to get an abundant yield of shoots, and to get them as strong as possible—and hence, in time, each plant may be 1 ft. or more in diameter. In planting, put the rows 18 inches apart, and the plants 1 ft. apart in the row. It is wild in some parts of England.

GOURDS.

Cucurbita, L. *Cucurbitaceæ.*

French, Courges. *German*, Speise-Kürbiss. *Flemish* and *Dutch*, Pompoen. *Danish*, Graskar. *Italian*, Zucca. *Spanish*, Calabaza. *Portuguese*, Gabaça.

The cultivation of Gourds dates from a very early period, and few vegetables are more extensively grown. The almost innumerable varieties of them which are met with have long since induced the conclusion that they could not all have possibly originated from a single type, but to M. Charles Naudin belongs the credit of having first thrown light upon the chaos of species and varieties, and of having ascertained the origin and parentage of the different forms, all of which he refers to three very distinct species, viz. *Cucurbita maxima*, Duch., *C. moschata*, Duch., and *C. Pepo*, L. We shall describe in succession the varieties which have sprung from each of the different botanical types, following the classification of M. Naudin, and we may remark that we do not know any form of Gourd that should necessarily be considered a hybrid between any two of these species. Although the various forms of cultivated Gourds have, as we have just observed, originated from plants which differ in their botanical characteristics and also in their native habitats, they nevertheless, in their mode of growth and in their fruit, exhibit a striking resemblance, from which it is easy to understand how it was that they were for a long time supposed to be mere varieties of a single species. They are all annual climbing plants, furnished with tendrils; their stems are perfectly herbaceous, very long, pliant, and tough, angular and rough ; the leaves are broad, with hollow stalks, and roundish or kidney-shaped lobes, sometimes more or less incised or deeply cut; the flowers are large, yellow, and monœcious ; and the fruit is round or elongated, almost always ribbed, and with the seeds in a central cavity, surrounded by usually thick flesh. The plants grow very rapidly, and heat is indispensable for their development. Being originally natives of warm climates, they cannot be sown in France before May without the aid of artificial heat, and their growth is completely stopped by the early frosts, which make havoc of all their green parts.

CULTURE.—The seed is usually sown in the open ground in May. In order to forward the growth, round or square holes, of various widths and about 20 inches deep, are filled with manure, upon which is placed a layer of soil or compost from 6 to 8 inches thick. In this the seed is sown, two or three seeds being usually given to each hole. The space to be left between the plants varies according as the variety grown is of a more or less spreading habit of growth. For an early crop, the seed may either be sown in a hot-bed, and the seedlings pricked out into another hot-bed before they are finally planted out, or it may be sown in pots placed on a hot-bed, in which the plants are left until they are finally planted out. When very large fruit are desired, only two or three should be left on each plant, the best being selected, and the branches should be cut a few leaves beyond the last fruit. The readiness with which the stems of Gourds take root may also be turned to account by covering those stems which bear the finest fruit here and there with soil at the joints, where they soon strike root, especially if watered now and then, if needful. The effect of this is to increase the size of the fruit, in consequence of the additional supply of nutriment. USES.—The fruit, whether young or fully grown, is cooked and sent to table in an infinite variety of ways, and there are also some varieties which are eaten raw, like Cucumbers. The only Gourd generally cultivated in England is the Vegetable Marrow, and the people do not even know the importance and the distinct value of the others, especially the keeping kinds grown in America and France.

I. Cucurbita maxima, Duch., and Varieties.

This species is the parent of the largest-sized Gourds; amongst others, of those known by the name of *Pumpkins.* All the cultivated varieties of *Cucurbita maxima* exhibit in common the following characteristics:—The leaves are large, kidney-shaped, rounded, and never deeply divided; the numerous stiff hairs which cover all the green parts of the plant never become spiny; the segments of the calyx are united for a certain portion of their length, and the whole of this portion is devoid of well-marked ribs and presents only a few veins or nerves; the segments of the calyx are narrowed from the base to the extremity; lastly, the stalk of the fruit is always roundish and without ribs, often thickens considerably after the flower has fallen, becomes cracked, and sometimes attains a diameter twice or three times that of the stem. The seed is rather variable in size and colour, but always very smooth. On an average, a gramme contains only three seeds, and a litre of them weighs about 400 grammes. Their germinating power lasts for six years. The principal varieties which have sprung from *Cucurbita maxima* are the following:—

PUMPKINS.

French, Potirons. *German,* Melonen-Kürbiss. *Danish,* Centner-Grœskar. *Italian,* Zucca. *Spanish,* Calabaza totanera.

Under this name, which does not correspond to any botanical division, are grouped a certain number of varieties of *Cucurbita maxima* which are remarkable for the great size of their fruit. In France they are grown on a large scale for market, and also on farms for home use. At the Central Market in Paris, Pumpkins may often be seen which weigh over 110 pounds each.

Mammoth Pumpkin (*Potiron Jaune Gros*).—Stems climbing, from 16 to nearly 20 ft. long; leaves very large, roundish, or with five faintly marked angles, and of a dark-green colour; fruit very much flattened at the ends, and with well-marked ribs; skin of a salmon-yellow colour, and slightly cracked or netted when ripe; flesh yellow, thick, fine flavoured, sweet, and keeping good for a long time. In the United States, under the name of the *Connecticut Field Pumpkin,* a variety is grown which resembles the present one, except in having a somewhat finer skin.

Large White Pumpkin (*Potiron Blanc Gros*).—Fruit very large, approaching much more to the spherical shape than that of the pre-

ceding kind, and with a very smooth, creamy-white skin; flesh fine
flavoured, not so deep in colour nor so strong tasted as that of the
Mammoth Pumpkin, which
the plant resembles exactly
in its habit of growth. This
variety is very distinct and
remarkable for the colour
and the enormous size of the
fruit, yet it is not very much
grown.

Étampes Pumpkin (*Po-
tiron Rouge Vif d'Étampes*).
—Fruit of medium size, not
so broad as that of the Mammoth Pumpkin, but relatively
thicker; ribs broad and well
marked; skin of a very bright
and distinct orange colour.
The cultivation of this variety
has been very much extended
of late years, and it is now
the kind which is most frequently seen in the Central
Market at Paris. In its habit
of growth it resembles the
Mammoth Pumpkin, but its
leaves are rather paler. There
are two forms of it, one of

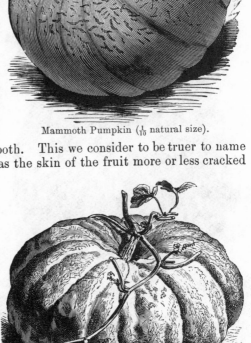

Mammoth Pumpkin (¹⁄₁₀ natural size).

which has the fruit quite smooth. This we consider to be truer to name
than the other form, which has the skin of the fruit more or less cracked
and netted. Some culti-
vators prefer the latter,
saying that it has thicker
flesh. It appears to us to
be a reversion towards the
Mammoth variety.

Large Green Pumpkin
(*Potiron Vert Gros*).—Fruit
large, rather flattened, with
a dark-green skin, which is
often cracked or netted when
ripe. It is a good hardy
variety, but the following
kind is now rather more in
favour.

Spanish Gourd or
Pumpkin (*Potiron Vert
d'Espagne*).—Stems 10 to

Étampes Pumpkin (¹⁄₁₀ natural size).

13 ft. long; leaves of medium size, roundish, of a dark green slightly
tinged with ash-colour; fruit of medium size or even comparatively
small, very much flattened, hollowed on both ends; skin green, often

very finely netted, which gives it a grayish tint; flesh bright yellow, very thick, and keeping good for a very long time. This excellent

Spanish Gourd or Pumpkin.

variety, which is in very great demand in the markets, has the advantage of producing fruit of a moderate size, which are generally more convenient for family use than the very large kinds, which often become spoiled before the whole of them can be eaten, all kinds of Gourds being very difficult to keep after the skin is cut. When growing, the plant will carry two or three fruit well.

Boulogne Gray Pumpkin (*Potiron Gris de Boulogne*).— The size of this fine variety approaches that of the old Large Green Pumpkin, but the colour and appearance of the skin, and the quality of the flesh, cause it to resemble the Spanish Gourd particularly. The plant is of vigorous growth, pretty early, and very productive, with large broad leaves, and fruit which are often from $2\frac{1}{2}$ to 3 ft. across, and about half as thick. The skin is of a dark olive colour, sometimes a little bronzy on the side next the sun, and marked with longitudinal bands of a slightly paler colour; the whole surface is also covered with a great number of very fine short parallel lines, which give it the gray tint from which

Boulogne Gray Pumpkin ($\frac{1}{10}$ natural size).

the variety is named. The flesh is yellow, thick, and floury. The fruit of this variety keeps at least as long as that of the Étampes Pumpkin. It was raised only a few years ago, at Boulogne-sur-Seine, and has already come extensively into cultivation, being in high repute with the market gardeners about Paris.

Warted Marrow Squash ($\frac{1}{5}$ natural size).

Warted Marrow Squash (*Courge Brodée Galeuse*).—A vigorous-growing plant, with stems from 13 to over 16 ft. long. Leaves large, of a dark-green colour, roundish, or sometimes undulated in outline. This variety, raised in the neigh-bourhood of Bordeaux, is evi-dently very closely allied to the Turk's-Cap or Turban Gourd, but differs from it in some very marked characteristics. In the first place, the enlargement in the upper part of the fruit is very slight, and sometimes altogether wanting ; and in the next, the whole surface of the skin, when ripe, is covered with excrescences of a corky appearance, somewhat like those seen on the skin of Netted Melons. This pecu-liarity gives the variety a very

Chestnut Squash (⅛ natural size).

distinct character. The flesh of the fruit is orange-coloured, very thick and sweet, and of excellent quality.

Chestnut Squash (*Courge Marron*).—A vigorous-growing plant, with stems from 13 to over 16 ft. long. Leaves roundish, entire, most usually undulated at the edges. This is an ex-cellent variety, with medium-sized or small fruit, which is somewhat flattened at the ends, but not concave there, as Pumpkins often are. Ribs barely defined, or altogether wanting ; skin smooth, of an intense brick-red colour; flesh deep yellow, very thick, sweet, and floury, and keeping well. A plant may carry three or four fruit well.

Valparaiso Squash (*Courge de Valparaiso*). — Stems trailing, from 16 to nearly 20 ft. long. Leaves entire, somewhat elongated, toothed and spiny at the edges, of a clear-green colour, sometimes silvery gray on the upper surface ; fruit ob-long, narrowed at both ends, about 16 to 20 inches long, and 12 to 14 inches in dia-

Valparaiso Squash (⅙ natural size).

meter in its widest part, and shaped something like a Lemon ; ribs faintly defined, or altogether wanting; skin white, slightly tinged with gray, covered, when ripe, with a great number of small cracks or very fine tracings; flesh orange-coloured, sweet, and of delicate flavour. A plant, unless it is exceptionally strong, should not be allowed to carry more than two fruit. These often weigh from 27 to 33 pounds each, and even more, and are rather difficult to keep.

Ohio Squash, or Californian Marrow (*Courge de l'Ohio*).—A variety of American origin. Stem creeping, 16 to nearly 20 ft. long; leaves entire, roundish, kidney-shaped, or with five faintly marked lobes, sometimes wavy at the edges. The fruit somewhat resembles that of the preceding variety in shape, but is not so long in proportion to its width, which is sometimes 10 inches, while the length seldom exceeds 12 to 14 inches; ribs very faintly marked; skin almost

Ohio Squash, or Californian Marrow (⅙ natural size).

quite smooth, of a light salmon-pink colour. The flesh is very floury, and in high repute in the United States, where this variety and the following one are two of the most extensively grown kinds. A plant should not be allowed to carry more than three or four fruit.

Hubbard Squash (*Courge Verte de Hubbard*).—A very vigorous-growing kind, with trailing, branching stems often 16 to nearly 20 ft. long. Leaves roundish, slightly sinuated, and very finely toothed at the edges. The fruit has a slight resemblance to that of the preceding variety, but it is often shorter, more pointed at the stalk end, and is quite different in colour, being of a dark green, sometimes marbled with brick-red. The flesh is dark yellow, very floury, not very sweet, rather dry, and, in America, is considered to be of excellent quality; it also keeps good for a very long time. The skin is so

Hubbard Squash (⅙ natural size).

hard and thick that it cannot always be cut with an ordinary knife. A plant will carry and ripen five or six fruit well.

The *Marble-head Squash*, another American variety, differs from the *Hubbard* only in the colour of the skin, which is of an ashy gray.

Olive Squash (*Courge Olive*).—This Gourd, which belongs to the section of *Cucurbita maxima*, derived its name from the shape and colour of the fruit, which exactly resembles an unripe Olive magnified a hundred times.   The swollen fruit-stalk and the rounded, almost uniform, leaves surely indi-cate its origin from *Cucurbita maxima.*   The plant is re-markably vigorous in growth, and productive, but rather late, however.   The fruit is of moderate size, generally not exceeding from six to about eleven pounds in weight, with golden-yellow flesh of excellent quality.   It keeps well if properly ripened.   This variety comes nearest to the Hubbard Squash, from which, however, it entirely differs in its more diffuse and exuberant habit of growth, and also in the more elongated form of the fruit.

Olive Squash.

Valencia Squash (*Courge de Valence*).—The fruit of this variety is of a peculiar shape, being swollen at the base, then almost cylindrical, and ending in a roundish point. Ribs very strongly marked ; skin grayish green, resem-bling that of the Green Pumpkins in colour ; flesh bright yellow, rather abun-dant, and of good quality. The stems attain a length of from 16 to nearly 20 feet. This is a rather late variety, and ripens with difficulty in the northern parts of France, but it is a productive and vigorous-growing kind.

Valencia Squash ($\frac{1}{6}$ natural size).

Turk's-cap, or **Turban, Gourd** (*Giraumon*).—A very distinct kind of Gourd, well known everywhere from its peculiar shape, from which it has received the common name of Turk's-cap, or Turban, Gourd.   There is an almost infinite number of forms of it, all of which in common pre-serve the characteristic turban shape of the variety, but differ from one another in the size and colour of the fruit.   The kind which is most commonly grown, and which may be considered the type of the variety, produces fruit weighing

Turk's-cap, or Turban, Gourd ($\frac{1}{8}$ natural size).

s

from about six to nine pounds each, bearing on the end farthest from the stalk a cap-shaped enlargement, which is sometimes hemispherical, and sometimes with four or five deeply cut ribs. The fruit is hardly ever uniform in colour, being often variegated in a variety of ways, most frequently with dark green, yellow, and red. One of these colours is often absent, and sometimes the fruit is entirely of a dark-green hue. The flesh is of a fine orange colour, and is thick, floury, and sweet.

Small Chinese Turban Gourd (*Giraumon Petit de Chine;* Chinese, *Hong-nan-koua*).—This pretty

little Gourd has been quite recently introduced from China by the authorities of the Museum of Natural History at Paris. It is a very distinct plant, and appears to possess a considerable degree of merit. It differs from the Gourds hitherto known in Europe, in the small size of its fruit, which do not usually exceed two or three pounds each in weight. They are generally of a bright-red colour, marked longitudinally with yellow and dark green. The crown is well marked, but usually not very prominent.

Small Chinese Turban Gourd ($\frac{1}{6}$ natural size).

Flesh yellow, firm, floury, and sweet. A plant may carry ten fruit or even more. They ripen pretty early, and keep admirably. This is one of the few kitchen-garden vegetables which we have received ready-made from China.

OTHER VARIETIES OF *Cucurbita maxima.*

Sometimes, under the name of *Courge de Chypre* (Cyprus, or Musk, Gourd), a variety is met with, which is of medium size, slightly flattened, with very faintly marked ribs, and with a smooth grayish skin, variegated or marbled with pale green or pink. This kind does well in the south of France, but is rather late for the climate of Paris. To *Cucurbita maxima* must also be referred a variety of Gourd which does not climb or creep, and was introduced from South America, fifteen or twenty years ago, under the name of *Zapallito de Tronco.* It is not a productive kind, and seems to have gone out of cultivation. In North America, under the name of *Essex Hybrid Squash,* or *American Turban,* a variety is grown which has thick, almost cylindrical fruit, with the crown hardly defined, and of a uniform salmon-pink colour, almost exactly resembling the tint of the *Ohio Squash.*

II. Cucurbita moschata, Duch., and Varieties.

The varieties which have sprung from this species have all long running stems, which readily take root, and are covered (as are also the leaves and leaf-stalks) with numerous hairs, which never become spiny. They are also distinguished by having the fruit-stalk (which is pentangular or sexangular, like that of *Cucurbita Pepo*) swollen where it joins the fruit. The leaves are not cut, but exhibit well-marked angles, and are of a dark-green colour relieved by blotches of silvery white produced by a thin layer of air under the skin, which rises here and there between the principal veins or nerves. The calyx has the segments divided almost as far as the stalk, and often broader at the extremity than at the base; they sometimes become leafy. The seed is variable in size, but always of a dirty-white colour, and margined and covered by a loosely adhering membrane or skin, which often becomes detached here and there, giving the seed a shaggy appearance. A gramme contains, on an average, seven seeds, and a litre of them weighs about 420 grammes. Their germinating power lasts for six years. This species derives its name from the musky flavour which all the varieties of it possess, to a greater or less extent, in the flesh of the fruit.

Carpet-bag Gourd, or Naples Squash (*Courge Pleine de Naples*).— Stems trailing, 10 to 13 ft. long; leaves medium sized, entire, roundish or five-angled, of a deep and rather dull green, with veins and spots of whitish gray, clearly relieved on the green ground; fruit large, 20 inches to 2 ft. long, and 6 to 8 inches broad in its widest part. The part next the stalk is nearly cylindrical, but the lower part is more or less swollen, and it is only in this part that seeds are found, the upper part being solidly filled with flesh without any central cavity. Skin smooth, dark green, becoming yellow when the fruit is quite ripe; flesh orange coloured, very abundant, sweet, perfumed, and keeping well. This variety is very productive, and the fruit is of excellent quality. It has no fault except that it ripens rather late. The *Courge Pleine d'Alger* and the *Courge des Bédouins* appear to be identical with this kind. In Italy a truly gigantic variety is grown, the fruit of which, usually

Carpet-bag Gourd, or Naples Squash (⅓ natural size).

slightly curved, often measures upwards of 3 ft. in length, and weighs from thirty-three to forty-four pounds.

Early Carpet-bag Gourd, or Early Neapolitan Squash (*Courge Portmanteau Hâtive*).—This variety resembles the preceding one in all the particulars of its habit of growth, and only differs from it in the smaller size of its fruit, and its considerably greater earliness, which renders it a very valuable plant, and one to be recommended for the climate of the north of France in preference to the previous variety.

Canada Crook-neck, or Winter, Gourd (*Courge Cou Tors du Canada*). —This pretty little Gourd is closely allied to the preceding variety, but differs from it chiefly in having the portion of the fruit which is next the stalk completely filled with flesh (as in the Naples Carpet-bag Gourd), and usually curved like the neck of a swan, in which respect it resembles the Siphon Gourd. It possesses the good qualities of earliness and excellent flavour, and also keeps well. The plant is of small size, the stems seldom exceeding 5 or 6 ft. in length. It is therefore well adapted for gardens of moderate extent.

OTHER VARIETIES OF *Cucurbita moschata.*

There are also some forms of this species, in which the fruit is not of

Canada Crook-neck, or Winter, Gourd
(⅙ natural size).

Yokohama Gourd (⅙ natural size).

an elongated shape, but roundish or even flattened. Among the first of these we may mention the Bordeaux Melon Squash— a vigorous-growing plant, bearing great numbers of fruit, which are nearly cylindrical, flattened at both ends, something like a drum, as broad as they are long, and with faintly defined ribs. It is a productive variety, with fruit of excellent quality, but rather late in ripening. The *Courge à la Violette* of the south of France and the *Courge Pascale* are two varieties closely allied to the preceding one, and, like it, have almost spherical fruit.

Yokohama Gourd (*Courge de Yokohama*). — The only flat-fruited variety of *Cucurbita moschata* that we know of is the Yokohama Gourd, a Japanese variety that has often been introduced into Europe. It is a plant of very rampant habit and somewhat late in ripening. Fruit flattened in shape, especially on the portion surrounding the eye, generally twice as broad as long, sometimes even more so, of a very dark green colour, with irregularly formed ribs, and the skin indented and wrinkled, like that of the Prescott Cantaloupe Melon.

III. Cucurbita Pepo, L., and Varieties.

This species is the parent of a very great number of cultivated varieties, all of which exhibit the following characteristics of the type : —Leaves with lobes always well defined, and often deeply cut ; hairs becoming spiny here and there; fruit-stalks pentangular or five-ribbed, never swollen under the fruit, and becoming exceedingly hard when the fruit ripens; segments of the calyx united for some part of their length, and often slightly contracted below the commencement of the divisions; the part between the stalk and the contractions usually has five prominent ribs, and the segments of the calyx are narrowed from the base to the extremity. The seed varies very much in appearance, but is always winged or margined, and is seldom as large as that of the varieties of *Cucurbita maxima.* It may be observed that the seed of genuine varieties of *Cucurbita Pepo* weighs, on an average, 425 grammes to the litre, a gramme containing from six to eight seeds, while the seed of the Custard and Fancy Gourds is much smaller. The germinating power of the seed of all kinds of Gourds, except the Large Tours Pumpkin, lasts for six years or more.

Vegetable Marrow (⅛ natural size).

Vegetable Marrow (*Courge à la Moelle*). —A plant with long, slender, running stems. Leaves of medium size, deeply cut into five lobes, which are often undulated or toothed at the edges, of a dark-green colour, sometimes variegated with grayish spots, and very rough to the touch; fruit oblong in shape, 10 to 16 inches long, and 4 or 5 inches in diameter, with five or ten ribs more or less well marked, but most prominent on the part next the stalk; skin smooth, of a dull yellow or yellowish-white colour. The fruit is generally eaten when it is less than half grown, as the flesh is then very tender and marrowy; when ripe, it is rather dry. It should be used always in a young state.

CULTURE.—Little need be said in this respect, as the Marrow will grow anywhere if supplied with plenty of manure and moisture at the root. For early Marrows the seed should be sown in pots and placed in a gentle heat any time in April; when they have made two pairs of rough leaves they may be hardened off ready for planting early in June. Hand-lights should be placed over them for a few days after planting, until they become established. It is a bad practice to keep the lights on too long, inasmuch as the plants do not grow any faster and they are liable to mildew—the latter disease being the only drawback to growing Marrows in pits or frames. Some gardeners sow earlier and plant earlier, but there is seldom anything gained by it unless in exceptionally favour-able seasons. Marrows are generally planted on old refuse-heaps, or old manure beds, which places are well suited to their growth. We have seen them planted on great heaps of decayed leaf-mould; on this they grow and fruit amazingly. They may, however, be successfully grown in any ground by taking out a few spits of earth and digging in a barrow-load of manure. Summer Marrows do well planted in old ditches or dykes that are comparatively dry during the summer months. The usual time for sowing seed of Marrows is in May and June, and it is sown where it is to remain, having a flower-pot or hand-light placed over it until it has germinated. It is a good plan to soak the seed in water for a few hours previous to sowing. The same remarks as to culture apply to all the tribe of Gourds. For a full account of the culture of this very impor- | tant vegetable in London market gardens, the reader is referred to Shaw's "London Market Gardening."

Long White Bush Marrow (*Courge Blanche non Coureuse*).—This variety is very distinct in its habit of growth. The stems, instead of running, remain very short and rather thick, bearing closely set leaves of a dark-green colour with a few grayish blotches, and deeply cut and toothed at the edges. Fruit longer than that of the Vegetable Marrow, being from 14 to 20 inches in length, with a diameter of $5\frac{1}{2}$ or 6 inches, narrowed towards the stalk, and traversed by five ribs. Like the

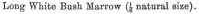

Long White Bush Marrow ($\frac{1}{6}$ natural size).   Italian Vegetable Marrow
($\frac{1}{8}$ natural size).

Vegetable Marrow, the fruit of this variety is usually eaten before it is fully grown, the plant continuing to produce new fruit in succession.

Italian Vegetable Marrow (*Courge d'Italie ;* Italian, *Cocozella di Napoli*).—An extremely distinct variety. Stems not running, very thick and short, producing numerous leaves of a dark-green colour, very large, and very deeply cut into five or six lobes, which are also more or less notched. The luxuriant foliage forms a regular bush. Fruit very much elongated, being 20 inches or more in length, with a diameter of 3 to 4 inches, furrowed by five ribs, which are most prominent on the part next the stalk, where the fruit is also narrowest; skin very smooth, of a dark green, marbled with yellow or with paler green. All through Italy, where this Gourd is very commonly grown, the fruit is eaten quite young, when it is hardly the size of a small Cucumber, sometimes even before the flower has opened, when the ovary, which is scarcely as long or as thick as the finger, is gathered for use. The plants, which are thus deprived of their undeveloped fruits, continue to flower for several months most profusely, each producing a great number of young Gourds, which, gathered in that state, are exceedingly tender and delicately flavoured. This should be tried in England, and the same excellent way of gathering young adopted.

Brazilian Sugar Gourd (*Courge Sucrière du Brésil*).—A plant with long, slender, running stems. Leaves lobed, rough, of a very dark green colour, and finely crimped and puckered; fruit oblong, rather short, swollen in the middle, with five faintly marked ribs, and sometimes slightly warted; skin green, turning orange when ripe; flesh yellow, thick, and very sweet. This variety is highly to be recommended, on account of its earliness, and the abundance and good quality of its fruit, which keeps for a long time. It ripens half-early.

Brazilian Sugar Gourd (⅛ natural size).

Patagonian Squash (*Courge des Patagons*).—A plant with very long running stems, and large, lobed, dark-green leaves. Fruit from 12 to 20 inches long, and 6 to 8 inches across, traversed from end to end by five very regular ribs, which form so many prominent rounded flutings; skin smooth, of an extremely dark green, almost black, a colour which it retains when ripe; flesh yellow, of medium quality. This variety is remarkable for its hardiness and productiveness.

Under the name of Alsatian Gourd, a variety has been highly spoken of, which resembles the Patagonian Squash, except that the fruit is less angular and of a

Patagonian Squash (⅛ natural size).

lighter green colour. When the fruit of this variety is full grown, but before it is ripe, it is used in salads, cut in slices and seasoned in the same way as Gherkins. With care, it will keep for some time in winter.

Geneva Bush Gourd (*Courgeron de Genève*).—Stems not running; leaves long-stalked, of medium size and clear-green colour, rather deeply cut into elongated lobes which are toothed at the edges; fruit numerous, small, very much flattened, 5 or 6 inches in diameter and

2 or 3 inches in depth; skin smooth, brownish-green, turning orange when ripe; flesh yellow, and not very thick. The fruit is eaten young, before it is fully grown, like the Vegetable Marrow.

Bush, or **Crook-neck, Gourd** (*Courge Cou Tors Hâtive*).—This plant is not a climber or trailer, but forms a tuft like the Elector's-cap Gourd. Leaves of a clear green, large, toothed at the edges, and more or less divided into three or five rather pointed lobes; fruit of a very bright orange colour, elongated, covered with numerous roundish excrescences, narrowed and most usually curved in the part next the stalk, and swollen at the other end, which, however, always terminates in a point. This variety, if cut while young, is not without some merit for table use,

Geneva Gourd,

but it is chiefly grown for ornament, like the Fancy Gourds. From the hardness of its skin, the fruit is easily kept all through the winter, and never loses the fine orange colour which is peculiar to it.

Large Tours Pumpkin (*Citrouille de Touraine*).—Stems creeping, 16 to 20 ft. long; leaves very large, of a dark-green colour with a few grayish blotches, sometimes entire, but most usually divided into three or five lobes; fruit roundish or elongated, generally flattened at both ends, with faintly marked ribs, and a smooth skin of a pale or grayish green colour marked with deeper bands and marblings. The fruit often weighs from 90 to 110 pounds. Its flesh is yellow, not very thick, and of middling quality. The seed is very large. A gramme contains only three

Bush, or Crook-neck, Gourd (⅕ natural size).

seeds, and a litre of them weighs about 250 grammes. Their germinating power lasts for only four or five years. This variety is generally grown for feeding cattle only.

Elector's-cap, or **Custard, Marrow** (French, *Patissons;* American, *Scollop Gourd;* German, *Bischofsmütze;* Flemish, *Prinsenmuts*).—The Custard Marrows are some of the most curious varieties which have sprung from *Cucurbita Pepo.* They are not climbing or creeping plants, and have large leaves, of a clear-green colour, entire, or with five faintly marked lobes. The fruit is very much flattened transversely, so that it is much broader than long, and the outline, instead of being rounded, exhibits five or six projections or blunt teeth, which are either diverging from, or more or less curved back towards, the stalk end of the fruit. The fruit of all the Custard Marrows is pretty solid, and the flesh is firm, not very sweet, but rather floury; the skin is very smooth, and variable in colour and thickness. The seed is very small, compared with that of the other varieties of *Cucurbita Pepo*. A gramme contains about 10 seeds, and a litre of them weighs about 430 grammes.

The following are the most commonly grown varieties:—
Yellow Custard Marrow (*Patisson Jaune*).—This seems to be the original variety or type of the cultivated Custard Marrows. The skin of the fruit is of a uniform butter-yellow colour, and the teeth or divisions of the crown are very prominent and curved back in the direction of the stalk. **Green Custard Marrow** (*Patisson Vert*).—Fruit (unripe) dark green, nearly entirely so, or faintly marbled. The colour is very deep at first, but turns yellow as the fruit ripens. **Orange-coloured Custard Marrow** (*Patisson Orange*).—Like the preceding kind in shape, but of a far more vivid colour, resembling that of a ripe Orange. **Striped Custard Marrow** (*Patisson Panaché*). — Stems often running; fruit rather small, with faintly marked teeth, and very prettily variegated with green and white. **White Flat Warted Custard Marrow** (*Patisson*

Large Tours Pumpkin ($\frac{1}{6}$ natural size).

Elector's-cap, or Custard, Marrow ($\frac{1}{6}$ natural size).

Yellow Custard Marrow ($\frac{1}{6}$ natural size).

Blanc Plat Galeux).—Fruit with faintly marked lobes or teeth; skin creamy white, covered all over with roundish warts. All these varieties produce numbers of small fruit. A strong plant may be allowed to carry ten or twelve. **Improved Variegated Custard Marrow** is distinguished from the preceding kinds by the much greater size of its fruit, which often weighs seven or eight pounds. A plant should not, as a rule, be allowed to carry more than three or four. In shape and colour the fruit resembles that of the Common Variegated Custard Marrow.

Improved Variegated Custard Marrow
(⅛ natural size).

FANCY GOURDS.

French, Coloquintes.　*German*, Kleine Zierkürbiss.　*Dutch*, Kawoerd appel.　*Italian*, *Spanish*, and *Portuguese*, Coloquintida.

The true Colocynth (*Cucumis Colocynthis*, L.), an exclusively medicinal plant, is seldom met with in cultivation, and it is a misapplication of the name, only sanctioned by usage, when it is employed to denote a large number of varieties of Gourds with small fleshy fruit, the chief merit of which consists in the elegance or singularity of their shape, and the handsome colours which they exhibit when ripe. The skin of these fruit usually becomes very hard, and the pulp in the interior dries up rather quickly, in consequence of which they keep much longer than most of the edible kinds. In all the particulars of their habit of growth, the Fancy Gourds, or Colocynths, resemble the varieties of *Cucurbita Pepo*. The stems, leaves, flowers, and fruit are generally of smaller size than those of any of the kinds hitherto described in this volume, but the characteristics of all those parts, and also of the calyx and flower-stalk, indicate the origin of the varieties clearly enough; and yet the Custard Marrows, which all are agreed to consider the undoubted off-spring of *Cucurbita Pepo*, may be said to form, by their small hard-skinned fruit, a true connecting link between the Fancy Gourds and the edible kinds described in the Vegetable Marrow section. The seed of these plants is small, numbering about 20 to the gramme, and weighing about 450 grammes to the litre. The Fancy Gourds have generally, if not always, long climbing or creeping stems, and, on this account, are very often grown as ornamental plants on trellises, arbours, etc. As they grow very rapidly, they are very useful for quickly covering bare surfaces with verdure, and their numerous and usually prettily variegated fruit are highly ornamental late in autumn and up to the first appearance of frosty weather. The number of varieties is almost unlimited, and new kinds are constantly being raised from seed. As it would be impossible to enumerate them all here, we shall confine ourselves to the description of the best established and most generally cultivated kinds.

Pear Gourd (*Coloquinte Poire*).—One of the most common forms
of Fancy Gourds is the elongated shape, with a spherical or ovoid
swelling at the end farthest from the stalk. The varieties which
have fruit of this shape are known by the general name of Pear
Gourds, and differ more or less from one another in colour, as the
White Pear Gourd, the skin of which is smooth and entirely milk-
white; the Striped Pear Gourd, which is of a dark-green colour.
marked with irregular longitudinal bands, or rows of spots, which are

Striped Pear Gourd ($\frac{1}{12}$ natural size; detached fruit, $\frac{1}{5}$ natural size).

Ringed Pear Gourd ($\frac{1}{12}$ natural size; detached fruit, $\frac{1}{5}$ natural size).

either white or of a much paler green than the rest of the fruit; the
Two-coloured Pear Gourd, one half of which is yellow, and the other a
uniform green; the Ringed Pear Gourd, in which the green colour,
instead of covering half the fruit, only forms a ring round it of greater
or less width. These different variegations may also be found combined with one another in various ways, as in some two-coloured fruits
which have the yellow part of a uniform tint, while the green part is
striped or banded with different colours. All the varieties of Pear
Gourds generally exhibit the following characteristics :—The plants
are of medium size, the stems seldom exceeding from $6\frac{1}{2}$ to about
$10\frac{1}{2}$ ft. in length. Leaves of moderate size,
dark green, nearly entire, with five roundish
angles, or divided into five faintly marked
lobes.

Several varieties of Fancy Gourds have
fruit almost spherical in shape or slightly
flattened at the ends, like an Apple or an
Orange. Of these the following are the
most commonly grown kinds :—

Early Apple Gourd (*Coloquinte Pomme
Hâtive*).—Stems of moderate length, not
exceeding from $6\frac{1}{2}$ to about 10 ft.; leaves
medium sized, grayish green, cut into

Orange Gourd ($\frac{1}{12}$ natural size).

five lobes with toothed edges; fruit nearly spherical, flattened at the
ends, especially at the end farthest from the stalk; skin very smooth
and entirely white.

Orange Gourd (*Coloquinte Orange*).—The fruit of this variety is similar in shape to that of the preceding one, but of a fine orange colour. Leaves largish, divided into five lobes more or less deeply cut, of a dark-green colour, and often slightly crimped. The fruit exactly resembles a ripe Orange in size and colour.

Miniature Gourd (*Coloquinte Miniature*).—A small plant with thin slender stems, seldom more than about 6½ ft. long. Leaves dull green, with grayish blotches, sometimes nearly entire, but most usually divided into three (rarely into five) roundish lobes; fruit generally rather flat at the ends, about 2 inches in diameter, and variegated with pale green on a darker green ground, almost like the Striped Pear Gourd.

White-striped Flat Fancy Gourd (*Coloquinte Plate Rayée*).— A vigorous-growing variety, with stems 10 to 14 ft. long. Leaves largish, divided into five lobes, which generally terminate in rather

White-striped Flat Fancy Gourd (1/10 natural　　Warty Fancy Gourd (1/13 natural
size; detached fruit, 1/8 natural size).　　　　　size).

sharp points; fruit very much flattened transversely, much broader than long, 2 or 3 inches in diameter, and striped or marbled with various shades of green. The peculiar shape and regular markings of this Gourd give it quite a unique appearance, and would lead one to think, at first sight, that it belonged to some species very different from *Cucurbita Pepo*. There are, in fact, some small kinds of wild Melons to which it bears a considerable resemblance.

Egg Gourd (*Coloquinte Oviforme*). — A vigorous-growing plant, with stems often 13 ft. long. Leaves large, of a rather dark green colour, entire, five-angled, or divided into five faintly marked lobes. Fruit entirely white, and of the shape and size of a hen's egg.

Warty - skinned Fancy Gourd (*Coloquinte Galeuse*). — Stems thickish, but not very long, seldom exceeding about 6½ ft. in length; leaves of a clear-green colour, shining, slightly crimped, entire, roundish, or divided into three lobes faintly toothed on the edges; fruit usually spherical, and having the skin entirely covered with numerous roundish excrescences, of variable colour, sometimes green, but most usually white or orange. The stems of this variety, instead of being slender and pliable like those of the other kinds of Fancy Gourds, are stiff and stout, as if the plant had a tendency to grow without any support. The plant does not branch much.

BOTTLE GOURDS.

Lagenaria vulgaris, Ser. ; *Cucurbita Lagenaria*, L.   *Cucurbitaceæ.*

Courge bouteille.

Natives of South America.—Annual.—Like the Fancy Gourds, or small varieties of *Cucurbita Pepo*, the different varieties of *Lagenaria vulgaris* are much more grown for ornament than for any use that is made of them.   The Common Bottle Gourd (*Courge Pèlerine*), the double swollen fruit of which is familiar to most people, is almost the only kind that is turned to any account in the way of practical utility, its dried fruit, when the flesh is removed, forming an excellent substitute for bottles and other vessels.   The very rapid growth of this plant, the abundance and beauty of its large white flowers, and the shape and extraordinary dimensions of the fruit of some of its forms, render it a valuable ornamental climbing plant.   As it is easily grown, it appears to be cultivated in every part of the world where the climate is warm or temperate.   From an early period it has been grown by the Chinese and the Japanese, who possess some varieties of it differing somewhat from those grown in Europe.   Culture.—This is exceedingly simple.   The seed is sown, where the plants are to stand, in May, or plants previously raised in hot-beds or frames may be planted out in the open ground that month. These, of course, will bear sooner than the others. The plants like good, rich, well-manured soil, and plentiful waterings, although not absolutely necessary, will help to increase the size and

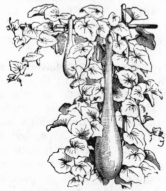

Club Gourd (¹⁄₁₅ natural size).   Long Club Gourd (¹⁄₁₂ natural size).

beauty of the fruit.   No variety of Bottle Gourd ripens its fruit regularly in the climate of Paris.   Uses.—The young fruit is eaten in some countries, like the Vegetable Marrow, but it does not appear to us to be very desirable for table use, and the plant should be regarded as a purely ornamental one.   Its rapid growth renders it valuable for quickly covering trellises, arbours, trunks of trees, dead walls, and other bare places.   The leaves and all the green parts of the plant, when bruised, give out a very strong and disagreeable odour, but the flowers, on the contrary, are scented almost like Jasmine.

Club Gourd (*Lagenaria clavata.   Courge Massue d'Hercule*).—Fruit very long, sometimes over 3¼ ft. in length, almost cylindrical, but only about half as thick in the half next the stalk as it is in the other half. Sometimes the extremity is greatly swollen. All the forms of this plant, however, are extremely variable, and as changeable as the whims of amateurs.

Siphon Gourd (*Lagenaria Cougourda. Courge Siphon*).—The fruit of this variety is swollen at the extremity into a spherical or slightly flattened enlargement, 8 to 12 inches broad, and about one-third less in depth; the rest of the fruit forms a long thin neck, which is curved

Siphon Gourd (¹⁄₁₂ natural size).

Common Bottle Gourd (¹⁄₁₂ natural size).

into a semicircle in the part next the stalk. When growing, the fruit should rest on the ground or some other support, otherwise the neck will be broken by the weight of the enlarged lower part.

Common Bottle Gourd (*Courge Pèlerine*).—Fruit contracted about the middle, and presenting two unequal divisions, of which the lower one is larger and broader than the other, and sometimes flattened at the base, so as to allow the fruit to rest firmly upon it; the upper division, next the stalk, is almost spherical. There is a certain number of forms of this variety, all of which bear fruit of nearly the same shape, but of extremely variable dimensions, some of them being nearly 20 inches long and capable of containing at least two gallons, while others are seldom more than 5 or 6 inches in length, with a capacity of less than a pint, and they are found of all sizes between these extremes.

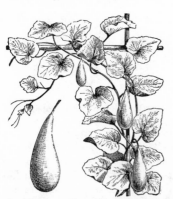

Powder-horn Gourd (¹⁄₁₂ natural size).

Powder-horn Gourd (*Courge Poire à Poudre*).—Fruit of a more or less elongated Pear-shape, with a well-marked neck, and variable in size. They can be applied to the same kind of purposes as the fruit of the preceding kind, and are sometimes used as powder-horns in country places.

Flat Corsican Gourd (*Lagenaria depressa. Courge Plate de Corse*).—

A remarkably distinct variety, with rounded and exceedingly flat fruit, rather like that of the Yokohama Gourd in shape, but quite smooth and without ribs. It is from 6 to 8 inches in diameter and 3 or 4 inches thick.

WAX GOURD.

Benincasa cerifera, Savi.   *Cucurbitaceæ.*

Courge à la cire.

Native of India and China.—Annual.—A creeping plant, which spreads on the ground, like a Cucumber plant, with slender sharply five-angled stems from 5 to 6½ ft. in length. Leaves large, slightly hairy, rounded, heart-shaped, and sometimes with three or five faintly marked lobes; flowers axillary, yellow, with five divisions, which extend almost

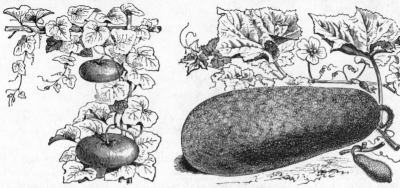

Flat Corsican Gourd (½₂ natural size).   Wax Gourd (⅛ natural size).

to the base of the corolla, broadly cup-shaped, and 2 inches or more in diameter; calyx reflexed, rather large, and often petaloid. Fruit oblong, cylindrical, very hairy up to about the time of ripening, when it attains a length of from 14 to 16 inches, with a diameter of 4 or 5 inches. It is then covered with a kind of whitish bloom, like that which is seen on Plums, but much whiter and more abundant, and constituting a true vegetable wax. Seeds flat, grayish, truncate, numbering about 21 to the gramme, a litre of them weighing about 300 grammes. Their germinating power lasts for ten years. Their culture is similar to that of other kinds of Gourds. The fruit is eaten like that of other Gourds. The flesh of it is extremely light, slightly floury, and intermediate between that of a Gourd and a Cucumber. The fruit will keep pretty far into the winter.

HERB PATIENCE, or PATIENCE DOCK.

Rumex Patientia, L.   *Polygonaceæ.*

French, Oseille épinard.   *German,* Englischer Spinat.   *Flemish,* Blijvende spinazie.
Danish, Engelsk spinat.   *Italian,* Lapazio.   *Spanish,* Romaza.   *Portuguese,* Labaça.

Native of Southern Europe.—Perennial.—Leaves slender, flat, oval lanceolate, pointed, narrowed abruptly into the leaf-stalk, which is long and channelled on the upper surface; stem 4 to 6½ ft. high, with

ascending branches; flowers in thick clusters, forming a rather close branching panicle at the top of the stem; seed triangular, pale brown, much larger than that of the Common Sorrel. A gramme contains about 450 seeds, and a litre of them weighs about 620 grammes. Their ·germinating power lasts for four years. This species is not so acid as the other kinds of Sorrel, but it is exceedingly productive, and has the advantage of yielding a supply of leaves immediately after winter, ten or twelve days, at least, before any other kind. It is grown exactly like the Common Sorrel.

Herb Patience, or Patience Dock (1/30 natural size).

HOP.

Humulus Lupulus, L.   *Urticaceæ.*

French, Houblon.   *German,* Hopfen.   *Flemish,* Hop.   *Italian,* Luppolo.   *Spanish,* Lupulo.

Native of Europe.—Perennial.—This is not, properly speaking, a kitchen-garden plant, but as, in some countries, the young shoots are often used as table vegetables, we think it should be noticed in the present volume. When the plants commence to shoot in spring, most of the shoots are pinched off, so as to leave only two or three of the strongest to each plant. The shoots thus removed are used as vegetables. In Belgium the young shoots are much used as a table vegetable, prepared in the same way as Asparagus or Salsafy.

HOREHOUND.

Marrubium vulgare, L.   *Labiatæ.*

French, Marrube blanc.   *German,* Andorn.   *Italian,* Marrubio.

Native of Europe.—Perennial.—A common roadside plant, often occurring on slopes with a southern aspect. Stems numerous, erect, entirely covered with a white down ; leaves almost square, with roundish angles, toothed and netted, and of a grayish-green colour; flowers white, in compact rounded whorls, growing in numerous tiers to the top of the stem ; seed small, oblong, brownish, pointed at one end and roundish at the other, compressed, and with two or three faces. A gramme contains about 1000 seeds, and a litre of them weighs about 680 grammes. Their germinating power lasts for three years. The seed is sown, where the plants are to stand, in spring ; or they may be propagated by division of the tufts at the same time. The plants are perfectly hardy and require no attention while growing. The leaves are used for seasoning, or as a popular cough remedy.

HORSE-RADISH.

Cochlearia Armoracia, L.   *Cruciferæ.*

French, Raifort sauvage.   *German,* Meerettig.   *Flemish,* Kapucienen mostaard.   *Dutch,*
Peperwortel.   *Danish,* Peberrod.   *Italian,* Rafano.   *Spanish,* Taramago.   *Portuguese*
Rabao de cavalho.

Native of Europe.—Perennial.—Root cylindrical, very long, penetrating deeply into the ground, with a slightly wrinked yellowish-white
skin ; flesh white, somewhat fibrous, very hot to the taste, something like
mustard ; radical leaves long stalked, oblong oval, about 16 inches
long and 5 or 6 inches broad, toothed, of a clear-green colour, and
shining. The first leaves, which make their appearance immediately
after winter, are reduced to mere nerves and resemble a small comb. As
the season advances, the blade of the leaf becomes developed and
assumes its ordinary size and appearance.
Flower-stems 20 inches to 2 ft. high, branching
at the top, and smooth ; flowers white, small, in
long clusters ; seed-vessels small, rounded, and
almost always barren.

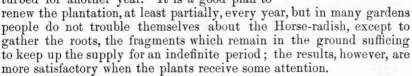

CULTURE.—The plant delights especially in
good, deep, moist soil. It is propagated from
pieces of the root, which are planted, immediately after winter, in rows 20 inches to 2 ft.
apart, and with a distance of about 10 inches
from piece to piece in the rows. The ground
should be very deeply dug and well manured
before planting. The better the soil is prepared, the more abundant will be the produce
and the better the quality of the roots. They
may be used in the autumn succeeding the
spring in which they were planted, but the
yield will be greater if they are left undis-   Horse-radish (⅕ natural size).
turbed for another year. It is a good plan to
renew the plantation, at least partially, every year, but in many gardens
people do not trouble themselves about the Horse-radish, except to
gather the roots, the fragments which remain in the ground sufficing
to keep up the supply for an indefinite period ; the results, however, are
more satisfactory when the plants receive some attention.

CULTURE. — A correspondent of
the *Garden* gives the following
method of growing Horse-radish, by
which he claims to have produced in
ten months sticks that measured from
5 to 8 inches in circumference :—
" During February, take small
straight pieces of the roots about the
size of, or somewhat smaller than, the
little finger ; from these remove all
the side-shoots and roots, and form
them into straight sets from 8 to 14

inches long. Prepare a piece of
ground by deeply digging and well
manuring it, and plant the sets in it
in rows 3 ft. apart and from 12 to 18
inches in the rows. The sets must
be planted in a slanting position, and
must not be more than 2 inches beneath the surface. The ground at all
times must be kept free from weeds,
and should be well watered in very
dry weather. Planting the set at an
angle — in fact, in nearly a hori-

T

zontal position—is, no doubt, the great secret of success : for, being placed so near the surface, it has the full benefit of the sun's heat, which causes it to make rapid growth long before that which is planted according to the old method—*i.e.* from 18 to 20 inches deep, and in a perpendicular position—reaches the surface. I am certain that want of success is to be attributed to this alone, and that the experience of any of your readers who may think fit to adopt my plan will be the same as my own." Mr. Bradley, Preston Hall, grows his Horse-radish by placing a common round drain-tile with it, sunk 2 inches in the ground, filling the tile with fine earth, and planting a set near the top of the tile and 10 inches above the surface. He says it is an admirable plan ; digging for the product is saved, and a fine clean stem is the result. Mr. R. Gilbert says that by placing leaves or litter on the tops of Horse-radish crowns 2 ft. or so thick, the plants grow through them in the course of the summer, making small white roots the thickness of one's finger, which are as tender as spring Radishes, and a great step in advance of the tough

stringy stuff often supplied with our roast beef. During the winter months a supply of Horse-radish should always be at hand, stored away in sheds, and covered with dry soil or sand, in the same way as Carrots, etc.

Horse-radish is not grown to a very great extent in London market-gardens, but where it is found in them it is always in deep, rich, open soil. Crowns such as are not marketable are planted deeply in trenches 2 ft. apart; the plants stand 1 ft. asunder in the row. Manure is then applied on and about the crowns, which lie in a slanting position in the bottom of the trench, and they are at first not deeply buried. Early in spring, after they have started fairly into growth, the ridges between the trenches are levelled down lightly, and a crop of Radishes is sown on the surface, the latter being off in May, and by the time the Horse-radish appears in full row, the Radishes are cleared off the ground, which is hoed and afterwards kept clean. Covent Garden is, however, now chiefly supplied with Horse-radish from Holland.

The root is grated or scraped and used as a condiment, like mustard.

HYSSOP.

Hyssopus officinalis, L. *Labiatæ.*

French, Hyssope. *German,* Isop. *Flemish* and *Dutch,* Hijsoop. *Danish,* Isop. *Italian,* Issopo. *Spanish,* Hisopo.

Hyssop ($\frac{1}{12}$ natural size).

Native of Southern Europe.—Perennial. —An evergreen under-shrub with oblong-lanceolate leaves. Flowers usually blue, sometimes white or pink, in whorled spikes ; seed small, brown, shining, oval three-angled, with a small whitish *hilum* placed near the point. A gramme contains about 850 seeds, and a litre of them weighs about 575 grammes. Their germinating power lasts for three years. All the parts of this plant, especially the leaves, have a very aromatic odour and a rather hot and bitter taste. The Hyssop prefers rather warm, calcareous soil. It withstands ordinary winters in England and Northern France, and is generally propagated by division of the tufts, which readily take root. It may also be raised from seed, as it usually is in cold climates. The seed is sown in the open ground, in April, and the seedlings are planted out in July, most commonly as an edging to beds of other plants. It is advisable to renew the plantation every three or four years. The leaves and the ends of the branches are used as a condiment, especially in the countries of the North.

ICE-PLANT.

Mesembryanthemum crystallinum, L.　*Ficoideæ.*

French, Ficoïde glaciale.　*German,* Eiskraut.　*Flemish* and *Dutch,* Ijsplant.　*Italian,* Erba ghiacciola.　*Spanish,* Escarchosa.

Native of Greece or the Cape of Good Hope.—Perennial, but grown in gardens as an annual.—A spreading, round-stemmed plant. Blade of the leaf widened towards the extremity, and contracted towards the stalk ; flowers whitish, small, with a swollen calyx, which is covered, as are all the green parts of the plant, with small, very transparent, membranous bladders, which give the plant the appearance of being covered with frozen dew; seed very small, black, and shining. A gramme contains about 5700 seeds, and a litre of them weighs about 760 grammes. Their germinating power lasts for five years. The culture is exceedingly easy. The seed is sown like Spinach seed, and the plants bear hot and dry weather admirably. This quality and the thickness and slightly acid flavour

Ice-plant (1/12 natural size).

of the fleshy part of the leaves have caused it to be used as a fresh table vegetable for summer use in warm, dry countries. However, it is rather a plant to be grown as a curiosity in the gardens of amateurs, and it is also not without merit as an ornamental plant. The leaves are eaten minced and boiled.

JERUSALEM ARTICHOKE.

Helianthus tuberosus, L.　*Compositæ.*

French, Topinambour.　*German,* Erdapfel.　*Flemish,* Aardpeer.　*Danish,* Jordskokken *Italian,* Girasole del Canada, Tartufoli.　*Spanish,* Namara.　*Portuguese,* Topinambor.

Native of North America.—Perennial.—A tall plant, with annual stems, but producing, year after year, underground shoots which are swollen into genuine tubers. It was introduced into Europe some centuries ago, and is very generally cultivated on a large scale. The stem is erect and very stout, sometimes over 6½ ft. high, often branching in the lower part, and bearing oval-acuminate leaves, which are long stalked and very rough to the touch ; flower-heads comparatively small, seldom opening in the north of France before October; florets yellow; tubers violet red, slender at the bottom, and swollen in the upper part, where they are about 2 inches in diameter, marked with hollows and scale-like enlargements. They form very late, and should not be dug until the stems have nearly ceased growing. The flesh is sweet and rather watery. CULTURE.—The tubers are planted in the open ground, in March or April, in rows 2½ to 3 ft. or more apart, and with a distance of 12 to 14 inches between the tubers. The plants require no attention beyond the occasional use of the hoe, and the tubers are dug as they are wanted. They are not affected by frost as long as they are left in the ground, but are very liable to be injured if exposed to it after they are taken up. In warm countries the plant produces

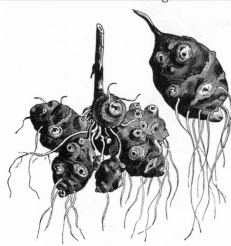

Jerusalem Artichoke (⅓ natural size).

seed, from which it can be propagated. Experiments made with the view of raising improved varieties from seed have hitherto been attended with very unsatisfactory results. From one of these experiments we obtained a variety with yellow tubers which have a finer and more agreeable flavour than the common kind, but the plant is far less productive. This variety may answer as a kitchen-garden plant, but is not suitable for extensive or field culture.

As this vegetable may be grown in almost any place, it is generally planted on gravelly pieces of ground that would be too dry for other crops. Knolls or mounds are usually cropped with it, and it is also grown along the sides of hedges and in shady places. A few growers, however, grow it on good soil in open and somewhat exposed positions, and the result is an abundant crop of fine tubers. After preparing the ground by manuring and digging or trenching it, the tubers are planted in February, in rows like Potatoes, and are allowed to grow unchecked, and without being earthed up, till November. It has not become very popular perhaps owing to its resemblance to the Potato, to which it is, no doubt, inferior, if looked at only from the Potato standard. But it never should be so regarded, being very distinct from any Potato, and having distinct uses in cookery. It is excellent as baked by French and Italian cooks, the flavour being richer and better this way.

JEWS' MALLOW.

Corchorus olitorius, L.   *Tiliaceæ.*

French, Corette potagère.   *German*, Gemüse-Corchorus.

Native of Africa.—Annual.—Stem cylindrical, smooth, more or less branched at the base, and about 20 inches high; leaves alternate, broadish near the base, narrowed for a considerable length to a point, and sharply toothed ; flowers yellow, axillary ; seed-vessels cylindrical, rather elongated, and smooth ; seed very angular, pointed, greenish, and very small. A gramme contains about 450 seeds, and a litre of them weighs about 660 grammes. Their germinating power lasts for five years. As this plant is a native of a very warm country, it does not succeed very well in the climate of Paris. The seed is sown in the open ground, in a warm position, in May, or may be sown earlier in a hot-bed. The plant, however, is more valued in tropical countries, where it can be grown in the open air without any trouble. The leaves are used for salad while they are young and tender.

LAB-LAB, or EGYPTIAN KIDNEY-BEAN.

Lablab vulgaris, Savi. *Leguminosæ.*

French, Dolique Lablab. *Italian,* Fagiuolo d'Egitto. *Spanish,* Indianella. *Portuguese,* Feyas da India.

Native of India.—Annual.—A climbing plant, with stout branching stems, which are sometimes from 13 to over 16 ft. long. Leaves compound, with three large broad leaflets of a dark-green colour, and slightly puckered or crimped ; flowers sweet-scented, largish, in long dense clusters ; pods rather short, wrinkled, and very flat, growing sometimes seven or eight together on the same stalk ; seed short, oval, tolerably flat, three or four in each pod ; *hilum* white, very prominently marked, occupying nearly one-third of the circumference of the seed. A litre of the seed weighs about 810 grammes, and 100 grammes contain about 520 seeds. There are two principal varieties, one with white flowers and white seed, and the other with violet-coloured flowers and black seed. They are grown in the same way as Tall Kidney-Beans. In France they are only grown as ornamental plants, but the seeds are eaten in those countries where they are grown for table use.

Lavender (¹⁄₁₂ natural size).

LAVENDER.

Lavandula Spica, L. ; *Lavandula vera,* DC. *Labiatæ.*

French, Lavande officinale. *German,* Lavendel. *Flemish,* Lavendel. *Danish,* Lavendel. *Italian,* Lavanda. *Spanish,* Espliego.

Native of Southern Europe.—Perennial.—An undershrub, not exceeding from 2 to about 2½ ft. in height. Stems very numerous, forming compact tufts or clumps ; leaves linear, grayish ; flower-stems slender, square, bare with the exception of one pair of opposite leaves ; flowers violet blue, in a short terminal spike ; seed brown, shining, oblong, with a well-marked white spot at one end, denoting its point of attachment to the bottom of the calyx. A gramme contains about 950 seeds, and a litre of them weighs about 575 grammes. Their germinating power lasts for five years. CULTURE. —The Lavender plant delights especially in light and rather calcareous soil. It is generally grown as an edging to beds of other plants, and is propagated by division of the clumps, or from cuttings, rarely from seed. A plantation of it should be remade every three or four years. The leaves are sometimes used for seasoning, but the plant is chiefly grown for its flowers, which are used in the manufacture of perfumery.

In Surrey alone there are supposed to be no fewer than 350 acres of land devoted to its culture, and almost as large a space may be found under Lavender in Hertfordshire. At Mitcham both cottagers and market gardeners grow Lavender for sale, and when the fields of it are in bloom its fragrance pervades the air for miles. Lavender is increased by means of rooted slips, obtained by division of the old roots. The young plants are put out in March or April, 18 inches apart, in rows half that distance asunder, the space between the rows being the first year planted with Lettuce, Parsley, or some similar crop. When the Lavender becomes crowded, each alternate row and plant are lifted and transplanted to another field to form a new plantation. The remaining plants then stand 3 ft. apart each way, and in-

tercropping is discontinued. During the first two or three weeks in August the flowers are harvested. The stalks are cut off with a sickle, bound up in sheaves similar to Wheat, and carried to the homestead for distillation or for other purposes. In Hertfordshire a somewhat different method is practised. The young plants are put out in November, 3 ft. apart each way, no other crop being grown between them, and the ground is well tilled and attended to. When three years old, the plants are considered at their best, and after they have been planted seven years they are dug up and the ground is replanted. A new plantation is, however, made every year or so, and thus there are always young, vigorous plants upon which dependence for a crop of flowers can be fully placed.

LEAF-BEET, or SWISS CHARD BEET.

Beta vulgaris, L. *Chenopodiaceæ.*

French, Poirée. *German,* Beisskohl. *Flemish* and *Dutch,* Snij beet. *Danish,* Blad bede. *Italian,* Bieta. *Spanish,* Bleda. *Portuguese,* Acelga.

Native of Southern Europe.—Biennial.—This appears to be exactly the same plant as the Beet-root, except that in its case cultivation has developed the leaves instead of the root. The botanical characteristics, especially those of the flowers and the fructification, are precisely alike in both plants. The root of the Leaf-Beet is branched and not very fleshy, while the leaves are large and numerous, and, in some varieties, have the stalk and its continuation, the midrib, developed to a remarkable extent. The seed resembles that of the Beet-root, but is usually somewhat smaller. A gramme contains about 60 seeds, and a litre of them weighs about 250 grammes. Their germinating power lasts for six years or more.

CULTURE.—The Leaf-Beet is grown in precisely the same way as the Beet-root, except that it does not require the soil to be so deeply dug. The seed is sown in April or May, in drills 16 to 20 inches apart. The seedlings are thinned out to a distance of 14 to 16 inches from plant to plant, and after that require no further attention beyond occasional waterings. At the close of the summer, the leaves of the Chard varieties may commence to be gathered, the best-grown leaves only being then selected. The leaves of the Common White Leaf-Beet, or Spinach Beet, may be cut for use even earlier. The varieties of Leaf-Beet are pretty hardy, and will continue to yield, in the open ground, until late in the season. However, in order to be sure of having a supply all through the winter, it is advisable to remove a sufficient number of plants to a vegetable-house, where they are treated in the same way as Cardoons or Turnip-rooted Celery.

USES.—The leaves of the Silver Leaf-Beet, or Spinach Beet, are used, minced and boiled, like Spinach leaves. They are also often mixed with Sorrel, to modify its acidity. In the Chard varieties, besides the green part or blade of the leaf, the stalk and midrib are also eaten. These are very broad, tender, and fleshy, and have a very agreeable and quite peculiar flavour.

White Leaf-Beet, or **Spinach Beet** (*Poirée Blonde ou Commune*).— The leaves of this variety are very numerous, broad, slightly undulated, and of a very light or yellowish green colour. The leaf-stalks are somewhat larger than those of the Beet-root, and are of a paler colour than the blade of the leaf. This kind is chiefly grown in the eastern districts of France, where it is highly esteemed as a fresh vegetable for table use in summer and autumn, the leaves being boiled and minced like Spinach. They are also mixed with Sorrel, as mentioned above.

White Leaf-Beet ($\frac{1}{10}$ natural size).

Sea-kale Beet, or **Swiss Chard** (*Poirée à Carde Blanche*).—Leaves broad, short, and stiff, of a rather dark green colour, spreading rather than erect, with very white stalks, from about $1\frac{1}{4}$ to $1\frac{3}{4}$ inches broad, and continued into a midrib which is equally white, and narrows rather abruptly. This variety is hardy, and is chiefly grown in the countries of the North. It may be considered a drawback that the chards or midribs have almost always an earthy flavour, and in this variety these are the only parts of the plant that are used.

Silvery Sea-kale Beet, or **Silvery Swiss Chard** (*Poirée Blonde à Carde Blanche*).—A very fine and good kind, with large broad leaves,

which are very much undulated, half erect, and remarkable for the
size of their stalks and midribs, which are often 4 inches broad or
more. This variety is not quite so
hardy as the preceding kind, but it
is much more productive, and the
chards are of far better quality,
being quite free from any trace of
earthy flavour, and having a very
delicate, slightly acidulous taste.
Moreover, the blade of the leaf may
also be used, like that of the Common Spinach Beet. In these plants
a light and pale colour in the leaves
appears to be accompanied by a
mild flavour, while leaves of a dark-
green colour have always a strong
acrid taste, There are few vegetables which require less care during
their growth or yield a more certain
crop than this variety of Chard-

Silvery Sea-kale Beet ($\frac{1}{10}$ natural size).

Beet. Well-grown chards may be gathered from it in July, and the
plants will continue to bear all through the summer and autumn, and
even far into winter, if the precaution is taken of removing them to a
vegetable-house, In France this
excellent vegetable is hardly
used, except in some of the departments of the north and east.

White Curled Swiss Chard
(*Poirée à Carde Blanche Frisée*).
—This is almost as vigorous and
productive a variety as the preceding one, with leaves equally
white, but crimped and curled
in a remarkable manner. The
chards and stalks are not so
broad as those of the preceding
kind, but they are of quite as
good quality,

White Curled Swiss Chard ($\frac{1}{10}$ natural size).

**Chilian Beet, or Red-stalked
Swiss Chard** (*Poirée à Carde du
Chili*).—A very large kind, with long, stiff, almost erect leaf-stalks, 2
or 3 inches broad. Leaves rather large, undulated, almost curled, of a
dark-green colour with a metallic lustre, and 2 to 2½ ft. long, including
the stalk. This variety is much less grown as a table vegetable than
as an ornamental plant. There are two forms of it, one with bright
red, and the other with deep yellow leaf-stalks.

LEEK.

Allium Porrum, L.   *Liliaceæ.*

French, Poireau.   *German*, Lauch.   *Flemish* and *Dutch*, Prei.   *Danish*, Porre.   *Italian*,
Porro.   *Spanish*, Puerro.   *Portuguese*, Alho porro.

Said to be a native of Switzerland.—Biennial.—Notwithstanding
the different names given by botanists to the two plants, the Leek and
the Great-headed Garlic are probably identical, the only difference
between them being that, in the case of the latter, cultivation has
developed the production of cloves, while with the former the object
has been to develop the leaves in such a manner that they may both
be numerous and cover one another at the base for the greatest distance
possible.   In the Leek, as in the Onion, during the first year, the stem
is reduced to a simple plate or very flat cone, from the under side of
which the roots issue, while the leaves spring from the upper part,
sheathing one another at the base, and then forming a long blade, which
is usually folded longitudinally and narrowed to a point. These leaves,
of greater or less length and breadth, according to the variety, are
arranged in two opposite rows, so that they spread one above another
on both sides evenly from the central axis, in a kind of fan-shape.   The
flower-stem, which does not appear before the second year, rises from
the centre of the leaves, dividing the fan into two equal parts.   It is
smooth, solid, of nearly the same thickness throughout its entire
length, and not swollen like that of the Onion.   The flowers, which are
white, pink, or lilac, form a large, almost spherical, simple cluster on
the top of the stem, and are succeeded by three-valved, roundish three-
angled seed-vessels, which are filled with black, flat, wrinkled seeds,
very like Onion seeds.   A gramme contains about 400 seeds, and a
litre of them weighs about 550 grammes.   Their germinating power
usually lasts for three years.

CULTURE.—The Leek is a true biennial plant; that is, it requires
nearly a whole year to grow before it prepares to flower and ripen its
seeds, which it does in the course of the following year.   The seed is
usually sown in March in a seed-bed.   In May or early in June, when
the plants (which should have been previously thinned if sown too
thick, and watered when necessary) are about as thick as a good-sized
goose-quill, they are planted out in good, moist, rich soil, which should
have been prepared beforehand by being manured with well-rotted
stable manure, if possible.   It is best to plant in moist, cloudy weather,
or else to moisten the soil well a few days before.   The plants are
generally set in drills or rows, 16 to 20 inches apart, and with a distance
of 10 to 12 inches from plant to plant in the drills.   They should not
be planted deeper than they were growing in the seed-bed, but soil
should be laid on to cover the stalks, so as to blanch them for as great
a portion of their length as possible.   Another mode of planting is to
make small circular holes in the rows, about 4 inches wide and the
same in depth, in each of which a young plant is set, the holes being
afterwards gradually filled up by rain and watering washing into them
the soil which was taken out in making them and left beside them.

Leeks planted out in May will commence to be fit for use about
September, or they may be had earlier by sowing in February and
planting out in the latter end of April. Some market gardeners about
Paris are able to send them to market in July, by sowing in a hot-bed
in December. If the supply is required to be continued through the
winter or until spring, when full-grown plants are preparing to run to
seed, late sowings should be made in the latter end of April or May,
and the plants should not be planted out before August.

Large quantities of Leeks are
grown in the valley of the Thames,
where the soil is moist. The first
sowing is made towards the end of
January in a frame set on a gentle
hot-bed, on which has been placed a
few inches of light, rich soil. The
seed is sown rather thickly and
afterwards slightly covered with fine
soil. The sashes are then kept close
until the young plants appear, when
abundance of air is admitted both
night and day on all favourable
opportunities. If severe weather
sets in the sashes are covered with
litter or mats. On fine days plenty
of water is supplied to the plants,
and the soil is kept frequently
stirred. If the seedlings are too
thick they are thinned out to 1 inch
or so apart, and those that remain
are gradually hardened off until towards the end of March, when they
are carefully lifted and planted out-
of-doors in rows about 1 ft. apart,
the plants in the row being about
6 inches asunder. Between the rows
Lettuces are planted, and these,
being of quick growth, are removed
long before they can in any way
injure the Leeks. The next sowing,
which takes place about the end of
February, is made out-of-doors in
beds, and when large enough the
plants are put out, in a similar manner to the former sowing, in heavily
manured, deeply dug soil. Another
sowing is made six or eight weeks
later, and the last one generally
about the first week in May. In all
cases drills are drawn to a depth of
4 or 5 inches, in which the plants
are put. These in some measure
protect the plants in the early stages
of their growth, and serve as re-
ceptacles for water. The frequent

hoeing of the ground, which is considered a very important matter, fills
in the drills and blanches the necks
of the Leeks—one of the main things
to be considered in their culture.
During dry weather abundance of
water is applied, and some growers,
after taking a crop of Lettuce from
between the rows, heavily mulch the
ground with manure. The produce
from the first sowing is ready for
market by the beginning of August,
when it is quickly removed and the
vacant ground cropped with other
vegetables. The latest sowing keeps
up a constant supply of Leeks far
into the winter, when they are most
in request. The fine qualities of
this vegetable are much better
known to the Welsh, Scotch, and
French than to the English or Irish.

A good mode of growing fine
Leeks is to form trenches for them
in the same way as for Celery,
though not so wide—9 or 12 inches
being quite sufficient. Fill each
trench at the bottom with about
6 inches of well-rooted, rich, light
manure; surface this with a few
inches of soil, and leave the top from
6 to 12 inches deep. Plant the
Leeks out of the seed drills or beds
into the trench in dull, showery
weather, taking care to preserve all
their roots. This will be found a
most convenient method to allow of
the easy application of water and
manure; see that the plants are
kept clear of weeds. As they advance in growth fill in the earth a
little at a time; this will refresh
and stimulate the plants. By the
end of the season the trench will be
level with the surface or probably
converted into a slight ridge on
either side of the Leeks, which will

be from 12 to 18 inches long, thoroughly blanched, and of the finest quality. Leeks are sometimes planted with a dibble in newly dug, highly manured ground, in the same way as Cauliflowers or Cabbage plants, and simply left to shift for themselves.

Another method of planting is that adopted for setting Potatoes with spade and line. The ground is dug and manured in the autumn, and again dug early in April. When 1 ft. or more is dug, set the line against the work and cut it down straight with the spade; then plant the Leeks carefully against the straight cut along the face of the dug ground, spreading out the roots and covering them with some of the fine soil already cut down; dig another foot of ground—taking care not to bury the Leeks too deeply— and proceed to plant another row, and so on until all are completed; by this mode the plants will have a fresh, soft, untrodden root-run in which to start, and often thrive remarkably well. The subsequent management consists in merely keeping the surface clear of weeds, and in copiously watering should the weather prove dry. This style of planting is termed " digging in."

Uses.—The blanched lower part of the leaves, improperly called the stem of the plant, is extensively used in culinary preparations. In the south of England and in Ireland, the great value of this vegetable is little known except to good cooks; it is not always to be had in the best condition in these parts.

Long Winter Leek (*Poireau Long d'Hiver de Paris*).—This kind is very distinct from all others. Its leaves are consolidated for a considerable portion of their length, and, in the free part, are longer and narrower than those of any other variety; they are also of a paler and grayer green. The lower part of the leaves, where they overlap one another, and which is generally termed the stalk, measures, in well-grown plants, about 12 inches long and about 1 inch in diameter. This variety withstands the winter well, and is particularly suitable for planting out late in autumn. It is the only kind which produces those fine, very long, slender Leeks, which are seen in long bundles in the Central Market at Paris; at the same time, it is true that the market gardeners help Nature a little by earthing up the plants while they are growing.

Long Winter Leek (⅛ natural size).

Broad, or London, Flag Leek (*Poireau Gros Court*).—This kind should rather be called the Long Flag Leek, as it has a very long as well as comparatively broad stem. It is often, in fact, 10 inches long, with a diameter of nearly 2 inches. The leaves are large, pliant, often drooping backwards, rather variable in colour, but most commonly of a rather dark clear green. It is a very fine, good, rather early, and very productive variety, but not very hardy. In the climate of Paris, it can only be used for an autumn crop, as it is unable to bear any winter that is not exceptionally mild.

Large Yellow Poitou Leek (*Poireau Jaune du Poitou*).—This variety, as its name indicates, originated in the west of France, and the climate of its birthplace seems to have influenced its constitution to the extent of rendering it rather too delicate to endure a Paris winter always without injury. It is, probably, a local variety of the Broad Southern Leek, but it differs from it very plainly in several characteristics. The stem is shorter, but quite as thick, at least, being often 2 inches or more in diameter, and from 8 to 10 inches long. The leaves are larger and more fan-like in their arrangement; they are also longer and softer, and often have nearly one-half pendent so as sometimes to reach the ground. The colour, too, is very distinct, being a light, almost yellowish green, totally different from the glaucous or grayish tint of the leaves of almost all other kinds of Leek. As before observed, this is not a very hardy variety, but it is early and swells rapidly, which renders it very suitable for an autumn crop.

Large Rouen Leek (*Poireau Très Gros de Rouen*).— Stem short, very thick, seldom

Broad, or London, Flag Leek.

Large Yellow Poitou Leek (½ natural size).

exceeding 6 to 8 inches in length, with a diameter of 2 inches or more, and growing almost entirely covered by the soil; leaves commencing to separate, fan-shape, almost at the level of the ground, numerous, closely overlapping one another, folded into a spout-shape, stiff, of moderate length, and usually pendent at the extremity. The blade of the leaf is broad, and of a dark-green colour, with a grayish or slightly glaucous tinge. This is a very fine and productive variety, equally good for a winter as for an autumn crop, swelling less rapidly than the preceding kind, but, on the other hand, very slow in running to seed, and therefore yielding a more prolonged supply for table use.

Large Rouen Leek (⅙ natural size).

Giant Carentan Leek (*Poireau Monstrueux de Carentan*).—The characteristics of this variety are nearly the same as those of the preceding one, of which it is, very probably, only an improved form, but a very distinct one, on account of its much greater size and the very dark colour of its leaves. The length of the stem, in this kind, seldom exceeds 6 to 8 inches, but it is often 3 inches or more in diameter in well-grown plants, and we have not unfrequently seen it of still larger dimensions. Like the Rouen Leek, it is very hardy, and is not at all affected by Parisian winters.

In addition to the foregoing, we may mention the following varieties :—

Brabant Short Broad Leek (*Poireau Gros Court de Brabant*).—This is indeed a very short and very hardy kind, but of small size, the diameter of the stem seldom exceeding about 1 inch. In its general appearance as to the colour and arrangement of the leaves, it is tolerably like the Rouen Leek, but is far inferior to it in size.

Musselburgh, or **Scotch Flag, Leek** (*Poireau de Musselbourg*).—An improved form of the Common Long Winter Leek (raised near Edinburgh), with a longer and thicker stem and broad leaves. It comes very near the Giant Carentan Leek, if not identical with it. The Ayton Castle New Giant (Henry's Prize Giant) Leek is also a very superior large variety.

Small Mountain Leek (*Poireau Petit de Montagne*).—A half-wild kind, grown in the southern and central districts of France. It has narrow leaves, which are folded longitudinally and of a dark glaucous-green colour, and a very short and small stem, which frequently sends up shoots or suckers. Its only merit is that it is a very hardy kind.

LENTILS.

Ervum Lens, L.; *Lens esculenta*, Mœnch. *Leguminosæ.*

French, Lentille.　**German**, Linse.　*Flemish* and *Dutch*, Linze.　*Danish*, Lindse.　*Italian* Lente.　*Spanish*, Lenteja.　*Portuguese*, Lentilha.

Native of Southern Europe.—Annual.—A small and very branching plant, forming a tuft 14 to 16 inches high. Stems slender and angular; leaves winged, composed of a great number of small oval leaflets, of a clear-green colour, and terminating in a simple tendril; flowers axillary, small, white, produced in pairs, and succeeded by very flat pods, each of which usually contains two very flat seeds, which are rounded in outline and convex on both sides. The germinating power of these seeds lasts for four years. The seed is generally sown in drills or lines, in March. The plant usually prefers light soil; at least, it seeds most plentifully when grown in soil of that description. It requires no attention until the seeds are gathered in August or September. These keep better in the pods than they do after they are threshed, so the crop is only threshed out as a supply is required. The seeds are eaten like Haricot Beans, and of late years their use has been very much more frequent in England. It is excellent for soups and stews, and a capital addition to our food supplies.

Large Yellow Lentil (*Lentille Large Blonde*).—Plant of rather small size, but very branching, and of rather pale green colour; seed very broad, flat, and pale coloured. A gramme contains from 10 to 15 seeds, and a litre of them weighs about 790 grammes. This is the most commonly cultivated variety, and is grown extensively in the eastern and central districts of France, and also in Germany.

Like the Pea, the Lentil is often attacked by a small beetle or weevil, the grubs of which feed on the seed, in which they remain until they change into the form of a perfect insect; and it is probably owing to the ravages of these insects that the cultivation of Lentils has greatly fallen off in the northern districts of France.

The two commercial names of *Lorraine* and *Gallardon* Lentils merely indicate the districts from which the seeds are supplied, but both refer to the same Large Yellow Lentil, just described.

Large Yellow Lentil (⅟₁₀ natural size; detached branch, natural size).

Puy Green Lentil (*Lentille Verte du Puy*).—A very distinct kind, with small seed, which is only about ¼ inch in diameter, but very thick, and of a pale-green colour, spotted and marbled with dark green. A gramme contains about 40 seeds, and a litre of them weighs about 850 grammes. This variety is almost exclusively grown in the departments of Haute-Loire and Cantal, where it is highly esteemed both for table use, and as green fodder for cattle.

Small Winter Lentil (*Lentillon d'Hiver*).—This variety is chiefly grown in the northern and eastern districts of France, and is sown in autumn, either among corn, or more commonly by itself. It is seldom used as fodder for cattle, as the seed is highly esteemed for table use, many persons preferring it to that of the Large Yellow kind. It is of small size, comparatively thick in shape, and of a rather deep reddish colour, which distinguishes it at first sight. A gramme contains about 44 seeds, and a litre of them weighs about 800 grammes.

Small March Lentil (*Lentillon de Mars*).—The seed of this kind resembles that of the Large Yellow Lentil in colour and shape, but is only about half the size. A gramme contains, on an average, 35 seeds, and a litre of them weighs about 825 grammes. It is sown in spring, like the Large Yellow variety. The name Small Queen Lentil (*Lentille à la Reine*) is sometimes given to this kind, and also to the preceding one. Both varieties are very highly esteemed for table use, on account of their delicate flavour and the remarkable thinness of the skin of the seed.

Auvergne Lentil, or **One-flowered Tare** (*Ervum monanthos,* L. *Leguminosæ. Lentille d'Auvergne*).—Native of Southern Europe.— Annual.—A small plant, with slender stems, which require support. Leaves compound, formed of numerous, very small, oval leaflets; flowers axillary, solitary, whitish, and long-stalked, succeeded by broad flat pods, each containing two or three seeds. The plant will grow about 2 or 2½ ft. high, if the stems have something to support them; otherwise they sprawl on the ground, the extremities only standing erect. Seed irregularly rounded, tolerably convex, intermediate in shape between the seed of a Lentil and that of a Vetch, of a grayish-brown colour, streaked or marbled with black, about ¼ inch in diameter, and about ½ inch thick, floury, and rather agreeable in flavour. A gramme contains from 15 to 20 seeds, and a litre of them weighs about 800 grammes. Their germinating power lasts for three years. The seed may be sown in autumn or in spring. The plant is much more frequently grown to furnish green fodder than for its seeds, and is mostly sown along with Rye or Oats, which furnish a support for its climbing stems. The seed is sometimes eaten boiled, like Lentils.

LETTUCE.

Lactuca sativa, L. *Compositæ.*

French, Laitue cultivée. *German,* Lattich. *Flemish* and *Dutch,* Latouw. *Danish,* Salat. *Italian,* Lattuga. *Spanish,* Lechuga. *Portuguese,* Alface.

Native of India or Central Asia.—Annual.—The origin of the cultivated Lettuce is not known for certain, any more than the time when it was first introduced into Europe; neither can we be sure that the ancients knew anything about it. However, the great number of varieties of it which now exist in cultivation, and the very permanent

manner in which some of these varieties appear to be established, afford
good grounds for the opinion that the plant has been cultivated for a
very long time.

The different varieties present such a diversity in the shape and
colour of the leaves, that it is difficult to give a general description of
the plant which will be applicable to all its forms. We may suppose,
however, and especially from the fact that some Chinese varieties do
not form a head, that in its original or natural state the Lettuce forms
a rosette of large, longish leaves, which are somewhat spoon-shaped,
and more or less undulated and toothed at the edges. From the centre
of the rosette springs a nearly cylindrical stem, which narrows very
rapidly and becomes branching at about one-third of its height, furnished with clasping leaves, which are auricled, and become narrower
as they approach the top of the stem. The flower-heads are numerous,
longer than broad, with pale yellow florets. Seed small, of a long
almond-shape, pointed at one end, marked with pretty deep longitudinal furrows, and usually either white or black, but sometimes brown
or reddish yellow. A gramme contains about 800 seeds, and a litre of
them weighs, on an average, 430 grammes. Their germinating power
lasts for five years.

Good authorities appear inclined to refer all the cultivated varieties
of Lettuce to two distinct botanical types, from one of which have been
derived the Cabbage Lettuces, properly so called, which have roundish
or flattened heads, while the other has been the parent of the Cos
Lettuces, in which the head is tall and elongated in shape. We find
it difficult to assent to this view of a twofold origin; in the first place,
because the two kinds pass into each other through almost imperceptible
gradations; and secondly, because as soon as they run to seed they
present no difference from each other, which is the most conclusive
proof of the identity of their origin.

We have described the Cultivated Lettuce as an annual plant,
because the growth of the flower-stem uninterruptedly succeeds that of
the radical leaves which form the rosette, and because the rosette itself
is completely formed in a few weeks, or, at most, in a few months.
Nevertheless, several varieties are so hardy, that they may be sown in
autumn, and, after withstanding the winter, will not run to seed until
spring. All the varieties are by no means amenable to this treatment.
On the other hand, there is a great deal of inequality in the degrees
of readiness with which the different varieties run to seed under the
influence of warm summer weather. These differences of constitution
and suitability for various seasons have led to the division of the
varieties of Lettuces into three classes, from a cultural point of view,
viz.:—

1. WINTER LETTUCES, which, with a little care, will withstand
ordinary winters.

2. SPRING LETTUCES, which head rapidly when sown immediately
after winter.

3. SUMMER LETTUCES, which are usually larger than the spring
kinds, and do not run to seed too fast in hot weather.

Although this division is not very precise, we shall adopt it here,
as affording a means of indicating the mode of culture suitable for each

variety, without falling into endless repetitions. We shall accordingly first point out the treatment suitable for winter Lettuces in general, after which we shall enumerate and describe the varieties which come under that head, doing the same in the case of the spring and summer varieties.

CABBAGE LETTUCE.

Lactuca capitata, D.C.

French, Laitues pommées. *German,* Kopfsalat. *Flemish* and *Dutch,* Kropsalad. *Italian,* Lattuga a cappucio. *Spanish,* Lechuga acogollada. *Portuguese,* Alface repolhada.

I. Winter Varieties.

These are sown from the middle of August to the middle of September. About the end of October, when the plants form a rosette 2 to 3 inches in diameter and have each five or six pretty strong leaves, they are planted out permanently in as warm and favourably situated a position as possible—preferably at the bottom of a south wall or in a thoroughly well-drained bed. In very frosty weather the plants should be protected with straw mats, which are to be taken off when the weather becomes mild. Winter Lettuces are not injured by snow— so far from it, that we sometimes see varieties which are not very hardy pass through the winter in safety when well covered by it. In February the growth of the winter Lettuces becomes more active, and the heads begin to form at the end of April or early in May, the plants continuing to yield for six weeks to two months, until the spring Lettuces come in.

Madeira, or **Large Winter, Cabbage Lettuce** (*Laitue Passion*).— This variety, when the plant is young, has the leaves very much rounded and entire in outline, the blade being slightly twisted and faintly crimped in the lower part, of a rather dark, clear-green colour, with brown spots interspersed. The colour becomes much lighter as the plant increases in size. The full-grown plant is of medium size, broadish, and of low growth, the leaves resting on the ground and forming a rosette somewhat irregular in outline, and 8 to 10 inches in diameter; the outer leaves are not crimped, and are entire at

Madeira, or Large Winter, Cabbage Lettuce (⅙ natural size).

the margin, but are broadly folded and twisted, and of a clear, lightish-green colour, marked with a few brown spots. The head is roundish, pretty thick, and of a pale-green colour, tinged with red on the top. The leaves immediately surrounding it are crimped, rumpled. and tinged with red on the edges. Seed black. This is considered one of the hardiest of all Lettuces, and is generally only used for winter culture in the open ground. If sown in spring, it runs to seed very quickly.

U

White Boulogne Lettuce (*Laitue Blonde de Boulogne*).—In many respects this variety resembles the preceding one, like which, it has leaves of a very decided light tint, with a few brown or russet spots, but it forms a larger head in proportion to the size of the outer leaves, and also heads more speedily. It is, in fact, a superior kind, both in appearance and productiveness, but is, perhaps, not quite so hardy. However, it usually withstands the winter in the neighbourhood of Paris without any injury. The seed is white.

Hammersmith, or Hardy Green Winter, Cabbage Lettuce (*Laitue Morine*).—The leaves of the young plant are nearly round, shortly spathulate, finely toothed near the base, entire on the rest of the margin, generally folded in the direction of the midrib, frequently hollowed out like a spoon, and of a light, pale, or yellowish green colour. The full-grown plant is rather thick-set, not exceeding 7 or 8 inches in diameter, and somewhat irregular in outline. Outer leaves green, not very large, longer than broad, twisted considerably without being exactly folded, and partially crimped near the midrib, but not at the edges; head rather close and tallish, tolerably solid and compact, and surrounded by leaves which are generally folded in two, almost like a twisted paper bag, and are very much crimped and a little paler in colour than the outer leaves; seed white. This variety is only used for winter culture. It is hardy and of good quality, and can be planted pretty close, which makes up in some degree for the small size of the individual plants.

Hammersmith Cabbage Lettuce.

Large White Winter Cabbage Lettuce (*Laitue Grosse Blonde d'Hiver*). —The leaves of the young plant are spathulate, slightly puckered or folded, faintly toothed near the base, spreading very much, and of a light, almost whitish, green colour. The full-grown plant is stout, broad, and tallish, 10 to 12 inches in diameter, and very irregular in outline. The outer leaves are green, entire at the edges, but very much twisted and folded into broad undulations; head roundish, thick, of a pale, light-green colour, composed of and surrounded by leaves which are very much crimped, folded, and twisted, the margins, however, being entire or nearly so; seed white. This is very suitable for winter culture, being hardy, early, and very productive. It may also be sown in spring, and when raised at that time, it keeps the head very long for a winter Lettuce.

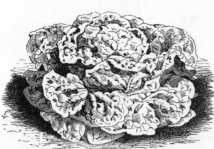

Large White Winter Cabbage Lettuce
(⅛ natural size).

Brown Winter Cabbage Lettuce (*Laitue Brune d'Hiver*).—The young plant of this variety is very considerably deeper in colour than the young plant of the Red Winter Lettuce. Its leaves are shortly oblong, and angular in outline rather than really toothed; the blade, which is sometimes slightly undulated, is hollowed out like a spoon, and blotched and plentifully tinged with brown. The full-grown plant is compact and rather thick-set. Leaves all more or less spoon-shaped, the outer ones almost smooth; head rounded, rather

Brown Winter Cabbage Lettuce
(⅙ natural size).

solid, composed of and surrounded by coarsely crimped, rather rumpled leaves of a delicate green colour. The whole plant seldom exceeds 7 or 8 inches in diameter. This is a very hardy variety, excellent in quality, and taking up but little space when growing; but it is only right to say that it runs to seed rather faster than the following kind.

Hardy Red Winter Cabbage Lettuce (*Laitue Rouge d'Hiver*).— The leaves of the young plant are oblong, slightly narrowed at the extremity, and having very much the appearance of Cos Lettuce leaves; edge nearly entire, faintly undulated, only toothed on the lower third part; colour palish green, slightly tinged and blotched with light brown. The full-grown plant is medium sized or stout, tallish, does not spread much on the ground, and is 9 or 10 inches in dia-meter. Outer leaves rounded, not much crimped or undu-lated, sometimes spoon-shaped, and slightly tinged with red-dish brown; head tallish, thick, very solid, forming quickly and lasting for a pretty long time, of a pale

Hardy Red Winter Cabbage Lettuce
(⅙ natural size).

green colour, very deeply tinged with reddish brown. The leaves sur-rounding the head exhibit the same colour on their edges and crimpings, which last are very coarse and prominent. Seed white. The Red Winter Lettuce is a very hardy kind. We consider it to be both earlier and more productive than the Madeira Lettuce, and recommend it as a good variety for winter culture.

Roquette Cabbage Lettuce (*Laitue Roquette*).—Under this name, a variety of winter Lettuce is grown which is remarkable for its dwarf size and the firmness of its head. The plant is very small and compact, with pale-green leaves deeply tinged with bronzy red where-ever it is exposed to the light, and in shape and general appearance it somewhat resembles a miniature Batavian Lettuce. When fully grown, it does not exceed 4 inches in diameter, and its small size makes it very suitable for growing in frames or under bell-glasses. The seed is white.

The Silesian Winter Lettuce is a rather large and pretty hardy kind, somewhat resembling the White Batavian Lettuce. The leaves are large and twisted, and of a pale-green colour tinged with red. Head rather large, but flabby. This variety does not answer for summer culture.

II. Spring Varieties.

These are sown in March, on a spent hot-bed, or simply on compost, at the foot of a south wall. The seedlings are planted out in April, and the plants may commence to be cut for use about the end of May or early in June. They may also (as is usually the practice with market gardeners) be sown, where the crop is to stand, about the end of February, among other vegetables growing in pure compost, or in soil covered with a thick layer of compost. In this case the small varieties should be grown, as being less likely to interfere with the other vegetables among which they are sown.

The spring varieties, especially the Crisped and Tennis-ball kinds (*Laitue Crêpe* and *L. Gotte*), are those which are used for forcing. These two kinds, and especially the Black-seeded Crisped (*L. Crêpe à Graine Noire*), are sown in October in hot-beds, and are entirely grown either in frames or under bell-glasses. The last-named kind (the "*petite noire*" of the Paris market gardeners) has the peculiarity of being able to grow almost entirely without air, so that it can be quickly raised with the help of a little artificial heat. The Tennis-ball is a more productive kind, but requires fresh air to be admitted from time to time. The sowings made in frames during winter may be finished off by a sowing made on the hot-beds with the frames and lights removed. The plants thus raised, and not transplanted, will come in some days earlier than the first of those planted out in the open air.

Black-seeded Crisped Cabbage Lettuce (*Laitue Crêpe à Graine Noire*).— Young plant rather compact, with leaves nearly round in outline, but angularly indented. The young leaves begin very soon to fold themselves like a twisted paper bag.

The full-grown plant is small, low, resting on the ground, of a very pale, almost whitish, green colour, somewhat irregular in outline, and 6 or 7 inches in diameter. Outer leaves largish but short, slightly undulated at the edges, twisted, and very partially crimped ; head round, slightly flattened, formed of leaves which are paler in colour, but much less crimped and curled,

Black-seeded Crisped Cabbage Lettuce (⅕ natural size).

than those of the White-seeded Tennis-ball Lettuce; it is firm and forms quickly, but does not last long. This variety is chiefly grown for an early crop under bell-glasses and in frames, in winter and early spring.

White-seeded Crisped Cabbage-Lettuce (*Laitue Crêpe à Graine*

Blanche).—The leaves of the young plant are broad and short, with an angular or bluntly toothed outline, and of a lightish-green colour, which changes almost to a butter yellow in the parts exposed to the sun. The full-grown plant is of medium size, about 8 inches in diameter, with leaves of a light-green colour, very much curled and undulated. Outer leaves very much folded and waved at the edges, broadly and bluntly toothed, and coarsely crimped here and there; head of medium size, tallish, formed of leaves which are paler and much more crimped than the outer ones, and also more curled than those of the Black-seeded Tennis-ball Lettuce. It is generally soft, although very full, forms quickly, but is soon put out of shape by the quick growth of the flower-stem. This variety is well adapted for spring culture, especially in the open air. When sown in autumn, it bears the winter well.

White-seeded Tennis-ball, or Boston Market, Cabbage Lettuce (*Laitue Gotte à Graine Blanche*).—The young plant of this variety has leaves of a very light green colour (which become yellow where it is exposed to the sun), and of an outline which is angular rather than decidedly toothed, except at the base. The young leaves begin very soon to become crimped and rumpled, and plants which have not made a dozen leaves will sometimes exhibit the rudiments of a head. The full-grown plant is small and thick-set, about 6 inches in diameter, and roundish in its outlines. Outer leaves roundish and partially crimped, with edges almost entire, but very much folded and sinuated; head small, but rather compact, of a light pale, almost yellowish green, and formed of leaves which are much more crimped and sinuated than the outer ones. This variety, notwithstanding its small size, is a very productive one. It grows rapidly, keeps the head well, and may be planted very close. It is especially suitable for a spring crop, that is, to be sown immediately after winter, and cut for use before summer. When sown in autumn it bears the winter well, but for this purpose we have other varieties which are hardier and much more

White-seeded Tennis-ball, or Boston Market, Cabbage Lettuce (⅙ natural size).

productive. For summer culture also, although this kind is not particularly liable to run to seed, the true summer Lettuces are to be preferred.

There is another form of White-seeded Tennis-ball named *Laitue Gotte Dorée*, or *L. Gotte Jaune d'Or* (the Golden Tennis-ball), which is very like the variety next described, but runs to seed sooner.

Spring Black-seeded Cabbage Lettuce (*Laitue Gotte à Graine Noire*).—The young plant differs very little from that of the preceding variety, except that its leaves are more crimped and folded. The full-grown plant is smaller than that of the preceding kind, and has the head flattened and never very firm. In all other respects it is exceedingly like it, and is grown in the same way.

Tom Thumb Lettuce (*Laitue Gotte Lente à Monter*).—The leaves of the young plant are of a rather dark, clear-green colour, roundish, entire, hollowed like a spoon, and with one-half almost always folded back. The central leaves begin to become crimped very early. The full-grown plant is low and rather thick-set, irregular in outline, and

6 or 7 inches in diameter. Outer leaves falling back on the ground, rather short and stiff, of a dark-green colour, generally folded along the

midrib, with one-half flat and the other turned up, and pretty well crimped; central leaves also more or less folded, with numerous and prominent crimpings, forming a head of medium size, very firm and compact, quite green on the outside, but very tender, and keeping for a long time, even in summer; seed black. This variety, which is rather small, but comparatively very productive

Tom Thumb Lettuce.

and early, and keeps the head well, is one of the best for spring and summer culture. The head is tender and of excellent quality.

Green Tennis-ball Cabbage Lettuce (*Laitue Tennis-ball*).—Leaves of the young plant broad, very entire, roundish, not toothed, except merely at the base, and of a vivid green colour. The head is slow in forming. Full-grown plant small, 7 or 8 inches in diameter, with an erect head; leaves comparatively narrow, and of a very dark-green colour, by which this variety is distinguished from all other Lettuces; the outer ones almost flat, very like those of the Lettuce-leaved Spinach, the central ones tolerably crimped, and forming a head which is at least as tall as it is broad, and is never very solid; seed black. This is an old variety, without any great merit except its hardiness.

Red-edged Victoria, or Paris Market, C. L. (*L. à Bord Rouge*).— Leaves of young plant roundish, folded in the lower part, and flat or slightly hollowed like a spoon in the rest of the blade, of a light-green colour, faintly tinged with yellow in the parts exposed to the sun. Full-grown plant compact, 8 or 9 inches in diameter; outer leaves roundish, nearly flat, resting on the ground; those surrounding the

head slightly crimped, and of a very pale, yellowish-green colour, tinged with red at the edges; head very solid, and compact, looking as if twisted, and of a light, pale-green colour, but yellow and tinged with red on the top; seed white. This is the most productive of all the spring Lettuces. It is also slower in forming the head than any other kind, and may

Red-edged Victoria Cabbage Lettuce.

be regarded as the connecting link between the spring and the summer varieties. The head is very tender and, at the same time, very firm. It is one of the best kinds either for the private kitchen garden or for market-gardening purposes.

The following varieties are only occasionally met with in cultivation:—

Laitue Bigotte.—Head medium sized or large, roundish, very light-coloured green, deeply tinged with red. A fine, early, and productive kind.

L. Cocasse à Graine Noire.—Leaves of a light glaucous green, crimped; those around the head folded back; head very firm and solid. The white-seeded form of this kind exhibits hardly any difference from it.

Coquille Cabbage Lettuce (*Laitue Coquille*).—A small variety, with a tall head. Leaves stiff, crimped, folded in two, and turned back at the ends. The appearance of the plant is almost intermediate between that of a Cabbage and a Cos Lettuce. It is a pretty early kind, but not very productive.

Green Crisped Cabbage Lettuce (*L. Crêpe Dauphine*).—Leaves large, undulated, curled at the edges, and of a clear-green colour; head medium sized, somewhat flattened, and tinged with brown on the top. A hardy kind, but not very tender or well flavoured.

L. Dauphine (*L. Grosse Brune Hâtive*).—Leaves large, marked with a few red spots; head tallish, not very solid, of a light-green colour, slightly tinged with red on the top. In appearance this variety somewhat resembles the Large or White Summer Cabbage Lettuce, except that it is of a darker green. Seed black.

George Early White Spring Cabbage Lettuce (*L. Georges*).— Leaves large, roundish, and not much undulated; head round, light coloured, of medium size, composed of broadly crimped leaves. This variety is not so good as the Crisped or Tennis-ball kinds, and is most commonly grown as a Cutting Lettuce. Seed white.

L. Grasse de Bourges.—A rather compact kind, nearly the whole of the plant forming the head, with short spoon-shaped leaves. Head round and close. This is an early and tender variety, but is liable to rot very easily.

Mousseronne Cabbage Lettuce (*L. Mousseronne*).—Leaves medium sized, curled and toothed, slightly crimped, and of a light-green colour edged with brown; head small and loose, tinged with brownish red; seed white. This variety is very early, but heads badly. It may also be grown as a Cutting Lettuce, like the George Lettuce.

Some foreign varieties of spring Lettuces may be here mentioned, of which the best and most commonly grown are the following:—

Early Cabbage, or **Dutch Butter-head, Lettuce.**—A small and very distinct American variety, with crimped leaves, blotched with pale brown. Head firm and compact, tinged with red on the top, and scarcely as large as that of the Tom Thumb Lettuce; seed white.

Earliest Dwarf Green Lettuce.—A pretty little green variety, very thick-set and distinct, although evidently not far removed from the Tom Thumb Lettuce. Seed black.

Laitue Empereur à Forcer.—This small variety, which is very early, very much resembles the White-seeded Tennis-ball Lettuce, but is somewhat lighter in colour, and runs to seed sooner.

Earliest Dwarf Green Lettuce
(⅙ natural size).

Hubbard's Forcing Lettuce.—A largish, light-coloured, American kind, something like the White-seeded Tennis-ball and the White Summer Cabbage Lettuce. It is forced under glass in spring.

III. Summer Varieties.

The culture of these is of the most simple kind. The seed is sown in a seed-bed from March to July, and the seedlings are usually pricked out once before they are planted out permanently, which is done when they have made five or six good leaves. After this, they require no further attention except frequent and plentiful waterings. A good mulching of manure spread amongst them will keep the soil cool and moist and stimulate the growth of the plants.

White-seeded All-the-Year-Round Lettuce (*Laitue Blonde d'Été*).— Leaves of young plant light green, short, entire, roundish, very faintly

toothed at the base, and slightly undulated. Full-grown plant with a round, compact, very solid head, of a very pale, almost whitish, green colour; outer leaves short, roundish, very entire at the edges, but finely crimped and slightly undulated; the plant is 6 to 8 inches in diameter; seed white. This excel-

White-seeded All-the-Year-Round Lettuce (⅕ natural size).

lent variety is one of the most commonly grown, as shown by the great number of names which it bears. It is hardy and very productive, being, as the gardeners say, "all head." It makes a fine, tender, crisp salad, and grows well in almost any soil, so that it is found in cultivation almost all over the world.

Black-seeded All-the-Year-Round Cabbage Lettuce (French, *Laitue Blonde de Berlin;* German, *Grosser Berliner Gelber Fester Kopf-Lettich*).—Young plant of a light-green colour; leaves roundish, entire

Black-seeded All-the-Year-Round Cabbage Lettuce.

Large Versailles Cabbage Lettuce.

at the edges, and with a tendency to become twisted in the shape of a paper bag. Head of full-grown plant round, soft, but very full; outer leaves broadly crimped, roundish, entire, and of a very pale or almost yellowish green; those surrounding the head are more erect and less folded than they are in the preceding kind. The head is also somewhat taller. The plant is seldom more than 8 inches in diameter; seed black.

Large Versailles Cabbage Lettuce (*Laitue Blonde de Versailles*).— Young plant of a rather light-green colour; leaves roundish, entire, with visible veinings. It resembles the young plant of the Large White Cabbage Lettuce, but is larger at the same age. Head of full-grown plant round or somewhat elongated, very firm and solid, and of a rather pale, clear-green colour; outer leaves very large, entire, of a rather dark green, folded and crimped, especially about the midrib; those surrounding the head are broadly undulated and twisted in all directions, giving the plant a somewhat irregular appearance. The plant is 10 or 11 inches in diameter; seed white.

Chavigny White Lettuce (*Laitue Blonde de Chavigné*).—Young plant of a clear-green colour, and exceedingly like the young plant of the White Summer Cabbage Lettuce, only not so light coloured; the leaves also are rather narrower towards the base. Head of full-grown plant large, full, and compact, of a pale green, almost yellow, on the top; outer leaves very much rounded in outline, with a few coarse, broad crimpings, and not nearly so pale in colour as the leaves which

Chavigné White Lettuce (⅛ natural size).

form the head; plant 8 to 10 inches in diameter; seed white. This is a very fine variety, regular in shape, quick in forming the head, slow in running to seed, and yielding, with less bulk, quite as heavy a crop as the Large Versailles Lettuce. It is highly to be recommended.

White Stone, or **Nonpareil, Cabbage Lettuce** (*Laitue Grosse Blonde Paresseuse*).—Young plant of a pale green, rather light coloured; leaves roundish, or shortly spathulate, flat, toothed and undulated on the lower half. Head of full-grown plant large and tallish, but flattened on the top, of a very pale green and very light coloured, almost the colour of wax or butter; outer leaves large, very much rounded, slightly crimped, and not quite so pale in colour as the head; plant about 12 inches in diameter;

White Stone, or Nonpareil, Cabbage Lettuce (⅛ natural size).

seed white. This fine Lettuce is large-sized and productive. It grows well and keeps the head perfectly in very hot weather.

Turkish or **Butter, Russian** or **Asiatic, Cabbage Lettuce** (*Laitue Turque*).—Young plant of a uniform dull, pale-green colour; leaves short, rounded, spathulate, and slightly toothed on the whole of the margin. Head of full-grown plant roundish, slightly flattened, of a very pale green, almost whitish; outer leaves resting on the ground, roundish, very entire, scarcely crimped, of an exceedingly pale green, and of an appearance betokening great thickness. The outside face of the leaves is of a still lighter tint and sometimes quite silvery. All the leaves are very entire, and those which form the head and also those which immediately surround it are rather crimped. Plant 8 or 10 inches in diameter; seed black.

Imperial, or **Asiatic, Cabbage Lettuce** (*Laitue Impériale*).—
Young plant of a uniform palish and rather dull-green colour; leaves

roundish, short, flat, and
bluntly toothed on the whole
of the margin. This variety
only differs from the preceding one in the colour of its
seed, which is white. Both
kinds are only suitable for
summer culture, for which
they are highly to be recommended, as they are very productive and bear hot dry
weather well.

Imperial, or Asiatic, Cabbage Lettuce
(⅙ natural size).

The *Laitue Caladoise* and
the German variety named
Perpignaner Dauerkopf have always appeared to us to come exceedingly
close to the Imperial Lettuce.

Fat Green Cabbage Lettuce (*Laitue Verte Grosse*).—Young plant

of a dark-green colour; leaves
short, roundish, or bluntly spathulate, very slightly toothed on the
margin, the lower ones crimped
and sinuated. Head of full-grown
plant roundish or slightly flattened,
close, firm, and surrounded by
leaves with entire edges, all broadly
crimped, of a clear-green colour,
dark on the upper surface and
almost silvery on the under side;
outer leaves very round, small,

Fat Green Cabbage Lettuce (⅙ natural size).

entire, and smooth. All the leaves are stiff and of a dense texture,
somewhat resembling Spinach leaves. The plant is from about 7 to
9 inches in diameter; seed black. This is a good summer Lettuce,
yielding a heavy crop with small bulk, and keeping the head very well.

Black-seeded Dutch Cabbage Lettuce (*Laitue Monte à Peine
Verte, à Graine Noire*).—Young plant of a uniform very dark-green
colour; leaves short, roundish, flat, slightly toothed near the base, the

inner leaves crimped and sinuated. Head
of full-grown plant small, round, very close
and hard, of a pale-green colour, and surrounded by entire, crimped, and slightly
undulated leaves, which form a very compact rosette. The plant is, at most, from
6 to 8 inches in diameter. Its general
appearance resembles that of the Large
White Cabbage Lettuce, with which,
however, it cannot be confounded, if the

Black-seeded Dutch Cabbage
Lettuce (⅙ natural size).

difference in the colour of the leaves and of the seed is taken into
consideration. Small-sized Lettuces, like this variety, are often valuable
to gardeners for growing amongst other vegetables.

Mortatella Cabbage Lettuce (*Laitue Mortatella*).—A very distinct and highly-to-be-recommended variety, of Italian origin. A peculiarity which belongs almost exclusively to this Lettuce is that the stem becomes elongated in a very striking manner from the base, like that

of many round-headed Cabbages (especially those sown in autumn), in consequence of which the large outer leaves, instead of forming a rosette, so to say, close to the ground, grow in tiers one above another, the head forming at some distance above the surface of the soil. These outer leaves are of a dark and somewhat dull green, short, rounded in shape, and often hollowed like a spoon.

Mortatella Cabbage Lettuce.

The head is compact, of medium size, a little longer than broad, and frequently tinged with red on the upper part; it preserves its shape for a remarkably long time. The axillary buds of the lower leaves sometimes become developed into sprouts or shoots, which are rarely of any great size. In Italy this Lettuce is said to grow well all the year round, but, from our experience of it, it is chiefly valuable as an autumn and winter Lettuce in the neighbourhood of Paris.

Large Normandy Lettuce (*Laitue Grosse Normande*).—Young plant dark green; leaves elongated spathulate, usually twisted, toothed towards the base, and angular on the remainder of the margin, almost more like the leaves of the Batavian Endive than Lettuce leaves. Head of full-grown plant roundish or slightly elongated, rather thick, very solid, slightly crimped, and of a pale-green colour; outer leaves roundish, of a dense texture, very entire at the edges, of a uniform dark-green colour, and coarsely crimped here and there. Some of the leaves spread on the ground and others stand erect around the head. The diameter ranges from 10 to 12 inches; seed yellow. This variety is something like the Large Versailles Lettuce in appearance, but its leaves are considerably darker in colour, and it is unmistakably distinguished by the colour of the seed.

Mogul Cabbage Lettuce (*Laitue Grosse Brune Paresseuse*).—Young plant of a rather pale dull green, marked with brown spots; leaves

short, roundish, entire at the end and toothed along the sides. This is a large strong-growing kind, the full-grown plant being about a foot in diameter. Outer leaves very large, of a clear-green colour, much paler on the inner side, folded rather than crimped, and marked, as are all the other leaves, with brown spots; head tallish, compact, tinged with brownish red on the top, and

Mogul Cabbage Lettuce (⅕ natural size).

composed of leaves which are tolerably crimped, and become spoon-shaped as they overlap one another. Seed black. This is a very hardy and exceedingly productive kind, very suitable for field culture. The

Berlaimont Lettuce (*Laitue de Berlaimont*), which is in high repute in the north of France, appears to us to be identical with it.

Pas de Calais Cabbage Lettuce (*Laitue Julienne d'Été*).—Young plant of a uniform dark-green colour; leaves elongated spoon-shaped, slightly angular at the margin, and toothed and undulated towards the base. The full-grown plant is stout, and rather like the preceding variety, but differing from it notably in the total absence of brown spots from the leaves. It is also somewhat taller, and the head is more ovoid in shape and of a bronzy, rather than a red, colour in the parts exposed to the sun. Seed black.

White-seeded Brown Dutch C. L. (*Laitue Monte à Peine, à Graine Blanche*).—Young plant of a dull green tinged with brown on the veins; leaves roundish spathulate, slightly toothed towards the base, the central ones soon becoming crimped and undulated. Head of the full-grown plant roundish, or slightly elongated, very full and firm, of a very pale green, and deeply tinged with red on the top; outer leaves roundish, with entire margins, tolerably crimped, of a grayish-green colour, edged and tinged with light brown; those which surround the head are very much crimped, and tolerably folded and twisted. All the parts exposed to the sun, whether on the upper or lower side of the leaves, become tinged with coppery red. This is a very good kind; it is hardy, keeps the head well, and does not take up too much space when growing. The plant does not exceed from 8 to 10 inches in diameter.

Brown Geneva Cabbage Lettuce (*Laitue Palatine*).—Young plant green, tinged with brown; leaves rather short, roundish spathulate,

entire at the margin, except towards the base, where it is toothed; veinings reddish. Head of full-grown plant of medium size or large, roundish, very solid without being hard, and deeply tinged with brownish red on the top; outer leaves rather large, entire at the edges, but tolerably crimped, folded, and twisted, tinged with red and with dark-brown blotches interspersed; plant 10 to 12 inches in diameter; seed black. This variety is one

Brown Geneva Cabbage Lettuce (⅕ natural size).

of the hardiest and least troublesome to grow. No other kind is superior to it for summer or autumn culture, either in productiveness or the certainty of the crop. It heads very quickly, keeps the head well, and withstands the early frosts in the latter end of autumn. During the latter part of summer and all through the autumn it furnishes more than half of the Cabbage Lettuces which are sent to the Central Market at Paris.

Black-seeded Brown Dutch C. L. (*Laitue Rousse Hollandaise*).— Young plant of a dull-green colour, slightly tinged with light brown; leaves short, roundish or spathulate, finely toothed towards the base, where they are of a reddish colour, as are also the veins. This variety differs from the preceding one chiefly in having no spots on the leaves, and the plant altogether is not so brown. In other respects the two kinds are much alike in size and general appearance. Seed black.

The Dutch Capucine Cabbage Lettuce (*Laitue Capucine de Hollande*) is barely distinguished from the Brown Dutch Lettuce by being a trifle paler in colour.

Red Besson Cabbage Lettuce (*Laitue Merveille des Quatre Saisons*). —Young plant of vigorous growth, tinged all over with brownish red; leaves short, almost round, very entire, with the edges turned up in a

Black-seeded Brown Dutch Cabbage Lettuce (⅙ natural size).

Red Besson Cabbage Lettuce (⅙ natural size).

kind of spoon-shape. The plant is easily recognized from its earliest age by its colour. The full-grown plant is stout and rather thick-set, and of rapid growth. Head roundish, slightly flattened on the top, where it is deeply tinged with bright red, which contrasts in a striking manner with the very pale tint of those parts of the plant which are not exposed to the sun. The outer leaves are similarly coloured with red on the exposed parts. All the leaves are roundish in outline, more or less undulated, and coarsely crimped here and there. This is the most highly coloured of all the Lettuces which are commonly grown about Paris, and is of a still deeper red than the old variety known as the *Rouge Chartreuse*. The plant is about 1 ft. in diameter; seed black. This variety may be grown almost all the year round, as one of its French names indicates, but it does best in spring and summer. The head forms very quickly and keeps firm for a long time, even in very hot weather.

Small Dark-red Cabbage Lettuce (*Laitue Sanguine Améliorée*).— Young plant marked with very small and fine red spots and streaks; leaves roundish, entire, undulated or folded like a paper bag. In the central leaves the green colour disappears altogether under the numerous small spots of reddish brown with which they are covered. In the full-grown plant the head is exceedingly close, of medium size, round, or slightly flattened on the top, the inner leaves being very much folded and of an ivory white, very finely and plenti- fully streaked with carmine. The top of the head is of a deep copper colour. The outer leaves, which are small,

Small Dark-red Cabbage Lettuce (⅙ natural size).

numerous, and less crimped as they are nearer to the ground, are covered with a vast number of small red spots, which give the whole plant a bronzy tinge. The plant seldom exceeds from 7 to 9 inches in diameter; seed white. This variety, although small, is productive. It is also early and keeps the head well. The very lively colour of the spots forms a pleasing contrast on the leaves when they are blanched, making a nice-looking salad, which is at the same time tender and of excellent quality.

Trocadero Cabbage Lettuce (*Laitue Lorthois*).—This is a very good summer Lettuce, but may be equally well grown in winter or spring.

Trocadero Cabbage Lettuce.

It is a very distinct variety, so well marked, indeed, that it cannot be mistaken for any other. In general appearance it resembles a Crisped Lettuce (*Laitue Crêpe*), but, in addition to being larger than either the black-seeded or white-seeded varieties of that Lettuce, its leaves are not nearly so light coloured, but are of a duller green; the head, also, and the leaves which surround it are tinged with russet, the former on the upper part and the latter on the margin. It is both a hardy and an early kind of Lettuce, and the head forms quickly and keeps its shape well. It is equally well adapted for field culture and for the kitchen garden. Seed white.

Early Simpson Cabbage Lettuce (*Laitue Hâtive de Simpson*).— Young plant pale green, light coloured, and almost yellow; leaves

Early Simpson Cabbage Lettuce (⅛ natural size).

angular, very much undulated at the margin, curled and rumpled. Head of full-grown plant seldom well formed; leaves large, light green, with a shining surface, as if varnished, very fresh and pleasing to the sight, very much curled and undulated, finely crimped, very numerous, and tender even when they do not form a head. This is one of the best summer Lettuces, and is very suitable for growing in warm climates. All it requires is to be plentifully watered. Seed white.

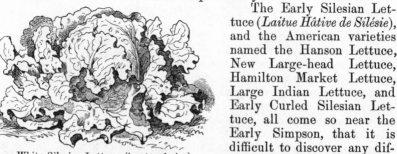

White Silesian Lettuce (⅛ natural size).

The Early Silesian Lettuce (*Laitue Hâtive de Silésie*), and the American varieties named the Hanson Lettuce, New Large-head Lettuce, Hamilton Market Lettuce, Large Indian Lettuce, and Early Curled Silesian Lettuce, all come so near the Early Simpson, that it is difficult to discover any difference between them.

White Silesian Lettuce (*Laitue Batavia Blonde*).—Young plant of a light or yellowish green colour; leaves slightly toothed, undulated, and tinged with pale red on the margin. Head of full-grown plant very large, but not very firm, of a very pale-green colour tinged with light red, roundish, or slightly flattened; outer leaves largish, curled, finely crimped, very much undulated and broadly toothed at the edges, where they are also slightly tinged with red. The plant is 12 to 14 inches in diameter; seed white.

The variety named *Laitue Belle et Bonne de Bruxelles* comes very near the White Silesian. Sometimes it is almost entirely without the red tinge, and then it very much resembles the following kind.

Curled German Batavian, or **Curled Silesian**, **Cabbage Lettuce** (French, *Laitue Batavia Frisée Allemande*; German, *Grüner Früher Montrée Lattich*).—Leaves of the young plant broad and short, with the edges scalloped and undulated, and of a light, slightly yellowish, green colour. Head of full-grown plant large, softish, roundish or slightly flattened, and of a very pale-green colour; outer leaves crimped, curled, and slightly cut at the edges. The plant is 11 or 12 inches in diameter; seed white. With the

Curled German Batavian Lettuce
(⅙ natural size).

exception of its pale and very light colour, this variety is not unlike the Neapolitan Cabbage Lettuce. It is a vigorous-growing kind, very easily grown, and yields a sure crop in summer.

Brown Batavian, or **Marseilles**, **Cabbage Lettuce** (*Laitue Batavia Brune*).—Young plant of a very dark-green colour; leaves very long, narrow, sharply toothed at the edges; midrib and margin of the leaves tinged with brown. Head of full-grown plant very tall and elongated, more like the head of a Cos than that of a Cabbage Lettuce, almost always soft, and seldom well formed; outer leaves very large, erect for some portion of their length, then turned backwards, crimped, very much undulated and puckered at the edges, and of a dark-green colour tinged with brown on all the parts that are most exposed to the sun.

Brown Batavian, or Marseilles, Cabbage
Lettuce (⅙ natural size).

The plant is about 16 inches in diameter, and nearly the same in height; seed white. This variety does not succeed well in the climate of Paris, but is in high repute in warm climates, and even in the south of France.

American Curled, or **Gathering**, **Lettuce** (*Laitue Frisée d'Amérique*).—This variety of summer Lettuce is characterized by having its leaves twisted, puckered, and folded at the margin, and especially by the wine-lees-red tint which suffuses the edges and all the raised parts of the leaves that are more especially exposed to the direct rays of the sun, giving the plant a very striking and pleasing appearance. The leaves, however, are rather flabby in texture, and the variety would not much deserve to be recommended, if it did not possess the advantage of succeeding remarkably well in very warm climates. The head does not usually form very well. It is used as a green salad, like the Early Simpson Lettuce, and sometimes the first leaves are merely plucked off and thrown away, with the view of making a later gathering of the new leaves which are produced, or of the sprouts or shoots which grow from the axils. From this it derives its name of "Gathering Lettuce."

American Curled Lettuce.

Neapolitan Cabbage Lettuce (*Laitue Chou de Naples*).—Young plant of a dark-green colour; leaves shortly spathulate, wavy at the edges, toothed, and slightly crimped. Head of full-grown plant large, depressed, sometimes almost flat, of a very pale whitish green, and slightly crimped; outer leaves of a rather dark green, spreading on the ground, finely crimped, very much curled and undulated at the edges. The plant is often 12 to 14 inches in diameter; seed white. This variety keeps the head better, perhaps, than any other kind of Lettuce. It often happens that the flower-stem is unable to make its way through the head, unless the latter is cut so as to give it a passage.

Neapolitan Cabbage Lettuce (⅕ natural size).

Large Bossin Cabbage Lettuce (*Laitue Bossin*).—Young plant of a light green, almost yellow, colour, with some brown spots; leaves longish, toothed, and tinged with brown on the veins and edges. Head of full-grown plant large, flattish, of a pale light green, tinged with brown; outer leaves very large and luxuriant, spreading widely on the ground, and forming a rosette 16 inches or more in diameter, very much toothed and undulated at the edges, slightly crimped, and irregularly shaded

Large Bossin Cabbage Lettuce (⅕ natural size).

and spotted with reddish brown; seed black. This is a very vigorous-growing and hardy kind, bearing hot weather well, but the weight of the produce is not in proportion to the extent of ground covered by the plants.

Malta, or Ice, Drumhead Lettuce (*Laitue de Malte*).—Young plant of a uniform light-green colour; leaves spathulate, longish, veined, very much toothed, and slightly undulated on the whole of the margin, and somewhat twisted. Head of full-grown plant composed of pale-green leaves, which are folded and marked with elongated crimpings. When the head is commencing to form, it is tolerably like that of a Cos Lettuce, but it widens and becomes nearly round when fully grown. The midribs of the leaves are thick, and often project from the head. Outer leaves very large, of a pale light-green colour, with the edges folded, slightly cut, and sometimes rolled inwards on the under side. The plant is 12 to 14 inches in diameter, and about the same in height;

Malta, or Ice, Drumhead Lettuce
(⅙ natural size).

Lebœuf Lettuce.

seed white. The Malta Lettuce grows rapidly, and bears hot weather well, but it does not keep the head long. It is especially suitable for warm climates.

Lebœuf Lettuce (*Laitue Lebœuf*).—Young plant of a dark-green colour; leaves very large, the first spathulate and flat, the succeeding ones shorter, crimped at the base, with broad white midribs, and more like the leaves of a Cos than those of a Cabbage Lettuce. Head of full-grown plant tolerably like that of a Cos Lettuce, composed of leaves pressed close to, but not regularly overlapping, one another; outer leaves elongated, erect for a portion of their length, and then turned backwards near the end, all more or less folded in the direction of the midrib, and folded, crimped, and often twisted at the edges. The plant is 7 or 8 inches in diameter, and as much, or even more, in height; seed white. Except that its leaves are somewhat stouter and larger, this variety is tolerably like a Cos Lettuce in the ground. It has the peculiarity of frequently producing shoots at the base of the head.

In addition to the summer Lettuces already described, the following varieties appear to us the best and most distinct :—

Bellegarde Cabbage Lettuce (*Laitue de Bellegarde*).—A tall, broad plant, having the head surrounded with large leaves, which are cut and deeply toothed on the edges. In general appearance it resembles the

X

Large Bossin Cabbage Lettuce (*L. Bossin*), but is smaller and rather more deeply coloured.

White Stone Cabbage Lettuce (*Laitue Blonde Trapue*).—A compact plant, with crimped, wavy leaves of a light-green, almost yellow, colour, tinged with light brown on the top of the head, which is of medium size, close, and somewhat flattened. It is a good summer variety, hardy, and slow in running to seed. The only fault it has is its slightly bitter flavour. Seed white.

California Lettuce, or Royal Summer Cabbage Lettuce.—A fine and good American summer Lettuce, well headed and productive, re-

Curled Californian Lettuce (⅛ natural size).

sembling the Large White Cabbage Lettuce (*L. Blonde d'Été*), but rather more thick-set, and lighter in colour. The leaves are spotted with brown, and bronzy at the edges.

Under the name of Curled Californian Lettuce (*Laitue Frisée de Californie*), two varieties, differing from each other, and entirely distinct from the preceding kind, are grown. Both have the leaves quite green, spreading on the ground in a rosette, like the Endives, and seldom or never forming a head. They differ from each other in this respect, that in one of them, which is also called the Beauregard Curled Lettuce, the leaves are simply toothed, and cut on the margin almost like those of the Winter Batavian Endive

Beauregard Lettuce (⅙ natural size).

(*Scarole en Cornet*), while in the other the leaves are very much puckered and folded at the edges, and are not so deeply cut, but far more curled. This latter kind forms a broad and well-furnished rosette, and is remarkably slow in running to seed.

Laitue de Fontenay.—A fine variety of Cabbage Lettuce, very slow in running to seed, of large size, and productive. It has some resemblance to the Turkey Cabbage Lettuce (*Laitue Turque*), but is larger. It is very pale and light coloured in all its parts.

Laitue de Néris.—A fine summer Lettuce, very much resembling the Mogul Lettuce, except that it is much lighter in colour. It is very much grown and highly thought of in the central parts of France.

New Gem Cabbage Lettuce.—A pretty little kind, with a compact head, almost devoid of outer leaves. It take up very little space when growing, and produces a comparatively large and very solid head. In general appearance the plant is rather like the Roquette Lettuce, but it is somewhat larger growing, and does not bear the winter.

Laitue Rose, ou *Rouge d'Été.*—A very distinct variety, not spotted, but very deeply tinged with brownish red on the edges of the leaves and on the head. It is something like a brown winter Lettuce, but is more deeply coloured, and the head is taller. It is very suitable for growing in the latter end of spring, and in summer and autumn, and is often to be met with in the Central Market at Paris.

Large Red Cabbage Lettuce (*Laitue Rouge Chartreuse*).—This fine variety has the same shape and, to a certain extent, the same appearance as the Palatine Lettuce, but it is not spotted, and the colour of the leaves is a much more decided red. It is a good summer variety, and will also bear the winter, if not too severe. Seed black.

Yellow-seeded Brown Cabbage Lettuce (*Laitue Rousse à Graine Jaune*).—This variety comes very near the Brown Dutch Lettuce in shape, colour, and general appearance, but differs from it in having the leaves more crimped and of a rather redder tinge, and differs entirely from it in the yellow colour of the seed. In Anjou there is another yellow-seeded kind grown, which must not be confounded with this one. The Anjou variety is small, entirely green, and is chiefly adapted for winter culture, but it is not very extensively distributed, nor does it seem deserving of being more so.

White-seeded Spotted Cabbage Lettuce (*Laitue Sanguine à Graine Blanche*).—A rather compact variety, with roundish, sinuated, twisted leaves, forming a close and very tender head. The inner leaves are almost white, and are streaked with bright red; the outer ones are of a dark green, with brown blotches.

Black-seeded Spotted Cabbage Lettuce (*Laitue Sanguine à Graine Noire*).—This variety differs from the preceding one in the fineness of the red streaks with which the leaves are marked, which gives the whole plant a bronzy tinge. The inner leaves appear as if dusted with red on a white ground. Both this and the preceding kind have been superseded by the new Improved White-seeded variety.

Laitue Tannhäuser.—A compact variety, with thick roundish leaves and round head, rather like the Large Normandy Lettuce, but differing from it entirely in the colour of its seed, which is black.

Laitue de Zélande (Seelander Latouw).—A handsome and compact variety of Cabbage Lettuce, of a very pale, light-yellow colour, remarkably like the Berlin White Summer Lettuce, except that the head is almost ovoid in shape, being longer than broad. Seed black.

A variety is grown in the United States, under the name of *Boston Market Lettuce,* which appears to come very near this variety, or to be intermediate between it and the Berlin White Summer Lettuce.

COS LETTUCES.

French, Laitues romaines. *German,* Römischer *oder* Bind-Salat. *Flemish,* Ezelsoor salat. *Dutch,* Roomsche latouw. *Italian,* Lattuga romana. *Spanish,* Lechuga romana. *Portuguese,* Alface romana.

The Cos Lettuces are distinguished from the common Cabbage Lettuces by the shape of their leaves, which are elongated and almost always somewhat spoon-shaped, and also by the usually large size of the midrib, which in some varieties forms a regular white, tender, and very thick chard.

They are grown in exactly the same manner as the Cabbage Lettuces, only that, as they do not naturally form a head so well as these, gardeners are in the habit of tying up the leaves together in order to blanch the inner ones. There are winter, spring, and summer varieties of Cos Lettuces. For forcing, and for early sowing in the open air, the preference is given to the White Paris Cos, next to which come the Green Paris Cos and the Gray Paris Cos, all of which are closely allied kinds. For summer culture the same varieties may be employed, and also the Florence Cos, or Magnum Bonum (*Romaine Alphange*), the Giant Cos (*Romaine Monstreuse*), and the Brown, or Bath, Cos (*Romaine Brune Anglaise*). Lastly, for winter culture in the open air, the Green Winter Cos, the Royal Green, and the Blood-red Winter Cos are the kinds most commonly selected.

I. WINTER VARIETIES OF COS LETTUCE (*Romaines d'Hiver*).

Green Winter Cos Lettuce (*Romaine Verte d'Hiver*).—Leaves of young plant smooth, of a dark-green colour, rather flat and roundish, but narrowed towards the end ; margin entire, with the exception of a few teeth on the lower third part. Full-grown plant compact, with the leaves closely pressed against one another, erect, and slightly turned back at the ends ; blade of the leaf shortly spathulate or oval, smooth, and of a very vivid, clear-green colour, with a glazed or glossy appearance ; veins numerous and very distinctly marked. The head forms of

Green Winter Cos Lettuce
(⅙ natural size).

Royal Green Winter Cos Lettuce
(⅙ natural size).

itself without being tied up ; it is not very tall, but is firm, compact, and very solid. Seed black. This is a very old and very excellent variety ; it is very little affected by frosty weather, and yields a heavy crop for the moderate size of the plants.

Royal Green Winter Cos Lettuce (*Romaine Royale Verte*).—Leaves of young plant shortly spathulate, slightly crimped and twisted towards the base, rather deeply toothed on the lower two-thirds of the margin, and of a uniform dark-green colour. Full-grown plant vigorous growing ; leaves of a clear green, shining almost as if varnished, oblong, slightly crimped, somewhat turned back at the edges until the head begins to form, when they turn the other way, becoming spoon-shaped as they overlap one another; head tallish, tolerably solid, and blanching itself without being tied up; seed black. This variety is chiefly distinguished from the preceding one by the rosette which it forms before heading being less spreading, stiffer, and of a paler and more glistening green colour.

Red Winter Cos Lettuce (*Romaine Rouge d'Hiver*).—Young plant deeply tinged with brownish red; leaves spathulate, flat, smooth, and slightly toothed at the base. Head of full-grown plant tall, long, entirely green, with the exception of a brownish-red tinge on the top; outer leaves long, rounded at the ends, very entire, nearly flat, and very deeply coloured with reddish brown. It is only in the centre of the plant, near the head, that any green colour is visible. Seed black. This variety generally heads very well without being tied up. It is hardy, productive, and remarkably slow in running to seed. It is also so constant in character that it is hardly ever found to vary or degenerate.

Red Winter Cos Lettuce
(⅙ natural size).

The English *Hardy Winter White Cos* is only a paler-coloured sub-variety of this kind.

II. Spring and Summer Varieties of Cos Lettuce.

Green Paris Cos, or Buckland Cos, Lettuce (*Romaine Verte Maraîchère*).—Young plant dark green; leaves erect, with white midribs, elongated, spathulate, and very much toothed towards the base. Head of full-grown plant elongated, pointed or slightly blunt, showing three well-marked faces; outer leaves erect around the head, comparatively narrow, of a rather dark green, almost as if varnished, and with very white midribs. This is a fast-growing kind, not so large as the White Paris Cos, but somewhat earlier. Seed white.

Gray Paris Cos Lettuce (*Romaine Grise Maraîchère*).—The young plant of this variety hardly differs from that of the White Paris Cos, except that it is decidedly darker in colour. Head of full-grown plant well rounded at the top, and more thick-set than that of either the preceding or the following kind; outer leaves large, rounded at the end, and not so light-coloured as those of the White Paris Cos; those forming the head are very much hollowed out like a spoon; seed white. This variety is chiefly grown under cloches or bell-glasses, and for that mode of culture it is generally preferred by the Paris market gardeners to all other kinds.

A sub-variety, which is somewhat shorter, lighter coloured, and earlier, is grown under the name of *Romaine Courte Blanche.*

The Paris market gardeners grow, under the name of *Romaine Plate*, a variety which appears to be intermediate between the Green and the Gray Paris Cos Lettuces. It is not so pale-coloured as the Gray variety, and might be described as a large-leaved Green Paris Cos. It forms a broad head, very full and broadly arched at the top, whence it has obtained the name of *plate,* or " flat." It is grown under bell-glasses along with the Gray variety.

White Paris Cos Lettuce (*Romaine Blonde Maraîchère*).—Young plant pale green; leaves rather erect, spathulate, toothed and slightly crimped towards the base, and broad and rounded at the ends. Head

of full-grown plant long and tall, but very thick, blunt or rounded at the top, and with the faces or angles less marked than those of the Green Paris Cos; outer leaves spathulate, large and luxuriant, of a light-green colour, and tolerably crimped; those forming the head are always folded, of a very pale-green colour, and with the midrib white and very prominent; seed white. This variety is undoubtedly the most extensively grown of all the Cos Lettuces, and perhaps of all other kinds. It appears to be very well adapted for all temperate climates, and even for warm ones, as it is grown all over the world. It likes rich soil and plentiful waterings, and is grown under bell-glasses or cloches for

White Paris Cos Lettuce
(⅛ natural size).

an early crop, and in the open air from April to the end of autumn. When carefully attended to, it heads in seven or eight weeks after being planted out in the open air, and keeps the head firm for a remarkably long time. A well-grown plant will often weigh over six pounds and a half.

Ground Cos Lettuce (*Romaine Pomme en Terre*).—Young plant short and compact, of a uniform, rather dark, clear-green colour; leaves

stiff, short, oval, slightly spoon-shaped, erect, and with a very prominent white midrib. Full-grown plant very thick-set, and of a dark, shining green colour; head short, very close and hard, commencing so low down that it appears to be partially buried in the ground; outer leaves very stiff, somewhat pointed, almost always folded in two and curved back outwardly, slightly crimped, with the midrib stout, stiff, and very large for the size of the leaves; seed black. The leaves of this variety are very crisp, and leave a slightly bitter after-taste which is not disagreeable. The

Ground Cos Lettuce
(⅛ natural size).

plant bears frosty weather well, if slightly protected. As the head is very solid, the crop is pretty heavy for the small size of the plants.

III. Summer Varieties of Cos Lettuce.

White-seeded Florence, or **Magnum Bonum, Cos Lettuce** (*Romaine Alphange à Graine Blanche*).—Young plant of a dull, pale-green colour;

leaves broad, oval, slightly toothed, and faintly tinged with light brown
at the base, and also on the margins and veins. The full-grown plant
does not head well unless it is tied up. Outer leaves very large, and
especially very broad, rounded in
outline, broadly crimped, with the
edges turned backwards, and forming a large and very open rosette;
they are of a palish and grayish
green colour, very slightly tinged
with light brown at the edges and on
the parts exposed to the sun. The
average diameter of well-grown
plants is 16 inches or thereabout.

Florence, or Magnum Bonum, Cos Lettuce
(⅛ natural size).

**Black-seeded Florence, or Mag-
num Bonum, Cos Lettuce** (*Romaine
Alphange à Graine Noire*).—Leaves
of young plant spathulate, large,
longish, bluntly toothed, and tinged
with pale brown at the base and on
the veins and edges. The whole
plant is considerably paler in colour
than the young plant of the preceding variety. Head of full-grown
plant elongated, seldom forming unless tied up; outer leaves very
long and broad, of a light pale-green or yellowish colour, slightly
tinged with russet on the parts exposed to the sun, finely crimped,
more pointed, and apparently thinner in texture than those of the
preceding kind. They also form a broader rosette, this being often
20 inches in diameter.

Giant Pale-green Cos Lettuce (*Romaine Monstrueuse*).—
Young plant vigorous growing, half-spreading; leaves largish, broad
from the base, of a pale dull green, tinged with light brown on
the veins and edges; margin slightly sinuated or bluntly toothed.
Head of full-grown plant oblong, not forming well unless tied up;
outer leaves large, numerous, in a broad and very open rosette, almost
spreading on the ground; they are entire in outline, but the edges are
twisted and waved, and the surface is crimped
and puffed from the midrib towards the edges.
All the parts exposed to the sun are very deeply
tinged with russet, while the rest of the plant
is of a wan dark green. The general appearance of the plant is shining, as if varnished,
not dull and heavy, like the Alphange varieties. It is often 20 inches in diameter.

Brown, or Bath, Cos Lettuce
(⅙ natural size).

Brown, or Bath, Cos Lettuce (*Romaine
Brune Anglaise à Graine Blanche*).—Young
plant of a dull-green colour; leaves spathulate,
deeply toothed to the very end, and tinged
with red on the edges and veins. Head of
full-grown plant oblong, almost pointed, of a pale-green colour, slightly
tinged with dull brown; outer leaves rather spreading, entire, not
much crimped, finely toothed on the edges, and tinged on all the parts

exposed to the sun with pale brown on a grayish-green ground. A well-grown plant is about 14 inches in diameter. This is an exceedingly hardy kind, and does well under summer or autumn culture; it sometimes also withstands the winter. Although it heads tolerably well when left to itself, it is usually tied up to increase the number and expedite the production of tender blanched leaves. The contrast of colour in the parts of the leaves which are bronzed by being exposed to the sun and those parts which are covered is very striking in this variety. This, and the following variety, are especially suitable for winter Lettuces in England.

Black-seeded Bath Cos Lettuce (*Romaine Brune Anglaise à Graine Noire*).—Young plant somewhat

Black-seeded Bath Cos Lettuce
(⅙ natural size).

paler than that of the Common or White-seeded Bath Cos, but similar in other respects. The full-grown plant does not differ very materially from the preceding kind, except in the colour of the seed; however, there is a very apparent disparity between the two varieties in the habit of the plants and the manner in which the leaves overlap one another, those of the black-seeded kind being shorter, forming a rosette, which speads more broadly on the ground, and being slower in standing erect to form the head; they are also more toothed at the edges. The two varieties are alike in productiveness, earliness, and quality.

Spotted, or Aleppo, Cos Lettuce (*Romaine Panachée à Graine Blanche*).—Leaves of young

Spotted, or Aleppo, Cos Lettuce (⅙ natural size).

plant half-erect, stiff, oblong, toothed at the edges of the lower half, of a clear-green colour, which is almost entirely hidden by a multitude of brownish-red spots, which are usually very small and often confluent. The full-grown plant does not head, unless tied up. Outer leaves entirely spreading, almost always folded along the midrib, very much plaited, undulated, and twisted, and very plentifully tinged with deep brownish red. When artificially blanched, the leaves of this variety exhibit the same red variegation on a white ground as those of the Dark-red Cabbage Lettuce (*Laitue Sanguine*). The plant is about 16 inches in diameter.

Black-seeded Spotted Cos Lettuce (*Romaine Panachée Perfectionnée à Graine Noire*).—Young plant deeply tinged with brownish red on a green ground; leaves rather short, entire, rounded spathulate. It is much dwarfer and more compact than the young plant of the preceding variety, and also not so red-coloured. The full-grown plant has erect leaves, closely pressed against one another, and surrounding an oblong, short, and rather compact head. Outer leaves stiff, rounded or blunt at the ends, not much crimped, and of a deep-green colour, with brown spots and blotches. This Lettuce heads of itself, but the produce is better when it is tied up, and it then yields a large quantity of salad for the small size of the plant, which does not exceed 10 or 12 inches in diameter. This variety differs entirely from the preceding one, in having all its leaves erect before they form the head, giving the plant somewhat the shape of a funnel, while in the other kind the leaves are spreading, and even turned backwards.

Balloon Cos Lettuce (*Romaine Ballon*).—Young plant of a palish, clear - green colour; leaves erect, rather narrow, toothed on the entire margin, the teeth on the lower half being long and sharp, while those towards the end of the leaf are faintly marked; the veins of the leaf, also, are not very clearly defined there. Full-grown plant very vigorous growing, with a large, broad, roundish head, slightly flattened at the top, full and firm; outer leaves not so much crimped as those of the White Paris Cos, but greener in hue and more rounded at the ends. The White Paris Cos heads sooner than the Balloon Cos, but the latter is considered hardier,

Balloon Cos Lettuce (⅙ natural size).

and is very suitable for sowing in autumn. It is also a remarkably productive variety.

We shall now proceed to mention a few other varieties, which, although inferior in importance to those already described, nevertheless possess a certain amount of merit.

Brunoy White Cos Lettuce (*Romaine Blonde de Brunoy*).—A rather leafy plant, not heading unless tied up; leaves somewhat folded, entire at the edges and turned back at the ends. This variety grows to a considerable size, but runs to seed rather rapidly. There are both a white-seeded and a black-seeded form of it, the latter of which appears to be the same as the English variety named Ivery's Nonesuch.

Romaine Blonde de Niort.—This fine, large variety is grown in Vendée, where it is highly esteemed. It very much resembles the Black-seeded Alphange Cos, but runs to seed rather sooner. The seed is white.

Romaine de Chalabre.—A very good kind of winter Cos for the south of France, and even at Paris it bears ordinary winters well. In appearance it rather resembles the Green Paris Cos, but it grows much larger, and has the leaves tolerably toothed in the lower half.

Romaine Epinerolle.—A variety almost intermediate between the Green and the White Paris Cos Lettuces, and apparently hardier than either, but at the same time not so tender or delicate in flavour. It is especially suitable for the south of France, where it can be grown in winter.

Romaine Frisée Bayonnaise; R. Parisienne; R. du Mexique.— Under these three names two or three kinds of Cos Lettuce are grown which are rather like the Brown Batavian Lettuce. Like it, they are of vigorous and rapid growth, but somewhat leathery in texture. They are suitable for warm climates, and should be tied up in order to blanch the leaves and make them tender.

Romaine Chicon Jaune Supérieure.—This may be considered as merely a sub-variety of the Florence Cos or White-seeded Alphange Cos, from which it is distinguished by having a shorter and entirely light-coloured head.

Magdalena Cos Lettuce (*Romaine de la Madelaine*).—Closely allied to the Giant Cos, but taller and lighter in colour. The leaves are large, pale, and tinged with red, especially at the edges. The plant almost heads of itself without being tied up. The head is not very solid. Seed black.

ASPARAGUS LETTUCE.

Lactuca angustana, Hort.

Romaine asperge.

Leaves long, very narrow, lanceolate, never forming a head. The plant soon runs to seed, and it is the thick swollen stems that are used as a table vegetable, gathered when they are about a foot high. This plant is very distinct, and resembles no other Cos Lettuce. The *Lactuca cracoviensis*, Hort., is a form of the Asparagus Lettuce with reddish stems and bronzy leaves. It is grown and used in the same way as the common form. Notwithstanding their very peculiar appearance and the Latin names which they have received from horticulturists, these two plants are nothing but modified forms of the cultivated Lettuce (*Lactuca sativa*, L.). The indications obtained from the flowers and seeds leave no doubt whatever on this point.

SMALL or CUTTING LETTUCES.

French, Laitues à couper. *German*, Schnitt-Salat. *Dutch*, Snij salade. *Italian*, Lattuga da taglio. *Spanish*, Lechuguino.

A certain number of varieties of Lettuce never form a head, but compensate, as it were, for this by producing a great abundance of leaves, which grow again after being cut, thus furnishing a large supply of green vegetables in a limited space. These are known by the general name of Cutting Lettuces (*Laitues à Couper*), and a certain number of kinds are in cultivation. Sometimes some of the Early White Cabbage Lettuces are treated as Cutting Lettuces, especially the Crisped Lettuce (*Laitue Crêpe*) and the Georges Lettuce (*L. Georges*), but the varieties which we are about to describe never form a head, and consequently can never be grown except as Cutting Lettuces.

White Cutting Lettuce (*Laitue Blonde à Couper*).—A variety with spathulate leaves, which become shorter and rounder as the plant advances in growth, with almost entire edges, slightly waved and toothed towards the base. If the leaves are not cut when the plant is young, the central ones become folded and rumpled so as to form a kind of heart, but not a true head. The plant soon runs to seed. Seed white. This variety is chiefly grown in frames.

Black-seeded Cutting Lettuce (*Laitue Frisée à Couper, à Graine Noire*).—A very distinct variety, forming a tuft 10 to 12 inches broad, dense and matted, and somewhat resembling a Curled Endive. Leaves cut into roundish lobes, twisted and puckered, of a rather dark green on the upper surface and somewhat grayish underneath. This is a hardy and very productive kind, and is well adapted for growing in the open air. The leaves are entirely green at the

Black-seeded Cutting Lettuce (⅙ natural size).

ends and edges where they are exposed to the sun and air, but elsewhere they are white, like Endive leaves.

Oak-leaved Cutting Lettuce (*Laitue Épinard*).—The plant forms a tallish rosette, tufty and rather full in the centre, 12 to 14 inches broad, composed of very numerous leaves, which are rather long, of a very light-green colour, divided into roundish lobes, sinuated, and something broader and far less undulated than those of the preceding kind. This variety is hardy and bears the winter well. It grows very well again after being cut. Seed black.

A variety named Artichoke-leaved Cos Lettuce (*Romaine à Feuille d'Artichaut*) is sometimes grown. This is very like the Oak-leaved variety, differing from it chiefly in the brown tint of its leaves.

Endive-leaved Cutting Lettuce (*Laitue Chicorée*). — Leaves spreading in a rosette, light coloured, curled and crisped like those of the Small Green Curled Winter Endive. This variety is tender to eat, very hardy, and very good for cutting. It bears the winter well. The seed is black, and is the smallest of all kinds of Lettuce seed.

There is another variety which has a fuller heart, but the leaves are not so much curled, and are of a light grayish or silvery hue. It is named the English Endive-leaved Cutting Lettuce (*Laitue Chicorée Anglaise*).

There is an American variety of Cutting Lettuce which is very distinct from any of the preceding kinds, named the Boston Curled Lettuce. The leaves of this variety are of a light-green colour, spreading into a rosette, and are cut, curled, and puckered at the edges like the leaves of a Curled Endive. It is a summer Lettuce and has black seed.

PERENNIAL LETTUCE.

Lactuca perennis, L.　*Compositæ.*

Laitue vivace.

Native of Southern Europe.—This plant, which is common in the wild state on light or calcareous soils all over the central districts of France, has been highly spoken of as a vegetable for table use. The part eaten is the leaves, which are very much cut and form their rosettes in the early part of spring. The plants are gathered where they grow naturally (as Dandelion plants are gathered in the meadows in various parts of France), but not in sufficient quantity to be sent to market. They do not make a bad salad, but the produce of the plant is so trifling that it is hardly worth cultivating. The seed is black, elongated, and small. A gramme contains about 800 seeds, and a litre of them weighs about 260 grammes. Their germinating power lasts for three years.

Perennial Lettuce (⅛ natural size; detached leaf, ⅓ natural size).

LOVAGE, or LOVACHE.

Levisticum officinale, Koch; *Ligusticum Levisticum*, L.　*Umbelliferæ.*

French, Ache de montagne.　*German,* Liebstock.　*Spanish,* Apio de monte.

Native of Southern Europe.—Perennial.—A very tall plant with large, shining, dark-green, radical leaves, which are twice or thrice divided into pinnate segments, entire and wedge-shaped at the base and incised lobed in the upper part. Stem thick, hollow, erect, dividing at the top into opposite whorled branches; flowers yellow, in umbels; seed strongly aromatic, hollow and boat-shaped on one side, and convex on the other, with three prominent ribs. A gramme contains about 300 seeds, and a litre of them weighs about 200 grammes. Their germinating power lasts for three years. CULTURE.—The plant is propagated either from seed, or by division of the roots. The seed is sown as soon as it is ripe, that is, about August. The young plants are planted out permanently, either in autumn or early in spring, in good deep, moist, well-manured soil. The division of the roots should be made in spring. A plantation will last several years without requiring to be renewed. When growing, the plants are treated exactly like Angelica plants. USES.—At the present day Lovage is almost exclusively used in the manufacture of confectionery; formerly the leaf-stalks and bottoms of the stems were eaten, blanched like Celery.

MAIZE, or INDIAN CORN.

Zea Mays, L. *Gramineæ.*

French, Maïs sucré. *German,* Maïs. *Flemish* and *Dutch,* Turksche tarwe. *Italian,*
Grano turco. *Spanish,* Maiz. *Portuguese,* Milho.

Native of America.—Annual.—The Maize plant, or Indian Corn,
was introduced in the sixteenth century from America into Europe,
where its cultivation soon became very general, and where it now
occupies an important place
among the cereal crops
which furnish food for man.
In many places the heads
or "cobs" are gathered while
the seeds are young and
tender, and are parched and
eaten as a delicacy, but it
is almost exclusively in the
United States of America
that the Maize is regarded
as a regular table vegetable
and grown specially for that
purpose. Almost all the
varieties may be eaten as
they are in America, that
is, boiled before the seeds
have become hard and
floury, and while the pulp
of the interior is still in
the condition of a soft

Maize, or Indian Corn (⅓ natural size).

paste, but there are some kinds which are superior to the rest for this
purpose, their seeds being sweeter and more tender, and which are
known by the general name of Wrinkled Sweet Maize (*Maïs Sucrés
Ridés*). These are distinguished by the very peculiar appearance of
the seed, the skin of which is wrinkled, shrunken, and almost transparent when ripe, instead of being hard, swollen, and smooth, like that
of other kinds. A gramme contains about four or five seeds, and a
litre of them weighs about 640 grammes. Their germinating power
lasts for two years.

In the United States, where this plant is highly esteemed as a table
vegetable, there are at least a dozen distinct varieties grown, differing
from one another chiefly in size and earliness. Most of these have
white seed. The best varieties are:—

The **Early Minnesota.**—A very early kind, growing from 3 to 4
feet high.

The **Early Crosby** (*Maïs Hâtif de Crosby*), and the **Large Early
Eight-rowed** (*M. Hâtif à Huit Rangs*).—These are somewhat larger
kinds than the preceding one, with a longer head, but about ten days
later.

The **Concord.**—A stronger growing kind, of excellent quality.

Stowell's Evergreen Late (*M. Sucré Toujours Vert*).—A later kind, but a good bearer, and keeping the heads tender and delicate for a longer time.

Besides these may be mentioned the Early Narraganset Dwarf, the ripe seeds of which are red, and the Sweet Mexican, which has black seeds.

CULTURE.—The Maize is sown in the open air about the same time as Kidney Beans ; that is, as soon as the ground has become somewhat warmed, and there is no longer any danger of frost. All the attention it requires is the occasional use of the hoe when the plants are commencing to grow, and occasional waterings when they have become pretty strong. The earliest kinds sometimes yield a few well-grown heads about the end of July, and heads may be had somewhat earlier, if a sowing is made in a hot-bed and the young plants put out in the open ground about the 24th of May. By making successional sowings, and employing varieties of different degrees of earliness, fresh heads may be had up to the arrival of the first frosts.

USES.—The head or " cob " is boiled and served up, either entire, or the seeds are taken off and served up like Kidney Beans. The heads are also gathered when very young and small and before the flower opens, and are pickled in vinegar like Gherkins.

MALABAR NIGHTSHADE (WHITE).

Basella alba, L.   *Chenopodiaceæ.*

French, Baselle blanche.   *German*, Indischer grüner Spinat.   *Flemish*, Meier,   *Italian*, Basella.   *Spanish*, Basela.

Native of the East Indies.—Biennial, but cultivated as an annual.

—A plant with creeping stems from 4 to over 6 ft. long, bearing alternate, oval-heart-shaped, slightly undulated, fleshy, green leaves. Flowers small, greenish or red, in spikes; seed round, bearing the remnants of the pistil and calyx, which are persistent. A gramme contains about 35 seeds, and a litre of them weighs about 460 grammes. Their germinating power lasts for five years at least. CULTURE.— The seed is sown in a hot-bed in March. In the end of May, or early in June, the seedlings are planted out at the foot of a south wall, and the plants will yield all through the summer without any care except occasional waterings. USES.—The leaves are eaten like Spinach, and are abundantly produced all through the summer, growing in greater profusion the warmer the weather becomes. Care should be taken, however, not to strip a plant of

Malabar Nightshade (White)
(1/10 natural size).

all its leaves at once, as this necessarily checks its growth.

MALABAR NIGHTSHADE (RED).

Basella rubra, L.

Baselle rouge.

Native of China.—Biennial, but cultivated as an annual.—This species only differs from the preceding one in having all its parts tinged with purplish red. Its seed is like that of the White Malabar Nightshade, and the plant is grown and used in the same manner.

Another species, which was introduced from China in 1839 by Captain Geoffroy, and which has been referred by botanists to the *Basella cordifolia* of Lamarck, is certainly a better kind than either of those just described, as its leaves are larger and more abundantly produced. It does not appear, however, to be much grown, probably on account of the difficulty which is found in getting it to seed in France. It is usually known under the name of the Very Broad-leaved Chinese Malabar Nightshade (*B. de Chine à Très Larges Feuilles*).

CURLED, or CURLED-LEAVED, MALLOW.

Malva crispa, L.   *Malvaceæ.*

French, Mauve frisée.   *German,* Krausblättrige Malve.   *Italian,* Malva crespa.

Native of the East.—Annual.—A large plant, with an erect, simple, or slightly branched stem, 4 to over 6 ft. high, and leafy to the top. Leaves large, roundish, of a clear-green colour, very elegantly curled and puckered at the edges; flowers white, small, in long leafy terminal clusters; seed brown, kidney shaped, with a rough and irregular surface. A gramme contains about 300 seeds, and a litre of them weighs about 530 grammes. Their germinating power lasts for five years. The seed is sown in April, either where the plants are to stand or in a seed-bed, from which the young plants are transplanted when they are from 2 to 4 inches high. They require no particular attention. When this plant is once grown in a garden it generally continues to reproduce itself from self-sown seed. No part of the plant is eaten,

Curled, or Curled-leaved, Mallow
(⅒ natural size).

but the leaves are sometimes used for garnishing desserts, etc., and a few plants may be worth having in the kitchen garden.

MARIGOLD (POT).

Calendula officinalis, L.   *Compositæ.*

French, Souci des jardins.   *German,* Ringelblume.

Native of Southern Europe.—Annual.—Leaves lanceolate oblong, entire, rough, and of a rather grayish green; stems short, branching from the base, and bearing broad orange-coloured flower-heads; seed grayish, very much wrinkled, covered with small round protuberances, almost spiny, and curved into the shape of a bow or ring. A gramme contains about 150 seeds, and a litre of them weighs about 180 grammes. Their germinating power lasts for three years. The seed is sown where the plants are to stand, in March or April, in drills 14 to 16 inches apart, and the seedlings are thinned out to a distance of 10 to 12 inches from one another in the drills. The plants com-

Marigold (Pot) ($\frac{1}{20}$ natural size).

mence to flower in July, and continue to bloom all through the summer and far into autumn. The flowers are used in some culinary preparations, for which purpose they are gathered during the summer, dried in the shade, and kept until wanted. They are also used for colouring butter.

POT, or PERENNIAL, MARJORAM.

Origanum vulgare, L. *Labiatæ.*

French, Marjolaine vivace. *German*, Perennirender Englischer Majoran. *Flemish*, Orego. *Danish*, Merian.

Native of Europe.—Perennial.—This is a very common wild plant in France, especially on the borders of woods. It forms a branching

Perennial, Marjoram ($\frac{1}{10}$ natural size; detached branch, natural size).

tuft or clump, 20 inches to 2 ft. high, bearing terminal clusters of pink or lilac flowers. Seed very small, oval, and of a reddish or dark-brown colour. A gramme contains about 12,000 seeds, and a litre of them weighs about 675 grammes. Their germinating power lasts for five years. Culture.—This is a very hardy plant, and will grow in almost any kind of soil, so that it is as easily cultivated as Thyme. The seed is sown in spring or in autumn, in drills, or to form edgings, which will last for many years without requiring any attention. Uses.—The leaves are used for seasoning.

There is a variety which has short erect stems, bearing large clusters of almost white flowers, and forming a very compact tuft not more than from 12 to 14 inches high. This kind, which is named Dwarf Pot Marjoram (*Marjolaine Vivace Naine*), is especially adapted for forming edgings, and always comes true from seed.

SWEET, or ANNUAL, MARJORAM.

Origanum Majorana, L. ; *Majorana hortensis*, Mœnch.   *Labiatæ.*

French, Marjolaine à coquille.   *German*, Majoran.   *Flemish* and *Dutch*, Marjolijn.   *Italian*, Maggiorana.   *Spanish*, Mejorana.   *Portuguese*, Manjerona.

Native of the East.—Perennial, but grown in gardens as an annual.
—A plant with an erect, square, branching stem.
Leaves opposite, roundish, of a grayish-green colour; flowers small, whitish, in roundish clusters with spoon-shaped bracts; seed small, roundish or slightly oblong, of a more or less dark-brown colour. A gramme contains about 4000 seeds, and a litre of them weighs about 550 grammes. Their germinating power lasts for three years. Culture.— The seed may be sown in the end of March or early in April. The plant springs up rapidly, so that the leaves may commence to be gathered in the course of May. The flowers appear about the end

Sweet, or Annual, Marjoram ($\frac{1}{12}$ natural size; detached branch, natural size).

of June or early in July. Uses.—The leaves and the ends of the shoots are used for seasoning, for which they are highly esteemed, especially in the south of France.

MEADOW CABBAGE.

Cirsium oleraceum, Scop.   *Compositæ.*

German, Wiesenkohl.

Native of Southern Europe.—Perennial.—A spiny plant with swollen taproots, which often branch or divide. Radical leaves large, entire or cut, pinnate, and spiny at the edges; stem erect, stiff, furrowed, bearing sessile clasping, auricled leaves up to the top; flower-heads nearly sessile, of a pale-green or yellowish colour, collected together at the top of the stem and on the ends of the branches, and

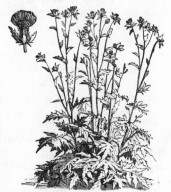

Meadow Cabbage ($\frac{1}{10}$ natural size).

surrounded with large spiny yellowish bracts; seed of a long oval shape, whitish, smooth, finely striated, not so pointed at the base as the

Y

seed of the Lettuce, which it somewhat resembles in appearance. A gramme contains about 500 seeds, and a litre of them weighs about 300 grammes. Their germinating power lasts for six years. This plant does not appear to have ever been brought into cultivation, those who use it contenting themselves with gathering it in the meadows, where it grows naturally. The swollen root-stock, gathered before the plant flowered, was formerly used as a table vegetable.

MELON.

Cucumis Melo, L. *Curcurbitaceæ*.

French, Melon. *German*, Melone. *Flemish* and *Dutch*, Meloen. *Italian*, Popone.
Spanish, Melon. *Portuguese*, Melão.

Annual.—A native of the warm parts of Asia, and cultivated from a very remote period of antiquity, the Melon is not now certainly known to exist in the wild state, but it is supposed that the original or typical plant, if it is still to be found anywhere, must have an oblong fruit like that of the Persian Melon.

It is a plant with herbaceous, slender, flexible, almost cylindrical stems, furnished with tendrils, by means of which they attach themselves to surrounding objects, and climb when they meet with a suitable support; otherwise they creep along the ground. The leaves, leaf-stalks, and stems are rough, with short thick hairs, which have almost the texture of true spines. The shape and size of the leaves are very variable, and there is no unvarying relation between the size of the leaves and that of the fruit in any one kind or variety. Most usually the leaves are kidney-shaped, rounded, and often folded or waved on the margin; frequently they are distinctly cut into three or five lobes, and sometimes the divisions even reach the depth of half the leaf; the margin is smooth and unbroken in some varieties, and toothed and spiny in others. The Melon is a monœcious plant; that is, male and female flowers, distinct from each other, are produced on the same plant. These flowers are rather small, and have a yellow corolla with five divisions and from $\frac{4}{5}$ to about $1\frac{3}{4}$ inches in diameter. The female flower is situated on the top of the ovary, which, in almost all the varieties, is ovoid at the time when the flower expands, and is then about as big as a good-sized hazel-nut, at least. Insects, especially hive-bees and humble-bees, visit the flowers in great numbers, and are almost always effectual in insuring their fertilization; but when the plants are forced, or when it is desired to preserve a certain variety free from any intermixture with others, it is better to fertilize the flowers artificially, by applying the pollen with a camel-hair pencil, or direct from the male flower stripped of its corolla. The fruit exhibits so much diversity of shape, size, and colour, that it is difficult to give any general description of it. It is met with under a variety of round, flat, and elongated shapes, ranging from the form of a Pumpkin to that of a Cucumber. The colour is equally diversified, from white to black, and passes through every shade of green and yellow, not to mention variegations of all kinds. The skin is often marked with wrinkles or creases, which become, as it were, corky, and stand out in bold relief on

the surface. The fruit in this case is termed " netted," or " net-veined."
In other instances the fruit is covered with protuberances, more or less
large and prominent, and known as " scabs " or " warts." Lastly, the
skin of the fruit is sometimes perfectly smooth, and sometimes marked
by a number of furrows, extending from the stalk to the eye of the
fruit. These furrows have between them a certain number of ribs,
usually from nine to twelve, which are more or less prominent, according to the variety. The seeds, which are smooth, usually white or
yellowish, flat and oblong, are collected together in the centre of the
fruit, and surrounded by a very watery pulp, full of soft filaments,
which are the umbilical cords of the seeds. The flesh, properly so
called, of the fruit is always watery, sweet, and usually highly perfumed ; its colour is green, white, or orange. A litre of the seed weighs
about 360 grammes, and a gramme contains, on an average, 35 seeds,
a few more in the case of the small-fruited kinds, and a few less in
the case of the very large-fruited varieties, although the relation between the size of the fruit and that of the seed is not always constant.
The germinating power of the seed lasts for five years at least, and
often for more than ten years.

CULTURE.—Melons, like most other plants of the same natural
family, require good soil, in order to grow well and produce fine fruit.
They do not succeed well in the open air, except in very rich alluvial
soil, or in ground that has been abundantly manured. All through
the north of Europe they are only grown in the open air in exceptional
cases, and, as a rule, are cultivated exclusively under glass. We shall,
therefore, dwell more particularly upon this mode of culture.

The Melon requires for its growth a moderately high temperature.
This should almost always exceed 12° Centigrade (53½° Fahrenheit);
and the quality of the fruit is always better if the mean temperature
is kept raised while they are ripening. Under the most favourable
conditions, the plant requires four or five months to complete its
growth, from which it may be seen that in the climate of Paris there
is no positive certainty of ripening the fruit without the aid of artificial
heat, and consequently they are almost always grown there in hot-beds.
During nine or ten months of the year the market gardeners about
Paris have the plants under cultivation, and these furnish a supply of
ripe fruit for six full months. The frames or Melon-pits being lined
with manure, the plants are, in a manner, forced, as they thus receive
a greater amount of heat than they would in the open air. Custom,
however, has restricted the meaning of " forcing," in the case of Melons,
to this mode of culture when commenced in January with the object of
obtaining ripe fruit in May, while an " early " crop is that which ripens
in June and early in July, and Melons " of the season," or the general
crop, are those which are gathered from the end of July up to October.
The details of the mode of culture are not exactly the same for these
three periods, nor are the same varieties of plants grown in succession.

FORCING.— Melon-forcing commences, as we have just said, in
January, and the kinds usually forced at Paris are the Prescott Small
Early Frame and the Early Black Rock Melon. The seed is sown on
a warm hot-bed during the month of January, and the fourth week after
sowing the young plants are pricked out into another hot-bed, from twenty-

eight to thirty plants under each light. During the whole of this early period of their growth the plants require continual attention in giving them air as often as that can be done with safety, occasionally watering them from a fine rose, and especially in guarding against the condensation of too much moisture on the lower part of the lights. In March they are planted out on another hot-bed. Before doing so, they should be stopped; that is, the main stem should be cut above the second leaf. After they have taken root, two lateral branches are quickly produced, and these are allowed to grow until they have made eight or ten leaves each, when they are cut above the sixth leaf, and at this time fresh branches are growing, which almost always bear fertile or female flowers. Various modes of stopping the plant have been suggested, all of which may be useful under certain circumstances, but the method which we have just described has been generally adopted in the neighbourhood of Paris, as the most simple and usually the most sure. There are two things which should not be lost sight of in growing Melons. One is, that vigorous, healthy, well-grown leaves are indispensable for the production of fine and good fruit. Care should therefore be taken to grow and maintain as many leaves as can find room in the portion of the frame where the plant is, without depriving one another of a due share of air and light. The other important point is, that it is almost always necessary to expedite the branching of the plants, in order to cause the fruit to set as soon as possible; for if the plant is allowed to follow its natural mode of growth, it may only commence to produce fertile or female flowers too late for the fruit to ripen properly. As soon as there are a few fruit set, the best of them, or that which, from its strength and position, promises the best growth, should be selected, and all the rest pinched off. In forcing Melons, only one fruit is left on each plant. The last thing to be done is to cut away any useless branches that may make their appearance, and to insure the symmetrical growth of the fruit by raising it off the hot-bed on a tile or small board, turning it so that it may, as far as possible, rest on the part where it is united to the stalk. Melons forced in this way sometimes ripen in April, but cannot be expected to do so with certainty until May.

EARLY CROP.—For this, the seed should be sown in the course of February, up to the end of the month, and the plants are treated in the same way as those which have just been described as " forced," the same operations being simply repeated three or four weeks later. This is a more certain crop than the previous one, as there is less danger of frosty weather and a better supply of light. The same varieties are now sown, and also the *Cantaloup Prescott à Fond Blanc,* a kind which is somewhat larger and more esteemed at Paris than the other two varieties.

GENERAL CROP.—This crop is grown on by far the most extensive scale at Paris, and is one in which the market gardeners excel. The seed is sown in the usual way in a hot-bed, and the plants are planted out during May in hot-beds, which are generally arranged in great numbers one before another, occupying a whole square, or section of a garden. The varieties generally grown are the Cantaloups *Prescott à Fond Blanc, Fond Gris,* and *Fond Blanc Argenté ;* sometimes the Rock, or Algerian, Cantaloup (*Cantaloup d'Alger*), and (rarely now) the Common Melon (*Melon Maraîcher*). When the plants are well rooted, the lights are completely removed, sooner or later, according to the prevailing temperature, and thenceforward, until the fruit ripens, the plants are grown entirely in the open air. The stopping, selection of the fruit, etc., are just the same as in the two previous seasons ; however, the plants are generally allowed to push a little more, and two fruit are often grown on the same plant, but the second one is not started until the first is nearly full grown. In this way the remaining strength of the plant is turned to account without injuring the first fruit, which requires no further supply of nutriment to increase its size, and has only to ripen the quantity of matter which it has already assimilated.

OPEN-AIR CULTURE.—This method, which, as we have seen, is very little used in the north of France, is, in fact, only a simplification of what has just been described. The plants are raised in the same way in a hot-bed, and planted out in rows of holes containing a good fork-full of manure, covered with mellow soil or compost. For the first few days they are protected with cloches or bell-glasses, or, in some places, with oiled paper or calico, supported by thin rods bent in the form of an arch. As soon as the weather becomes quite warm these coverings are removed, and the plants are grown on in the open air without any protection.

In gathering Melons, it is not necessary to wait until the fruit is perfectly ripe ; for if they are gathered a few days before that time and kept in a dry warm place, they will ripen there more or less speedily, according to the temperature. It is not always easy to know the exact time when a Melon ripens, as the indications vary with the species, and are often not very plain. In a great many varieties, when the fruit is near ripening, the stalk exhibits a number of cracks (often deep ones), as if the fruit were about to separate from the plant. In almost all kinds of Melons, ripeness is indicated by the softening of the part of the fruit which surrounds the eye, and which yields to the pressure of the finger. A change in the colour of the fruit to a more or less decided yellow tinge, is also a sign of ripeness. When this change makes its appearance, the fruit may be gathered and kept for a few days in the fruit-room. Lastly, the perfume, which Melons commence to give out almost as soon as they have attained their full size, becomes stronger and more perceptible as they grow ripe ; so that it is sometimes one and sometimes another of these indications, according to the variety, that must be taken as a guide in fixing upon the proper time for gathering the fruit.

Strictly speaking, Melons are fruits, and among the best, but in the Paris market gardens they are commonly cultivated among the vegetable crops. It is also the custom to eat before dinner, or in the early part of it, the common Melon of the market with pepper and salt, which explains their presence in this book. With us the difference in the kinds and the greater difficulty of the culture make our garden Melons among our very choicest " dessert " fruit. Slight though the distance be between North France and London, it is sufficient to cause a considerable difference in Melon culture, and as this book is mainly intended for

English use, we give here an account of the English culture. There are various methods of Melon culture in England, more especially since it has become the rule to devote a house or houses to their production, and an interesting modification of the common practice is suggested by Mr. Iggulden in the *Garden :*—" Where they are grown principally in frames, certain rules have of necessity to be followed, but in houses the case is very different. Much of this variance in practice may be due to the construction of the houses. As a rule, I believe that the majority of Melon-growers have a fixed routine from which they do not deviate any more than they can avoid, let the conveniences be what they may. Some prefer to cultivate Melons in large pots, not only the earliest, but also throughout the season. Others there are who plant in mounds of soil placed on a slate staging or iron gratings not far from the hot-water pipes, some of the latter, perhaps, being enclosed to afford bottom-heat; while many more, probably the majority of cultivators, make a good hot-bed with fermenting material, and on this place a continuous ridge of soil in which to start the plants. If all plans were alike successful, there would be no necessity nor room for criticism, but, as it happens, the reverse is the case, and really good fruits are by no means plentiful. Let those who doubt the truth of this assertion taste all the fruits in a well-filled Melon class at any exhibition, and after that probably they will change their opinion. Several reasons for Melon failures may be given, foremost among which should be placed premature ripening; this may be brought about either by the drying process or by the actual collapse of the plant. The fruits may be well coloured and otherwise tempting enough, but unless they are cut from a healthy plant they are certain to be unfit to eat. If we treat Melons much as we should some species of Orchids, that is to say, almost stew

them at one time and bake them at another, we ought to expect failure. Treat Melons as Cucumbers are generally treated, and not only will they yield a succession of crops, but the fruits will be certain to be good. One set of plants may be easily made to perfect three crops of fruit, or I might say a continuous crop, and the last fruits to ripen may be as fine, both as regards size and quality, as the first. Two, or maybe three or four, Cucumber plants are by many good cultivators considered ample for an average-sized house, and a similar number of Melons is also quite enough. Instead of this, we oftener see them planted 2 ft. and even less distances apart, and confusion is not unfrequently the consequence. If the cultivator is fortunate enough to set the first four fertile flowers, or at any rate a fair crop on the laterals thrown out by the main stem, the result may be satisfactory enough, but should he miss the chance it is very doubtful if another good one will offer. In the case of the plants allowed to extend freely and naturally, these will be constantly developing healthy, fertile, and easily set blossoms. Melons grown like Cucumbers, and in a house with them if need be, will be continually gaining strength, and, almost incredible as it may appear to some, will set fruit naturally and at different times. Instead, therefore, of a glut we may secure a succession from the same plant, and this is one strong recommendation in favour of the practice which I recommend. True, these liberally treated plants are apt to produce rather large fruit, which for market purposes especially are not desirable, but this difficulty may be obviated, and need not deter any one from adopting the plan.

"BOTTOM-HEAT.—Many cultivators lay much stress upon the necessity for bottom-heat, this being afforded either by fermenting material or enclosed hot-water pipes, or the two combined. I shall try to prove that not only are these not absolutely necessary, but they are also not unfrequently a source of danger and a cause of failure. At the outset a bed of heating material composed, say, of stable manure and leaves will give the plants an excellent start, and they will be apparently altogether superior to those started without such bottom-heat. All the while the heat lasts and the material is still in good condition the progress is satisfactory, but when the mass of material is decayed and gets sodden with moisture the temperature is materially lowered, and other evils follow. When the plants stand in most need of assistance, viz., when heavy crops are being matured, they get much less than at the earlier stages. A collapse is frequently the consequence, and the plants are either necessarily " dried off," or the fruits are cut and placed on hot shelves to colour or ripen where the bottom-heat is principally afforded by enclosed pipes ; these, with the assistance, perhaps, of a small bed of heating material, answer very well for a time, but later on the material in contact with the gratings or slates, as the case may be, becomes very dry and non-conducting—the bottom-heat thus being wasted. This is by no means an imaginary case, as I have several times opened the chambers formed over hot-water pipes in order, if possible, to discover why we obtained insufficient bottom-heat, and they have proved unbearably hot. Then, again, unless the valves are so regulated as to admit of all the heat being turned on to the bottom-heat, the chances are that during warm weather they are not heated at all. In this case the difference between the top and bottom heat may be much too divergent for the well-being of the plant. A healthy root action should be maintained as long as possible, and the bottom-heat should be equal to the top heat. Without at present going into details, I may state that our Melons are planted in raised square mounds of soil enclosed by loose bricks. The bottom-heat is not enclosed or concentrated in any way on the mounds, but these being well exposed share more or less in the fluctuations of the top heat. This plan entails more labour in the shape of very frequent waterings, varied with liquid manure, and the progress at the outset is rather slow, but in the end the stems become strong and woody and it rarely happens that they fail.

" Soil.—It may be a difficult matter for some to completely change their practice, even if they are disposed to do so, but there is nothing to prevent a modification, especially with regard to the disposition of the soil. Many seem to think that the poorest and heaviest loam procurable is the correct compost for Melons, this being placed in a rounded ridge on the top of the hot-bed and heavily beaten down in that position. In this case the loam has but little to do with an ultimate success, but may be partly blamed for a failure. It cannot be kept properly moistened, and the consequence is the roots quickly leave it and find their way down into the too rich manure underneath. Given a square ridge of fairly stiff turfy loam, made tolerably firm (this will render watering an easy matter), and occasional slight top-dressings with good soil to which has been added a sprinkling of manure, and no difficulty will be experienced in maintaining a healthy surface root action. The best varieties to cultivate ought in every case to depend upon circumstances— whether green-fleshed or scarlet-fleshed, large, medium, or small, ought to be settled in accordance with what may be required. Some think the exigencies of the case are met by growing as many varieties as there are plants, but this, although an interesting experiment, is far from being politic. At the present time I have seeds of upwards of twenty varieties in a seed drawer, but of these only three varieties will be grown, and one of these only by way of experiment."

USES.—The fruit are eaten raw. In the south of France, some white-fleshed or green-fleshed kinds are preserved, or made into jam. The young fruit which are pinched off may be eaten like young Gourds or Cucumbers, or may be pickled in vinegar, like Gherkins.

There are numerous classifications of Melons. Of these we shall follow the simplest and most common one, which divides them into the two groups of the Netted and the Cantaloup or Scabby-skinned Melons.

I. NETTED MELONS.

French, Melons brodés.   *German,* Netz-melone.   *Italian,* Popone primaticcio.
Spanish, Melon escrito.

Red-fleshed Pine-apple Melon (*Melon Ananas d'Amérique à Chair Rouge*).—A vigorous-growing, branching plant, with medium-sized or small, entire, roundish leaves of a slightly glaucous green colour. Fruit very long stalked, with slightly marked ribs, and of a delicate green colour, very plentifully dotted with blackish green; the furrows between the ribs are very shallow and of a clear-green colour, and the ribs themselves are slightly netted when the fruit is quite ripe; rind thin. The fruit is from about 3 to 4 inches in diameter, and weighs from about ten ounces and a half to over one pound. The flesh is red, rather firm, sweet, juicy, and highly perfumed. In this variety the central cavity seldom exceeds the size of a walnut.

Red-fleshed Pine-apple Melon (⅓ natural size).

Green-fleshed Pine-apple, or Jersey Green Citron, Melon (*Melon Ananas d'Amérique à Chair Verte*).—The principal difference between this and the preceding variety is in the colour of the flesh, which is of a pale green, with a yellowish tinge in the vicinity of the seeds; the leaves also are somewhat larger and lighter coloured. The plant continues growing for a longer time, and the skin of the fruit is rather more netted when ripe. Both this and the preceding kind will readily carry and ripen from six to eight fruit on each plant.

Red-fleshed Cavaillon Melon (*Melon de Cavaillon à Chair Rouge*). —A large vigorous-growing plant, with large grayish - green leaves which have distinctly marked and very rounded lobes. Fruit oblong, sometimes almost spherical, blunt at both ends, and with well-marked ribs. When ripe, the skin becomes orange-coloured, and is broadly and densely netted, resembling the Tours Sugar Melon in this respect. The furrows between the ribs are very narrow, and, when the fruit is ripe, become reduced to mere lines. The stalk of the fruit is remarkably thick and strong. The flesh is of a bright red colour, thick, a little coarse, juicy, and of a high vinous flavour. The fruit ripens slowly. This variety is hardy, and is grown in the open air in the south of France, almost without any attention. The fruit has a tendency to become

Red-fleshed Cavaillon Melon (⅓ natural size).

slightly modified in shape, and, at the present day, is more elongated than it was twenty-five years ago. The district about Cavaillon is one of the great centres of Melon-growing in the south of France, and there are many distinct varieties in cultivation there, so that the name " *Cavaillon* Melon " is rather an indication of the place in which the fruit has been raised than a true specific name. The variety which we have just described is at the present time far less commonly grown in its native district than the various forms of Malta Winter, and especially of Malta Summer Melons, such as the following.

Green-fleshed Cavaillon Melon (*Melon de Cavaillon à Chair Verte*). —A vigorous-growing plant, with very long stems. Leaves largish, rounded, toothed on their entire margin, and of a palish-green colour. Fruit oblong, 5 or 6 inches in diameter, and 9 or 10 inches in length ; skin smooth, of a dark-green colour, thinly and loosely netted when ripe ; flesh pale green, rather firm, but very juicy, sweet, and perfumed in warm climates; seldom good, however, in the climate of Paris.

Honfleur Melon (*Melon de Honfleur*).—A very vigorous-growing plant, with very branching, long, and remarkably slender stems. Leaves large and luxuriant, folded and waved at the edges, of a light-green colour, usually distinctly lobed, and toothed on the entire margin, and especially so towards the extremity. The plant continues to flower for an exceedingly lengthened period, producing blooms in succession on the branches, even after the fruit which set first have almost attained their full size. Fruit very large, elongated, with tolerably well-marked ribs, finely netted all over, and becoming of a yellowish, slightly salmon, colour when ripe; flesh orange coloured, thickish. The fruit is sometimes 14 to 16 inches long and 8 to 10 inches in diameter. When it is well grown, the quality is often excellent. It ripens half-late.

Honfleur Melon (⅓ natural size).

This and the Black Rock Melon are the largest of all Melons in cultivation, the Honfleur being equally remarkable for its great hardiness.

Red-fleshed Malta Winter Melon (French, *Melon de Malte d'Hiver à Chair Rouge*).—A plant of moderately vigorous-growing habit, with slender and very branching stems. Leaves slight, of a grayish and palish green, usually entire, but slightly twisted at the margin; fruit oblong, blunt at both ends, only about one-fourth or one-third longer than broad, seldom exceeding 9 or 10 inches in length, and weighing from three and a quarter to four pounds and a half. The ribs are marked, but not very prominently, the furrows between them being of a grayish green and the top of the ribs pale green spotted with dark green, and covered, when ripe, with very short, almost entirely longitudinal, tracings. The fruit-stalk is longish and very slender for the size of the fruit. Flesh red, rather thick, juicy, very sweet and musky. If the fruit is gathered before the proper time, it remains firm and almost hard. This variety succeeds well in the open air, but requires a southern climate to grow it to perfection.

Red-fleshed Malta Winter Melon (⅛ natural size).

Green-fleshed Malta Winter Melon (*Melon de Malte d'Hiver à Chair Verte*).—A vigorous-growing plant, with long trailing stems and numerous long branches. Leaves erect, of a dark and rather dull green, roundish and bluntly toothed; leaf-stalks very stiff. The leaves are usually of no great size, and remain rolled up, in the shape of a funnel. Fruit oblong, roundish, blunt at both ends, and particularly so at the end farthest from the stalk; skin greenish white, entirely smooth, or with a few tracings on the part next the stalk. The fruit is from 7 to 9 inches long, and 5 or 6 inches in diameter, and weighs from three and a quarter to four

Green-fleshed Malta Winter Melon (⅛ natural size).

pounds and a half. A plant may carry two or three fruit. In the south of France, this variety is very much grown for a late autumn crop. The fruit gathered at that time are kept in a fruit-room for winter use. They are also preserved in sugar or converted into jam.

Round Netted Paris Market-Garden Melon (*Melon Maraîcher*).

—A branching, vigorous-growing plant, with numerous roundish leaves of a clear-green colour, and slightly toothed on the margin. Fruit nearly spherical or more or less flattened at the ends, entirely devoid of ribs, and very uniformly covered with regular and very fine tracings, forming a very close network which completely hides the natural colour of the skin; flesh orange coloured, thickish, and firm. The fruit is about 8 or 10 inches in diameter, and weighs, on an average, from four and a half to six pounds and three-quarters. A well-grown plant may carry two fruit.

Paris Market-Garden Melon
(⅓ natural size).

The Saint-Laud Market-Garden Melon and the Mazé Market-Garden Melon (from the neighbourhood of Angers) are somewhat like the preceding kind, but differ from it in being oblong in shape, having the ribs rather well marked, and the skin more coarsely netted. The flesh is orange coloured, firm, and usually very sweet.

Nutmeg Melon (*Melon Muscade des États-Unis*).—A medium-sized, branching plant. Leaves largish, waved at the edges, and of a rather dark, clear-green colour; fruit oval, almost pear-shaped, narrowed to a point at the stalk end and bluntly rounded at the other; skin dark

Saint-Laud Market-Garden Melon
(⅓ natural size).

Nutmeg Melon (⅓ natural size).

green, almost black, marked with whitish tracings forming a rather loose network. The length of the fruit varies from about 6 to 8 inches, and the diameter from 4 to about 6 inches. The average weight is about two pounds and a quarter. Flesh green, not very thick, but juicy, sweet, and highly perfumed. This is a hardy and easily grown kind, ripening half-late. Three fruit may be left on each plant.

Tours Netted Sugar Melon (*Melon Sucrin de Tours*).—This is a rather variable kind, having several sub-varieties which differ from one another in the shape of the fruit. One form of it is often met with, of which the fruit is oblong, but the best form appears to be that which we are about to describe. This is a vigorous-growing plant, but

of medium size, and tolerably branching. Leaves large, entire or not very deeply lobed, slightly folded at the edges, and of a rather dark, clear-green colour; fruit spherical, about 6 inches in diameter, devoid of ribs or having them very faintly marked, and completely covered with very coarse, broad, and prominent tracings, crossing one another at right angles and surrounding the fruit like a network of cords; flesh orange red, thick, firm, and generally very good. The fruit ripens half-late. A plant may carry three fruit.

Tours Netted Sugar Melon (⅕ natural size).

Persian, or Odessa, Melon (*Melon de Perse*).—A rather vigorous-growing plant, with long and somewhat

slender stems. Leaves of medium size, tolerably lobed and cut on the edges, and of a lively green colour; fruit devoid of ribs, very much elongated, and narrowed to a point at both ends, especially at the stalk end; skin smooth, of a very dark-green colour, with yellowish bands, which are themselves spotted or striped with green; flesh very thick, almost without any rind and almost entirely filling the fruit, rather firm but very finely flavoured, juicy, sweet, and highly perfumed. This Melon requires a great deal of heat, and seldom ripens very well in northern countries. The fruit, if gathered a short time before ripening, may be kept for several weeks, and sometimes even for a part of the winter, provided they are stored

Persian, or Odessa, Melon (⅕ natural size).

in a place where the frost cannot get at them.

In Persia and Turkestan there is a great number of varieties of Melons which are highly esteemed for their quality in those countries, and of which travellers speak in terms of admiration. The climate must have a great deal to do with this, as the very same kinds, when grown in France, are always inferior to the French varieties, both in quality and especially in the certainty of the crop.

Green Climbing Melon (*Melon Vert à Rames*).—A vigorous-growing, branching plant, with long slender stems. Leaves of a dark-green colour, sometimes five-lobed, especially those near the ends of the stems; fruit oblong, with ribs faintly marked, of a deep green

Green Climbing Melon (⅕ natural size).

colour slightly dotted with pale green, 4 or 5 inches long and 3 or 4 inches in diameter, and weighing from about one pound to one pound and a half; flesh green, very melting, exceedingly juicy and sweet, with an agreeable perfume, although not so delicate as that of the Cantaloup Melons. It cannot be said that this variety requires a different mode of culture from that which is commonly employed for the other varieties of Netted Melons, yet its earliness renders it more suitable for growing in the open air than most other kinds, and the small size of the fruit allows of the stems being grown on a slight trellis, which would be impossible in the case of a large heavy-fruited variety. By planting it in pockets filled with manure covered with good soil, it may be easily brought to climb on espalier stakes, or

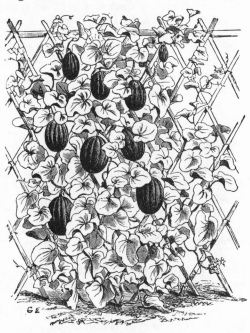

Green Climbing Melon (1/10 natural size).

even on a wall, if it has something to which it can attach itself. When grown in this way, the fruit ripens more quickly and better.

There is no doubt that some other kinds of Melon might be grown in the same way. The American Pine-apple Melons, which have very long and branching stems, are particularly well adapted for growing on trellises. The conditions most favourable to success in this way exist in those kinds which grow rapidly and ripen early, and the fruit of which does not require the artificial heat of a hot-bed along with the natural heat of the sun to render it very sweet.

Green-fleshed Sugar Melon (*Melon Sucrin à Chair Verte*).—A vigorous-growing plant, with long branching stems, and very large flat leaves which are hardly toothed. Fruit oblong, narrowed at both ends, of a pale-green colour, finely netted

Green-fleshed Sugar Melon (1/6 natural size)

when ripe, and bearing some pointed protuberances; ribs well marked, but not very prominent; flesh of a pale-green colour, exceedingly melting and sweet. The length of the fruit varies from about 9 to 11 inches, with a diameter of 4 to 6 inches. It usually weighs from about four and a half to six pounds and a half. Two, or even three, fruit may be grown on each plant. This is especially a summer Melon, and only attains its full quality in very warm weather. It should, therefore, be grown in such a manner that the fruit may ripen in August or early in September.

OTHER VARIETIES OF NETTED MELONS.

Melon Blanc de Russie.—Fruit small and round, without ribs; skin smooth, and entirely white; flesh white, with not much flavour.

M. Blanc à Chair Verte.—A very distinct kind. Fruit medium sized, very much flattened at the ends, and weighing from two to three pounds; skin white, smooth; ribs pretty well marked; flesh very thick, excellent in quality, and green throughout.

M. Boulet de Canon.—A small and rather early variety, with spherical fruit 5 or 6 inches in diameter; skin smooth, green, marked here and there with a few fine tracings; flesh pale green.

M. de Cassaba, or *de la Casba.*—This kind, which is in high repute in the East, appears to require a warm climate to bring it to perfection. In appearance it is tolerably like the Green-fleshed Malta Summer Melon.

Cyprus Melon (*M. de Chypre*).—Fruit oblong, with ribs faintly marked, of a grayish-white colour, very slightly netted, the furrows being of a dark green; flesh orange coloured, firm, very thick, and high flavoured.

Composite Melon (*M. Composite*).—Fruit oblong, with prominent ribs and a thinnish rind, of a dark-green colour, almost entirely covered with network of medium thickness; flesh red, firm, sweet, and well tasted.

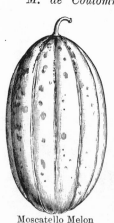

Moscatello Melon
(⅓ natural size).

M. de Coulommiers.—Fruit large, oblong, with tolerably well-marked ribs, and very like the Honfleur Melon, of which it appears to be a sub-variety. A rather late kind.

M. d'Esclavonie.—A very distinct variety, with large fruit of a long oval shape, rounded at both ends, and with a white, smooth, and thickish skin; flesh nearly white, sweet but rather insipid.

M. de Langeais.—A variety of the Paris Market-Garden Melon, with oblong fruit, almost twice as long as broad; ribs pretty well marked and very much netted, while the furrows are smooth; skin thin; flesh red, watery, and rather insipid. Ripens half-late.

Moscatello Melon (*M. Moscatello*).—Fruit very much elongated, and almost pointed at both ends; ribs rather well marked, of a pale grayish or silvery green, and very seldom netted; flesh red, very juicy, and highly perfumed.

Quito Melon (*M. de Quito*, or *de Grenade*).—Fruit small, oblong, scarcely larger than a hen's egg, and citron coloured when ripe; flesh white and acidulous.

Siam Netted Melon (*M. de Siam*).—Fruit nearly spherical, rather small; ribs tolerably well marked and of a dark-green colour, almost black in the furrows, and covered with close coarse network; flesh red.

Early Green Japanese Melon (*M. Vert Hâtif du Japon*).—Fruit rather small, almost spherical; ribs regular, not very prominent; skin nearly smooth, slightly downy, deep green, hardly marked by a very few small tracings here and there; flesh red, firm, and perfumed.

ENGLISH AND AMERICAN VARIETIES.

The English varieties of Netted Melons are very numerous. In this country Melons are mostly grown with the aid of artificial heat and more frequently as fruits than as vegetables. The varieties cultivated are generally rather small, and most usually round-fruited kinds with a very thin skin. Many of these varieties do not succeed very well when grown in the open air.

I. *Red-fleshed Varieties.*

Blenheim Orange Melon.—Fruit shortly oval, netted and thin skinned; flesh orange coloured, rather thick, and very highly perfumed.

Christiana Melon.—An American variety. Fruit spherical, with a smooth dark-green skin, hardly marked by a few very fine tracings; flesh red, very thick, and exceedingly fine flavoured and perfumed.

Crawley Paragon Melon.—Fruit very small, spherical, netted; flesh red, firm, tolerably like that of the *Windsor Prize Melon.*

Hero of Bath Melon.—Fruit small, round, netted; flesh red and firm; skin very thin.

Munroe's Little Heath Melon.—A very handsome and distinct little Melon, with slightly marked ribs flattened a little at the ends, and netted; flesh red, thick, nearly filling the fruit, juicy and sweet.

Read's Scarlet-flesh Melon.—Fruit medium sized, round; skin dark green, netted; flesh scarlet, melting, sweet, and good.

Scarlet Gem Melon.—A pretty little fruit, almost spherical, about the size of a large Orange, with a smooth grayish skin covered with fine and rather close tracings; flesh red, juicy, sweet, and highly perfumed.

Windsor Prize Melon.—This appears to be only a sub-variety of the preceding kind, with still smaller fruit, but sweeter and more highly perfumed, if possible.

Surprise Musk Melon.—An American variety. This is a form of the Orange Cantaloup Melon, which has the fruit somewhat larger than that of the ordinary variety. It is slightly oblong in shape, and netted a little on the ribs; flesh orange coloured and firm.

Victory of Bristol Melon.—Fruit quite spherical, something like that of the Tours Sugar Melon, but more finely netted; flesh orange coloured, thick, sweet, and rather juicy. The skin becomes almost yellow when ripe.

II. *White-fleshed Varieties.*

Bay-View Musk Melon.—An American variety. Fruit oblong, olive-shaped; skin green, netted; flesh white, sweet, and not very thick.

Colston Bassett Seedling Melon.—Fruit slightly oblong, blunt at both ends; skin netted, yellow when ripe; flesh white, melting, very juicy, and very delicately perfumed.

Hero of Lockinge Melon.—Fruit medium sized, roundish; skin bright yellow, netted; flesh almost white, very tender, melting, rich, and excellent. One of the best of Melons.

Longleat Perfection Melon.—Fruit large, roundish; skin smooth, greenish yellow; flesh white, very melting, juicy, and high flavoured.

Queen Emma Melon.—Fruit rather large, almost round; skin thin; flesh white, very melting. A productive kind.

III. *Green-fleshed Varieties.*

Bailey's Green-flesh Melon.—Fruit medium sized, roundish ovate, smooth, greenish yellow; flesh green, very tender, sweet, and richly flavoured.

Beechwood Melon.—Fruit oval, netted, yellowish green when ripe; flesh pale green, melting, sweet, and perfumed. Ripens half-late.

Eastnor Castle Melon.—Fruit slightly oblong, nearly smooth, scarcely marked by a few tracings when ripe, and then becoming pale yellow, having been previously of a perfectly uniform dark green; flesh very tender, sometimes a little clammy. A productive kind.

Egyptian Green-flesh Melon.—Fruit roundish, blunt at both ends, slightly netted; skin grayish or silvery; flesh sweet and perfumed.

Gilbert's Green-flesh Melon.—Fruit rather large, oval, yellowish when ripe; flesh juicy and melting. A good and productive variety.

Golden Perfection Melon (⅓ natural size).

Gilbert's Improved Victory of Bath Melon.—Fruit rather large, shortly oval, not much netted, and with ribs slightly marked; flesh pale green, melting, and highly perfumed. This variety somewhat resembles the Green-fleshed Sugar Melon, but its fruit is not so large.

Golden Perfection Melon (*Melon Brodé Boule d'Or*).—Fruit spherical or slightly oblong, rather loosely netted, and becoming of a fine golden-yellow colour when ripe; flesh pale green, rather thick, very sweet, and agreeably perfumed. A very good, productive, and comparatively hardy variety.

Golden Queen Melon.—A vigorous-growing kind, probably a sub-variety of the preceding one, with somewhat larger and well-netted fruit; flesh firm, juicy, and highly flavoured.

High Cross Hybrid Melon.—Fruit medium sized, spherical, and of a uniform white colour; flesh quite green, rather thick and melting.

William Tillery Melon.—Fruit oval, with ribs very feebly marked; skin dark green, slightly netted when ripe; flesh very green, not very thick, quite melting and exceedingly sweet, but deficient in delicacy of flavour.

II. CANTALOUP, or ROCK, MELONS.

French, Melons cantaloups.   *German,* Cantalupen Melone.   *Italian,* Zatta.
Spanish, Meloncillo de Florencia.

Algerian Cantaloup Melon (*Melon Cantaloup d'Alger*).—A rather dense-growing plant, with numerous short branches. Leaves dark green, slightly cut, and very much folded at the edges, which gives them the appearance of being five-lobed. They are almost turned round in the shape of a funnel, and are very variable in size, those on the lower parts of the stems being three or four times as large as those at the ends of the branches. Fruit slightly elongated, sometimes spherical, bearing roundish warts or scabs, which, as well as the bottoms of the furrows, are of a very dark green, almost black, colour, contrasting strongly with the light silvery hue of the other parts of the ribs. The dark-green parts eventually change to an orange colour, but this is not fully developed until the fruit is over-ripe, so that it should be gathered before the change takes place. The length of the fruit varies from 6 to 10 inches, and

Algerian Cantaloup Melon
(⅕ natural size).

the diameter from about 5 to 8 inches, the weight ranging from about four and a half to six and three quarter pounds. A plant may carry two fruit.

It is surprising that this Melon is not grown by the Paris market-gardeners, as it is one of the hardiest summer Melons, and surpasses all of them, perhaps, in uniform goodness of quality. The flesh is thick, juicy, perfumed, and always very sweet. Ripens half-late.

Green-fleshed Cantaloup Melon (*Melon Cantaloup à Chair Verte*). —A medium-sized, branching, rather slender-stemmed plant. Leaves medium-sized or small, dark green, folded at the edges, and often rather deeply cut into five lobes; fruit spherical, or slightly flattened at the ends, with faintly marked ribs, of a light-green colour at the bottom of the furrows, and slightly warted on the convexity of the ribs, which are marbled with white and with dark green. The length of the fruit varies from about 5 to 6 inches, the diameter slightly exceeding those dimensions, and the weight ranging from about 2 lbs. 10 oz. to 3 lbs. 5 oz. A plant may carry two, and sometimes three, fruit. Flesh pale green,

z

very thick, melting, juicy, sweet, and delicately perfumed. This is one of the finest flavoured of all the Cantaloup Melons.

Early Black Rock, or **Des Carmes Cantaloup, Melon** (*Melon Cantaloup Noir des Carmes*).—A medium-sized, rather branching plant. Leaves largish, of a dark, shining green colour, very distinctly five-lobed, folded at the edges, and almost turned round in the shape of a funnel; leaf-stalk short and thick; fruit nearly spherical, but slightly flattened at the ends, with ribs clearly but not very deeply marked; skin usually smooth and without warts, of a very dark green colour, almost black, turning orange coloured when ripe; flesh orange coloured, thick, sweet, perfumed, and of excellent quality. The diameter of the fruit varies from about 6 to 7 inches, and its length (from stalk to eye) from about 5 to 6 inches; it weighs from about two pounds and a quarter to three pounds and a half. A plant may carry two fruit for the general crop. This is one of the best and most easily grown of the early Melons.

Early Black Rock, or Des Carmes Cantaloup, Melon (⅓ natural size).

Black Portugal, or **Rock Cantaloup, Melon** (*Melon Cantaloup Noir de Portugal*).—A very vigorous-growing, branching plant, with very large, soft, roundish, entire leaves, of a clear-green colour, more like the leaves of a Netted Melon than those of a Cantaloup. Fruit very large, slightly oblong, very blunt, and almost flat at the end farthest from the stalk; ribs deeply marked; skin irregular, knobby, and marked with spots of very dark green on a lighter green ground; stalk very long, and swollen to a remarkable degree close to the fruit. The shape of the fruit is somewhat variable, the length sometimes exceeding the diameter, and sometimes the reverse. The extreme diameters range from about 10 to 12 inches, and the fruit often weighs from eleven to thirteen pounds. A plant should not be allowed to carry more than one fruit.

Black Portugal, or Rock Cantaloup, Melon (⅓ natural size).

Orange-fleshed Cantaloup Melon (*Melon Cantaloup Orange*).—A medium-sized branching plant. Leaves of a slightly grayish-green colour, entire, slightly toothed at the edges; fruit small, oblong, numerous, with ribs rather well marked, of a pale-green colour, dotted and marbled with darker green; flesh orange coloured, not very thick, remarkably firm, almost hard, not very juicy, but sweet and perfumed. The length of the fruit seldom exceeds 5 or 6 inches, and the diameter is about 4 inches. The average weight is from seventeen ounces and a half to twenty-one ounces. A plant may generally carry from seven to nine fruit. This variety sometimes exhibits, on the convexity of the ribs, cracks or fissures very much resembling the tracings which are characteristic of the Netted Melons. This feature, together with the elongated shape of the fruit, would lead us to regard it as intermediate between the Netted Melons and the Cantaloups, properly so called.

Bellegarde Cantaloup Melon (*Melon Cantaloup de Bellegarde*).—Plant of medium size, rather slender, with a thin, long, branching stem; leaves medium sized, entire, but folded at the edges, and of a light-green colour; fruit slightly elongated in shape, with not very prominent ribs, and borne on a remarkably long and slender stalk; skin thin, and of a silvery-white colour, spotted with green; flesh thick, of a deep orange colour, sugary, perfumed, and melting. The fruit is between 5 and 6 inches in length, and 4 or 5 inches in diameter, and weighs about one pound and a half.

Orange-fleshed Cantaloup Melon (⅛ natural size).

This Melon, which in its habit of growth somewhat resembles the Netted Melons, is especially remarkable for its very great earliness. For several years we have seen it ripen its fruit sooner than any other variety, including even the Early Black Rock Melon and Prescott Early Frame Melon.

Prescott Early Frame Melon (*Melon Cantaloup Prescott Petit Hâtif à Châssis*).—A medium-sized plant. Leaves largish, rounded or slightly angular, of a light, slightly grayish, green colour, and

Bellegarde Canteloup Melon.

almost always folded in the shape of a funnel; fruit spherical, or slightly flattened at the ends, with the ribs marked, faintly warted, marbled with dark green on a pale-green ground, and with the bottom of the furrows of a uniform olive-green colour; flesh orange coloured, thick, juicy, and melting. The diameter of the fruit is from about 5 to 6 inches, and its length (from stem to eye) from 4 to 5 inches. Its weight ranges from twenty-six ounces to over two pounds. A plant should carry only one fruit for the early crop, and two for the general crop. This variety is a remarkably early one, and its quality is almost invariably excellent. It and the

Prescott Early Frame Melon (⅛ natural size).

Early Black Rock Melon are the best two kinds for forcing under frames.

Passy Cantaloup Melon (*Melon Cantaloup de Passy*).—This Melon almost exactly resembles the Prescott Early Frame Melon in all the parts of the plant, differing clearly from it, however, in the fruit, which in the Passy Melon is smoother, more regularly spherical, and considerably smaller. The skin is not warty, but simply spotted with

darker green on a light-green ground, especially on the parts of the fruit which are exposed to the sun. The fruit seldom exceeds 4 inches, or a little more, in diameter, and the average weight is from one pound and a half to one pound and three-quarters at the most. The flesh is red, thick, remarkably sugary, and of a very uniformly good quality, even in fruit which ripen late in autumn.

Passy Cantaloup Melon.

Large Paris White Prescott Cantaloup Melon (*Melon Cantaloup Prescott Fond Blanc de Paris*).—A rather vigorous-growing and branching plant. Leaves medium sized, folded at the edges, often five-lobed, and of a rather deep, clear-green colour; fruit large, and very much flattened at the ends; ribs broad, very much wrinkled, covered with knobs and protuberances of all shapes, and irregularly variegated with dark and pale green on a whitish ground. The ribs are separated by very deep, narrow furrows. Flesh orange coloured, very thick, exceedingly fine flavoured, juicy, and melting. The skin also is thick, but, owing to the shape of the fruit, that does not prevent the flesh

Large Paris White Prescott Cantaloup Melon (⅕ natural size).

from being very abundant. The length of the fruit—that is, the distance from the stalk to the eye—varies from about 5 to 6 inches, and the diameter from 9 to 11 inches, while the weight ranges from five pounds and a half to nearly nine pounds. A plant is generally allowed to carry only one fruit, or, in rare cases, two.

Silvery Prescott Cantaloup Melon (*Melon Cantaloup Prescott Fond Blanc Argenté*).—This variety only differs from the preceding one in the colour of the ribs being somewhat more metallic, and in the fruit being a little larger, but of just the

Silvery Prescott Cantaloup Melon (⅕ natural size).

same quality. The two varieties are those which are the most extensively grown by the Paris market gardeners, who supply them in abundance from July to the end of October. As the large Prescott Melons are grown to an enormous extent, new varieties of them are of frequent occurrence. Whenever a particularly good fruit possesses any exterior characteristic which distinguishes it, even in a slight degree, from others, the cultivators aim at reproducing this characteristic as indicative of the quality, and that is how a new variety is often established.

Sugar Cantaloup Melon (*Melon Cantaloup Sucrin*).—A medium-sized, very branching, vigorous-growing, and hardy variety. Leaves rather large, very distinctly lobed, and of a dark grayish-green colour; fruit nearly spherical, or slightly flattened at the ends, with ribs not very strongly marked, of a uniform silvery-gray colour, not very distinguishable from the colour of the bottom of the furrows, which is a pale gray; flesh orange coloured, very thick, sweet, juicy, and perfumed; skin remarkably thin. The diameter of the fruit is about 5 or 6 inches, and the weight usually ranges

Sugar Cantaloup Melon
(⅓ natural size).

from about 2 lbs. 10 oz. to 3 lbs. 13 oz. A plant may easily carry two fruit. This is one of the varieties which succeed the best in the open air.

Vaucluse Cantaloup Melon (*Melon Cantaloup de Vaucluse*).—Plant of rather vigorous growth, with stems and leaves quite like those of a Cantaloup Melon. The leaves are slightly cut and of a rather dark-green colour. The fruit is borne on a long stalk, is deeply ribbed, and remarkable for its very flattened shape, being little more than 2 inches deep, while it is often 6 inches in its transverse diameter. Its weight is more frequently under than over two pounds and a quarter. The skin is nearly smooth, and is marbled

Vaucluse Cantaloup Melon.

with dark green on a pale-green ground. This little Melon is remarkable for its very great earliness, and is sent to the Paris markets in June and July from the department of Vaucluse. It does not appear to differ very appreciably from a variety of Melon peculiar to the neighbourhood of Lyons, named *Cantaloup de Pierre-Bénite*.

Other Varieties of Cantaloup Melons.

Archangel Cantaloup Melon (*Cantaloup d'Arkhangel*).—A handsome, medium-sized variety. Fruit nearly spherical, or slightly flattened at the ends, with ribs faintly marked, and a grayish-green, not very warty, skin, almost intermediate in appearance between the White Prescott and the Sugar Cantaloup Melon; flesh red, thick, juicy, sweet, and high flavoured.

Épinal Cantaloup Melon (*C. d'Épinal*).—This appears to be a sub-variety of the *Prescott Early Frame Melon,* which it somewhat exceeds in size. The fruit is almost spherical, with ribs pretty well marked, and a pale-green skin variegated with gray. Flesh red, and very thick.

Early English Cantaloup Melon (*C. Fin Hâtif d'Angleterre*).—This variety, which is now not much grown, is distinguished by its small size and great earliness. The fruit is slightly flattened at the ends, and does not exceed 4 or 5 inches in diameter. Flesh red, fine flavoured, and good.

Mogul Cantaloup Melon (*C. du Mogol*).—Fruit almost pear-shaped, twice as long as broad, with very prominent ribs; skin wrinkled, velvety, and covered with warts; flesh red and thick, but deficient in fineness of flavour. Ripens very late.

Black Dutch Cantaloup Melon (*C. Noir de Hollande*).—Fruit very large, oblong, sometimes almost pear-shaped; ribs well marked, warty, of a dark-green colour, almost black, more or less marbled with paler green; skin thick; flesh orange red, comparatively scanty, and rather coarse. Ripens late.

C. Prescott à Écorce Mince.—A handsome variety, more spherical in shape than most of the Prescott Cantaloups commonly grown about Paris, and yet coming very near the Sugar Cantaloup, which is also distinguished by the thinness of the skin.

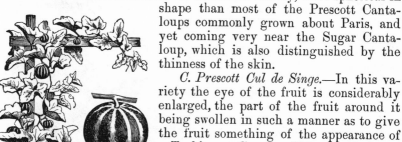

Sweet-scented, or Queen Anne's Pocket, Melon (¹⁄₁₅ natural size; fruit, ¼ natural size).

C. Prescott Cul de Singe.—In this variety the eye of the fruit is considerably enlarged, the part of the fruit around it being swollen in such a manner as to give the fruit something of the appearance of a Turk's-cap Gourd. This peculiarity of shape being sometimes found to be accidentally accompanied with a remarkably good quality in the fruit, has caused it to be much sought after by some amateurs, but there is really no necessary connection between the two things, since quite as good fruit are found amongst the ordinary varieties of Prescott Melons. The peculiar shape, moreover, is not confined to this variety, as it occasionally occurs in the Sugar and other Cantaloup Melons, and even in the Netted Melons, and is never found to be accompanied with an invariable improvement of quality in any variety.

SWEET-SCENTED, or QUEEN ANNE'S POCKET, MELON.

Cucumis Melo, L. var.

Melon Dudaim.

A slender branching plant, with slight foliage. Leaves more or less deeply cut into five lobes; fruit numerous, very small, flattened at the ends, without ribs, but marked with bands either of green or of broad blotches of greenish yellow; flesh not very thick, pale orange coloured, not edible; seed oval, small. The transverse diameter of the fruit does not exceed about 3 inches, and its length (from stem to eye) is about 2 inches. The average weight is seven ounces. The perfume, which resembles that of other Melons without being so strong, is rather agreeable as the fruit ripens, but the taste is not equally pleasant, and the plant is, consequently, only grown as a curiosity, or as an ornamental climber on trellises and arbours, or for covering bare slopes where the climate is warm enough.

WATER-MELON.

Citrullus vulgaris, Schrad.; *Cucumis Citrullus*, Ser.; *Cucurbita Citrullus*, L.
Cucurbitaceæ.

French, Melon d'eau Pastèque. *German,* Wasser-Melone. *Italian,* Cocomero.
Spanish, Sandia. *Portuguese,* Melamia.

Native of Africa.—Annual.—The Water-Melon is a climbing plant with slender and very long stems, particularly suitable for warm climates, where the watery but insipid pulp of the fruit is considered very refreshing. The whole of the plant is covered with long, soft, grayish hairs. The leaves are rather large, and divided into numerous segments, which are also cut or lobed. All the divisions of the leaves, as well as the spaces between the divisions, are rounded in outline, which gives the foliage of the plant a very peculiar appearance. The flowers are rather like Melon-flowers; they are monœcious, and the female flowers are placed on the top of the ovoid and very hairy ovaries, which, as they grow, become changed into perfectly smooth, spherical, or oblong fruit. The colour of the fruit is sometimes a uniform more or less dark green, and sometimes variegated and marbled with grayish green on a darker ground. The fruit is filled with flesh or pulp, the colour of which varies from greenish white to dark red. The seeds are in longitudinal rows, and are flat, oval, short, and of various colours—white, yellow, red, brown, or black. A gramme contains five or six seeds, and a litre of them weighs about 460 grammes. Their germinating power lasts for six years. The varieties of Water-Melons are almost without number, the plant being very extensively cultivated in countries where little importance is attached to pureness of variety, and where different kinds may be seen growing and flowering side by side.

CULTURE.—The Water-Melon, being a native of warm countries, is not much grown in Europe, except on the shores of the Mediterranean and in the south of Russia, where it forms an important article of food. In all tropical countries it is one of the commonest fruits, and is grown there, like the Melon, in the open air and without any trouble. In the climate of Paris it requires, like the Melon, the aid of artificial heat; but it is only grown there as a curiosity, the fruit being always insipid. The only difference in the culture of it from that of the Melon is, that the Water-Melon plants are never pinched or stopped, the produce being always better the more freely the stems are allowed to grow. We have never known it to be well grown in England.

Uses.—The ripe pulp of the fruit is eaten raw, like a Melon. Sometimes the fruit is sliced, and preserved either alone or mixed with other kinds of fruit. It is also made into jam. Before it has ripened, it may be boiled and eaten like a Vegetable Marrow. It is of great value in hot countries.

Red-seeded Water-Melon (*Pastèque à Graine Rouge*).—A vigorous-growing plant, but not so branching or luxuriant in growth as the black-seeded variety. The stems spread along the ground, and are seldom more than about 8 ft. long; they have comparatively few branches. The leaves are largish, with the lobes broader and less cut than those of any other Water-Melon. Fruit spherical, 12 to 16 inches in diameter, of a rather pale green colour, variegated with grayish bands marbled with green; flesh watery, but rather firm, and of a greenish-white colour; seed pink or red. The fruit of this variety requires nearly four months' heat to ripen it, and is chiefly used preserved or made into jam.

Red-seeded Water-Melon (⅛ natural size).

Black-seeded Water-Melon (*Pastèque à Graine Noire*).—Fruit oblong, 20 inches to 2 ft. long, and 12 to 14 inches in diameter; skin smooth, dark green; flesh red, very melting, slightly sweet, and filling the whole of the fruit; seed varying from dark red to black. This variety is most usually eaten raw, and, along with its sub-varieties, is the kind most commonly grown on all the shores of the Mediterranean.

Black-seeded Water-Melon (⅛ natural size),

There is a small-sized variety of this Melon, named the Seikon

Water-Melon, which is remarkable for being an extremely early kind. The fruit ripens perfectly in the climate of Paris, and it is the only kind of Water-Melon that can be grown with any chance of success in the north of France.

The *Helopa* Water-Melon is a vigorous-growing plant, with very large, spherical, or slightly flattened fruit; skin thin, pale green, marbled with still lighter green; flesh greenish white, firm, but not very sweet; seed black. The fruit sometimes weighs nearly five pounds. It ripens half-late, and is seldom eaten except preserved. It is sometimes used for feeding cattle.

AMERICAN VARIETIES.

In the United States Water-Melons are very highly esteemed and very extensively grown. The chief varieties are the following :—

Black Spanish Water-Melon.—Fruit large, roundish, or shortly oblong, with ribs slightly marked; skin nearly black; flesh dark red; seed brown or blackish. A hardy and productive kind.

Citron W.-M.—A kind only used for preserving. Fruit small, spherical, marked with alternate bands of dark green and silvery white; flesh white, very firm, almost hard, scarcely edible in the raw state. It is cut in slices, and preserved like Citrons.

Gipsy W.-M.—An enormously large kind. Fruit oblong, dark green, marked with paler spots in longitudinal bands; flesh red; seed brown or black.

Ice-cream W.-M.—Fruit roundish, large, often flattened at the ends; skin thick, of a very pale green; flesh white and sweet; seed white.

Iceing, Ice-rind, or Strawberry W.-M.—A sub-variety of the White-seeded Water-Melon, remarkable for the red colour of the flesh of the fruit, which is of moderate size, very sweet, melting, and agreeably perfumed.

Mountain, or Mountain Sweet, W.-M.—Fruit large, elongated, oval, sometimes slightly contracted like a Gourd, and without ribs; skin marked with faint bands, some pale, others darker in colour; flesh red, entirely filling the fruit; seed more or less dark brown. A hardy and productive kind.

Mountain Sprout W.-M.—This variety comes exceedingly close, in every respect, to the preceding one, but is a little later.

Orange W.-M.—Fruit medium sized, oval; skin smooth, marbled with dark green on a paler green ground; flesh red, tender, and sweet.

Rattlesnake W.-M.—A fine form of the Black-seeded Water-Melon. Fruit oblong, elongated, and of a uniform dark-green colour; flesh very red.

Many other varieties of Water-Melons might be mentioned, as they are perhaps as numerous as those of Melons properly so called, but we limit ourselves to the number just described, as this work is chiefly written for countries in which the cultivation of Water-Melons seldom succeeds well.

MINT, or SPEARMINT.

Mentha viridis, L. *Labiatæ.*

Menthe verte.

Native of Europe.—Perennial.—A plant with a creeping root-stock. Stem erect, with spreading branches at the top; leaves nearly sessile, lanceolate-acute, slightly rounded at the base, and with distantly placed teeth on the edges; flowers pink or lilac, in cylindrical spikes; seed very scanty, exceedingly fine, roundish, brown. CULTURE.—This plant is usually propagated by division in spring. It prefers a cool moist soil, and a plantation of it will last for several years, if the stems are cut off close to the ground every autumn, and a layer of good soil or compost placed over the plants. USES.—The leaves and the ends of the shoots are used for seasoning, and Mint sauce is considered indispensable for some dishes, especially in England.

MUGWORT.

Artemisia vulgaris, L. *Compositæ.*

French, Armoise. *German*, Beifuss. *Dutch*, Bijvoet. *Italian*, Santolina.

Native of Europe. — Perennial.—An exceedingly hardy plant, forming very long-lived tufts or clumps. Leaves dark green on the upper surface, whitish underneath, pinnate, with oval-lanceolate segments, the lower ones stalked, the stem-leaves sessile and auricled; stems from 2 to over 3 ft. high, reddish and furrowed; flower-heads small, greenish, in large, erect, pyramidal, irregular clusters on the ends of the stems and branches; seed very small, oblong, grayish, and smooth. A gramme contains about 8000 seeds, and a litre of them weighs about 600 grammes. Their germinating power lasts for three years. CULTURE.—Exactly the same as that of Wormwood (see Wormwood). USES.—The leaves have a strong, bitter, aromatic taste, and are sometimes used for seasoning.

MUSHROOMS.

Agaricus campestris, L. *Fungi.*

French, Champignon comestible. *German*, Schwamm. *Flemish* and *Dutch*, Kampernoelie. *Italian*, Fungo pratajolo. *Spanish*, Seta.

The cultivated Mushroom is the same kind as that which grows naturally in meadows and pastures, and in the wild state is known in France by the names of *Champignon Rose, C. des Prés,* and *C. de Rosée.* In this species, as in the case of most other Mushrooms, people generally suppose that the parts which in reality are only the organs of fructification are the entire plant. The true plant, however, which feeds, grows, and finally prepares to flower, is the network of whitish threads which form what is commonly called the "spawn," or, botanically, the "*mycelium*," of the Mushroom. The growth of this spawn, which is suspended in dry weather, becomes active under the influence of moisture accompanied with a sufficient degree of heat, and is developed in an especial degree in horse-manure, which appears to be the most favourable medium of all for the growth of this species. When the Mushroom-plant is on the point of flowering, it swells and produces small whitish excrescences, which soon assume the shape of a miniature parasol, usually white on the upper surface, and covered underneath with a number of very thin radiating plates or "gills," which are at first of a pale pink colour, and gradually change to brown. This parasol or cap is borne on the top of a cylindrical, fleshy, white stalk. The colour of the "gills" is an index whereby the Edible Mushroom is distinguished from the poisonous, and happily rare, kinds with which it might be confounded.

In the neighbourhood of Paris several varieties of the Edible Mushroom are in cultivation. These differ from one another in the colour and general appearance of the skin. It has been found from experience that these varieties (of which there are three principal ones, viz. the White, the Gray, and the Yellowish-white) are not invariably constant, and that after some time, and when removed from the special conditions under which they were produced, they lose their distinctive character, and revert to the Common White kind. After several comparative trials, the White variety appears to us to be the best for the table. The Yellowish-white is not so tender nor so well

Mushrooms (natural size).

scented, while the Gray variety, although of a stronger flavour, has the drawback of discolouring the sauces made with it, even when it is not nearly full grown.

CULTURE.—Mushrooms may be easily grown everywhere, and at all seasons, by following some directions which we shall endeavour to give as briefly and clearly as possible. The conditions essential to success in cultivating Mushrooms consist in growing them in very rich artificial soil and in a steady temperature. And it is for the purpose of securing the last-named requisite that cellars and old subterranean quarries are often utilized for their culture. Any other kind of place would answer equally well, provided that, either naturally or by the use of artificial means, its temperature never rose above 86° Fahr. nor fell much below 50° Fahr.

After selecting a suitable place, the first thing to attend to is the making of the bed or beds in which the Mushrooms are to grow. The indispensable ingredient of this is horse-manure, if possible that of strong well-fed animals, and as free from straw or other litter as it can be obtained. It will not do to make the beds with this manure just as it comes from the stable, as the fermentation would be too great and would give out too much heat. It should, therefore, be tempered down by mixing it as thoroughly as possible with a fourth or a fifth part of good garden soil. As soon as this is done, the beds should be at once made with the mixture, which will ferment slowly and give out a moderate constant heat. Care should be taken to place the beds in a very well-drained place, rather dry than damp; and when they are made, all projecting straws, etc., should be removed and the surfaces made level and very firm.

If the manure is used pure, as it is by some Mushroom-growers about Paris, it should be allowed to spend some of its heat before employing it. For this purpose it is brought from the stables to a place of preparation, where it is put into a square heap, about a yard or more high, formed of successive layers, from which all foreign substances are carefully extracted, and which have been well mixed together, so as to render the whole mass as homogeneous as possible. Any parts that seem too dry are slightly moistened; the sides are then trimmed and trodden down well, so as to reduce the height to about 2 ft. 8 inches. The heap is then left until the heat produced by the fermentation threatens to become excessive, which is denoted by the hottest parts commencing to turn white. This usually occurs in from six to ten days after the making of the heap. The whole heap must then be taken down and made up again exactly as before, taking care to make the interior of it consist of the manure which was previously on the outside, and which was consequently less fermented. It generally happens that within a few days after the heap has been thus re-made, the fermentation becomes so violent that the heap has to be thrown down and re-made a third time.

Sometimes after the second re-making, the manure will be fit for forming the beds. It may be known when this can be done without any danger by the manure having become of a brown colour, having entirely lost its usual consistence and being elastic and greasy to the touch, and having no longer the smell of fresh horse-manure. It is difficult to obtain a good preparation of horse-manure unless a sufficient quantity is operated upon at once. The heap should be at least a yard, or a little more, every way. This is a frequent cause of failure with amateurs, and should be avoided. Even if a less quantity is required for the beds, the manure should be prepared in a heap of at least the dimensions we have just mentioned, and any of it that is not required for the Mushroom-beds will be very useful for any other kind of vegetables.

When the manure is in a proper condition, it is brought to the place where the Mushrooms are to be grown and made into beds at once. The beds may be of any shape or size desired, but experience has shown that both the manure and the space at disposal will be employed to the best advantage by making the beds from 20 to 24 inches high, and about as wide at the base. An excessive rise of temperature from a fresh fermentation is less to be apprehended in beds of this size than in larger ones. When there is a good deal of room to spare, the best plan is to make the beds sloping at both sides and of any length that may be thought fit, but always of the same height and the same width at the base as we have just mentioned. When the beds, however, are made up against a wall or other perpendicular support, and have but one sloping side, the width at the base should be less than the height. Beds may also be made in old tubs, in casks sawn in two, or on plain flat boards, in which cases the beds should be of a conical shape, or in the form of the heaps of broken stones or road-metal often seen on road-sides. In this way it is possible to carry beds ready-made into cellars or other parts of dwelling-houses, where one would not like to bring in a lot of rough manure and litter the place by making the beds there.

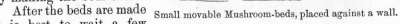

After the beds are made it is best to wait a few

Small movable Mushroom-beds, placed against a wall.

days before spawning them, in order to see whether any excessive fermentation will ensue. This may generally be pretty well ascertained by thrusting the finger into the bed, but the surest way is to use a thermometer. As long as the temperature is over 86° Fahr., the bed is too hot, and must be allowed time to cool down. The cooling process will be expedited by making a few holes here and there in the bed with a stick, to allow the heat to escape. When the temperature stands pretty steadily at about 78° Fahr., it is time to put in the spawn. This may sometimes be

Mushrooms grown in a tub.

found growing naturally in old hot-beds, or on the edges of manure-heaps, and may be used for this purpose; but it is far better to employ the dried spawn sold by seedsmen, which may be obtained at all seasons, and which grows much quicker, is more to be depended on, and will keep good from one year to another. For a few days before it is used, it should be kept in a moderately warm, moist atmosphere, which has the effect of stimulating it into a more speedy and certain growth.

The beds are spawned in the following manner:—The " bricks " or cakes of spawn are broken into pieces about the length and thickness of the hand, but only half the breadth. These are put into the sides, ends, and top of the bed at a distance of from 10 to 12 inches from one another in every direction. In beds of the usual height (from 20 inches to 2 ft.), two rows of pieces are generally set, in such a way that those

of the upper row may be opposite the intervals between those in the lower row. The pieces should be only buried their own depth in the bed, and they are commonly put in with the right hand, while the left is employed to excavate holes for their reception. If the bed has been made in a place with a sufficiently

Movable two-sided Mushroom-bed.

high and steady temperature, there is nothing further to be done but to wait until the Mushrooms appear. But if it has been made in the open air, or in a place exposed to a change of temperature, it should be covered with straw, long manure, or hay, which will serve to confine a certain amount of uniformly warm air around the bed.

If the work has been properly done, and the conditions are favourable, the spawn should commence to grow in seven or eight days after it was placed in the bed. At the end of that time the beds should be examined, and any pieces which have not germinated should be re-

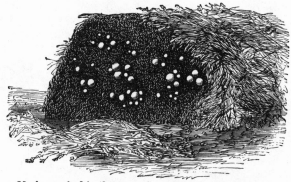

Mushroom-bed in the open air, protected with straw, etc.

placed by fresh ones. The failure of a piece to germinate is indicated by the absence of white threads from the manure which surrounds it. In a fortnight after spawning, the spawn should have permeated the entire bed, and should begin to show itself at the surface, in which case the sides and top of the bed should be covered with a thin layer of soil. This soil should be light rather than too stiff, slightly moistened without being wet, and would be all the better for containing a little nitre. If it does not do so naturally, some finely pulverized old lime plaster should be added to it, or it should be watered well beforehand with liquid manure. It should be put on the bed in a layer of nearly 1 inch thick, and should be well pressed down so as to adhere firmly to the surface of the bed in every part. It must be understood that, if the bed was previously covered with straw, etc., this covering must be replaced after the layer of soil has been added. It is often possible to dispense entirely with watering in the case of Mushroom-beds; and whenever they are watered, it should be very moderately, and only when the surface becomes quite dry.

In a few weeks after the layer of soil has been added, sooner or later according to the temperature, the Mushrooms begin to appear, and, in gathering them, care should be taken to fill the cavities left with the same soil which covers the bed. The bed will of itself continue to yield for two or three months, and for a longer time if watered with liquid manure, guano, or saltpetre; the results being much better if the liquid is of the temperature of from 70° to 86° Fahr. when applied. Watering, however, should be done carefully, so as not to dirty the Mushrooms or interfere with their growth. By making three or four beds under cover in the year, a continuous supply may be secured; and besides, during summer, beds may be made in the open air, which will yield abundantly at a trifling expense. Hot-beds, in which other plants are grown, might have their sides and the spaces between the plants spawned, and would often yield well, provided their temperature was suitable for the purpose, and that care was taken to protect the young Mushrooms with a slight covering of soil as soon as they commenced to grow.

The very interesting Paris culture of Mushrooms is fully described, and illustrated with a variety of original woodcuts, in " The Parks and Gardens of Paris," second edition; and the English market-garden culture is fully treated of in Shaw's " London Market Gardens."

MUSTARD (WHITE or SALAD).

Sinapis alba, L.   *Cruciferæ.*

French, Moutarde blanche.   *German,* Gelber Senf.   *Flemish,* Witte mostaard.   *Dutch,* Gele mosterd *or* mostaard.   *Italian,* Senapa bianca.   *Spanish,* Mostaza blanca.

Native of Europe.—Annual.—A plant of rapid growth. Stem thickish, often angular, branching, bearing incised leaves with rounded segments; flowers yellow, in terminal spikes; seed-vessels slightly hairy, terminating in a flat, membranous kind of beak, and swollen at the sides over the seeds. There are usually from three to four seeds in each side of the silique or pod, which is divided into two parts by a thin membranous partition. The seeds are white, quite spherical, and about the size of a Millet-seed. A gramme contains about 200 seeds, and a litre of them weighs, on an average, 750 grammes. Their germinating power lasts for four years. The seed may be sown in pots, either in the open air or in a frame, and is cut as soon as the seed-leaves are well grown and of a good green colour, which is usually about six or eight days after the seed is sown. The leaves of this plant are generally only sent to table while they are quite young, when they are used in salads and for garnishing.

MUSTARD (BLACK, BROWN, or GROCER'S).

Brassica nigra, Koch ; *Sinapis nigra,* L.   *Cruciferæ.*

French, Moutarde noire.   *German,* Schwarzer *oder* Brauner Senf.   *Flemish,* Zwarte
mostaard.   *Dutch,* Bruine mosterd *or* mostaard.   *Spanish,* Mostaza negra.

Native of Europe.—Annual.—A plant with a rather slender stem.
Radical leaves oblong, lyrate ; stem-leaves becoming narrower as they
approach the top of the stem ; flowers yellow, in terminal spikes ;
siliques or seed-vessels long and slender, each containing about twenty
small, almost spherical, reddish-brown seeds. A gramme contains
about 700 of these seeds, and a litre of them weighs about 675 grammes.
Their germinating power lasts for four years.

The Large-seeded Black Mustard (*M. Noire d'Alsace*) is remarkable for the large size of its yellowish-green leaves. The Small-seeded
Black Mustard of Sicily (*M. Noire de Sicile*) appears to come nearer
the wild form of the plant. Its leaves are about one-third smaller
than those of the Alsace variety, and are also of a darker green colour.

Like the White Mustard, this plant is only grown in kitchen-
gardens for the sake of its young leaves, which are similarly used,
and it is grown in precisely the same way. The ground seeds form
the mustard of commerce or grocer's mustard.

CHINESE CABBAGE-LEAVED MUSTARD.

Native of China.—Annual.—A large plant, attaining the height
of from 4 to 5 ft. when in flower. Radical leaves very large, often
14 to 16 inches long, lyrate, undulating in outline, and with the
edges often turned in underneath. The blade of the leaf is of a
delicate or yellowish-green colour, and netted and sometimes almost

crimped like that of a Savoy
Cabbage. The first leaves,
which are produced on the
lower part of the stem, are
also long and wide, but those
higher up become smaller, until
they are almost linear near the
top of the stem when the plant
is in flower, being a little
broader at the base which clasps
the stem. Flowers yellow,
largish, in terminal clusters ;
siliques almost cylindrical, each
containing about twenty brown
seeds, a little larger than those

Chinese Cabbage-leaved Mustard ($\frac{1}{10}$ natural size).

of the Black Mustard. A
gramme contains about 650
seeds, and a litre of them weighs about 660 grammes. Their germinating power lasts for four years. The seed is sown, where the crop
is to stand, in August, in the open air, either in beds or in drills

from 16 to 20 inches apart.   After sowing, the beds or drills should be watered a few times to ensure germination, but when the cool nights of September arrive, the plants will require no further attention.   In about six weeks from the time of sowing, the leaves may commence to be gathered, and the plants will continue to yield until very frosty weather sets in.   The seed may also be sown immediately after winter, but the plants soon run to seed, and never yield as fine leaves as those which are sown in autumn.   The leaves are eaten boiled, like Spinach.   They are not much diminished in substance by cooking, and have a very agreeable flavour.   In warm countries they form one of the most highly esteemed green vegetables.

NASTURTIUM, or INDIAN CRESS (TALL or LARGE).

Tropæolum majus, L.   *Tropæolaceæ.*

French, Capucine grande.   *German*, Kapuciner Kresse.   *Flemish* and *Dutch*, Capucine-kers.
Italian, Nasturzio maggiore.   *Spanish*, Capuchina grande.   *Portuguese*, Chagas.

Native of Peru.—Annual.—Stems climbing, sometimes nearly 10 feet long when they find a suitable support; leaves alternate, long-stalked, peltate, entire or bluntly five-lobed, almost smooth; flowers long-stalked, large, with five orange-coloured petals spotted with purple, especially the two upper ones; seed large, triangular, almost kidney-

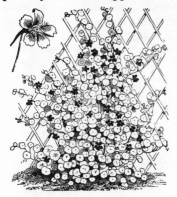

Nasturtium, or Indian Cress (Tall or Large) ($\frac{1}{20}$ natural size; detached flower, $\frac{1}{3}$ natural size).

Nasturtium (Dwarf) ($\frac{1}{10}$ natural size; detached flower, $\frac{1}{3}$ natural size).

shaped, convex on one side, furrowed and wrinkled, and of a yellowish colour.   A gramme contains 7 or 8 seeds, and a litre of them weighs about 340 grammes.   Their germinating power lasts for five years. The plant flowers continuously almost all through the summer.

NASTURTIUM (DWARF).

Tropæolum minus, L.   *Tropæolaceæ.*

French, Capucine petite.   *German*, Kleine indianische Kresse.   *Italian*, Nasturzio
caramindo minore.   *Spanish*, Capuchina pequeña.

Native of Peru.—Annual.—A smaller plant, in all its parts, than the preceding kind.   Stem not so slender and requiring no support;

2 A

leaves nearly round ; flowers yellow, with five petals, the three lower ones especially marked with a purple spot ; seed of the same shape as that of the Tall Nasturtium, but usually smaller, more wrinkled, and browner. A gramme contains about 15 seeds, and a litre weighs about 600 grammes. Their germinating power lasts for five years. Sometimes dwarf varieties of the Tall Nasturtium are confounded with this species. The culture of Nasturtiums is of the simplest description. If sown during spring and summer in the open ground where the plants are to stand, they flower and seed profusely in about two or three months after sowing. The flowers are used for garnishing salads. The flower-buds and the seeds, while young and tender, are pickled in vinegar and used for seasoning, like Capers. For this latter purpose the Dwarf Nasturtium is to be preferred, as it flowers more abundantly than the Tall kind, and does not require stakes or any other kind of support.

NASTURTIUM (TUBEROUS-ROOTED).

Tropæolum tuberosum, R. and P. *Tropæolaceæ.*

French, Capucine tubéreuse. *German*, Peruanische Knollen-Kresse. *Flemish*, Knoll-kapucien. *Spanish*, Capuchina tuberculosa.

Native of South America.—Perennial.—Roots tuberous, conical, as large as a hen's egg, with scale-like swellings, of a yellow colour striped with red, and pleasing in appearance ; stems very branching,

Nasturtium (Tuberous-rooted)
(tubers ½ natural size).

weak, about 3 ft. long ; leaves peltate, divided into three or five blunt lobes ; leaf-stalks red ; flowers medium sized, with a long spur and rather small petals of a yellow colour shaded with orange. The seeds seldom ripen in the climate of Paris, and the plant is propagated from the tubers. The tubers are planted in April or May, in the open ground, 20 inches apart in every direction. The hoe should be used occasionally until the stems, spreading on the ground, cover it entirely. The tubers should not be taken up for use before the latter end of autumn, after the early frosts, as they do not form until late in the season, and are not affected by frost as long as they remain in the ground. When boiled like Carrots or Potatoes, the tubers are watery and have a rather unpleasant taste, although the perfume is agreeable. In Bolivia, where the plant is extensively cultivated in high mountain districts, the people freeze the tubers after boiling them, and they are then considered a delicacy and are largely consumed. In other places they are eaten in a half-dried state, after having been hung up in nets and exposed to the air for some time. It is, therefore, not surprising that the quality of the fresh tuber appears to us to be very indifferent, since, even in its native country, it is not eaten until it has undergone special preparation.

BLACK-BERRIED NIGHTSHADE.

Solanum nigrum, L. *Solanaceæ.*

French, Morelle noire. *German,* Nachtschatten Spinat. *Italian,* Erba mora.
Spanish, Yerba mora.

Native of Europe.—Annual.—A well-known wild plant, generally regarded as a weed, growing most usually near dwelling-houses and in cultivated ground. It has an erect branching stem from 1½ to about 2½ ft. long, with simple, broad, oval leaves, often wavy at the edges. Flowers white, star-shaped, growing in small axillary clusters, and succeeded by round berries, about the size of a pea, of a black or, rarely, amber-yellow colour, and filled with a greenish pulp, mixed with very small lenticular seeds, of a pale-yellow colour. A gramme contains about 800 seeds, and a litre of them weighs about 600 grammes. Their germinating power lasts for five years. The kind which is cultivated in the Isle of France, under the name of *Brède,* does not differ, botanically, from the common kind, but is more vigorous growing and larger in all its parts. The seed is sown where the plants are to stand, in April, in beds, or, preferably, in drills 12 to 14 inches apart. After being thinned out, the plants require no further attention, and are quite proof against dry weather. The leaves, however, are more tender and more plentifully produced if the plants are occasionally well watered when they appear to need it. This plant is not as yet used in France as a vegetable, but in warm countries the leaves are sometimes eaten as Spinach, and apparently without any injurious result, although the plant belongs to the dangerous family of the *Solanaceæ.*

OKA-PLANT.

Oxalis crenata, Jacq. *Oxalidaceæ.*

French, Oxalis crénelée. *Flemish,* Zuerklaver. *Spanish (American),* Oka.

Native of Peru.—Perennial, but cultivated as an annual.—Stem fleshy, reddish, prostrate, bearing very numerous leaves, composed of three roundish-triangular thickish leaflets; flowers axillary, with five yellow petals striped with purple at the base; tubers swollen, elongated ovoid, marked with hollows and protuberances (like some kinds of Potatoes, especially the *Vitelotte* variety), and narrowed at the end which joins the stem; skin very smooth, and of a yellow, white, or red colour. CULTURE.— The Oka-plant is easily propagated from the tubers, which are planted in May, in light rich soil, in rows which should

Tubers of Oka-plant (⅓ natural size).

not be less than 3 ft. apart, on account of the spreading growth of the stems of the plant. As it continues to grow for a long time and is very sensitive to cold, it is better, if possible, to start the tubers in a hot-bed in March, and plant them out in May, at which time they will be pretty forward. As the stems lengthen, they should be covered with light soil or compost, in order to promote the formation of new tubers, taking care to leave 6 or 8 inches of the end of the stem uncovered. The tubers do not commence to swell until rather late in the season, and are not gathered until the ends of the stems have been killed by frosty weather. In France they seldom grow as large as a hen's egg. USES.—The tubers are highly esteemed in Peru and Bolivia, where they are used in great quantities. When they have been recently gathered, they have a very acid, and therefore not very agreeable, taste. The people of South America get rid of this acidity by putting them into woollen bags and exposing them to the action of the sun, the effect of which is that in a few days they become floury and sweet. If they are kept thus exposed for several weeks, they dry up, become wrinkled, and acquire a flavour which somewhat resembles that of dried Figs. In this condition they are known by the name " *Caui.*" In addition to the tubers, the leaves and young shoots may be eaten as salad or as Sorrel.

Two varieties of this plant have been introduced into France, namely, the Yellow and the Red, differing from each other only in the colour of the tubers. The Yellow variety has spontaneously produced a sub-variety, with pure white tubers, which reproduces itself exactly, but appears to be inferior to the other two kinds in vigour and quality for table use.

OKRA, or GOMBO.

Hibiscus esculentus, L. *Malvaceæ.*

French, Gombaud. *Italian,* Ibisco. *Spanish,* Gombo ; (*American*), Quimbombo.

Native of South America.—Annual.—Stem stout, erect, branching but little or not at all, from 20 inches to over 3 ft. high, according to the variety ; leaves very large, five-lobed, toothed, dark green on the upper surface, slightly grayish underneath, and with very prominent veins ; flowers solitary in the axils of the leaves, with five straw-coloured petals, brown or violet coloured in the centre ; fruit pyramidal, ending in a point, with five prominent ribs, and divided into five cells or compartments filled with largish gray or greenish seeds, nearly spherical in shape and rough skinned. A gramme contains from 15 to 18 seeds, and a litre of them weighs about 620 grammes. Their germinating power lasts for five years. CULTURE. — Like the Egg-plant and the Tomato, the Gombo requires artificial heat in the climate of Paris, while in warmer climates it may be sown and grown in the open air. The seed is usually sown in a hot-bed in February, the seedlings are pricked out into another hot-bed, and are finally planted out in May, after which the plants only require plentiful watering to attain their full growth. USES.—In the colonies the young and tender seed-vessels are very extensively used as a table vegetable. They are exceedingly mucilaginous, and when cut into thin slices are made into soups and sauces, which are highly esteemed by the

Creoles. The ripe seeds also are parched and used instead of Coffee. The infusion which is obtained from them is not inferior to that made from Chicory, Sweet Acorns, *Astragalus bæticus*, and other substitutes for Coffee.

Long-fruited Green Okra (*Gombo à Fruit Long*).—Stem short, seldom exceeding 20 inches in height; leaves very deeply cut; seed-vessels 6 to 8 inches long, slender, long pointed, and about 1 inch in diameter. This is the most commonly cultivated kind. There is a sub-variety in which the seed-vessels are pendent.

Round-fruited Okra (*Gombo à Fruit Rond*).—Seed-vessels short, and comparatively thick, being about 2 inches long, and nearly 2 inches in diameter, and blunt at the ends rather than pointed. This variety is dwarfer and earlier than the preceding kind.

Long-fruited Green Okra (seed-vessels ⅓ natural size).

OLLUCO.

Ullucus tuberosus, Lozano. *Basellaceæ.*

Spanish (*American*), Ulluco.

Native of Chili.—Perennial.—A plant with a branching, creeping stem, which takes root wherever it touches the ground. Leaves alternate, thick, spathulate, glistening, and of a lively green colour; leaf-stalk rather long, and reddish coloured. The plant does not seed in the climate of Paris. The tubers are produced on runners which issue from the base of the stem, and are of an oblong-roundish shape, very smooth, and of a bright yellow colour. In the climate of Paris they seldom grow larger than a good-sized walnut. These tubers appear to be swollen underground stems, like the tubers of the Potato. The flesh is yellow, mucilaginous, and starchy when they are fully grown. Culture.—The tubers are planted about the same time as Potatoes, in the latter part of April, the plant being sensitive to frost. It likes a light rich soil, and grows remarkably well in leaf-mould. It is a good plan, when the stems are pretty well grown, to cover the lower part of them, where the tubers are produced, with soil or compost. The tubers are gathered in October or November, after the stems have been killed by frosty weather. Uses.—The tubers are eaten in Chili. In Europe the plant has never been cultivated with satisfactory results.

ONION.

Allium Cepa, L.　*Liliaceæ.*

Native of Central or Western Asia.—Biennial, sometimes perennial.
—The original native country of the Onion is not known with certainty;
within the last few years, however, M. Regel, jun., discovered, south
of Kouldja, in Turkestan, a plant which had every appearance of
being the wild form of *Allium Cepa,* and we believe the same plant has
also been found on the Himalayas.

The Onion has no stem, or rather the stem is reduced to a mere
plate, from which issue, on the lower side, numerous white, thick,
simple roots, and on the upper side leaves, the fleshy, swollen, and
overlapping bases of which form the bulb of the Onion. The form,
colour, and size of the bulb are very much varied in different varieties
of the plant. The free portion of the leaves is elongated, hollow, and
swollen in the lower part for about one-third of their length. The
flower-stems, which are very much longer than the leaves, are erect,
hollow, and swollen in the lower part for about one-third of their length.
The flowers, which are white or lilac, are severally borne on very slender
stalks, and are collected in a very dense spherical head on the top of
the flower-stem. Sometimes, instead of flowers, a head of small bulbs
is produced. This may occur exceptionally in any of the varieties, but
is an invariable characteristic of the Tree Onion, which is thence named
the Bulbiferous Onion. The flowers are succeeded by capsules of an
almost triangular shape, filled with black, angular, flattish seeds. A
gramme contains about 250 seeds, and a litre of them weighs about
500 grammes. Their germinating power lasts for two years.

Usually, the plant, after seeding, dies and disappears entirely; but
sometimes we find Onions which produce cloves as well as seeds. Such
plants may be considered perennial, as well as the Potato Onion, which
never seeds and is propagated by division of its bulbs.

The culture and use of the Onion date back to a very remote
period of antiquity. The strong odour and flavour of all parts of the
plant caused it to be valued in very early times as a seasoning, and
being easily grown, man has carried it with him into almost every
climate in the world. Hence a great number of varieties have resulted,
the best of which have become fixed, and form the various kinds which
are now in cultivation.

Culture.—The Onion, considered only with a view to the production of bulbs for household consumption, is generally grown as an
annual plant, whether sown for a summer crop or sown in autumn.
For a summer crop, the seed is sown in spring, and the crop is
gathered in the end of summer or in autumn. In this case, the entire
growth of the plant is completed in the course of the same year. This
mode of culture is the general one in the central and northern
districts of France, where Onions are grown very extensively and as a
field crop. The seed is sown in the latter part of February, or in

March, in good, moist, but well-drained soil, which has been well manured and well pulverized at the surface, at the same time that it is somewhat firm and compact underneath. The seed, being rather small, should be only slightly covered. In gardens, Onion-beds, after being sown, are often simply strewn with leaf-mould or with grape skins from the wine-presses. When the seedlings have grown pretty strong, they are thinned out more or less, according to the size of the variety, and after that require no further attention until they are fully grown. Watering is not necessary except in unusually dry weather.

When the seed is sown in autumn, the growth of the plants is extended from one year into the next. This mode of culture is most common in districts where the winter is mild, as in the west and all through the south of France. The seed is sown from August to October, and the young plants are planted out either in the course of the same autumn or as soon as the winter is over. This way of growing Onions is not so simple as that first mentioned, but the crop is finer and earlier. It is generally practised, as we have just said, in southern districts, and it is in this way that the enormous Onions which are sent during winter to our markets from Spain, Italy, and Africa are raised. At Paris, too, it is almost the only way in which the Early White Silver-skinned Onion is grown. This is sown in August or September, and the seedlings are generally pricked out in October (the roots and leaves being trimmed at the same time), and they are slightly sheltered during the winter when the frost is severe. The bulbs are fit for use in May. By sowing the New Queen variety in the same way, a crop could, no doubt, be obtained in April.

Sometimes the Onion is grown as a biennial, that is, its culture extends over nearly two whole years. In this case, the growth is retarded by planting out, not young seedlings, but small bulbs raised the year before by sowing very thickly in spring and growing them on like summer Onions, but without thinning them. These small bulbs, which are about as big as a Hazel-nut, easily keep through the winter, and when planted out in spring increase in size rapidly, and in a few months become as fine bulbs as those obtained from plants grown on through the winter in the usual way. This mode of culture was recommended a very long time ago by MM. Lebrun and Nouvellon, who applied it to Onions of every kind. At the present day it is generally practised, especially in the east of France, with a yellow variety, the small bulbs of which form an important article of commerce, under the name of *Mulhouse Onions.* When the bulbs of this variety are fully grown, it is very difficult to distinguish them from those of the Strasburg Onion. The Brown Spanish Onion may also be grown in the same way.

For good Onions there is always a large demand, and late in the season they fetch high prices. In nearly all market gardens round London Onions are grown to a large extent both as summer and winter crops. In the neighbourhood of Lea Bridge large fields are devoted to them, and from this district come large quantities of the finest produce brought to market. Great breadths of Onions are also grown at Fulham, Chiswick, Deptford, and Mitcham, the land thereabouts being light and rich and well suited for their culture. The main spring sowing, which consists usually of the Deptford and Reading varieties, is made as soon after the middle of February as the condition of the soil and weather permits. If the seed be good and is sown broadcast, nine to twelve pounds per acre are used, but if sown in lines only eight pounds to the acre are needed. Land intended for Onions is generally roughly trenched during winter and thrown into ridges, so as to become thoroughly pulverized and sweetened by the action of the frost. During dry weather in February the ridges are levelled and the surface rendered smooth by raking and rolling, after which the seed is sown either broadcast or in drills 9 to 10 inches apart. If small pickling bulbs be desired, seed is sown broadcast at the rate of twenty pounds per acre. After sowing, the seed is raked or harrowed in, and the operation is completed by rolling the surface firm and even. After the young Onions appear above the ground, weeding and thinning are proceeded with as may be required. Broadcast sowing is considered the best for spring-sown crops, as involving less labour; and as the bulbs, after thinning, stand at regular distances apart over the whole area, the produce per acre is considerably more than when sown in beds or lines. Seed sown in the autumn is, however, sometimes drilled on beds 4 or 5 ft. wide, these being divided by narrow alleys which serve as walks for labourers who weed the beds and draw the crop as required for market; but this crop is also often sown broadcast.

Onion seed takes a long time to germinate, but if the ground be clean and well tilled, weeds will not appear much sooner than the Onions, or, at least, not so thickly as to choke them. As soon as the Onions have fairly come up, women or men accustomed to Onion cleaning are set to work amongst them. These operators are furnished with the short-handled 2½-inch wide hoes, with which they hoe down the weeds and thin the whole crop with wonderful certainty and expedition. The field is marked off into strips for the guidance of the hoers, to each one of whom there is a space of 6 ft. given, so that were four cleaners employed the strips would each be 24 ft. wide. People accustomed to this work do not trample carelessly about; nor, indeed, can the crop be materially damaged by doing so, for the Onions that are thus prostrate to-day are nearly erect to-morrow. Each plantation is generally cleaned by this means three times during the season, the last cleaning being made about the end of June or early in July, and any large weeds that appear after that time are pulled out by the hand. Towards the end of August or early in September the Onions, being ripe, are harvested when dry. Those that are green and thick-necked are laid aside for immediate sale; but the firm and sound bulbs, particularly of the Deptford kind, are either cleaned of any loose scaly skins and spread out a few inches deep over the floor of a loft, or tied into bunches and strung in pairs over poles or pegs in a loft or shed, so that they can be marketed at any convenient season during winter and spring.

The profits on a good crop of spring-sown Onions are comparatively large, although the prices vary considerably in some seasons. Sometimes as much as £45 per acre is made of them by the grower, the purchaser being at the expense of harvesting the crop. At other times, however, £30 per acre is considered a good price. The Silver-skinned Onion, which is grown largely for pickling, is sown on good land, the plants being left as thickly as they come up, as the closer they are together the sooner they will cease growing in summer and the better they will ripen their bulbs. Good clean bulbs realize from 8s. to 10s. per bushel in the market. The autumn sowing of Onions is made on ground cleared of Cauliflowers, Cabbages, or other early crops, in the end of July for drawing in a young state from September onwards, but the main sowing is not made till about the middle of August. The autumn sowings are, as a rule, made in beds about 5 ft. wide, and the seeds are covered deeper than those of the spring sowings. Autumn sowings of Onions are not often made broadcast on fields, as they must be weeded, not hoed, in the process of cleaning; the hoeing would thin them too much. As they are only required for drawing when young they do not need to be more than one-third of the distance asunder required in the case of the summer Onions. They are weeded soon after they come up, and once, or perhaps twice, during the winter time. Weeding is performed by women in dry weather, each of whom takes a small round basket to put the weeds into, rather than throw them on the alleys. In marketing these Onions they are cleared off the beds in large patches, and not by picking out the strongest and leaving the weakest, as is generally done, and they are washed, which makes them look white. If a portion be intended for transplanting, a piece of well-prepared rich ground is made ready for them, rolled firmly, and lined off into rows about 9 inches apart, and into these lines the young plants are dibbled about 6 inches apart. These make large saleable bulbs early in July. The kinds used for autumn sowings consist of White Spanish and White Tripoli or Lisbon. Some growers save large quantities of Onion seed, for which purpose well-formed bulbs are selected and planted in spring in rows which vary from 2 to 6 ft. apart, Lettuce, Radishes, Spinach, or other low-growing vegetables being grown as intermediate crops. After the flower-stems make their appearance they are staked at intervals, and twine or cord is strained on either side the rows to prevent the stems being beaten down by hail, rain, or wind. Ordinary Onion seed fetches from 2s. to 5s. per lb., according to the season; but the best seed, or that from improved or rare sorts, is more valuable. In Hertfordshire large breadths of seed Onions may be seen in July, and on good deep land it is considered one of the most profitable of crops.

Uses.—The bulbs are eaten boiled, raw, or pickled with vinegar.

New Queen Onion (*Ognon Blanc Très Hâtif de la Reine*).—Bulb small, very much flattened, silvery white, from 1⅕ to 1⅗ inch in diameter, and from ⅗ to ⅘ of an inch thick; neck fine, soon becoming green, if the bulbs are stored in the expectation that they will keep; leaves very short, of a dark and slightly glaucous green, three or four, or at most five, in number when the plant is fully grown. It is not uncommon to find, amongst plants sown in spring, some bulbs growing as large as walnuts, and ripening without forming more than two leaves. This variety is an exceedingly early one. If sown in March, the bulbs begin to swell in the course of the following May; but, on the other hand, it is not at all a productive kind, nor does it keep well.

New Queen Onion
(⅓ natural size).

Early White Nocera Onion (*Ognon Blanc Hâtif de Nocera*).—This variety is probably only a form of the preceding one which has been

so modified by long-continued cultivation in a colder climate than that
of its native district, as to have become larger in size and a little later
incoming to maturity. Bulb silvery

white, flattened, broader and comparatively flatter than that of the
preceding kind, being from 2 to
over 3 inches in diameter, and
from ⅘ to 1 inch thick ; neck fine ;
leaves few, dark green. An almost
invariable feature in this variety
is that, in spite of every care
taken in the selection of plants
for seed, a small percentage of

Early White Nocera Onion (⅓ natural size).

light-brown or chamois-coloured bulbs will almost always be produced.
It is a very early kind, but at least three weeks later than the New
Queen Onion, and, like that variety, keeps badly.

Early Paris Silver-skinned Onion (*Ognon Blanc Hâtif de Paris*).—

Bulb silvery white, flattened,
and of about the same diameter as that of the preceding kind—that is, from 2 to
over 3 inches—but thicker,
and formed of more nume-
rous and more closely set
coats ; neck fine ; leaves of
a rather deep, slightly
glaucous, green colour, and
not very numerous. This
variety is not so early as
the preceding one, but keeps
better ; yet the bulbs are

Early Paris Silver-skinned Onion (⅓ natural size).

almost always sent to table quite fresh, and most frequently before
they are fully grown. It is one of the best early Onions, and very
probably originated from one of the early South Italian varieties,
which, when grown in the climate of Paris, exhibit a tendency to
become identical with this variety.

Early White Valence Onion (*Ognon Blanc Hâtif de Valence*).—

Bulb not so broad as that
of the preceding kind, but
thicker and larger, being
less than 3 inches in diameter, and from 1⅗ to 2
inches thick ; leaves rather
numerous, of a slightly yellowish-green colour. This
variety is rather early and
productive, and the bulbs
are tender, but do not keep
well. It is more suitable

Early White Valence Onion (⅓ natural size).

for the southern than for
the northern parts of France. As regards its origin, it is more likely

that it is a smaller and earlier form of the White Lisbon Onion than
that it has sprung from any of the kinds which have been previously
described.

White Portugal Onion (French, *Ognon Blanc Rond Dur de Hollande;*
Dutch, *Zilverwitte Winter Uijen*).—Bulb
of a dull-white colour, medium sized, very
firm, with thick tough coats, and varying
from 2 to nearly 3 inches in diameter,
and from $1\frac{1}{5}$ to $1\frac{3}{5}$ inch in thickness. It
is not so much flattened as that of either
the Early White Nocera or the Early
Paris Silver-skinned Onion, and is also
somewhat later than these varieties, but,
on the other hand, it keeps remarkably
well. In this respect it will bear comparison with the good yellow or red
varieties of Onions. It is notably distinguished from the white varieties
hitherto described by the outer coats of
the bulb being firm and tough, instead
of being of a delicate, brittle, and almost
transparent texture. In consequence of

White Portugal Onion
($\frac{1}{3}$ natural size).

this peculiarity the bulbs keep better, and are never disfigured by the
greenish tinge which exposure to the sun often produces on the bulbs
of the very early white varieties of Onions.

Neapolitan Maggiojola White Onion (*Ognon Blanc de Mai*).—An
early and very large kind. Bulb silvery white, 4 or 5 inches in
diameter, and about 2 inches thick; flesh tender; neck a little
stout; leaves numerous, and of a peculiar light tint. This variety
derives its name from the circumstance that in Italy it attains its full
growth in the month of May, but it does not do so in France until
August. However, it is a comparatively early kind, considering its
large size and great productiveness. It does not keep well.

Italian Tripoli Onion (French, *Ognon Blanc Gros Plat d'Italie;*
Italian, *Cipolla Agostena*).—
It is rather difficult to procure this variety perfectly
true to name, and it does
not appear to be very ex-
tensively grown, even in
Italy. It is in all points
an exaggerated form of the
preceding kind, being one-
third broader, often exceeding 6 inches in transverse
diameter, with a depth of
about 3 inches. The neck is
thick, and the leaves stout
and of a dark-green colour.

Italian Tripoli Onion ($\frac{1}{3}$ natural size).

The coats of the bulb are
of a pearly white when dried, but more or less greenish as long as

they retain any moisture. This is a half-late and productive variety, and keeps tolerably well.

White Lisbon Onion (*Ognon Blanc Gros*).—Bulb round, more or

less flattened, sometimes irregular in shape, 3 to 4 inches in diameter when well grown, and from about 2 to over 3 inches thick, often slightly Pear-shaped in the lower part; neck rather thick; leaves numerous, and of a yellowish-green colour. The flesh is not very firm, and, although it ripens rather late, this variety does not keep very well. It is most usually sent to table fresh from the ground, even in the south of France. In England it is grown in immense quantities for use

White Lisbon Onion (⅓ natural size).

while quite young and hardly formed, the bulbs being scarcely larger than a Walnut.

Globe Silver-skinned Onion (*Ognon Blanc Globe*).—Bulb silvery

white, almost exactly spherical, with a diameter of from 2⅖ to 3⅕ inches every way, very firm, with a fine neck, and keeping remarkably well; leaves dark green, slender, and rather numerous. This variety is about as early as the preceding one.

Como Flat Yellow Onion (French, *Ognon Jaune Plat de Côme*; Italian, *Cipoletta di Como*).—Bulb extremely flat, being usually only from ½ to ¾ inch deep, with a transverse diameter of about 2 inches;

Globe Silver-skinned Onion (⅓ natural size).

outer coats very thin, almost transparent, and of a coppery or salmon-

tinted yellow colour; neck fine; disc exceedingly small. This variety, which originated at Como, in Lombardy, is remarkable for its very great earliness, and keeps very well, provided it is stored in a place free from damp. It is only suitable for spring sowings, and should not be sown too early, otherwise it has a tendency to run to seed in the first year.

Como Flat Yellow Onion.

Danver's Yellow Onion (*Ognon Jaune de Danvers*).—Bulb spherical or slightly flattened, of a coppery-yellow colour, a little more reddish tinted than that of the Brown Spanish or Portugal Onion, usually from 2⅖ to 3⅕ inches in diameter, and nearly the same in thickness; coats numerous and closely set; neck very fine, as is also the disc or plate from which the roots issue; leaves medium sized, and of a clear-green colour. This is an excellent early kind, and keeps remarkably well. It is as well adapted for field culture as for the kitchen garden, but should always be sown in spring. When sown in autumn, we have always found it to run to seed in the following spring without bulbing to any extent. It is an American variety, and when first introduced into France (about 1850) was quite spherical in shape, but now it grows almost always more or less flattened, not only in European gardens, but also in its native country.

Danver's Yellow Onion (⅓ natural size).

The varieties of the Globe Onion known as Brown Globe, Bedfordshire Champion, James's Long Keeping, and Magnum Bonum, differ from one another mainly by the care taken in maintaining their distinctive shapes. They are all excellent keepers, but Magnum Bonum is the largest and keeps the longest.

Brown Spanish, or **Oporto, Onion** (*Ognon Jaune des Vertus*).—Bulb very much flattened, 3 to 4 inches in diameter, and about 2 inches thick, of a coppery-yellow colour, with firm thickish coats, which do not easily come asunder, and are deeper coloured in the part of the bulb which is covered by the soil than in the upper and exposed part; neck rather fine; leaves numerous, largish, and of a dark-green colour. This is a rather early and exceedingly productive variety, and keeps to perfection. It is the kind most commonly used for field culture about

Brown Spanish Onion (⅓ natural size).

Paris, and is grown in very large quantities in the neighbourhood of Saint-Denis, and as far as Normandy. The winter supply of Paris and of a great part of Europe consists chiefly of this variety, which may be often seen hanging up in dwelling-houses in long hanks formed by interlacing and plaiting the withered leaves together.

Strasburg, or **Essex, Onion** (*Ognon de Cambrai*).—This variety is very closely allied to the preceding one, but is a little more reddish coloured and usually of smaller diameter. It is a productive and pretty early kind, and keeps well. The general practice is to sow it in spring; but it is often grown from small bulbs, raised in the previous year from thick sowings. These small bulbs form an important article of commerce under the name of Mulhouse Onions (*Ognons de Mulhouse*). The Brown Spanish, or Oporto, Onion is also frequently grown in the same way.

Strasbourg, or Essex, Onion (small bulbs for planting out, natural size).

White Spanish, or Reading, Onion (*Ognon Jaune-soufre d'Espagne*).—Bulb quite flat, 3 to 4 inches in diameter, and 2 inches or less thick, very much resembling that of the Brown Spanish, or Oporto, Onion, but of a far less coppery colour, and very perceptibly not so thick; coats firm, rather thick, very closely set, of a bright and slightly greenish yellow colour, almost like that of brass; leaves of a clear green, pretty large sized, and long. This is a mid-season variety, very hardy and productive, and keeps remarkably well. This is the sort most generally grown and cultivated in England. There are many varieties of it grown, of which Nuneham Park, Banbury Improved, Naseby Mammoth, and Cantello's Prize are the principal.

White Spanish, or Reading, Onion (⅓ natural size).

Yellow Trébons Onion (*Ognon Jaune de Trébons*).—Bulb usually pear-shaped, more or less elongated, about as long as broad, generally 3 to 4 inches every way, narrowed at the neck, and very often at the other end; inner coats of a bright-yellow colour, outer ones of a slightly coppery hue; neck narrow; leaves numerous, but slender, and of a dark-green colour; flesh tender, sweet, and of an agreeable mild flavour. This is a half-late variety, of remarkably good quality, but rather difficult to keep, and answers equally well for sowing in spring or in autumn. It was raised in the neighbourhood of Tarbes (Hautes-Pyrénées).

Giant Zittau Onion (*Ognon Géant de Zittau*).—Bulb large, flattish, 4 to nearly 5 inches in diameter,

Yellow Trébons Onion (⅓ natural size).

and a little over 2 inches thick; outer skin very smooth and almost silky, of a pale salmon-colour, forming the connecting link between the yellow-skinned and the pale-red-skinned varieties; leaves pretty numerous, of a light, slightly yellowish, green; neck fine, as is also the disc, or part from which the roots issue. This is a fine mid-season variety, and is both productive and keeps very well. It does best in light, well-drained, but at the same time rich and well-manured soil.

Common Pale-red Onion (*Ognon Rouge Pâle Ordinaire*).—Bulb medium sized, flattened, 2 to nearly 3 inches in diameter, and from ⅘ to 1⅗ inches thick, somewhat irregular in shape; outer coats of a coppery pink colour; inner ones of a darker shade, changing to a purplish colour; neck rather thick; leaves pretty numerous, but short, and of a clear-green colour. This is a hardy variety, and is very generally grown. It is a half-early kind, and keeps tolerably well, although it readily parts with its outer coats, like the kinds which start to grow too soon. It is only suitable for spring culture. There are very many local forms of it which hardly differ from one another. That which is

Giant Zittau Onion (⅓ natural size).　　　Common Pale-red Onion
　　　　　　　　　　　　　　　　　　　　　　　　(⅓ natural size).

most frequently met with in commerce is grown in the neighbourhood of Bourgueil, in Touraine. The Pale-red Strasburg, or Dutch, Onion is closely allied to the Common Pale-red Onion, differing from it only in being a little more coppery in colour, and not quite so much flattened in shape.

Early Flat Red Onion (*Ognon Rouge Plat Hâtif*).—An exceedingly early variety, which bulbs almost as soon as the Early White Silver-skinned Onion, like which it has but scanty and slightly glaucous leaves. The bulb is very broad and flat in proportion to its depth, and is of a decided red colour when dried a little, but while growing, and also underneath the outer coats, it is more of a purplish colour. It is a good first-crop Onion, but, like most very early varieties, does not keep very well.

Niort Pale-red Onion (*Ognon Rouge Pâle de Niort*).—Bulb broad and flat, 3 to 4 inches in diameter (sometimes more), and from 1⅕ to 1⅗ inches thick, of a pale pink, slightly tinged with copper-colour, and with something of a purplish shade on the inner coats; leaves numerous, erect, large, and of a clear green; neck rather fine. The outer coats of the bulb are thin and brittle, but it keeps well notwithstanding. This is an excellent, early, and very productive variety, and is very highly esteemed in the west of France. It answers well for sowing in spring, but succeeds best in its native district when sown in autumn, and transplanted either at the beginning or the end of winter. As the winters are mild in Brittany, Vendée, and Poitou, where it is chiefly grown, this mode of culture can be successfully practised. The Lencloître Onion, a great favourite in Poitou, is only a form of the present variety which has a somewhat flatter and harder bulb. The Saint-Brieuc Pale-red Onion differs from the Niort variety in having the bulb not so much flattened, and of a yellower colour, less tinged with red. It is also not so hardy.

Niort Pale-red Onion
(⅓ natural size).

Of the two varieties the Niort is preferable in every respect, and it has almost entirely superseded the Saint-Brieuc even in Brittany.

Bright-red Mézières Onion (*Ognon Rouge Vif de Mézières*).—Bulb flat, very broad, sometimes 4 or 5 inches across, and about 2 inches thick, of a fine intense red colour, slightly tinged with purple on the inner coats; neck rather stout; leaves large, numerous, erect, and of a dark-green colour. This is a very handsome and exceedingly productive variety, and deserves to be more extensively cultivated. It keeps well, and is very suitable for sowing in spring. It is one of the good old local varieties of the north of France, where it has been cultivated for a very long period, and derives its name from Mézières, a village in the neighbourhood of Pontoise.

Bright-red Mézières Onion (⅓ natural size).

Bright-red August Onion (*Ognon Rouge Vif d'Août*).—This handsome variety is not unlike the preceding one, but is distinguished from it by the bulb being somewhat smaller, seldom exceeding 4 inches in diameter, and about 1¾ inch in thickness. It is usually somewhat thicker in comparison with its diameter than the Mézières variety, and is also less flattened at the ends; its colour, too, is a little darker on the outer coats, and of a violet red on the inner ones. A very essential difference between the two kinds, however, is that the August variety is especially suitable for sowing in autumn. It is chiefly grown in the south-eastern parts of France, where it is sown in August and transplanted in October, the crop coming in in the course of the following summer. It is a productive kind, and keeps well.

Dutch Blood-red, or St. Thomas's, Onion (*Ognon Rouge Foncé ;* Dutch, *Platte Bloedroode Uijen*).—Bulb very much flattened, seldom exceeding about an inch in thickness, with a diameter of from $2\frac{2}{5}$ to $3\frac{1}{5}$ inches; coats firm, closely set, of a deep wine-red on the outside; inner ones of a fine, intense, brilliant red; neck fine; leaves rather stiff, compact, and of a dark-green colour. This is a mid-season variety, not very productive, but keeps very well. It is hardy and easily grown, and is most in favour in the northern districts of France.

In the south-west of France, especially about Bordeaux, a very fine variety of Onion is sometimes met with under the plain name of the Red Onion (*Ognon Rouge*). The bulb of this variety is as highly coloured as that of the

Bright-red August Onion ($\frac{1}{3}$ natural size).

Dutch Blood-red Onion, but in shape and size it more resembles the Flat Tripoli. It is sometimes nearly 5 inches in diameter, and is very much flattened at top and bottom. The flesh is tender and mild-flavoured, but the bulb does not keep well.

It is to be observed that, in all the Red Onions which we have just described, the red colouring is superficial. When the bulbs are cut across, two or three of the outer coats are seen to be pretty highly coloured, while the interior ones are hardly pink. The

Dutch Blood-red, or St. Thomas's, Onion ($\frac{1}{3}$ natural size).

colour is stronger, and extends deeper in the following variety.

Dark-red Brunswick Onion (French, *Ognon Rouge Noir de Brunswick ;* German, *Dunkelrothe Braunschweiger Zwiebel*).—Bulb very flat, rather small, seldom exceeding about $2\frac{1}{2}$ inches in diameter, and about an inch or less thick, hard and firm, of such a deep-red colour that it verges on black; neck fine; leaves short, rather slender, and of a dark, slightly glaucous, green colour. This is a moderately productive kind, but keeps remarkably well.

Wethersfield Onion (*Ognon Rouge de Wethersfield*).—A very handsome American variety, with a very smooth, clean-skinned bulb, almost spherical, or slightly flattened at the ends. In shape and size it comes very near the Danver's Yellow Onion, and, like that variety, has an exceedingly fine neck; but it differs entirely from it in colour, being of a bright red, like the Mézières Onion. The leaves are slender, long, and of a clear-green colour. This is a half-early kind, and keeps well. In its original form the bulb was quite spherical, but at the present

2 B

day it is seldom found, even in America, without having the ends somewhat flattened, and wherever the primitive form occurs it is known as the Large Red Globe Onion.

Globe Tripoli, or Madeira, Onion (½ natural size),

Globe Tripoli, or Madeira, Onion (*Ognon de Madère Rond*).—This is the largest of all varieties of Onion. The bulbs are almost spherical, and it is not uncommon to see some of them 6 or 7 inches in diameter. The outer coats are very thin and brittle, and of a salmon-pink colour, while the inner ones have a tinge of lilac. The flesh is very tender, sweet, and mild flavoured. The neck is rather fine for the size of the bulb; leaves stout, numerous, and of a clear-green colour. This variety does best in warm climates, and in the south of Europe is highly valued for its size and agreeable flavour. It only attains its full development when sown in autumn. In the climate of Paris it is very sensitive to cold, and does not keep well.

Flat Tripoli Onion (⅓ natural size).

Flat Tripoli Onion (*Ognon de Madère Plat*).—Bulb of large size, broad, and very much flattened, from 6 to 8 inches in diameter, and about 2 inches thick, of the same colour as the preceding kind, or a little more reddish. The flesh, like that of the Globe Tripoli, is tender, and the bulb keeps equally badly. Both varieties are grown in exactly the same manner.

In order to obtain the enormous specimens of Tripoli Onions which may be sometimes seen exposed for sale by dealers in southern produce, the seed is sown in August, and the young plants are planted out in October and November. In the following year their growth is stimulated by continual supplies of water and manure, until July or August, when watering is discon-

Blood-red Flat Italian Onion (⅓ natural size).

tinued, and in about a month afterwards the bulbs are gathered, some of them weighing two pounds each or even more.

Blood-red Flat Italian Onion (*Ognon Rouge Gros Plat d'Italie*).— Bulb flat, rather thick, from 4⅖ to 5¾ inches in transverse diameter and a little over 2 inches thick ; outer coats rather thick and of a dull-red colour ; inner ones of a brighter shade slightly tinged with violet ; flesh tender and not very close ; leaves numerous, stout, and of a dark-green colour. This is a half-late variety, and rather difficult to keep. It does better when sown in autumn than when sown in spring, and is especially suitable for warm climates. When grown in northern localities, it quickly becomes altered in character, losing much of its size, and at the same time becoming closer in texture and stronger in flavour. In order to have the variety quite pure, seed must be procured every year from the south of Europe.

Giant Rocca Onion (*Ognon Géant de Rocca*).—A very handsome and good variety, of Italian origin. Bulb somewhat smaller than that of the Tripoli Onion, and still further distinguished from it by being of a chamois colour rather than decidedly

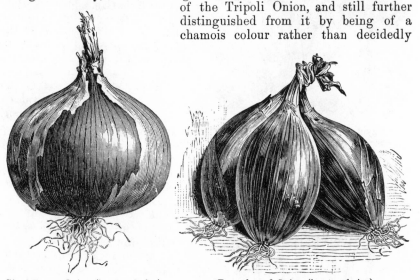

Giant Rocca Onion (⅓ natural size).   Pear-shaped Onion (⅓ natural size).

pink, and by being very perceptibly flattened on the top. The neck is fine for the size of the bulb, and the outer coats are firmer and tougher than those of the Tripoli Onions. The leaves are stout (but not excessively so), stiff, and of a clear-green colour. A well-grown bulb will have a diameter of nearly 5 inches, with a thickness of about 3½ inches. This is a half-late variety, very productive, keeps well, and, for a southern kind, does not do badly when sown in spring, although it succeeds far better when sown in autumn. It is one of the best kinds that have been introduced within the last fifteen years.

Pear-shaped Onion (*Ognon Piriforme*).—There are numerous varieties of long-bulbed Onions, which differ from one another in colour and earliness. In these, the broadest part of the bulb is usually found nearer to the neck than to the roots, so that the bulb narrows more abruptly at the neck end than it does towards the roots, and resembles a Pear with its stalk downwards. In Spain a White Pear-shaped Onion is cultivated. This is a late and large-sized kind, often growing nearly 5 inches long and about 3 inches in diameter. In France and Germany there are several other varieties of Pear-shaped Onions with a red or yellow skin, one of which grows so long that it is named the Ox-horn, or Spindle-shaped, Onion (*Ognon Corne de Bœuf*). These varieties, however, are more curious than useful.

To the Pear-shaped Onions may be referred the variety grown in England under the name of James's Keeping Onion (*Ognon de James*). The bulb of this variety is nearly as long as broad. It is not spherical, however, but it is almost flat at the top and narrows gradually towards the roots. It is of small or medium size, seldom exceeding a little over 2 inches in length. The outer coat or skin is of a coppery red, the neck is exceedingly fine, and the bulbs keep most remarkably well.

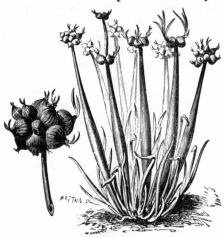

Tree, Egyptian, or Bulb-bearing, Onion (¹⁄₁₅ natural size; detached bulblets, ⅓ natural size).

Tree, Egyptian, or **Bulb-bearing, Onion** (*Ognon d'Egypte*).— Bulb rather flat, of a coppery colour. Instead of seeds, the stem produces at the extremity a cluster of bulblets, or small bulbs, of a brownish-red colour, and about the size of Hazel-nuts, from which the plant is propagated. When planted in spring, these small bulbs form large ones by the end of the year, but do not produce any bulblets until the following year. The flesh of the Tree Onion is tolerably agreeable to the taste, but rather deficient in delicacy of flavour. The bulbs soon decay, but the bulblets keep very well.

Catawissa Onion.—A few years since, a variety was introduced from America under the name of the *Catawissa Onion*, which appears to us to be only

Catawissa Onion (⅕ natural size).

a slight modification of the Tree Onion, from which it is distinguished by the great vigour of its growth and the rapidity with which the bulblets commence to grow without being detached from the top of the stem. These have hardly attained their full size, when they emit stems which also produce bulblets, and in favourable seasons this second tier of bulblets will emit green shoots, leaves, or barren stems, bringing the height of the plant up to over 2½ feet. Only a small number of bulblets (two or three on each stem) are thus proliferous. The rest do not sprout in the first year and can be used for propagating the plant. The plant is perennial, and may be propagated by division of the tufts, like the Welsh Onion.

Potato Onion (*Ognon Patate*).—Bulb rather large, from 2 to over 3 inches in diameter, and about 2 inches thick; skin thickish and of a coppery-yellow colour. This variety more frequently forms a cluster of underground bulbs of irregular shape than a single round bulb. It produces neither seeds nor bulblets, and is propagated only from the cloves or bulbs which are formed underground. If pretty strong cloves are planted immediately after winter, well-grown Onions may be gathered from them in the following June; but if the plants are allowed to attain full maturity, instead of a single bulb from each, seven or eight will be produced of various sizes. The strongest of these will also in their turn produce a number of bulbs or cloves, while the weaker ones generally grow into a single large bulb. The flesh of the Potato Onion is very agreeable to the taste and of good quality. The larger the bulbs are the worse they keep.

WELSH ONION, or CIBOULE.

Allium fistulosum, L.   *Liliaceæ.*

French, Ciboule. *German,* Schnittzwiebel. *Flemish,* Pijplook. *Dutch,* Bieslook. *Danish,* Purlog. *Italian,* Cipolletta. *Spanish,* Cebolleta. *Portuguese,* Cebolinha.

Native of Siberia or the East.—Perennial, but cultivated as an annual or biennial.—A plant very closely allied to the Common Onion in its botanical characteristics, although it does not form a bulb, properly so called, but only a small enlargement at the base of each shoot. Leaves numerous, hollow, of a rather dark-green colour, somewhat glaucous, and 10 to 14 inches long. In the second year, the flower-stem makes its appearance and grows about 20 inches high; it is swollen about the middle and terminates in a spherical cluster of flowers like those of the Common Onion. Culture.—The plant may be propagated by division, as each of the stems which are swollen at the base will speedily produce a new tuft; but, as it seeds abundantly, and the plants are apt to suffer in a severe winter, it is most usually raised from seed in preference. The soil should be good, and both well manured and well dug. The seed is sown, where the plants are to stand, from February to April or May. The only attention afterwards required is to water the plants and keep the beds free from weeds, as with Onions. In three months' time after sowing, the first cuttings of the leaves for use may be made. Uses.—The leaves, which have a strong Oniony flavour, are used for seasoning.

Common Welsh Onion, or Ciboule.—Bulbs or enlargements very long, of a coppery-red colour, and covered with dry membranes, like the outer coats of the Common Onion, which also cover the bases of the leaves for some distance overground; seed black, angular, flattened and concave on one of the sides or faces, and quite like the seed of the Common Onion. A gramme contains about 300 seeds, and a litre of

them weighs about 480 grammes. Their germinating power lasts for two or three years. This is the variety which is most commonly grown. It is productive and comparatively hardy.

Early White Welsh Onion (*Ciboule Blanche Hâtive*).—A very distinct variety, having the bulbs or enlargements shorter than those of the preceding or ordinary kind, and with pinkish-white coats, the overground part of which is of a silvery-white tint. Leaves short and stiff, of a dark glaucous-green colour, not so strong tasted as those of the ordinary kind, which they excel in delicacy of flavour. The seed also is

Common Welsh Onion, or Ciboule (⅓ natural size; detached stem, ¼ natural size).

smaller. A gramme contains 500 seeds or more, and a litre of them weighs about 520 grammes. Their germinating power continues for the same length of time. This variety appears to be sensitive to cold. In winter it loses its leaves entirely, but sends out new ones early in spring.

PERENNIAL WELSH ONION.

Allium lusitanicum, Lamk. *Liliaceæ.*

Ciboule vivace.

Bulbs numerous, very long, of a rather deep reddish-brown colour, attached to a common disc at the base; leaves of a very glaucous green colour, stiff, thick, and numerous. The plant sometimes produces flower-stems, which terminate in a globular cluster of pale violet-coloured flowers yielding no seed. This Onion is always multiplied by division of the tufts, and with this exception its culture is exactly similar to that of the ordinary variety.

Among the very numerous varieties of Onions which exist in addition to those just described, the following are the most noteworthy :—

Ognon d'Aigre.—A local variety, grown in the Department of Charente, which may be regarded as a sub-variety of the Niort Pale-red Onion, but has a flatter bulb.

Bedfordshire Champion Onion.—A fine English variety. Bulb nearly spherical, and of the colour of the White Spanish Onion. It is a little thicker than the Naseby Mammoth and its allies, which are mentioned further on.

Ognon Cabosse.—Bulb very flat and rather firm, with a very fine satiny skin of a slightly coppery or salmon-pink colour. The neck is very fine, and the disc or plate from which the roots issue is remarkably small. This fine variety is well adapted for sowing in autumn.

Cantello's Prize Onion.—Intermediate between the White Spanish and the Strasburg Onion. It comes near the numerous English varieties which are referred to the Deptford Onion. (See Strasburg Onion.)

Ognon Chamois Glatter Wiener.—A handsome coppery pink-coloured variety, with a fine neck and somewhat irregular shape. The Zittau Giant Onion appears to be an improved form of it.

Two-bladed Onion.—A very early small-sized kind, of a coppery-red colour, with a fine neck, which is almost sunk in the bulb. When this variety comes true from seed, most of the plants have only two or three leaves each, from which peculiarity it takes its name.

Yellow Russian Onion.—An exceedingly distinct kind. Bulbs rather small and thick, with the fault of frequently splitting into cloves, but still keeping better than any other kind. We have seen bulbs of this variety which were gathered in autumn keeping good for use until the September of the following year. The outer skin is very leathery; it is of a coppery colour, like that of the Strasburg Onion, but with age becomes as brown as the skin of a Tulip bulb.

Early Flat Red Onion.—An American variety. Bulb very flat, of the same size and earliness as the Early White Silver-skinned Onion, but of a dark-red colour, slightly tinged with violet. It is a very distinct kind, and bulbs remarkably early.

Ognon de Gênes.—Bulb red, of medium size, often splitting into several cloves. It is earlier and smaller than the Blood-red Flat Italian Onion.

Yellow Lescure Onion (*Ognon Jaune de Lescure*).—A handsome kind, much grown in the vicinity of Toulouse, and all through Langue-doc. It is chiefly adapted for sowing in autumn. The bulb somewhat resembles that of the Niort Pale-red Onion, but is not so flat, and its colour is much more of a yellow or coppery tinge.

Large Yellow Dutch Onion.—An American variety. Bulb yellow, of medium size, nearly the same shape as that of the Brown Spanish Onion, but of a more coppery colour, like that of the Danver's Onion.

Ognon Monteragone.—An Italian variety. Bulb medium sized, thickish, with a coppery-red skin, and rather like that of the Strasburg Onion.

Naseby Mammoth, Nuneham Park, and **Improved Reading Onion.**—These three varieties are so like one another that they may be considered identical. They are a form of the White Spanish Onion with the bulb thicker and somewhat darker coloured than that of the ordinary variety.

Ognon Nürnberger Zwiebel.—A German variety of the Common Pale-red Onion, from which it is distinguished by the smallness of the bulbs, which are also somewhat firmer and better shaped.

O. Paille Gros de Bâle.—A rather handsome, half-early variety, with a flat, well-shaped bulb, and a very fine neck, intermediate in colour between the White Spanish and the Strasburg Onion.

O. Paille de Château-Renard.—The bulb of this variety is more of a coppery or salmon colour than a true yellow, which its name would appear to indicate. It bears a considerable resemblance to the Lescure Onion.

O. de Puyrégner, or *O. Rouge Rosé d'Angers.*—In Anjou this variety is considered different from the Niort Pale-red Onion. We mention it here merely to state this, as from all the comparative trials we have made with it, it appears to us to be exactly the same.

Red Globe Onion.—An American variety, apparently only a spherical-bulbed form of the Wethersfield Onion.

Ognon Rouge de Castillon.—A handsome red flat Onion of large size, which is brought to Bordeaux in considerable quantities in autumn. It is tolerably like the Mézières Onion, but is often larger—more about the size of the Flat Tripoli. Like most large tender-fleshed Onions, it keeps badly.

O. Rouge Monstre.—A kind of Tripoli Onion, intermediate in shape between the Globe and the Flat varieties, and of a very decided red colour.

O. Rouge Pâle d'Alais.—A southern variety, suitable for sowing in autumn. It is tolerably like the Niort Pale-red Onion, but is thicker in the bulb.

O. Rouge Pâle de Tournon.—A very handsome, pink-tinged, yellow Onion, of rather large size, flat, and early. It greatly resembles the *O. Jaune de Lescure* mentioned above.

O. Rouge de Salon.—A southern variety, with a large but rather soft bulb, like that of the Tripoli Onions. In colour it quite resembles the Blood-red Flat Italian Onion, but it is notably thicker.

O. de Ténériffe.—A very distinct small-sized variety, with a very flat bulb of a grayish, pink colour. This is the earliest of all varieties next to the New Queen Onion, being even some days earlier than the Early White Nocera. It may be here remarked that in sowings of the last-named variety some coloured bulbs are almost always found which bear a marked resemblance to the Ténériffe Onion.

O. de Vaugirard.—This name is sometimes given to a somewhat earlier form of the Early Paris Silver-skinned Onion, but the variety is not well established nor very constant.

O. de Villefranche.—A handsome, medium-sized, very flat, and fine-necked variety, of a yellowish-pink or salmon colour. It is an early kind, keeps well, and is not unlike the Lescure Onion.

White Globe Onion.—Under this name is grown in England a variety with a spherical bulb of the colour of the White Spanish Onion, that is, a pale or greenish yellow. It is important not to confound this variety with the Globe Silver-skinned Onion, which is really white.

ORACHE.

Atriplex hortensis, L.　*Chenopodiaceæ.*

French, Arroche.　*German*, Gartenmelde.　*Flemish* and *Dutch*, Melde.　*Italian*, Atreplice.
Spanish, Armuelle.　*Portuguese*, Armolas.

Native of Tartary.—Annual.—A plant with broad, arrow-shaped, slightly crimped, soft, pliable leaves. Stems 5 to 6½ ft. high, angular, and furrowed; flowers apetalous, very small, and greenish or red, according to the variety; seed flat, russet coloured, surrounded by a leafy membrane of a light-yellow colour. The plant also produces some seeds, which are black, small, and disc-shaped, without any membranous appendage. These are not always fertile. The good seeds weigh about 140 grammes to the litre, and a gramme contains about 250 seeds. Their germinating power lasts for six years. CULTURE.—The seed is sown, where the plants are to stand, in the open ground in the beginning of March, usually in drills. When the seedlings have made three or four leaves they should be thinned out, after which they require no further attention, except occasional watering in very dry weather. The plants bear hot weather pretty well, but soon run to seed, on which account it is advisable to make successional sowings from month to month. USES.—The leaves are eaten boiled, like Spinach or Sorrel, and are often mixed with the latter to modify its acidity.

Orache ($\frac{1}{35}$ natural size).

The following are the three principal kinds of Orache which are most commonly cultivated in France:—

White Orache (*Arroche Blonde*).—This variety is more commonly grown than any other kind. The leaves are of a very pale green, almost yellow.

Dark-red Orache (*Arroche Rouge Foncé*).—The stems and leaves of this variety are of a dark-red colour, which gives it a very distinct appearance. The red colour disappears in cooking.

Green Orache, or Lee's Giant Orache (*Arroche Verte*).—A very vigorous-growing kind, with a stout, angular, branching stem. The leaves are rounder and less toothed that those of the White variety, from which they especially differ in being of a dark-green colour.

There is also a variety grown which has pale-red or copper-coloured leaves. This, however, does not possess any special merit.

Within the last few years some persons have spoken very highly of *Chenopodium auricomum*, Lindley—a tall, branching plant, with rather small leaves. This does not appear to be in any way superior to the Common Garden Orache, except perhaps for warm climates.

PARSLEY.

Apium Petroselinum, L. ; *Petroselinum sativum*, Hoffm.   *Umbelliferæ.*

French, Persil.   *German,* Petersilie.   *Flemish* and *Dutch,* Pieterselie.   *Danish,* Petersilje.
Italian, Prezzemolo.   *Spanish,* Perejil.   *Portuguese,* Selsa.

Native of Sardinia.—Biennial.—During the first year of its growth the Parsley plant only forms a more or less full rosette of long-stalked leaves, which are two or three times divided, and of a dark-green colour ; the divisions are toothed, more or less entire, or, in some varieties, finely cut. The flower-stem, which does not appear until the second year, is erect, branching, furrowed, and from 2 to over $2\frac{1}{2}$ ft. high. Flowers small, of a greenish-blue colour, in terminal umbels ; seeds three-sided, grayish or light brown, flat on two sides and convex on the third, where they are marked with five prominent ribs. They are strongly aromatic, like all the other parts of the plant. A gramme contains about 350 seeds, and a litre of them weighs a little over 500 grammes. Their germinating power lasts for three years at least.

CULTURE.—The seed may be sown in the open air, from March to August or September, either on the edges of beds containing other plants or in separate beds, in drills 10 or 12 inches apart. It is usually rather slow in germinating, seldom doing so in less than a month. If the seedlings are properly thinned, and the beds kept free from weeds and frequently watered, some leaves will be fit to cut in about three months after sowing. It is a good plan to cut only the best-grown leaves one by one, as Sorrel leaves are gathered, as when this is done the plants yield a more prolonged supply than when whole tufts are cut off at once. As Parsley is somewhat sensitive to cold, it is advisable, in order to keep up the supply in winter, to put a frame over a bed in full bearing, choosing, if possible, one containing young plants which were sown about August. Old well-established plants also might be taken up and forced in a plant-house or a hot-bed, in the same way as Asparagus stools.

Simple as the matter is to many, others find it difficult to secure a constant supply of good Parsley, owing to haphazard ways of sowing and to subsequent neglect. The following extracts from *Gardening*, written in reply to a question on the subject, furnish good general cultural directions: "An open plot should be selected, but it should be protected from the northern and eastern winter's blast. This should be trenched, or at least deeply dug, and liberally manured. The seed should be sown the first week in June, so that the plants may get large and strong before winter sets in. When the seedlings are large enough, they should be thinned out to at least a foot apart each way. I should have stated that, as the plants grow but slowly in winter, a much larger piece of land must be sown than would be required for a summer's supply. It would be advisable to make a sowing in a pit or frame for use when frost and snow are on the ground; or if four short stakes were driven into the ground, and connected with cross-pieces, so as to be in readiness for laying boards, faggots, or wattle hurdles across on the approach of hard frost, the same end would be attained. A sowing should be made in July for late spring use. March is the time to sow

for a summer supply. Sometimes failure ensues, not from defective cultivation, but because the young seedlings are destroyed by vermin as soon as they appear; or, as is often the case, as the seeds must not be buried deep, and are a considerable time germinating, when dry weather sets in after sowing, the seeds perish. To guard against failure from either of these causes, at the same time the seeds are sown in the open ground some should be sown in a box or pan, so that should failure arise in the first instance, there would be a supply of young seedlings that could be potted into small pots. These young plants, when ready, should be put out in the ground where the seeds failed to germinate. It is safer to shift the young seedlings into small pots than to prick them into boxes, because, when, in the latter case, they are taken up with balls of earth and put into the ground, the injury done to the roots in the operation causes flagging, and makes the plants very palatable to slugs. Nor is the potting so formidable a matter as to some it might appear. Old potting stuff or common garden soil would do for the purpose, and a man of ordinary quickness would pot off a hundred plants in an hour."—L. C. R.

"Sow thinly in March and again at

the end of July for succession on land that has been heavily manured for the previous crop, and which should be deeply trenched. Sow in beds broadcast when the ground is dry, and well tread in. By doing so, some of the seeds will be in the exact depth to germinate freely and make nice healthy plants, which should be left when thinning out, say 12 inches apart if large specimens are required. A slight dressing of soot will be of service when plants are thinned, which put on when damp. If your soil is light in texture, well roll or tread, as I find Parsley does well with me on light soil when ground is so treated. Sutton's Giant Curled is a very robust and well-curled variety."—E. T. P.

" In preparing a Parsley bed, the soil should be removed to the depth of 6 or 8 inches, and filled in with stones, brick-rubbish, and similar loose material ; on the top a good depth of rich soil should be placed, which should be raised above the level of the ground. Sow at the end of May seed of the most early variety. If the weather continues dry, water frequently until the plants are up, which will be in five or six weeks. When large enough, thin them out to 4 or 5 inches apart. Parsley when well up requires very little water ; the roots should be kept in a rather dry state."—A. N.

" It is thought that Parsley will grow anywhere, but I have found that in some classes of soil the roots are attacked by canker of some kind. The main stem has a rusty appearance, and many of the fibrous roots decay. You should work the ground to the depth of a foot, giving it a good dressing of rotten stable manure. Sow the seeds in March. To make sure of Parsley in winter, the leaves must be cut off about the first week in September ; this will be the cause of a sturdy late autumn growth, which will stand best through the winter."—J. D. E.

MARKET-GARDEN CULTURE.— Parsley is grown to a large extent in some market gardens about London, whilst in others none can be found. The seed is sown in successional batches from March to August in rich soil, and generally where the plants are to remain, transplantation being considered detrimental to its producing good foliage ; it also induces the plants to run to seed sooner than they otherwise would do. When up, the young plants are thinned out to a proper distance apart by means of hoes, and some growers protect a large bed of it during winter ; but, as a rule, this kind of treatment is not considered sufficiently remunerative to be carried out on a large scale.

USES.—The leaves, which are aromatic, are much used, raw or boiled, for flavouring, garnishing, etc.

Common, or **Plain, Parsley** (*Persil Commun*).—The characteristics of this plant being exactly the same as those of the typical species described above, we need not repeat them here, and shall merely observe with respect to this form of Parsley, that it is the only one that might be easily confounded with Fool's Parsley (*Æthusa Cynapium*, L.), a native and virulently poisonous plant. The leaves of the two plants are so much alike that even

Common, or Plain, Parsley (⅓ natural size).

a practical gardener cannot distinguish one from the other with certainty unless he tests them by taste and smell. When Parsley is grown for flavouring sauces, etc., it is a matter of great importance that every precaution should be taken to prevent a poisonous plant being mistaken for it. This could be done most effectually and easily by making it a rule never to grow any kind except the Curled-leaved or Fern-leaved varieties, which are quite as good for flavouring as the Common Parsley, and much better for garnishing. As these kinds do not seed very plentifully, and require some care to keep the varieties pure, the seed is rather dearer than that of the Common Parsley, but so little of it is sufficient for a garden, and the perfect security from danger which is ensured by growing only these kinds is so precious, that the matter of cost is really hardly worth mentioning.

Neapolitan, or **Celery-leaved Parsley** (French, *Persil Grand de Naples*; Italian, *Prezzemolo di Spagna*).—This variety differs from the Common Parsley in the large size of its leaves and leaf-stalks, which are thick and stout in proportion to their length. It may be grown just like the common kind, or the stalks may be blanched and used like Celery. In the latter case, the plants are grown in the same manner as Celery, being planted out in trenches which are gradually filled up in autumn in order to blanch the stalks. These, it is said, taste like Celery, and are more easily grown, as the plant requires less water than Celery, and is not so liable to suffer from "rust." This mode of growing the Neapolitan Parsley, however, has not yet been practised in France, and we must confess that we speak of it from hearsay and not from our own experience.

Double-Curled Parsley (*Persil Frisé*).—In this variety, the divisions of the leaves are rather deeply cut, and each of the small segments thus formed is more or less turned back on the upper side, giving the whole leaf a crisped or curled appearance which has a rather pleasing effect.

In some forms of Curled Parsley, the segments of the leaf are

turned back so much as to show almost the whole of the under side, which is of a paler and more grayish green than the upper side. Of this kind are the forms known as the *Windsor Curled Parsley* and *Smith's Curled Parsley*. These kinds are not so pleasing in appearance as the Common Curled Parsley, as their leaves always have something of the look of being blemished or diseased.

Double - curled Dwarf Parsley (*Persil Nain Très Frisé*).—A sub - variety of Curled Parsley, remarkable

Double-curled Dwarf Parsley (⅓ natural size).

for the fineness of the cutting and the great number of the divisions of the leaves. The segments touch one another, and give the leaf the appearance of a piece of very dense Moss. In this form the leaf-stalks are exceedingly short, so that the leaves almost lie upon the ground, forming a very low thick tuft. This is the best Parsley of all to use as "greenery" for decorative purposes, and for garnishing dishes. It is also quite as aromatic as the other kinds.

Fern-leaved Parsley (*Persil à Feuille de Fougère*).—In this variety the leaves are not curled, but are divided into a very great number

Fern-leaved Parsley (⅕ natural size).

Early Hamburgh Parsley (⅕ natural size).

Late Hamburgh Parsley
(⅕ natural size).

of small thread-like segments, giving the whole plant a very light and graceful appearance. The plant is also distinguished by the very dark colour of the leaves, which are of an almost blackish green. It is one of the most difficult kinds to preserve quite pure.

Hamburgh, Large-rooted, or Turnip-rooted Parsley (*Persil à Grosse Racine*).—In this kind of Parsley it is not the leaves, but the thick fleshy roots, which form the edible part of the plant. These roots, which are of a dingy-white colour, and almost like Parsnip roots, often grow 6 inches long, with a diameter of about 2 inches in the thickest part, which is usually close to the neck. The flesh is white and somewhat dry. In flavour, it resembles the Celeriac, or Turnip-rooted Celery, but is not so delicate. The leaves are exactly like those of the Common Parsley. In Germany, where this plant is rather extensively cultivated, there are two varieties grown, viz. a late one, which has long slender roots, and an early one, the roots of which are shorter and thicker. These varieties do not appear to us to be very constant, and the difference in the weight of their respective produce is rather slight. The early or thick-rooted variety is grown like the Parsnip. The seed is sown immediately after winter in well-dug soil, and the roots may commence to be gathered in September. They are not affected by frost, and may be left in the ground until it arrives. This plant is not one of the old-fashioned vegetables, but, like the Bulbous-rooted Chervil, was taken in hand and introduced into cultivation at a comparatively recent date.

It is very probable that, amongst plants which are not yet in cultivation, and especially amongst the biennial Umbelliferous plants, it would be possible to bring some of them to produce fleshy roots of sufficient size to form useful vegetables. The result of one experiment which was undertaken by us for a purely scientific purpose, confirms us in this opinion. The Beaked Parsley (*Anthriscus sylvestris*, L.), a wild plant of our woods, at the end of ten years' repeated sowings and methodical selection, produced in some sowings a proportion of one-half or more of simple, clean-skinned, fusiform roots, as regular in shape as the best roots of the Hamburgh Parsley. Now, in the wild state the root of this plant is as forked and divided as that of the Celery. The progress made, therefore, was considerable, and it is to be observed that the plants thus improved represented only the fifth generation from the wild plant, as the *Anthriscus*, being a biennial, does not seed until the second year.

PARSNIPS.

Pastinaca sativa, L.   *Umbelliferæ.*

French, Panais.   *German*, Pastinake.   *Flemish* and *Dutch*, Pastenaak.   *Dutch*, Pinkster nakel.   *Danish*, Pastinak.   *Italian*, Pastinaca.   *Spanish*, Chirivia.   *Portuguese* Pastinaga.

Native of Europe.—Biennial.—Root a very long tap, white, swollen, and fleshy ; radical leaves divided, as far as the midrib, into irregular toothed segments ; leaf-stalks overlapping, and often violet coloured at the base ; stem hollow, furrowed, branching, bearing at the extremity broad umbels of greenish flowers, succeeded by very flat, almost circular seeds, which are winged at the margin, of a light-brown colour, and marked with five raised lines or ridges. A gramme contains about 220 seeds, and a litre of them weighs about 200 grammes. Their germinating power lasts for two years.

CULTURE.—Parsnips are grown in the same manner as Carrots, only they may be sown earlier in the year—about the end of February or early in March. The seed cannot always be depended on for germinating, and, in dry climates, often fails to do so, from the want of atmospheric moisture. Being a very hardy plant, the crop may be left in the ground until late in autumn, or even all through the winter, and taken up as the roots are required.

SOIL.—Although the Parsnip will grow in almost any kind of soil, it succeeds best in land that is neither over-light and sandy on the one hand, nor too heavy and adhesive on the other. The form of the root, penetrating as it does for a considerable distance straight down, at once shows the necessity for a sufficient depth of soil to admit of its extending; consequently the ground should be well and deeply dug, so as to readily allow its descent whilst the root is young and delicate. The soil should be moderately rich for Parsnips to grow to a large size, in which condition they are quite different, both in flavour and texture, from the stunted, starved productions resulting from poor hungry land and negligent cultivation. But although the Parsnip likes to be well nourished, it is not advisable to grow it in land that has immediately before received a heavy dressing of manure, as so treated the roots are liable to be cankered or affected with grub. It is best to grow it after some other crop that has been well manured, such as Onions, Cauliflowers, or Lettuce, trenching or deeply digging the ground over in the autumn, and leaving it as rough as possible on the surface. Should the soil not be suitable for the crop on account of its poverty, some manure ought to be added in the autumn, which will be much better than adding it at the time of sowing; mixing it regularly with the soil as the work proceeds.

SOWING AND THINNING. — About the middle or latter end of March, according as the locality may be early or late, as soon as the land is sufficiently dry, let it be well forked, reducing all the hard lumps that exist—not merely making it smooth on the surface, but quite as deep as the fork or spade goes. This is necessary for most plants, but particularly so for Parsnips, or the roots are liable to grow forked. With this, as with all other spring-sown crops, never be guided by a certain date, even to a week, in the time of sowing, if the state of the land be such as not to favour the sowing of the seed; it is always better to wait than sow when the soil is too wet—the effect of which is that it does not germinate freely, and the land gets compressed and never works kindly throughout the whole season. Sow in drills 1 inch deep, and from 15 to 18 inches apart, according to the more or less rich condition of the land. All that is afterwards required is timely thinning, leaving the plants 10 or 12 inches apart in the rows, and the careful destruction of weeds by frequent hoeings throughout the season.

STORING.—With the view of being handy to get at, many take up the roots towards the end of October and store them in sand or ashes; but they are vastly superior if left in the ground. In this way they are not liable to get spongy or strong flavoured, which they sometimes do when stored under cover. If the ground occupied by the crop is required for other purposes the roots may be dug up and stuck in mounds or clamps, in the same manner as Potatoes, or a deep trench may be dug and the roots placed perpendicularly in it close together, afterwards covering them over with soil to a depth of 6 inches.

In the London market gardens, Parsnips are always sown as soon after the middle of February as possible, provided the ground is moderately dry and warm, and crumbles freely with the fork. Preparatory to sowing, the ground is levelled, and the soil well broken in the operation, and finished off by raking the surface smooth with a wooden rake. Shallow drills are then drawn for the seeds at about 18 or 20 inches apart; and after being sown they are covered in by the feet or the back of a rake, and the whole is smoothly rolled. Sometimes white or green Cos Lettuces have been planted in rows at the above distances, and the Parsnips are sown in lines between them. In either case, Lettuces are planted—if not first, they are put in afterwards; and as the Parsnips take a long time to germinate, the Lettuces are removed before they can injure them. As soon as the Parsnips are fairly up and growing, they are thinned out a little, and when well established, they are finally thinned to 9 inches apart. The Lettuces, when marketable, are tied up and removed before they can choke or otherwise injure the Parsnips, which afterwards soon grow rapidly, no further care than occasional hoeing being then bestowed upon them. The bulk of roots per acre is enormous, many of the specimens measuring individually 7 and 8 inches in diameter at the shoulder, and 20 to 24 inches in length. The variety grown in market gardens is the Hollow Crown, a capital sort, that produces roots from 4 to 6 inches in diameter at top, and from 10 to 20 inches in length; and the crowns are, as a rule, buried a little below the surface soil. Parsnips are not brought to market much before November, unless the demand for them is great and prices high. But from that time until the middle of February, they are in fine marketable condition, and, being always left in the land where they grow, are lifted as required. Being thus left undisturbed, they preserve their flavour much better than they do when lifted and stored in pits.

Long Parsnip (⅕ natural size).

USES.—The roots are eaten boiled, and are often used for flavouring broth or soup without being eaten. They also form an excellent food for horses, and are extensively used for that purpose in districts where Parsnips are easily and successfully grown, as in Brittany.

Long Parsnip (*Panais Long*).—This form, which comes the nearest to the Wild Parsnip, is now very little grown. It is characterized by having a very long root, often 16 inches in length, deeply sunk in the ground, and an elongated conical neck.

The **Improved Brest Parsnip** (*Panais Amélioré de Brest*) is a thicker and shorter form of the old Long Parsnip. It also has a conical neck and a wrinkled skin. It has the advantage of being productive, while the roots are more easily pulled than those of the old variety; however, the following kind is far superior to it.

Hollow Crown, or **Student, Parsnip** (*Panais Long de Guernesey*).—Root handsome, long, thick, very clean skinned, with a fine neck surrounded by a circular gutter-like depression, from the centre of which the leaves issue, the root being swollen all round it. The root is generally only about three or four times as long as broad, and has a smooth white skin, whereas that of the Common Long Parsnip is wrinkled and furrowed. The leaves also of the Hollow

Crown Parsnip are much smaller and fewer for the size of the root. There is quite as great a difference between this variety and the Common Long Parsnip as there is between a variety that has been modified and improved by cultivation and one that is almost wild. The Hollow Crown Parsnip is the best and the most productive of the Long Parsnips. The English variety, *Sutton's Student,* is a superior-flavoured local form of it, and El-combe's Improved is a first-class variety, of excellent flavour. Although it is both large enough and hardy enough to be grown for cattle-feeding, the Hollow Crown Parsnip is essentially a table vegetable, and as such it is chiefly cultivated.

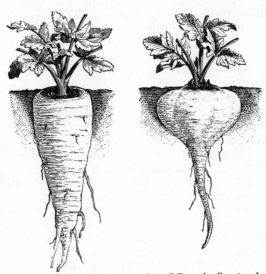

Hollow Crown, or Student, Parsnip (⅓ natural size).

Round Parsnip (⅓ natural size).

It is not quite so early as the Round Parsnip, but is more productive.

Round Parsnip (*Panais Rond*).—Root top-shaped, broader than long, often 5 or 6 inches across and 3 or 4 inches in depth. The leaves of this variety are fewer and slighter than those of the Long Parsnips; the root also swells much sooner. It is the best kind for kitchen-garden culture.

PEAS.

Pisum sativum, D.C. *Leguminosæ.*

French, Pois. *German,* Erbse. *Flemish* and *Dutch,* Erwt. *Danish,* Haveœrt. *Italian,* Pisello. *Spanish,* Guisante. *Portuguese,* Ervilha.

The Pea is an annual plant, of uncertain origin, but probably a native of Central Europe or the mountainous region of Western Asia, as it is hardy enough to withstand the winter generally in the climate of Paris. The cultivated Pea has slender hollow stems which require some support to enable them to grow erect. The leaves are compound, pinnate without an odd one, the leaf-stalk terminating in several tendrils which take the place of the odd leaflet, and enable the plant to climb by attaching themselves to any object within their reach. The base of the leaf-stalk is surrounded by a very broad clasping stipule, which is larger than any of the leaflets. The flowers are produced in the axils of the leaves, commencing almost regularly at a certain height from the ground in each variety, either in pairs, or often solitary, and very rarely three together, at each joint of the stem. The market gardeners about Paris give the name of "*mailles*" to the

2 c

flower-bearing joints of the Pea-stem, and when they want to describe a variety as one-flowered or two-flowered, they say that it " has one or two flowers to the '*maille.*' " The flowers are sometimes white, and sometimes violet coloured, with the wings and keel of a darker shade than the standard. The varieties which have coloured flowers may be distinguished, long before they come into bloom, by having a small reddish circle around the stem where it is clasped by the stipules.

The seeds of the violet-flowered Peas are always more or less tinged or spotted with brown. When boiled, they turn to an unattractive grayish colour, and have a rather strong rough flavour, in consequence of which they are not grown for table use. The varieties of Gray Peas which have tough leathery pods are only grown for feeding cattle, and the kitchen-garden varieties of these have pods without any leathery or parchmenty inner lining.

Most of the varieties which are grown for table use have white flowers, and the seed also is white or green when ripe. The size and weight of the seed vary too much in the different varieties to permit us to treat of them here in a general manner, but we shall mention these matters in detail in the description of each variety. We shall only observe that the germinating power of the seed lasts good for three years, after which it speedily declines, although it is not unusual to find some seeds germinating well after seven or eight years. Wrinkled Peas usually do not germinate so well as the Smooth-skinned, or round, Peas, nor does their germinating power last so long.

Among the very numerous varieties of Peas, a distinction is made between those of which only the seeds, whether green or dried, are eaten, and which are termed Shelling Peas (*Pois à Écosser*), and those of which the pods are eaten entire when the seeds are hardly formed in them; these are called Edible-podded, or Sugar, Peas (*Pois sans Parchemin*).

Among the varieties of Shelling Peas, a distinction is made between the Smooth or Round-seeded and the Wrinkled kinds, the latter of which are now nearly as numerous as the others. And lastly, both the Edible-podded and the Shelling Peas are divided into the three classes of Tall, Half-dwarf, and Dwarf Peas (*Pois à Rames, P. Demi-Nains, and P. Nains*). All these differences, without taking into account the green or white colour of the seeds, have caused the cultivated varieties of Peas to be grouped into several classes or subdivisions, under which we shall describe each kind in succession.

CULTURE.—The cultivation of Peas presents no great difficulty, and in the vicinity of Paris and other large towns it is carried on in the open fields on a large scale, and usually very profitably. The soil in which they are grown should be, as far as possible, well drained, rich, and of a medium consistence. The seed is sown in drills, from the middle of November to March. The Early Frame Pea (*Pois Michaux Ordinaire*) is the kind most used about Paris for sowing in autumn, on which account it has obtained the name of St. Catherine's Pea (*Pois de Sainte-Catherine*). These November sowings might also be very advantageously made in kitchen gardens, in which case the seed should be sown in a border at the bottom of a wall with a south aspect, using the earliest kinds of all, such as Ringleader (Prince Albert, Sangster's No. 1), Caractacus, or the Early Dwarf Frame

Pea. The last-mentioned kind, as its name indicates, is most suitable for growing in a hot-bed. It is exceedingly early, very dwarf, takes up very little room, and there is no need to bend down its stems with laths or cross-bars, as was formerly done when, before its introduction, tall or half-dwarf varieties were grown in frames.

Successional sowings in the open air should be made all through the spring, in order to ensure a continuous supply through the summer. After the early varieties, the next sowings consist of tall kinds, which are later, more productive, and less liable to suffer from mildew during hot weather. The Clamart Pea (*Pois de Clamart*) and the tall varieties of Wrinkled Peas are particularly good kinds for late sowings, the crop from which comes in at the end of summer or early in autumn.

In kitchen gardens, tall Peas are staked with branches of trees, chestnut-loppings being mostly used for this purpose in the vicinity of Paris; but when grown in the open fields, they are seldom staked, on account of the cost and labour which the operation would involve. In the absence of stakes, the stems of the Peas are pinched off just above the third or fourth joint, after which they grow sufficiently stiff and firm to support themselves. This treatment, however, which answers very well for varieties of moderate height, such as the Michaux Peas, does not suit the tall kinds, such as the Tall Wrinkled Peas, and these, accordingly, are not employed for field culture.

When Peas are once well up and staked (if they require it) they need no further attention except occasional watering in dry weather. Transplanting is only practised with very early Peas, which are raised in pots in a plant-house or under frames, to be planted out as soon as winter is over, and its advantages are not quite certain.

With every suitable appliance the Pea season may extend from the beginning of July till the end of October, and I have, in exceptional seasons, gathered a dish of Peas as late as the 10th of November. But those Peas gathered early in May are grown under glass, and the very late Peas are, of course, mainly dependent upon the season. The best months for Peas are June and July. In warm situations the produce of the early south border begins to turn in about the end of May, and green Peas are common enough in June, but July is the month for excellent Marrow Peas. In August and September, unless the land is good and the treatment very liberal and first-rate in every respect, the Peas are very likely to fall away, and if they do not cease to bear, the pods lose their fresh green colour, and the peas in the coshes are infested with maggots, and if mildew makes its appearance the chapter of ills is complete. Most of these evils may be successfully combated, as I shall show presently. But we will begin with

THE FIRST EARLY PEAS.—These, where glass can be had sufficient for our needs, will comprise several small supplies in pots of some approved dwarf kind, which should be sown in 8-inch pots in November, and be brought on steadily in a pit close to the glass with just the smallest amount of artificial warmth, as Peas do not force well in heat; and therefore it will not do to be impatient. A steady, regular growth, in a very light position, with a temperature never exceeding 45° to 50° at night, will be best. Ventilation must be given at every suitable opportunity. The first sowing in the open air may take place any time from the beginning of November till March, and the probabilities are that if the same kind of Peas are planted at both these extreme limits of time, there would not be more than ten days' difference in the time of gathering! But even then the week or ten days gained is thought much of. In cold, wet districts it is as well not to sow till after Christmas, as in such situations the early sown crops are not unfrequently cut off by cold winds. Very often the first early Peas are raised under glass, and when hardened planted out early in March. The seeds of a white round early Pea, such as Sangster's No. 1, are sown in pots or troughs, or on sods of turf, and placed in heat, where they soon germinate, when they are hardened off and planted on a warm south border the first week in March. A ridge of earth is drawn up on each side as a shelter, and a few evergreen boughs are added as a further protection.

Mr. Muir advises sowing early Peas in cold frames, and not in warmer houses or pits :—" I like a frame about 2 ft. deep better than any other structure in which to raise early Peas. Fill some hundreds of small 3-inch pots half full of soil, then put in ten or a dozen seeds, finish off with more soil, and place them in a frame covered with a good sash; they will soon germinate and make fine, sturdy, dark green-leaved plants, which may be planted out almost at any time without receiving the slightest check. If a batch were placed in a cold frame and another in a warm house at the same time, by April the frame ones would be by far the best as regards robustness and fertility. There is no better place than a cold frame in which to raise early Peas, and I would advise everybody, especially amateurs, to try Pea-growing in this way. No expense is incurred in getting them up or anxiety in getting them put out and hardened off, as by judicious air-giving on fine days they may be grown from the first in a most natural way, and induced to pod some weeks earlier than any grown wholly in the open ground." The second early

Peas may be sown at the same time as the early kinds, when these are not sown before the end of February.

SUCCESSION.—To keep up a regular succession, there should be frequent sowings; taking account of and giving due weight to the fact that all Peas sown during the months of January, February, and the first half of March, will not vary more than a week or ten days at the time of turning in. There will not be much use in making successional sowings during these months. As a matter of fact I have often sown at intervals of a fortnight or so in order to test the matter, and I have always found that to obtain a succession from first sowing the best plan is to sow at least three or four distinct sorts at the same time, including an early kind, a mid-season one, and a late variety. After April comes in sow the succeeding crop as the preceding one is just through the ground. The following dates may be taken as approximately correct. They are founded upon a good deal of experience and careful note-taking; and, making due allowance for the effect of latitude upon climate, and the variations of soil and seasons, may be safely acted upon. Early white round Peas, sown before Christmas, or not later than the first week in January, should be fit to gather the last week in May. Those of a second early type, sown from the end of January to the end of February, should be fit to gather from June 10 to 20; Huntingdonian and Telephone, sown from February 20 to March 10, should be fit for use from June 20 to the middle of July, or later. Marrow Peas, such as Veitch's Perfection and Ne Plus Ultra, sown from middle to end of March, should be ready about the middle of July and onwards. The tall Marrows, sown first and third week in April and first and third week in May, should produce a supply from the middle of July till the close of the Pea season. But most people sow second earlies once or twice in June, and I have had the late Marrows do well sown as late as the middle of June. As to the manner of planting

THE LATE MARROW PEAS.—The crop is so important that every expedient should be adopted which can in any way enable it to pass through its difficulties without much suffering. Men may be seen labouring heavily with watering-pots in a dry, hot time, when less than half the time and labour in preparatory work at the right season would have given more satisfactory results. Mark out the sites, in January or February, open a trench, and fill in with a manurial compost—Peas dislike rank manure — of the usual decaying matters which accumulate about a garden, mixed with a proportion of manure from the stables or pigsty, with a little soot, etc.; blend the whole together and work into the trench, where the Peas will by-and-by be planted. When this is done early in the season, the added compost has become mellow and in a fit condition for the roots of the plants to work among at once. As much of the soil taken out of the trench may be thrown back and worked up with the compost as will fill the trench to the original level. The bottom of the trench will also be stirred up and incorporated. All the stations required for the late Peas should be got ready at the same time, and a stump driven down at the end of each row, so that when one wants to put in a row of Peas all he has to do is to place a line along the line of stumps, draw a drill about 3 inches deep, and plant the Peas.

SOWING AND GATHERING. — The large Marrow Peas should be allowed room to branch out, not only below the surface, as the preparation of the site suggested above will provide for, but also above the ground, as must be provided for by thin planting. From 2 to 3 inches apart all over the drill will not be too much space to allow; and this will necessitate the careful distribution of the seeds individually by hand. In dry weather the drills should be soaked with water, and then covered with the dry soil drawn from the drills. If mice are likely to be troublesome, dress the seeds with red lead, or else keep traps set in the neighbourhood of the Pea row. To do the late Peas justice the rows should be isolated, with other dwarf crops between. Mulching with manure is a valuable expedient, and, in connection with a good preparation of the land at this season, should render watering, even in the driest weather, unnecessary. The mulch, which should consist of half-decayed stable manure, should be spread on both sides of the rows of Peas, 18 inches or so wide, and 3 or 4 inches thick. Gathering should be done carefully and as soon as they are fit for use, and in many cases a second crop of young shoots and blossoms will put forth, and a second crop of Peas, which will be very useful, will be produced.

TALL AND DWARF PEAS.—Dwarf Peas are very useful where sticks or supports cannot easily be obtained; but where sticks do not cost much, for the main crop tall Peas are best, as they are more prolific. In the case of all Peas requiring support—and, if possible, all Peas, even those of dwarf habit, should be supported— the sticks should be placed to the rows early, and the tops of the sticks should be levelled with the shears, and the pieces cut off be used between the large sticks at the base, to prevent the plants straggling through, and to give them an upward tendency.

Nearly all market gardeners near London grow Peas largely; and although French Peas are sent to market early in May, and sold at cheaper rates than English growers could afford to produce them, preference is always given to home-grown Peas, for which there is always a good demand until about September. Until the end of October, however, fine examples of the Ne Plus Ultra type may be obtained ready shelled in the market, the produce in many instances of the Surrey fields, Bedfordshire, Essex, and adjoining counties, from whence come the greater bulk of both early and mid-season Peas to Covent Garden. In making early sowings it is a practice with market gardeners to choose a fine day to break down the ridges (the ground having been previously manured and cast into ridges), measure off the lines and draw drills in the forenoon, and to leave them open till the afternoon, so that the soil in them may dry a little, and become thereby warmer; then to sow the seeds and cover all up before the evening. The drills vary from 2 to 3½ feet apart, according to the vigour of the sorts which are to be sown. In the close lines, Lettuces or Spinach are used as inter-crops, but in the more distant ones Cauliflower is the crop usually planted. In many instances the first sowing of Peas is made in December on a warm border; but, considering that they must be sown a little deeper than in January, and the risks to which the seeds are liable from mice, birds, insects, and damp, it is a much-disputed point among good growers whether the December sowing has any advantage over that made in January, many contending that the produce of the latter is quite as early as that of the former, and the crop less subject to risks. Different growers have a preference for different kinds; but the early dwarf kinds are universally the most desired, on account of their quick returns, the small space they occupy, and because they require no stakes.

Peas are seldom staked in market gardens, the haulm being allowed to lie on the ground. Gathering is a matter well attended to, as the oftener the pods are picked when full the longer do the plants continue to bear. Most market gardeners save their own seed, and some grow Peas for seed only; in this case the haulm is frequently shifted from one side of the row to the other in order to prevent the pods from rotting, or from being destroyed by snails, and to expose them to the air and sun, and thus cause them all to ripen alike. When ripe, the haulm is pulled up and dried, and taken indoors to be cleared of its seed during wet weather.

USES.—The seeds are eaten boiled, either in the green or the dried state, and the young pods of the Edible-podded kinds are used in the same way.

SHELLING PEAS.

French, Pois à écosser. *German*, Schal-Erbsen. *Flemish* and *Dutch*, Doperwten. *Danish*, Skalœrte. *Italian*, Piselli da sgranare. *Spanish*, Guisantes para desgranar. *Portuguese*, Ervilhas de grão.

I. Round or Smooth Peas.

A. TALL CLIMBING VARIETIES.

Pois à rames.

Tall Round or Smooth White-seeded Peas.

Sangster's No. 1, Ringleader, or **Prince Albert Pea** (*Pois Prince Albert*).—Stem slender, 2 to over 2½ ft. high, commencing to flower at the fifth or sixth joint, and producing from six to eight tiers of pods; flowers usually solitary, white, and of medium size; pods straight, about 2 inches long, somewhat square at the end, each containing from five to seven very round peas, which often remain slightly greenish or acquire a salmon-coloured hue when ripe. A litre of the peas weighs, on an average, 780 grammes, and 10 grammes contain about 50 peas.

Sangster's No. 1, or Ringleader, Pea
($\frac{1}{10}$ natural size).

Pods (natural size).

A remarkable peculiarity of this variety is that the flower, which makes its appearance lowest down on the stem, often withers without expanding, and sometimes, when it does open well, it is not until after the flower at the joint above it has come out. This variety is the earliest of all the kinds commonly grown in France. In England a sub-variety, named Dillistone's Early, is grown, which is three or four days earlier, but the plant is slenderer and less productive. The present variety is the best for an early crop in the open air.

Dickson's First and Best, Improved Early Champion, or Taber's Perfection Pea (*Pois Caractacus*).—This variety is probably the offspring of the preceding one, and is a somewhat larger and more productive kind, but not quite so early. It usually comes into flower two days later. It often produces the pods in pairs, and they are somewhat longer and broader than those of the preceding kind. The peas, which are white and round, weigh about 780 grammes to the litre, and there are about 45 of them in 10 grammes. This variety is very liable to degenerate, and it should be very carefully isolated,

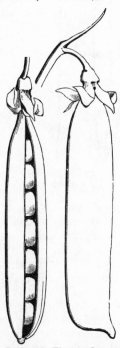

Dickson's First and Best
Pea (natural size).

when grown, to keep it true. In the vicinity of Paris it is rather extensively grown for market supply. It is not so productive as the Early Emperor Pea, but has the advantage of coming in four or five days earlier.

Daniel O'Rourke Pea (*Pois Daniel O'Rourke*).—Stem 2 to 2½ ft. high; leaves somewhat larger, rounder, and lighter coloured than those of Sangster's No. 1 Improved; flowers white, rather large, solitary, commencing to appear at the sixth joint of the stem; pods somewhat longer and broader than those of Sangster's No. 1 Improved; peas rather large, becoming of a greenish-white or salmon-colour when ripe. A litre of them weighs, on an average, 790 grammes, and 10 grammes

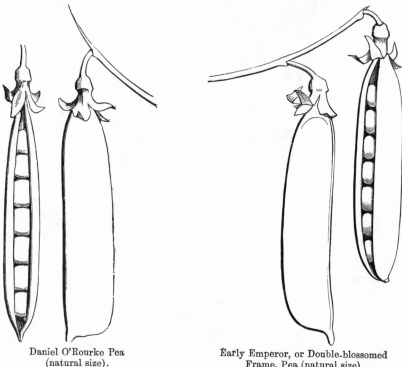

Daniel O'Rourke Pea
(natural size).

Early Emperor, or Double-blossomed
Frame, Pea (natural size).

contain about 45 peas. This variety is quite as early as the preceding one, and about equally good. The two kinds are very closely allied, and are sometimes confounded with each other, although a well-marked difference may be observed by any one who studies them carefully. The Daniel O'Rourke may be infallibly recognized by the stems terminating abruptly above a leaf which is nearly as large as the others, instead of having at the end one or two small-sized leaves, as is usually the case in the two preceding varieties.

Early Emperor, or Double-blossomed Frame, Pea (*Pois Michaux de Hollande*).—Stem something over 3 ft. in average height; leaves and stipules larger than those of Sangster's No. 1 Improved, and notably of a much darker and more glaucous green colour; flowers white, medium sized, almost always in pairs, and commencing to bloom at about the eighth joint of the stem, which usually carries from six to eight tiers of them ; pods shortish, seldom over about two inches in length, but very well filled, each containing eight or nine medium-sized, nearly round peas, which become very white as they ripen. A litre of them weighs, on an average, 820 grammes, and there are about 50 peas in 10 grammes. This variety is one of the most suitable for growing in the fields for market supply. It is comparatively early, very productive, and very hardy. In the neighbourhood of Paris it is not usually staked by those cultivators who grow it on a large scale. They sow it in drills about 20 inches apart, and leave the plants to themselves. The tendrils of the leaves become intertwined, so that a whole drill is like one plant, and, should it incline to right or left, the stems turn and grow erect, mutually supporting one another. The flowers soon make their appearance, when the cultivators pinch the stems above the third flower. This forwards the growth of the first pods and increases their size. When stakes are scarce, the same might be done in kitchen gardens.

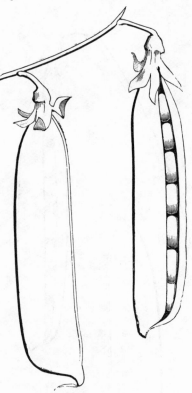

Ruelle Michaux Pea (natural size).

Ruelle Michaux Pea (*Pois Michaux de Ruelle*).—Stem usually simple, rather thick, 3 to 4 ft. high. The leaves and stipules are much larger than those of the preceding kind, and of a lighter green. The flowers are very white, large, and pretty often solitary. They begin to open at the ninth or tenth joint of the stem, which carries about ten tiers of them. Pod straight, broad, somewhat blunt at the end, and containing seven or eight white, round, largish peas. A litre of them weighs, on an average, 810 grammes, and there are about 42 peas in 10 grammes. This variety requires a little more attention, when growing, than the preceding one. Its peas are larger and handsomer, but it is not so early.

Early Frame Pea (*Pois Michaux Ordinaire*).—At first sight, this variety does not seem to differ much from the Early Emperor. It might even be described as a sub-variety, which is hardier, a little earlier, and continues bearing for a longer time. The leaves are exactly like those of the Early Emperor, except that they are a little larger ; but the flowers, which are always produced in pairs, do not commence to open before the tenth joint, and the stem carries twelve tiers of them. Pods straight, rather narrow and smallish, but very well filled ;

peas very round, white, slightly tinged with salmon colour, and of medium size. A litre of them weighs about 810 grammes, and there are about 45 peas in 10 grammes. This variety is almost always branched; that is, it produces shoots from the axils of the leaves immediately under the first flowers, which soon flower themselves. These branches or secondary stems grow particularly strong when, from any cause, the main stem above them has been either wholly or partially destroyed, but they always produce fewer pods than the main stem.

Within the last few years a variety was much grown, and still exists

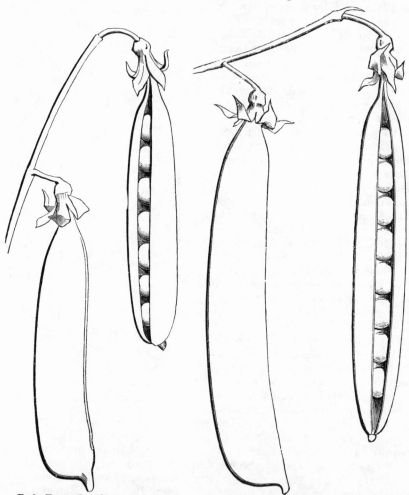

Early Frame Pea (natural size).   Leopold II. Pea (natural size).)

in certain localities, under the name of White Branching Pea (*Pois Remontant Blanc*). This comes very near the Early Frame Pea, but is especially remarkable for the vigorous growth of its secondary shoots, or branches, and their abundant and continuous yield of pods. If the Early Frame Pea, however, is sown rather thinly, and the pods are

gathered only as they are fit for use, it will yield almost as abundantly
and as long as the *Pois Remontant Blanc.*

Leopold II. Pea.—Stem usually simple, about 3 ft. high; leaflets
and stipules pale green, finely spotted with gray, oval, and rather
elongated; flowers white, almost always produced in pairs, and rarely
commencing to open before the twelfth joint; there are seldom more
than six tiers of them on a
stem; pods long, straight, pale
green, each containing seven
or eight white, very round,
medium-sized peas. A litre
of the peas weighs about 780
grammes, and there are about
42 peas in 10 grammes. This
variety comes into flower five
or six days after the Early
Emperor Pea. A remarkable
peculiarity of it is the rapidity
with which the pods form and
fill. It seldom continues to
flower longer than a fortnight,
and the pods are all gathered
in about the same time, after
which the plants may be cleared
off and replaced by something
else—a great advantage in
market-garden culture.

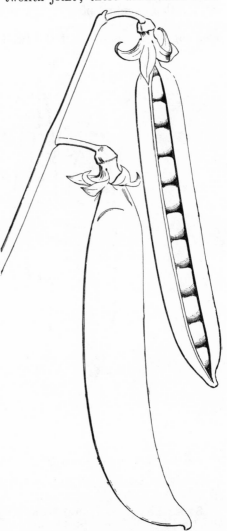

Étampes Wonder Pea
(*Pois Merveille d'Étampes*).—
Stem usually simple, long
jointed; leaves largish, and of
a very light green; stipules
exceedingly large and broad.
The general appearance of the
plant resembles that of Laxton's Supreme Pea, but it is
not quite so tall. Flowers
generally in pairs, commencing
to bloom at the tenth joint of
the stem, large, white, often
having the standard scalloped
or toothed on the margin. The
pods grow very rapidly, and in
a few days become long, broad,
and slightly curved towards   Étampes Wonder Pea (natural size).
the end. They swell con-
siderably before the peas are fully grown, in which respect the plant
very much resembles Laxton's Supreme; but the two varieties differ
entirely in the seed or peas, these being large and green in Laxton's
Supreme, while in the Étampes Wonder they are medium sized and
white. The pods of the latter variety are well filled, each generally

containing from ten to twelve peas, which become very round and white when ripe. The plant usually carries from seven to twelve tiers of pods. A litre of the peas weighs about 735 grammes, and there are about 46 peas in 10 grammes.

White Scimitar Pea (*Pois d'Auvergne*).—Stem almost always branching, and averaging about 4 ft. in height; leaflets and stipules oval, rather pointed, of a clear green, sometimes faintly tinged with yellow; flowers almost always in pairs, white, medium sized, commencing to bloom at about the twelfth joint of the stem ; pods long and slender, at first slightly curved backwards, then becoming straight, and finally curved forwards in the shape of the blade of a pruning-knife. The concave curved line, corresponding to the edge of the knife-blade, is that along which the peas are attached inside the pod. This is regarded as the front part of the pod. The opposite or convex part is termed the " back " of the pod, and the peas are never attached to the pod on that side. The pod of the White Scimitar Pea is very well filled, and contains from nine to eleven, and sometimes twelve, medium-sized peas, which are remarkably round, rarely flattened, and, when ripe, are white, slightly tinged with salmon colour. A litre of them weighs, on an average, 790 grammes, and there are about 48 peas in 10 grammes. This variety comes into flower from eight to ten days later than the Early Emperor, and yields a very constant supply of pods for more than a month. It is a very good kind, remarkable for the fine quality of the peas, and grows well in ordinary soil.

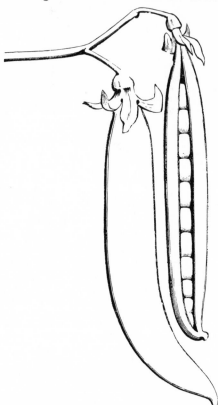

White Scimitar Pea (natural size).

Sabre Pea (*Pois Sabre*).—Stem stout, very often branching, from about 4 to 4½ ft. high; leaflets and stipules very large, rather roundish, somewhat blunt, and of a glaucous and grayish green ; flowers both solitary and in pairs, large, white, usually only commencing to bloom at the twelfth or fourteenth joint of the stem. The plant comes into flower at the same time as the preceding variety. Pods broad, pale green, curved backwards in an opposite direction to that of the White Scimitar Pea ; that is, having the peas attached along the inside of the convex line formed by the front of the pod, the back of the pod in this variety being concave. This Pea does not continue bearing so long as the preceding one, its period being about three weeks. The stem carries ten or more tiers of pods. The peas are white, large, and somewhat oblong in shape. A litre of them weighs about 790 grammes, and there are about 35 peas in 10 grammes. This variety was some

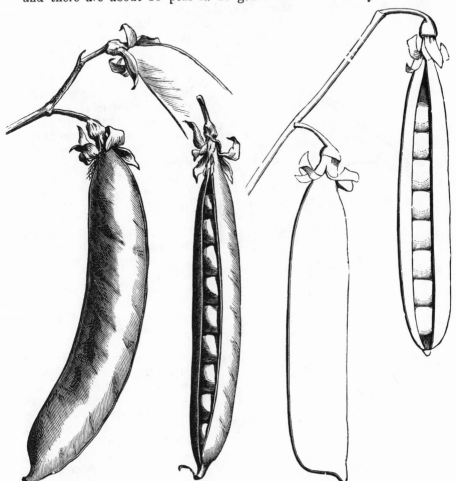

Sabre Pea (natural size).　　　　Marly Pea (natural size).

years ago in great request in the Central Market at Paris, but it does not appear to be so much in favour there at the present day.

Marly Pea (*Pois de Marly*).—A vigorous-growing plant, often branching, and in its general appearance rather like the Ruelle Michaux Pea, but almost always producing the flowers in pairs, and only commencing to bloom at about the twelfth joint of the stem. Pods straight, about 3 inches long, each containing seven or eight large round white peas, of a slightly oblong shape, rather like those of the preceding variety. A litre of them weighs about 780 grammes, and there are about 30 peas in 10 grammes. The variety is moderately productive and early, but is chiefly distinguished for the large size of the peas, as are also several other varieties which are closely allied to it, but are seldom found in cultivation at the present day. Of these varieties we may mention the following :—**Gouvigny Pea.**—The pods of this variety are longer and narrower than those of the Marly Pea. **Lady's-finger Pea.**—In this variety the outside of the pods is swollen over each of the peas. Lastly, the **Square White Pea** (*Pois Carré Blanc*).—The peas in this variety, being closely pressed together in the pod, are usually flattened on two sides, like those of the Clamart Pea. In their habit of growth the three varieties just mentioned very much resemble the Marly Pea. They have thick stout stems and very large leaves and stipules. They come in about the same time as the White Scimitar, that is, half late. Of the four kinds mentioned in this article, the Marly Pea is the earliest.

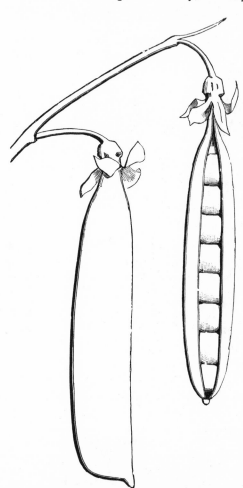

Late Clamart Pea (natural size).

Late Clamart Pea (*Pois de Clamart*).—Stem tall, tufty, branching, 5 to 6 ft. high; leaves medium sized, light green, not so glaucous as those of most other varieties; flowers white, medium sized, almost always in pairs; pods straight, or very slightly curved, of uniform width, and abruptly narrowed at both ends. The stem is simple up to the fourteenth or fifteenth joint, after which it divides into two or three, rarely four, branches. The flowers first appear at about the sixteenth or eighteenth joint. The pods are seldom more than about 2 inches in length; they are generally well filled, and the peas are pressed so closely together that they are quite flat on two sides. They retain this shape when ripe, and are then white or slightly greenish. There are usually from five to eight peas in each pod. A litre of them weighs about 800 grammes, and there are about 32 peas in 10 grammes. The main stem carries from seven to nine tiers of pods, and the branches have seldom more than four tiers.

Early Clamart Pea (*Pois de Clamart Hâtif*).—Stem 4 to 5 ft.

high, generally branching above the first pods, which are produced at the tenth or twelfth joint. The pods are usually in pairs, and are preceded by very white medium-sized flowers. They are distinguished from the pods of the ordinary Clamart Pea by being somewhat longer, of a paler colour, and pretty considerably curved. There are, on an average, ten tiers of them on a stem. They are very well filled, each containing from seven to nine peas, which very soon swell so large as to touch and mutually flatten one another on two sides. They

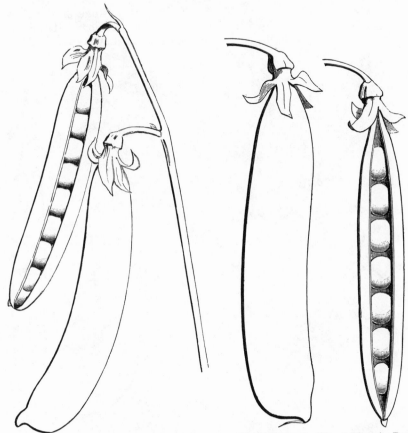

Early Clamart Pea (natural size).

Giant Marrow, or Royal Victoria, Pea (natural size).

retain this shape when ripe, at which time they become almost wrinkled, and of a white colour with a very faint greenish tinge. This variety comes in almost at the same time as the Early Frame Pea, and continues to yield nearly as long. The two kinds are very easily distinguished from each other by the difference in the shape of the pods and in the shape and colour of the peas.

Giant Marrow, or **Royal Victoria, Pea** (*Pois Victoria Marrow*). —A very tall variety, 5 to 6½ ft. high. Stems thick and stout; leaves large, numerous, light green; flowers white, large, almost always in pairs ; pods usually commencing to appear at about the fifteenth joint of the stem, rather large, broad, square at the end, and very slightly curved. The stem carries about ten tiers of pods, and does not usually branch. Each pod contains from five to seven peas. These are somewhat elongated in shape, white, and, when ripe, are flattened or more or less hollowed, as if they had a tendency towards the shape of the Wrinkled Peas. A litre of them weighs about 800 grammes, and there are about 20 peas in 10 grammes. This variety is one of the latest. It comes into flower at the same time as the Late Clamart Pea.

Laxton's William the First Pea
($\frac{1}{10}$ natural size).

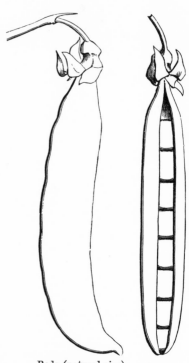

Pods (natural size).

In England the name of *Marrow Peas* is applied to all the varieties which have very large tender peas, including the Wrinkled as well as the Smooth or Round-seeded kinds.

Tall Round or Smooth Green-seeded Peas.

Laxton's William the First Pea (*Pois William*).—A rather slender climbing Pea, with slight yellowish-green leaves. Stems thin, rather long jointed, almost always simple, commencing to flower at the seventh or eighth joint, and carrying from seven to ten tiers of pods. Pods mostly solitary, of a dark-green colour, from 2 to nearly 3 inches long, narrow, curved like a pruning-knife blade, generally very well filled, and borne on very long stalks. Each pod contains from seven to ten peas, which are of a deep, clear-green colour, very closely pressed against one another, and remain flattened on two sides when ripe. A litre of them weighs 800 grammes, on an average, and there are about 42 peas in 10 grammes. This variety is not so early as Sangster's No. 1 Improved, but it is earlier than the Early Emperor, and continues bearing for a remarkably long time. Its fresh green peas are of a fine colour and excellent flavour. In England this variety is one of the most highly esteemed of early Peas.

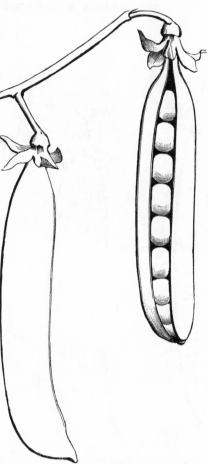

Laxton's Supreme Pea (*Pois Serpette Vert*).—This variety was one of the first raised by Mr. Laxton, and it remains one of the best. It is hardy, rather productive, and remarkable for the handsome appearance of the pods and peas. It quickly came into favour with the cultivators around Paris soon after its introduction in 1869. Stem about 4½ ft. high, usually simple and glaucous in colour; leaflets and stipules rather large, and of a pale, yellowish green; flowers generally solitary, greenish at first, then white, and commencing to bloom at about the twelfth joint of the stem, which usually carries from six to eight tiers of them; pods from about 3 to nearly 4 inches long, dark green, straight, with a short and abruptly curved point; peas large,

Laxton's Supreme Pea (natural size).

somewhat oblong in shape, sometimes misshapen from the great pressure which they undergo in the pods, and remaining of a dark-green colour after they are ripe. A litre of them weighs, on an average, 760 grammes, and there are about 34 peas in 10 grammes. This variety comes into flower a day or two earlier than the White Scimitar Pea, but does not continue bearing so long,—usually not longer than three weeks. A peculiarity, which is confined to this Pea, is the remarkable manner in which the pods swell, long before the peas attain any size, and, while these are very small, become,

2 D

as it were, inflated to such an extent that the width is greater than the depth.

Prizetaker Green Marrow Pea (*Pois Prizetaker*).—A rather slender climbing Pea. Leaves medium sized, of a glaucous green; stipules very broad, dark green, very distinctly blotched with grayish green; stem slender, tolerably long jointed, sometimes simple and sometimes with one or two branches; flowers almost always solitary, usually commencing to bloom at the twelfth joint of the stem; pods dark

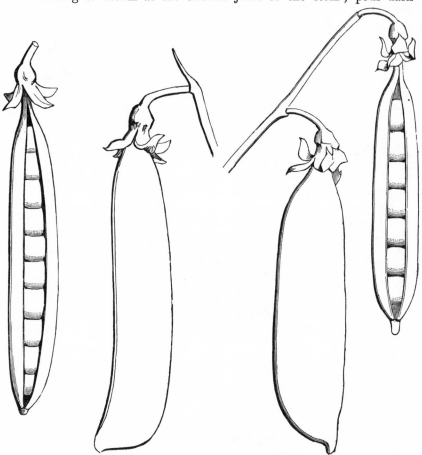

Prizetaker Green Marrow Pea (natural size).   Tall Square Mammoth Pea (natural size).

green, from about 3 to nearly 4 inches long, faintly curved like a pruning-knife blade, and quite square at the end. Each pod contains from eight to eleven smooth green peas, which completely fill it, and are usually misshapen by being pressed against one another. When ripe, they are of a clear-green colour, somewhat oblong in shape, or irregularly flattened, and rarely quite round. A litre of them weighs about 785 grammes, and there are about 40 peas in 10 grammes. The main stem carries up to ten or twelve tiers of pods, and the branches seldom have more than two or three tiers.

Tall Square Mammoth, or **Normandy, Pea** (*Pois Vert Normand*).
—Stems thick, very stout, almost always branching, from 5 to 6½ ft.
high; leaves large, rather closely set, and of a dark, somewhat glaucous,
green; flowers largish, always in pairs, of a slightly greenish-white colour;
pods very broad, between 2 and 3 inches long, very slightly curved, and
narrowed from the middle to both ends. They do not commence to
appear lower than at about the eighteenth or twentieth joint of the
stem. Each branch seldom carries more than five or six tiers of
pods, but, as the plant usually has three or four branches, the produce
is considerable. Each pod generally contains from four to six peas,
which are large, very much flattened at the sides, somewhat wrinkled,
and of a grayish-green colour when ripe. A litre of them weighs
about 790 grammes, and there are about 36 peas in 10 grammes.

B. HALF-DWARF VARIETIES.

Smooth or Round White-seeded Peas.

Bishop's Early Dwarf Pea (*Pois Lévêque*).—A dwarf, yet not very
dwarf, variety, 20 inches to 2ft. high. Stem rather thick-set, thin at
the base, and somewhat zigzag in growth; leaves medium sized, and of
a rather dark green; stipules rather small than large, and very much
toothed at the base; flowers white, medium sized, sometimes solitary
and sometimes in pairs, commencing to open at about the tenth or
eleventh joint of the stem; pods
comparatively large and broad,
from about 2 to over 3 inches long,
slightly curved, each usually containing from five to seven peas,
which are white, sometimes greenish, large, and slightly square in
shape. A litre of them weighs, on
an average, 800 grammes, and there
are about 36 peas in 10 grammes.
The stem usually carries seven or
eight tiers of pods, and occasionally has one or two branches
which are often sterile.

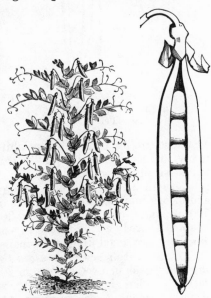

Blue Dwarf English Pea (*Pois
Nain Hâtif Anglais*).—This variety differs from the Common
Early Dwarf Pea in having leaves
of a somewhat more yellowish tint,
stem a little taller, flowers almost
always in pairs, and pods not
quite so long, but more pointed.
The stem very rarely branches, but
there are usually several spring-

Bishop's Early Dwarf Pea   Pod
(1/10 natural size).   (natural size).

ing from the same root, the main one becoming abortive at an early
date, and producing from its lower joints two or three others of about

equal size, each carrying from six to eight tiers of pods. This kind is suitable for growing in the same way as the Common Early Dwarf Pea. A litre of the peas weighs, on an average, 780 grammes, and there are about 34 peas in 10 grammes.

Bishop's Long-pod Pea (*Pois Nain Bishop à Longues Cosses*).—This variety seldom grows higher than from 20 inches to 2 ft., the stem having one or two branches immediately below the twelfth joint, at which place the flowers usually

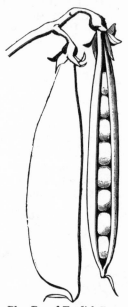

Blue Dwarf English Pea
(natural size).

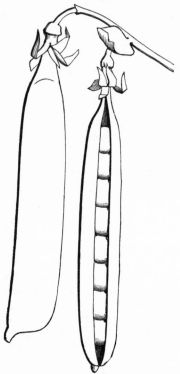

Bishop's Long-pod Pea
(natural size).

commence to appear. Flowers white, medium sized, opening not very freely, and as often solitary as in pairs; pods rather long—3 inches or more—straight, somewhat pointed, each containing from six to eight peas, which are nearly round, pale green, becoming white, quite round, and of medium size, when ripe. A litre of them weighs, on an average, 790 grammes, and there are about 36 peas in 10 grammes. This variety is about as early as the preceding one, from which it differs but little. Both are very good kinds for a main crop in the open air.

Dwarf Dutch Pea (*Pois Nain Ordinaire*).—A dwarf, compact-growing kind, seldom exceeding from 20 inches to 2 ft. in height. Stems rather slender, zigzag in growth, with numerous closely set joints, and usually branching; leaves numerous, small, stiff, and slightly twisted; flowers almost always in pairs, and commencing to open at about the twelfth joint of the stem; pods seldom more than 2 inches long, slender, square at the end, very slightly curved, each containing from six to eight peas, which are very closely pressed against one another, and are consequently flattened on two sides when ripe. They are remarkably small, somewhat angular in shape, and of a slightly greenish tint. A litre of them weighs about 800 grammes, and there are about 54 peas in 10 grammes. The main stem carries about eight tiers of pods, and the branches have from two to four tiers each. This variety has a remarkably compact appearance when growing, and the very numerous white flowers are effectively relieved by the very green and tufted foliage.

Smooth or Round Green-seeded Peas.

Imperial Dwarf Blue Pea (*Pois Nain Vert Impérial*).—A half-dwarf kind, from 2 to 2½ ft. high. Stem stout, rather thick-set, and of

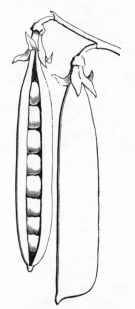
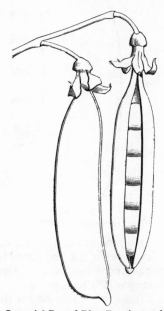

Dwarf Dutch Pea (natural size).   Imperial Dwarf Blue Pea (natural size).

zigzag growth, especially at the base; leaves rather slender, with oval-pointed leaflets, of a clear-green colour, entirely free from any glaucous tint or grayish markings; flowers usually in pairs, almost green, commencing to bloom at about the twelfth joint of the stem, and above one or two branches which are seldom of any great size; pods about 2 inches long, rather narrow, well filled, faintly curved like a pruning-knife blade, each containing six or seven peas, which, when ripe, are large and closely pressed against one another. They continue quite green, and are generally very full, but slightly square or angular. A litre of them weighs about 800 grammes, and there are, on an average, 32 peas in 10 grammes. The main stem carries from six to eight tiers of pods, and the branches rarely have more than three tiers. This variety may be infallibly distinguished from all others, when it comes into bloom, by the peculiar, almost greenish, colour of its flowers, which, even when quite fully expanded, are veined and tinged with green, like the unexpanded flowers of all kinds of Peas.

Dwarf Blue Prussian Pea (French, *Pois Nain Vert Gros ;* German, *Grüne Prussische Zwerg-Erbse*).—A half-dwarf variety, from 2 ft. to 2 ft. 4 inches high, thick-set, and very branching. Leaves rather large, roundish, and glaucous; stipules very much blotched with gray; stem stout, of zigzag growth, with very close joints, beginning to branch at the fourth or fifth joint, and showing the first flowers at about the tenth joint; flowers white, medium sized, sometimes solitary, but most usually in pairs; pods broad, between 2 and 3 inches long, slightly pointed at the end, and seldom very well filled, each usually containing not more than five or six peas, which are large, very much flattened, slightly irregular in shape, and of a pale-green colour, turning bluish when ripe. A litre of them weighs, on an average, 800 grammes, and there are about 30 peas in 10 grammes. The stem generally carries seven or eight tiers of pods, and the principal branches have four or five tiers. This is a very

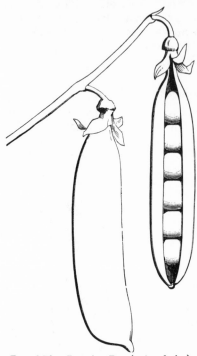

Dwarf Blue Prussian Pea (natural size).

hardy and productive variety, but rather late than early. It is grown on a large scale for the dried peas, which are usually met with in commerce under the name of Green Noyon Pea (*Pois Vert de Noyon*).

Laxton's Fillbasket Pea (*Pois Fillbasket*).—A half-dwarf kind, 2½ to 3 ft. high. Stem rather thick-set, short jointed, often producing two or three branches which grow nearly as tall as the main stem, and generally issue from about the tenth or twelfth joint. The first flowers appear at about the thirteenth or fourteenth joint, and are greenish white and pretty often solitary. The main stem carries six or seven tiers of them, and the branches only from three to five tiers. Pods about 3¼ inches long, rather narrow, tolerably curved like a pruning-knife blade, very much pointed at the end, and almost always exceedingly well filled, each containing from seven to ten peas, which are dark green, large, squarish, and, when ripe, becoming of a clear, rather pale green. A litre of them weighs, on an average, 785 grammes, and there are about 32 peas in 10 grammes. This variety is easily enough distinguished by its leaves being of a light yellowish green, narrow, slight, and very much waved at the edges, especially those at the top of the stem.

Laxton's Supplanter Pea (*Pois Supplanter*).—A half-dwarf variety, with large, rather dark, but very glaucous leaves. Stem usually simple, commencing to flower at the seventh or eighth joint; flowers white, seldom opening fully, and usually in pairs; pods about 3¼ inches long, dark green, remarkably broad, especially at the lower end, each containing from six to eight very green peas, flattened at the sides and squarish in shape. They retain their deep green colour when ripe, at which time they are flattish in shape, somewhat angular, and sometimes

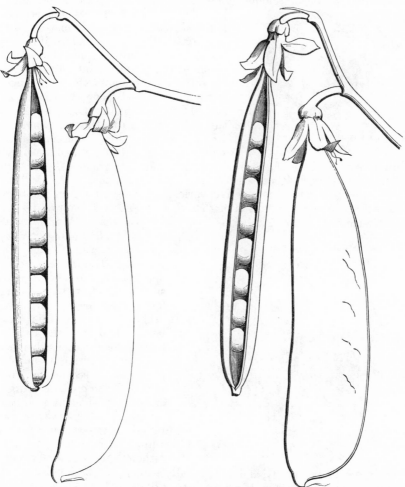

Laxton's Fillbasket Pea (natural size).   Laxton's Supplanter Pea (natural size).

slightly hollowed on the faces. A litre of them weighs, on an average, 780 grammes, and there are about 36 peas in 10 grammes. The stem usually carries from eight to twelve tiers of pods. This is a productive variety, continuing to yield for a long time. A greater number of tiers of pods will be produced on plants from which the pods are pulled as they are required. The number which we have given above was taken from plants grown for observation, from which the pods were not removed.

C. Dwarf Varieties.
Smooth or Round White Peas.

Early Dwarf Frame Pea (*Pois Nain Très Hâtif à Châssis*).—Stem exceedingly short, seldom more than from 8 to 10 inches high;

joints very close; leaflets and stipules roundish, dark green, finely marbled with a grayish tinge; flowers white, very small, usually solitary, commencing to bloom at the seventh joint, seldom opening fully, and often not extending outside of the leaves; pods about 2 inches long, straight, rather slender, nearly square at the end, and very like those of Sangster's

Early Dwarf Frame Pea
(1/10 natural size).

No. 1 Improved Pea, each containing seven or eight white, round, medium-sized peas. A litre of the peas weighs about 790 grammes, and there are, on an average, 42 peas in 10 grammes. Notwithstanding its dwarf size, this is a rather productive variety, excellent for frame culture, and only two or three days later than Sangster's No. 1 Improved.

Couturier Dwarf Pea (*Pois Très Nain Couturier*).—A truly dwarf

and very branching variety, somewhat resembling the Brittany Dwarf Pea in its appearance, but not so early as that kind, and producing larger-sized peas. The stem usually branches from the base, dividing into two or three branches of nearly equal size, each bearing from four to six tiers of pods, which grow in pairs. The pods are straight and rather slender, each containing from six to eight very round peas, which become white when ripe. This Pea,

Couturier Dwarf Pea.

although dwarf, is very vigorous growing and hardy, and is especially suitable for field culture. It seldom grows more than 12 or 14 inches high, and consequently does not require stakes.

Brittany Dwarf Pea (*Pois Très Nain de Bretagne*).—A very dwarf Pea, with slender, rather dark green leaves. Stems very short jointed, of zigzag growth, commencing to flower at about the twelfth joint. The two joints immediately below generally produce branches which are often sterile. Flowers in pairs, white, well opened, but very small; pods seldom over 2 inches long, of a dark-green colour, very slender, and slightly curved like a pruning-knife blade, each containing from five to seven peas, which are square from pressure and fill the pods com-

pletely. A litre of the peas weighs, on an average, 810 grammes, and
there are about 80 peas in 10 grammes.
The main stem carries from six to ten
tiers of pods, and the branches seldom
have more than two tiers. This variety
is about as early as the Early Frame Pea.
The peas, when ripe, are small, squarish,
slightly tinged with salmon colour, and
sometimes greenish.

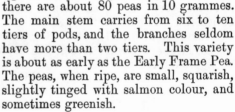

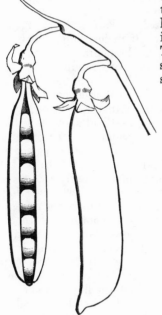

Brittany Dwarf Pea (natural size).

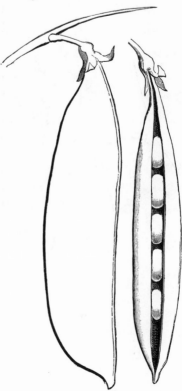

MacLean's Blue Peter Pea				Pods (natural size).
($\frac{1}{10}$ natural size).

Smooth or Round Green Peas (*Dwarf*).

MacLean's Blue Peter Pea.—A very dwarf variety, but not so
compact in growth as the preceding one. The joints of the stem are
longer, being about equal in length to the stipules. Leaves of a very
dark glaucous green, those at the end of the stem being very much
reduced in size, closely crowded together, and of a very dark green;
flowers rather small and slightly tinged with green, sometimes solitary
and sometimes in pairs, and commencing to bloom at the seventh or
eighth joint of the stem, two or three days later than the Early
Dwarf Frame Pea; pods rather broad, a little over 2 inches long,

each containing from five to eight peas, which are somewhat oblong in shape, very large, and, when ripe, retain their pale-green, slightly bluish tint. A litre of the peas weighs, on an average, 780 grammes, and there are about 34 peas in 10 grammes.

St. Michel's Dwarf Green Pea (*Pois Nain Vert de St. Michel*).—A very productive variety, growing about 20 inches high, with stiff, thick-set, branching stems. The pods, which are produced in pairs, are well filled with medium-sized, round, green-coloured peas.

Crown, Cluster, or Mummy Pea (*Pois Turc*).—Plant about 4 ft. high ; stem usually simple, bearing medium-sized leaves of a rather pale green, rather far apart at the base of the stem, and more closely set towards the upper part, where the flowers make their appearance, not in regular tiers one over another, as in other kinds of peas, but in a kind of cluster, the stem becoming broader here, and generally fasciated by producing a number of leaves, from the axils of which the flowers issue ; peas smooth, regular in shape, and of a light-yellow colour. A litre of them weighs, on an average, 800 grammes, and there are about 40 peas in 10 grammes. There are two forms of this Pea, one with white and the other with two-coloured flowers. Neither of them is of much interest for the kitchen garden.

Purple-podded Pea (*Pois à Cosse Violette*).—This variety very much resembles the Marly Pea in its habit of growth, but is distinguished from it and from all other varieties of Peas by the very deep purple colour of its pods, which they retain when dried. The flowers are bluish violet, not so deeply coloured on the stan-

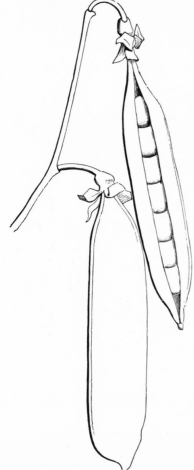

Purple-podded Pea (natural size).

dard as on the wings. Peas greenish gray, large, and irregular in shape. A litre of them weighs about 700 grammes, and there are, on an average, 42 peas in 10 grammes. Like the preceding kind, this variety is more curious than really useful. The peas have the serious defect of becoming brownish when cooked, like Field Peas and all violet-flowered Peas. This greatly diminishes their value for table use. The pods, on the contrary, when boiled, lose their purple colour and become almost green ; but they can only be eaten when very young, as they become tough and leathery, and unfit to eat, before they are fully grown.

II. Wrinkled Peas.

Pois ridés.

A. Tall Climbing Varieties.

White-seeded Peas.

Laxton's " The Shah " Pea (*Pois Shah de Perse*).—A climbing Pea with a very slender stem, which is almost always simple or with one or two small branches, and rather long jointed. Leaves slight, clear green, faintly tinged with gray; stipules a little darker coloured than the leaves, and distinctly marked with grayish blotches; flowers white, medium sized, solitary, or rarely in pairs, and commencing to bloom at the sixth or seventh joint of the stem; pods very slender at first, about 2 inches long, quite square at the end, and becoming very much swollen before ripening, each containing from five to seven peas, which are very closely pressed together, and consequently flattened at the sides, and, when ripe, are square in shape, very much wrinkled, and of a pure white colour. A litre of the peas weighs, on an average, 740 grammes, and there are about 48 peas in 10 grammes. The stem usually carries six or seven tiers of pods. In all its characteristics of growth, habit, and foliage, this variety

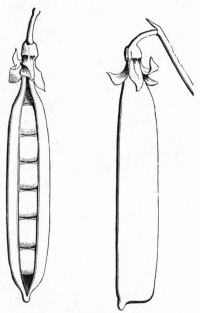

Laxton's " The Shah " Pea (natural size).

comes very close to Sangster's No. 1 Improved Pea, but differs from it entirely in the appearance of the seeds or peas. It was raised by Mr. Laxton, about the year 1875.

Carter's Telephone Pea (*Pois Téléphone*).—A climbing Pea, from about 3 to 4 ft. high. Leaves very large, pale yellowish green, veined and marbled with white; stipules quite remarkable for their large size; stem generally simple, but occasionally with one or two branches, rather long jointed, and commencing to flower at about the twelfth joint; flowers white, rather large, and often solitary; pods very large and broad, sometimes 4 inches long, straight, and slightly curved towards the end like the blade of a pruning-knife, rather swollen, each containing from eight to ten very large green peas, squarish in shape, and, when ripe, either perfectly white or more or less tinged with green. A litre of the peas weighs, on an average, 710 grammes, and there are about 30 peas in 10 grammes. This variety is a little later than Laxton's Supreme, and a plant seldom carries more than twelve pods.

Knight's Tall Marrow Pea (*Pois Ridé de Knight*).—A tall-growing
late variety, 6½ ft. or more high. Stems rather strong, but not very
thick, long jointed, unbranched up to the twelfth joint, and commencing
to flower at about the sixteenth joint; flowers white, very large, almost
always in pairs; pods long stalked, large, broad, perceptibly curved,

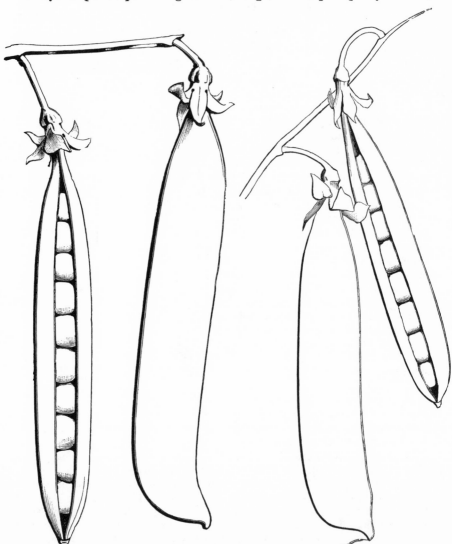

Carter's Telephone Pea (natural size).　　　Knight's Tall Marrow Pea (natural size).

and from about 2 to over 3 inches long. The main stem carries from
eight to ten tiers of pods, and the branches from three to five tiers. It
is to be remarked that the joints immediately below the first flower do
not all produce branches, and that the same stem does not usually produce more than two. Each of the pods contains from six to eight large

elongated peas, which, when ripe, become very much wrinkled, almost flat, and generally either white or slightly greenish. A litre of the peas weighs, on an average, 730 grammes, and there are about 26 peas in 10 grammes. In this variety one of the two flowers in the pairs is often accompanied by a small roundish leafy bract at the base.

Green-seeded Peas.

Laxton's Alpha Pea (*Pois Laxton's Alpha*).—This variety very much resembles Sangster's No. 1 Improved in height, habit of growth, and earliness, but is distinguished from it by the paler and more yellowish tint of the leaves. The flowers are generally solitary, but occasionally in pairs, and begin to open at the seventh or eighth joint of the stem. Pods very long stalked, rather pointed, and very slightly curved, about 2 inches long, each con- taining from six to eight peas, which are small, very much wrinkled, and remaining green when ripe. A litre of the peas weighs, on an average, 690 grammes, and there are about 40 peas in 10 grammes. A stem carries from five to seven tiers of pods. This Pea is one of the best known and most extensively cultivated of the varieties raised by Mr. Laxton, whose name we have had frequent occasion to mention. In raising new varieties, he has given his attention to a well-directed crossing of the old ones, and owes his suc- cess in a great measure to his intelligent choice of seed-bearing plants, and to his discreet propagation of distinct and really good varieties from among the very numerous forms which his extensive ex- perimental sowings have yielded him, thus avoiding a useless multiplication of names and varieties.

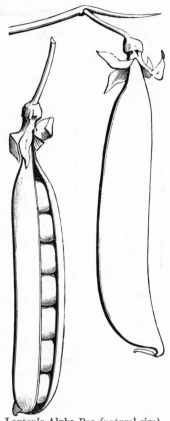

Laxton's Alpha Pea (natural size).

Standish's Criterion Pea (*Pois Cri- terion*).—A climbing Pea with rather slender stems, between 3½ and 4 ft. high. Leaves clear or yellowish green, with hardly any glaucous tinge; stems whitish, slender, simple up to the tenth joint, and commencing to flower at about the twelfth joint; flowers usually solitary, medium sized, greenish white. One or two slender branches issue from underneath the lowest or first flowers, and these sometimes grow as high as the main stem. Pods dark green, very straight, square at the end, and of uniform breadth, very well filled, each containing from six to eight peas, which are very green, large, and closely pressed against one another, becoming square, wrinkled, and of a pale grayish-green colour when ripe. A

litre of the peas weighs, on an average, 680 grammes, and there are
about 40 peas in 10 grammes. The main stem carries seven or eight
tiers of pods, and the branches only from three to five tiers. This
variety is about as early as Laxton's Supreme, but continues bearing
for a very considerably longer time. Although it is of recent introduction, it is already a great favourite in England. It grows well in
almost any kind of soil, and its pods, although narrow, are exceedingly
well filled.

Knight's Tall Green Wrinkled Marrow Pea (*Pois Ridé Vert à
Rames*).—A tall-growing variety, but
having a comparatively slender stem.
Leaves rather far asunder, medium
sized, and of a clear-green colour.
The stem commences to branch at the

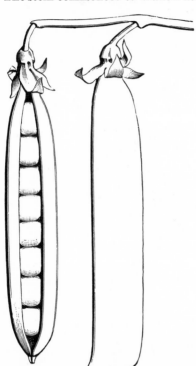
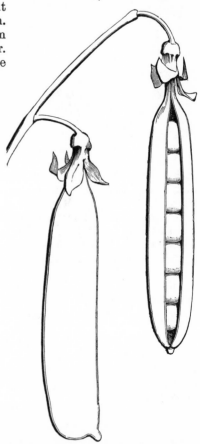
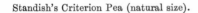

Standish's Criterion Pea (natural size).   Knight's Tall Green Wrinkled Marrow
                                                Pea (natural size).

eleventh or twelfth joint, and to flower at the fourteenth. Flowers
white, medium sized, on long slender stalks, and usually in pairs, but
not unfrequently solitary; pods at least 3 inches or more in length,
rather narrow, but blunt at the end, each containing seven or eight
medium-sized peas, with some interval between them, which, when
ripe, become wrinkled and of a slightly bluish-green colour. A litre
of the peas weighs, on an average, 670 grammes, and there are about
30 peas in 10 grammes. This is a rather early variety, coming in at

least four or five days earlier than Knight's Tall Marrow. It is also rather productive, the stem usually carrying from eight to ten tiers of pods, and the peas are of very good quality. It is not known where it originated, but it has been cultivated in France for a very long time. We have not been able to identify it very closely with any English variety, but it comes nearest to Standish's Criterion.

Champion of England Pea (*Pois Champion d'Angleterre*).—A climbing Pea, of medium height, seldom exceeding from 4 to 5 ft. Leaves pale glaucous green; stem rather stout, whitish, unbranched up to about the twelfth joint, and seldom producing pods below the fifteenth or sixteenth joint. The intermediate joints send out two, three, or four branches, which sometimes become nearly as large as the main stem. Flowers rather small than large, often solitary, but generally in pairs, and sometimes, but very exceptionally, three together; pods medium sized, 2 or 3 inches long, the lower ones sometimes containing only three or four peas, while some of the upper ones have as many as nine. The peas are small, very much wrinkled, and of a pale bluish-green colour. A litre of them weighs, on an average, 700 grammes, and there are about 36 peas in 10 grammes. The main stem carries six or seven tiers of pods, and the branches from two to five tiers.

Duke of Albany Pea.—A tall, stout-stemmed, vigorous-growing Pea, 5 to nearly 6 ft. high, with usually only one or two branches, which are produced at about the tenth or eleventh joint of the stem. Leaves large and rounded in shape, giving the plant somewhat of the appearance of the Telephone Pea, although they are of a deeper shade of green. The pods, which usually grow in pairs, are exceedingly long and thick, of a deep-green colour, straight, and abruptly curved at the end; they are often 4 inches long, and are well filled with

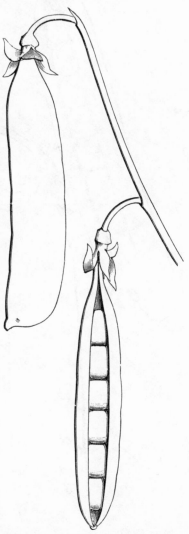

Champion of England Pea (natural size).

large round peas, which become wrinkled when ripe, and retain a rather decided green tint. This is a half-late variety, and bears from twelve to fifteen pods on each plant.

Tall Green Mammoth, or **King of the Marrows, Pea** (*Pois Ridé*

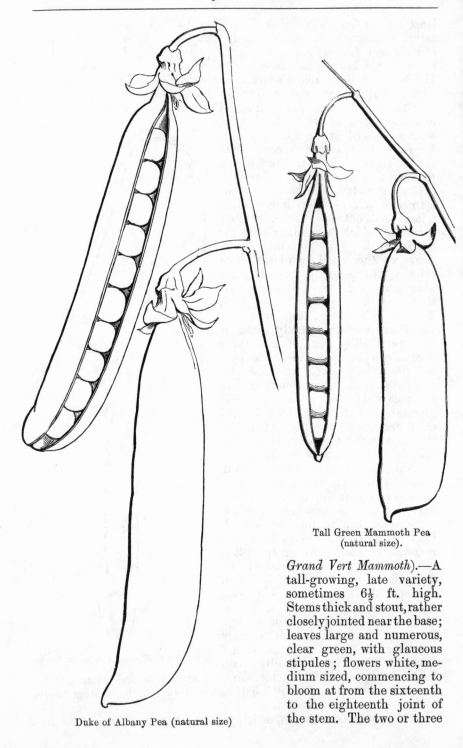

Tall Green Mammoth Pea
(natural size).

Duke of Albany Pea (natural size)

Grand Vert Mammoth).—A tall-growing, late variety, sometimes 6½ ft. high. Stems thick and stout, rather closely jointed near the base; leaves large and numerous, clear green, with glaucous stipules ; flowers white, medium sized, commencing to bloom at from the sixteenth to the eighteenth joint of the stem. The two or three joints immediately below the first flowers generally produce rather long branches. Pods usually in pairs, very broad, between 2 and 3 inches long, and bluntly rounded towards the end. The main stem carries from eight to ten tiers of pods, and the branches from two to five tiers. Each pod contains from five to eight peas, which are large, rather oblong in shape, and of a light-green colour. A litre of the peas weighs, on an average, 750 grammes, and there are about 30 peas in 10 grammes. The flowers of this variety, like those of Knight's Tall Marrow, often have a small leafy bract at the base. It is one of the latest of all cultivated Peas, and requires a cool, temperate climate to grow well. In France very hot weather sometimes checks its growth and diminishes its yield, which, under favourable conditions, is very abundant. In that climate, however, successional sowings of early Peas are generally more satisfactory in their results than sowings of late varieties.

B. HALF-DWARF VARIETIES.

White Wrinkled Peas.

White Eugénie Dwarf Wrinkled Marrow Pea (*Pois Ridé Nain Blanc Hâtif*).—A half-dwarf variety, 2 ft. to 2 ft. 8 inches high. Stem rather slender, almost always unbranched, commencing to flower extremely low, often at the fifth joint; flowers white, medium sized, always solitary towards the lower part of the stem, and often in

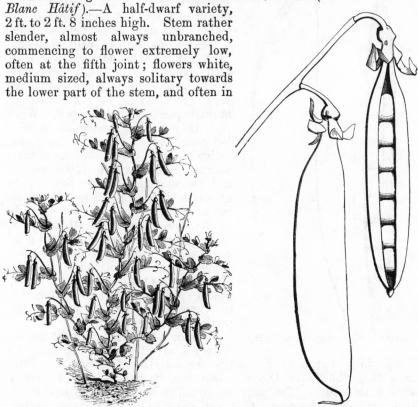

White Eugénie Dwarf Wrinkled Marrow Pea
($\frac{1}{10}$ natural size).

Pods (natural size).

2 E

pairs a little higher up; pods rather variable in size, usually 2 or 3 inches long, pointed towards the end, slightly curved like the blade of a pruning-knife, and very unequally filled, those at the lower part of the stem often containing but one pea, and seldom more than three or four, while later pods will often have seven or eight. While in the green or unripened state, the peas are large, square, and somewhat flattened at the sides; when ripe, they become very wrinkled, somewhat unequal in size, and of a slightly salmon-tinted white colour. The stem carries from twelve to fifteen tiers of pods. A litre of the peas weighs, on an average, 670 grammes, and there are about 36 peas in 10 grammes. This would be one of the most productive early varieties if the first pods were better filled. It will bear for six weeks or more if the pods are gathered as they become fit.

Laxton's Marvel Pea (*Pois Prodige de Laxton*).—A half-dwarf

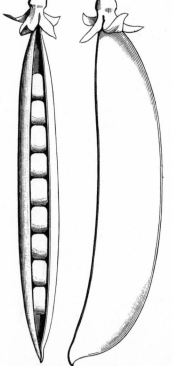

variety, seldom exceeding 2 or 2½ ft. in height. Stem often branching; leaves large, of an exceedingly dark-green colour, slightly spotted with gray; flowers white, rather large, but almost always opening imperfectly, as often solitary as in pairs, and commencing to bloom at about the tenth joint of the stem; pods dark green, between 3 and 4 inches long, rather broad, somewhat curved in the shape of a pruning-knife blade, pointed at the end, each containing from seven to nine peas, which are very green, large, and flattened by mutual pressure in the pod. When ripe, they become somewhat angular, but remain very full, and of a very pale, yellowish-green colour. A litre of them weighs, on an average, 750 grammes, and there are about 36 peas in 10 grammes. The main stem usually carries not more than four or five tiers of pods, as the flowers are frequently abortive. Although it has some undoubted good qualities, this variety cannot be regarded as one of the best of those raised by Mr. Laxton, as the flowers do not always produce pods, and the plant is altogether too vigorous growing and leafy in proportion to its yield of peas.

Laxton's Marvel Pea (natural size).   **Laxton's Minimum Dwarf Pea.**— A very dwarf variety, growing about 10 inches high, but very productive for its size. Coming in a little later than the Early Dwarf Frame Pea, it may be advantageously sown to succeed it. The pods are small, straight, and very well filled, each containing from six to eight peas, which, when ripe, become wrinkled and white. This is a very good kind for forcing, or for growing on the edges of beds.

Premium Gem Pea.—A variety growing from 2 to over 2½ ft. high, and coming into bloom nearly at the same time as Knight's Marrow Pea. The flowers are abundantly produced in pairs. The pods are straight and well filled with pretty large peas, which are wrinkled and of a pale-green colour.

Green Wrinkled Peas.

Knight's Dwarf Green Wrinkled Marrow Pea (*Pois Ridé Nain Vert Hâtif*).—This variety only differs from the Early White Dwarf Wrinkled Pea in having the leaves somewhat marbled and undulated, and the peas of a pale-green colour. It exhibits precisely the same characteristics of growth, and especially the peculiarity of the lower pods being usually small and badly filled, while those growing from the middle of the stems are much larger and generally well filled. A litre of the peas weighs, on an average, 700 grammes, and there are about 34 peas in 10 grammes. It is very difficult to obtain this variety quite pure at the present time, and among the numerous varieties which resemble it, and which are often sold for it, there is, perhaps, not one that possesses the same combination of good qualities, and especially such great earliness along with such very great and continuous productiveness.

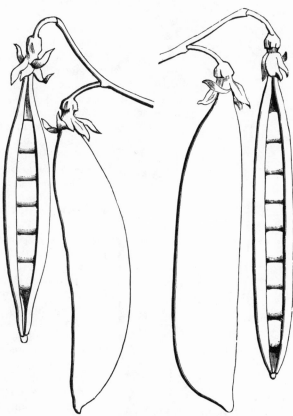

Knight's Dwarf Green Wrinkled Marrow Pea (natural size).

MacLean's Best of All Pea (natural size).

MacLean's Best of All Pea.—This is a half-dwarf kind, growing about 2½ ft. high, very thick-set, and with a short-jointed stem. Leaves stiff, medium sized, and of a very dark, glaucous-green colour; flowers medium sized, white, in pairs; pods broad, from 3 to nearly 4 inches long, gradually narrowed at both ends, and usually not completely filled ; stems simple to the eighth or ninth joint, then producing three or four branches, and bearing the first pods at about the twelfth joint. The main stem carries from five to seven tiers of pods, and the branches have seldom more than two or three tiers. Each pod contains from three to eight very large peas, somewhat oval in shape, and, when ripe, becoming very wrinkled, very much flattened, and of a pale, grayish-green colour. A litre of the peas weighs, on an average, 690 grammes, and there are about 30 peas in 10 grammes. This is a productive, half-late variety, of good quality.

Turner's Dr. MacLean Pea (*Pois Docteur MacLean*).—A half-dwarf, compact-growing variety, with broad and numerous leaves, of a rather glaucous, dark-green colour up to the middle of the stems, and becoming much smaller and toothed towards the top. Stems short jointed, thick-set, simple to about the eighth joint, then producing three or four rather unequal branches, and bearing the first flowers at about the twelfth joint; pods very long and broad, generally solitary, and between three and four inches in length. The main stem carries from five to seven tiers of pods, and the branches only two or three tiers. The pods are usually quite as well filled as they are handsome in appearance, each containing from seven to ten very large peas, squarish in shape, and, when ripe, becoming very much wrinkled, flattened, and of a pale-green colour, inclining to yellow rather than blue. A litre of the peas weighs, on an average, 700 grammes, and there are about 48 peas in 10 grammes. This variety is considerably earlier than the preceding one, but does not continue bearing for so long a time. Although quite distinct from Laxton's Marvel Pea, it bears a marked resemblance to it, especially in its habit of growth, but its pods set more regularly than those of that variety.

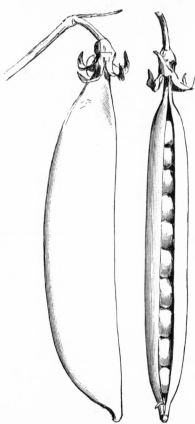

Turner's Dr. MacLean Pea (natural size).

G. F. Wilson Pea (*Pois Wilson*).—A half-dwarf variety, growing from 2 to 2½ ft. high. Stem thick and stout; leaves very large, glaucous green, especially remarkable for the great size of the stipules and the absence of grayish spots; flowers white, rather large, generally in pairs, but often solitary also, and commencing to open at about the tenth joint of the stem ; pods from about 2¼ to over 3 inches long, at first very flat and exceedingly broad, but becoming narrower as the peas increase in size. The stem carries from six to eight tiers of pods. They are seldom very well filled, each usually containing not more than five or six peas, but these, it is true, are nearly as large as field-beans; they are oblong and somewhat flattened in shape, and, when ripe, become exceedingly wrinkled, flat, and of a pale-green colour. A litre of them weighs, on an average, 720 grammes, and there are about 26 peas in 10 grammes. The thickness and strength of the stalks which bear the pods are a particularly distinctive characteristic of this variety.

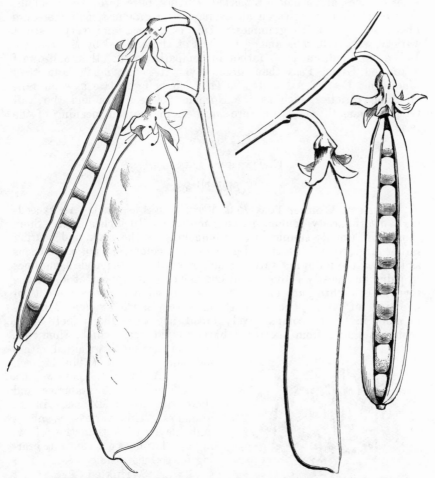

G. F. Wilson Pea (natural size).   Laxton's Omega Pea (natural size).

Laxton's Omega Pea (*Pois Omega*).—A half-dwarf variety, seldom growing higher than about 2½ ft. Leaves rather numerous and tufty, dark green, uniform in colour, with the exception of the ribs or veins, which are whitish and very apparent; stem thick, compact, and short jointed, usually having two branches below the first flower, which generally opens at about the thirteenth or fourteenth joint. The flowers are of a greenish white, rather large, and very frequently open imperfectly; they are almost always in pairs. Pods rather narrow, from about 2½ to over 3 inches long, of a dark-green colour, and exceedingly well filled. The main stem carries from five to eight tiers of pods, and the branches only one or two tiers, when they are not entirely sterile. The peas are of a rather dark green colour, and are very closely set together in the pods, which they fill completely, each pod usually containing eight or nine peas. When ripe, they are not very much wrinkled, but are rather square and hollowed on the sides or faces, and are of a remarkably lively, pure, light-green colour. A litre of them weighs, on an average, 725 grammes, and there are about 36 peas in 10 grammes. This is a good and very distinct variety, worthy to rank among the best of those raised by Mr. Laxton. It is a late kind, but is so rather in comparison with other half-dwarf Wrinkled Green Peas than absolutely. It is not much later than MacLean's Best of All, and it is far from being so late as some tall-climbing varieties, such as the Normandy Green Pea and the Tall Green Mammoth Pea, which are *late* Peas in the full meaning of the term.

C. DWARF VARIETIES.

Wrinkled Peas.

American Wonder Pea (*Pois Merveille d'Amérique*).—An exceedingly dwarf variety, seldom growing more than 10 inches high. Stem short, stiff, usually simple, or only branching at the neck, and bearing rather large, roundish leaves of a dark-green colour, and not so glaucous as those of the following variety; flowers small, white; pods sometimes in pairs, but mostly solitary, and commencing to appear at about the seventh or eighth joint of the stem, which seldom carries more than five tiers of pods. These are straight, very much swollen, 2 inches or more in length, comparatively broad, and exceedingly well filled, each containing from six to eight large flat peas, which, when ripe,

become very much wrinkled, rather flat, and of a pale bluish-green colour. A litre of the peas weighs, on an average, 720 grammes, and there are about 42 peas in 10 grammes. This variety is about eight days earlier than the following one, but does not continue bearing for so long a time.

Dwarf Wrinkled Pea (⅒ natural size).

Dwarf Wrinkled Pea (*Pois Ridé Très Nain à Bordures*).—A very dwarf variety, seldom exceeding 10 or 12 inches in height. Stems very thick-set, commencing to flower at about the seventh joint, below which they branch once or twice; flowers small, white, generally solitary; leaves very closely set, small, stiff, and of a dark-green colour; pods from six to eight in number on the main stem and two or three on the branches, straight, square at the end, 2 inches or a little more in length, and usually very well filled, each containing from five to eight rather large peas, which are very much flattened by pressure against one another, and, when ripe, become square, moderately wrinkled, and of a pale bluish-green colour. A litre of the peas weighs, on an average, 700 grammes, and there are about 45 peas in 10 grammes. This variety is admirably adapted for forcing and for growing as an edging to beds of other vegetables.

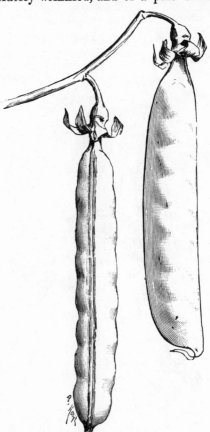

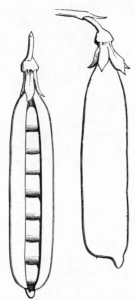

Pods of Dwarf Wrinkled Pea (natural size).

Forty Days' Edible-podded Pea (natural size).

EDIBLE-PODDED, or SUGAR, PEAS.

French, Pois sans parchemin. *German*, Zucker-Erbsen. *Dutch*, Peulen. *Italian*, Piselli di guscio tenero. *Portuguese*, Ervilhas de casca.

In all the varieties of Peas of which we have hitherto spoken, the pod is lined on the inside with a thin but hard and tough membrane which gives it a certain amount of solidity, and which, contracting as the pod ripens and dries, causes it to open into two equal parts, which become twisted spirally and often project the peas to some distance. We are now about to describe a class of varieties, the pods of which are destitute of this membrane, and consequently always remain soft and tender, and do not open when ripe, so that they may be eaten entire, the tender fleshy part of the pod becoming more fully developed in the absence of the tough parchment-like membrane.

A. Tall Climbing Varieties.

Forty Days Edible-podded Pea (*Pois sans Parchemin de Quarante Jours*).—A climbing variety, from 3¼ to 4¼ ft. high. Stems slender, rather long jointed, and commencing to flower at about the fifth or sixth joint; flowers usually in pairs, white, and rather large ; pods straight, slender, somewhat pointed at the end, very free from membrane, each containing from six to eight medium-sized peas of roundish or slightly compressed shape, becoming round and white when ripe. A litre of the peas weighs, on an average, 790 grammes, and there are about 34 peas in 10 grammes. This variety very seldom branches, but carries from fifteen to eighteen tiers of pods, which are produced in succession, so that some of them may be quite ripe and dry at the base of the plant, while flowers continue to appear on the upper part of the stem. The flowering is often prolonged for more than two months.

Butter Pea (*Pois Beurre*). —This variety is very clearly distinguished from all other kinds of Edible-podded Peas by the swollen appearance and thickness of the pods, which very soon grow to be thicker than they are broad. They are from 2 to nearly 3 inches long, and the sides, which are very fleshy and succulent, are nearly ⅕ of an

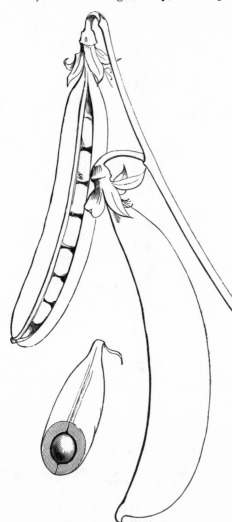

Butter Pea (natural size).

inch thick. The pods are pretty deeply curved, and are sometimes solitary, but most usually in pairs. The stems grow from 3¼ to about 4 ft. high, and are rather slender and long jointed. The leaves are of a rather dark green, with whitish veins, and are almost devoid of spots. The flowers, which are large and white, are only solitary at the base and at the top of the stem. The stalks which bear the pods are slender, very stiff, and of medium length. The great thickness of the sides or walls of the pods causes them to remain smooth on the outside, *i.e.* not bulged by the swelling of the peas, as is usually the case with most other varieties of Edible-podded Peas. The peas are white, very round, and rather large. A litre of them weighs, on an average, 800 grammes, and there are about 30 peas in 10 grammes. This variety is almost as early as the Ruelle Michaux Pea. In the growth of the pod of the Butter Pea, that which we have already remarked regarding Edible - podded Peas in general appears to take place, namely, the soft portion or parenchyma of the pod seems to be developed at the expense of the parchment-like membrane, which is wholly wanting, as if the elements or nutrimental juices intended to form this membrane were diverted to the adjacent parts of the pod. There is, however, this difference between the pod of the Butter Pea and those of all other Edible-podded kinds, that it is the *thickness* or *depth* of the pod which takes on the greatest development, while in the other kinds, as, for example, the Large Crooked Sugar Pea and the Giant Sugar Pea, it is the *breadth* of the pod which is abnormally enlarged.

Large Crooked, or Scimitar, Sugar Pea ($\frac{1}{10}$ natural size).

Large Crooked, or Scimitar, Sugar Pea (*Pois Gourmand Blanc à Large Cosse*).—A tall climbing variety, 4 to over 4½ ft. high. Stem of medium thickness, usually branching, long jointed; leaves rather large, of a pale, slightly yellowish green; flowers white, very large, well opened, commencing to bloom at the twelfth or thirteenth joint of the stem, and almost always solitary; pods very large, whitish, entirely free from membrane, often twisted—

whence the variety derives its name—sometimes from 4 to nearly 5 inches long and 1 inch or more broad, each usually containing from five to eight rather large round peas, set at some distance from one another, and of a very pale green colour, becoming white and perfectly round when ripe. A litre of the peas weighs, on an average, 780 grammes, and there are about 26 peas in 10 grammes. The main stem usually carries from eight to ten tiers of pods, and the branches have only from three to five tiers. This is an exceedingly productive variety. It comes in in mid-season, commencing to yield soon after the Forty Days Edible-podded Pea, but continuing to bear for a much longer time, and the size and fine appearance of its pods cause it to be always more sought after than any other kind, so that it is more extensively grown than any other variety of Edible-podded Peas, especially in the eastern parts of France and in Switzerland. It is rather surprising to see the comparatively low estimation in which the Edible-podded Peas are held in the vicinity of Paris.

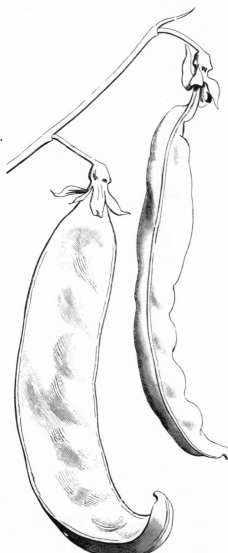

Pods of Large Crooked, or Scimitar, Sugar Pea
(natural size).

An attentive study shows that two different forms are grown under the same name of Large Crooked Sugar Pea. The commonest is that which we have just described. The other, which is sometimes known as the Lyons variety (*race de Lyon*), is not quite so tall, is five or six days earlier, and the pods are generally solitary, but large and very fleshy.

Giant Sugar Pea (*Pois Géant sans Parchemin*).—A climbing variety with large, broad, light-coloured leaves. Stems tinged with purple, and usually from 3½ to 4½ ft. high; flowers purplish coloured, sometimes solitary and sometimes in pairs; pods very large, of a pale-green colour, very much twisted, sometimes over 6 inches in length and more than 1 inch broad. The two sides or halves of the pod are generally, as it were, glued together,

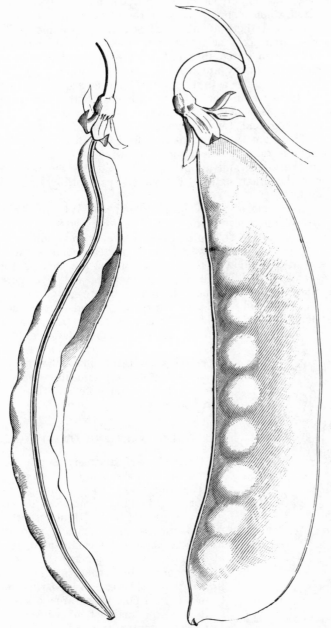

Giant Sugar Pea (natural size).

with no space between them except that which is completely filled by the peas, the positions of which are distinctly marked on the outside of the pod, where it bulges over each pea. Each pod contains from six to ten peas of large size, slightly angular or flattened in shape, and of a clear-green colour, becoming grayish and finely spotted with brownish red, when ripe. A litre of the peas weighs, on an average, 760 grammes, and there are about 24 peas in 10 grammes. The main stem carries from six to eight tiers of pods, and the branches, which are usually two or three in number, have hardly half that number. The pods of this variety are best for table use when young, as when they are near ripening both they and the peas acquire the somewhat strong hot taste which characterizes all Peas with purplish-coloured flowers. The peas, which in the raw state are perfectly green when they are young and tender, even then turn gray or brownish in cooking. There are two very distinct forms of the Giant Sugar Pea, one of which is taller, more vigorous growing, and at the same time later than the other, and almost always produces the pods in pairs. The pods of the other, or earlier form, are perceptibly larger, but are usually solitary.

Under the name of the White-flowered and White-podded Sugar Pea, a variety is grown in Germany which is very late, very branching, with stems from 5 to 6 ft. high, almost white or wax yellow in colour, and bearing large broad leaves, of a clear-green colour; the stipules are marked with a circle of the same colour as the stem at the place where they clasp it. The flowers are in pairs and of a pure white colour; they do not commence to bloom before about the sixteenth joint of the stem. The pods are straight, pointed at the end, about 3 inches long, and of a pale-yellow colour, almost like that of fresh butter. Each of them contains seven or eight peas, which become white and round when ripe. This is a rather productive variety, but very late and of only middling quality. It is very liable to degenerate, and then has stems and pods of a greenish colour.

B. Half-Dwarf and Dwarf Varieties.

Early Dwarf Brittany Sugar Pea (*Pois sans Parchemin Nain Hâtif Breton*).—A half-dwarf variety, from 2 to 2½ ft. high. Leaves rather slight, small, and of a grayish and glaucous green; stem rather short jointed towards the base; flowers white, medium sized, usually in pairs, and commencing to bloom at about the twelfth joint of the stem, immediately below which there are generally two branches of no great size, bearing from two to four tiers of pods which are most commonly solitary. The main stem ordinarily carries from seven to ten tiers of pods, which are produced in pairs, are of a pale, slightly grayish, green colour, and are not much over 2 inches in length; they are narrow, tolerably swollen and fleshy, quite free from membrane,

Early Dwarf Brittany Sugar Pea (1/10 natural size).

each containing from five to seven white peas,
squarish in shape, and, when ripe, becoming
of a grayish-white colour and irregular in
shape, but rather roundish. A litre of the peas
weighs, on an average, 800 grammes, and
there are about 54 peas in 10 grammes.
The stems of this variety are very stiff, and
as they are also numerous and short jointed,
the tendrils interlace the plants together in
such a manner that they mutually support
one another and grow quite erect without
needing any stakes, although they attain
some height. This property is worthy of
note, as many other varieties which are of
dwarfer growth are very much inferior to it
in this respect.

Capuchin Dwarf Sugar Pea (*Pois sans
Parchemin Nain Capucin*).—This variety is
very much grown in the north of France,
where it is highly esteemed. It somewhat resembles the Early Dwarf Brittany
Pea, and is hardy, exceedingly productive,
very free from membrane, and comes in half-
early. The plant grows from 20 inches to
2 ft. high, and the peas are round, white, and
very smooth.

Dwarf Dutch, or **Dwarf Crooked, Sugar
Pea** (*Pois sans Parchemin Très Nain Hâtif*).
—A very dwarf variety, not exceeding 8 to
10 inches in height.
Stem very zigzag in
growth, and with joints
so short that it is difficult
to count them exactly;
it usually commences to
branch at about the
seventh joint, and to
flower from the eighth to
the tenth joint. Flowers of
medium size, very white,
and often solitary. The
pods, which are borne in

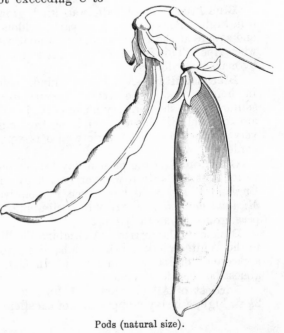

Pods of Early Dwarf Brittany
Sugar Pea (natural size).

Dwarf Dutch, or Dwarf Crooked,
Sugar Pea ($\frac{1}{10}$ natural size).

Pods (natural size).

from five to seven tiers on the main stem and in from two to four tiers on the branches, are of a pale, whitish-green colour, rather narrow, and well filled with white and largish peas, from five to seven in each pod. With the exception of the " strings," which are rather tough, the pod is thick, fleshy, and quite free from membrane. A litre of the peas weighs, on an average, 750 grammes, and there are about 48 peas in 10 grammes. This variety is almost as early as the Early Frame Pea, and, like it, is especially adapted for forcing. There is a sub-variety of it, which most usually produces solitary pods somewhat larger than those of the ordinary kind, and has larger and darker-coloured leaves, but it possesses no special merit to recommend it in preference to the form which has just been described.

OTHER ENGLISH VARIETIES.

A. *Round or Smooth-skinned Peas.*

Batt's Wonder.—A half-dwarf, rather thick-set kind, with large dark-green leaves. Flowers in pairs; pods long and slender, slightly curved and pointed ; peas round, sometimes square from pressure, and of a dark-green colour. A productive, hardy, and somewhat late variety.

Beck's Gem.—A dwarf variety, seldom exceeding a foot in height. Stem stiff, often branching; flowers white, in pairs ; pods rather short, and comparatively broad ; peas large, palish in colour. A half-early and, notwithstanding its dwarfness, a rather productive variety.

Bedman's Imperial.—A climbing variety, about 4 ft. high, with flowers sometimes solitary, and sometimes in pairs. Pods long, and very slightly curved, but blunt at the end ; peas large, somewhat oblong in shape, green. Ripens half-early.

Blue Prussian.—A half-dwarf kind, growing from about 2½ to over 3 ft. high. Pods generally in pairs, seldom solitary, almost straight, and square at the end ; peas large, round, very green, becoming bluish when ripe. This is one of the kinds which are most extensively grown by market gardeners.

Blue Scimitar.—A half-dwarf kind, seldom exceeding about 2½ ft. in height, and of a very vigorous growth. Pods pretty often solitary, long, slender, very much curved, and pointed at the end ; they are very well filled, each containing from eight to ten rather large and very green peas. This variety also is very much grown by market gardeners.

Charlton.—At the present day this variety is almost lost to cultivation, but formerly it was very much grown and highly valued. In England it seems to have been the equivalent of the French *Pois Michaux de Hollande.* It was a climbing variety, with white round peas, grown for an early crop.

Dickson's Favourite.—A climbing Shelling Pea, very closely allied to the White Scimitar Pea in its habit of growth, its earliness, and the appearance of its pods and peas. In fact, the two varieties might almost be considered identical.

Earliest of All (Laxton).—A first-class early blue Pea, growing 2½ ft. high, a heavy cropper, and of excellent quality.

Early Kent.—This is almost exactly the same kind which was formerly grown in France under the name of *Prince Albert*. At the present day the latter name is applied to a variety which comes in somewhat earlier and almost corresponds to Dillistone's Early Pea.

Fairbeard's Surprise.—A climbing variety, about 5 ft. high. Flowers white, large, generally solitary; pods long, rather broad, faintly curved, and roundish at the end; peas large, very green, and slightly oval in shape. A very early kind.

Flack's Imperial.—A half-dwarf kind, usually not more than about 3 ft. high. Pods pretty often solitary, but most usually in pairs, long and rather broad, slightly curved, and square at the end; peas large, and somewhat oval in shape, becoming slightly bluish in colour when ripe.

Harbinger.—This is the earliest of all Shelling Peas. It is a small-sized and exceedingly slender climbing Pea, remarkably like Dillistone's Early· Pea, but coming in two or three days earlier. Flowers solitary; pods short and very slender; peas small, round, and green when ripe.

Kentish Invicta (*East's Kentish Invicta*).—This may be described as a green-seeded Daniel O'Rourke Pea. It grows to nearly the same height, is equally early, and almost equally productive. The first flowers are often abortive.

Laxton's Evergreen.—Having for a time enjoyed a certain amount of favour, this variety appears to be now almost entirely neglected. It is a tall climbing Pea, with a rather slender and very branching stem, bearing slender, slightly curved pods of medium length. The peas are round and small, and, when ripe, assume a peculiar olive-green tint, by which they are easily recognized.

Laxton's Prolific Long-pod.—A tall climbing variety, 5 ft. or more in height. Leaves very large, and remarkably light coloured; flowers in pairs; pods almost like those of the White Scimitar Pea in shape, fully one-third longer and thicker, but far less numerous; peas white, somewhat irregular in shape; they are not perfectly smooth, without however being actually wrinkled.

Laxton's Superlative.—A tall climbing, thick-stemmed Pea. Leaves broad and luxuriant, but not tufty; pods almost always in pairs, often nearly 5 inches long, very much curved, pointed, and greatly swollen when ripe. They are not, however, very well filled, each pod only containing from six to eight small round peas, which, when ripe, become of a pale-green colour.

Laxton's Unique.—This is a very dwarf variety, growing from 12 to 14 inches high, with a usually branching stem. Pods in pairs, rather broad, tolerably curved, of medium length, and pointed at the end; peas round, rather small, and half white and half pale green when ripe.

Paradise Marrow (*Champion of Paris, Excelsior Marrow, Stuart's Paradise*).—A vigorous-growing climbing Pea, 5 to 6 ft. high, usually branching. Pods sometimes in pairs, but generally solitary, 4 inches long at least, broad, square at the end, and very slightly curved, well filled; peas seven to nine in each pod, large and sweet, becoming round and white when ripe.

Peruvian Black-eye Marrow.—An American variety resembling the *Pois de Madère.* It is also very like the Marly and Gouvigny Peas, but is distinguished from them by having a black spot on the *hilum.*

Philadelphia Extra Early.—Another American kind. A handsome climbing, very early Shelling Pea, very much resembling Daniel O'Rourke. Peas white.

Princess Royal.—A very productive, fine variety, 4 ft. high, with long well-filled pods.

Royal Dwarf (*White Russian*).—A half-dwarf variety, about 2½ ft. high, branching. Pods generally solitary, rather broad, very faintly curved, each containing five or six large peas, somewhat oval in shape, and very white when ripe.

Shilling's Grotto.—A climbing Pea, about 4 ft. high, not branching. Pods long, comparatively narrow, and slightly curved, each containing seven or eight peas, which become white and round when ripe.

Sutton's Emerald Gem (*Danecroft Rival*).—A very early climbing Pea, very distinct on account of the colour of its leaves, which are of a clear green without any trace of glaucousness. It is in every respect very like Sangster's No. 1 Improved (*Pois Prince Albert*).

Woodford Marrow.—A half-dwarf variety, with a stout, often branching stem, about 3 ft. high. Leaves dark green, glaucous; pods sometimes solitary, sometimes in pairs, long, rather slender, and of a dark-green colour. Each pod contains seven or eight peas, which, from being closely pressed against one another, are squarish in shape, and, when ripe, are of an olive-green colour, like those of Laxton's Evergreen Pea.

B. *Wrinkled Peas.*

Advancer.—A fine-flavoured, heavy-cropping, early variety, 3 ft. high, coming in about seven days after Alpha.

British Queen (*Hair's Defiance, Erin's Queen, Thorn's Royal Britain, Rollisson's Victoria, Shanley Marrow, Wonder of the World*).— A tall climbing Pea, 5 ft. and upwards in height. Stem branching; leaves large and luxuriant; pods generally in pairs, very long, broad, and nearly straight; peas large and tender, becoming white and wrinkled when ripe.

Connoisseur.—A vigorous-growing kind, rather late, but productive, and considered to be of exceptionally fine quality. Notwithstanding its high character, it does not appear to be very much grown.

Dr. Hogg.—An excellent, early, and tolerably productive climbing variety, with a slender stem, seldom exceeding 4 ft. in height. Leaves slight; pods usually solitary, long, very much curved, and exceedingly well filled; peas large, square, and remaining green when ripe. This variety is at least as early as the Early Emperor.

Early Maple.—A small slender variety, with purplish-coloured flowers, remarkable for nothing except its very great earliness. It comes into flower about the same time as Sangster's No. 1 Improved.

Evolution (Laxton).—A very productive variety, 3 ft. high, with very handsome pods, which are larger and of a deeper green than those of Telephone, and of superior quality.

Giant Emerald Marrow.—Very closely allied to Knight's Tall

Marrow, but distinguished from it by the clear-green colour of its leaves, which glisten like those of Sutton's Emerald Gem. It is a rather late kind, with large white wrinkled peas.

Giant Marrow (Culverwell's).—This grand and exceedingly productive Pea, like Telegraph and Telephone, has monstrous pods (7 inches long and 1 inch broad), which are slightly curved, of a dark-green colour, and crowded with large peas of the finest quality. It grows to a height of 5 ft.

Gladiator.—A distinct main-crop Pea, 3 ft. high, very robust and branching, with an abundance of long curved pods in pairs, closely filled with peas of delicious flavour and deep-green in colour.

Hair's Dwarf Mammoth.—A half-dwarf variety, of exceedingly vigorous growth. Stem thick and strong, about 2½ ft. high, and often branching; pods in pairs, long and broad, very slightly curved, and well filled; peas green, wrinkled.

Hay's Mammoth (*Tall White Mammoth, Ward's Incomparable*).—A vigorous-growing climbing Pea, attaining a height of 6½ ft. Stem thick and stout, generally branching; pods usually in pairs, long, broad, nearly square at the end, but very much narrowed towards the stalk; peas white, wrinkled. This is a late variety, but continues bearing for a long time, often until very late in autumn.

John Bull.—A very handsome, half-dwarf Wrinkled variety, with fine long pods and green peas. It comes in a little earlier than MacLean's Best of All Pea.

Little Gem.—A very dwarf kind, 12 to 16 inches high, vigorous growing, and usually very branching. The pods are rather small, but broad, straight, and well filled. The peas, when ripe, are pale coloured, bluish, and wrinkled.

MacLean's Wonderful.—A rich-flavoured, free-cropping, productive variety, growing 3 ft. high, and bearing large pods.

Multum in Parvo.—A very dwarf kind, about 1 ft. high, of compact and thick-set growth. Leaves broad and rather numerous, of a deep bluish green; pods usually solitary, short and rather broad, and narrowed towards the end; peas pale green or greenish white when ripe. A rather early variety.

Ne Plus Ultra (*Payne's Conqueror, Cullingford's Champion*).—A very tall-growing late Pea, sometimes over 6½ ft. high. Pods numerous, commencing at about one-third the height of the plant, usually in pairs, long, broad, perceptibly curved, and very much narrowed towards the stalk; peas very large, somewhat oval in shape, and green and wrinkled when ripe. First-class quality.

Nelson's Vanguard.—A half-dwarf Wrinkled Pea. Leaves rather large; pods borne in pairs, of medium length, but rather broad. This variety comes into use about the same time as the Early White Dwarf Wrinkled Pea, but is of a more compact and thick-set habit of growth.

Nutting's No. 1.—A branching, rather vigorous-growing, but really dwarf variety. Stem stiff, about 20 inches high; pods numerous, in pairs, of moderate length, but well filled, nearly straight, and bluntish at the end; peas white, wrinkled. A very early kind, and one of the best Dwarf White Wrinkled Peas.

2 F

Pioneer.—A small climbing variety, with fine slender stems, like those of Sangster's No. 1 Improved. Pods of medium size, usually solitary, straight, palish coloured, each containing five or six peas, which become white and wrinkled when ripe.

Pride of the Market.—This is a half-dwarf kind. Leaves very large, and of a light-green colour; pods of enormous size, being almost like those of Carter's Telephone Pea, but not very numerous. They set very irregularly, and the plant is rather delicate. Peas indented, green.

Premier.—A remarkably fine Pea, growing 3 ft. high, very productive, rich in flavour, and of fine constitution.

Prince of Wales.—An improved variety of the White Eugénie Pea, 3 ft. high, producing a heavy crop of fine-flavoured peas.

Princess of Wales.—A half-dwarf variety, seldom exceeding 2½ ft. in height. Leaves pale coloured, rather numerous; pods shortish, broad, blunt, whitish, growing very close together at the top of the stem owing to the shortness of the joints; peas wrinkled, pale green, and sometimes almost white.

Robert Fenn.—A splendid main-crop Pea, 2½ ft. high (a cross between Multum in Parvo and Premier), bearing abundantly broad straight pods, each containing eight or nine peas.

Standard.—A half-dwarf kind, about 2 ft. 8 inches high. Stem stout, and very leafy; leaves pale green, pods long, pointed, very much curved, rather swollen, each containing about ten large round peas, which become wrinkled when ripe, some of them remaining green, while others turn perfectly white.

Stratagem.—This variety closely resembles the Pride of the Market in every respect except in the colour of its leaves, which are of a dark green. Peas wrinkled, pale green.

Telegraph.—This variety comes near Telephone, but is distinct. It grows 4 ft. high, and bears very numerous long, broad pods, containing large peas, which, when cooked, are of a deep-green colour and of excellent flavour.

Veitch's Perfection.—This is a first-class variety, growing 3 ft. high, and bearing large well-filled pods, which are freely produced. Flavour superior.

Walker's Perpetual Bearer.—A first-class variety, 3 ft. high, a heavy cropper and continuous bearer. Flavour excellent. Should be sown very thin.

William Hurst (Laxton).—The most prolific, largest podded, earliest, and handsomest of all the Dwarf Wrinkled Marrow Peas. Requires no stakes.

OTHER FRENCH VARIETIES.

Shelling Peas (Pois à Ecosser).

Pois Bivort.—A climbing variety, of moderate height and early, with smooth white peas. It hardly differs from the Early Emperor Pea.

P. Blanc d'Auvergne.—A late kind, with a tall, very branching stem. Flowers white; pods very small and narrow, but well filled; peas white, squarish in shape. This is a good variety for feeding cattle, but comes in too late in the season to be of any great use as a kitchen-garden plant.

P. Café.—A Canadian variety of the cattle-feeding class, tall and late, with red flowers and brown peas, which are somewhat elongated and flattened in shape.

P. de Cérons Hâtif.—A climbing and rather early kind, resembling the Early Emperor-in its earliness, and the Early Frame Pea in its vigorous growth and great productiveness.

P. de Commenchon.—This is a good early Pea, coming in several days before the Early Emperor, but still not so early as Sangster's No. 1 Improved. It has rather large leaves and broad pods, which latter are as often solitary as in pairs. The peas are smooth, white, and large.

P. Dominé.—A sub-variety of the Early Frame Pea, later and more productive than the ordinary form. It has now almost entirely gone out of cultivation.

P. Doré.—A climbing variety, coming in nearly at the same time as the White Scimitar Pea. Leaves large and very light coloured; flowers white ; pods in pairs, long and narrow, and of a yellowish-green colour, as are also the peas.

P. Fève.—In its habit of growth this variety rather resembles the Marly Pea and its allies, but is distinguished from them by the shape of its peas, which are somewhat oblong and are marked with a black spot on the *hilum.*

P. Géant.—A large late Pea, with a very tall stem. Flowers violet coloured ; pods large, in pairs ; peas squarish in shape, grayish in colour, or slightly speckled with black ; *hilum* black.

P. le Plus Hâtif Biflore, de Gendbrugge.—An early kind, coming very near the Early Emperor, from which it is distinguished by being a little earlier and not quite so vigorous in growth.

P. Gros Jaune.—A very distinct variety, of a very light, almost yellowish, green colour in all its parts; often one-flowered. The pods and peas resemble those of the *Pois Carré Blanc.*

P. Gros Quarantain de Cahors.—This is a climbing variety, coming very near the Marly Pea, but a little earlier. The peas are white and large.

P. de Lorraine.—This is more a cattle-feeding than a kitchen-garden Pea. It is very late and has very small pods.

P. de Madère.—A climbing kind, rather like the Marly Pea in its habit of growth, but distinguished from it by its peas having a black spot on the *hilum.* It differs from the *Pois Fève* in the whiteness and. well-rounded form of the peas.

P. Michaux à Œil Noir (Black-eye Pea).—This variety is very distinctly characterized by the black spot on the *hilum* of the pea. It comes in about the same time as the Ruelle Michaux Pea, is productive, and is said to succeed very well in warm climates.

P. Michaux de Nanterre.—This is a sub-variety of the Early Frame Pea, a little later than the ordinary form, but not quite so late as the *Pois Dominé* mentioned above.

P. Michemolette.—A climbing, half-late kind, with large long pods, but only moderately productive. It comes very close to the *Pois de Gouvigny.*

P. Migron.—A good, very early, and productive climbing Pea, very closely allied to the English varieties, Dickson's First and Best and Daniel O'Rourke.

P. Nain Gros Blanc de Bordeaux.—A variety very much esteemed in its native district for growing on a large scale in market gardens. It is half-dwarf, two-flowered, and a little later than the Common Dwarf Pea, but has larger pods and peas.

P. Nain Gros Sucré.—A very dwarf variety, scarcely as high as the Brittany Very Dwarf Pea. Leaves narrow and of a light green; flowers in pairs; pods short and rather narrow, each containing from six to eight palish, smooth, very regular-shaped peas. This variety appears to be at present lost to cultivation.

P. Nain de Joseph.—A really dwarf kind, seldom exceeding from 14 to 16 inches in height. Pods medium sized, well filled; peas smooth and white. It comes very near Bishop's Early Pea, of which it may be considered as simply a sub-variety with a dwarfer habit of growth.

P. Nain Vert Petit.—A half-dwarf, very distinct kind, about $2\frac{1}{2}$ ft. high, with a branching stem. Leaves rather slight and of a dark-green colour; flowers very white; pods narrow, slightly curved; peas small, green, and very round. This variety is a trifle later than the Blue Prussian and the Imperial Dwarf Green Pea.

P. Quarantain.—A variety which is very generally grown in the neighbourhood of Paris, especially in the direction of St. Denis. It is a very early climbing kind, usually with solitary flowers, and in point of earliness does not differ much from the English variety, Dickson's First and Best.

P. Quarante-deux.—This is grown in the same localities as the preceding variety, and comes in later. It is a good variety, with short but well-filled pods. The stems are rather slender. It is somewhat earlier than the Early Emperor. Some growers distinguish two forms of it—one as early as the Early Emperor, but yielding for a shorter period, and the other almost as early as Sangster's No. 1 Improved. This latter form seems to be confounded with the *Pois Quarantain.*

P. Remontant Vert à Rames (Green Branching Pea).—A rather slender and tall-stemmed variety, almost as early as the White Scimitar Pea. Flowers often solitary; pods long and slender, each containing seven or eight round dark-green peas.

P. Remontant Vert à Demi-Rames.—A half-dwarf, very branching kind, which continues bearing for a long time. It is pretty closely allied to the *Pois Nain Vert Petit* (mentioned above), but is distinguished from it by the somewhat larger size of the peas.

P. Vert Nain du Cap.—This is rather a half-dwarf than a really dwarf variety, with stiff branching stems, and flowers in pairs, exhibiting a considerable resemblance to the Blue Prussian Pea, but with peas of smaller size and not so blue in tint. It is not a very productive kind.

B. *Edible-podded, or Sugar, Peas.*

Pois de Commenchon Sans Parchemin.—A climbing variety, not more than from $3\frac{1}{2}$ to 4 ft. high, almost as early as the Early Emperor. Flowers white, large; pods medium sized, whitish.

P. Friolet Sans Parchemin.—A climbing kind, very much like the Ruelle Michaux Pea, but entirely free from membrane. Pods straight, somewhat swollen, and pale coloured.

P. Mange-tout Demi-nain à Œil Noir.—A half-dwarf early variety, coming in a few days earlier than the Breton Early Dwarf Sugar Pea. Flowers violet coloured; pods smallish, slightly twisted; peas gray, not spotted, and with a black *hilum.*

P. Sans Parchemin à Cosse Jaune.—A half-early climbing variety, with large light-green leaves. Flowers white, tinged with yellow, in pairs; pods long, rather broad, entirely free from membrane, and of a greenish-yellow colour; peas somewhat elongated in shape, and of a light-yellow colour.

P. Sans Parchemin à Fleur Rouge (Tall Red-flowered Sugar Pea).— A tall late Pea, with the stem usually branching. Flowers pale red, not violet coloured, in pairs; pods medium sized, comparatively narrow, somewhat curved, and sometimes slightly twisted; peas pale brown marbled with red.

P. Sans Parchemin Très Hâtif à Fleur Rouge.—A climbing variety, almost as early as Sangster's No. 1 Improved. Stem thin and slender, seldom exceeding about 3 ft. in height; flowers violet coloured, with a red keel, commencing to bloom very low down on the stem; pods small, whitish, and very free from membrane.

P. Sans Parchemin Nain Gris (Dwarf Gray Sugar Pea).—A distinct, half-dwarf, branching variety, with violet-coloured flowers and smallish and very numerous pods. It has been very generally superseded by the early white-flowered varieties.

P. Sans Parchemin Nain Hâtif de Hollande.—A dwarf variety, growing from about 20 inches to 2 ft. high, and a true early kind, as it flowers about the same time as the Ruelle Michaux Pea. Pods rather small, between 2 and 3 inches long and $\frac{3}{5}$ inch broad, slightly curved, and quite free from membrane.

P. Sans Parchemin Nain Ordinaire (Common Dwarf Sugar Pea).— This variety differs very little from the preceding one. It comes in a day or two later, but is hardier and somewhat more productive. Both varieties are now superseded in cultivation by the Breton Dwarf Sugar Pea.

P. Sans Parchemin Ridé Nain (Knight's Dwarf Marrow Sugar Pea).— This is rather a half-dwarf than a really dwarf kind, as it grows from about 2½ to upwards of 3 ft. high. Flowers white, in pairs; pods small, numerous, generally curved, and very free from membrane; peas quite wrinkled, small, square or flattened in shape. This is a very distinct variety, but it has the fault of being somewhat late. The peculiarity of the pea being wrinkled adds nothing to the merit of the variety as a Sugar Pea.

GERMAN VARIETIES.

Buschbaum-Erbse.—A very dwarf Shelling Pea, rather like the Brittany Dwarf Pea, but coming in a little earlier and having somewhat larger pods. The name is also applied to a very dwarf and thick-set Edible-podded Pea.

Grosse Graue Florentiner Zucker-Erbse.—This variety is almost exactly the same as the old Giant Sugar Pea. It is a very tall-growing, somewhat late kind, and usually produces the flowers in pairs. The pods are nearly the same size as those of the Large Crooked Sugar Pea, and are generally straighter than those of the Giant Sugar Pea, which is now commonly grown, and which has been already described.

Pois Jaune d'Or de Blocksberg.—A Shelling Pea, rather like the White Scimitar Pea, but of a more slender habit of growth, not quite so tall, and somewhat earlier. It is particularly distinguished by the wax-yellow tint of its pods and fresh peas, but, as a fine green colour is generally a *desideratum* in Peas, this peculiarity is rather a defect than otherwise.

Kapuziner-Erbse.—In Germany, and especially in Holland, this name is given to all kitchen-garden peas which have red flowers, and is chiefly applied to the Edible-podded Peas, as these are almost the only kinds with coloured flowers which are grown. There are both climbing and dwarf varieties of these Peas.

Ruhm von Cassel Erbse.—A variety which is very closely allied to the White Scimitar Pea, and might almost be considered identical with it, only that its pods are straighter or less curved than those of that kind.

Pois Sans Parchemin de Henri (Frühe Heinrich's Zucker-Erbse).—A climbing Sugar Pea, of moderate height, rather like the Ruelle Michaux Pea. Flowers often solitary. A good and rather early variety, but not so productive as the good half-dwarf kinds, such as the Breton Sugar Pea.

Pois Sans Parchemin de Hollande (Holländische Grünbleibende Späte Zucker-Erbse).—A very tall late kind, with white flowers in pairs. Pods of medium size, much smaller than those of the Large Crooked Sugar Pea. This variety does not commence to bear until late in the season, but it continues bearing for a long time. It requires very tall stakes.

Pois Sans Parchemin Très Nain de Grâce.—A very dwarf variety, with small, grayish, slender, scanty leaves. The pods are not always quite free from membrane.

Pois Très Hâtif à Châssis de Grâce.—This pea may, at the most, be considered only a sub-variety of the ordinary Dwarf Dutch or Dwarf Crooked Sugar Pea, being merely a little more slender in habit, and growing a trifle taller. It is not a very productive kind, but very early and exceedingly dwarf.

FIELD, or GRAY, PEAS.

Pisum sativum, L. var. *arvense; Pisum arvense*, L.

French, Pois gris. *German,* Feld graue Erbsen. *Italian,* Piselli grigi da foraggio. *Spanish,* Guisantes pardos, Chicharos.

Notwithstanding the authority of Linnæus, we find it very difficult to regard the violet-flowered Peas which are commonly grown for feeding cattle as belonging to a different botanical species from the white-flowered Peas which are grown in the kitchen garden ; or rather, we doubt whether the solitary-flowered Pea which is found growing wild in cultivated ground is really the Gray Pea which in all its characteristics comes so near the kitchen-garden Pea, presenting, in fact, all the same peculiarities of growth from germination to maturity, varying exactly like other Peas, and, in fine, only differing from them in the colour of the flower, which has reddish wings and a violet-coloured standard. Now, a difference in the colour of the flowers, especially if the flowers of one of the two forms in question are white, cannot be regarded as a specific difference. Modifications of this kind may be seen every day in most cultivated plants, and, without going beyond the *Leguminosæ* family for examples, we may point to the Kidney Beans and Broad Beans as constantly exhibiting similar variations in the colour of their flowers and seeds.

The violet-flowered Peas, like the others, embrace a number of varieties which are climbing or dwarf, early or late, producing flowers solitary or in pairs, and, finally, some of them have the pods lined with a parchment-like membrane, while others have the pods free from membrane. The colour of the peas also is variable, being sometimes greenish or russet coloured, and uniform in tint, and sometimes speckled with red or brown on a lighter ground. For cattle-feeding purposes, the tallest, most vigorous-growing, and most branching kinds are most in request. The three varieties which are most generally grown in France are the Spring Gray Pea (*Pois Gris de Printemps*) and the Partridge Pea (*Pois Perdrix*), which are sown immediately after winter ; and the Winter Gray Pea (*Pois Gris d'Hiver*), which may be sown in autumn. It is hardly necessary to say that no one ever thinks of staking these Peas. They are usually sown along with Rye or strong-stemmed kinds of Oats, on which they climb, and when the Peas are sown in autumn, it should be along with a hardy variety of Oats that will bear the winter well.

The germinating power of the Peas of the violet-flowered kinds lasts for the same time as that of the white-flowered kinds, that is, for three years at the least.

Spring Field, or **Gray, Pea** (*Pois Gris de Printemps*).—A very vigorous-growing and very branching kind, with long slender stems of a pale-green colour, growing up to 6½ ft. high, and bearing numerous leaves of medium size and plentifully spotted with light gray. The flowers, which are violet coloured, with a violet-gray standard, are always in pairs ; they are small sized, and turn green in fading. The first flowers appear at about the eighteenth or twentieth joint of the stem, just above the branches, which are three or four in number, and sometimes grow almost as high as the main stem. A well-grown plant will produce from sixty to eighty pods. These are small and narrow, and often open spontaneously when ripe. Each pod contains from five to seven peas, which are somewhat angular in shape, and of a reddish or faint bronzy colour. A litre of the dried peas weighs, on an average, 790 grammes, and there are about 70 peas in 10 grammes. We have seen, in Auvergne, a sub-variety which rather frequently produces the flowers in threes, but is remarkable for nothing else but this peculiarity.

Partridge, Maple, or Marlborough Pea (*Pois Perdrix*).—This variety is entirely distinct from the preceding one, although it is grown much in the same way. It is almost as tall, but has much larger, thicker, longer-jointed, and less branching stems. The leaves, and the stipules especially, are very large. The flowers have light violet-coloured wings and a bluish-gray standard veined with dark violet; they are large sized, and sometimes, but rarely, solitary. They commence to open at about the fifteenth or sixteenth joint of the stem, and therefore somewhat earlier than those of the preceding variety. The pods are longer and broader than those of that variety, and contain broad, flat, squarish peas, plentifully speckled with brownish red on a chamois-coloured ground. A litre of the dried peas weighs, on an average, 680 grammes, and there are about 50 peas in 10 grammes. As a forage-plant, this variety yields more heavily than the preceding one, but it is a more delicate kind, and requires richer soil and a more even temperature. It is chiefly grown in England and in the west of France.

Winter Field, or Gray, Pea (*Pois Gris d'Hiver*).—When this Pea comes into flower, having then attained its full development, it does not seem to differ from the Spring Field Pea, being of the same height, the same habit of growth, and apparently the same in all its characteristics; but, if examined at the commencement of its growth, it exhibits peculiarities which specially belong to it, and which distinguish it unmistakably from all other kinds of Peas. The young stem, instead of growing erect as soon as it issues from the ground, bends down and grows along the surface of the soil, speedily producing branches, which also sprawl upon the ground. All these young shoots are furnished with stipules situated at the base of rudimentary leaves, very close to one another, and so small that it is difficult, at first sight, to believe that they belong to a Pea. The plant remains in this condition all through the winter, and it is not until the month of March that the stems begin to grow erect, and to become furnished with leaves of the ordinary kind. It often happens that the main stem wastes away entirely, its place being supplied by shoots which issue from the root. From this time forward, the plant exactly resembles the Spring Field Pea, except that its peas are usually smaller, rounder, and of a greener tint. When sown in spring, the Winter Field Pea also commences its growth by spreading along the ground and producing slender stems with minute stipules, but it does not remain long in this condition, and the plant soon starts into growth like the common spring Peas. It comes in later, however, than any other kind. A litre of the dried peas weighs, on an average, 810 grammes, and there are about 80 peas in 10 grammes.

In France the three varieties of Field Peas just mentioned are almost the only kinds known, although there are some local varieties which differ very slightly from one or other of them. In England, on the contrary, there are some very distinct varieties, of which the following are the principal ones:—

Hastings Gray Pea.—A variety not much grown at the present day, resembling the Warwick Gray Pea, but coming in considerably later.

Rounceval Gray Pea.—The tallest-growing and latest kind of

Field Peas, but, at the same time, the most productive, next to the Partridge Pea. Its peas are flattened and almost wrinkled, chamois coloured, with a black *hilum*.

Warwick Early Gray Pea.—A sub-variety of the Spring Field Pea, coming in about three weeks earlier than the ordinary form, and very productive, although of dwarf habit. The peas are reddish coloured, speckled with brown.

TUBEROUS-ROOTED PEA.

Lathyrus tuberosus, L. *Leguminosæ.*

French, Gesse tubéreuse. *German*, Erdnuss. *Flemish*, Aardnoot. *Dutch*, Aardakker.
Italian, Ghianda di terra.

Native of Europe.—Perennial.—This wild plant, which is so common in some localities that it becomes a troublesome weed, is sometimes sought after on account of the tuberous excrescences which grow upon its roots, and which contain a large amount of white, starchy, sweetish matter of rather agreeable flavour, like that of chestnuts. The peas are largish, oblong, somewhat square or angular in shape, and of a brownish colour, slightly speckled with black. The plant is hardly ever cultivated, as it is apt to become too rampant, and the roots are gathered where it grows naturally.

WINGED PEA.

Lotus T. tragonolobus, L.; *Tetragonolobus purpureus*, Mœnch. *Leguminosæ.*

French, Lotier cultivé. *German*, Flügel-Erbse. *Flemish*, Vogelvitse. *Danish*, Asparges
œrten. *Spanish*, Bocha cultivada.

Native of South Europe.—Annual.—An almost creeping plant, with stems spreading on the ground, about 1 ft. long and of a pale grayish-green colour, of the same tint as the leaves, which are composed of three broad short leaflets. Flowers of a fine, slightly brownish red; pods square, with membranous wings at the angles, from about 2¼ to over 3 inches long, and tolerably fleshy when young; seed yellowish, almost spherical, or slightly flattened. A gramme contains from 15 to 18 seeds, and a litre of them weighs about 800 grammes. Their germinating power lasts for five years. This plant is grown in the same manner as Lentils or French Beans. The seed is sown in April where the crop is to stand, and the plants require no attention except watering in very dry weather. The pods, when young and tender, are eaten like Haricot Beans. The seed, when roasted, forms one of the many substitutes for coffee.

Winged Pea (1/10 natural size).

PEA-NUT, EARTH-NUT, or GROUND-NUT.

Arachis hypogæa, L. *Leguminosæ.*

French, Arachide. *German,* Erdnuss. *Italian,* Cece di terra. *Spanish,* Chufa.
Portuguese, Amenduinas.

Native of South America.—Annual.—A plant with weak, almost creeping, stems. Leaves consisting of two pairs of oval leaflets, with a broad emarginate stipule at the base of the leaf-stalk ; flowers yellow, solitary, in the axils of the leaves ; pods oblong, often contracted in the middle,

like a Bottle-Gourd, of irregular shape, reticulated, yellowish, each containing two or three nuts as large as good-sized peas, of an oblong shape, and covered with a brown or reddish skin. About 25 of these nuts weigh 10 grammes, and a litre of them weighs, on an average, 400 grammes. Their germinating power lasts for only one year. A remarkable peculiarity of this plant is that the flowers insert their ovaries into the ground, where they complete their growth, and where the seeds or nuts ripen, at a depth of from 2 to 4 inches. In America several varieties are grown, differing from one another in the size of the nuts and the number contained in each pod.

Pea-nut ($\frac{1}{10}$ natural size ; detached fruit, $\frac{1}{2}$ natural size).

CULTURE.—The seeds or nuts are sown in spring, as soon as the frosts are over, and the plant succeeds best in light soils. Being a tropical plant, it may sometimes live and ripen its fruit in the west of Europe, but cannot be profitably cultivated here. USES.—In warm countries the nuts are often eaten raw or parched. An oil, of the greatest value for economic purposes, is also extracted from them.

PENNYROYAL.

Mentha Pulegium, L. *Labiatæ.*

Menthe pouliot.

Native of Europe.—Perennial.—A plant with prostrate stems, which readily take root, bearing roundish-oval, slightly hairy leaves of a grayish-green colour. Flowers small, bluish lilac, in rounded whorled clusters rising one above another in tiers on the stem, sometimes to the number of ten or twelve ; seed exceedingly fine, oval, and of a light-brown colour. The whole plant gives out a very agreeable odour, which is somewhat more powerful than that of any other kind of Mint. The Pennyroyal prefers stiff moist soils. It is propagated by division, and a plantation of it will last for several years. The leaves are used for seasoning puddings and various dishes. It is seldom seen in English kitchen gardens.

PEPPERMINT.

Mentha piperita, L. *Labiatæ.*

French, Menthe poivrée. *German,* Pfeffermünze. *Danish,* Pebbermynte.

A native of North Europe.—Perennial.—A plant with a creeping stem, which readily takes root. Leaves stalked, oblong or lanceolate-acute ; flowers in a cylindrical-oblong spike and of a reddish-violet colour. This species does not produce seed. CULTURE.—The Peppermint plant is grown in the same manner as the Common Mint or Spearmint. Although, in the wild state, it is usually found in parts of meadows which are wet and almost under water, it nevertheless succeeds well in moist, deep garden soil. It is always propagated from cuttings of the stems, which take root with the greatest readiness. USES.—The leaves and stems are sometimes used for seasoning, but they are chiefly employed for the distillation of the essence of peppermint.

POTATOES.

Solanum tuberosum, L. *Solanaceæ.*

French, Pomme de terre. *German,* Kartoffel. *Flemish* and *Dutch,* Aardappel. *Danish,* Jordepeeren. *Italian,* Patata. *Spanish* and *Portuguese,* Patatas. *Spanish (American),* Papa.

Native of the high mountain regions of South America.—Annual, but virtually perennial through its tubers.—The history of the discovery and the introduction of the Potato into Europe is rather obscure. It appears certain, however, that towards the close of the sixteenth century the plant began to be generally cultivated and used as a table vegetable. It was first grown in the Netherlands, Lorraine, Switzerland, and Dauphiné, and its cultivation extended even to Spain and Italy before it became common in the central and northern districts of France. In fact, it was not until after Parmentier had laboured and written on the subject, that the Potato was appreciated at its true value in the neighbourhood of Paris and the adjoining localities. Almost about the same time, its culture began to acquire some degree of importance in England, and from that time forward it has extended most rapidly, and, in spite of the disease, which about the middle of the present century threatened complete ruin to its cultivation, the Potato still holds the first place amongst edible tubers.

The number of the varieties of the Potato is prodigious. They might be counted to the number of many thousands, if any one wished to record all that have been raised and recommended in different countries during the last hundred years. This extreme multiplicity of varieties has obliged us to pass over a very large number of them, and, not to make this volume too bulky, we shall confine ourselves to the description of forty varieties which appear to us to be the most distinct and, at the same time, the most worthy of note.

The stem of the Potato is generally solid, more or less quadrangular, and often furnished with membranous wings at the angles. The leaves are compound, formed of oval leaflets, between which are often found small leafy growths, like leaflets of smaller size. The flowers are produced in axillary and terminal clusters, and have an entire, wheel-shaped, five-pointed corolla, varying in colour from pure white to purplish. Many varieties do not flower, and of those which do flower, a very great number never bear fruit. The fruit is a roundish or very shortly oval berry, of a green colour or (rarely) tinged with violet brown, and averaging about 1 inch in diameter. It contains, in the midst of a green and very acrid pulp, small, white, kidney-shaped seeds. These are never sown except for the purpose of raising new varieties.

The tubers, which are only underground branches swollen and filled with starchy matter, exhibit very great differences in shape and colour, according to the varieties. They are usually divided into the four classes of Round, Oblong, Long Notched, and Long Smooth Potatoes. To these characteristics, and those which are derived from the colour, may be added those which are furnished by the buds or shoots which are produced by the tubers when kept in a dark place. These are very constant in appearance and colour, and afford the means of distinguishing one variety from another with a considerable degree of accuracy. We believe few characteristics are so important as these for determining varieties, and in a work* recently published we thus spoke of them : " Whether the tubers have attained their full growth, or, on the contrary, have remained exceedingly small and puny ; whether they have been fully ripened or not ; whether, even, they are sound or diseased, provided they have enough vitality left to enable them to commence to vegetate, the buds or shoots always develop themselves with the same appearance and the same colour in the same variety"—on condition, of course, that the tuber has not been exposed, either before or during the growth of the shoot, for any length of time to the influence of light.

CULTURE.—When grown in the open ground, Potatoes are usually planted in April, in holes or pockets at a distance from one another of from 16 inches to 4 ft., according to the vigour of growth of the variety. Entire tubers, of medium size, are the best for planting. They should be covered, at the time of planting, with soil to the depth of 4 or 5 inches, and the practice is to earth up as soon as the stems have grown to a height of 6 to 8 inches, the ground being then also hoed for the second time. The earthing-up is not absolutely necessary, but it has the advantage of causing the tubers to lie closer round the roots of the plant, so that they are more easily taken up. Potatoes ripen, or, at least, become good enough for use, from the beginning of June to the end of October, according to the varieties. When the tubers for planting have been exposed to the influence of light and air, they generally vegetate earlier and more vigorously ; but, in this case, much care must be taken, when planting, not to break off the shoots which have commenced their growth.

There is some advantage in planting Potatoes in autumn, as the yield is generally somewhat heavier than it would be on the same area and with the same quantity of " seed " potatoes, if planted in spring. On the other hand, there is the danger of the " seed " perishing in the

* *Essai d'un Catalogue Méthodique et Synonymique des Principales Variétés de Pomme de Terre,* par Henry Vilmorin. Paris, 1881.

ground in very cold or too damp winters, and, besides, the planting should be done in October or November—a time when there is almost always much to do in the gardens or in the fields.

Potatoes may be forced under frames on a hot-bed of greater or less strength. Forcing may be commenced in December or January, and monthly plantings in the hot-beds may be continued up to the middle of March. The *Marjolin* Potato, which has very scanty leaves, is chiefly employed for this purpose. New forced potatoes may be taken up in two and a half or three months after planting.

The culture of the Potato in the United Kingdom is so very extensive, and differs so much according to the district and the aim of the growers, that we have not space to do justice to it here. We therefore refer the reader to a small and handy book in which the culture in all its phases is carefully described, viz. Fremlin's " Potato in Farm and Garden," and the London market-garden culture is fully treated of in Shaw's " London Market Gardens."

Uses.—The tubers, either young or ripe, are eaten as a table vegetable. They are also used for feeding cattle and for the manufacture of starch.

I. Round Yellow Varieties.

Bonne Wilhelmine Potato (*Pomme de Terre Tige Couchée*).—Tuber roundish, bright yellow, smooth ; eyes faintly marked ; diameter rarely exceeding 2 inches ; flesh very yellow ; shoot of an intense violet colour. Stems of medium size, seldom more than 20 inches to 2 ft. long, more spreading than erect, slightly tinged with brown, very rarely branching. Lower leaves dark green, with oval, rather regular, almost flat leaflets ; those at the end of the stem lighter in colour, narrower, and much more curled. Flowers reddish violet, large, in clusters of from six to eight. Seed rather abundant. This variety is especially suitable for an early crop. The tubers, which are numerous and regular in shape, form and colour quickly. If planted in April, new Potatoes may be taken up in the beginning of July.

Model P. (*Pomme de Terre Modèle*).—Tuber pale yellow, very regularly rounded, slightly flattened in one part ; eyes faintly marked ; skin smooth or wrinkled, according to the kind

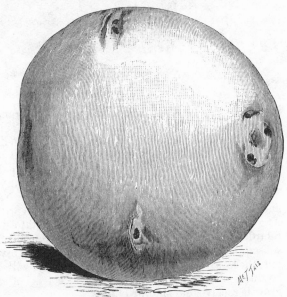

Model Potato (natural size).

of soil in which it is grown; flesh pale yellow; shoot violet coloured. Stems stiff, erect, tinged with violet brown, seldom more than 20 inches high. Leaves short and stiff, with almost round and very much reticulated leaflets of a very dark and dull green colour. Flowers very rarely produced. This variety is remarkable for the extremely regular shape and handsome appearance of the tubers. It also possesses much interest for us from the circumstance that it resists the Potato-disease better than any other kind that we know of.

Shaw, or Regent, Potato (*Pomme de Terre Chave*).—Tuber round, yellow, with a smooth or wrinkled skin, according to the kind of soil in which it is grown; eyes rather deeply sunk; flesh yellow and very floury; shoot of a wax-yellow colour, violet-coloured at the base and at the extremity. Stems rather long, sometimes 3 ft. or more, pliable, almost always drooping, quite green, or very slightly tinged with

Shaw, or Regent, Potato (natural size).

brown, faintly winged, and almost always branching. Leaves short, numerous, of a dark and rather dull green colour; leaflets crowded closely together, reticulated, and always curled and wavy. Flowers very rarely opening, as they almost always fall off when merely small buds; when they do bloom, they are of a pale bluish-lilac colour. This variety is more extensively grown than any other kind of Round Yellow Potato in the vicinity of Paris. It is very productive, floury, and of excellent quality. If planted in April, the crop ripens in August. When the growth of this Potato has been checked or retarded by very dry weather, it is not unusual for the tubers, in their subsequent growth, to become very considerably elongated in shape; but these same tubers, if used for "seed," will in the following year produce perfectly round Potatoes—that is, of course, provided their growth receives no similar check.

Early Round Yellow Potato (*Pomme de Terre Jaune Ronde Hâtive*). —This may be considered as a somewhat earlier form of the Shaw, or Regent, Potato, with usually rounder tubers, which also have fewer eyes. In its habit of growth it hardly differs from that variety. The stems, however, seldom exceed 2 ft. or 2 ft. 4 in. in length; the leaves are not so numerous, and are of a lighter-green colour, those at the top of the stem being paler and more yellowish than those at the base. The flowers fall off while in the bud state. This is a very fine and excellent variety. If planted in April, new potatoes, fit for use, may be taken up about the end of July.

Segonzac P. (*Pomme de Terre Segonzac*).—Tuber exactly like that of the Shaw, or Regent, Potato. The slight difference which exists between the two varieties is altogether in their habit of growth, the stems of the Segonzac Potato being somewhat stouter, with more erect and more numerous branches, and the leaflets being more curled and twisted. One of the most constant characteristics of this Potato is that it flowers pretty frequently. The flowers are rather small and of a bluish-gray colour. It is very extensively grown in France, under different names in different provinces, and is often called the St. Jean Potato, although it really does not ripen until August.

One of the most interesting features of this Potato is the very great length of time during which it has been in cultivation, and its sustained productiveness and vigour of growth, notwithstanding the remote date of its first introduction. It is a very general opinion, and probably a correct one in the main, that varieties of Potatoes, like most other varieties obtained by cultivation, have only a limited period of duration : that at the end of fifteen, twenty, thirty years, or more, they lose their vigour, cease to be productive, and finally become extinct from mere natural decay. In the Commission of Inquiry on the Potato-disease, which was opened by the English Parliament in 1880, this opinion was maintained by men of undoubted experience and authority on the subject, and we believe there is some truth in this view of the matter; nevertheless, it must be acknowledged that the Shaw, or Regent, and the Segonzac Potatoes, both of which have been in cultivation for more than sixty years, form a remarkable exception to this rule, and, moreover, an exception which does not stand alone.

Séguin P. (*Pomme de Terre Séguin*).—Tuber roundish, medium sized, and of a slightly grayish-yellow colour; skin usually wrinkled ; eyes not very deeply sunk; flesh yellow. Diameter generally ranging between 2 and 2$\frac{1}{5}$ inches. Stems erect, vigorous growing, 2 ft. to 2$\frac{1}{2}$ ft. high, quadrangular, deeply winged, marked with brown above the joints, and generally branching. Leaves rather distant from one another, large, composed of oval, stalked, large, flat leaflets, and of other leaflets which are small, sessile, and round. Flowers numerous, large, bluish lilac, in stout clusters, and produced in succession for a long time. This variety is very productive and floury, and keeps well. It does not ripen until September.

Scotch Champion P. (*Pomme de Terre Champion*).—Tubers very numerous, roundish, sometimes flattened; skin pale yellow, as is also the flesh ; eyes deeply sunk, but not very numerous; shoot violet coloured. Diameter seldom exceeding from 2$\frac{1}{5}$ to 2$\frac{2}{5}$ inches. The tubers are often longer than broad. Stems very vigorous-growing, very erect, 3 ft. or more high, quadrangular, winged, dotted with blackish brown, and comparatively slender. Leaves numerous, growing almost

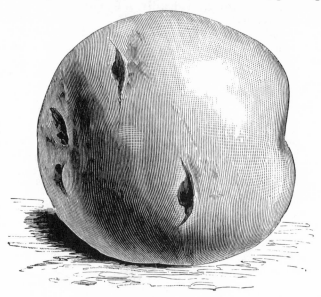

Séguin Potato (natural size).

erect, of medium size, and having the veins spotted with violet colour; leaflets elongated, very long pointed, very much reticulated, and covered with small stiff hairs. Flowers deep-violet colour, with white

Scotch Champion Potato (natural size).

points, in rather numerous clusters, and produced in succession for a long time. Seed very rarely formed. This is an exceedingly vigorous-growing and productive variety. During the last few years a great deal of noise has been made about it in England, on account of its resisting the disease. It is not, however, perfectly exempt from it, but, like the Chardon Potato, it continues to grow when attacked by the fungus, and ripens its tubers late in autumn, when the disease has spent much of its force.

Jeancé Potato (*Pomme de Terre Jeancé*).—Tubers roundish, somewhat irregular in shape in consequence of the eyes being very deeply sunk; skin of a slightly grayish yellow colour, and smooth or wrinkled, according to the kind of soil in which the plants are grown; flesh yellow; shoot pink. Diameter often $3\frac{2}{5}$ inches, and sometimes more. Stems vigorous growing, from $2\frac{1}{2}$ to $3\frac{1}{4}$ ft. long, quadrangular, rather deeply winged, often drooping, and very much branched. Leaves medium-sized, with short oval-rounded or heart-shaped leaflets, which are almost flat in the lower leaves and curled and folded in those at

Chardon Potato (natural size).

the end of the stem. Flowers rather numerous, of a pink-lilac colour, seldom succeeded by any fruit. The prevailing tint of the leaves is a rather pale, grayish green. This Potato, which is best known in the vicinity of Paris by the name of *Pomme de Terre Vosgienne*, is one of the most productive and best kinds. It is very floury and keeps well. If planted in April, the crop ripens in September.

Chardon P. (*Pomme de Terre Chardon*).—Tubers very large, roundish, often elongated, covered, so to say, with knobs and hollows, on account of the great depth to which the eyes are sunk; skin generally smooth and of a pale-yellow colour; flesh nearly white; shoot pink. The tubers may, generally, be easily distinguished from those of any other kinds; however, the roundest and yellowest of them are

2 G

sometimes hardly to be known from those of the Jeancé Potato. Stems very vigorous growing, 3 ft. or more high, very erect, quadrangular, deeply winged, tinged with brownish red, as are also the leaf-stalks, and especially the flower-stalks. Leaves rather large, with long, pointed, rather reticulated and slightly glazed leaflets. Flowers very numerous, in clusters of from fifteen to thirty, of a reddish-lilac colour, and produced in succession during nearly the whole season, but hardly ever succeeded by fruit. This variety is the kind which is most extensively employed for field culture, being the most productive, and, at the same time, one of the kinds which suffer least from the Potato-disease. It is usually grown for the manufacture of starch and for feeding cattle; nevertheless it is not a bad Potato for table use towards the end of winter, the flesh being then less watery than it is when newly taken up, and it remains firm and floury, owing to the slowness of the shoots to germinate.

Van der Veer Potato.—Tubers roundish or slightly elongated, from $2\frac{4}{5}$ to 4 inches in length by about $2\frac{1}{4}$ inches in diameter; skin smooth or slightly wrinkled; eyes rather deeply sunk; flesh pale yellow; shoot pink. Stems very erect, vigorous growing, quadrangular, stiff, bearing an abundance of large leaves with oval-acuminate leaflets,

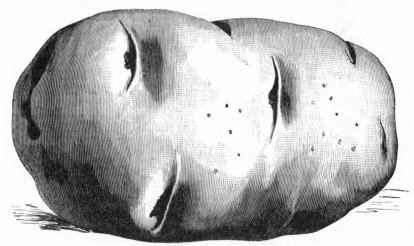

Van der Veer Potato (natural size).

of a pale, slightly yellowish, or grayish-green colour. Flowers white, rather large, usually producing no seed. This is a rather late, but extremely productive variety. It is particularly suitable for field culture, either for feeding cattle or for the manufacture of starch. There is a strong-stemmed form, which is more vigorous growing and more productive than the ordinary kind, and this improved variety is the only one of the two that should be propagated.

Paterson's Victoria P.—Tubers oblong or roundish in outline, but always perceptibly flattened; eyes very faintly marked; skin yellow, slightly tinged with salmon colour; flesh yellow; shoot violet coloured. Stems stout, quadrangular, very slightly tinged with brown near the joints, perfectly erect and $2\frac{1}{2}$ ft. or more in height. Leaves rather far apart, composed of large, oval-rounded and acuminate, rather flat, very much reticulated leaflets of a grayish-green colour. Flowers in rather close clusters, of a slightly reddish-violet colour, most usually falling off unfructified. This variety flowers rather late. An excellent Potato for table use, floury in the highest degree, and keeping to perfection. If planted in April, it ripens about the end of August. To us it has always appeared to be very seldom attacked by the disease, at least in the vicinity of Paris.

Alpha Potato.—Tubers roundish, rarely oblong, slightly flattened; skin smooth, pale yellow; flesh white; eyes moderately marked; shoot pink. Stems medium sized, seldom more than 20 inches long, half erect, quite green, diminishing abruptly in thickness from the base. Leaves rather long and large, composed of elongated-acute leaflets of a light-green colour and tolerably glazed. Flowers white, almost always abortive. A good early and, at the same time, productive variety. Flesh white, floury, and light in texture. If planted in April, the tubers ripen in July.

Snowflake P.—Tuber oval, always flattened, and quite remarkable for its neat symmetrical shape; skin pale yellow or grayish

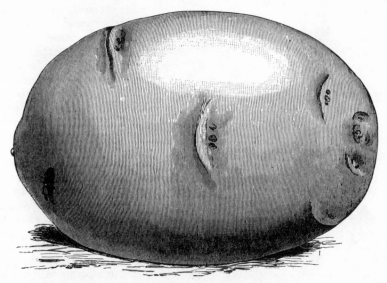

Snowflake Potato (natural size).

white, sometimes smooth, but most usually wrinkled; flesh white, very floury, and light in texture; eyes very faintly marked; shoot pale pink. Stem rather erect, seldom exceeding 2 ft. in height, more round than quadrangular, swollen at the joints, and quite green. Leaves rather numerous and large, and of a very pale, light-yellowish green; those at the base of the stem are much larger and flatter than those at the top. Flowers white, large, very often abortive. This is one of the best American varieties. It is a productive and rather early kind, and the flesh is of excellent quality. If planted in April, the tubers ripen about the middle of July.

Bresee's Prolific Potato.—Tuber very handsome, flattened, oblong, sometimes almost square at both ends; skin smooth, of a pale-yellow colour, more or less tinged with salmon colour; flesh white; eyes faintly marked; shoot pink. Stems half erect, about 2 ft. high, slightly twisted, quadrangular, winged, tinged with pale coppery red, as are also the leaf-stalks. Leaves pale green, slightly grayish, faintly reticulated. Flowers white, very often abortive. This variety is perhaps the best of all those which, up to the present, have come from America. It is as productive as the Early Rose Potato, keeps better, and is of finer quality.

II. Long Yellow Varieties.

Marjolin P. (*Pomme de Terre Marjolin.* English synonyms: Ash-leaf Kidney, Walnut-leaved Kidney, Sandringham Early Kidney).—Tubers elongated, often slightly curved, thicker and rounder at one end, and narrowed to a blunt point at the other, often marked with swellings about the eyes; skin yellow, smooth; flesh very yellow; shoot, when grown in

darkness, of a yellowish-white colour, and of a violet and greenish colour when grown exposed to the light. The tubers grow close together around the bottom of the stem. Stems short, seldom exceeding 16 to 20 inches in length, usually drooping, not branched, and slightly winged. Leaves medium sized, with roundish leaflets, of a dark-green colour on the upper surface, very much glazed, and almost always spoon-shaped. Flowers white, rather large, usually abortive, when the variety is very pure. This is the best known and most extensively grown early Potato, and forms tubers more quickly than any other kind. If planted in the open ground in April, the tubers ripen in June. It is the most suitable kind for growing in frames for an early crop, and

Walnut-leaved Kidney Potato (sprouting tubers, natural size).

is the variety which is most extensively used for that purpose. There is a form of it which has taller stems, leaves slightly reticulated, and numerous white flowers, and which resembles the Royal Ash-leaf Kidney. This, although not so early, is far more productive than the ordinary variety. It is grown in the open air. About Paris, the practice of sprouting "seed" potatoes before planting them is very common. For this purpose, the tubers are ranged on wickerwork screens (care being taken to place them with an eye uppermost), and kept in a dry place sheltered from frost until they are planted. When planting-time arrives, the screens are carried to the ground, and the tubers are taken from them one by one and carefully deposited each in the hole made to receive it. When the tubers are prepared in this way, the crop comes in from ten to fifteen days earlier than it would if they had been planted without being sprouted. Besides, the practice of sprouting is an almost certain preventive of a mishap which occurs more frequently with this variety than with any other, that is, the complete abortion of the overground stems. When this happens, no stems make their appearance above the surface of the ground, the tuber producing only a few underground stems bearing diminutive tubers which all together weigh less than the "seed" potato from which they have grown.

Tétard Marjolin Potato.—Tubers large, flattened, oblong or almond-shaped; skin smooth or faintly wrinkled, of a dark, somewhat coppery, yellow colour, assuming a peculiar and easily recognized tint after the tubers have been taken up out of the ground; flesh yellow,

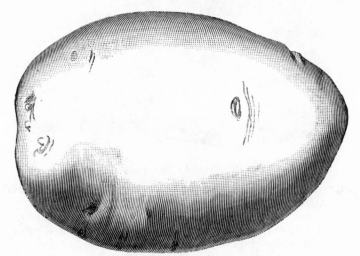

Tétard Marjolin Potato (natural size).

very fine and delicate in flavour; shoot yellowish white. The tubers are sometimes swollen around the eyes, like those of the preceding variety. Stems erect, quadrangular, slightly winged, very rarely branching, quite green, and from 20 inches to 2½ ft. high. Leaves rather curled and wavy, of a clear, slightly yellowish, green colour, and glistening. Flowers white, rather numerous, but hardly ever producing any seed. A very productive and, at the same time, early variety, of extremely and exceptionally fine quality for table use. If planted in April, new potatoes may be dug in the latter part of July. The Tétard Marjolin Potato was raised from seed, about the year 1873, by M. Tétard, of Groslay (Seine-et-Oise).

Nettle-leaved P. (*Pomme de Terre à Feuille d'Ortie.* English syno-

nyms : Early Bedfont Kidney, or Sutton's Early Racehorse, Potato).—
Tubers very like those of the Early Marjolin Potato, but distinguished
from them, as soon as they commence to sprout, by the pink colour of
the shoots, which are also hairy and covered with leaves ; flesh yellow.
Stems slender, generally unbranched and spreading along the ground,
from 20 inches to 2 ft. long, and slightly winged. Leaves rather far
apart, short, composed of a few oval-rounded, very much reticulated
leaflets of a dark-green colour. Flowers white, opening early, in not
very numerous clusters, and sometimes producing seed. A very good
variety for an early crop, coming in almost as soon as the Early Marjolin and quite as productive, but it keeps badly. It is very extensively
grown for an early crop in the open fields in the vicinity of Paris.

Yorkshire Hybrid Potato (*Pomme de Terre Quarantaine de Noisy*).
—Tubers medium sized, seldom more than from 3½ to 4 inches long by
2 inches in diameter, oblong or almond-shaped ; skin yellow, usually
smooth ; eyes hardly visible ; flesh very yellow and of excellent
quality ; shoot pink, slightly hairy, and slow in growth. Stems half-
erect, quadrangular, winged, sometimes branching, and from 2 to over

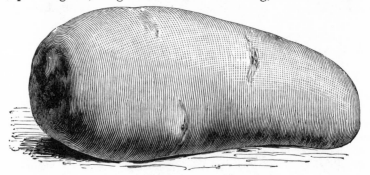

Yorkshire Hybrid Potato (natural size).

2½ ft. long. Leaves large and broad, composed of a great number of
leaflets of very variable dimensions ; in the lower leaves they are
broad, flat, and almost glazed ; in the upper ones they are narrower,
reticulated, and curled. Flowers numerous, violet pink, a pretty large
proportion of them producing seed. This variety, in fact, is one of
those which yield the most seed. In the Paris market it ranks
amongst the most highly esteemed kinds, and has completely superseded the old Long Yellow Dutch Potato. It is productive, of excellent quality, keeps very well, but, unfortunately, is very liable to be
attacked by the disease. If planted in April, new potatoes may be dug
in the course of August.

The Brie Long Yellow Potato is a sub-variety of this kind, from
which it does not differ essentially. Its tubers are generally a little
longer and yellower, and ripen somewhat later, but that is chiefly owing
to the circumstance that they are grown in richer, deeper, and colder
soils than those in which the Quarantaine de Noisy is usually planted.
The characteristic features of both forms—that is, the colour and
arrangement of the flowers, and especially the appearance and growing
period of the shoots—are, in fact, identical.

Princesse Potato.—Tuber very much elongated, almost as deep as broad, usually curved, and thicker at the top than at the bottom ; skin bright yellow, smooth ; eyes prominent rather than sunk ; flesh very yellow ; shoot smooth, copper coloured. Stems half-erect, 20 inches to 2 ft. long, quite green, thick, quadrangular, and winged. Leaves long and abundant, composed of numerous leaflets, large and small, of a

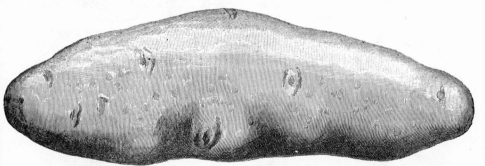

Princesse Potato (natural size).

pale, slightly yellowish, green colour. Flowers very large, reddish lilac, in not very numerous clusters, and seldom producing seed. This variety is particularly suitable for frying or for salads ; the flesh is very firm and compact. The tubers ripen middling early. If planted in April, new potatoes may be dug about the end of August.

Magnum Bonum P.—Tuber large, oblong, slightly flattened, sometimes irregular in shape ; skin pale yellow, smooth or wrinkled,

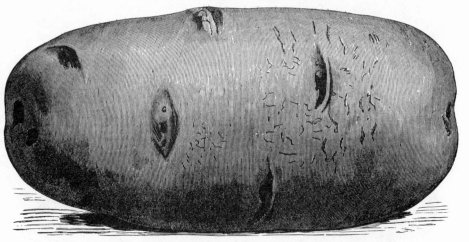

Magnum Bonum Potato (natural size).

according to the kind of soil in which the plants are grown ; flesh yellow ; eyes pretty well marked, and prominent rather than sunk ; shoot pink. Stems very erect, vigorous growing, quadrangular, winged, tinged with coppery red above the joints, and growing from about $2\frac{1}{2}$ to $3\frac{1}{4}$ ft. high. Leaves rather far apart, composed, especially those towards the base of the stem, of very broad, oval-rounded, not very numerous, almost flat, and broadly reticulated leaflets. The prevailing tint of the foliage is a rather pale, almost grayish green. Flowers reddish lilac, most frequently abortive. An extremely productive mid-season variety, coming in about the middle of September. In England it has the reputation of resisting the disease very well, but in France it does not appear to us to be anything remarkable in this respect. It is true that, at first, it remains green when other varieties have been attacked, but when it arrives at that period of its growth when the tubers commence to form, it takes the disease in its turn and soon succumbs to it.

Lapstone Potato (*Pomme de Terre Caillou Blanc.* English syno-

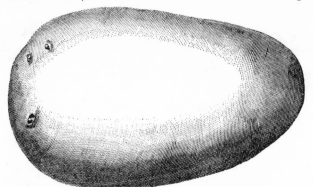

Lapstone, or Yorkshire Hero, Potato (natural size).

nyms: Ash-top Fluke, Perfection Kidney, Pebble White, Rixton's Pippin, Yorkshire Hero).—Tubers very regularly almond-shaped, sometimes short, sometimes very much elongated, and very smooth; eyes hardly marked; skin pale yellow, slightly grayish, becoming violet coloured when exposed to the light for any lengthened period; flesh pale yellow, very fine flavoured; shoot violet coloured. Stems half-erect, from 20 inches to 2 ft. high, thick at the base, but quickly becoming thinner, quadrangular, slightly winged, and of a very faint copper colour near the joints. Leaves broad, of a clear-green colour, almost flat, slightly glazed, and having a peculiar appearance which is easily recognized. Flowers numerous, large, pure white, seldom producing seed. A very handsome variety, with flesh of fine flavour, light texture, and excellent quality. If planted in April, new potatoes may be dug about the end of July.

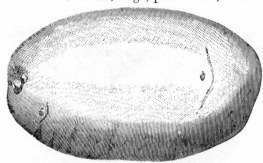

Royal Ash-leaved Kidney Potato (natural size).

Royal Ash-leaved Kidney P. (Synonyms: Early Alma Kidney, Carter's Early Race-horse, Harry Kidney, Royal Ash-top, Myatt's Ash-leaved Kidney, Veitch's Ash-leaved Kidney, or Rivers's Ash-leaved

Kidney).—Tuber elongated, very smooth, kidney-shaped, or like a Gherkin, almost resembling the Early Marjolin Potato; skin yellow; eyes faintly marked; flesh yellow; shoot violet coloured. Stems usually drooping, from 20 inches to 2 ft. long, rather slender, quadrangular, deeply tinged with a brownish-violet colour, especially near the angles. Leaves dark green; lower ones broad, almost flat, moderately reticulated; upper ones much more twisted and puckered, and with the leaflets more pointed. Flowers large, bluish lilac, very seldom blooming. An excellent kind for an early crop, more suitable for the open ground than for growing in frames. It is almost as early as the Marjolin Potato, but its tubers do not grow so close together around the base of the stem, and the foliage is more abundant. The flesh is very fine and of excellent quality.

King Potato (Synonyms: King of Potatoes, or King of Flukes).— Tubers oblong, often rather short, not much flattened; skin of a fine golden-yellow colour; eyes faintly marked; flesh very yellow, fine, and of excellent quality; shoot violet coloured. Stems generally drooping,

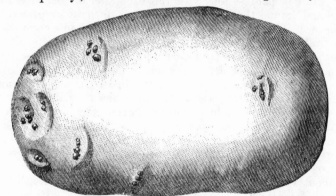

King Potato (natural size).

seldom exceeding 2 ft. in length, often twisted, winged, furrowed, usually unbranched, bearing a great number of short leaves composed of oval-rounded, closely crowded, slightly wavy, very much reticulated leaflets of a grayish-green colour. Flowers small, crumpled, reddish lilac, in not very numerous clusters, and very rarely producing seed. A rather productive mid-season variety, ripening about the end of August. Flesh yellow, exceedingly fine, and of quite superior quality. If planted in April, new potatoes may be dug about the end of August.

Marceau P.—Tubers flattened, oblong, often of enormous size, not unfrequently from 6 to over 7 inches long, and 3 inches or more in diameter; skin pale yellow, slightly wrinkled; flesh yellow; shoot violet coloured. Stems very vigorous growing, thick-set, and short, seldom exceeding 2 ft. in length, very branching, quite green, quadrangular, and winged; lower leaves large, broad, of a rather dark-green colour, flat, and reticulated; those at the middle and top of the stem of a paler green, very much curled and undulated. Flowers large, reddish lilac, in not very numerous clusters, and occasionally producing seed. This variety is especially remarkable for the very great size of the tubers, which ripen about the beginning of September.

III. Variegated Long Yellow Varieties.

Gleason's Late, or **New Hundred-fold Fluke, Potato** (*Pomme de Terre Rubanée*).—Tubers oblong or roundish, but always flattened ; skin very smooth, bright yellow, marked with a broad red band which contrasts very strongly with the colour of the rest of the tuber ; eyes hardly marked ; flesh yellow ; shoot red. Stems vigorous growing, erect, often over 2½ ft. high, frequently branching, of a coppery-brown colour, as are also the leaf-stalks and the veins of the leaves. Leaves rather abundant and broad ; leaflets roundish, pointed, rather reticulated. Flowers reddish violet, rather scanty, and hardly ever producing seed. A productive half-late variety. If planted in April, the crop seldom comes in until some time in September. The flesh of the tubers is firm and rather compact. The tubers keep well.

White Sausage P. (*Pomme de Terre Saucisse Blanche*).—Tubers flattened, oblong, often broader at the base than at the top, and almost entirely white or pale yellow, with the exception of some red spots at the base and around the point of attachment to the underground stem ; flesh yellow ; eyes faintly marked ; shoot pink. Stems vigorous growing, from about 2½ to over 3 ft. long, erect, branching, deeply tinged with coppery red, quadrangular and, generally, not winged. Leaves rather far apart, medium sized, very much reticulated, and of a grayish-green colour. Flowers in very numerous clusters, usually intermingled with the leaves, very often abortive, and, when they do bloom, rather small, crumpled, and violet coloured. Seed very seldom produced. This variety is very productive and keeps well. The crop is not taken up until September or October for winter use. The white colour of the tubers gives them an advantage over those of the old Sausage Potato, which this variety very much resembles in every other respect. It was raised about the year 1869, in the neighbourhood of Montlhéry, near Paris, and soon afterwards began to be very generally cultivated by the market gardeners, who grow it in large quantities for the supply of the Central Market.

IV. Round Red Varieties.

Red Regent, or **Gosforth Seedling, P.** (*Pomme de Terre de Zélande*). —Tubers round, medium sized, between 2 and 3 inches in diameter ; skin bright red, slightly wrinkled ; eyes faintly marked ; flesh yellow ; shoot red. Stems erect, very thick and very vigorous growing, quadrangular, winged, branching, from about 2½ to over 3 ft. high, plentifully tinged with coppery red. Leaves very large, appearing to be doubly compound, as they bear small leaflets not only on the main leaf-stalk, but also on the stalks of the large leaflets, which are oval-rounded, rather pointed, and reticulated. The prevailing tint of the foliage is a rather pale, grayish green. Flowers white, in strong long-stalked clusters, very seldom producing seed. A handsome and good half-late variety, and keeps well, its quality being better at the end than at the beginning of winter. The crop may be taken up about the end of September. It has been repeatedly remarked, and we have recently had the opportunity of noting the circumstance amongst our growing plants, that when tubers of this Potato are planted which are very true to name, un-crossed, and raised from white - flowered plants, a certain proportion of plants with larger flowers and of a bluish-violet colour will be produced from them. This is an instance of the dimorphism which is often seen in plants, and we only mention it here on account of its well-established fre-quent occurrence in this variety of Potato.

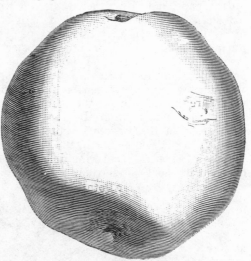

Red Regent, or Gosforth Seedling, Potato (natural size).

Red-skinned Flourball Potato (*Pomme de Terre Farineuse Rouge.* Syno-nyms: Garnet Chili, or Brinkworth Challenger).— Tubers large, deeply marked with hollows from the eyes being very much sunk, often 4 inches or more in diameter; skin usually wrinkled, of a palish-red colour;

Red-skinned Flour ball Potato (natural size).

flesh white; shoot white, with the point and base red. Stems erect, quadrangular, winged, of a coppery red, from about $2\frac{1}{2}$ to over 3 ft.

high, sometimes branched. Leaves medium sized, composed almost
solely of large oval-acuminate leaflets, which are nearly always folded
gutter-shape, and of a rather light, yellowish-green colour. The main
leaf-stalk is rather deeply tinged with brown, especially towards the
extremity. Flowers very abundant, of a slightly lilac-rose colour, in
numerous clusters, and produced in succession for a long time; they
very seldom bear seed. This is one of the good varieties for field
culture, and, although its introduction only dates back about twelve
years, it has already taken an important place among the varieties
which are grown both for the manufacture of starch and for table use.
It yields a pretty uniformly good crop, as it suffers comparatively
little from the disease, and is not too late in ripening, the crop being
usually dug in September in the vicinity of Paris. For table use, the
flesh is considered to have the defect of being too white and somewhat
deficient in fineness of flavour.

American Wonder Potato (*Pomme de Terre Merveille d'Amérique*).—

American Wonder Potato (natural size).

Tubers roundish, somewhat irregular in shape; eyes deeply sunk; skin
rather smooth, violet red; flesh white; shoot red. Stems erect, quadrangular, vigorous growing. Leaves broad, with dark-green leaflets.
Flowers numerous, in large strong clusters, of a rather vivid violet-red
colour. A half-late and very productive variety, but of only ordinary
quality.

V. FLAT PINK OR RED VARIETIES.

Early Rose P. (*Pomme de Terre Rose Hâtive*).—Tubers oblong,
rather flattened, often more pointed at the top than at the bottom; eyes

not very deeply sunk, but having a rather prominent ridge or wrinkle below them ; skin smooth, and of a pink colour slightly tinged with salmon colour ; flesh white ; shoot pink, and germinating remarkably soon. Stems medium sized, erect, from 2 to 2½ ft. high, rather thick at the base, but speedily becoming more slender, sometimes branching,

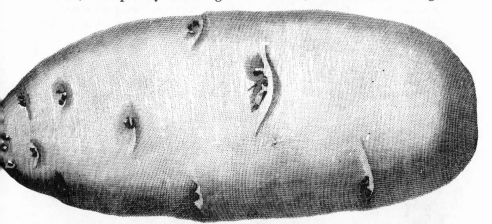

Early Rose Potato (natural size).

and slightly tinged with coppery red, especially near the joints. Leaves flat and smooth, composed almost solely of large oval-acuminate leaflets, of uniform size, slightly glistening, and of a light-green colour. Flowers white, large, in not very numerous clusters, and usually falling off abortive. A very productive and early kind, the crop ripening in the month of August. Flesh light in texture, and extremely variable in quality, according to the kind of soil in which the tubers are planted. These do not keep well, as they have too great a tendency to sprout.

Rosette Potato (*Pomme de Terre Rosette*).—Tubers very much flat-

Rosette Potato (natural size).

tened, round or oblong, scarcely longer than broad, and remarkably flat on both sides, very smooth, and, as it were, polished; eyes very faintly marked; skin of a bright pink colour; flesh white, sometimes slightly veined with pink; shoot pink. Stems of moderate height, seldom exceeding 2 ft. or 2 ft. 4 inches. Leaves rather large, roundish, and of a slightly grayish-green colour. This variety was raised by us, from seed of the Early Rose Potato. It was preserved in preference to a great number of other seedlings, on account of its very great productiveness and the remarkably regular shape of the tubers.

Cottager's Red Potato (*Pomme de Terre Saucisse*).—Tubers flattened, oblong, usually very regular in shape, from about $3\frac{1}{4}$ to 4 inches long, and about 2 inches in diameter; skin smooth, of a rather vivid red colour; eyes faintly marked, not sunk; flesh yellow; shoot pink. Stems tall,

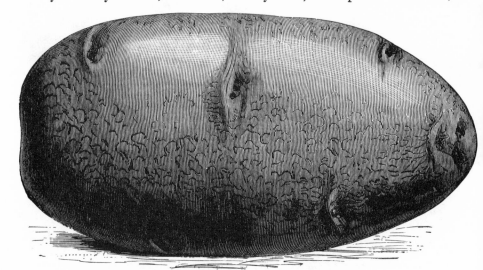

Cottager's Red Potato (natural size).

erect, very vigorous growing, almost always branching, often 3 ft. or more in height, quadrangular, slightly winged, and very deeply tinged with brownish red. Leaves large, composed of very unequally sized, quite oval-rounded, very much reticulated leaflets of a dark, slightly grayish and dull green. Flowers of a pale-violet colour, in very numerous clusters usually intermingled with the leaves, very rarely producing seed. One of the best kinds for winter use, and most extensively in request in Paris late in autumn. The flesh is somewhat compact, but becomes more floury as the season advances. This variety is rather free from the Potato-disease properly so called, but it often suffers from the affection known in France as "la Frisolée," which shrivels up both leaves and stems at the commencement of their growth. This is its only defect.

VI. Smooth Long Red Varieties.

Red Ash-leaf Kidney P. (*Pomme de Terre Kidney Rouge Hâtive*). —Tubers flattened, oblong or slightly kidney-shaped, rather blunt at both ends, from about $2\frac{1}{4}$ to $3\frac{1}{4}$ inches long, and between 1 and 2 inches in diameter at the broadest part; skin red, very smooth; eyes hardly marked; flesh pale yellow; shoot red. Stems half-erect, roundish, of a coppery-red colour, and seldom exceeding 20 inches in height. Leaves much more crowded than in the following variety, of a more glistening green, and not so grayish; all composed of pointed, rather roundish, and reticulated leaflets. Flowers white, in not very numerous clusters. A very handsome half-early variety, with floury flesh of good quality. The tubers ripen in the course of August.

Robertson's Giant Kidney Potato (*Pomme de Terre Rouge Longue de Hollande*).—Tubers very easily recognized, flattened, kidney-shaped or almond-shaped, usually very much elongated, with the base very much narrowed and often curved into a crook; skin smooth, of a rather dark red slightly tinged with violet colour; flesh yellow, fine in texture, and of good quality; shoot red. Stems erect, stiff, more round than quadrangular, of a coppery-red colour, and from 2 to $2\frac{1}{2}$ ft. high. Leaves rather scanty, and of a pale, grayish-green colour. In the lower leaves

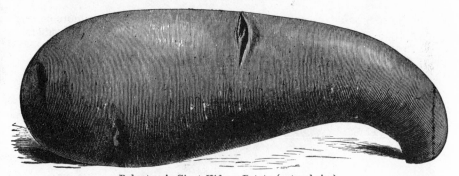

Robertson's Giant Kidney Potato (natural size).

the leaflets are often joined together so as to form one broad roundish leaf-blade; the leaves at the top of the stem are often curled and wavy, with pointed leaflets which are puckered at the edges. Flowers white, numerous, in rather strong clusters, and hardly ever producing seed. The haulms or stalks of this variety are remarkably slight and slender, and do not cover the ground beneath them. This is a remarkably distinct Potato; it was formerly a great favourite, but, at the present day, it has been, in a great measure, superseded by more productive kinds; nevertheless it always possesses the advantage of being of quite superior quality and an excellent keeper. If planted in April, new potatoes may be dug about the end of August. In the neighbourhood of Cherbourg, where it is very extensively grown, the mildness of the climate permits of its being planted in December, the crop coming in in June or July.

Pousse-debout P. (*Pomme de Terre Pousse-debout*).—Tubers almost cylindrical, narrowed at the ends, from about $3\frac{1}{4}$ to 4 inches long, and between 1 and 2 inches in diameter; skin pale red; shoot pink. Stems vigorous growing, erect, branching, generally short, seldom exceeding from 20 inches to 2 ft. in height, and tinged with coppery red, as are also the leaf-stalks. Leaves broad and large, of a dark-green colour, composed of broad, roundish, pointed leaflets. Flowers white, large, in rather numerous and compact clusters ; they usually produce no seed.

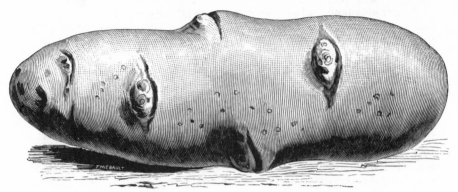

Pousse-debout Potato (natural size).

This is a productive variety and keeps well. The flesh is more compact than that of the preceding kind, and not so floury. The tubers ripen in September.

Belgian Kidney Potato (*Pomme de Terre Rognon Rose*).—Tubers flattened, usually almond-shaped or kidney-shaped, very smooth ; skin of a pale-yellowish or salmon-tinted pink ; eyes faintly marked ; flesh yellow ; shoot pink. Stems rather slender, tinged with brown, very

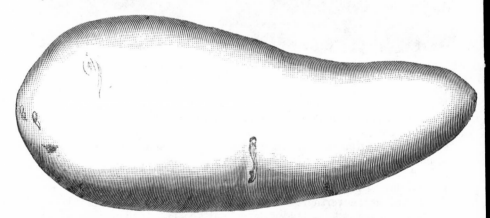

Belgian Kidney Potato (natural size).

often prostrate, frequently branching, and from 2 to over $2\frac{1}{2}$ ft. long. Leaves rather small, composed of few leaflets, which are reticulated, often folded, and of a rather pale, grayish-green colour. Flowers white, rather abundant, in not very numerous clusters, seldom if ever producing seed. A very good mid-season Potato for table use, productive, and keeping well. Flesh rather firm. The tubers ripen about the end of August.

VII. Notched Long Red Variety.

Vitelotte Potato (*Pomme de Terre Vitelotte*).—Tubers almost cylindrical, somewhat thicker towards the top than at the bottom; eyes numerous, each situated at the bottom of a deep wrinkle; skin red, rather smooth; flesh white, sometimes slightly zoned with red, especially at the

Vitelotte Potato (natural size).

end farthest from the point of attachment to the underground stem; shoot red. Stems erect, very stiff, vigorous growing, quadrangular and winged, tinged with brown, often branching, seldom more than from 20 inches to 2 ft. high, very thick-set and well furnished with leaves. Leaves short, of a slightly grayish-green colour; leaflets oval, rounded, rather pointed, especially those towards the top of the stem, very much reticulated, and often folded in two. Flowers white, very seldom seeding. This variety is not so highly esteemed nowadays as it was formerly; nevertheless it is of excellent

Peake's First Early Potato (natural size).

quality, rather productive, and keeps very well. It must be acknowledged that it has the defect of being difficult to peel, and that much of the tuber is wasted in that operation, as, in order to remove the skin which covers the hollows in which the eyes are sunk, a considerable portion of the flesh must be detached at the same time. The crop comes in in the course of September.

VIII. Violet-coloured and Variegated Varieties.

Peake's First Early P. (*Pomme de Terre Blanchard*).—Tubers round, sometimes flattened, yellow, plentifully variegated with violet, especially towards the top and around the eyes; skin smooth; flesh yellow; shoot violet coloured. Stems stout, usually prostrate, almost always branching, from about 2½ to over 3 ft. long, tinged with brown, especially towards the base. Leaves medium sized, composed of oval-acuminate, rather reticulated leaflets, of a clear-green colour. Flowers very numerous, large, bluish lilac, a large proportion of them seeding. This Potato seeds, perhaps, more abundantly than any other of the ordinary kinds. It is a good, early, productive variety, and keeps well. The flesh is floury and very yellow. The crop may be dug about the end of July. The tubers are never very large, but they are very plentifully produced, and of pretty uniform size.

Hundred-fold Potato (*Pomme de Terre Violette*).—Tubers roundish, often square at top and bottom, rather deeply notched by the hollows in which the eyes are deeply sunk; skin very deep violet colour; flesh yellow; shoot violet coloured. Stems erect, very branching, dark brown, and from 2 to 2½ ft. high. Leaves rather scanty, of medium

size, composed almost solely of large, oval-acuminate, slightly reticulated leaflets of a clear - green colour. Flowers violet coloured, with white-tipped divisions, abundant, in rather numerous but slight clusters; they often produce seed, but in small quantities. A good and productive variety, keeping well, of excellent quality, with floury and rather firm flesh. The crop comes in in

Hundred-fold Potato (natural size).

September. Of all the violet-coloured Potatoes, this is the variety which is most frequently seen in the Central Market at Paris. It is well known and highly esteemed there, and is one of those kinds which, like the Shaw, or Regent, and the Segonzac Potatoes, appear to maintain their vigour and productiveness, notwithstandng the very great length of time during which they have been in cultivation.

Compton's Surprise P. — Tubers flattened, oblong, narrowed at both ends; skin rather smooth, violet coloured; eyes not very deeply sunk, but having a long ridge or wrinkle below them, as in the Early Rose Potato; flesh white; shoot violet coloured. Stems more spreading than erect, rather stout, quadrangular and winged, often branching, and seldom exceeding from 2 to 2½ ft. in height. Leaves large, composed of very broad, oval-acuminate, broadly reticulated leaflets of a somewhat pale-green colour. Flowers white, large, not numerous, and seldom producing seed. A very productive and rather early American variety, coming in in the end of August. The flesh of the tubers is white, floury, and of very light texture.

Chandernagore P. (*Pomme de Terre Chandernagor*). — Tubers roundish or slightly elongated, as deep as broad, slightly notched, and of a blackish-violet colour; flesh deeply tinged with violet colour; shoot deep violet colour. Stems erect, vigorous growing, violet brown, quadrangular, and winged, and about 2 ft. high. Leaves rather short and compact; those at the base of the stem having very large and broad terminal leaflets, the others having the leaflets curled, puckered, and sometimes of a slightly grayish-green colour. The foliage, in its general aspect, is compact and dark coloured. Flowers white, rather large, most frequently falling off in the bud state, and seldom producing seed. A productive, half-late variety, coming in in September. The violet colour of the flesh of the tubers is not very agreeable to the eye, but the quality is excellent and the flavour of the finest.

Violet-coloured Quarantaine Potato (*Pomme de Terre Quarantaine Violette*).—Tubers flattened, smooth, kidney-shaped or almond-shaped, often from 4 to 6 inches long, and 2 inches or more in diameter at the thick end; skin exceedingly fine and thin, violet coloured, smooth; flesh yellow; shoot violet coloured. Stems rather slender, brownish,

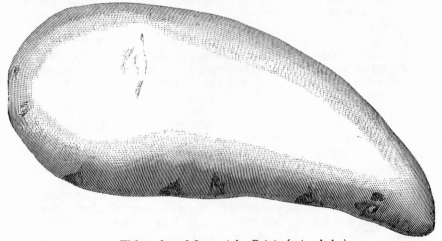

Violet-coloured Quarantaine Potato (natural size).

usually drooping, and seldom exceeding from 2 to 2½ ft. in length. Leaves medium sized or small, with rounded, grayish, very much reticulated leaflets. Flowers white, seldom appearing, and never seeding. This is a middling early variety, not productive in the highest degree, but of very good quality. It has especially the good property of keeping well and without sprouting, and is, perhaps, the best of all varieties for table use in spring, becoming more floury and improving in quality as the season advances.

A whole volume might be filled with the enumeration of all the varieties of Potatoes which have been raised and recommended since the commencement of the present century. We shall, however, confine ourselves to mentioning, in addition to those already described, some of the best known or most noteworthy English and other varieties.

I. ENGLISH VARIETIES.

Alice Fenn.—Tubers oblong, kidney-shaped, very regular in form; skin yellow, smooth; flesh pale yellow; shoot violet coloured. Stems of very scanty growth, slender and pliant. Leaves small and few. Flowers violet coloured. A handsome kind, rather early, but not very productive.

Bovinia.—Tubers very large, long, broad, flattened, rather deeply notched, and of a yellow colour variegated with red, especially towards the top and near the eyes; flesh yellowish white. Stems vigorous growing. Leaves large. A very late variety, producing tubers which sometimes weigh over two pounds each, but are not very numerous. The flesh is watery and of only middling quality. The variety is more curious than useful.

Coldstream, or Hogg's Coldstream.—Tubers round, small or medium sized; skin and flesh yellow; flowers and shoot violet coloured. Stems small and pliant, generally prostrate. Leaves roundish, grayish green. A very good hardy and early kind, but only moderately productive.

Dalmahoy.—Tubers round, small or medium sized, white; eyes rather well marked, but not very deeply sunk; shoot violet coloured. Stems erect, short, seldom exceeding 1 ft. in height. Leaves grayish, rather crumpled, with large pointed leaflets. The flowers fall off without opening. A selected form of the Regent.

Dawe's Matchless (Synonyms: Excelsior Kidney, Webb's Imperial, Early Bryanstone Kidney, Manning's Kidney, England's Fair Beauty, Chagford Kidney, Wormley Kidney, Champion Kidney).— A very fine and productive mid-season Potato. Tubers remarkably handsome, oblong, sometimes flattened, sometimes kidney-shaped, exceedingly smooth, nearly white, and often measuring 5 or 6 inches in length, by 2 inches or more in diameter; eyes hardly marked; flesh white; shoot violet-coloured. Stems rather vigorous growing, erect. Leaves roundish, reticulated, and of an almost blackish-green colour. Flowers white. This variety is not much grown in France, where we cultivated it for some time by mistake under the name of *P. Conféderée*. The true *P. Conféderée* (a synonym for *P. Marceau*), however, has violet-coloured flowers and broader and yellower tubers.

Early Emperor Napoleon.—Tubers almost quite spherical or slightly flattened, and entirely devoid of eyes; skin slightly wrinkled, red, and, in exceptional cases, variegated with yellow; shoot red; flesh yellowish white. Stems slender, usually trailing on the ground. Leaves exceedingly narrow, and quite grayish. Flowers reddish, in thin clusters. A half-early and not very productive kind, but remarkable for the handsome appearance and regular shape of the tubers.

Fenn's Early Market.—Tubers round, small, or medium sized, tolerably flattened; skin yellow, smooth; eyes not much sunk; shoot pink; flesh nearly white. Stems of very scanty growth, weak, and pliant. Leaves pale green. Flowers white, not numerous. This excellent small variety is one of the earliest of all the Round Yellow Potatoes, and is remarkable for the small size of its stems.

Golden Eagle and **Radstock Beauty.**—It is very difficult to distinguish these two varieties from each other, and they are probably identical. The tubers are yellow, variegated with red, roundish, and slightly flattened in one part; skin very smooth and having a very pretty and very peculiar appearance; shoot red. Stems of moderate height. Leaves dark green. Flowers reddish. Tubers rather late ripening and moderately productive.

Grampian.—This variety very much resembles the Early Emperor Potato, described above, but has somewhat darker and more numerous leaves and redder flowers. The tubers do not exhibit any well-marked difference. The Grampian Potato is especially distinguished by the remarkably regular and symmetrical shape of the tubers, which are spherical or flattened, but always rounded in outline. They are almost entirely devoid of eyes and are of a fine red colour; they are also hardy and rather productive, ripen half late, and keep very well.

International Kidney.—This variety has, undoubtedly, sprung from the Lapstone Kidney, from which it is distinguished by its more vigorous growth, by being later in ripening, and by its tubers being much larger and somewhat more elongated in shape. It also has the peculiarity of its tubers becoming violet coloured when exposed to the influence of daylight. It is one of the best kinds for exhibition, but is of inferior quality.

Lady Webster.—Tubers round, very smooth, somewhat flattened, yellow, and rather plentifully variegated with red; shoots red. Stems short and drooping, green. Leaves not numerous, with very glistening leaflets, resembling those of the Early Marjolin Potato.

Milky White.—Tubers white, slightly salmon tinted, very smooth, flat in one part, oblong, and without eyes or notches; shoot pink. Stems of scanty growth. Leaves slight, pale green. Flowers white. A handsome half-early variety, producing very clean-skinned tubers; but several American varieties have a still finer appearance, and are, at the same time, more productive.

Mona's Pride.—A variety very closely resembling the Early Marjolin Potato in its habit of growth, but differing entirely from it in the shape of the tuber, which is very short, or even round and flat. It is also somewhat later and somewhat more productive than the Marjolin Potato.

Porter's Excelsior.—One of the most perfect Potatoes, as regards shape, which has appeared up to the present. The tubers are quite round, yet flattened as pebbles are, being nearly twice as broad as they are thick; skin yellow, smooth; flesh pale yellow; shoot pink. Stems trailing on the ground. Leaves not numerous, dark green. Flowers white. This is a half-late variety; it is not very productive, and its chief merit consists in the handsome appearance of the tubers.

Prince of Wales.—This appears to be a form of the Royal Ash-leaf Kidney Potato, which it surpasses in productiveness, and is not much inferior to it in earliness. One defect it has is irregularity of shape in the tubers, which are sometimes almond-shaped, sometimes pear-shaped, and sometimes quite round. Flesh yellow; quality inferior.

Purple Ash-leaved Kidney (Synonyms: Jersey Purple, Black Kidney, Black Prince, Select Blue Ash-leaf, or Paterson's Long Blue).

—Tubers long or very long, flattened, more or less kidney-shaped, and very smooth; skin dark-violet colour, even, without wrinkles or hollows around the eyes. Stems rather slender, brownish. Leaves not numerous and of a dark grayish-green colour. Flowers lilac. A rather early kind, tolerably productive, and of good quality. Many people do not like the dark-violet colour of the tubers.

Rector of Woodstock.—Tubers exceedingly regular in shape, quite round, but tolerably flattened; skin somewhat wrinkled, grayish white, faintly tinged with yellow; eyes hardly marked; flesh white, very floury, and fine flavoured; shoot violet coloured. Stems very short. Leaves slight, slender, and few. Flowers violet coloured, rarely produced. This small variety is only moderately productive, but the tubers are of fine quality and exceptionally handsome. It is one of the best varieties raised by Mr. R. Fenn.

Saint Patrick.—A productive and vigorous-growing kind. Tubers white or pale yellow, oblong, not flattened, and rather irregular in shape; flesh white.

Schoolmaster.—Tubers large, round, generally even and regular in shape; skin rough, white; very handsome, and of first-rate quality; shoot pink. Flowers white. Great cropper; one of the best Potatoes grown.

Scotch Blue.—Tubers roundish, flattened in one part, smooth; eyes faintly marked; skin thin, and of a dark, almost blackish, violet colour; flesh white; shoot dark-violet colour. Stems rather short, but vigorous growing. Leaves rather broad, grayish. Flowers violet coloured. A half-late, rather productive, and very hardy variety, of fine quality.

Standard.—This variety is recommended for the handsome appearance of its smooth white tubers and the delicate flavour of the flesh, which is white and floury. It is a pretty early and very productive kind, and is highly esteemed for table use.

Turner's Union.—Tubers yellow, round, small or medium sized, and pretty regular in shape; eyes somewhat sunk; flesh pale yellow; shoot yellowish white, with a violet-coloured point. Stems of scanty growth. Leaves rather large, but not numerous. Flowers lilac, usually abortive. A good small-sized early variety, but there are many others of much more account.

Vicar of Laleham.—An exceedingly distinct kind. Tubers of a light-violet colour, large, oblong, faintly flattened; shoot violet coloured. A rather early and productive variety.

White Emperor.—A rather vigorous-growing, but short-stemmed variety. Tubers very smooth, nearly white, round, and slightly flattened, very like those of the Model and Schoolmaster Potatoes; shoot lilac. Leaves reticulated, and of a dull-green colour.

Woodstock Kidney.—A handsome and vigorous-growing variety. Tubers white, oblong, smooth, and well shaped; shoot violet coloured. Stems stout, brownish. Leaves broad, and of a clear-green colour. Flowers violet coloured, in strong clusters, and seeding abundantly. Somewhat subject to disease.

II. French Varieties.

Achille Lémon.—Tubers slender and elongated, usually curved, and much narrower at one end than at the other; skin very smooth, golden yellow, marked with broad dark-violet spots, especially at the end of the tuber and near the eyes, which are very slightly sunk; flesh deep yellow, rather firm, and very fine. A half-early, moderately productive variety.

Artichaut Jaune.—Tubers long, slender, almost cylindrical, very much notched, and like those of the Vitelotte Potato, only that they are yellow instead of red. A floury, half-late variety, now almost gone out of cultivation.

Belle Augustine.—Tubers pale yellow, oblong, flattened, usually somewhat kidney-shaped; skin smooth; eyes faintly marked; flesh yellow; shoot violet coloured. A rather dwarf, early, and productive kind, coming in eight or ten days earlier than the Yorkshire Hybrid Potato (*P. Quarantaine de Noisy*). It is grown to some extent in the vicinity of Paris for the supply of new potatoes.

Belle de Vincennes.—Tubers oblong, flattened, smooth, almost without eyes, remarkably handsome, and resembling the Snowflake Potato in appearance; shoot violet coloured. Stems stout, tinged with brown, usually twisted. Leaves broad, numerous, and of a dark-green colour. Flowers violet coloured, in rather crowded clusters. This variety seeds abundantly.

Blanche Longue.—A handsome main-crop variety, with white round tubers rather like those of the Magnum Bonum Potato in shape. The stalks, however, are not so stout as those of the last-named variety. The tubers are very productive, and their rough skin indicates the very floury character of the flesh.

Caillaud.—Tubers round, medium sized or large, yellow, slightly tinted with salmon colour; shoot pink; skin usually wrinkled. Flowers white. A stout-growing, productive, half-late variety, very good for field culture, and resembling the Jeancé Potato except in the flowers, but not so productive as that variety.

Comice d'Amiens.—A very handsome, small, early kind, with round, small, or medium-sized tubers, of a yellow colour variegated with pink; shoot pink. Flowers white. A very early, but not very productive variety, which might be suitable for forcing.

Des Cordillères.—Tubers yellow, round, very smooth, small, and very numerous; flesh yellow; shoot violet coloured. The plant is of tufty growth, with numerous stems. Foliage scanty. A very distinct kind, but of no great account for kitchen garden culture.

Descroizilles. — Tubers roundish or slightly oblong, somewhat irregular in shape; eyes rather deeply sunk; skin pink or very pale red, slightly wrinkled; flesh yellow; flowers white. A late variety, rather deficient in productiveness, but of good quality.

Excellente Naine.—A very handsome and good variety, tolerably resembling the earliest forms of the *Pomme de Terre Royale*. The stems are hardly longer than those of the Marjolin Potato, for which this variety might be substituted in frame culture, being quite as productive and quite as early.

Grosse Jaune Deuxième Hâtive.—This Potato is rather extensively grown in the fields in the vicinity of Paris. It is, properly speaking, only a sub-variety of the Shaw, or Regent, Potato, with somewhat larger tubers, and ripening from eight to ten days later.

Hâtive de Bourbon-Lancy.—Tubers medium sized, quite round or very slightly flattened, variegated with yellow and violet colour disposed in bands rather than in roundish marblings. A moderately vigorous-growing, early-ripening variety, with lilac flowers, which are generally abortive.

Jaune Longue de Hollande (*Parmentière, Cornichon Tardif*).— This was formerly the most extensively grown and the most highly esteemed Potato for table use, but, since the appearance of the Potato-disease, it has been almost entirely superseded by the *Quarantaine de Noisy* Potato and its sub-varieties. The following were its characteristics:—Tubers elongated, almost always greatly curved, and much thicker at one end than at the other; skin grayish yellow, slightly wrinkled; flesh yellow, very floury, and very fine in texture; shoot pink. Stems rather short, twisted. Leaves curled and reticulated. Flowers reddish lilac. This is a rather late kind, and never was very productive.

De Malte.—Tubers very large, round; eyes very deeply sunk, and rather like those of the Jeancé Potato; shoot pink. Stems usually trailing on the ground, green, and from about 2½ to over 3 ft. in length. Leaves clear green, curled, and reticulated. The flowers are constantly abortive.

Naine Hâtive.—Tubers small or medium sized, round; eyes faintly marked; skin yellow, rather smooth; shoot violet coloured; flesh yellow. Flowers lilac. Stem short and weak, seldom exceeding from 16 to 20 inches in length. An early variety, but a very poor cropper.

Noisette Sainville.—A miniature Potato, with a very appropriate name, as the size of the tubers is only about that of a hazel-nut (*Noisette*), very rarely exceeding that of a good-sized almond. They are ovoid and slightly flattened in shape, of a grayish-yellow colour, and with a slightly wrinkled skin. The eyes are hardly visible. Shoot violet coloured. Stems very small and weak. Leaves grayish. Flowers white. This variety has been recommended on account of the fine quality of the flesh of the tubers, but its produce is so trifling that it is hardly worth growing.

Oblongue de Malabry.—Tubers oval, pale yellow, not notched; flesh white; shoot white, faintly tinged with violet colour. A very productive and moderately early variety.

Patraque Blanche.—An exceedingly productive kind, with grayish-white, slightly pink-tinted tubers, which are oblong in shape, squarish at both ends, and tolerably notched; flesh white; shoot pink. Stems very long and very vigorous growing. Leaves grayish. Flowers pink, numerous. This variety produces a considerable number of tubers of medium size. It is a rather late kind, and is more grown for feeding cattle than for table use.

Quarantaine à Tête Rose.—Tubers oblong or almond-shaped; skin smooth, yellow, variegated with red near the eyes and especially at the end of the tuber; flesh yellow. Stems short, erect. Leaves grayish.

A half-late and rather productive variety. When grown in a light soil the tubers of this variety have an extremely handsome and quite distinct appearance.

Reine Blanche.—A handsome, rather late, variety. Tubers medium sized or large, very round, white, with a red spot around each of the eyes, which are rather deeply sunk; shoot pink. Stems erect, vigorous growing. Leaves abundant, dark coloured. Flowers reddish violet, in broad clusters. The tubers of this variety have a very handsome appearance, but are of only middling quality.

Reine de Mai.—Tubers oblong or almond-shaped, flattened, very smooth, and nearly white; shoot pink. Stem rather slender and bare of leaves. Flowers white. This is an early variety, and very handsome when well grown, but it is exceedingly delicate, and the tubers are very often spotted.

Rohan.—Very closely allied to the *Patraque Blanche* Potato, from which it is only distinguished by its tubers being more reddish coloured. It is a productive kind and well adapted for field culture.

Rosée de Conflans (*Rosace de Villiers-le-Bel*).—Tubers long, almost cylindrical, very slightly notched, usually pink coloured towards the top and salmon-tinted yellow at the bottom; shoot pink. Stems rather short and stiff. Leaves numerous, dark coloured. Flowers white. A half-late and rather productive kind. The flesh of the tubers is yellow, firm, and not easily bruised.

Rouge Ronde de Strasbourg (*Wéry*).—Tubers medium sized; skin usually somewhat wrinkled and of a rather deep-red colour; shoot red; flesh yellow. Stems very stiff and strong, brown. Leaves dark green. Flowers reddish lilac. A good common variety, productive, and coming in in mid-season.

Sainte Hélène.—Tubers handsome, yellow, very smooth, oblong, flattened, and slightly kidney-shaped; eyes very faintly marked; flesh yellow. Stems rather short and pliant. Leaves broad, dark green. Flowers violet coloured, not very numerous, but very large. Tubers ripen half-early. A fine kitchen-garden variety.

Tanguy.—This kind is rather extensively grown in Brittany. It comes very near the Segonzac or Saint-Jean Potato, but its tubers are of a paler yellow and rounder, its stems are thicker, and its leaves are of a paler green. When grown in the sandy or granitic soils of the coasts of Brittany, the tubers are very fine and floury. Large quantities of them are exported to England.

Tardive d'Irlande.—Tubers roundish or oblong, rather notched, and of a yellow colour variegated with red; flesh white; shoot pink. Stems scanty. Leaves rather slightly grayish. Flowers lilac, small. A late variety and a poor cropper. Its chief merit is that the tubers will keep for a long time without sprouting.

Truffe d'Août.—Tubers medium sized, roundish, bright red; eyes moderately sunk; flesh yellow; shoot red. Stems erect, rather stiff. Leaves dark grayish green. Flowers white. A mid-season variety, productive, and, many years ago, well known and highly esteemed.

Violette d'Islande.—This Potato can be recommended for both kitchen-garden and field culture. It is hardy, tolerably productive, and particularly remarkable for the regular and symmetrical shape of the tubers, which are roundish, slightly flattened, and without indentations or depressions. The skin is of a purplish colour; the flesh pale yellow, floury, and of a delicate flavour. This variety keeps well, as the eyes are late in starting into growth.

Xavier (*Patte Blanche*).—Tubers oblong, almost cylindrical, pale pink, slightly notched; flesh yellowish white; shoot pink. Stems rather long. Leaves grayish. Flowers white. This variety is worthy of recommendation on account of its good quality, but it is very liable to be attacked by the disease.

Yam, or **Igname.**—Like the preceding variety, this one also suffers greatly from the disease, and it is difficult now to meet with it in a perfectly healthy and vigorous condition. The tubers are oblong, rather large, almost cylindrical, and slightly notched; skin pale red, smooth; shoot red.

III. AMERICAN VARIETIES.

For the last twenty years the Americans have been very actively engaged in sowing Potato seed for the purpose of raising new varieties, and rival the English raisers in the success which has attended their efforts. A great number of their new varieties—such as the Early Rose, Snowflake, Bresee's Prolific, etc.—were at once adopted by Potato-growers, as well in Europe as in America. These varieties have already been described by us amongst those to which we assign the first rank, and we shall now mention some others, which, perhaps, only require to be better known in order to be equally appreciated.

Adirondack.—A vigorous growing mid-season variety. Tubers round or slightly flattened, smooth, pale red; flesh white; shoot pink. Stems erect. Leaves broad. Flowers reddish violet.

Bresee's Peerless.—Tubers handsome, very much flattened, almost as broad as long, oblong or sometimes heart-shaped, and almost always notched at the bottom; skin and flesh white; shoot pink. Leaves pale green, broad, and somewhat curled. Flowers white. A half-early and exceedingly productive variety.

Brownell's Beauty (*Vermont Beauty*). — Tubers oblong, rather flattened, and usually very broad; skin somewhat wrinkled, and of a dark, slightly vinous, red colour; flesh white; shoot pink. Stems erect, vigorous growing. Leaves rather broad, and of a slightly yellowish green. Flowers reddish lilac. A very productive mid-season variety, of great merit. The tubers are very handsome and generally very regular in shape.

Centennial.—Tubers bright red, spherical or slightly flattened, and very smooth; eyes hardly marked; shoot red. Stems of medium size. Leaves broad, pale green. Flowers reddish. A half-early and rather productive variety. The tubers keep well for an American kind.

Early Cottage.—A very productive variety. Tubers large or very large, roundish, and thick; eyes rather deeply sunk; skin often wrinkled, and of a very pale-yellow colour; flesh white. Stems rather scanty in growth compared with the weight of the crop of tubers. Leaves grayish green and rather curled. Flowers lilac, usually abortive.

Early Goodrich.—Tubers oblong, thick, not much flattened, often almost pointed at the top; flesh and skin white; shoot pink. Leaves

of a very light, almost yellowish green. Flowers white. A handsome
and productive variety, but too often attacked by the disease.

Early Ohio.—Tubers pink, smooth, oblong; eyes very faintly
marked; shoot red. Stems erect, stiff, slightly tinged with copper
colour. Leaves very broad, flat, with extremely large leaflets of a light
and somewhat grayish green. This variety does not flower.

Eurêka.—Tubers long, rather flattened, often square at the ends,
and sometimes slightly notched; skin white, hardly yellowish, and
very slightly wrinkled; flesh white; shoot pink. Stems of scanty
growth. Leaves of a very light green. Flowers white. A very productive and rather early variety. The tubers are rather irregular in shape,
and sometimes quite nondescript in this respect.

Extra Early Vermont.—There is only an exceedingly slight shade
of difference between this Potato and the Early Rose, so that they are
often mistaken one for the other. The tuber of the Extra Early Vermont
is a little broader and flatter, and ripens two or three days earlier than
that of the Early Rose.

Idaho.—A very productive, somewhat late, but vigorous-growing
variety, of hardy constitution, and resisting the disease tolerably well.
Tubers round or slightly oblong, white, having the eyes rather well
marked and tinged with pink. This Potato keeps for a very long time.

King of the Earlies.—Tubers somewhat angular or irregular in
shape, rounded and slightly flattened in their general outline, and with
the eyes rather deeply sunk; skin smooth, but dull in hue, of a salmon-
tinted and slightly grayish-pink colour; flesh white and floury; shoot
pink. Stems of very scanty growth. Leaves broad, of a pale grayish
green, and withering very early without any flowers making their
appearance. This is really one of the earliest of all Potatoes.

Late Rose.—In many respects this variety is very like the Early
Rose, and even the difference in earliness which exists between the two
varieties does not exceed ten days. The Late Rose, however, is distinguished by the greater size of its tubers, which, on the other hand, are
not so numerous as those of the Early Rose. They are also of a purer
pink, and not so much tinged with salmon colour.

Manhattan.—Tubers round, slightly flattened, and variegated with
yellow and violet colour; shoot pink, spotted with violet. Stems short
and stiff, about 2 ft. high. Leaves rather abundant, broad, roundish, of
a grayish green, and very much folded and reticulated. Flowers generally wanting.

Peach-blow.—Tubers roundish, exceedingly smooth, and of a fine
white colour, slightly tinged with pink around the eyes; shoot pink.
Stems erect, stiff, vigorous growing, and spotted with brown. Leaves
numerous, rather slender, and of a clear-green colour, with oval-acute
leaflets. Flowers numerous, violet red, hardly ever producing seed.
There is a sub-variety, named the White Peach-blow, in which the eyes
are not tinged with pink.

Queen of the Valley.—Tubers very handsome, large, oblong,
slightly flattened, and very smooth; eyes few and faintly marked; skin
very pale red; shoot pink. The tubers are very like those of Brownell's
Beauty, but are not so dark coloured.

Ruby.—Tubers oblong, tolerably flattened, smooth, regular in shape, and of a bright-red colour; flesh white. Stems of medium size, and rather vigorous growing. Leaves of a pale and somewhat grayish-green colour. A half-late variety.

Triumph.—Tubers round and of a rather bright-red colour; eyes slightly marked and not very deeply sunk; shoot pink. A half-early and productive variety.

White Elephant.—A large, late variety, of extremely vigorous growth. Tubers oblong, of enormous size, very long, flattened, white variegated with pink, especially towards the end remote from the point of attachment, and usually slightly notched; flesh white. Flowers white. This variety somewhat resembles the Van der Veer Potato in the tallness of its stalks and the broadness of its leaves.

Willard (*Red Fluke*).—Tubers oblong or pear-shaped, almost pointed at the top and thick at the bottom; skin rather smooth, bright red, sometimes marbled with yellow; shoot pink. Stems erect and stiff. Leaves light green. Flowers reddish lilac. A very distinct and rather handsome variety, but very subject to be attacked by the disease.

IV. GERMAN VARIETIES.

Achilles.—Tubers large, roundish; eyes somewhat sunk. Stems very vigorous growing, over 3 ft. high, quadrangular, winged, and spotted with brown. Leaves numerous, but small, very much reticulated, curled, and of a blackish-green colour. Flowers lilac, in numerous clusters, and yielding seed.

Alkohol.—Tubers round, somewhat flattened; eyes rather numerous and well marked. Stems about 2½ ft. high, stout, green, quadrangular, and erect. Leaves broad, clear green, and somewhat crimped. Flowers white, abortive.

Aurora.—Tubers oval, flattened; eyes numerous and pretty well marked. Stems thick, copper coloured, often trailing, and about 2 ft. 8 inches long. Leaves very abundant, flat, and of a clear, slightly grayish, green. Flowers white, abortive.

The three preceding varieties were raised by M. Paulsen, who has devoted his attention to the production of new varieties of Potatoes in Germany, as Mr. Fenn has in England, and Mr. Bresee in America.

Biscuit.—A vigorous-growing and rather productive variety. Tubers small and very numerous, yellow, roundish, and slightly notched; shoot pink. Stems rather long and slender. Leaves slight, pale green. Ripens half-early.

Euphyllos.—Tubers white or faint pink, round or oblong; eyes moderately sunk. A vigorous-growing, productive, half-late variety, particularly characterized by the large size and fine appearance of the leaves, which are smooth, even, and of a clear-green colour, whence the variety derives its name. It is one of the varieties raised by M. Paulsen.

Feinste kleine weisse Mandel.—Tubers ovoid, small, very numerous, nearly white, smooth, and without eyes; shoot violet coloured. Stems comparatively large. Flowers white. The quality of the tubers is good, but they are rather small sized.

Frühe rothe Märkische (*Dabers'che, de Poméranie*).—A good, hardy, and productive field variety. Tubers red, nearly round, and rather smooth; shoot red; flesh yellow. Stems vigorous growing, often trailing on the ground. Leaves grayish green. Flowers reddish. Ripens half-late.

Kaiser-Kartoffel.—A fine, vigorous-growing, and rather early kind, resembling certain American varieties, especially Bresee's Prolific; it is, however, somewhat later and produces larger tubers. In habit of growth it is much the same.

Kopsell's frühe weisse Rosen-Kartoffel.—Like the preceding kind, this variety very much resembles Bresee's Prolific, but differs from it in being somewhat earlier, and in having yellower tubers, with less of the pink tinge. The shade of difference, however, is exceedingly slight, and it would be no great mistake to consider the two names as perfectly synonymous.

Lerchen-Kartoffel.—Tubers yellow, round, rather small but numerous; eyes somewhat sunk; skin very smooth; shoot white. Stems medium sized, but rather vigorous growing. Leaves clear green. Flowers white. This handsome small variety is very distinct. The tubers are of good quality, but only moderately productive.

Mangel-Wurzel (Synonyms: Doigt de Dame, Constance Péraut, Catawhisa, Bush Potato).—Tubers long, broad, flattened, oblong, and most usually notched, entirely red, or variegated with red and yellow, and generally very large, sometimes weighing over two pounds each. Most commonly they ripen irregularly and keep badly. A late kind, more suitable for feeding cattle than for table use.

Richter's Imperator.—Tubers large, oblong or oval, slightly flattened, but still rather thick, and slightly notched; skin pale yellow, slightly tinged with salmon colour; flesh nearly white; shoot violet coloured. Stems vigorous growing, erect, stiff, and tall. Leaves rather far apart, with roundish plaited leaflets. Flowers lilac. A half-late variety, tolerably like Paterson's Victoria, but with larger and not so regularly shaped tubers.

Richter's Schneerose.—Tubers large, thick, oblong, white; eyes faintly marked; shoot pink. Stems vigorous growing, erect, about 2½ ft. high. Leaves stiff, broad, roundish, and of a dark and somewhat grayish green. Flowers pink, opening well, but falling off abortive.

Riesen Sand Kartoffel (*P. de Terre Géante*).—Tubers long, flat, yellow variegated with red, especially towards the top; eyes rather deeply sunk; shoot pink. Stems short, very stiff, thick, and green. Leaves very much curled and reticulated, rather broad, and of a dark-green colour. Flowers pink, abortive.

Rothe unvergleichliche Salat-Kartoffel.—Tubers nearly cylindrical, one and a half times or twice as long as broad, very much notched; skin red. They are easily distinguished from those of any other kind by the appearance of the flesh, which is variegated with red and yellow. Stems rather crowded together, vigorous growing, and very leafy. A somewhat late kind, but keeps well.

Sächsische Zwiebel-Kartoffel weissfleischige.—Tubers roundish, somewhat flattened, of medium and very uniform size; eyes slightly sunk; skin smooth, red; flesh white; shoot pink. Stems luxuriant, long, rather slender, and usually branching and trailing on the ground.

Leaves of a dark and slightly grayish green. Flowers generally abortive.

Sächsische Zwiebel-Kartoffel gelbfleischige (*Rouge de Bohême*).— Tubers round or somewhat elongated, not flattened, and rather notched; skin entirely red or red variegated with yellow; shoot pink; flesh pure yellow. Stems very vigorous growing, branching, sometimes nearly 6½ ft. long. Leaves very abundant, and of a dark-green colour. Flowers reddish violet. A late but very vigorous growing and very productive variety. The tubers keep well, and contain a considerable proportion of starch.

Spargel-Kartoffel (*P. de Terre Asperge*).—Tubers small, almost cylindrical, but short, being only twice as long as broad; skin and flesh yellow; shoot pink. Stems of medium height, rather slender. Leaves clear green. Flowers white. A half-late and very distinct small kind, esteemed on account of the firmness of the flesh, which is not easily broken, even when cooked.

SWEET POTATO.

Convolvulus Batatas, L. *Convolvulaceæ.*

French, Patate douce. *Italian*, Patata. *Spanish* and *Portuguese*, Batata.

Native of S. America.—Perennial, but cultivated as an annual.— Stems creeping, often 10 ft. long or more, with numerous heart-shaped leaves of a dark-green colour, sometimes glistening; flowers axillary, like those of a Convolvulus, seldom blooming in the climate of Paris; roots abundant, very much ramified, and bearing tubers more or less roundish or elongated in shape, according to the variety. The flesh of these tubers is tender, floury, sweet, and, in most cases, rather per-fumed. They are the edible part of the plant, and are produced in very great abundance in warm countries, where, as an article of food, they occupy, to a certain extent, the same place which the Potato does with us.

Culture.—As the Sweet Potato requires a rather long time to complete its growth, it is difficult to cultivate it in the climate of Paris without the aid of artificial heat; and as, moreover, the tubers keep badly in northern countries, gardeners are in the habit of starting some plants in the middle or end of winter, either in a plant-house or in a hot-bed. As soon as the shoots are strong enough, they are detached from the tubers and planted separately in pots, in which they remain until they are planted out. This is done from March to the end of May, according as it is desired to forward the growth of the plants. Those planted out in March and April should have the protection of a frame. In May this is not required, and the plants may then be simply put out on beds of dry leaves covered with from 4 to 6 inches of light soil or compost. Copious waterings are necessary as soon as the hot weather commences, and the stems quickly cover the whole bed, and even extend beyond it. In the South only, the Sweet Potato may be planted in the open air on sloping beds of rich mellow soil, and watered by means of trenches cut between the beds, which should be at least 6½ ft.

apart. The tubers are well grown in four or five months, and are taken up as late as possible in the climate of Paris, but care must be taken to lift the crop as soon as the stems and leaves have been touched by frost, as, the soil being no longer covered by the foliage, the frost would easily reach the tubers, which very often grow level with the surface of the ground, and are very sensitive to cold. The tubers are very difficult to keep, cold and damp being equally injurious to them; they should, therefore, be kept in a very dry place, the temperature of which should be as uniform as possible, and never fall below 40° or 42° Fahr. It is sometimes a good plan to store them in boxes, which are then filled up with dry sand, peat, or sawdust. The tubers should not be allowed to touch one another, and the boxes should be examined from time to time, and any tubers which have commenced to decay should be removed. Like the ordinary Potato, the Sweet Potato may be propagated from seed, but varieties are not reproduced true in this way, and it is only employed for the purpose of raising new varieties. However, the plant never seeds in the climate of Paris, and it is useless to attempt the culture of it in England.

Uses.—The tubers are prepared in various ways and eaten like those of the ordinary Potato. The flesh is sweet, very tender, and, in most varieties, has a perfume somewhat like the scent of violets. As in the case of the common Potato, there is a vast difference in the flavour of well-grown " mealy " and that of waxy roots.

Of Sweet Potatoes, an almost infinite number of varieties are cultivated. We shall only mention the earliest kinds, and those which succeed best in France.

Patate Igname.—Tubers very large, oval or oblong, blunt at the ends, and often channelled or furrowed; skin grayish white; flesh white, not very fine in texture, rather floury, and moderately sweet. This is one of the most productive kinds, the tubers sometimes weighing nearly nine pounds each.

Patate Jaune.—A somewhat late variety, but of excellent quality. Tubers long, slender, very thin, about 16 inches long, and 2 inches or less in diameter; skin yellow, smooth; flesh of a handsome yellow colour, very fine flavoured and sweet.

Patate Rose de Malaga.—Tubers oblong, somewhat variable in shape, often marked with longitudinal furrows, and thicker at one end than at the other; skin of a somewhat grayish pink colour; flesh yellow, very fine in texture, and moderately sweet. This is one of the earliest and most productive varieties.

" Rose de Malaga " Sweet Potato (⅓ natural size).

Red Sweet Potato (*Patate Violette*).—This is the sweetest, most highly perfumed, and least floury of all varieties. Tubers very long and slender, about 20 inches in length, by 2 inches or

less in the diameter of the thickest part, but much thinner at both
ends. They are almost always sinuated or undulated. Skin smooth,

red slightly tinged with violet; flesh
white in the interior, and light pink under
the skin. This is the variety which is
most generally grown by gardeners in the
vicinity of Paris.

Many other varieties of Sweet Potato
are cultivated in Algeria and other French
colonies, and even in the United States,
where this vegetable forms an important
article of commerce.

PURSLANE.

Portulaca oleracea, L.   *Portulaceæ.*

French, Pourpier. *German,* Portulak. *Flemish* and
Dutch, Postelein. *Danish,* Portulak. *Italian,*
Porcellana. *Spanish,* Verdolaga. *Portuguese,*
Beldroega.

Red Sweet Potato (⅓ natural size).

Native of India.—Annual.—The Purslane, which appears to be undoubtedly of
East Indian origin, has been naturalized
amongst us to the extent of having become a weed. It has a thick
fleshy stem, which sprawls on the ground when the plant grows alone,
but is unbranched and erect in plants grown closely together. Leaves
thick, shortly spathulate ; flowers very small, yellow, growing from the
axils of the leaves, and succeeded by roundish, slightly compressed
seed-vessels filled with very small, shining, black seeds. A gramme
contains about 2500 seeds, and a litre of them weighs, on an average,
610 grammes. Their germinating power lasts for seven years at least.
Culture.—The seed is sown, either in drills or broad-cast, in light
soil, from May to August, and the leaves and stems may begin to be
gathered for use in about two months after sowing. The same plants
will yield two or three gatherings, provided they are watered frequently.
Sowings are often made in frames or on hot-beds, in order to obtain
a winter or spring supply. In this case the seed is sown from December
to March on hot-beds, as the plant requires a pretty high temperature
to grow vigorously, and leaves may be gathered in two months or two
months and a half after sowing. Uses.—The leaves are eaten cooked,
or raw as salad.

Green Purslane (*Pourpier Vert*).—This is the wild plant developed
and increased in size by continuous cultivation of selected large-leaved
specimens. Even in the wild state some Purslane plants are met with
which have a more marked tendency than others to grow with the
stems erect instead of sprawling on the ground, and this form it has
naturally been sought to reproduce and improve by cultivation, as being
more productive on an equal area, and more easy to gather than plants
of spreading habit.

Golden Purslane (*Pourpier Doré*).—This variety is easily distinguished from the preceding one by the light and almost yellow tint of

its leaves. It is grown and used in exactly the same manner. Its peculiar tint appears to be less owing to a weaker colouring of the parenchyma of the leaf than to a greater thickness of the epidermis, which is of a yellowish hue. When cooked, the leaves do not differ very much in colour from those of the Green Purslane.

Large-leaved Golden Purslane (*Pourpier Doré à Large Feuille*).— This variety is very distinct on account of the size of the leaves, which are at least double as large as those of the two preceding kinds, and grow closer together on the stem. The plant does not grow quite so rapidly as either of the two other kinds, but it is quite as productive, being more thick-set and compact in habit.

Green Purslane (⅕ natural size; detached branch, ⅓ natural size).

Large-leaved Golden Purslane (⅕ natural size; detached branch, ⅓ natural size).

Winter Purslane (¼ natural size).

WINTER PURSLANE.

Claytonia perfoliata, Don.   *Portulacaceæ.*

French, Claytone perfoliée.   *Flemish*, Doorwas.   *Dutch*, Winter-postelijn.   *Spanish*, Verdolaga de Cuba.

Native of Cuba.—Annual.—Leaves all radical, very tender, thick, and fleshy, the earliest ones very narrow and lanceolate, the following

2 I

ones more or less broad, but always pointed; stems numerous, somewhat taller than the leaves, and bearing at the end a sort of broadly
funnel-shaped collarette of the same texture as the leaves, from the
centre of which issue short panicles of small white flowers; seed small,
black, slightly flattened, and lenticular in shape. A gramme contains
about 2200 seeds, and a litre of them weighs about 700 grammes.
Their germinating power lasts for five years. The seed is sown, where
the plants are to stand, all through spring and summer. The leaves
are eaten as salad, or cooked like ordinary Purslane or Spinach.

RADISHES.

Raphanus sativus, L. *Cruciferæ.*

French, Radis. *German,* Radies. *Flemish* and *Dutch,* Radijs. *Danish,* Haveroeddike.
Italian, Ravanello. *Spanish,* Rabanito. *Portuguese,* Rabao.

Native of South Asia (?).—Annual.—The type or original plant
from which the cultivated forms of Radishes have been derived is not
known with certainty. The question has given rise to many inquiries
and discussions, and probably will give rise to many more, as the highest
and most competent authorities on the subject hesitate to decide the
point in a positive manner. Up to the present, in fact, no wild plant
has been found possessing characteristics which would allow of its being
regarded unmistakably as the progenitor of cultivated Radishes. The
opinion that these have sprung from *Raphanus Raphanistrum* (the Wild
Radish of our fields) may be maintained, but there are very important
indications which appear to us to be opposed to it. Besides the
differences in the colour of the flowers (which, in the Wild Radish, are
often yellow, but never so in the cultivated varieties), and in the formation of the siliques or seed-vessels (which are jointed in the Wild
Radish, and not so in the others), it must be observed that the cultivated plants are much more sensitive to cold than our indigenous
Wild Radish, a fact which would appear to point to a more southern
clime as the native habitat of the first parents of these plants. Moreover, the stems of the cultivated plants grow erect, and not in an
inclined or almost prostrate position, as is frequently the case with the
Wild Radish. Now, there are two Asiatic forms of Radish which have
unjointed, fleshy, edible seed-vessels, viz. the Madras Radish (*Radis de
Madras*) and the Mougri, or Snake Radish, of Java (*Mougri de Java* ou
Radis Serpent), and it is towards the countries in which these forms,
resembling the cultivated Radish in the structure of the seed-vessel
and in all their characteristics of growth, are found, that we think we
should look for the original plant which was their common ancestor.

The cultivated Radish is looked upon as an annual, because the
growth of the flower-stems is not preceded by any period of repose in the
growth of the plant; the large late varieties, however, should rather
be considered biennial. The leaves are oblong in shape, the flower-
stems are branched, and the flowers are white or lilac, but never yellow.
The seed is reddish, roundish or slightly elongated, and usually somewhat flattened at the sides. A gramme contains about 120 seeds, and
a litre of them weighs about 700 grammes. Their germinating power
lasts for five years.

The French are such excellent Radish growers that those who care to be informed as to the best way of growing these roots can hardly do better than read the cultural notes given under the three divisions. For various reasons, however, it may be well to give here the culture usually pursued in our own country, both in private and market gardens. A small and constant supply of crisp, delicately flavoured bulbs should be the only aim. The earliest will be had from a hot-bed or from under some glass protection. It is seldom we grow a special frame of Radishes, but secure all we want from frames planted with other crops. In January and February we are frequently making up beds of manure and leaves for forcing Potatoes, Carrots, etc., and amongst these are sown a few Radishes. When the Potatoes, for example, are planted in rows 15 inches apart, a row of Radishes may be sown between, and they will be ready for use and cleared off before the Potato crop in any way interferes with them. In Carrot frames the same thing may be done, and sometimes a Radish seed is dropped in here and there amongst the Carrots, as they will push up and be cleared off before the Carrots require much top room. Thus young spring Radishes are obtained without any special attention; many, however, who try to grow early Radishes in this way make mistakes. One of these is sowing the seed too thickly. Under such circumstances, when the plants come up they are a mat at top and bottom, and when this is the case useful roots are never formed. Thinning out some of the plants as soon as they can be handled is one way of avoiding this, but it is a wasteful way; the better plan is always to sow thinly. One seed every few inches will give a much finer crop and better results altogether than close sowing. Many doubtless wonder why their Radishes do not all bulb, but allowing them to grow too close together is, as a rule, the cause of this. Many are

most particular, too, in getting their seeds in and the crop brought to maturity, but after the usable part of it has been gathered neglect follows, and where Radishes have been raised in a Potato or Carrot frame it is no uncommon thing to see worthless Radish tops overshadowing everything by the time the other crops should have been at their best. Cultivators should always be particular in clearing away all Radishes as soon as they become too old for use, and any which do not bulb early may be thrown away altogether.

Special Beds.—In making up a special bed for early Radishes, a very shallow bed of fermenting material is sufficient; about 1 ft. in depth is enough, and 6 inches of soil should be put on the top of this. They bulb fastest early in the year in a moderately rich sandy mixture. The seed should be sown broadcast, very thin, and it should not be covered more than $\frac{1}{2}$ inch deep. The earliest seed may be sown in frames in January and February, but in the latter month and throughout March seed may also be sown along the base of a south wall or in any sheltered sunny spot. Here the rule as to thin sowing should also be observed; in fact, this must be kept in mind throughout. When the little plants appear at first in the colder months of spring a slight protection will favour their free growth. A few branches or some similar covering is all that is needed.

Summer Radishes.—From April onwards throughout the summer select spots need not be chosen for Radishes, as they will do almost anywhere, their only requirements being a firm, rich, cool soil. Without this, especially in summer, the roots will become hot and stringy before they are well developed, and the period of their use will be very short. In general culture some may prefer having the seed in rows; others may sow broadcast, and good Radishes may be had in both ways. At no time should the seed be put more than $\frac{1}{2}$ inch below the surface; the soil should always be trodden firmly over it, as this induces the plants to bulb quicker and better than when in loose material.

WINTER RADISHES.—Our rule is to sow a small quantity of seed every three weeks from the middle of January until the beginning of September, when we stop all sowings and dealings with the summer varieties, and devote one good large piece of ground to the Chinese Scarlet for winter. This sowing is made on a south border which may have been previously cleared of Potatoes or some other crop. The seed is put in in rows 15 inches apart, in order that plenty of air and light may be admitted to them in winter, and if the young plants come up too close they are thinned out to 6 inches apart. Under this treatment a uniform crop of useful bulbs is the result. We generally gather some of these by the end of October, when they are no larger than filberts. To have Radishes in the best possible condition, they must be grown quickly; and to do this in dry soils, frequent waterings during dry weather must be given them, otherwise by the time the roots are of a usable size they will generally be stringy and ill-flavoured. Small sowings in quick succession are, therefore, preferable to large ones made at long intervals apart.

CULTURE FOR MARKET.—In the London market gardens, the first two crops of Radishes of the year are generally grown amongst fruit trees, if bush fruits or Roses do not occupy the ground. By sowing time, which is in November and December, the trees are leafless and pruned; therefore they do not offer much shade to the young Radish plants, but rather protect them from cold winds and severe frosts, and before the trees have made much growth in spring the Radishes are fit for market, and the ground when cleared of them is available for being planted with Lettuces or other plants that are best suited for a

shady situation. Crops of Radishes to succeed those under fruit trees are sown in open quarters, in 6-ft. wide beds with alleys between them. After sowing the seed is raked in with wooden rakes, and afterwards slightly covered with fine soil taken from the alleys. The surface of the beds is then rolled and, in the case of early sowings, slightly covered with long litter, which after the seeds have germinated is removed on every favourable opportunity, but immediately replaced on the appearance of frosty, snowy, or stormy weather. After the second week in February coverings are dispensed with if the weather is at all likely to continue mild for a time, as the plants have by this time become strong and better able to stand the cold. The litter is, however, kept in the alleys in case of emergency until all danger from frost is over, when it is removed entirely and converted into manure. Successional sowings are made in February, March, and April, in a manner similar to that just described, and in some cases during the summer. But, except in moist situations, Radishes do not succeed well in hot weather; therefore, where such situations do not exist, sowing ceases in spring, and recommences in August and September, if the weather be at all showery. A good crop of Radishes during the summer is profitable, and especially so in dry seasons. The ground chosen for them is usually that recently cleared of Celery, French Beans, Rhubarb, or Vegetable Marrows, which, after being deeply dug and heavily manured, is levelled and otherwise prepared to receive the seed. Sometimes Radishes are sown between Asparagus ridges, and in such positions they succeed remarkably well on account of the soil being deep and rich. When Radishes are required earlier in the spring than they can be gathered from the December outdoor sowing, they are obtained from frames placed on hot-beds, or trenches are dug out and filled with manure, on which a little soil is placed, and after sowing, the beds are covered over with litter. In March the first outdoor crops are usually ready for market. Birds are the worst enemies with which the Radish grower has to contend, and when large quantities are grown it is found necessary to employ boys to scare them away, otherwise they would devour all the seed, and even pull up the young plants in order to obtain the husks which adhere to the young leaves.

USES.—The roots are served up raw as a side-dish.

The varieties of Radishes are very numerous, and we shall divide them, according to their period of culture, into Small or Forcing, Summer or Autumn, and Winter Radishes, the mode of culture which is suitable for each of these divisions being very different from that which should be employed for the others.

I. Small, or Forcing, Radishes.

Radis de tous les mois.

These Radishes are sown in the open air from February to November, usually broad-cast in beds, and the seedlings are thinned out so as to allow the plants to grow evenly. The beds should be kept free from weeds, and frequently watered in hot dry weather. In about from sixteen to eighteen days, if the weather is favourable, and from twenty to twenty-five days if otherwise, the earliest plants will be fit for use. As for the rest, it may be four, five, or six weeks, according to the weather, before they are fit to be pulled. In spring, or late in autumn, the seed should be sown in a warm sheltered position; in summer a cool shady place is preferable. Sowings should be made in succession every fortnight or ten days, in order to keep up a supply of young tender Radishes. In December, January, and February, the seed is sown on hot-beds under frames or bell-glasses. The market gardeners of Paris grow Radishes in the depth of winter on hot-beds covered with leaf-mould or compost, without any protection except that of straw mats, which are placed over them at night and in frosty weather, and are taken off whenever the weather is not too severe. These Radishes are usually fit to be pulled in from five to six weeks after sowing.

A. ROUND, OR TURNIP-ROOTED, RADISHES.

Scarlet French Turnip Radish (*Radis Rond Rose* ou *Saumoné*).—Root nearly spherical, slightly top-shaped when very young; skin of a somewhat vinous red; flesh white, slightly tinged with pink; leaves rather roundish, cut at the edges, and of a somewhat glaucous green colour; leaf-stalks faintly bronzed. In fine weather, as in May, this

Scarlet French Turnip Radish (⅓ natural size).

Radish is fit for use in about twenty-five days after sowing. It is hardy, does not become hollow at the centre too quickly, and grows well in ordinary garden soil.

Early Scarlet Turnip Radish (*Radis Rond Rose Hâtif*).— Root more flattened than that of the preceding kind, well rounded underneath, having only a very slender, small tap-root, and resembling the ordinary Scarlet Turnip Radish in the colour of the skin; flesh very white; leaves short and close growing. This variety is fit for use in about twenty days after sowing, and can be grown in ordinary garden soil, but compost or leaf-mould suits it much better. It becomes hollow at the centre sooner than the preceding kind.

Early White-tipped Scarlet Turnip Radish (*Radis Rond Rose à Bout Blanc*).—A handsome and exceedingly early variety. Root

roundish, of a very bright carmine pink, but quite white in the lower fourth part. It is the only garden Radish that is really pink coloured, the two preceding kinds being more of a carmine-red tint; but in this variety the upper part of the root is of a true bright pink, which makes a pleasing contrast with the white of the lower part. The root of this Radish swells more speedily than that of any other variety, but it also quickly becomes hollow at the centre, and should be pulled for use as soon as it is fully grown.

Early White-tipped Scarlet Turnip Radish (⅓ natural size).

It grows really well only in compost or leaf-mould, and is sometimes fit for use in from sixteen to eighteen days after sowing. The market gardeners about Paris grow it in preference to all other kinds for an early crop.

Deep Scarlet Turnip Radish (*Radis Rond Écarlate*).—Root of the same shape as that of the Scarlet Turnip Radish, but of a much more

brilliant red, without any tinge of violet colour; flesh very white; leaves very green, medium sized, roundish. The root of this Radish swells as quickly as that of the ordinary Scarlet Turnip Radish, and the plant is grown in the same manner. There is no great difference between the two kinds, except in colour, that of the present variety causing it to be much sought after in some countries, as in Belgium, and rejected in others. This, however, like many other things, is a matter of fashion. The Deep Scarlet Turnip Radish is an early variety,

Deep Scarlet Turnip Radish (⅓ natural size).

and has the advantage of not becoming hollow at the centre too soon, when left in the ground a little longer than usual. It has a pretty strong pungent flavour.

Early Deep Scarlet Turnip Radish (*Radis Rond Écarlate Hâtif*). —A very handsome variety. Root very round, or slightly flattened, and of an exceedingly lively colour; flesh white, firm, crisp, and very pleasant to the taste; leaves very like those of the preceding kind, and of a somewhat lighter green than those of the pink-skinned

Radishes. This variety is often fit for use in about twenty days after sowing. It grows well in ordinary garden soil, and still better in compost or leaf-mould.

Small Early White Turnip Radish (*Radis Rond Blanc Petit Hâtif*).—Root roundish, usually flattened above and underneath, often twice as broad as deep; leaves short, rather spreading, very much cut or divided, somewhat grayish, and tinged with brown on the veins and in the middle. In this variety the roots do not swell very quickly, as they take at least from twenty to twenty-five days from the time of sowing before they are fit to be pulled for use. It is, however, employed for forcing, especially in northern countries. Even when quite small, this Radish is remarkably pungent to the taste, and its flavour is sometimes so strong as to be hardly endurable.

Small Early White Turnip Radish (⅓ natural size).

White Turnip Radish (*Radis Rond Blanc*).—A handsome variety. Root nearly round, not so much flattened as that of the preceding kind; leaves greener, broader, and more erect. Although it is only two or three days later than the Early White Turnip Radish, this kind is more suitable for open-air culture than for forcing. The flesh is firm and very pungent.

Early Purple Turnip Radish (*Radis Rond Violet*).—Root slightly top-shaped, of a fine clear violet colour; flesh white, almost transparent; leaves rather large, cut or divided, erect, and of a clear-green colour. The roots of this variety take about a month to swell, but they remain a long time without becoming hollow at the centre. It is a true "all-the-year-round" Radish.

White-tipped Purple Turnip Radish (*Radis Rond Violet à Bout Blanc*).—A handsome, small kind, with an almost spherical root, of a dark-violet colour around the neck, becoming gradually paler towards the lower extremity, which is pure white. Leaf-stalks and veins of the leaves violet coloured or brownish; leaves rather slight. Like the Early White-tipped Scarlet Radish, this variety should be sown at intervals of about a fortnight, as it becomes hollow at the centre very speedily.

Small Early Yellow Turnip Radish (⅓ natural size).

Small Early Yellow Turnip Radish (*Radis Jaune Hâtif de Tous les Mois*).—Root roundish or slightly elongated, sometimes ending in a tap-root of some thickness; skin rather smooth, and of a somewhat dull-yellow colour; flesh fine and compact, rather pungent; leaves half-erect, and distinctly lyrate in shape. The roots of this Radish take about a month to swell. Although early and small sized, they have not the fine quality which the other varieties of this section possess.

A new variety, named the Golden Yellow Turnip Radish (*R. Rond Jaune d'Or*), has for some years been gradually superseding the Early Yellow variety, which it excels in being earlier, and having the root better shaped, very smooth and round, and of a much brighter and purer yellow. Of all the Yellow Radishes, this comes the nearest to the small early White or Scarlet varieties.

B. Intermediate, or Olive-shaped, Varieties.

Olive-shaped Scarlet Radish (*Radis Demi-long Rose*). — Root

ovoid, slightly elongated, usually olive-shaped, sometimes almost cylindrical for a good part of its length, and rounded at both ends, of a very deep carmine-red colour; flesh white, firm, and crisp; leaves roundish, of a clear-green colour, rather broad, and not quite so large as those of the Scarlet Turnip Radish. This is one of the kinds which are most extensively grown in kitchen gardens and for market supply. It grows well in the open ground, and remains a pretty long time without becoming hollow at the centre. The market gardeners of Paris often try to raise it with the roots long and slender, rather than ovoid in shape, and they succeed in doing so by covering the beds with compost or leaf-mould as soon as the young plants are pretty well up.

Olive-shaped Scarlet Radish (⅓ natural size).

French Breakfast Radish (*Radis Demi-long Rose à Bout Blanc*).—A very handsome variety, of the same shape as the preceding kind, or not quite so much elongated; skin of a florid and rather lively pink colour on the upper three-fourths of the root, and pure white on the lower part. Like the White-tipped Scarlet Turnip Radish, this variety is exceedingly early; but the root very soon becomes hollow at the centre, if it is not pulled as soon as it is fully formed. It grows much better in a hot-bed, or in compost or leaf-mould, than in ordinary garden soil. It is essentially a market-garden Radish.

French Breakfast Radish (⅓ natural size).

Deep Scarlet Intermediate Radish (*Radis Demilong Écarlate*).—This variety is as distinct in the colour of the skin as it is in the shape of the root, which is more elongated, and terminates in a longer and finer point than that of any other Intermediate variety. Leaves of a clear-green colour, rather large, and erect; flesh very white, firm, crisp, very juicy, and with a tolerably strong and pungent flavour. This is a pretty hardy and very suitable kind for growing in the open air. The roots take about twenty-five days to swell, and do not become hollow too speedily.

Short-leaved Early Scarlet Intermediate Radish (*Radis Demi-long Écarlate Très-hâtif à Courte Feuille*).—This very handsome, small Radish is evidently a seedling variety of the preceding one, from which it only differs in the still greater rapidity with which the root swells, and in the small size of the leaves, which

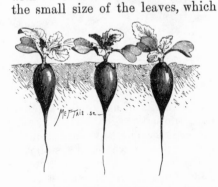

Deep Scarlet Intermediate Radish
(⅓ natural size).

Short-leaved Early Scarlet Intermediate
Radish.

are scarcely larger than the seed-leaves when the roots are quite fit to pull for use. It comes in almost as early as the Early White-tipped Scarlet and the French Breakfast Radishes, like which, it succeeds best when grown in compost or leaf-mould.

Early Deep Scarlet Olive-shaped Radish (*Radis Demi-long Écarlate Hâtif*).—This is, from every point of view, one of the handsomest and best of all the Small or Forcing Radishes. The root is regularly olive-shaped, very symmetrical, and very smooth skinned; flesh white and firm; leaves short, stiff, and extremely few for the size of the root. The plant grows admirably in the open air. The roots take about twenty to twenty-two days to swell. Its earliness and scanty foliage render it equally suitable for forcing. This variety is easily distinguished from the preceding one, by the roots being shorter and terminating more abruptly at the base, instead of gradually diminishing in a long point. The

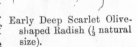

Early Deep Scarlet Olive-
shaped Radish (⅓ natural
size).

flesh is tender, and of a mild cool flavour, with hardly any pungency.

White Olive-shaped Radish (*Radis Demi-long Blanc*).—When this variety is grown true to name, the root is very handsome, very regularly olive-shaped, and of a very fresh pure white colour; flesh very white and crisp, and not too strong flavoured; leaves medium sized, rather erect, and of a light-green colour. This Radish may be grown equally well in a hot-bed and in the open air. The roots take about twenty-five days to swell. Their colour forms a pleasing contrast to that of the other Intermediate varieties. It is not long since the variety was firmly established in the olive-shape repre-

sented in the accompanying illustration. Formerly it had the defect of being elongated in the lower part, almost like a Long Radish—a defect which, even yet, it sometimes exhibits when the seed is not very pure.

Purple Olive - shaped Radish (*Radis Demi-long Violet à Bout Blanc*).—Root ovoid, almost pear-shaped, the thickest part being near the base. The

White Olive-shaped Radish (⅓ natural size).

upper half is of an almost blackish-violet colour, which, in the lower half, gradually becomes paler until it passes into pure white at the extremity. The leaves are scanty, rather cut at the edges, and tinged with violet brown on the stalks, veins, and sometimes on the blade of the leaf itself, giving the foliage a rather pleasing appearance. The flesh is white, hardish, and strong flavoured. The roots take about a month to swell. This variety is especially suitable for open-air culture, but is also well adapted for forcing.

C. Long Radishes.

Long Scarlet, or Salmon-coloured, Radish (*Rave Rose Longue ou Saumonée*).— Root extremely long and slender, often 5 or 6 inches in length and only about ⅖ inch in diameter, the upper part of an elongated cone-shape, narrowed towards the base of the leaves; skin smooth, of a vinous-red colour; flesh almost transparent, and slightly tinged with pink or lilac. This peculiar appearance of the flesh easily distinguishes the variety from all others which resemble it. This Radish is most usually grown in the open air in well-dug and well-manured soil. It is very seldom employed for forcing, on account of the great length of the root, which would require the hot-beds to be covered with too deep a layer of compost or leaf-mould. The roots take about a month to become fully formed. The flesh is tender, crisp, and fresh to the taste, but has not the pungent flavour of the Turnip Radishes or the Intermediate varieties.

Long Scarlet, or Salmon-coloured, Radish (⅓ natural size).

Long Scarlet Short-top Radish (*Rave Rose à Collet Rond*).—Root somewhat thicker and one-third shorter than that of the preceding variety, of a carmine-red colour, like that of the Intermediate Scarlet

Radish; flesh white; leaves rather large, half-erect, and of a clear green colour. This variety is more suitable for forcing than the preceding one, but the following kind is generally preferred for that purpose.

Wood's Early Frame Radish (*Radis Long Rose*).—This variety might be described as coming between the Long and the Intermediate kinds. The roots, which are of a very elongated-ovoid shape, are usually from $2\frac{3}{5}$ to $2\frac{4}{5}$ inches long, and about $\frac{4}{5}$ inch broad in the thickest part, which is not far below the base of the leaf-stalks. The skin is of a very lively carmine red, which becomes gradually paler towards the lower end of the root. The flesh is very white, firm, juicy, very crisp, fresh and pleasant to the taste, with a slightly pungent flavour like that of the Scarlet Intermediate Radish. The leaves are broad, but rather short, compact, and roundish in shape, and having the stalks and veins tinged with coppery red. This Radish, which may also be very well grown in the open air, is almost exclusively cultivated in frames, especially in England. A layer of compost or leaf-mould 4 inches deep over the hot-bed is deep enough to grow it in. Of all the early Radishes this variety yields the heaviest weight of produce in the same space of time.

Wood's Early Frame Radish
($\frac{1}{3}$ natural size).

The roots take from twenty to twenty-two days to become fully formed.

Long Purple Radish (*Rave Violette*).—Root very long and slender, resembling that of the Long Scarlet Radish, with a long conical top, of an almost blackish-violet colour, which becomes paler on the portion of the root buried in the soil; flesh almost transparent, lilac; leaves erect, rather long and broad, with brown stalks and veins. This variety is only grown in the open air. The roots take about a month to swell.

Long White Naples Radish (*Rave Blanche*. Synonyms: White Transparent, or White Italian, Radish).—Root long and slender, pure white, resembling the Long Scarlet Radish in shape, but somewhat thicker; the upper part is conically tapered and tinged with pale green. This variety is almost exclusively grown in the open air. The roots take about a month to become fully formed. A sub-variety of it is sometimes met with, in which the neck of the root is tinged with violet colour, but in every other respect it is exactly the same as the common variety.

Long White Vienna Radish (*Rave de Vienne*).—Root white, very smooth and clean skinned, straight, spindle-shaped, from 2 to nearly 3 inches long, and from $\frac{4}{5}$ to 1 inch broad at the top; neck short, rounded, tinged with green, and very narrow at the insertion of the leaf-stalks; leaves rather large, broad, and of a light-green colour. This is an early variety. The roots take four or five weeks to become

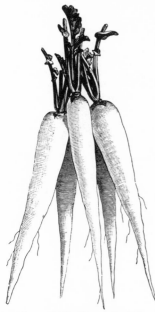

Long White Vienna Radish
(⅓ natural size).

fully formed; the flesh is very tender, crisp, and juicy. Amongst the Japanese varieties of Radishes, of which we shall have occasion to speak at the end of this article, there is one which, in its appearance, bears a tolerable resemblance to the present variety. It has long slender roots, which at first are quite under the surface of the soil, but afterwards the top of the root rises a little overground and becomes tinged with green at the neck. The flesh of this variety is very white, rather strong flavoured, and of very good quality.

Long Normandy, or Marsh, Radish (*Rave de Marais*).—A very distinct long-rooted variety, remarkable for its habit of protruding from the ground and becoming twisted like the Ox-horn Beet-root. The part of the root which remains underground is white, and the portion which is exposed to the light becomes violet coloured. This Radish is usually sown in the open air, and the roots are pulled for use when they are about ⅖ inch in diameter and 4 inches in length; they are then very tender. They attain this size and condition in less than a month from the time of sowing, after which they rapidly increase in size, and become twisted and hollow at the centre.

White Crooked, or Mans Corkscrew, Radish (*Rave Tortillée du Mans*).—An exceedingly distinct variety. Root very long, cylindrical in the upper part, over 1 inch in diameter, and frequently more than 1 ft. in length. About one-fourth or one-fifth of the root protrudes overground, and this part is of a dull white colour, more or less tinged with pale green. The underground portion is pure white, seldom straight, but most usually twisted in a zigzag manner, like a corkscrew, in consequence of which the root can rarely be pulled up without breaking off and leaving a part behind in the ground. The flesh is white, not very compact, and of pungent flavour. The leaves are very broad and the neck of the root often badly formed. The roots of this Radish should be pulled for use about six weeks after sowing, as, if left in the ground longer, they become only fit for feeding cattle.

The Ardèche Field Radish (*Raifort Champêtre de l'Ardèche*), which is grown in the south of France more for feeding cattle than for table use, has some resemblance to the present variety. Like it, it is a very long-rooted and rather late Radish, and yields a heavier crop of leaves than of roots. It is a plant of no account for kitchen-garden culture, and even for cattle-feeding purposes neither it nor the Corkscrew Radish is very extensively grown. Experience has shown, however, that they are not without merit in this respect, and we think that in many cases it would be found advantageous to cultivate some of the larger varieties of Radishes for cattle-feeding purposes, as is done in the case of Beet-roots, Carrots, and Turnips. We shall return to this subject when we come to describe some of the Winter Radishes.

II. Summer and Autumn Radishes.

Radis d'été ou d'automne.

Under this name are grouped a certain number of varieties, the roots of which are of larger size than those of the varieties belonging to the preceding section, and take a longer time to form, but, nevertheless, grow rapidly, so that, by making successional sowings, a continuous supply of fresh tender Radishes may be kept up all through the summer and autumn. These varieties do not usually keep long. They are sown in drills, which are from 16 to 20 inches apart, and the seedlings are thinned out to a distance of from 6 to 8 inches from one another, according to the size of the variety sown. They require no attention except occasional waterings. The roots of most of the varieties are fully formed in from six weeks to two months from the time of sowing. Sowings may be made from March until August.

Large White Summer Turnip-Radish (*Radis Blanc Rond d'Été*). —Root roundish or top-shaped, 2 inches or more in diameter and length when well grown; skin white; flesh white, rather tender, and slightly pungent in flavour; leaves rather long, broad, half-erect, considerably more abundant and larger than those of the Small or Forcing Radishes, especially exceeding them in the size of the midribs or stalks, which form a rather broad neck at their junction with the root.

Large White Summer Turnip Radish (⅓ natural size).

Stuttgard Early Giant White Turnip Radish (⅓ natural size).

The roots of this variety form pretty soon, and are generally fit for use in from thirty-five to forty days after sowing.

Stuttgard Early Giant White Turnip Radish (*Radis Blanc*

Géant de Stuttgart).—A larger variety, and somewhat more flattened in shape than the preceding one. It is regularly top-shaped, and often 3 or 4 inches in diameter, and over 3 inches in depth. Skin and flesh white; leaves somewhat broader and stiffer than those of the preceding variety, but not so erect. The roots may be pulled for use about six weeks after sowing, although they will continue to increase in size for some time longer without becoming deteriorated in quality. When they have attained their full size, they are too large to be served up entire, and are cut into slices like the Winter Radishes.

Yellow Summer Turnip Radish (*Radis Jaune ou Roux d'Été*).— Root almost spherical or slightly top-shaped, sometimes longer than

Yellow Summer Turnip Radish (⅓ natural size).

broad, good for use when it has attained the diameter of about 1¾ inch, but often becoming hollow when it exceeds that size; skin dark or grayish yellow, veined longitudinally with small white lines produced by fine longitudinal cracks; flesh white, compact, and very pungent in flavour; leaves broad and long. This Radish grows rather rapidly, the roots being fit for use in about five weeks after sowing. With the exception of the Black Spanish Radish, no other variety, perhaps, has so strong a flavour. It must be observed, however, that the flavour of the flesh is not always invariable in any variety of Radish, and that the conditions of soil and climate have a very great influence in increasing or diminishing its pungency.

Gray Summer Turnip Radish (*Radis Gris d'Été Rond*).—Root almost spherical or slightly top-shaped. Except in colour, it is very like the preceding kind, being of the same size, equally early, and having the skin cracked longitudinally in the same manner.

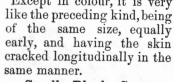

Small Black Summer Turnip Radish (*Radis Noir Rond d'Été*).—A variety which comes pretty near the preceding one, but is more deeply coloured, and from eight to ten days later. The skin is black, but is cracked and furrowed with whitish lines. The flesh is very white and firm, and of very pungent flavour.

White Strasburg Radish (⅓ natural size).

White Strasburg, or **White Hospital, Summer Radish** (French, *Radis Demi-long Blanc de Strasbourg;* German, *Weisser Halblanger*

Strassburger oder *Spitalgarten, Rettig*).—A comparatively early and, at the same time, very productive variety. Root pointed at the extremity, from 4 to nearly 5 inches long, and 2 inches or less in diameter; skin white; flesh white, rather tender, and not too pungent in flavour; leaves large, broad, half-erect, deeply lobed, and of a clear-green colour. The roots of this variety may commence to be pulled for use in about six weeks after sowing, at which time they will have attained two-thirds of their full size. They will continue to increase in size for a month or more without deteriorating in quality.

III. Winter Radishes.

French, Radis d'hiver.   *German*, Winter-Rettig.   *Flemish* and *Dutch*, Rammenas.
Spanish, Rabano.

The name of Winter Radishes is applied to those kinds which have such compact and firm-fleshed roots that they will keep through a great part of the winter without sprouting or becoming hollow at the centre. They are usually pretty large varieties, and require several months to attain their full growth. The seed is sown in May or June (that of some varieties up to the beginning of August), usually in drills from 16 to 20 inches apart. The roots are pulled in November, and will keep up to a more or less advanced part

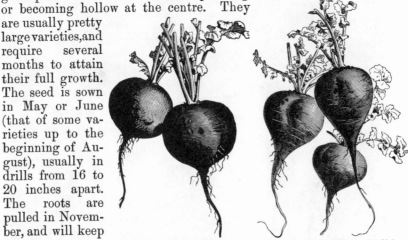

Black Spanish Winter Turnip   Large Purple Winter Radish
Radish (⅓ natural size).   (⅓ natural size).

of the winter, simply stored in a dry cellar or in a vegetable house.

Black Spanish Winter Turnip Radish (*Radis Noir Gros Rond d'Hiver*).—Root roundish, often top-shaped, 3 or 4 inches in diameter, and about 3 inches long; skin black, cracked in longitudinal lines; flesh white, very compact, and firm; leaves rather broad, very deeply cut into numerous lobes. This is not a very late kind for a Winter Radish; the seed may be sown up to the end of July. The roots keep well, and are the strongest-flavoured of all varieties of Turnip Radish.

Large Purple Winter Radish (*Radis Violet Gros d'Hiver*).—Under the name of Large Purple Winter Radish, a sub-variety of the Black Spanish Winter Turnip Radish is grown. It is much the same in shape, size, and earliness, but is distinguished by the purplish tint of the skin.

Long Black Spanish Winter Radish (*Radis Noir Long d'Hiver*).
— Root cylindrical, very regular in shape, from about 7 to 10
inches long, and between 2 and 3 inches in diameter; skin very
black, and somewhat wrinkled; flesh white, firm, and compact; leaves
stout, broad, and long.   Two forms of this variety are in cultivation—
one having the root abruptly rounded and shortened off at the lower
extremity, while in the other form the root is tapered at the same
place into a long point.   The latter is a somewhat later kind, and the

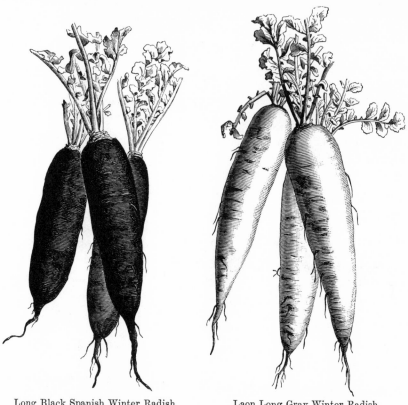

Long Black Spanish Winter Radish   Laon Long Gray Winter Radish
(⅓ natural size).   (⅓ natural size).

flesh of the root is very pungent to the taste.   The other is much
more clean skinned, and the flesh is often quite mild in flavour.

The Laon Long Gray Winter Radish (*R. Gris d'Hiver de Laon*),
and the Gournay Large Purple Winter Radish (*R. Violet d'Hiver de
Gournay*), are very closely allied to the Long Black Spanish Winter
Radish, which they resemble in the size and shape of the root, and are
only a little thicker in proportion to the length; they are distinguished
from it by their colour, which in the *Laon* variety is an iron gray, and
purplish in the *Gournay.*   Both are grown and used in the same way
as the Black Spanish Winter Radish.

Large White Spanish Winter Radish (*Radis Gros Blanc d'Augs-
bourg*).—Root spindle-shaped, nearly cylindrical in the upper two-

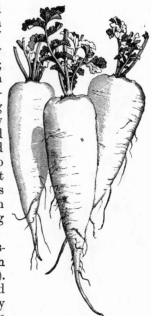

thirds of its length, and narrowed to a point in the lower part, 6 or 7 inches long, and nearly 3 inches in diameter; neck rounded; skin white; flesh white, compact, and very strong flavoured; leaves very broad. This is a good Winter Radish, and keeps well. It grows so quickly, however, that it may be cultivated as a Summer or Autumn Radish, the seed being sown in June.

Large White Russian Winter Radish (*Radis Blanc de Russie*). —Root elongated ovoid in shape, exceedingly large, being often from 12 to 14 inches long, and 5 or 6 inches in diameter; skin rather wrinkled,

Gournay Large Purple Winter Radish (⅓ natural size).

Large White Spanish Winter Radish (⅓ natural size).

and of a grayish-white colour; flesh white, not very compact, and rather strong flavoured; leaves numerous, rather broad, very much divided, and forming very dense rosettes spreading on the ground. This is an exceedingly productive Radish, but for table use the roots should be pulled before they are fully grown. In order to keep them well in winter, the seed should be sown in the end of June or in July. If sown earlier, the roots often become hollow at the centre, and are then only fit for feeding cattle. For this last-named purpose, the large Winter Radishes, and especially the present variety, might be more extensively employed than they are at present. In the same space of time, in fact, they produce in leaves and roots a greater quantity of cattle-feeding material than Turnips, and, from the large size of the seed, young Radish plants are from

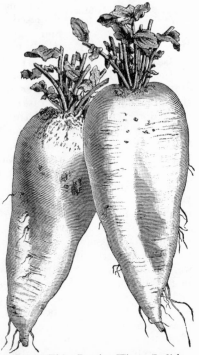

Large White Russian Winter Radish (⅓ natural size).

2 K

their earliest growth more vigorous than young Turnip plants, and suffer far less from the attacks of insects.

Chinese Scarlet Winter Radish (*Radis Rose d'Hiver de Chine*).— A very distinct variety. Root elongated, thicker at the lower extremity than at the neck, blunt at both ends, and very closely resembling the Jersey Turnip in shape; skin very bright red, marked with some small semicircular white lines, which usually extend half-way round the root; flesh white, very firm and compact, with a pungent and sometimes slightly bitter flavour; leaves rather broad, divided, and spreading; leaf-stalks bright pink. The roots are of moderate size, usually 4 or 5 inches long, about 2 inches in diameter at the thickest part of the lower extremity, and about 1¾ inch below the neck. This variety is chiefly grown for autumn and winter use. It may be sown up to August, and much thicker than the other Winter Radishes. There is a pure white sub-variety of this Radish, and also a violet-coloured one, both of which only differ in colour from the present variety. If we had to admit that any variety of cultivated Radishes is derived from the Wild Radish (*Raphanus Raphanistrum*), the present variety is the one of all others to which we should be disposed to assign that origin; its leaves, root, and *tout ensemble* presenting a peculiar appearance which makes it entirely distinct from any other cultivated kind.

Chinese Scarlet Winter Radish (⅓ natural size).

Californian, or **Mammoth White, Winter Radish** (*Radis Blanc de Californie*).—This Radish bears a still greater resemblance to the Jersey Turnip than the preceding variety, as, in addition to being similar in shape, it is also like it in colour. The root is, in fact, pure white, long, cylindrical, and thickest at the lower extremity; it is from 6 to 8 inches long, about 2¼ inches in diameter at the thickest part, and about 2 inches for the remainder of its length. When growing, the root projects between 1 and 2 inches above the ground. The leaves are large, broad, and of a pale and very light green colour. This is a productive variety, and forms a good autumn or winter vegetable. The roots take two or three months to form; the flesh is mild, with not much pungency of flavour.

The Japanese cultivate a great many kinds of Long White Radishes which they esteem very highly for table use. Some of these, according to credible authorities, produce roots attaining the almost fabulous weight of from thirty-three to forty-four pounds each. When grown in Europe, most of these Japanese Radishes run to seed very rapidly, and consequently are not of much value here. We shall make an exception, however, in favour of the variety which the Japanese call *Ninengo daikon*, which is as remarkable for the length and symmetry of its root as it is for its slowness in running to seed. The root is white, cylindrical, blunt-pointed and sometimes slightly thickened at the lower extremity, and often 16 to 20 inches long, and 3 to 4 inches in diameter. The leaves are large, very long, divided into a very great number of almost triangular lobes, and of a very dark green colour; they spread upon the ground, forming a broad flat rosette. This Radish, to be grown to its greatest perfection, should be sown in April. It requires the soil to be very deeply dug and plentifully manured.

OTHER VARIETIES.

Radis Blanc Demi-long de la Meurthe et de la Meuse.—A white Summer Radish, of rather variable shape, almost always pear-shaped or top-shaped, but of unequal length. It grows to a pretty large size, but is usually pulled for use when half-grown, being then about the size of a hen's egg. The flesh is white, firm, and rather pungent in flavour.

R. Früher Neuer Zwei-Monat (Rettig).—A late variety of the White Olive-shaped Radish, like which, it is ovoid or olive-shaped, and is an intermediate kind between the Summer Radishes and the Small or Forcing Radishes.

R. Gris d'Été Oblong.—A pear-shaped or ovoid form of the Gray Summer Turnip Radish, but not so regular in shape and not superior to it in any respect. The flesh is somewhat more pungent in flavour.

R. Gros d'Hiver de Ham (R. Gros Gris d'Août).—A true Winter Radish. Root long, cylindrical, ending in a bluntish point, and about the size of the Long Black Winter Radish, but of a grayish-white colour. It presents a good deal of resemblance to the Laon Gray Winter Radish. It derives its name of *Gris d'Août* from the circumstance that the roots are generally first pulled for use in August, but it is more to be recommended as an Autumn or Winter Radish.

R. de Mahon.—An exceedingly distinct kind, appearing to be peculiar to the Balearic Islands and some districts in the south of France. It is a kind of Long Red Radish, the root being often angular (especially when it grows to a large size), and projecting from the ground for one-half or two-thirds of its length, like the Mangel-Wurzel. Its growth is remarkably rapid. The leaves are broad and stout. The flesh of the root is of a pinkish white, and very juicy, firm, and solid while the root is young. The root does not begin to grow hollow at the centre until it has attained the size of a small Beet-root.

R. Rond Rouge Foncé.—This is a particular variety of small Turnip Radish, which has a very dark, almost violet-coloured skin. It is in rather high repute in the southern provinces of France, where it is said to resist the heat better than the Common Scarlet Turnip Radish.

RAT-TAILED RADISH.

Raphanus caudatus, L.

Radis serpent.

Native of South Asia.—Annual.—The edible part of this Radish is not the root, but the silique or seed-vessel, which is gathered before it is fully grown. This, instead of being short and thick, as in other Radishes, is very much elongated, often twisted, scarcely as thick as a lead-pencil, and often 8 to 10 inches long. It is frequently violet coloured, and has a somewhat pungent flavour, like that of the Small or Forcing Radishes. CULTURE.—This plant is extremely easy to grow. The seed is sown in May, where the plants are to stand, in a warm position if possible, and in about three months the plants commence to flower and yield pods or seed-vessels. USES.—The fresh pods are eaten raw, like Radishes, or they may be pickled in vinegar.

In warm countries, another kind of Radish, named the Madras Radish (*Radis de Madras*), is sometimes grown for its pods, which are used like those of the Rat-tailed Radish. They are almost of the same shape as the pods of the common kinds of Radish, but are far more fleshy and tender.

RAMPION.

Campanula Rapunculus, L.　*Campanulaceæ.*

French, Raiponce.　*German*, Rapunzel-Rübe.　*Flemish* and *Dutch*, Rapunsel.　*Italian*, Raperonzolo.　*Spanish*, Reponche.　*Portuguese*, Rapunculo.

Native of Europe.—Biennial.—Root white, spindle-shaped, and nearly ½ inch in diameter for 2 inches or more of its length ; flesh white, very firm, but crisp ; leaves sessile, rather numerous, of a long oval-spathulate shape, narrowed at the base, somewhat resembling those of the Common Corn-salad, but more slender and of a lighter green colour ; flower-stems slender, hard, somewhat angular, sometimes

branching, and bearing a few linear leaves ; flowers lilac, bell-shaped, with five sharp-pointed divisions, and borne in long spikes ; seed-vessels small, top-shaped, surmounted by the five teeth of the calyx ; seed oblong, flattened, light brown, and exceedingly small. They are the smallest of all kitchen-garden seeds, a gramme containing more than 25,000 of them, and a litre of them weighing about 800 grammes. Their germinating power lasts for five years. CULTURE.—The seed is sown in the open ground early in May, either broadcast or in drills from 8 to 10 inches apart. As it is exceedingly small, it is a good plan to mix it with a little fine soil or sand, in order to avoid sowing it too thick.

Rampion (⅓ natural size).

The first waterings should be given carefully, so as not to wash away the seed, which should not be deeply buried, but merely pressed firmly into the soil, on account of its extreme fineness. If the seedlings come up too thick, they should be thinned out, and they should also be frequently watered in hot weather. As plants sown early in the season are apt to run to seed, it is advisable to make a fresh sowing in June, using the same precautions. The roots may commence to be gathered for use in October or

November, and they will continue to yield a supply through the
winter; and in order that this may not be interrupted by severe
frosty weather, a sufficient quantity of the roots should be taken up
beforehand and stored in sand in a cellar or vegetable-house. Uses.—
The roots and leaves are eaten as salad.

RHUBARB.

Rheum, L. *Polygonaceæ.*

French, Rhubarbe.   *German*, Rhabarber.   *Flemish* and *Dutch*, Rabarber.   *Danish*,
Rhabarber.   *Italian*, Rabarbaro.   *Spanish* and *Portuguese*, Ruibarbo.

The cultivated varieties of Rhubarb are generally referred by
botanists to *Rheum hybridum*, Ait., a native of Mongolia. These
varieties, however, are far from exhibiting any constant characteristics,
and it is not impossible that some of them may have sprung, either
directly or as the result of crossing, from the *Rheum undulatum* of
North America, or even from other species.

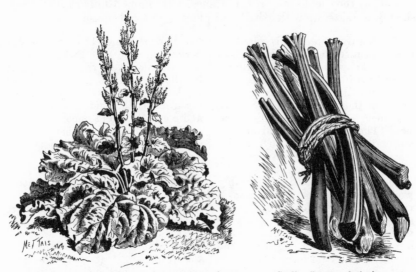

Rhubarb (*Rheum hybridum*) ($\frac{1}{20}$ natural size).   Stalks ($\frac{1}{4}$ natural size).

The plant, as it is grown in gardens, is remarkable for its very
large heart-shaped radical leaves, which measure over $2\frac{1}{2}$ ft. in length
and 2 ft. or more in breadth, and are borne on stalks which are rounded
underneath and flat or channelled on the upper surface, about 2 inches
in diameter, and from 1 ft. to 16 inches in length—dimensions which
by special culture may be increased to nearly double the size. The
flowering stems are large, cylindrical, hollow, and furrowed, and bear
small, short, erect branches, covered with small greenish flowers, which
are succeeded by triangular seeds with a membranous wing on each of
the angles. A gramme contains about 50 seeds, and a litre of them
weighs only from 80 to 120 grammes, according to the variety. Their
germinating power lasts for three years.

CULTURE.—Rhubarb may be propagated from seed; but as, in this case, the plants are liable to exhibit much diversity in their habit of growth, the more common practice is to divide the root-stock of the plants which produce the thickest and longest stalks. The roots so divided are planted at the end of winter in good, moist, deep, very mellow, and well-manured soil, and about a yard apart in every direction. The stalks are not pulled for use until the spring of the year following that in which the roots were planted, and the same plants will continue to yield for four years at least, and sometimes for ten years or longer, without the plantation requiring to be renewed. The only attention necessary is to keep the ground free from weeds, and to apply a good dressing of manure every two or three years. In order to increase the length of the stalks, a large bottomless flower-pot, a chimney-pot, or a small barrel with the ends knocked out, is sometimes placed over each plant in spring when the leaves are starting into growth. Striving to reach the light, the leaves naturally grow longer and the stalks at the same time become longer and more tender. The flowering stems, which would otherwise exhaust the plants, should be cut off as they make their appearance. To force Rhubarb, the roots should be taken up with a ball and planted in a hot-house or a hot-bed.

The cultivation of this plant, as yet unpractised on the Continent, as far as we know, is of much importance in Great Britain and North America. Rhubarb will grow in many kinds of soil; but the richer and deeper it is, the finer will be the quality and size. The situation should also be moderately dry, or made so by drainage. It will grow in clay, peat, or the bog-earth of the Fens. We have seen it succeed remarkably well in mud cleaned out from a river. When the leaves get fairly into growth, they need plenty of food to keep them growing. The larger the leaves of one season the stronger will be the crown for the next; hence the importance of rich feeding all through the growing season. It is a good plan, in small gardens, to plant Rhubarb near the depôt for house sewage, so that it may be nourished with this as well as solid manure; 4 ft., at least, of a rich root-run should be provided for it. For new plantations the ground should be thoroughly trenched and manured. Its productive force should be kept up afterwards by an annual dressing, from 2 to 3 inches in thickness. No plant is more easily increased and multiplied than Rhubarb; plants two or more years old seed freely if permitted to do so. Unless seed be required, however, they should not be allowed to do so, as seed-bearing weakens the crowns. The seeds ripen about the end of September, and may be sown at once in shallow drills a yard apart, or they may be sown in February. As soon as they are well up, thin the plants to 18 inches or 2 ft. asunder, according to the size of the kind and the intention of the cultivator. If intended to remain where they are, a yard apart is close enough—indeed, too close for some varieties. Some, however, prefer rows 2 ft. apart, and thinning the plants to 1 ft. only the first season; then in the October or February following fresh ground is prepared, and the Victoria transplanted at distances of from 4 to 6 ft. by 4 ft., and the Defiance 3 ft. by 18 inches or 2 ft. The best plan is to sow Rhubarb where it is to remain, as it forms immense roots that are easily broken,—and to break it is to injure it more or less. Nevertheless, a very common mode of propagating Rhubarb is by root division. The huge stool or fleshy root is sliced into as many portions as there are crowns to it with a sharp knife or spade, and each slice forms a new plant. Gathering Rhubarb, and when to cease gathering, are matters which require more attention than they generally receive. In gathering, the proper method is to give the leaf-stalk a twist outward, and a sudden jerk down at the same moment. From want of attention to this, many tear off the crown with the base of the leaf-stalk. Again, too many leaves should not be gathered at once. If a plant have only a dozen leaves, do not gather more than six of them, and let these be the lowest. Some prefer Rhubarb when the leaves are freshly unrolled, others when they are half-grown, and others when they are fully grown. Of course there is great waste if the stalks be gathered before they have reached their full length. Rhubarb is at its best just when the leaf has reached full size. It can hardly be too old for preserving, and is seldom gathered till the end of August for that purpose. As to the time of ceasing to gather Rhubarb, it should certainly be not later than August if the gathering is to be annual : this leaves but little time for the last leaves to ripen good crowns for the next year's crop. All the leaves removed have doubtless been a loss to the plant : they did much to weaken and nothing to strengthen it ; it is only the leaves left on that recoup it for its loss in those taken off. Hence the importance of rich food to replenish the plant, and time for the maturation of the later growth ; and it need hardly be said that no weed must be permitted to grow at the expense of the Rhubarb plants.

There are various ways of forcing this useful plant, which may briefly be divided into two distinct methods, No. 1 consisting of lifting the roots and placing them in artificially heated structures ; or No. 2, by covering the crowns where they are grown with pots or boxes, and applying fermenting material, composed of stable litter, leaves, etc., or, in fact, anything that will generate warmth enough to excite growth. There is much to be said in favour of both systems, for they are both good under certain conditions, and gardeners, in private gardens, as a rule, find lifting the roots and placing them in heat the best plan for the earliest crops during December and January ; for where heated glass structures are in use, a supply of Rhubarb may be procured without any additional outlay, or even occupying any space useful for any other purpose, as under stages, or in the boiler-shed, or, in fact, any position near the hot pipes. The roots may be placed on the floor, or in pots or boxes, and covered with soil, keeping it moist, and the crowns may be covered with hay, fern fronds, or litter, to blanch it. The only objection to this plan is that it weakens the crowns more than by forcing them in the ground, as the roots get very much mutilated in removal, so that if the quantity of Rhubarb roots is limited, it is preferable to adopt the plan of forcing the roots where they are grown. Procure the requisite number of pots, with movable covers, and place them over the crowns ; then cover them over with fresh stable litter, or a coating of leaves and litter mixed together. The leaves of deciduous trees are most useful for many purposes, as they can be used for forwarding crops of Rhubarb and then placed in pits or frames for supplying bottom heat for Cucumbers and other early crops. To have Rhubarb fit for use at Christmas, cover the crowns in the middle of November, and as soon as the first batch gets fairly started into growth, cover a few more pots in succession until it comes on naturally in March, when any large tubs or boxes turned over the crowns to shelter from cold winds will forward the growth at least a fortnight before the crowns left uncovered. Rhubarb, unlike many other crops, is better when forced than from the open air, being more tender and succulent.

MARKET GARDEN CULTURE.—Rhubarb forcing in market gardens is very simple, and is done in hot-beds covered with hoops and mats. In making young plantations, the sets are sometimes planted about 18 inches apart each way; and, at forcing time, every other row, and the alternate plants in the row left, are lifted for forcing; old plantations, too, are cleared entirely for forcing. The leaves will be decayed enough to be raked off by the middle of October, by which time the first portion is usually lifted for forcing. For this purpose trenches are cast out, about 4 ft. wide and 2 ft. deep, and filled with fermenting manure. Over this a thin layer of common soil is placed, and in it the crowns, after being trimmed of some of their rougher roots, are planted. Over the crowns some loose litter is strewed, and then the beds are hooped over and covered with mats, over which another layer of straw or litter is placed during winter. In the outside covering, apertures are made at gathering time, and closed again when done. In February, if the weather be mild, the hoops and mats are commonly dispensed with. In some gardens excellent Rhubarb is produced in pits, with some heating material underneath, and some loose straw merely shaken loosely over the roots. Some force Rhubarb in fruit houses; the roots are packed closely together on the floors, a little leaf-mould or other soil is cast over them, and they are afterwards covered with mats, which remain on them until the stalks are fit to gather. Rhubarb forced in this way is not so good in colour as that produced in darker places, and which we see in the markets early in the season; but it is greatly superior to it in flavour.

Whole fields in Surrey are devoted to Rhubarb culture, but the bulk of it from London market gardens is grown under fruit trees—positions in which it grows well. In spring, when the produce is most wanted, the trees are leafless, and therefore they do not shade it much, but afford slight protection, and the produce comes naturally fit for use about a week sooner than from the open field. In making permanent plantations, divisions of the old stools are used, and they are planted in rows 2½ or 3 ft. apart, and from 2 to 2¼ ft. asunder in the rows. No leaves are cut away from them the first year, but the space between the lines is planted with Lettuces or Coleworts. During the second season many stalks are not cut, but in the third year a fair crop is gathered. As soon as time can be spared in winter, and before the leaves begin to grow, the ground between the rows is dug over roughly, and a large forkful of rank litter placed over each crown. Under the litter the stalks come up clean, tender, and crisp—very much more so than if none were used.

USES.—The fleshy stalks are used for making tarts, pies, and preserves, especially in England and America.

The following are the principal varieties which are considered to be derived from *Rheum hybridum* :—

Mitchell's Royal Albert (*Early Red*).—A very early variety, with thick long stalks of excellent flavour, equal in length (when not drawn) to three-fourths of the length of the blade of the leaf, plentifully spotted with red over their entire surface, and more angular than channelled. Leaves heart-shaped, broad, with blister-like swellings on the upper surface, but not much crumpled; blade of the leaf clear green and smooth. This variety flowers abundantly, and has a very thick, smooth, and very branching flower-stem, of a uniform green colour.

Myatt's Victoria.—A later kind than the preceding one. Stalks

red, very thick, considerably longer than the blade of the leaf, channelled underneath, and of good quality; leaves broader than long,
heart-shaped or roundish, pointless, very wavy at the edges, very much
crumpled, and of a rather dark and somewhat glaucous green colour.
This variety flowers very scantily.

Stott's Monarch.—A giant variety, greatly recommended by some
for its fine quality, and an excellent preserving sort. Leaves heart-
shaped, over 3 ft. long, and nearly the same in breadth, with a dark
green, even-surfaced blade; stalks exceedingly thick, scarcely half the
length of the blade, but 3 or 4 inches broad, and of a somewhat bronzy
green colour.

Hawke's Champagne.—This has now become the favourite sort in
the London market gardens. Comes early into use. Stalks of a deep
crimson colour, large, and of fine quality; leaves deep green, slightly
pubescent, the younger ones having an almost heavy appearance.

Myatt's Linnæus.—A second early sort, resembling Royal Albert,
but a much larger and stronger grower. Stalks deep green, roundish,
of good quality.

The *Rheum undulatum* of North America (*Rh. Ondulée d'Amérique*)
is sometimes cultivated as a vegetable. This is a distinct and early
species, the stalks of which are not so acid as those of other kinds of
Rhubarb. The leaves are of a clear-green colour, very wavy at the
edges, of a rather elongated heart-shape, but almost blunt pointed;
stalks slender, about as long as the blade of the leaf, smooth, and
green, except at the base, which is tinged with red for a short distance;
flower-stems very numerous, of a uniform pale-green colour, and with
erect branches. The other cultivated kinds of Rhubarb are grown for
ornament or for medicinal purposes, but are not suited for the kitchen
garden. A description of them will be found in "Les Fleurs
de Pleine Terre." The finest of them are *Rheum officinale*, H. Bn.;
Rheum Emodi, Wall.; and *Rheum palmatum*, L., with its variety, *Rh.
p. Tanguticum.*

ROCAMBOLE.

Allium Scorodoprasum, L.

French, Ail Rocambole. *German*, Roccambol. *Danish*, Rokambol. *Italian*, Aglio
d'India. *Portuguese*, Alho de Hespanha.

Native of South Europe.—Perennial.—The stem, which is twisted
spirally in the upper part, bears at the top a cluster of bulblets, from
which the plant may be propagated; they are seldom, however, used
for this purpose, as more speedy results are obtained by planting the
cloves of the underground bulb. The cloves should be planted in
autumn, or not later than February. Uses.—The same as those of the
Common Garlic.

ROCKET-SALAD.

Eruca sativa, Lamk.; *Brassica Eruca*, L. *Cruciferæ.*

French, Roquette. *German*, Rauke. *Flemish*, Krapkool. *Dutch*, Rakette kruid.
Italian, Ricola, Ruchetta. *Spanish*, Jaramago. *Portuguese*, Pinchão.

Native of South Europe.—Annual.—A low-growing plant, with the
radical leaves thickish, oblong, and divided, like the leaves of Radishes

or Turnips, into several segments, of which the terminal one is oval and much larger than the others.   Stem erect, smooth, and branching ;

flowers rather large, white or yellow, veined with violet; seed-vessels cylindrical, with three not very prominent ribs on each side ; seed brown, smooth, and somewhat flattened.   A gramme contains about 550 seeds, and a litre of them weighs about 750 grammes. Their germinating power lasts for four years.   Culture.—The seed is sown in the open ground from April to the end of summer, and in about six weeks or two months the leaves may commence to be cut.   In spring or autumn fresh leaves are abundantly produced after cutting.   In summer the

Rocket-salad (⅙ natural size).

plants run to seed rapidly.   Frequent waterings are useful in keeping the leaves tender, and in modifying the flavour, which is very strong and somewhat like that of the Horse-radish.   The young leaves are eaten as salad.

TURKISH ROCKET.

Bunias orientalis, L.   *Cruciferæ.*

Native of Western Asia, but naturalized in France.—Perennial.— A hardy and very long-lived plant, with numerous entire, elongated leaves, which in shape somewhat resemble those of the Horse-radish. Stem about 3 ft. high, very much branched; flowers yellow, and resembling those of the Mustard-plant ; seed-vessels hard, very short, resembling those of the Chick-pea, but smaller.   A gramme contains from 35 to 40 seeds, and a litre of them weighs about 500 grammes. Their germinating power lasts for three years.   Culture.—This plant is as easily grown as the Chicory.   The seed is sown in drills in autumn or spring, and the plants will continue vigorous and productive for several years.   Uses.—The young and tender leaves and shoots are eaten either boiled or as salad.   This plant has been highly spoken of as a kitchen-garden plant.   It commences to grow very early in spring, when other fresh green vegetables are exceedingly scarce, and it resists both cold weather and drought remarkably well.

ROSEMARY.

Rosmarinus officinalis, L.   *Labiatæ.*

French, Romarin.   *German,* Rosmarin.   *Flemish* and *Dutch,* Rozemarijn.   *Danish,* Rosmarin.   *Italian,* Rosmarino.   *Spanish,* Romero.   *Portuguese,* Alecrim.

Native of South Europe.—Perennial.—An under-shrub, common on the calcareous hills of the south of France and in the vicinity of the sea-coast. Stem branching, woody, with erect branches bearing an abundance of linear obtuse leaves, of a lively green colour on the upper surface and silvery gray underneath; flowers axillary, forming long leafy clusters on the upper part of the stems, labiate, and of a somewhat grayish-blue colour; seeds light brown, oval, with a large whitish *hilum* on one end. A gramme contains about 900 seeds, and a litre of them weighs about 400 grammes. Their germinating power lasts for four years. CULTURE.—The Rosemary does not require any culture, so to say. Tufts of it planted in good well-drained soil, and, if possible, at the

Rosemary ($\frac{1}{15}$ natural size; detached branch, $\frac{1}{3}$ natural size; detached flower, natural size).

foot of a south wall, or on a slope with a southern aspect, will continue productive for many years without requiring any attention. USES.—The leaves are used for seasoning.

RUE.

Ruta graveolens, L.   *Rutaceæ.*

French, Rue.   *German*, Raute.   *Dutch*, Wijnruit.   *Spanish*, Ruda.

Native of South Europe.—Perennial.—A plant growing from 16 inches to 2 ft. high and forming a small roundish bush. Stem woody, very much branched; leaves all stalked, twice or thrice divided, and winged; divisions almost triangular, or oval-obtuse; flowers largish, with four petals of a greenish-yellow colour, and produced in short, corymbose, terminal clusters; seed-vessels roundish, four or five lobed; seeds black, crescent-shaped or kidney-shaped. A gramme contains about 500 seeds, and a litre of them weighs about 580 grammes. Their germinating power lasts for two years. CULTURE.—This plant is easily propagated in spring from seed, or from divisions of the tufts, which, as soon as they are well rooted, are planted out 20 inches apart in every direction in good and well-drained, rather than moist, soil, where they may live for many years without requiring any care. It is advisable to cut the plants short every two or three years in order to promote the growth of young stems. USES.—The leaves, which have an exceedingly strong odour, very disagreeable to most people, are nevertheless sometimes used for seasoning. They have a bitter and very pungent flavour. In old cookery books Rue is frequently mentioned amongst the seasonings then in common use.

RUSH-NUT, or CHUFA.

Cyperus esculentus, Gouan. *Cyperaceæ.*

French, Souchet comestible. *German,* Erdmandel. *Flemish,* Aardmandel.
Italian, Mandorla di terra. *Spanish,* Chufa.

Native of South Europe.—Perennial.—A plant forming tufts of stiff, pointed leaves, which are almost triangular, like those of most plants of the *Cyperaceæ* family.

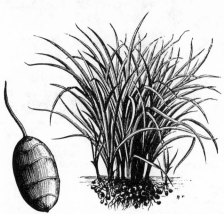

Roots brownish, very numerous, tangled, and intermixed with underground shoots, which are swollen into a kind of small, scaly tubers of a brownish colour, and with white, floury, sweet flesh. CULTURE.—The plant is propagated in April or May, either from the tubers, or from divisions of the tufts. The divisions so planted increase in size, and spread very much during the summer, and the tubers or "nuts" are gathered in October or November. They may be easily kept all through the winter, if stored

Rush-nut, or Chufa ($\frac{1}{10}$ natural size; detached nut, natural size).

in a dry place, sheltered from frost, and in drying become sweeter and more agreeable to the taste than when eaten newly gathered. The tubers are eaten raw or parched.

SAFFRON-PLANT.

Crocus sativus, L. *Iridaceæ.*

French, Safran. *German,* Safranpflanze. *Italian,* Zafferano. *Spanish,* Azafran.

Native of the East.—Perennial.—A bulbous plant, with long, narrow leaves, like those of a Grass, of a glistening dark-green colour, with

a white line running longitudinally through the middle of the blade. Flowers violet coloured, of a very elongated-ovoid shape, and not much opened at the mouth; pistils extremely large, divided into numerous strips, and of a handsome orange or saffron colour. Their weight causes them to droop over the side of the flower, producing a rather peculiar effect. The bulbs or corms are covered with brownish, wrinkled coats.

CULTURE.—The Saffron-plant is not propagated from seed, although it occasionally bears some, but is always multiplied by

Saffron-plant ($\frac{1}{8}$ natural size).

means of the bulbs or corms. These are planted from June to August.

in good, free, light soil, containing, if possible, a plentiful proportion of calcareous matter, and in a position well exposed to air and sunshine. The flowers bloom in September; they are gathered as soon as they open, and the pistils are picked off with the hand. The cultivation and preparation of Saffron require an enormous amount of manual labour, and, consequently, the plant is very little grown for economic purposes in gardens.

Uses.—The pistils, when dried, are used for flavouring and colouring certain dishes. Saffron, being expensive in proportion to its purity, is often adulterated with Turmeric, which is obtained by pulverizing old roots of *Curcuma longa,* an East Indian plant of the *Zingiberaceæ* or Ginger family, and is of a deep-yellow colour, with a slightly peppery and aromatic flavour.

SAGE.

Salvia officinalis, L. *Labiatæ.*

French, Sauge officinale. *German,* Salbei. *Flemish* and *Dutch,* Salie. *Italian* and *Spanish,* Salvia. *Portuguese,* Molho.

Native of South Europe.—Perennial.—A plant with an almost woody stem, at least at the base, and forming broad tufts seldom more than 14 to 16 inches high. Leaves whitish green, oval, toothed, very finely reticulated, and wrinkled; lower leaves narrowed into a stalk, upper or stem-leaves narrow and long pointed; flowers in heads of three or four, in terminal clusters, usually bluish lilac, sometimes white or pink; seed nearly spherical, and of a blackish-brown colour. A gramme contains about 250 seeds, and a litre of them weighs about 550 grammes. Their germinating power lasts for three years.

Culture. — The Sage-plant is as easily grown as Thyme. The seed is sown in spring or autumn, in rows or as edgings, which will last for many years without requiring attention. Care

Sage (⅛ natural size).

should be taken, however, to have the plants in a well-drained and rather dry position, for it should not be forgotten that the plant is a native of Southern Europe, and that it grows naturally on dry, calcareous hills. Nevertheless, it withstands our ordinary winters. The leaves are used for seasoning.

SALAD-BURNET.

Poterium Sanguisorba, L. *Rosaceæ.*

French, Pimprenelle petite. *German,* Garten-Pimpinelle. *Flemish* and *Dutch,* Pimpernel.
Italian, Pimpinella. *Spanish,* Pimpinela. *Portuguese,* Pimpinella.

Native of Europe.—Perennial.—Radical leaves pinnate, with an
odd leaflet; leaflets oval-rounded, very much toothed; stems usually
very erect, 16 inches to 2 ft. high, angular, branching, and ending in

spikes of female flowers, the
flower at the base being male
or hermaphrodite; seed oval,
four-angled, with more or less
prominent ridges on the angles,
and reticulated on the sides. A
gramme contains about 150
seeds, and a litre of them weighs
about 280 grammes. Their
germinating power lasts for
three years. The Salad-Burnet
is an exceedingly hardy and
long-lived plant, and grows wild
through the greater part of
France. CULTURE.—The seed
is sown in spring or at the end
of summer, usually in drills 10
to 12 inches apart. It is often

Salad-Burnet ($\frac{1}{10}$ natural size).

grown as an edging to beds of other vegetables, and may also be sown
in beds by itself. The plants do not require any attention. The
leaves are cut for use with a knife or sickle, and successional cuttings
are made so as to have a constant supply of fresh young leaves.
Leaves are produced in greater abundance and for a longer time if the
plants are not allowed to flower. USES.—The young, tender leaves
are used as salad; they have a peculiar flavour, resembling that of
the Green Cucumber.

SALAD MILK-VETCH, or "WORMS."

Astragalus hamosus, L. *Leguminosæ.*

French, Vers. *German,* Würme.

Native of South Europe.—Annual.—A half-sprawling plant, from
1 ft. to 20 inches high, with furrowed, spreading or half-erect stems.
Leaves slight, composed of from eight to twelve pairs of oval-oblong,
obtuse leaflets; flowers whitish, very small, in short, globular clusters;
pods cylindrical, about $\frac{4}{5}$ inch long, and curved like a fish-hook; seeds
brown, glistening, kidney-shaped, and square at both ends. A gramme
contains six or seven of the pods, and a litre of them weighs about
210 grammes. The germinating power of the seeds lasts for three
years. The seed is sown in the open ground in April, and the plants
are grown exactly in the same manner as dwarf Kidney Beans. The

young pods begin to appear in June or July.   This plant is chiefly
grown on account of the peculiar appearance of the pods, which, before
ripening, resemble some kinds of worms.   Like the seed-vessels of
Caterpillars, they are, as a harmless practical joke, sometimes put into
salads to startle the unwary, but their flavour is poor.

SALSAFY, or VEGETABLE OYSTER.

Tragopogon porrifolius, L.   *Compositæ.*

French, Salsifis.   *German,* Haferwurzel.   *Flemish,* Haverwortel.   *Danish,* Havrerod.
Italian, Barba di becco.   *Spanish,* Salsifi blanco.   *Portuguese,* Cercifi.

Native of Europe.—Biennial.—A plant with a long, fleshy tap-root,
6 to 8 inches in length, and 1 inch or less in diameter, and with a
yellowish and rather smooth skin.   Leaves straight, very long and
narrow, half-spreading at first, afterwards erect,
and of a somewhat glaucous and grayish-green
colour, with a white line running through the
middle ;   stem smooth, branching, 3 ft. or
more high ;   flower-heads terminal, very much
elongated, swollen at the base, and contracted

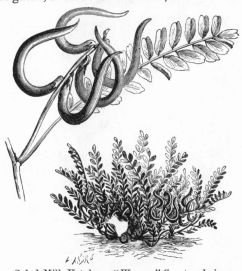

Salad Milk-Vetch, or " Worms " (¼ natural size ;   Salsafy, or Vegetable
detached branch, natural size).   Oyster (⅓ natural size).

at the top at the time of blooming; florets violet coloured ; seed long,
generally curved, pointed at both ends, and with the whole surface
furrowed and wrinkled.   A gramme contains about 100 clean seeds,
and a litre of them weighs about 230 grammes.   Their germinating
power lasts two years for certain, and often continues longer.

Culture.—The seed is sown in spring, where the plants are to
stand, in drills 10 to 12 inches apart.   If the weather is dry at the
time of sowing, the drills should be watered a few times to assist the
germination, which is always somewhat uncertain.   The seedlings should

be thinned out to about 4 inches apart in the drills, and the hoe and the watering-pot should be used when necessary. The roots may commence to be gathered for use about October, and will yield a supply all through the winter. They are always finer and smoother in proportion as the ground has been well dug and prepared before sowing. Uses.—The roots are sent to table boiled, and the tenderest leaves form a very good salad.

In some localities a yellow-flowered variety of Salsafy is grown, which probably originated from a botanical species different from *T. porrifolius.* This might be either *T. pratensis,* L., which is common in meadows throughout the whole of France, or *T. orientalis,* which is larger than *T. pratensis* in all its parts, and consequently comes nearer to the size of the cultivated plant ; or it might be *T. major,* Jacq., which in all its characteristics of growth, except the colour of the flowers, bears a perceptible resemblance to the Common Salsafy (*T. porrifolius*). It appears certain, moreover, that *T. porrifolius* itself was first brought into cultivation at a comparatively recent date

SAMPHIRE.

Crithmum maritimum, L.   *Umbelliferæ.*

French, Perce-pierre.   *German,* Meer-Fenchel.   *Flemish* and *Dutch,* Zeevenkel.
Italian, Bacicci.   *Spanish,* Hinojo marino.   *Portuguese,* Funcho marino.

Native of Europe, including Great Britain.—Perennial.—Samphire usually grows on rocks or the steep sides of cliffs by the seaside, but

always above high-water mark of the highest tides. It is a plant with a creeping rootstock ; the stems are short and stout, finely striated, and often branched, the branches being very widely forked. The leaves are twice and thrice divided into linear, thick, swollen, fleshy segments. Flowers small, whitish, in terminal umbels; seed oblong, elliptical, yellowish, flattened on one side, and convex, with three prominent ribs, on the other. They are remarkably light in proportion to their size. A gramme contains about 350 seeds,

Samphire ($\frac{1}{10}$ natural size).

and a litre of them seldom weighs more than 120 grammes. Their germinating power is quite gone after the first year. By the sea-shores the Samphire is gathered from the rocks where it grows naturally, but it may be grown in gardens by sowing the seed in autumn, as soon as it ripens, in good, light, well-drained soil. It is advisable to cover the seedlings in the winter with some protection from frost, to which the plants are rather sensitive. It grows still better when planted in crevices at the bottom of a wall with a warm aspect. The leaves are pickled in vinegar and used as a seasoning.

SUMMER SAVORY.

Satureia hortensis, L. *Labiatæ.*

French, Sarriette annuelle. *German,* Bohnenkraut. *Flemish* and *Dutch,* Boonenkruid. *Danish,* Sar. *Italian,* Santoreggia. *Spanish,* Ajedrea comun. *Portuguese,* Segurelha.

Native of South Europe.—Annual.—A small-sized plant, 8 to 10 inches high, with an erect, branching, herbaceous stem. Leaves soft, linear, slightly obtuse, and narrowed into a short leaf-stalk; flowers pink or white, borne in clusters of from two to five; seed brown, ovoid, very finely shagreened. A gramme contains about 1500 seeds, and a litre of them weighs about 500 grammes. Their germinating power lasts for three years. The whole plant is highly odoriferous. The seed of the Summer Savory is sown in the latter end of April, or in May, in good, warm, light soil; or plants may be forwarded by sowing in March in a hot-bed, and planting out in the open air about the end of May. In June the ends of the stems may be gathered for use; the

Summer Savory (⅓ natural size; detached branch, natural size).

plants then form branches, and continue to produce new shoots for several weeks. The leaves and young shoots are used for flavouring, especially with boiled Beans.

WINTER SAVORY.

Satureia montana, L.

French, Sarriette vivace. *German,* Perennirender *oder* Winter Bohnenkraut. *Spanish,* Hisopillo.

Native of South Europe.—Perennial.—A low-growing plant, spreading on the ground. Stems woody, at least at the base, slender, very branching, and from 1 ft. to 16 inches high; leaves narrow, linear, very acute, and slightly channelled on the upper surface; flowers white, pink, or pale lilac, in small axillary clusters; lower lip divided into three segments; seed brown, of a triangular-ovoid shape, and very finely shagreened. A gramme contains about 2500 seeds, and a litre of them weighs about 430 grammes. Their germinating power lasts for

2 L

Winter Savory ($\frac{1}{8}$ natural size; detached branch, natural size).

three years on an average. The seed may be sown in spring or the latter end of summer, on the edges of beds of other vegetables, or in drills 14 to 16 inches apart. The plant is sufficiently hardy to withstand ordinary winters in the climate of Paris, provided it is grown in well-drained soil free from stagnant moisture. It requires no attention; but if the stems are cut down every spring to about 4 inches from the ground, a much more abundant supply of vigorous young shoots will be produced. The leaves and young shoots are used for flavouring, like those of the Summer Savory.

SCORZONERA.

Scorzonera hispanica, L. *Compositæ.*

French, Scorsonère. *German*, Scorsoner. *Flemish* and *Dutch*, Schorseneel. *Danish*, Schorsenerrod. *Italian*, Scorzonera. *Spanish*, Escorzonera. *Portuguese*, Escorcioneira.

Scorzonera ($\frac{1}{5}$ natural size).

Native of Spain.—Perennial.—This plant is cultivated as an annual or a biennial. It has a fleshy tap-root, resembling that of the Salsafy in size and flavour, but distinguished from it by the black colour of the skin. The leaves also of the Scorzonera are much broader than those of the Salsafy; they are lanceolate-oblong in shape and pointed at the extremity; the stem-leaves are sessile and are also of some breadth. Flowers bright yellow; seed white, smooth, very long, blunt at one end and more or less pointed at the other. A gramme contains about 90 seeds, and a litre of them weighs about 260 grammes. Their germinating power lasts for two years, at least. The Scorzonera is grown in exactly the same manner as the Salsafy, with this difference, that it is not absolutely necessary to pull up all the plants that remain after the first year's growth, as the roots will continue to increase in size without becoming less tender or less fit for use, even though the plants may have produced some stems and flowers in the course of the summer. The roots are eaten boiled, like those of the Salsafy; the leaves also may be used as salad.

FRENCH SCORZONERA.

Scorzonera picroides, L. ; *Picridium vulgare,* Desf. *Compositæ.*

French, Picridie cultivée. *Italian,* Caccialepre.

Native of South Europe.—Annual.—Radical leaves sinuated, or cut into entire or toothed lobes, generally obtuse, and forming a rather full rosette 10 to 12 inches in diameter. Stems numerous, branching, smooth, bearing a few long narrow leaves, which are clasping at the base and usually toothed; flower-heads terminal, largish, swollen at the base, and composed of yellow florets; seed brown, small, long, marked with four furrows and four prominent transversely notched ridges. A gramme contains about 1200 seeds, and a litre of them weighs about 220 grammes. Their germinating power lasts for five years. The seed is sown in drills, like Parsley seed or Chicory seed, and the leaves are cut for use as small green salad, like those of the Chicory. After being cut, the plants send out fresh leaves, and several successive cuttings may be made in the course of the season. In hot weather frequent waterings are serviceable. The young leaves are used as salad, especially in Italy.

SCURVY-GRASS.

Cochlearia officinalis, L. *Cruciferæ.*

French, Cochlearia officinal. *German,* Löffelkraut. *Flemish,* Lepelkruyd. *Dutch,* Lepel-blad. *Danish,* Kokleare. *Italian* and *Spanish,* Coclearia. *Portuguese,* Cochlearia.

Native of Europe.—Perennial, but cultivated as an annual.—This plant has some resemblance to the Water-cress. Leaves roundish, numerous, shining, and of a dark-green colour; radical leaves long-stalked and heart-shaped; stem-leaves sessile, oblong, and more or less toothed; stems numerous, bearing small white flowers; seed small, oval, slightly angular, rough skinned, and of a reddish-brown colour. A gramme contains from 1500 to 1800 seeds, and a litre of them weighs about 600 grammes. Their germinating power lasts for four years. All the green parts of the plant have a strong acrid taste and a very de-

Scurvy-grass (⅒ natural size).

cidedly tarry flavour. The seed is sown where the plants are to stand, and, if possible, in a cool, shady position. Scurvy-grass requires no special attention. The leaves are sometimes eaten as salad, but the plant is more usually grown for medicinal purposes, its antiscorbutic properties being well known.

SEA-KALE.

Crambe maritima, L.   *Cruciferæ.*

French, Crambé.   *German,*' Meer-*oder* See-Kohl.   *Flemish* and *Dutch*, Zeekool.
Danish, Strand-kaal.   *Spanish*, Soldanela maritima.

Native of Europe.—Perennial.—Leaves broad, thick, fringed, often twisted and cut at the edges into roundish segments, and of a very peculiar glaucous-green colour, which is almost the same on both sides of the leaf; stems stout, branching, from 20 inches to 2 ft. high; flowers very

numerous, white, and broad, succeeded by seed-vessels, which are almost spherical in shape, a little less than $\frac{2}{5}$ inch in diameter, white, rather hard, never opening when ripe, and each containing only a single seed. A gramme contains from 15 to 18 of the unshelled seeds, and a litre of them weighs about 210 grammes. Their germinating power declines rapidly after the first year.

The Sea-kale, which is found in the wild state on most of the sea-coasts of Western Europe, is very little used as a vegetable in France, although it has been for many years very extensively culti-vated in England. The leaves, or rather the leaf-stalks, of the

Sea-kale (⅓ natural size).

plant are prepared for table use by blanching them in a dark place, by which means tender shoots of an agreeable flavour and only a slightly bitter taste are obtained, whereas if they were grown exposed to the light, they would become intolerably acrid.

Culture.—Sea-kale may be propagated either from divisions or cuttings of the root or from seed. By the first-named method, in February or early in March, the roots of old plants are cut into pieces about 4 inches long, which are at once planted, where the crop is to stand, in good, well-dug, and well-manured soil, and at a distance of 2 ft. 8 inches from one another in every direction, as the plants grow to a pretty large size. In the first year the young plants attain a certain degree of strength, and may be cut for use in the ensuing

winter, if a supply is badly needed. It is better, however, not to commence cutting until the second year. In raising plants from seed, the
seed is sown either in a seed-bed or where the plants are to stand. In
either case, it should be sown as soon as possible after it ripens and
without being shelled. When the young plants in the seed-bed have
made four or five leaves, they are planted out permanently, at the
same distance from one another as the cuttings of the roots above
mentioned. In sowing where the plants are to stand the seed is placed
in holes or pockets, which also should be the same distance apart as the
root-cuttings. These pockets should be well filled with compost, and
the ground should be kept very free from weeds. The growing plants
should be frequently watered until they have attained their full size.
When they are sufficiently strong, and out of danger from the black
flea (*Haltica nemorum*), all the seedlings in each pocket are pulled up
except the strongest one, which is left to grow, and during the remainder
of the year and the whole of the following years the plants are treated
in exactly the same way as plants raised from root-cuttings. They will
not be fit to cut for use until the spring of the third year, and after
that they will continue to bear for eight or ten years.

In order to blanch Sea-kale, each crown of the plant is covered with
an inverted flower-pot, care being taken to stop the hole in the bottom
so as to entirely exclude the light, and the pot is also more or less
covered with soil or dry leaves. If it is desired to force the plants, the
pots should be completely covered with suitable manure, and in a few
weeks the shoots will be sufficiently grown for use. In gathering them,
there need be no hesitation in cutting them at some distance below the
blanched part, as the root-stock has always a tendency to grow overground. Plants may also be forced in a hot-house, hot-bed, or any
other place supplying artificial heat. For this purpose the plants are
taken up entire, and replanted close to one another in fresh sand. As
with plants grown in the open air, the shoots should be covered, either
with more sand, or in any other way so as to exclude the light. Caro
should be taken to cover the plants with soil every year, to prevent the
roots from becoming bared. In order to maintain the vigour of the
plants, some shoots should be left uncut on each plant, and these should
not be allowed to flower, as the plant would thereby be more or less
exhausted for nothing. It is advisable to go over the plants every
autumn and remove all dead leaves and weak and superfluous shoots,
and also to spread some light soil or compost over any parts of the
ground where the roots of the plants are becoming bared. As the Sea-
kale is a seaside plant, a little common salt, mixed with the soil, can
hardly fail to be beneficial to its growth.

Like Rhubarb, the use of Sea-kale
is at present almost confined to the
English people at home and abroad.
It has gone to America and the antipodes, but has not crossed the
Channel! We speak of its general
use—in a few gardens in France
it may be seen, but they belong to
those who have learned to care for
the plant in England or who have
English gardeners.

Forced Sea-kale fit for use can be
had early in December, and by
growing a sufficient number of
plants a constant supply may be
maintained till late in the spring.
The crop of roots may either be
grown from seed sown in the spring,

or by selecting roots from plants lifted in the autumn to be prepared for forcing, which may be easily accomplished in any warm structure kept dark for blanching purposes. Seeds of Sea-kale may be sown in March or early in April, in drills 9 inches apart, or broadcast upon beds 4 feet wide, covering them with fine soil. When large enough the young plants should be thinned out to several inches apart to afford ample room for growth. The following spring they will be large enough to transplant into a piece of ground deeply trenched and dressed with rotten farmyard manure. Some time in March lift the plants carefully with a fork, and plant them in rows 12 inches asunder and 9 inches plant from plant, *i.e.* when grown for lifting in autumn for forcing. But if to be planted to make stools for forcing in the open air—which may be done by covering them with hot manure and leaves—plant the rows 3 feet apart and 2¼ feet clump from clump. This will give plenty of room to cover the plants with heating material. Three or four plants may be placed in each clump, allowing 3 or 4 inches between each plant. Take care that the plants are 3 inches clear of the rims of the Seakale pots which are placed over them when ready for forcing. Where the plants are grown from roots or thongs, when lifted in autumn for forcing, the strongest should be selected; but where the stock of roots is scarce, thongs may be used about the thickness of a quill pen, when they will be strong enough to force the following spring. Cut the roots 9 inches in length, leaving the top or thick end level, and the thin end slanting about ½ inch, when it will emit a number of fibres. Tie the roots thus prepared in bundles, and lay them in some fine sandy soil, covering them 2 inches in thickness.

Ground intended for Sea-kale should be deeply trenched during autumn, and enriched by several inches in thickness of rotten manure. If ridged as the trenching proceeds, the ridges must be levelled down in spring before planting. Early in April is a good time to plant the roots or thongs; they will then be found to have formed crowns, and will be pushing out young fibres. Rake the ground level after levelling down the ridges, tread it firmly, and plant the sets in rows 12 inches asunder and 9 inches plant from plant. The ground will require to be frequently hoed between the plants during summer to keep down weeds and the surface open. Liquid manure will be found of great benefit to the plants during summer, and if at hand, a dressing of artificial manure may be given, for by feeding well during the growing season fine strong roots will be the result. As soon as frost kills the leaves in autumn the plants intended to be lifted for forcing should be taken up and laid in some light soil. Open a trench at one end of the plantation and lift the plants, with as many roots attached to them as possible. After taking off the thongs for next year's crop, lay the roots in some light dry soil, covering their crowns over with some dry litter to keep frost from them. Thus a few roots may be had during winter for forcing when required. From 55° to 60° will be heat enough, and the roots may be planted either in large flower-pots or boxes. If in pots, invert another the same size over the one in which the roots are planted. Thus circumstanced and placed in the temperature just named, fine, crisp, well-blanched Kale will be produced. If required soon after being put in warmth, place a few barrow-loads of hot manure in the house, and on that set the pots. The warmth induces quick growth and superior heads. If in boxes, they should be deep enough for the roots to stand upright, and there should be depth for the Kale to grow to its full length before it reaches the lid of the box.

If more convenient, the roots may

be planted in light soil in the Mushroom house, covering them over with some light material to keep the crowns in darkness. Fine crops may also be grown upon ordinary hot-beds covered with frames and wooden sashes; if glass sashes are used, they must be covered with straw and double mats to exclude light and keep the temperature of the frames equable, *i.e.* about 60.° The roots may be planted in light soil or in pots placed upon the heated material, which should be covered with sifted ashes or some light material to keep down the rank steam. Where Kale is required in large quantities a Cucumber or Melon house with bottom heat at command will be found to be one of the best structures in which to produce it. Put a few inches of soil over the slates or boards forming the bottom over the pipes or hot-water tank; in this set the roots upright several inches apart, running some soil in between them, and water well, and as soon as the crowns show signs of growth, give another soaking, and cover them to the depth of 9 inches or 1 ft. with dry, sifted leaf-mould or cocoa-nut fibre. Thus treated, in a very short time the tips of the leaves will appear above the covering, when the Kale will be fit for use.

When forced in the open air, Sea-kale pots or boxes having wooden covers must be placed over the clumps of plants, and the pot or boxes must be covered with fermenting material, consisting of hot stable manure and leaves well mixed together. Care must be taken that the manure does not overheat, or the crowns will get scorched and the crop lost for the season. When planted in rows, if a covering of ashes or light, loose soil is placed over the crowns from 9 inches to 1 ft. in depth just before the crowns start into growth in spring, the heads of Kale will grow up through the covering, and when uncovered the result is often a very

superior crop, which being late is generally very acceptable, especially if, after a severe winter, other crops are scarce.

SEA-KALE ON THE COAST.—Between Calshot Castle and Leap, Hampshire, Sea-kale grows wild luxuriantly on the beach, just above high-water mark, and those who live close to the shore claim so much of it as is opposite their domain. In autumn, when the stems die down, they cover each stool with shingle, to the depth of 18 inches or so, which answers two purposes : it keeps the crown from being trodden underfoot in winter, and when the Kale commences to grow in spring it blanches it. The shoots are ready for use about the middle of March. A good harvest is made of it when fit to cut, which is just before it peeps through the shingle. The latter is carefully removed by the hand, so as not to break the tender stalks, which turn out quite clean and well blanched. It is sent to Southampton and Cowes, where it finds a ready market. Although all the crowns are covered at the same time they do not all come in at one time; for the cutting generally lasts three weeks. There is no reason why Sea-kale should not be grown on the coast in many places—that is, where any waste space is left above high water for its accommodation. Where any beach exists above high-water mark, seed may be sown in the following manner :—With a shovel open a trench 1 ft. deep, if shingly; but, if sandy, half that depth will do : sow the seed in it as you would Peas, but more thinly ; then fill it up, which is all that is necessary until the roots are large enough to be transplanted, which, if the seed be sown in March, will be in the succeeding March. Take the roots up as carefully as possible, and plant them four in a 9-inch square, leaving a space of 3 ft. between the squares, and, if in lines, there should be a space of 6 ft. between the lines. When covering the crowns for blanching, the shingle may be heaped up over them in ridges along the lines. This Kale is generally well blanched, stout in growth, and in every way excellent; when cooked, the flavour is more delicate than that of ordinary forced Sea-kale, and it often produces stems 9 inches long, each of which weighs one pound, and some twenty ounces. The reason of its quality is the use of the clean shingle. There is too much direct use of manure in the common way of forcing Sea-kale, and used in a way, too, which can contribute very little to the nourishment of the plant. Manure is for the roots, not the tops. Therefore we prefer the clean forcing which is possible in any heated and darkened structure to the old way of piling fresh manure over the Sea-kale plot in the garden.

MARKET-GARDEN CULTURE.—Some growers raise Sea-kale plants from seed, but the majority propagate them from root-cuttings. It is, however, advisable once in every few years to raise plants from seed in order to infuse fresh vigour into the stock. The best way of increasing Sea-kale is from the trimmings or cuttings of the fleshy roots cut away from the plants when they are lifted for forcing. These thongs or roots, when removed, are thrown into a heap in a shed, there to remain until all the plantations that are to be lifted for forcing have been dug up and trimmed. The best of the trimmings are then selected, cut up into pieces about 4 inches long, and laid in a heap by themselves, and the remainder thrown away. In January beds are prepared for the cuttings, about 4 ft. in width, any length, and raised 6 inches higher than the surrounding level, to keep the Sea-kale roots healthy and free from damp. The cuttings are laid thickly on the surface of the bed and covered with soil. At planting time, which is in March, the beds are uncovered, when the roots will have formed several eyes, all of which are rubbed off, excepting the strongest top one. Some growers do not cut the roots until planting time, but lay them on the beds as selected from the shed. In March, when the beds are uncovered, they select the best eye, then cut the roots at the required length below it, and rub off all other eyes, as in the previous case. The Sea-kale cuttings, being thus prepared for planting, are inserted with iron-shod dibbles into ground which was well manured and deeply dug or trenched in winter, levelled in February, and lines drawn along it 3 ft. apart and planted with Cauliflowers, keeping them at the same distance asunder in the rows. Between the lines of Cauliflowers, other lines are drawn precisely in the middle, and in them are planted White or Green Paris Cos Lettuces 18 inches apart. In the rows occupied by the Cauliflowers, too, Lettuce plants are inserted alternately. A Sea-kale plant is now placed alternate with the Lettuces and Cauliflowers, but in the same lines. The Lettuces are first ready for market, and are removed before they injure the Cauliflowers, which by the end of June are marketed, leaving the Sea-kale, which will be coming up strongly by this time, in sole possession of the soil. Some growers plant Sea-kale sets 15 to 18 inches apart amongst spring Cabbages, which are all removed before they can materially injure the Sea-kale. Others plant them between Asparagus ridges; but in this case they must all be lifted at the end of the first season, as is also the case when they are planted between fruit bushes and Moss Roses. Some market gardeners who grow roots for sale plant their sets at 18 inches apart each way, and never intercrop the ground amongst them, but take great care of them; and, under such management, they get finer roots than those produced among other crops. No care is necessary among Sea-kale plantations throughout the summer and autumn, beyond frequently hoeing the surface soil, cutting away all flower-spikes, and rubbing off all small shoots that may chance to spring around the main one.

When forcing-time arrives, if the field is to be kept to yield what is termed " natural " Kale, *i.e.* without being forced in any way, every third row of roots is lifted as required for forcing, and thus the rows are left in pairs with a space of 3 ft. between them. The surface of the soil is then raked clean, and from this wide space the rows are earthed over to the depth of 6 inches to prevent the frost penetrating the ground amongst the crowns and thus rendering it cold and late. The Kale begins to push about the second week in March, and, according to the position of the field and nature of the soil and weather, a supply may be gleaned therefrom till the end of April. As soon as the point of a shoot of Kale is discerned above the ridge the head is fit for cutting.

For early forcing, the very best crowns, and such as the leaves die away from earliest, are selected and trimmed, so that 4 or 5 inches of the main stem, with the crown on the top, only remain. These are then placed closely together in an upright position in a hot-bed prepared for starting them in, which, in the case of the earliest batch, consists of a manure-bed covered with frames and sashes, and a few inches deep of soil levelled within the frames for planting the roots amongst. A heat of 65° or 70° is kept up inside the frames, if possible, by applying hot linings of manure and by placing litter or mats on the surface over the glass, which latter also keeps all dark and blanches the Kale. Sea-kale growers try to have a good cutting on Lord Mayor's Day; but this is considered too early for regular forcing.

Forcing commences in earnest about the first fortnight in November, and large trenches or beds, on which Cucumbers were grown during the summer, are cleared out and re-filled with hot manure, over which 8 inches of soil is placed, and therein the Sea-kale is planted thickly in lines across the bed, which are about 5 inches apart, and about the same

space for a margin is left empty on each side. Amongst the roots, and all round the beds, rows of stakes are inserted, 18 inches of their length being left above the soil, after which some 6 or 7 inches deep of short litter is strewed over the whole surface of the beds, which are then covered over with mats supported on the ends of the stakes. Hoops and mats are often used instead of stakes. In about three or four weeks after the beds are made up, cutting begins, when it is necessary to uncover the beds as the operation proceeds, drawing the short litter off the crowns to get at them, and replacing it as speedily as possible, as all the crowns are not fit to cut at the same time.

Beds for later crops are prepared on a well-sheltered plot of ground as near home and the manure-heap as possible. The ground is marked off into spaces either 4 or 5 ft. wide, with alleys 2 ft. wide between them. These spaces are used as beds, over which the soil from the alleys is placed, after finely breaking it, until the alleys are 20 inches deep. The Sea-kale crowns are then all lined into these beds as described in the case of earlier beds, and thus the beds are left uncovered until they are required for forcing; but, as a rule, two or more of them are always being forced, and others started to succeed them. As these beds have no bottom-heat, it is not necessary that they should be immediately covered, as in that case they, being incited at the bottom, would grow, no matter whether their crowns are cared for or not; but, in this instance, having no exciting agent, and being in a dormant state, they await the grower's convenience. In forcing them, the alleys between the beds are firmly filled with fermenting manure, and, the beds being covered, as formerly stated, with short litter and mats supported on the upright stakes, all is finished. The Kale takes a longer time to push into growth by this means than when forced on a manure-bed, and it does not come quite so regularly. This method, however, has the advantage of less trouble and risk, and great convenience in keeping up a supply until it can be produced from the open-air beds, after which the forced roots are removed to a heap by themselves, or to the piggery, where their vitality is sure to be destroyed. If conveyed to a field at once, with the manure which formed the beds, and dug in, they would grow again, and prove a future annoyance.

There are two varieties of Sea-kale in cultivation.

1. The Common, the young blanched leaves of which have a purplish tinge when they are exposed to the light.

2. The Lilywhite, the young leaves of which are totally devoid of this purple colour, becoming green under similar conditions. In other respects they are identical.

USES.—The blanched stalks are eaten boiled, almost in the same way as Asparagus. When properly cooked, they preserve all their firmness, and have a very fine and agreeable flavour, like that of hazelnuts, with a very slight amount of bitterness.

SHALLOT.

Allium ascalonicum, L. *Liliaceæ.*

French, Échalote. *German,* Schalotte. *Flemish* and *Dutch,* Sjalot. *Danish,* Skalottelog. *Italian,* Scalogno. *Spanish,* Chalote. *Portuguese,* Echalota.

Native of Palestine.—Perennial.—Although botanically very closely allied to the cultivated Onion, the Shallot, in its manner of growth, differs from it completely from a horticultural point of view. It is a plant which seldom produces seed, but has a profusion of leaves, and its bulbs, when planted in spring, speedily divide into a great number of cloves, which remain attached to a common disc, and in a few months become as strong as the parent bulb. It has been in cultivation from a very remote period, and there are now several rather distinct forms of it in existence. [It may be well to note that the plant commonly sent in quantities to the London market is not the True Shallot, but a small roundish Onion with a rich brown skin. The True Shallot has a pale-gray skin, and is elongated in shape.—R.]

CULTURE.—The cloves are planted immediately after winter in good, rich, well-manured soil. Well-rotted farmyard manure suits the Shallot better than that which is fresh and strawy. It is still better, when possible, to plant the cloves in ground that was plentifully manured in the previous year. They should not be deeply buried, and the cloves of the Common Shallot should be placed about 4 inches apart. They may be grown either in beds by themselves, or on the edges of beds containing other vegetables. When the leaves commence to wither, about July, the tufts of plants are pulled up and left to dry for a few days, after which they are divided and the bulbs stored in a dry place. Those bulbs which are intended for planting may be left in the ground some time longer. USES.—The bulbs, which keep for the whole year, are used as seasoning, and give a more delicate flavour than most Onions. The leaves are also eaten, cut when they are green.

True Shallot (*Échalote Ordinaire*).—Bulb the size of a small Walnut, sometimes larger, pear-shaped, narrowed in the upper part into a rather long point, and covered with a russet-coloured skin, of a coppery-red colour in the lower part, shading off into gray towards the upper extremity, and often wrinkled longitudinally. The outer skin is thick and tough. When the dried coats are taken off, the bulb is greenish at the base, and violet coloured at the top. Leaves small, very green, and 10 to 12 inches long. This variety, which is more extensively grown than any other, has the advantage of keeping very well. At the Central Market, in Paris, some sub-varieties of it are met with, viz.—

Échalote Petite Hâtive de Bagnolet.—Somewhat smaller than the type or true variety, and produces a great number of cloves to each plant.

E. Grosse de Noisy.—Bulb the size of a small fig. This variety keeps well, and has a very thick tough skin. It does not multiply so much as the other kinds.

É. Hâtive de Niort.—This is somewhat larger than the True Shallot, which it very much resembles in other respects, but commences to grow sooner.

It is easy to perceive that these three forms are only slight modifications of the True Shallot.

In England a large-bulbed, vigorous-growing variety is cultivated under the name of *Russian,* or *Large Brown,* or *Large Red* Shallot. Bulbs nearly twice the size of the True Shallot. The outer skin is of a reddish-brown colour, the inner scales deep violet or purple. Cloves grow in tufts of from three to seven. Leaves erect, 18 inches long, deep green in colour.

Jersey, or **False, Shallot** (*Échalote de Jersey*).—Bulbs short, almost always irregular in shape, but sometimes perfectly rounded and broader

True Shallot (½ natural size).   Jersey, or False, Shallot (½ natural size).

than long, when they quite resemble a small Onion; skin coppery red, thin, and easily torn. The bulb, when stripped of the dried coats, is entirely violet coloured, the tint being somewhat paler than that of the True Shallot. The leaves are distinguished by their very peculiar glaucous hue. The bulbs do not keep so well as those of the True Shallot, and commence to grow sooner in spring. The Jersey Shallot flowers and seeds pretty regularly, the seed exactly resembling Onion seed. Indeed, in all the characteristics of its growth, the plant is an Onion, and has nothing to do with the True Shallot.

SKIRRET.

Sium Sisarum, L.   *Umbelliferæ.*

French, Chervis.   *German,* Zuckerwurzel.   *Flemish,* Suikerwortel.   *Danish,* Sukkerrod.
Italian, Sisaro.   *Spanish,* Chirivia tudesca.   *Portuguese,* Cherivia.

Native of China.—Perennial.—Authors generally concur in describing the Skirret as a native of China.   It must be acknowledged, at any rate, that it was introduced into France at a very early period, as it is mentioned by Olivier des Serres as a plant commonly cultivated in his time.   He considered it a native of Germany, and that it was introduced from that country into Italy by the Emperor Tiberius. However that may be, the plant appears to have been more generally cultivated two or three centuries ago than it is at the present day.

It is a plant with numerous swollen roots, forming a bundle from

the upper part of the neck, somewhat like Dahlia roots, but much longer and more slender. Leaves composed of largish, shining leaflets, of a dark-green colour; stems 3 to 4 ft. high, channelled, smooth, usually produced in the second year, but often in the first; flowers small, white, in umbels; seed brown, oblong, curved, often cylindrical, and marked with five longitudinal furrows.   A gramme contains about 600 seeds, and a litre of them weighs about 400 grammes.   Their germinating power lasts for three years. Roots of a grayish-white colour; flesh firm, very white, and sweet. The centre of the root consists of a woody core, of greater or

Skirret ($\frac{1}{20}$ natural size; detached roots, $\frac{1}{8}$ natural size).

less thickness, which, if not removed before cooking, is very detrimental to its quality as a table vegetable, and, moreover, is not easily separated from the fleshy part of the root.

Culture.—Skirret may be propagated either from seed, offsets, or divisions of the roots.   The seed is sown in autumn or early in spring. When the seedlings have made four or five leaves, they are planted out permanently, in good, moist, rich, well-manured soil, and will commence to yield abundantly in the ensuing autumn.   As the plants delight in abundance of moisture, they should be plentifully watered all through the summer.   Divisions of the roots or offsets of old plants are planted in March or April, and the plants raised in this way are treated exactly like those raised from seed.   It has been asserted that the roots of plants which have been raised from divisions or root-cuttings have the core less woody than those of plants raised from seed.   This, however, is only true when a careful selection has been made of the roots used for propagating. Plants raised in the same seed-bed differ very much from one another in the size of the woody core, and it is evident that, by means of a judicious selection, the best may be propagated to the exclusion of all the others. As the Skirret is a very hardy plant, the roots may be left in the ground all the winter, and only taken up as they are wanted for use. USES.—The roots, which are tender, sweet, and slightly floury, are used in the same manner as Salsafy or Scorzonera roots.

SNAILS.

Medicago scutellata, All.   *Leguminosæ.*

French, Limaçon.   *German,* Schnirkelschnecke.   *Spanish,* Caracol

Native of South Europe.—Annual.—A creeping, spreading, slender-stemmed plant. Leaves winged, composed of oval leaflets, broad at the top; flowers small, yellow; seed-vessels smooth, twisted spirally with six turns, and bearing a good resemblance to a snail-shell; seed largish, kidney-shaped, flattened, and of a brownish-yellow colour, three or four in each seed-vessel. A gramme contains four full seed-vessels on an average, and a litre of them weighs about 150 grammes. The germinating power of the seed lasts for five years. This plant is not edible, but, like the Cater-

Snails (⅓ natural size; detached seed-vessels, natural size).

pillar-plant, is grown on account of the singular shape of its seed-vessels.

SORREL.

Rumex, L.   *Polygonaceæ.*

French, Oseille.   *German,* Sauerampfer.   *Flemish* and *Dutch,* Zuring.   *Italian,* Acetosa.
Spanish, Acedera.   *Portuguese,* Azedas.

A considerable number of species of *Rumex* are cultivated in gardens, all of which are perennial plants, and characterized by the acidity of their leaves. Of these, the principal varieties which are grown have sprung from *Rumex Acetosa, R. montanus, R. scutatus,* and *R. Patientia,* all of which grow wild in France. The garden Sorrels may be ranked among the plants which have been least modified by cultivation, as most of them are little, if anything, better than wild plants of the same species growing under favourable conditions.

COMMON SORREL.

Rumex Acetosa, L.

Oseille commune.

Native of Europe.—Perennial.—Leaves oblong, hastate at the base, with long-pointed auricles directed downwards almost parallel with the leaf-stalk, which is longish and channelled; stem hollow, striated, and often of a reddish colour; flowers dioecious, in terminal and lateral clusters; seed small, triangular, brown, and shining. A gramme contains about 1000 seeds, and a litre of them weighs about 650 grammes. Their germinating power lasts for four years. CULTURE.—The plant may be propagated by division of the tufts in March or April. This method is employed when, for instance, it is desired to form edgings of male-flowered plants alone, as these are not liable to be exhausted by bearing seed. The more usual way, however, is to raise the plants from seed sown in spring, in drills, and, if possible, in good, deep, moist soil. The seedlings, when strong enough, are thinned out to the distance of 6 to 8 inches from one another in the drills. In about two months after sowing, some leaves will be fit to gather. Some persons, when gathering, cut off the whole plant with a knife, but the Parisian market gardeners, who are well skilled in the cultivation of this plant, always gather the leaves one by one, selecting only those which are fully grown; a more abundant and continuous supply is obtained in this way than by cutting off all the leaves, large and small, at the same time. A plantation of Common Sorrel will last for three or four years; when its productiveness begins to decline, new plants, raised either from seed or divisions of the tufts, should be substituted. The leaves are very extensively used, and are sent to table boiled.

FRENCH SORREL.

Rumex scutatus, L.

Oseille ronde.

Native of South Europe.—Perennial.—A plant of very peculiar

Common Broad-leaved French Sorrel
(⅛ natural size).

appearance, and impossible to be mistaken for any other kind of Sorrel. Stems slender, usually prostrate, and bearing small leaves of a glaucous or grayish green colour, gene-rally roundish or heart-shaped, and having narrow, divergent auricles at the base; flowers in spikes, and hermaphrodite and unisexual on the same plant. The leaves of this Sorrel are extremely acid. Its chief recommendation is that it withstands dry weather very well. It is principally grown as a summer Sorrel.

Common Broad-leaved French Sorrel (*Oseille de Belleville*).—This is the most extensively grown variety of the Common Sorrel, and is almost the only kind which is cultivated in the vicinity of Paris. It differs from the type in the greater size and paler colour of its leaves, and comes very true from seed. The market gardeners around Paris often have whole fields under this plant, and, by growing it under frames, keep up a constant supply of fresh leaves nearly all the year through.

The following kinds have also been recommended :—

Virieu White Sorrel (*Oseille de Virieu*).—This is a broad-leaved variety, said to be somewhat earlier than the Common Broad-leaved French Sorrel.

Lettuce-leaved Sorrel (*O. à Feuille de Laitue*).—A variety with broad, roundish leaves of a very light-green colour.

O. Blonde de Sarcelles.—This kind is distinguished from the Common Broad-leaved French Sorrel by having longer leaves, and the leaf-stalks entirely green, without any tinge of red.

All these varieties, in short, differ very little from one another, and, when propagated from seed, revert more or less to the Common Broad-leaved French Sorrel.

MAIDEN SORREL.

Rumex montanus, Desf. ; *Rumex arifolius*, All.

Oseille vierge.

Native of South Europe.—**Perennial.**—Leaves oval oblong, hastate at the base, almost smooth, of a rather deep green, with short auricles of an almost bluntly rounded or shortly pointed shape and directed outwards ; leaf-stalks pink coloured at the base ; stem resembling that of the Common Sorrel ; flowers diœcious, usually barren. The leaves of this species are somewhat larger than those of the Common Sorrel, and not so acid, and the plant is slow in running to seed. As it is diœcious, it may be employed, like the Common Sorrel, for making edgings consisting of male-flowered plants alone. Two forms of this Sorrel are distinguished, viz. the Common or Green-leaved and the Crimped-leaved Maiden Sorrel ; the leaves of the latter being larger, slender, very much crimped, and marked with small red spots on the midrib and larger veins at the lower part of the stem. The wild form of the Maiden Sorrel (*Rumex arifolius*) is often met with in France. It is especially common in the pine forests on the high mountain districts of Central and Eastern France from the Vosges to the Alps.

In addition to the foregoing three species, another (*Rumex alpinus*, L.) is sometimes grown in gardens under the name of Pyrenean Sorrel (*Oseille des Alpes*). It has soft, wrinkled, reticulated leaves, and is especially characterized by the width of the sheathing part of the leaf. As a table vegetable it does not appear to possess any quality in which it equals the Patience Dock, or Herb Patience (*Rumex Patientia*), which see.

WOOD SORREL.

Oxalis Acetosella, L.   *Oxalidaceæ.*

French, Oxalis oseille.   *Italian,* Acetosella.   *Spanish,* Acederilla.

Native of Europe.—Perennial.—This plant, which grows wild in woods and cool, shady places, is sometimes gathered and eaten as salad, the leaves being acid and similar in flavour to those of the Common Sorrel. It is not often cultivated, and if any one desires to have a few tufts of it in his garden, the best way is to dig them up where they grow naturally and transfer them to a cool, shady part of the garden. By cutting them frequently a continuous supply of tender leaves may be obtained, and the plants will also be prevented from seeding. If allowed to seed, they sometimes multiply to such an extent as to become troublesome weeds.

Deppe's Wood Sorrel (*Oxalis Deppei,* Lodd).—Native of Mexico.—Perennial.—Roots fleshy, white, semi-transparent, and resembling small Turnips ; leaves very long stalked, composed of four rounded leaflets of a very light-green colour, each marked with a brown spot ; flowers large, carmine pink, greenish at the base of the petals. CULTURE.—This plant is easily multiplied from the bulblets which grow in large numbers near the neck of the root. These are planted in April, in good light soil, either on the edges of beds, or in rows 12 to 16 inches apart. The plants will continue growing until late in autumn without requiring any attention except watering in very dry weather. It is advisable to take the roots up before the approach of frosty weather, but if some of the plants can be conveniently covered with frames and, in this way, kept growing until November, they will produce much finer and larger roots. USES.—The roots, which are tender and juicy, but very insipid, may be eaten. The leaves, used like those of the Common Sorrel, appear to be a better table vegetable than the roots. They are tender, with an agreeably acidulous flavour, and, after being cut, the plant speedily sends out fresh leaves, which are fit for use in two or three weeks.

SOUTHERNWOOD.

Artemisia Abrotanum, L.   *Compositæ.*

French, Aurone.   *Danish,* Ambra.   *Italian,* Abrotano.

Native of South Europe.—A shrubby perennial plant, about 3 ft. high, grown in gardens either singly or as an edging. Branches very numerous ; leaves pale green, grayish, and divided into exceedingly narrow segments ; flowers numerous, small, yellowish ; seed very small, resembling that of the Wormwood. Southernwood is propagated from seed, or more usually from cuttings, which strike root very readily, especially in the early part of summer. It is a good plan always to keep a plant or two of it in an orchard-house or plant-house, as it is sensitive to cold. The plant is cultivated on account of its agreeable flavour and its medicinal properties, which are similar to those of the Wormwood.

SOY BEAN.

Soja hispida, Mœnch.   *Leguminosæ.*

French, Soja.   *German*, Soja-Bohne.

Native of China.—Annual.—In China the varieties of this plant are almost as numerous as those of the Kidney Bean are in Europe. There are dwarf kinds and also tall ones which, if not exactly climbers like our tall Kidney Beans, at least trail along the ground for a con-siderable distance.   Up to the present time, only one or two dwarf early varieties have been cultivated in Europe and considered of any importance for table use, and to the de-scription of these we shall here confine ourselves.   One great recommendation of this plant is that, so far, it does not appear liable to be at-tacked by any insect, nor to suffer from any parasitical fungus, while its vigorous habit of growth, its great productiveness, and the rich-ness of its beans in nutritive properties cause it to be justly esteemed as a valuable plant for agricultural and economic purposes.   CULTURE. — The Soy Bean is grown in exactly the same manner as Kidney Beans.   It requires nearly the

Soy Bean (⅕ natural size ; detached pods, ⅓ natural size).

same degree of heat, and ripens at the same time as the mid-season varieties of these plants.   All the pods on a plant, however, do not ripen together, those which set first being often full-grown and nearly ripe while the plant still continues to flower on the upper part of the stem.   USES.—The beans are eaten, either green or dried, like Kidney Beans.   The dried beans should be steeped in water for some time before they are cooked, otherwise they will remain almost as hard as they were when uncooked.

Common Yellow Soy Bean (*Soja Ordinaire à Grain Jaune*).—A dwarf thick-set plant, forming small compact tufts from 10 to 20 inches high, according to the richness of the soil and the time of sowing.   Flowers exceedingly small, greenish or lilac, in axillary clusters, and succeeded by hairy pods, each containing two or three small beans, which are pale yellow when ripe, and are scarcely larger than those of the Rice Kidney Bean (*Haricot Riz*).   A litre of these beans weighs about 720 grammes, and there are about 80 beans in 10 grammes.   Their germinating power lasts for two years.   This is

2 M

Étampes Yellow Soy Bean (⅛ natural size ; detached pods, ⅓ natural size).

the earliest variety of Soy Bean yet known. The beans ripen in three or four months after sowing.

Étampes Yellow Soy Bean (*Soja d'Étampes*).—This variety is not so early as the preceding one, but is far more productive. The plant forms branching tufts from 2 to over 2½ ft. high, which become laden with pods growing from the axils of all the leaves. The beans are considerably larger than those of the preceding variety, being almost as large as those of the China, or Robin's-egg, Kidney Bean, and sometimes a little more elongated in shape. A litre of them weighs about 725 grammes, and there are about 70 beans in 10 grammes. Their germinating power lasts for two years. This plant requires at least four or five months to complete its growth and come to maturity; however, in ordinary seasons, it ripens the greater part of its pods in the climate of Paris.

SPINACH.

Spinacia oleracea, L.   Chenopodiaceæ.

French, Épinard.   *German,* Spinat.   *Flemish* and *Dutch,* Spinazie.   *Danish,* Spinat.
Italian, Spinaccio.   *Spanish,* Espinaca.   *Portuguese,* Espinafre.

A plant of rapid growth, the wild form having arrow-shaped, pointed leaves, while in the cultivated varieties the leaves are broader and rounder and are remarkable for the thickness of the parenchyma. In cooking they lose nearly all their savour, but preserve their green colour in a notable manner. When growing, these leaves form a rosette, from the centre of which the flower-stem makes its appearance more or less speedily, according to the variety. The Spinach, being diœcious, bears only male flowers on some plants and only female flowers on others. The seed, which, of course, is only found on the female plants, varies very much according to the variety, that of some kinds being armed with three very sharp points, while in other kinds the seed is round and without points.

CULTURE.—The seed is best sown where the plants are to stand, in drills 10 or 12 inches apart. It is advisable, in order to have a continuous supply, to make successional sowings every fortnight, or at least every month, especially in spring and summer, when the plants run to seed quickly. Frequent and plentiful waterings are indispensable to ensure an abundant growth and good quality in the leaves. The market gardeners around Paris have for a long time preferred the Prickly-seeded varieties for spring sowings, reserving the Round-seeded kinds for late summer and autumn sowings. At the present day, however, we have Round-seeded varieties which are quite as hardy and as slow in running to seed as any of the Prickly-seeded kinds.

The first sowing for summer use should be made early in March, as a rule ; but in warm soils and situations a small sowing may be made in February.

SUMMER SPINACH.—Owing to the Summer Spinach being so liable to run to seed, it is advisable to make small sowings often rather than to make large sowings at long intervals,—as by the former plan a regular supply of fine young leaves is ensured, whereas in the latter case small tough leaves have often to be used in consequence of successional crops not being sufficiently advanced to give a supply. It is therefore obvious that a sowing should be made once a fortnight, or at longest every three weeks, during the summer months. These sowings may consist of the Round Spinach for the first two or three sowings, and the Flanders or the Lettuce-leaved varieties for sowing through the summer. These two last-named kinds are far superior, both in quality and cropping, to the Round Spinach. For summer sowings it is best to choose as shady and moist a situation as possible, to save watering, as well as to prevent the plants from running to seed too quickly. All Spinach seed is benefited by being soaked in water for a few hours previous to sowing, inasmuch as it germinates more quickly and the growth is often stronger. Sowing in drills is by far the best mode of sowing the seed, as then the crop is more easily kept free from weeds, and watering or mulching can be effectually done when desired, as well as rendering it much easier to gather the crop. The drills should be about 1 ft. apart,

and the plants, after thinning, at least 6 inches asunder. The Lettuce-leaved and Flanders require even more room than this, if the production of fine large leaves be aimed at. The last summer crop should be sown on a well-prepared border or quarter about the middle of July, in drills about 18 inches apart; this will yield a good supply of fine large leaves till October is out.

For the late or winter crop, prepare about the end of July a border or sheltered quarter ; apply a good coating of thoroughly decayed manure, trench the ground well and cast it up into ridges, so as to expose as great a surface as possible to the influence of the atmosphere. Every dry day till August 10th or 12th cast down the ridges and pulverize with a steel fork, so as to sweeten and incorporate all together. Then draw lines 1 ft. apart and sow the hardy Prickly variety. As the plants advance, thin them out from 6 to 9 inches apart, and maintain a healthy and vigorous growth by constant surface stirrings in suitable weather : this, if attended to, prevents canker, and encourages the production of an abundance of fine leaves for use every day throughout the winter. Timely forethought should be taken to shelter a portion with a row of short stakes about 18 inches high, interwoven with fern, straw, evergreen branches, furze, heath, or other material, which should be neatly applied, and also made wind-proof. Thatched hurdles or frames, cheaply made, of battens backed together and thatched, might also be used for the purpose of protecting from frost.

The last sowing, to supply leaves in the spring, generally consists of the Prickly variety. The time to sow this crop, however, depends upon the locality. If sown too soon, it runs to seed the same season and is useless. To sow it late enough to have a crop of leaves without the plants throwing up their flowering stems is what has to be aimed at, and for this reason many sow twice for the winter crops. In some parts of Scotland and the north of England the middle of August is not too soon, while in the south it is not often safe to sow before the end of September; but a practical acquaintance with the climate and locality will generally be the best guide. This crop is often sown after Potatoes or Onions. The winter crop will generally afford a good supply of leaves till nearly the beginning of June, by which time the Round or Summer Spinach will be coming in in abundance.

A deep, rich, moist soil is necessary to grow good Spinach; and if liberal supplies of liquid manure be given to summer crops, a great advantage will be gained thereby. Some care is required in picking Spinach, especially in winter, when the growth is often not equal to the demand. Indiscriminate picking will soon ruin the crop; the largest leaves should therefore be taken first, and picked off singly, so as to avoid injuring the plants.

CULTURE FOR MARKET.—English market gardeners seldom grow Spinach as a summer crop, as it " bolts " or runs to seed before many leaves have been gathered from it, and in that case it is by no means a profitable crop. The Round-leaved sort is that which is used for spring sowings, the first of which is made in February, a second about the 1st of March, and another sowing or two

at an interval of three weeks or thereabouts, just as space and convenience permit. The latest spring sowings are made on a damp, cool piece of ground, provided such can be obtained, as, thus circumstanced, better leaves are produced in hot weather than on dry and warm soils. In July, if the weather be moist, a sowing of the Round-leaved variety is usually made on a spare piece of ground for autumn use. Early in August a large sowing of the Prickly-seeded or the Flanders is made broadcast on fields or in rows about 8 inches apart. Some growers prefer the Flanders on account of its large fleshy leaves and hardy constitution, and it sells in the market better than the Prickly sort. By sowing in the first and last week of August and the middle of September, a succession of Spinach from October till May is easily kept up. Coleworts are frequently planted in a field of late Spinach, at 3 or 4 ft. apart. In damp winters a large proportion of the roots may die, but in ordinary winters they survive, and produce an abundance of large fleshy leaves in spring. No care is taken with this crop from the time of sowing till gathering, beyond hoeing and thinning once or twice. Spaces under fruit trees are also covered with Spinach sown broadcast; and as the trees are not furnished with leaves, they do not shade the plants. Open fields are also often sown with Spinach in beds, which are covered by throwing soil over them from the alleys; on these beds Cauliflowers are also planted, at the usual distances apart. By the time the Spinach has come well up the Cauliflowers will have become well established, so that the Spinach, which as soon as ready is removed for market, does not injure the Cauliflowers.

USES.—The leaves are eaten boiled.

COMMON SPINACH.

Spinacia spinosa, Mœnch.; *Spinacia oleracea, a.* L.

Épinard ordinaire.

This form, which appears to come nearer than any other to the wild plant, is now very rarely cultivated, at least in France. It is distinguished by its rather narrow, pointed, and very pronounced arrow-shaped leaves, by having the leaf-stalks tinged with red, and the seed armed with sharp, horn-like prickles. It is not a kind to be recommended. A gramme contains about 90 seeds with the prickles on, and a litre of them weighs about 375 grammes. Their germinating power lasts for five years.

Large Prickly, or **Winter, Spinach** (*Épinard d'Angleterre*).—Resembling the preceding kind in the seed, this variety is distinguished from it by the broadness of its leaves (which, however, are distinctly arrow-shaped) and by its very great productiveness. When sown thin, it often forms broad spreading tufts, with numerous branches, plentifully covered with leaves and rather slow in flowering. This habit of growth is peculiar to the plant. The Round-seeded varieties usually form only a simple rosette, from which, at flowering-time, one or more vertical stems issue, bearing from their earliest growth well-developed organs of fructification. These stems also are hollow at the centre and much thicker, being sometimes $1\frac{1}{5}$ to $1\frac{3}{5}$ inches in diameter, while the stems of the Prickly-seeded kinds are seldom thicker than one's finger. This is a good, vigorous-growing, and hardy variety, and, as we have already observed, is preferred by the Parisian market gardeners to all other kinds for spring sowings.

Large Prickly, or Winter, Spinach ($\frac{1}{6}$ natural size).

There is a Prickly-seeded variety with roundish leaves, which bears a tolerable resemblance to the Lettuce-leaved Spinach, and is known by the name of *Épinard Camus de Bordeaux,* or *É. Rond à Grain Piquante.* It is very clear that, of two varieties which are equally good in other respects, the preference will always be given to the Round-seeded kind, the seed being more convenient to handle and more easily sown.

ROUND-SEEDED SPINACH.

Spinacia glabra, Miller; *Spinacia oleracea,* β. L.

Épinard à graine ronde.

The opinion of botanists that the Round-seeded Spinach is a distinct species from the Prickly-seeded appears to be well founded, as the shape of the seed is a very permanent characteristic in these plants. From a horticultural point of view also, the two kinds are clearly different, the Round-seeded always growing more thick-set and forming more compact and less spreading tufts than the Prickly-seeded varieties. A gramme contains about 110 of the round seeds, and a litre of them weighs about 510 grammes. Their germinating power lasts for five years.

Round-seeded Round-leaved Large Dutch Spinach (*Épinard de Hollande*).—A good, vigorous-growing, and hardy kind, with leaves which, although considerably arrow-shaped, are large and broad. They are of a clear-green colour, tolerably crimped, especially while young, and have blunt points which are generally slightly turned underneath. The leaf-stalks are, on an average, about as long as the blades of the leaves. Seed round. This form may be considered the type of the

Viroflay Giant Spinach (⅙ natural size).

Round-seeded varieties, which are improved modifications of it. At the present time, the Spinach which is most frequently sold under the name of Dutch Spinach, especially in Germany, is nothing but the Lettuce-leaved Spinach.

Round-seeded Flanders Spinach (*Épinard de Flandre*).—This is the best-known and most extensively cultivated Round-seeded Spinach. Its characteristics are almost the same as those of the true Dutch Spinach, but it is of somewhat greater size, and the leaves are rounder and less arrow-shaped. It is an excellent and productive variety, and may be sown nearly all the year round. When sown in autumn, it yields a very considerable crop in spring, and in this respect it and the following variety have a marked advantage over the Late-seeding Spinach (*Épinard Lente à Monter*), the growth of which is not so vigorous at the end of winter. The latter, however, in its turn, surpasses them in the summer months, when it yields a continuous supply of broad tender leaves, after the earlier varieties have entirely run to seed.

Viroflay Giant Spinach (*Épinard Monstrueux de Viroflay*).—This
variety, which is a rather
new one, resembles the Flanders Spinach in the shape of
its leaves and in its habit of
growth, but is of much greater
size, as it is not uncommon
to see tufts of it measuring
2 to nearly 2½ ft. in diameter,
with leaves 10 inches long
and 8 inches wide at the base.
Like all extremely vigorous-
growing and large-sized varieties, this requires a plentiful supply of nutriment, and
is worthy of recommendation,
being especially suited for
well-manured and well-kept
gardens.

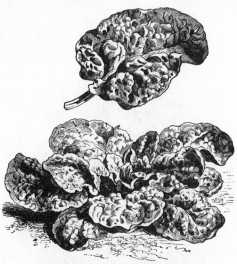

Lettuce-leaved Spinach
(*Épinard à Feuille de Laitue*).
—This is a very distinct variety, having oval leaves,
which are rounded both at
the base and the upper extremity, are of moderate size,
spreading on the ground,
and of a very dark-green
colour. Leaf-stalks short and

Lettuce-leaved Spinach (⅙ natural size).

stiff. The name of this variety does not convey a very
accurate idea of its appearance, and it might, perhaps,
be more appropriately styled
the Sorrel-leaved Spinach,
only that this name has been
already applied to another
variety which is now seldom
met with in cultivation, and
of which the leaves, with their
short and partially violet-
tinged stalks, very closely
resemble Sorrel leaves, not
only in shape, but also in
their light, pale colour. The

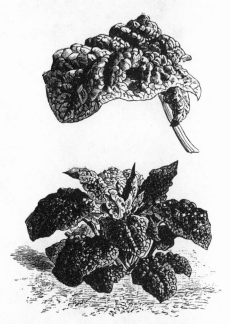

Savoy-leaved Spinach.

Lettuce-leaved Spinach is a
rather productive variety, notwithstanding its low and thick-set habit
of growth. It answers well for summer, and autumn sowings, and,
when sown before winter, is one of the latest kinds to run to seed
in spring.

Savoy-leaved, or Curled, Spinach (*Épinard à Feuille Cloquée*).—The distinguishing feature of this Spinach is that it has the leaves crimped like those of a Savoy Cabbage. This peculiarity does not, in itself, present any marked advantage, and, as the plant is very prone to run quickly to seed, it may be looked upon as more curious than really useful. The leaves are long, rather broad, and generally hastate in shape. It is disposed to run to seed somewhat early.

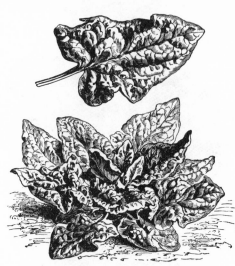

Late-seeding, or Long-stander, Spinach (⅙ natural size).

Late-seeding, or Long-stander, Spinach (*Épinard Lente à Monter*).—We are indebted to M. Lambin, Secretary-general of the Soissons Horticultural Society, for our acquaintance with this excellent variety, which surpasses all others in the length of time during which it continues bearing. The plant forms compact thick-set tufts, with numerous leaves of a dark-green colour, somewhat more crimped and less rounded in shape than those of the Lettuce-leaved Spinach, but yet resembling them more than those of any other variety. The leaf-stalks are very short, their length rarely exceeding that of half the blade of the leaf. The distinguishing quality of this variety is, as its name indicates, that it runs to seed more slowly and later than any other kind. The difference of time in its favour may be estimated at from fifteen to twenty days at least, according to circumstances, and is especially marked in spring sowings, which are so often liable to run to seed too soon.

NEW ZEALAND SPINACH.

Tetragonia expansa, Ait.
Mesembryanthemaceæ.

French, Tétragone cornue. *German*, Neuseeländischer Spinat. *Flemish*, Vierhonk. *Danish*, Nyseelandsk Spinat. *Italian*, Tetragona.

New Zealand Spinach (1/12 natural size; detached branch, ¼ natural size).

Native of New Zealand.— Annual. — Stems spreading, branched, from 2 to over 3 ft. long, bearing numerous alternate, thick, fleshy leaves, resembling Orache leaves in shape; flowers axillary, small, greenish, and without petals, succeeded by hard horned seed-vessels somewhat like the Water Chestnut in shape, and of an almost woody texture in the interior, where the seeds are enclosed. A gramme contains from 10 to 12 of these seed-vessels, and a litre of them weighs about 225 grammes. The germinating power of the seeds lasts for five years. This plant is grown to supply the place of the ordinary Spinach during the hottest months of the year, or in dry, arid localities where the ordinary Spinach does badly. The seed is sown, where the plants are to stand, in May, either in a hot-bed or in the open ground, and the plants will continue to yield a supply of leaves during the whole summer, requiring hardly any attention. The leaves are eaten boiled and minced like ordinary Spinach.

STRAWBERRIES.*

Fragaria, L.   *Rosaceæ.*

French, Fraisier.   *German,* Erdbeere.   *Flemish* and *Dutch,* Aardbezie.   *Danish,* Jordbeer.
Italian, Fragola.   *Spanish,* Fresa.   *Portuguese,* Moranguoiro.

Several species of *Fragaria* have been introduced into cultivation at different times, and, either through the improvement of the wild forms themselves, or by being crossed with one another, have contributed to produce the diversified varieties which are now found in gardens. The number of these varieties has become so great, that it is absolutely impossible to mention them all in this work, and we have been obliged to make a selection comprising only those kinds which appeared to us most worthy of note, either as possessing in a high degree a combination of various good qualities, or as being specially adapted for some particular purpose. Earliness, productiveness, perfume, and fine flavour are qualities which every one will appreciate in a Strawberry, and it is according to the merit of varieties in these different respects that the amateur who grows them in his own garden for his own use will select the kinds of Strawberries which suit him best to plant. But the private gardener who forces them for an early crop, or the market gardener who grows them on a large scale to supply the markets, must look for other qualities in the kinds which he takes in hand, especially if the fruit which he intends to sell has to be carried to a distant market. In the latter case, the property of bearing carriage without being damaged is one of such high importance that very often the possession of it is sufficient to decide the selection of the kinds which make their appearance in the markets.

All the varieties of cultivated Strawberries have in common the advantage of being remarkably early, and they supply the first fruit that ripens in spring. As the attentions which their culture requires vary to some extent according to the species from which the varieties have sprung, we shall, in this page, give only some very general instructions on the subject.

* Strictly fruit, these owe their presence here to the fact that they are generally cultivated with kitchen-garden crops. Our neighbours have raised some of the best sorts grown, and have a knowledge of Strawberries which we have pleasure in making more fully known to English readers.—W. R.

CULTURE.—Almost all the varieties of Strawberries suffer from dry and excessively warm weather; it is therefore advisable to plant them in cool, moist ground, and in a position somewhat sheltered from the burning rays of the sun. If a little is thereby lost, as regards earliness, the produce, on the other hand, will be more abundant and more prolonged. The hardiness of Strawberries is such that they will withstand the winter without any protection from frost, but almost all the varieties are injured by an excess of moisture at that time of the year, and are liable to rot at the root if planted in badly drained ground. Once the warm weather has arrived, however, Strawberry plants, on the contrary, require to be plentifully watered, and it will generally be found advantageous to give them a good mulching with stable manure or straw, which, by preventing evaporation, will keep the roots cool and moist, so that the plants will not require to be so frequently watered.

USES.—The fruit, which is excellent and very wholesome, is eaten fresh, and is also used for making preserves, ices, etc.

WILD, or WOOD, STRAWBERRY.

Fragaria vesca, L.

Fraisier des bois.

Native of Europe.—Perennial.—A herbaceous stoloniferous plant. Leaves composed of three folded toothed leaflets, which are hairy on the lower part; flower-stem erect, branching, hairy, a little taller than the leaves; divisions of the calyx reflexed after the flower has faded; hairs on the flower-stalks adpressed; fruit small, pendent, and roundish or conical in shape; seeds prominent, small, numbering about 2500 to the gramme. This species is common in the woods of the whole northern hemisphere, and especially so in mountainous districts. It has seldom been seen in gardens since the introduction of the Red Alpine Strawberry. We must, however, mention some forms of it which have been preserved up to the present day in the neighbourhood of Paris, from an adherence to old practices in the first instance, and also because the fruit of the Wood Strawberry possesses a quite peculiar perfume and delicacy of flavour. In low-lying districts its season lasts hardly a month, but on the mountains, on account of the difference in the time of ripening at different altitudes, Wood Strawberries may be gathered from June to September.

Fontenay Early Small Strawberry (*Fraise Petite Hâtive de Fontenay*).—A variety differing very little from the Wood Strawberry. It is a very early kind, ripening seven or eight days before the Red Alpine Strawberry. Fruit small, round, and of a dark-red colour when very ripe. The plant is not a continuous bearer, and only produces fruit in spring.

Montreuil Strawberry (*Fraise de Montreuil*).—A very distinct variety, with rather narrow, very light-coloured, folded leaves, which have a quite peculiar appearance. The plant is vigorous growing and productive. Fruit of a rather elongated-conical shape, but sometimes broad and of a cock's-comb form, and dark red when well ripened, which occurs somewhat late, namely, about the end of June or early in July. This variety is very productive, but it only bears once in the year. It was raised in the neighbourhood of Montlhéry, by a horticulturist named Montreuil, in the early part of the eighteenth century.

The *Fraise Monophylle*, or *F. de Versailles*, which has only a single leaflet in each leaf, is another variety of the Wood Strawberry, raised by Duchesne, the author of the celebrated "Monographie du Fraisier."

RED ALPINE STRAWBERRY.

Fragaria alpina, Pers. ; *F. semperflorens*, Duch.

Fraisier des Alpes.

Native of the Alps.—Perennial.—A very different plant from the Wood Strawberry, and distinguished from it by the greater size of all its parts—the fruit, in particular—and especially by the property (which is peculiar to it) of producing flowers and fruit continuously all through the summer. The introduction of this Strawberry into cultivation is of no very distant date, as it was brought into France from Mont Cenis by Fougeroux de Bondaroy, in 1754; but it speedily attained a very important position in horticulture, on account of its valuable quality of producing fruit at a season when all other varieties of Strawberries have long ceased bearing. The fruit has nearly the same appearance and flavour as that of the Wood Strawberry, but is generally larger, longer, and more pointed in shape. The seed also is perceptibly larger and longer. A gramme contains only about 1500 seeds. CULTURE.—As this Strawberry reproduces itself exactly in every respect from seed, many gardeners are in the habit of raising it in this way instead of from runners, and they generally agree in the opinion that plants raised from seed are more vigorous growing and more productive than the others. In order to ensure a very prolonged and very abundant supply late in autumn, it is a good plan to rest the plants which are intended to bear at that time, by not allow-

Red Alpine Strawberry (natural size).

ing them to flower in spring, or at least by discontinuing to gather the fruit at an early period, and by cutting off the flowering stems and the runners, but continuing to water the plants all the time. Alpine Strawberries, when properly taken care of, ought to yield almost as abundantly in September as in spring. The greatest difficulty in their culture is to make them fruit plentifully in July and August.

White Alpine Strawberry (*Fraisier des Alpes à Fruit Blanc*).—There are numerous varieties of Alpine Strawberries. One of the oldest known is the White-fruited kind, which differs from the ordinary kind in the colour of the fruit, which is also not quite so acid. The plant is an equally continuous bearer.

Janus Alpine Strawberry (*Fraisier Janus Amélioré*).—A very fine variety of the Alpine Strawberry, characterized by the fruit being conical, large, and well-shaped, and becoming almost blackish when perfectly ripe. It is very productive, a very continuous bearer, and highly worthy of recommendation in every respect. The variety comes very true from seed.

Improved Red Alpine Strawberry (*Fraise Améliorée Duru*).— Another improved variety of Alpine Strawberry has been pretty much grown for some years past under the name of *Fraise des Quatre Saisons Améliorée Duru.* This is distinguished from the other varieties by the peculiar shape of the fruit, which is very long and slender; it is lighter in colour than the Janus Strawberry. The size of the fruit of the Alpine Strawberry might be much increased by a careful selection of seed-plants,

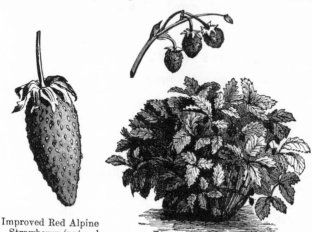

Improved Red Alpine Strawberry (natural size).

Bush Alpine Strawberry (¼ natural size).

but it must not be lost sight of that every increase in the size of the fruit is usually gained at the expense of their number or the continuous production which is the real and greatest recommendation of the Alpine Strawberry.

Meudonnaise Perpetual Strawberry (*Fraise La Meudonnaise*).— This variety, which formerly was rather commonly grown in the neighbourhood of Paris, but at present is somewhat neglected, is distinguished at first sight from all others by its rather light-coloured leaves, which exhibit the peculiarity of being, so to say, crimped or puffed in the middle, instead of being flat or folded in two, like those of most other varieties of the Alpine Strawberry. The fruit is large, conical, and very dark-coloured when quite ripe. It ripens rather late.

Bush Alpine Strawberry (*Fraisier des Alpes Sans Filets*).—This very distinct variety has the advantage of growing without producing any runners, which often render it troublesome to keep Strawberry beds in order, and, on this account, it is peculiarly adapted for planting as edgings. There is one form of it with red, and another with white fruit. Both are hardy, productive, continuous bearers, and reproduce themselves from seed with hardly any variation. They may also be multiplied by division of the tufts.

SHORT-RUNNERED WILD STRAWBERRY.

Fragaria collina, Ehr.

Fraisier étoilé.

Native of France.—Perennial.—This species, at first sight, resembles both the Common Wild, or Wood, Strawberry and the Alpine
Strawberry in its habit of growth, but is distinguished from the former
by having the runners simple or not composed of successive joints, and
from the latter by not fruiting continuously. Its fruit is rounder and
much more obtuse at the end than that of the Wood Strawberry; it is
also somewhat larger, and often narrowed into a sort of neck close to
the calyx; in colour it is much duller and less shining than the fruit
of other Strawberries, except the Hautbois, like which it often has the
shaded side of the fruit hardly coloured at all. The flesh is rather
firm, buttery, very solid, and with a very peculiar musky flavour.
The seed is comparatively large, a gramme containing not more than
about 1100 seeds. They are far apart on the surface of the fruit, in
which they are rather deeply sunk. In short, this species very much
resembles the Wood Strawberry, except in the fruit, which is more like
that of the Hautbois than any other kind.

According to the latest investigations of M. J. Gay, the *Fraisier de
Bargemont* (*F. Majaufea,* Duch.) is only a form of *Fragaria collina.*
These two Strawberries, which formerly were now and then met with
in gardens, are at present only to be found in botanical collections.

HAUTBOIS STRAWBERRY.

Fragaria elatior, Ehr.

Fraisier capron.

Native of Europe.—Perennial.—A stoloniferous plant, with folded
leaves, of a dull dark-green colour, and somewhat hairy. Flowers most
usually dioecious through abortion; fruit of a very deep violet red;
seed black, deeply sunk, and numbering about 1200 to the gramme.
In some plants, the pistils only are developed, and in others the
stamens, so that fructification will not occur with certainty unless both
forms of the plant grow within a short distance from each other.
CULTURE.—The Hautbois, like most Strawberries, is almost always
propagated from runners, which it produces in abundance. All the
cultivated varieties of this Strawberry, being derived from a plant
which grows wild in France, are perfectly hardy and easily grown;
nevertheless, since the appearance of the large or Pine-apple Strawberries which have now become so common, the Hautbois Strawberries
have lost much of the favour which they formerly enjoyed. The
peculiar and exceedingly strong flavour of their fruit is disagreeable to
many persons, and they have not the advantage of producing a second
crop in autumn, like the Alpine Strawberry. Any good well-drained
soil suits them, and the plants may be left growing in the same place

for several years, but it is necessary to plant male and female plants together in order to ensure complete fructification.

Common Hautbois, or Musky, Strawberry (*Fraise Capron Framboisé*).—This variety exhibits all the characteristics which we have

described as belonging to the species from which it is derived, with a vigorous habit of growth and abundant foliage. The fruit are very numerous, nearly spherical, slightly shortened at the point, elongated at the neck, and without seeds on the part next the calyx. They do not ripen until about the end of June, and are then of a violet or wine-red colour. The flesh is very solid, juicy, buttery, and melting, white or faintly yellow, or, sometimes, somewhat greenish, and with a very strong flavour, which is something like that of Raspberries, or rather of Black Currants. The leaf-stalks are very hairy, especially when young.

Common Hautbois, or Musky, Strawberry (natural size).

Belle Bordelaise Strawberry.—A plant of smaller size than the preceding kind, but more thick-set and compact in growth. Leaves of a light, almost grayish green; leaflets elongated oval, with well-marked veins and sharp, deeply cut teeth; flower-stems erect, well raised above the leaves; flowers largish, pure white, with very round petals; fruit rather elongated, often conical, considerably larger than that of the Common Hautbois Strawberry, and ripening about the middle of June.

SCARLET STRAWBERRY.

Fragaria Virginiana, Ehr.

Native of North America.—Perennial.—A stoloniferous plant. Leaves long, not folded, and almost perfectly smooth, as are also the leaf-stalks; fruit numerous, small, roundish, with very slender stalks; seed deeply sunk, rather small, brown, and numbering about 1500 to the gramme. This Strawberry is very easily grown, and is early, hardy, and very durable, but the fruit, unfortunately, is very small. It is nearly spherical in shape, narrowed near the neck (where there are no seeds), and of a rather bright scarlet colour even when ripe. The plant is not a continuous bearer, and this, together with the small size of the fruit, has caused it to be set aside, like many other kinds, in favour of the large-sized and the continuous-bearing Strawberries.

Old Scarlet, or Scarlet Virginia, Strawberry (*Fraisier Écarlate de Virginie*).—This variety represents the botanical type of the species scarcely modified by cultivation, and exhibits no characteristic in addition to those which we have just described as belonging to the species. Pure seedling varieties, raised from *Fragaria Virginiana*, have almost disappeared from cultivation, but there are several others grown which have been obtained by crossing the species with the Pine-apple Strawberry (*Fraisier Ananas*), and these retain all the characteristics of the Scarlet Strawberry.

CHILI STRAWBERRY.

Fragaria chilensis, Duch.

Fraisier du Chili.

Native of Chili.—Perennial.—A stoloniferous plant, of thick-set habit of growth, and very hairy on all its parts. Flowers diœcious by abortion, very broad, yellowish white at first and changing to pure white; leaf-stalks short and thick, tinged with red; leaflets nearly round, with very large and very blunt teeth; fruit large, usually irregular in shape, orange-coloured, and more or less hairy even on the skin; seed black, prominent, comparatively large, numbering from 800 to 900 to the gramme. The fruit ripens late. Even in the wild state in Chili, this Strawberry exhibits rather diversified forms. Sometimes the fruit is white, bearing black seeds, and sometimes it is salmon-coloured or pale orange. The flowers are sometimes pure white, and sometimes sulphur yellow, changing to white when the flower is well opened. The Chili Strawberry is not perfectly hardy in all parts of France. It succeeds very well in seaside districts, especially in Brittany, where it is grown on a large scale at Plougastel, in the neighbourhood of Brest. At Paris it rather suffers in severe or damp winters, and there it is grown more as a curiosity than anything else. Like other Strawberries, it is propagated from runners. It was introduced from Chili in 1714, by Frézier.

True Chili Strawberry (*Fraisier du Chili Vrai*).—A very hairy plant, with large orange-coloured fruit, ripening rather late in the season, with a peculiar, somewhat insipid flavour, not very highly perfumed. Seed black, prominent, retaining the persistent pistils. This Strawberry, as already mentioned, is not very hardy about Paris, and only grows well in the vicinity of the sea.

PINE-APPLE STRAWBERRY.

Fragaria grandiflora, Ehr.

Fraisier Ananas.

The origin of this large-fruited form of Strawberry is very obscure. At the time of its introduction into cultivation, about the middle of the last century, it was not exactly known how it originated. Moreover, two kinds of Strawberry have borne this name—one, described by Poiteau, which is not the true Pine-apple Strawberry; the other, which is much more extensively grown, especially in England and Holland, appears to have produced, either by variation or perhaps from crossing, most of the large-fruited kinds known as "English" Strawberries. It is very possible that the Pine-apple Strawberry itself is the offspring of a cross between the Chili Strawberry and some other botanical species. The typical plant, as preserved in some collections, is of a vigorous and rather thick-set habit of growth. The leaves are tolerably like those of the Scarlet Virginia Strawberry; the flower-stems are stout, not very tall, and somewhat hairy, and the flowers are very large ; the fruit is round or slightly heart-shaped, and of a pale-pink colour, with a faint yellowish or salmon-coloured tint; the flesh is very white and often hollow at the centre ; the seed is brown, medium-sized, and not very deeply sunk. A gramme contains about 1100 seeds.

From the seed of this Strawberry thousands of distinct varieties have been raised, and of these we shall now describe the best and most noteworthy.

Hybrid Strawberries.

French, Fraises hybrides. *German,* Grossfrüchtige Erdbeeren. *Spanish,* Fresones.

The varieties which are comprised under the name of Hybrid or Large-fruited Strawberries are far from presenting an identity of character, so that we shall not endeavour to give any general description of plants which exhibit so many points of difference from one another. To give some idea of the diversity which exists amongst them, we may observe that the colour of the fruit varies from white to blackish red, while the weight ranges from less than a quarter to over three ounces. The flavour also of the fruit, the size of the seed and the depth to which it is sunk in the surface of the Strawberry, the size of the flowers, the time of ripening, and the number of runners produced exhibit equally strongly marked differences.

CULTURE.—The Hybrid Strawberries like well-drained, deep, substantial soil, but they readily accommodate themselves to soils of various kinds, provided they are not brought into contact with stagnant moisture, which injures them more than anything else. Any kind of garden-soil, by being moderately well dug and properly manured, can be brought to produce good Strawberries, unless the climate is excessively dry. The seed of Hybrid Strawberries is rarely sown except for the purpose of raising new varieties, and they are almost always propagated from runners—a method so prompt and easy that a better could hardly be desired. The runners are long, slender, bare, and cord-like branches, the swollen extremity of which bears a cluster of leaves, and from its under surface speedily sends out roots and attaches itself to the soil at a short distance from the parent plant. The runners of the Hybrid Strawberries do not terminate with the rooting of the first cluster of leaves, but produce four or five joints in succession, each bearing at its extremity a cluster of leaves which grows and roots itself like the first, under favourable conditions. The runners begin to appear when the plant comes into flower, and continue to increase in length all through the summer, during which time the plant will also produce fresh ones, should the first have been cut off. About August, the earliest plants of the runners will be well rooted and strong enough to be planted out, either as edgings or in beds, each containing three or four rows of plants, which should be about 20 inches apart in every direction. Before planting, the ground should have been well dug, well manured, and covered with a good litter of manure or dead leaves. The young plants will begin to bear in the following spring, and the fruit will be more abundant and finer if all runners are carefully removed. As soon as the first fruits are formed, it is advisable to place a layer of long straw, or else slates or tiles, on the ground under the young fruit, to keep them from coming into contact with the damp soil. When this is done, the fruit ripen sooner, and are always clean, even after heavy rain. A bed of Strawberry plants usually continues to bear well for two or three years. In the second year, preparations should be made to replace the plants with new ones, so as to have the beds always in full bearing. The weakest runners and those produced latest in autumn may be transplanted into a nursery-bed, in order to be planted out in spring, but these must not be expected to bear fruit until the year after they are planted out. Strawberries are sometimes forced in hot-houses, but more usually in frames or pits heated by hot-water pipes. Plants for forcing are raised in pots and placed in artificial heat from the end of October until Strawberries begin to ripen in the open air. By pinching off the first runners of plants growing in the open air beyond the first joint, and rooting each of the young plants in a flower-pot filled with good soil, plants may be obtained sufficiently well grown to be repotted in autumn and forced in the ensuing winter. The same method may be employed to forward plants which are to be planted out in the open air. The varieties of Hybrid Strawberries which are best adapted for forcing are :—*Princesse Royale, Marguerite, Vicomtesse Héricart de Thury,* and *La Constante ;* and, of English varieties, *Black Prince, Keen's Seedling,* and *British Queen.* USES.—The fruit is eaten raw, and is also made into sweetmeats and preserves.

Admiral Dundas Strawberry.—Plant rather vigorous growing; leaves dark green ; leaf-stalks long, reddish, hairy ; leaflets elongated oval, rather frequently in fours, spoon-shaped and sharply toothed; flowers broad, white, not very numerous ; flower-stems stout, branching, often leafy; fruit conical, elongated, sometimes square at the end, dark red when ripe ; flesh pinkish-white, firm, and sugary ; seeds numerous, nearly black, half-sunk in the fruit. A productive late-ripening variety. This Strawberry produces very stout, thick, hairy runners, slightly tinged with red. They are also sufficiently numerous to allow the plant to be easily and quickly propagated. Notwithstanding all its good qualities, this is rather an amateur's Strawberry than one suitable for growing on a large scale, and although it has been known for the last twenty years in the neighbourhood of Paris, it has never been generally adopted by the market gardeners there.

Admiral Dundas Strawberry (natural size).

Barnes's White Strawberry (*Bicton Pine*).—Plant of moderately vigorous and rather thick-set habit of growth ; leaves roundish, of a dark, shining-green colour, deeply and rather sharply toothed ; veins very distinctly marked; leaf-stalks long, slender, and green ; flowers numerous, comparatively small, and borne on short branching stems which are scarcely taller than the leaves; fruit roundish or conical, blunt pointed, white slightly tinged with pink ; flesh very white, some-

2 N

what flabby, sugary, juicy, and with a rather strong musky flavour; seeds half-projecting, red or brown. Fruit ripens mid-season. A very productive variety, especially notable for the white colour of the fruit. After fruiting, the plant remains remarkably compact and thick-set. It produces few runners, and these are short, stiff, and thickish, and bear the clusters of leaves closer together than the runners of most other Strawberries.

Two-coloured Strawberry (*Fraise Bicolore* [*de Jonghe*]).—Plant rather vigorous growing; leaves numerous, of a clear shining green; leaflets of a very long oval shape, and somewhat flabby; leaf-stalks long and green; flowers almost pendent; flower-stems tall, very branching, often leafy; fruit very numerous, small, nearly spherical, with a narrow well-marked neck, which is without seeds, of a very pale orange colour, and sometimes remaining perfectly white on the side not exposed to the sun; flesh yellowish white, exceedingly buttery, juicy, sugary, and perfumed. This variety is one of those which have least outside show. It is deficient in size and colour, but, on the other hand, it possesses a peculiarly delicate flavour, differing completely from that of all other Hybrid varieties; one might almost say that it is inter-mediate between the flavour of a Hybrid and a Hautbois Strawberry. It begins to fruit very early and continues bearing for a very long time.

British Queen Strawberry.—Plant of medium height, and some-what delicate; leaves oval, rather long; leaf-stalks hairy, often red-dish; leaflets oval, nearly round, with very large short teeth; flowers very broad; flower-stems stout, usually taller than the leaves; pedicels thickish and hairy; fruit very large, oblong, often flat-tened, conical or square at the end, of a vermilion-red colour which never becomes very dark; flesh white, firm, very juicy, sugary, highly per-fumed, and very fine flavoured; seeds brown, rather project-ing. This is certainly one of the best of all Strawberries as regards quality, and is especially to be recommended for stiff moist soils. It would, undoubtedly, be more extensively grown if it were hardier, and if its propagation was not rendered tedious and difficult from the circumstance of its producing very few runners, and these thin and slender ones.

British Queen Strawberry
(natural size).

Carolina Superba Strawberry
(natural size).

Carolina Superba Strawberry.—Plant rather vigorous growing, hairy on all its parts; leaves dark green, shining on the upper surface; leaflets oval, folded or twisted, often spoon-shaped; flowers medium sized, numerous; flower-stems rather stout, but scarcely taller than the leaves; fruit large, heart-shaped, shortish, and of a vermilion-red colour; flesh very white, melting, buttery, perfumed, slightly musky; seeds half-projecting. A very good and rather productive, but somewhat tender variety. Fruit ripens mid-season. Although coming near the British Queen Strawberry in other respects, this variety differs from it in producing stout, thick, hairy runners. These are not very numerous, and we have sometimes seen them flower in the same year, but such an occurrence is exceptional.

Doctor Hogg Strawberry.—Plant very much like the British Queen in habit of growth, but somewhat more compact and with rounder leaflets. The fruit also is larger, heart-shaped, and of a fine scarlet-red colour, with yellow or brown half-projecting seeds; flesh very solid, firm, pinkish white, juicy, and buttery, with a delicate perfume, sometimes musky. Ripens mid-season.

Docteur Morère Strawberry.—A very vigorous-growing variety. Leaf-stalks and flower-stems rather hairy; leaves large, broad, and of a very dark-green colour; leaflets broad, almost always folded on the midrib, slightly puckered and twisted, and with very large, rather deep

Docteur Morère Strawberry (natural size). Docteur Nicaise Strawberry (natural size).

and sharp teeth; flowers large, rather numerous; calyx very large; flower-stems stout, erect, often leafy; fruit very large, shortish, of a very deep-red colour when ripe, and rapidly diminishing in size from those first produced to the last; flesh pink, melting, sugary, juicy, and rather perfumed, but often hollow at the centre; seeds black and rather projecting. The flavour of the fruit somewhat resembles that of the Chili Strawberry. This variety, which was raised not long since, is already grown on a large scale in the neighbourhood of Paris for market supply.

Docteur Nicaise Strawberry.—Plant rather dwarf and of medium vigour and productiveness; leaves not very hairy; leaflets of a lively shining green, longer than broad, and rather sharply but not very deeply toothed; flowers large; flower-stems very short, branching, almost creeping; fruit very large, usually of cock's-comb shape, and weighing from an ounce and a half to an ounce and three-quarters; flesh pale red, softish; seed half-sunk in the fruit, which ripens half-late, and is more remarkable for its size than its quality. This variety was raised by Dr. Nicaise, of Châlons-sur-Marne. He was a persevering raiser, and we are indebted to him for having brought out a great number of new varieties of Strawberries. Several of these have been set aside, such as *Alexandra, Amazone, Gabrielle, Melius, Passe-partout, Pauline,* and *Perfection;* but others will hold their ground, and especially the present variety, which is distinguished for the enormous size of the fruit—all the more remarkable because it is produced by a small and apparently not very vigorous plant. The Châlonnaise, which is not inferior in delicacy of flavour or in perfume to any other Hybrid Strawberry, will also be preserved in collections (see p. 551).

Duke of Edinburgh Strawberry.—Plant of rather vigorous growth; leaves erect; leaf-stalks hairy; leaflets oval, toothed, and of a bright, glistening green colour; flower-stems taller than the leaves; fruit conical or heart-shaped, and of a very bright scarlet colour; seeds half-projecting; flesh pale red, slightly acid, rather sugary, and agreeably perfumed. The chief merit of this variety is the handsome appearance of the fruit, which is symmetrical in shape, and grows to a considerable size without becoming irregular in form. It is a half-late and rather productive kind.

Duc de Malakoff Strawberry.—Plant exceedingly vigorous grow-

ing, with large broad leaves of a deep, almost blackish, green colour; leaflets oval rounded, with very large short teeth; leaf-stalks, flower-stems, and runners very hairy, and often tinged with red; flowers large, pure white; flower-stems stout but shortish; fruit large and short, and of a peculiar brownish tint when ripe; flesh yellow,

Eleanor Strawberry (natural size).   Duc de Malakoff Strawberry (natural size).

something like the colour of the flesh of an apricot, juicy, melting, and with somewhat of the flavour of the Chili Strawberry. This is a very productive and very hardy variety, and ripens mid-season.

Eleanor Strawberry.—Plant rather vigorous growing; leaf-stalks hairy; leaflets medium sized, usually spoon-shaped, almost smooth on the upper surface and silky-haired underneath, oval, with rather long sharp teeth on the upper two-thirds of the margin and without teeth towards the base; flowers very broad, pure white, with the petals far apart from one another; flower-stems stout, usually leafy, and generally longer than the leaves; fruit oblong, very handsomely shaped, and of a fine deep-red colour; flesh pale scarlet red, softish, not very juicy, but sugary and perfumed. Ripens late.

Elisa Strawberry.—Plant rather vigorous growing and productive, but somewhat fastidious as regards soil, preferring that which is stiff and clayey; leaf-stalks hairy, thick, and long; leaflets large, almost always twisted or puckered, deeply and sharply toothed, and of a dark shining-green colour; veins on the under surface hairy; flowers medium sized, numerous; flower-stems very branching and usually shorter than the leaves; fruit medium sized or small, roundish, narrowed at the base into a rather well-marked neck, and of a rather pale vermilion-red colour even when quite ripe; flesh white, or slightly yellowish, very firm, juicy, and very agreeably perfumed. This is a half-early variety. It is not very productive, but has the advantage of continuing to bear for a considerable length of time.

Elton Improved Strawberry.—Plant very vigorous growing, with numerous large erect leaves of a lively green colour, which in the older leaves changes to a very dark tint; leaf-stalks stout, hairy, tinged with red; leaflets nearly round, with very prominent veins and blunt rounded teeth; flowers large, pure white; flower-stems very stout, erect, usually leafy and taller than the radical leaves; fruit heart-shaped, bluntish, and of a deep scarlet-red colour; flesh red, sugary, juicy, and tolerably acid; seeds brown, half-projecting. Ripens late. This excellent variety was raised from seed of the old Elton Strawberry, which was distinguished for the fine deep-red colour, and the very fine, perfumed, but exceedingly acid, flavour of its fruit.

Elton Improved Strawberry (natural size).

The new variety is a very decided improvement on the old.

General Chanzy Strawberry.—Plant very vigorous growing; leaves large and tall, and of a dark-green colour; leaf-stalks covered with an abundance of long hairs; flower-stems stout, erect, taller than the leaves, or partially so; fruit generally very large and long, narrowed at both ends, sometimes hollow at the centre, and of an exceedingly dark-red colour, which becomes nearly black when the fruit is fully ripe; flesh blood red throughout, sugary, vinous, and sometimes perfumed to a surprising degree. This variety ripens rather late and continues bearing for a considerable time.

Gloire de Zuidwyck Strawberry (German, *Ruhm von Zuidwijck Erdbeere*).—Plant very vigorous growing, with very hairy leaf-stalks and flower-stems, and forming strong broad tufts of foliage; leaves medium sized, and of a slightly grayish-green colour; leaflets sometimes spoon-shaped, and with large and rather long teeth like those of the Jucunda Strawberry; flowers medium sized or nearly small; flower-stems very stout, erect, branching, very stiff, and equal to the leaves in length; fruit large, of a regular conical or sometimes cock's-comb shape, and of a deep orange or very bright scarlet colour; flesh orange coloured, melting, juicy, agreeably acidulous, sugary, and not very highly perfumed. This is an excellent, very productive, and middling early variety, well adapted for market supply. It has the advantage of being easily multiplied from its runners, which are numerous, of average vigour, and usually remain quite green even on the parts exposed to

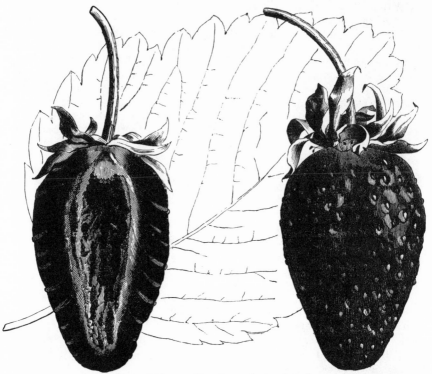

General Chanzy Strawberry (natural size).

the sun. It has also another good quality, namely, that the fruit is not very liable to be injured by damp and does not rot easily.

Gloire de Zuidwyck Straw-
berry (natural size).

Jucunda Strawberry
(natural size).

Jucunda Straw-berry.—Plant very vigorous growing and thick-set; leaf-stalks tall; leaves medium sized, of a clear-green colour, almost glazed; leaflets nearly round, with short and rather roundish teeth and well-marked veins; flowers medium sized, very numerous; flower-stems stout, erect, often leafy, always very branching, and taller than the leaves; fruit very abundant, heart-shaped, of a bright vermilion-red colour, becoming darker when over-ripe, and sometimes slightly hollow at the centre; flesh red, juicy, rather perfumed, and not very sugary; seeds yellow, very slightly sunk. Ripens half-late. The vigour and hardiness of this variety, the abundance of its fruit, their fine colour, and their capability of bearing carriage without injury, render it one of the most valuable kinds of Strawberries for market gardens near large towns. It is in full bearing when the early kinds are on the decline.

La Châlonnaise Strawberry.—Plant of medium vigour of growth, somewhat tender; leaves rather slight; leaf-stalks long and hairy; leaflets oval, broadly toothed; flowers very large, pure white; flower stems branching, often leafy, and much taller than the radical leaves; fruit ovoid, medium sized; flesh very white, firm, solid, sugary, juicy, and highly perfumed; seeds half projecting. Ripens half-late. This is certainly one of the best Strawberries in cultivation. It resembles the British Queen.

La Constante Strawberry.—Plant of compact, thick-set growth; leaves short stalked; leaflets small, nearly round, of a dark and somewhat glaucous green, with large teeth, usually few in number, but long and sharp; flowers very numerous, small, and of a somewhat greenish-

La Châlonnaise Straw-   La Constante Strawberry   La Reine Strawberry
berry (natural size).   (natural size).   (natural size).

white colour; flower-stems branching, but very short, and almost hidden by the leaves; fruit large, conical, shortish, and of a rather deep scarlet colour when fully ripe; flesh pink or pale red, delicate in flavour, juicy, perfumed, and slightly deficient in sugar; seeds black, not deeply sunk. This variety is very highly to be recommended, as being productive, a very regular cropper, and taking up but little room.

La Reine Strawberry.—Plant small and slender in all its parts; leaf-stalks short and reddish; leaflets long, narrow, dark green, with usually rounded teeth; flowers large, yellowish at first, changing to pure white; flower-stems rather branching, but slender, and mostly hidden by the leaves; fruit long and slender, carmine red, often remaining pale and pink coloured on the side not exposed to the sun; flesh white, very firm, juicy, sugary, and perfumed; seeds small, black, and projecting. This variety has, perhaps, the most delicate and best flavour of all the Hybrid Strawberries, but it is also the least productive. Its slender, red-tinted runners are too scantily produced to allow the plant to be quickly multiplied.

Louis Vilmorin Strawberry. — Plant of rather low habit and medium vigour of growth; leaflets oval rounded, of a dark, shining-green colour, with very large and rather blunt teeth; flowers broad, pure white; flower-stems very short and very much branched, the branches being often tinged with red and partially hidden by the leaves; fruit heart-shaped, very regular, numerous, and of an extremely dark-red colour when ripe; flesh dark red, not very sugary, and somewhat deficient in delicacy of flavour and perfume, but very firm, juicy, and agreeable. This is a very hardy variety, bearing abundantly and for a long time, and is particularly remarkable for the deep-red colour of the fruit. Its runners are rather scantily produced, which hinders the speedy multiplication of the plant. It and the American variety named Wilson's Albany are the best two kinds for preserving; the preserves which are made of them having more flavour and a better colour than those made of any other Strawberries, even of those which are the best for eating raw.

Lucas Strawberry. — Plant of vigorous growth, second early; leaves rather large, of a clear-green colour, shining on the upper surface;

Lucas Strawberry (natural   Louis Vilmorin Straw-   Lucie Strawberry (natural
size).   berry (natural size).   size).

leaflets slightly oval, with very large, rather long teeth, which are somewhat variable in shape, being sometimes very acute and sometimes quite round; flowers medium sized, with round petals, and very numerous; flower-stems stout but short, often hidden by the leaves; fruit large, oblong, well shaped, and of a rather dark-scarlet colour; flesh pale pink, juicy, sugary, and highly perfumed. This excellent variety is both productive and of the very highest quality.

Lucie Strawberry. — Plant large, very vigorous growing, and hairy; leaves numerous, of a very deep green, shining on the upper surface; leaflets with broad round teeth, often spoon-shaped; flowers large, yellowish at first, changing to tolerably pure white when fully opened; leaf-stalks and runners very red; fruit large, of an elongated-ovoid shape, vermilion red, slightly hairy at the end; flesh white, sugary, rather perfumed, sometimes a little hollow at the centre; seeds projecting. This is a vigorous and productive variety. It ripens its fruit very late, and has the advantage of prolonging the season of Hybrid Strawberries after all the other kinds have ceased bearing.

Marguerite Strawberry.—Plant medium sized; leaf-stalks rather short and slender; leaflets long in comparison with their breadth, of a clear-green colour, very smooth on the upper surface, and with rather large sharp teeth on the margin of the upper half only of the leaflet; flowers medium sized; flower-stems short, extremely branching, and almost trailing on the ground; fruit very large, of an elongated-conical shape, and of a vermilion-red colour, which remains rather light even when the fruit is ripe; flesh pink, very juicy, melting, slightly deficient in sugar and perfume; seeds rather deeply sunk. This variety makes amends for its slight deficiency in sugar and perfume by being very productive, extremely early, continuing to bear for a long time, and being perfectly well adapted for forcing.

May Queen Strawberry. — Plant of medium vigorous growth, leafy, very like the Scarlet Strawberries in habit; leaf-stalks nearly smooth; leaflets of a very long oval shape, sharply toothed on the

Marguerite Strawberry
(natural size).

May Queen Strawberry
(natural size).

Napoleon III. Strawberry
(natural size).

upper two-thirds of the margin, the remainder of which is not toothed; flowers medium sized or small; flower-stems very branching, short, seldom rising above the leaves; fruit medium sized or small, short, blunt-pointed, rounded, and of a scarlet-red colour; flesh pink or pale red, tartish, perfumed, and rather sugary; seeds deeply sunk. The fruit of this variety is very agreeable to the taste, especially as it ripens in the latter end of May before any other Strawberry, thus redeeming its sole defect of smallness of size by its extreme earliness.

Napoleon III. Strawberry.—Plant vigorous growing, with large, erect, dark-green, shining leaves; leaf-stalks very hairy; leaflets large, nearly round, with broad blunt teeth; flowers medium sized, very round, in crowded clusters; flower-stems stout, leafy, rising well above the foliage; fruit large, rather short, and of a vermilion-red colour;

flesh very white, melting, buttery, well perfumed in warm seasons, sometimes a little hollow at the centre; seeds black, projecting. A hardy and productive variety, but ripening late, and liable to suffer much in dry seasons.

Premier Strawberry. — Plant rather vigorous growing, not very hairy; leaves medium sized and not very numerous; leaflets rather elongated, of a clear-green colour, with large and rather deeply cut teeth; flowers broad; flower-stems divided into long slender branches, and about the same height as the foliage; fruit of a short conical shape, often pointed, sometimes of cock's-comb shape, and of a fine bright-red colour; flesh pink or pale red, very juicy, sugary, very delicate in flavour, and very agreeably perfumed. A hardy, productive, and second-early variety. After fruiting, the plant assumes a quite peculiar stiff and firm appearance, as if the leaves were borne on stems of iron. Its runners are remarkably thick, stiff, and rather hairy.

Princesse Royale Strawberry.—One of the oldest varieties raised in France. Plant of medium height, but very vigorous growing and robust; leaves smooth, shining, and of a clear-green colour; leaflets elongated oval, with rather sharp teeth, which, as in the leaflets of the Marguerite Strawberry, only commence at some considerable distance

| Premier Strawberry (natural size). | Princesse Royale Strawberry (natural size). | Sabreur Strawberry (natural size). |

from the base of the leaflet; flowers very small, but very numerous; flower-stems stout, very branching, some of them taller than the leaves; fruit very numerous, conical, generally well shaped, and of a fine red colour; flesh perfumed, rather sugary and juicy, but somewhat hard in the centre. A very hardy, productive, and early variety. The fruit bears carriage well, and this good quality, added to all the others which it possesses, accounts for the tenacity with which the Parisian market gardeners have adhered to its culture, notwithstanding the introduction of new kinds which are superior to it in some respects. In the Central Market at Paris, the fruit of this Strawberry always command a higher price than those of any other varieties, except, perhaps, some choice kinds. They are especially esteemed for their fine colour and perfume.

Sabreur Strawberry.—A very distinct variety, easily known from all others by the violet colour of its runners and leaf-stalks. Leaflets

very long, with very large and deeply cut teeth, and of a rather dark
and slightly glaucous-green colour. The divisions of the calyx are
deeply coloured, like the leaf-stalks. The flowers have this peculiarity,
viz. that the petals, when about to fall, change to a very decided reddish
tint. Fruit ovoid, almost always regularly shaped, large, often very
large, and of a crimson colour more or less deep according to the temperature of the season ; flesh white, sugary, juicy, and rather perfumed ;
seeds very black and very prominent, giving the fruit a quite peculiar
appearance. This variety is certainly one of the best that has been
raised of late years. It does not produce fruit of the first quality, but
it is early, hardy, highly productive, and continues bearing for a long
time, being one of the earliest when it commences to yield and found
still fruiting amongst the latest kinds. The runners, which, as we have
remarked, are very deeply coloured, are very abundantly produced, and
the variety is, consequently, one of the easiest to multiply.

Sir Charles Napier (Smith).—Plant somewhat weak and delicate
in appearance, but, nevertheless, hardy and productive ; leaves pale
green ; leaf-stalks very hairy and rather slender; flower-stems short
and very much branched, bearing a large quantity of fruit, which is of
a short conical shape and deep-red colour, and covered with small,
projecting seeds; flesh pale pink, solid, juicy, and sugary. This variety
is one of the most productive and most suitable for field culture,
notwithstanding its delicate appearance. It ripens mid-season.

Sir Joseph Paxton Strawberry. — Plant of medium vigorous
growth ; runners slightly hairy ; leaf-stalks and
flower-stems somewhat more so ; leaves moderately numerous, and of a dark shining-green
colour; leaflets large, oval,
often puckered or twisted,
and with large and rather
deeply cut teeth ; flowers
broad, numerous, pure
white; flower-stems mode-
rately stout, and not always
taller than the leaves ;
fruit conical or heart-
shaped, well formed, and
of a rather dark scarlet
colour. This is one of the
best and most handsome
of all Strawberries, and is
very productive. Ripens
mid-season. In England
this variety is more largely

Sir Joseph Paxton Straw-
berry (natural size).

Souvenir de Kieff Strawberry
(natural size).

cultivated than any other by market growers. It is valued for its fine
colour, large size, and firm flesh, which enables it to bear carriage well.

Souvenir de Kieff Strawberry.—Plant of medium height, not very
leafy ; leaflets of a clear-green colour, nearly round or slightly oval,
with short roundish teeth ; flowers medium sized, with almost round
petals of very thin texture, soon becoming nearly transparent ; flower-
stems stout, branching, not taller than the leaves ; fruit of a long

conical shape, usually pointed, and of a fine scarlet colour; flesh pinkish white, very melting, perfumed, juicy, and sugary; seeds half-sunk. Ripens half-late. The fruit of this variety is of quite superior quality, and the plant is a very fair cropper, but rather tedious to propagate, as its runners are very scantily produced.

Vicomtesse Héricart de Thury Strawberry.—Plant vigorous growing, not very tall, but leafy, erect, and of a dark-green colour, indicating a robust constitution; leaflets oval, often narrowed at the base, which is without teeth, the rest of the margin bearing rather deep, large, and usually rounded teeth; flowers medium sized or small; flower-stems stout, very branching, and generally taller than the leaves; fruit conical or heart-shaped, and of a very dark-red colour; flesh red, very firm, sugary, juicy, sub-acid, and well perfumed; seeds half-projecting. The fruit of this variety bears carriage well. It ripens early, and is produced very abundantly and for a long time. It is, consequently, grown on a large scale for market supply, not only in France but also

Vicomtesse Héricart de Thury Strawberry (natural size).

Victoria Strawberry (natural size).

Wonderful, or Myatt's Prolific, Strawberry (natural size).

in England, and is a very suitable kind for forcing. The plant is one of those varieties from which, under proper treatment, a second crop may be most readily obtained in autumn.

Victoria Strawberry.—Plant of strong and vigorous growth, forming broad dense tufts; leaflets very broad, nearly round, with very large and very blunt teeth, and of a rather dark, shining-green colour; flowers numerous, medium sized; flower-stems long, stout, very branching, and rising well above the leaves; fruit large, very short, roundish, or slightly heart-shaped, of a palish vermilion-red colour, and with a very delicate skin; flesh pink, exceedingly juicy and melting, and tolerably sugary and perfumed; seeds very deeply sunk. The fruit of this variety bears carriage badly, and does not keep well, which detracts from its value as a market Strawberry; nevertheless, it is pretty largely grown for the Central Market at Paris, on account of its earliness and its very great and long-continued productiveness. It is a variety especially suitable for private kitchen gardens.

Wonderful, or Myatt's Prolific, Strawberry.—Plant vigorous growing and of medium height; leaves numerous; leaf-stalks slender, rather hairy; leaflets medium sized, nearly round, and of a clear, slightly grayish-green colour; flowers medium sized, very numerous; flower-stems very stout and very branching, not always rising clearly above the leaves; fruit long, usually flattened, almost always square at the end, and of a very dark crimson colour; flesh white, very firm, juicy, very sugary, and highly perfumed; seeds black, small, projecting, and very numerous. A mid-season and very productive variety, continuing to bear for a long time, and one of those which, in the highest degree, unite great productiveness with good quality; but, owing to the rather dark colour of the fruit, it is not much in request in the markets.

Like all other fruit-bearing plants, the Strawberry has been the parent of so many varieties that it would be almost impossible to enumerate them all. There would also be no great advantage in our attempting to give a complete list of them here, as there are special works on this subject which treat of it far more fully than we could possibly do. We shall, therefore, in addition to the kinds already described, only mention some American varieties which are not yet very well known in Europe, and which bear a high reputation in the United States. A rather considerable number of varieties have been raised in that country by various hands, and of these the following appear to be the most worthy of note:—

Wilson's Albany.—Plant vigorous growing; fruit medium sized, heart-shaped, of a bright-red colour, with a rather strong, acidulous flavour, and ripening in mid-season; flesh of a deep-red colour. It is good when eaten raw, but of quite remarkable quality when made into a preserve.

Crescent Seedling.—A good, productive variety. Fruit large, conical, squarish at the end, and of a bright-red colour; flesh firm and acid.

Monarch of the West.—Plant vigorous growing; leaves bright green; fruit large, heart-shaped, rather short; flesh very white, buttery; seeds brown, projecting. A productive, half-early variety.

Sharpless' No. 1.—Plant very vigorous growing; fruit large, often of cock's-comb shape, and of a dark-red colour; flesh red. A productive and early variety.

Sharpless' Seedling.—A half-late and rather hardy variety. Fruit blunt pointed, heart-shaped, often cock's-comb-shaped, and of a rather pale but lively red colour; flesh pink, juicy, and acidulous.

On account of the special purposes for which they are employed, we shall add the following few French and English varieties:—

Belle de Paris.—A very hardy and very productive variety. Fruit conical, large, bright red, ripening somewhat late; flesh white or red, sugary, and rather firm.

Black Prince.—Fruit small, round, becoming almost black when ripe. This is one of the earliest of all the Hybrid Strawberries.

Comte de Paris.—An old French variety with handsome heart-shaped fruit of a dark-red colour. Flesh red. A very productive kind, and well adapted for field culture.

Keen's Seedling.—A very good old variety. Fruit medium sized and of excellent quality. It is one of the best of all kinds for forcing.

La Grosse Sucrée.—Plant of thick-set growth, hardy, and vigorous, bearing rather abundantly and half-late ; fruit large, of an elongated heart-shape, and of a bright shining-red colour; flesh pinkish white, very melting, abundantly juicy, and very sugary.

Sir Harry.—A very fine variety, and really very rare, although many persons think they have it. Fruit large, heart-shaped, and of a bright-red colour ; flesh solid, juicy, sugary, and of a pale-pink colour. Ripens half-late. This variety does not continue bearing long, and produces but few runners.

STRAWBERRY BLITE.

Blitum virgatum, L., *and B. capitatum,* L. *Chenopodiaceæ.*

Epinard-fraise.

Natives of South Europe.—Annual.—Stems about 20 inches high, branching, and bearing triangular slightly toothed leaves, from the axils of which in the upper part of the stem are produced numerous clusters of flowers, succeeded by bundles of seeds surrounded by a fleshy pulp of a bright-red colour, and bearing a tolerable resemblance to small Strawberries ; seed very small, numbering about 5000 to the gramme, and weighing 800 grammes to the litre. These two plants, which very much resemble each other, and are known by the common name of Strawberry Blite, are distinguished from each other by the flower-spikes of *B. virgatum* being leafy, while those of *B. capitatum* are not so. The pulp which envelops the seeds may be eaten, although it is rather insipid. The plants are sometimes cultivated, but more as a curiosity than for table use.

SWEET CICELY.

Myrrhis odorata, Scop. *Umbelliferæ.*

French, Cerfeuil musqué. *German,* Grosser spanischer wohlriechender Kerbel. *Flemish,* Spaansche kervel. *Danish,* Spansk kjorvel. *Italian,* Finocchiella.

Native of Europe.—Perennial.—Leaves very large, winged, downy ; leaflets pinnatifid, lanceolate, or incised, and of a very pale grayish-green colour ; leaf-stalks and veins hairy, as are also the stems, which grow from 2 to over 3 ft. high ; flowers small, white, in broad umbels ; seed large, enveloped in a brown or blackish membrane, shining and folded into five prominent ridges. A gramme contains only about 40 seeds, and a litre of them weighs about 250 grammes. Their germinating power lasts for but a very short time. Culture.—It is advisable to sow the seed as soon as it is ripe, as it does not keep very well. When sown in autumn, it germinates in the ensuing spring, but if sown in spring, it usually does not germinate until the following year. When the seedlings have made four or five leaves they may be planted out from 20 inches to 2 ft. apart every way in a corner of the garden, where they will continue to grow for many years without requiring any attention except the occasional use of the hoe. It is easily increased by division. USES.—The leaves are sometimes used for flavouring; they have a sweetish taste, and a strong odour of Aniseed. The plant is not much cultivated, but it is interesting and graceful, and will grow in any corner or on a hedgebank.

TANSY.

Tanacetum vulgare, L.   *Compositæ.*

French, Tanaisie.   *German*, Gemeiner Rainfarn.   *Danish*, Reinfang.   *Italian*, Atanasia.
Spanish, Tanaceto.

Native of Europe.—Perennial.—A plant forming a clump of very permanent growth. Stems annual, erect, roundish, usually simple, and about 3 ft. high; leaves oval oblong in outline, but very much divided and very deeply cut into narrow segments, which are also divided into exceedingly slender toothed lobes; flower-heads small, numerous, in com-pound, terminal, and rather crowded corymbs; florets deep yellow; seed small, elongated, almost conical, bearing five prominent gray-ish ribs. A gramme contains about 7000 seeds, and a litre of them weighs about 300 grammes. Their germinating power lasts for two years. Two varieties of this plant are in cultivation, namely, the Common Tansy, which is the same as the wild plant, and a curled-leaved variety, the leaves of which, in addition to the ordinary use, may also be employed for garnishing, like those of the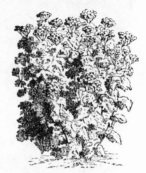

Tansy ($\frac{1}{25}$ natural size).

Curled Mallow. CULTURE.—The Tansy, like the Wormwood, demands no cultural care, and a plant or two of it growing in a corner of the garden is usually sufficient for all requirements. It is generally mul-tiplied by division in spring or autumn. By cutting off the flower-heads as they appear, the production of leaves is prolonged in the latter end of summer and in autumn. USES.—The leaves are used for season-ing, etc.

TARRAGON.

Artemisia Dracunculus, L.   *Compositæ.*

French, Estragon.   *German*, Dragon.   *Flemish* and *Dutch*, Dragonkruid.   *Danish*,
Estragon.   *Italian*, Dragoncello.   *Spanish*, Estragon.   *Portuguese*, Estragao.

Native of Siberia.—Perennial.—A plant with numerous branching stems, bearing lanceolate entire leaves, which, like all the green parts of the plant, possess a very delicate, aromatic flavour, on account of which they are very extensively used for seasoning. The flowers are whitish, very small and insignificant, and always barren, so that the plant must be propagated by division of the tufts or from root-cuttings.

If some old horticultural books are to be credited, the plant formerly produced fertile seeds, and if such was really the case, it might be hoped that some day or other such seed may again be regularly obtained from it; but it is certain that at present it does not usually produce any, and that the seed which is offered for sale from time to time only produces plants which resemble the Tarragon in all its botanical

characteristics, but which are entirely destitute of flavour. The Tarragon plant flowers frequently, and the flowers appear to be well formed. It would not be impossible, then, that some fertile seeds might be accidentally produced, and if these were carefully gathered and sown, a regularly seeding variety might be raised. As matters stand at present, however, if from any cause there should be a difficulty in multiplying Tarragon plants by division, an excellent substitute may be obtained by growing *Tagetes lucida,* a Composite plant, which, although belonging to a quite different genus, possesses in its green parts almost exactly the same flavour as the true Tarragon.

Tarragon (⅕ natural size; detached leaf, natural size).

CULTURE.—Being a perennial, the Tarragon requires no particular attention. It is advisable, however, in severe winters without snow, to cut down the stems and cover the necks of the plants with a litter of manure or withered leaves, as, although originally a native of Siberia, the cultivated Tarragon plant is somewhat liable to suffer in very frosty weather.

COMMON, FRENCH, or NARROW-LEAVED THYME.

Thymus vulgaris, L. *Labiatæ.*

French, Thym ordinaire. *German,* Französischer Thymian. *Flemish,* Thijmus. *Dutch,* Tijm. *Danish,* Thimian. *Italian,* Timo. *Spanish,* Tomillo. *Portuguese,* Tomilho.

Native of South Europe.—Perennial.—A very small under-shrub with slender, stiff, branching, woody stems, bearing small triangular leaves, which are of a more or less deep-green colour on the upper surface and gray underneath. Flowers small, labiate, pinkish lilac, in round or ovoid terminal clusters, which become elongated after flowering; seed small, round, of a reddish or dark-brown colour, numbering about 6000 to the gramme, and weighing about 680 grammes to the litre. Their germinating power lasts for three years.

CULTURE.—Thyme is usually planted as an edging in well-drained soil in a warm position. It may be propagated by division or cuttings,

but is generally raised from seed, which yields vigorous plants. The
seed is sown in April, either where the plants are to stand or in a seed-
bed, from which the young plants are planted out in June or July,
about 4 inches apart. It is advisable to re-make Thyme edgings every
three or four years.

Uses.—The leaves and young shoots are very often used for
seasoning.

Two varieties of this plant are cultivated, namely, the Narrow-leaved (*Thym
du Midi*), which has small grayish leaves
and a very aromatic flavour; and the
Broad-leaved Winter, or German, Thyme
(*Thym d'Hiver;* German, *Deutscher-* oder
Winter-Thymian), a somewhat taller and
stronger plant, with larger leaves, the
flavour of which is a little more bitter than
that of the other variety. The seed also
of the Broad-leaved kind is one-third larger.

Besides these, the Lemon Thyme (*Thymus
citriodorus*, Pers.), a small under-shrub with
trailing branches, the native country of
which is unknown, is sometimes cultivated.
Its flavour is very delicate and agreeable.

Common, French, or Narrow-
leaved Thyme (⅓ natural size;
detached sprig, ½ natural size).

Sometimes, also, especially in country places, the Wild Thyme, or
Mother-of-Thyme (*Thymus Serpyllum*, L.), is used for seasoning. This
is a native perennial plant, with a very slender creeping stem, bearing small oval-rounded leaves and erect terminal clusters of pink or
violet-coloured flowers.

TOMATO, or LOVE-APPLE.

Lycopersicum esculentum, Dun.; *Solanum Lycopersicum*, L.   *Solanaceæ.*

French, Tomate. *German*, Tomate. *Flemish* and *Dutch*, Tomaat. *Italian*, Pomo d'oro.
Spanish and *Portuguese*, Tomate.

Native of South America.—Annual.—The Tomato is a branching
plant with a flexible stem, requiring artificial support to enable it to
grow erect. The stem is thick, often woody, swollen, especially at the
joints, and covered with a green skin which is rough to the touch.
The leaves are pinnate, with oval-acuminate leaflets, which are slightly
toothed on the margin, grayish on the under surface, and often spoon-
shaped or even with the edges rolled upwards. Flowers yellowish, in
axillary corymbs; fruit large fleshy berries variable in shape and
colour; seed white, kidney-shaped, very much flattened, and shagreened
or rough on both sides. A gramme contains from 300 to 400 seeds,
and a litre of them weighs about 300 grammes. Their germinating
power lasts for four years.

Culture.—It is only in the south of Europe that the Tomato can
be perfectly well grown without the aid of artificial heat. In the
climate of Paris, the seed, for an ordinary or main crop, is generally
sown in a hot-bed, about the latter end of March. The seedlings are

2 o

pricked out into another hot-bed three weeks or a month afterwards, and are finally planted out about the end of May, from 20 to 32 inches apart, according to the variety. As soon as the plants have grown from 16 to 20 inches high, each of them should be supported either with a single stake, or with a series of stakes fastened together and forming a kind of trellis, upon which the branches of the plant are tied. The latest varieties would be all the better for being planted at the foot of a wall or other shelter with a warm aspect. In these varieties, too, it is advisable to limit the production of the fruit to a certain number, by pinching off all the late flowers. It is also a good plan, sometimes, to pinch some of the shoots ; but that should be done with discretion, so as not to leave the plant too bare of leaves. Under this mode of culture, the earliest varieties will commence to yield fruit in the course of August, and to produce them all through the autumn. When frosty weather approaches, any fruit that are full-grown but not yet coloured may be cut off, branches and all, and stored in a dry room, where they will duly ripen. Ripe Tomatoes may be obtained as early as the latter end of April by means of forcing. In this case the plants are grown entirely in hot-beds. The first sowings are made in September, but more usually in January. The seedlings are pricked out, and also permanently planted out in hot-beds, always under the same conditions, four plants to each light. As the plants require a good deal of heat, the beds should be surrounded with linings of manure, which can be renewed at pleasure. Plants thus formed are usually not allowed to bear more than two branches, which are attached horizontally to a wire or a strong cord running from one end of the bed to the other, and as near the glass as possible. Until the fruit is formed and commencing to ripen, other plants are usually grown in the hot-beds along with the Tomatoes, thus utilizing the heat and also the space which is not yet filled up by the principal crop.

In Great Britain of late years the culture of Tomatoes has spread very much, though far from, as yet, being able to meet the demand for the fruit. The climate is one of the worst possible for Tomatoes, yet, notwithstanding, our gardening resources and skill are such that much excellent fruit is grown. To raise it, however, is not so simple as in America, where over a vast range of the continent the Tomato is one of the most easily grown field crops. Some general idea of the most successful methods pursued in British gardens is therefore desirable here. Those situated in the southern counties of England and Ireland have a considerable advantage in Tomato culture over those in the north. Mr. Hobday, growing them in a by no means favourable district, may be

taken as a trustworthy guide for private garden practice, which, however, varies much and is improved year by year.

"Sow the seeds in February or early in March in pots or pans ; cover lightly with sand or sandy soil, and place in a hot-bed near the glass. When the young plants appear, move them to a warm house, where they will be near the glass, to get hardened by light and exposure. Pot off either singly or two in a pot, standing at opposite sides of the pot, so that when the time comes to plant out the ball may be divided through the middle, each plant taking its share ; and but little check need be given. After the plants are potted off they may either be taken back to the hot-bed for a few days, or be kept in a warm, close house till the roots begin work again, when they should be moved to a light place, in order to give strength. Plants that are well cared for in their youth begin to blossom and bear fruit weeks before those which are dragged up in vineries or in situations away from the full light, and in our short, often sunless, summers this is a very important matter. If necessary, the plants should be shifted on into larger pots, though a very little check when they have made some progress will do them no harm. It will simply have a hardening effect upon them. As soon as the weather is settled in May, or say about the third week, plant out. In the south of England Tomatoes will succeed in any warm position, but they cannot have too much heat in our climate, and though we may plant in any warm situation, even away from a wall, it must not be forgotten that the warmest positions at the foot of a south wall are the best.

"That mode of training is the best which insures early ripening rather than heavy crops that will not ripen, and this early ripening can be best attained by confining the growth to one or two main stems, and these main stems should have been started when the plants were young, by pinching out the leader. A two-stemmed plant will require 2 feet of space or a little more; a plant having only one stem will not require more than 15 inches. As soon as planted, and the soil settled round them by watering, a tie should be placed to each stem. If against a wall a nail and shred may be used, but the latter should be placed loosely round the stem to allow space for swelling, which it will do considerably. If planted on the open border, a strong stake 4 feet long should be placed near each stem, and a piece of matting placed round the stake and fastened to it first, and then the stem of the plant should be loosely fastened also. In the after training all side shoots should be rubbed off as they appear

(this will involve weekly attention), and all the strength of the plant directed upwards into the main stem. Sometimes the leaders are pinched when the first cluster of flowers appears. This throws strength into the blossoms and the next shoot, which breaks away from the leader and grows on till another cluster of blossoms is put forth, when another pinching of the leader takes place, and so on, a check to growth being given as each cluster of fruit is formed. I do not think it really matters much whether these pinchings or checks are given or not, for I have proved that a plant which is allowed to grow straight onwards, unstopped, will bear as much fruit as the one that is pinched. All that is gained by the pinching is the confining of the growth to a smaller space, and if the wall or the fence on which the plants are to be trained is a very low one, then pinching may be useful, but otherwise it is not of much value. Beyond the pinching and training the summer culture is almost nothing. Weeds, of course, must be kept down, and if the summer should be hot and dry, mulching and watering may be beneficial. In cold, wet districts the plants must occupy a south wall, and, if possible, lay a mound of soil (the sweepings of the potting-shed, or the old soil saved from the renovation or renewal of Vine or Peach borders will do) against the foot of the wall, and plant in the mound. When the fruits are swelling rapidly and approaching the ripening stage, gradually remove a few of the leaves to let in the sunshine, and in autumn, when frost is expected, the late fruits will ripen off if gathered and placed in a warm kitchen, or in a warm position anywhere.

"UNDER GLASS.—Given a light house and a night temperature of 60°, and the Tomato may be had all the year round. In the open air, in many places, it is a precarious crop. Very frequently the fruits refuse to ripen, and when they get the colour they lack the flavour of the fruits grown and ripened under glass; and very often, too, the fruits fall a prey to a disease not unlike in character and appearance to the disease which causes such destruction to its relative, the Potato. Under glass I have had one set of plants go through the year without renewal; but young plants should be raised at least every year, as young plants produce the finest fruit, and they are so easily raised that there is nothing gained by a prolongation beyond a year. The plants may be raised from seeds, but I like cuttings best, as I think they come into bearing earlier, and the plants are so healthy and strong in both cases that one need not consider the question as to whether we lose or gain in vigour. The seedlings are sometimes over-vigorous, and require curtailment at the roots in order to moderate their exuberance. The best time to take cuttings is in summer, say in August, and they will strike anywhere—in a shady place, in a frame, or under a hand-light best, or on the shelf in the greenhouse — in fact, anywhere. They are best put into single pots of small size, and shifted into larger pots as required, until the time comes to plant them out. If struck early in August and grown on steadily they may be taken to a fruiting condition in pots, and be transferred to the Tomato-house in time to begin bearing early in spring, when fruits are most valuable; so that really there need not be any break in the crop, as the crop in possession of the house will go on bearing till the time of its removal, if carefully managed. To do them justice they must have

"A Light House.—It may either be span-roofed or a lean-to, but it cannot be too light. In either case it should be wired, the wires being about as close to each other as would be necessary for vines, and about 9 inches from the glass. The provision for the roots may consist of narrow brick pits, or boxes, or large pots. Where convenient, I think the narrow pits are best, but they need not be more than 18 inches wide, and 2 feet in depth. Place 6 inches of drainage in the bottom, fill it with turfy loam, inclined to be rather sandy than heavy, and top-dress when necessary, giving manure water if it should be needful to swell off a crop readily.

"The best way to train is to pinch out the leader when the stems are 6 inches high, and from the shoots which break away train up two. These will form the main fruiting stems, and should be trained up the roof, 15 inches apart. All side shoots should be rubbed off, and when the first cluster of flowers show pinch out the leader. Select the next leader which breaks away, and nip out the point of that also when a truss of blossoms has been evolved, and so on till the shoot reaches the top of the house. The close pinching must be persisted in to throw the strength into the plant; and a few of the main leaves may be removed when the fruit begins to ripen, to let in the sun to colour them. As the bottom fruit begin to ripen and are taken off for use, a shoot here and there may be permitted to grow, and these in turn will develop blossoms, when, if the same pinching process be adopted, a successional crop will be started which will prolong the season."

Tomatoes without Manure.—Mr. Muir is inclined to think we use too much manure in the case of Tomatoes. "Almost every one who has anything to say on the culture recommends at least one part of the compost to be manure from the stable or cowshed, and plenty of plants, and fruit too, are produced under this treatment, but it must be owned that there is also a great deal of superfluous wood, and fruits in many instances are often neither so perfect in form, large in size, nor so numerous as they might have been. Three parts of the time spent in cultivating Tomatoes are often devoted to cutting back and thinning out the shoots, work which surely could not be over and above good for the plants. The majority of Tomatoes make a great deal of unnecessary wood before any fruits are formed, and many of them grow so freely that they do not fruit until their feeding supplies have become somewhat exhausted. My idea of a good bearing Tomato-plant is one which begins to fruit about 10 inches from the ground, and continues to bear closely as far up as the cultivator chooses to lead the main stems. The fruit should be numerous, and the superfluous growths in no way predominating. It is, however, a difficult matter to have Tomatoes in this condition where much manure is used, as the manure has a tendency to induce the plants to make wood rather than fruit. For some years we have been using less and less manure in Tomato growing, and in several instances we have dispensed with it altogether, and found the crops to be altogether more satisfactory than hitherto. The growths were short and robust, and the fruit formed in large quantities and swelled off and coloured beautifully. Early in summer we are in the habit of planting a Tomato here and there along the walls wherever a small vacancy occurs, and before planting we used to fork in a quantity of manure to assist them, but now no manure is employed, and the crops are good. The very poorest of soil without any manure might not answer, but ordinary potting turf will be found to grow them to the highest state of perfection."

Mr. Muir holds that, even in England and Wales, " Tomatoes, when properly managed, are far more prolific in the open air than under glass. They begin to bloom and fruit almost at the ground, and the stems throw out bunches of flowers every few inches and yield very fine crops. On some of our clusters we have counted as many as twenty, and where they were thinned out to single fruits some have weighed 14 ounces each. The flavour, too, of those grown and ripened during the harvest-time is much superior to that of those ripened under glass, especially in a close atmosphere. In short, open-air Tomatoes are so good and easily produced, that I would advise all who have a wall with any vacant spots on it to fill them up with this esculent. During May is the best time to plant. They may be grown and hardened off along with the bedding Pelargoniums, and be planted out at the same time. Many who know them to be gross feeders think they are doing right in giving them a rich mixture to root into; but that is a mistake. The harder and dwarfer the shoots are the better. When grown in poor soil they flower profusely, and become most prolific. As soon as plenty of fruits have been formed—as form they undoubtedly will on all plants grown in nothing but pure loam— supply them with doses of liquid manure. Pick off all young shoots as they form, and a heavy crop will be the result. Wherever we have a bare strip on any part of our walls— and these occur often between trees —we fork in a few shovelfuls of chopped-up turf, and in this plant Tomatoes. Many of the plants are pruned in to one stem only, and none of them are allowed to have more than two ; in fact, it is cordons and not bushes on which we depend for a profitable crop. When in poor soil they do not make side shoots rapidly, but they should be looked over frequently to take these off and to nail up the main stem."

In all the colder parts of these islands, and where Tomatoes do not thrive in the open air, we have a great, but often neglected, substitute for a good climate in the many pits and frames emptied of bedding and other plants during summer and early autumn. Mr. Iggulden's practice is as follows : — " I prefer pits with a single hot-water pipe round, and which are oftentimes devoted first or during the winter to Bouvardias, then to Kidney Beans during the spring months, and subsequently to Melons or Cucumbers.

If such a pit is available it may well be devoted to Tomatoes, and, failing this, a cold pit or ordinary Potato frame will do nearly as well, as it is protection from rain rather than heat that is indispensable during the summer and autumn. Supposing these pits and frames, in addition to perfecting the crops of Potatoes, are also required for the preparation of summer bedding plants, the best plan will be to have a number of strong Tomato plants, with perhaps a cluster of fruit already set, ready to plant, say, by the end of May.

"A bed previously devoted to early Potatoes just suits Tomatoes and needs no preparation beyond the addition of a little manure to the soil. If a bed has to be made specially for them a quantity of old heating material may be used, adding to this sufficient fresh to cause the whole to become just warm enough to give the Tomatoes a good start. Better, however, a small bed of half-decayed manure than a heap of material that has heated itself dry, as in the latter case the small amount of loamy soil on the surface of the bed is all the plants would have to support them. The depth of the manure in the pits must be regulated according to the depth of the walls, but any amount from 1 to 3 ft. will be ample, as the frames can be raised. The beds may be made of any height, so long as the heap does not become very hot. Over the manure place a layer about 1 ft. in depth of rich loamy soil, and if the loam is rough and fibrous so much the better. Keep the lights of the frames or pits on closely, and when the sunshine or bottom heat has warmed the soil, plant at once.

" In pits and deep frames a considerable number of plants may be fruited, these being grown with single stems and staked in a sloping direction ; while in shallow frames a few plants may be trained and fruited somewhat similar to Cucumbers or Melons. I prefer, however, in all cases where there is a depth of 2 ft. or more at the back, to adopt a combination of the two plans ; that is to say, to cover the back wall or boards, as the case may be, with a number of obliquely trained plants, and the beds with a few spreading or trailing plants. I find where numbers are in a pit or frame, say about 15 inches apart and necessarily staked in a slanting direction, they are apt to shade each other ; but if the back walls or boards are covered with plants, these yield surprisingly without interfering with or being injuriously affected by those spreading on the ground. In frame culture it is imperative that the cultivator be able to put on the lights at certain times, and for this reason the plants cannot well be too dwarf. Now, there are few or no really dwarf sorts to be had generally, with the exception of Vilmorin's Dwarf, but the plants may easily be dwarfed by burying the stems, and as these quickly emit roots, the plants are also strengthened by the process. I do not recommend burying the balls deeply ; the object is best attained by trimming off the lower leaves of the plants, and then, after some of the soil has been thrown out, lay them in different directions, so as to place all the heads where required, the soil being then returned. This will be found a better plan than either layering or striking the tops in order to secure dwarf plants, and laying them all in before covering the balls and stems is the only way to properly plant. The balls should be moist when planted, and are best slightly sunk and marked with pegs, so that they can subsequently be kept watered till such time as the roots are spread in all directions. The frames should be kept rather close till the plants have recommenced growth, when air should be given freely, throwing off the lights during hot weather. Close early in the afternoons till such times as the fruits are commencing to ripen, when a little may be left on during warm dry nights. A stout stake should be placed to each plant, the latter having all

side shoots kept rubbed out, and be
stopped beyond either the second or
third large cluster of fruit, or according to the head room. If what
I term the combination system is
adopted, those plants nailed or otherwise trained to the back of the frames
should be laid down or dwarfed;
while about two plants in the centre
of each light should also be planted
in a sloping direction, pegged down
and encouraged to spread, the former
to have all side shoots removed from
the one or more main stems that may
be laid in, and the latter must be freely
thinned out where at all crowded,
the laterals being depended upon for
fruiting, and are best raised from the
soil with short stakes, or the clusters
of fruit may be laid on pieces of slates
or roofing tiles. Wherever the stems
are pegged down they will strike
root, to the obvious benefit of the
crops.

"Disease and its Prevention.—It
is when the foliage is wet, and especially during dull showery weather,
that the fungus effects a lodgment
on it, and this happens whether the
plants be dry at the roots or not.
Consequently to withhold water from
the roots, or to increase the bottom
heat as a preventive of disease, is a
mistake. Keep the foliage dry with
the aid of the lights, never syringe
overhead, and do not leave air on
when the nights are what are termed
muggy—that is to say, warm and
moist. It is this kind of weather
that most favours the spread of the
Potato fungus, and during its preva-
lence those growing Tomatoes in
frames have the advantage over
open-air cultivators, as they can and
ought to keep their frames dry and
close. Where the pits are heated,
a little heat should be turned on
during cold or wet weather, and
again when it is desirable to hasten
the ripening of the late fruit. The
late fruit in cold pits and frames
will generally ripen if cut in bunches
and hung up either in a forcing or
warm house or in the kitchen of a
dwelling-house."

Market Garden Culture.—Outdoor Tomatoes in market gardens
are not planted against walls, as is
done in private establishments; but a
warm situation, convenient to water,
is selected for them in open positions,
and in such positions they produce
abundance of large, well-coloured
fruit. The earliest planted ones are
generally put in the most favourable
positions, such as a warm border, or
on either side of " spent" Mushroom
ridges, where they are well sheltered.
If planted too early, they are liable to
be cut down by late spring frosts,
in which case entire removal and
replanting is the remedy usually
applied; if the damage be not too
great, however, the sound eyes produce shoots that eventually carry
heavy crops.   Early in spring the
seeds are sown broadcast in a
frame, in which a bed of fermenting
manure, covered with 6 inches of
light soil, has been placed. These
frames are protected during cold
weather by a covering of litter or
mats placed over the sashes; but
during favourable weather this is
removed and air is given, in order to
render the young plants as strong,
healthy, and stubby as possible. If
the plants come up too thickly they
are thinned, and when they are about
2 inches high they are pricked out
into 4-inch or 6-inch pots, two plants
being generally put into each pot.
Frames are sometimes prepared by
placing in them fermenting manure
in the form of a bed to the depth of
15 inches, well trodden down, on
which are placed 8 inches of soil,
and in such beds pots filled with
mould are plunged up to the brim.
The plants are then dibbled into the
pots, and the frames shut up and
kept close for a time, until fresh root-
action has taken place. They are
afterwards kept freely ventilated
until May, when the sashes are entirely removed during the day, and
replaced and tilted up at night
and in wet weather. During the
last week in May the plants are
thoroughly hardened off, although
still unable to endure even a slight
frost, and they are planted in warm

positions, as before stated, on Mushroom ridges or similar places. As soon as the fruit has attained its full size, the leaves are turned aside so as to expose it to the sun, by which means it ripens more readily, and is of better colour than when shaded. The ripe fruits are generally picked off twice a week, leaving the greener ones a little longer, so as to mature themselves; but should frost come, all fruits are picked off, and spread out on hay in a frame under sashes, where they eventually become red.

The Potato disease has often played havoc with Tomatoes in the market gardens of London during recent years. The winter and early supply is to a great extent grown by special growers in the warmer parts of Sussex, and also in the Channel Islands.

Uses.—Every year Tomatoes are becoming more important for cooking and as the best of salads. The manufacture of Tomato preserves and Tomato sauce forms a very extensive branch of industry in the south of France.

Large Red Tomato (*Tomate Rouge Grosse.* English synonyms: Large Red Italian, Orangefield, Mammoth, or Fiji Island Tomato).— Plant vigorous growing; leaves rather broad, dark green; leaflets somewhat puckered and folded at the edges; fruit in bunches of from two to four, very large, flattened at the ends, irregularly ribbed, 3 to 4 inches wide, 2 inches or less deep, and of a fine deep-scarlet colour. A very productive variety, and the most extensively grown in the south of France, whence the fruit is sent to all the markets, while a considerable quantity is made into preserves. The fruit ripens rather late to suit the climate of Paris.

Large Early Red, or Powell's Early, Tomato ($\frac{1}{12}$ natural size; detached fruit, $\frac{1}{3}$ natural size).

Large Early Red, or **Powell's Early, Tomato** (*Tomate Rouge Grosse Hâtive*).— Plant rather slender, and characterized by the leaves being almost always curled, with the leaflets folded back on the upper surface, which gives the plant the appearance of being half-faded; fruit very numerous, in bunches of from three to six, ribbed like those of the preceding kind, but seldom exceeding $2\frac{1}{2}$ to $3\frac{1}{5}$ inches in diameter, and $1\frac{1}{5}$ to $1\frac{3}{5}$ inch in depth. It ripens a fortnight or three weeks earlier than the preceding kind, and is well adapted for climates similar to that of Paris. This variety, moreover, is one of those which are most extensively grown.

Early Dwarf Red Tomato (*Tomate Rouge Naine Hâtive*).—A sub-variety of the preceding kind, from which it differs in having the stem shorter and branching, and bearing fruit closer to the ground, while its other characteristics of growth are the same. Its dwarfer habit renders it easier to cultivate, and especially more suitable for forcing. When grown under the same conditions as the other, it commences to ripen its fruit two or three days earlier. The fruit is somewhat more flattened, more ribbed, and smaller than that of the preceding kind, but the difference is very slight.

Trophy Tomato (*Tomate Rouge Grosse Lisse*).—Plant large, tall, and vigorous growing, like that of the Large Red Tomato, but still later than that variety; fruit flattened at both ends, regularly rounded or faintly sinuated, from about 2½ to 4 inches in diameter, and from 1¾ to nearly 2½ inches in depth. It is difficult to keep this variety absolutely pure, the fruit

Early Dwarf Red Tomato (1/10 natural size).

Trophy Tomato (natural size).

always having a tendency to revert to the ribbed shape, and the same plant will often be found bearing at the same time some fruit which are smooth and others with ribs more or less distinctly marked.

The *Stamford* Tomato, raised by Mr. Laxton, the well-known English grower, comes very near this variety. It has somewhat smaller fruit, but they are still more regular in shape than those of the Trophy Tomato, and the flesh is thicker.

Tree Tomato ($\frac{1}{12}$ natural size; detached fruit, $\frac{1}{3}$ natural size).

To this variety should also be allied Livingston's Favourite Tomato, which is one of the handsomest smooth kinds in existence. In shape and size it bears a great resemblance to the Apple-shaped Purple Tomato, but its colour is a deep scarlet without any tinge of violet.

Smooth Red Curled-leaved Tomato (*Tomate Rouge Grosse Lisse à Feuille Crispée*).—A rather slender plant, with a tall, thin stem which does not branch much. Leaves entirely curled, like those of the Large Early Red Tomato; fruit broad and rounded in shape, usually without ribs, and remarkably flat in proportion to its transverse diameter. It ripens rather late, but, with a little care, does so without difficulty in the open air at Paris. The flesh is abundant, with few seeds, and keeps very well. This variety is at the present time one of the most highly esteemed by the Parisian market gardeners.

Tree Tomato (*Tomate à Tige Raide de Laye*).—This variety, raised in the gardens of the Count de Fleurieu at the Château

Apple-shaped Red, or Hathaway's Excelsior, Tomato (natural size).

de Laye, near Villefranche (Rhône), is distinguished from all others by having a very short stiff stem, which grows perfectly erect without any support and bears leaves which are very much curled, reticulated, and of an almost blackish-green colour. The fruit resembles that of the Large Red Tomato and ripens nearly as late. It would be very interesting, and, no doubt, would not be impossible, to raise different varieties of Tomatoes which would combine the best features of the ordinary kinds, as regards shape and earliness, with the stiff, firm, and thick-set habit of growth of the present variety.

Apple-shaped Red, or Hathaway's Excelsior, Tomato (*Tomate Pomme Rouge*).—Plant of medium vigour of growth, about the same size as the Large Early Red Tomato plant, but having the leaves less curled ; fruit almost perfectly spherical, quite smooth, 2 inches or more in diameter, and borne in bunches of from three to six. They ripen a little earlier than those of the Large Red Tomato, but some days later than those of the Large Early Red variety. The flesh of the present variety is more solid than that of the ribbed Tomatoes, and the fruit keeps well when the skin is not cracked or otherwise injured.

Rose-coloured Smooth Apple - shaped Tomato (*Tomate Pomme Rose*).—This very handsome variety differs from the preceding kind only in the colour of the fruit, which is pink coloured at first and changes, as it ripens, to a vinous, and in hot seasons to an almost violet, red colour. The fruit is produced in great abundance in bunches of

Greengage, or Yellow Plum, Tomato.

from three to six, and, like that of the preceding variety, is almost perfectly spherical in shape, very solid, and contains few seeds.

Apple-shaped Purple, or Acme, Tomato (*Tomate Pomme Violette*). —A very handsome, productive, and somewhat late variety, bearing some resemblance to the preceding kind in the colour and very regular shape of the fruit, but differing from it decidedly in the fruit being of larger size, and also of a darker, almost violet, tint when ripe. The bunches usually do not contain more than from two to four fruit each, and these, although very round, are somewhat broader than deep.

The American variety *Criterion*, which is almost of the same colour as the two preceding kinds, differs from them in being of a slightly elongated-ovoid shape. Its fruit is about 2 inches long and $1\frac{3}{4}$ inch in transverse diameter.

Greengage, Round Yellow, or **Yellow Plum Tomato** (*Tomate Jaune Ronde*).—This variety perfectly resembles the three preceding kinds, except in the colour of the fruit, which is of a fine golden yellow, nearly spherical, quite smooth, and exceedingly regular in shape. Yellow-fruited Tomatoes are not thought very much of, at least in France, so we shall only mention this variety, which is also the best of them.

Cherry Tomato (*Tomate Cerise*).—Plant comparatively hardy, very productive, and vigorous growing; stem about 4 ft. high, thick and stout, very branching, and bearing an abundance of very green leaves which are not at all curled. The flowers commence to appear a week later than those of the Large Early Red Tomato. Fruit spherical or slightly flattened, scarlet, only about 1 inch in diameter, and

Cherry Tomato (branch, ⅓ natural size).

growing in bunches of from eight to twelve. A well-grown plant may be allowed to carry more than twenty bunches, especially if the fruit are gathered as they ripen. This is a mid-season variety, and is very productive, notwithstanding the small size of the fruit.

Pear-shaped, or **Fig, Tomato.**—A very vigorous-growing and rather early variety. Stem 4 ft. to 4 ft. 3 inches high; leaves numerous, not curled, rather broad, and of a deep-green colour; fruit numerous, scarlet, pear-shaped, more or less contracted at the base, about 2 inches

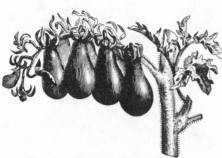

Pear-shaped, or Fig, Tomato (branch, ⅓ natural size).

long and $1\frac{1}{5}$ inch broad in the thickest part, borne in bunches of from six to ten. A well-grown plant may easily be allowed to carry from twenty to twenty-five bunches. In the south of Europe, especially near Naples, a great number of Pear-shaped varieties of Tomato are grown. We only mention the variety which appears to us most worthy of note for earliness and productiveness. The Pear-shaped kinds are considered to keep better than any others. The English variety named *Nisbett's Victoria* should be referred to the Pear-shaped section, although it is a rather distinct form of it. This Tomato is more of an elongated egg-shape, and broader at the lower extremity than a true pear-shape. The fruit are borne in bunches of from four to eight, and the plant, which is tall, stout, and half-late, is remarkable for the luxuriance of its foliage.

King Humbert Tomato (*Tomate Roi Humbert*).—This variety, which is very probably derived from the Pear-shaped Tomato, is distinguished by its rather peculiar form and appearance. The fruit, which grows in clusters of from five to ten, is of a pretty regular ovoid shape, but is frequently flattened on four sides, so that a section of it, especially near the end, presents a nearly square outline. It is about the size of a small hen's egg and of a very bright scarlet colour. The plant is of average height and earliness, and a most extraordinary cropper, with spreading leaves which are not curled. The new English variety named *Chiswick Red* comes so near this variety that we think one might be very easily mistaken for the other.

King Humbert Tomato.

RED CURRANT TOMATO.

Solanum racemiflorum, Dun.

Tomate groseille.

This is sometimes grown for table use, but more frequently as an ornamental plant. The fruit, which are very small, spherical, and scarlet coloured, are produced in long clusters of twelve, fifteen, or even more; they contain an acidulous pulp, which may be used like that of the Tomato.

Red Currant Tomato (branch, ⅓ natural size ; detached fruit, natural size).

Amongst the numerous varieties of Tomato which we have not described or enumerated, the following deserve to be mentioned:—

Tomate Belle de Leuville.—Fruit of the same shape as that of the Large Red Tomato, with faintly marked ribs, smooth, well shaped, and remarkable for its crimson tint, which becomes almost violet coloured when ripe. This variety was raised at Leuville, near Arpajon, in the vicinity of Paris. The new round-fruited kinds are at the present day preferred to it, but it appeared before any of the American or English varieties which are now so extensively grown.

Tomate Jaune Petite. — A yellow-fruited variety of the Cherry Tomato. Fruit numerous, golden yellow, and perfectly round.

Large Yellow Tomato (*T. Grosse Jaune*).—An American variety of the same shape and almost of the same size as the Large Red Tomato. The fruit is very deeply ribbed, and very inferior to that of the Round or Smooth Yellow Tomato (*T. Jaune Ronde*).

T. Scharlachrother Türkenbund (*T. Bonnet Turc*).—A curious red-fruited kind, with fruit under the average size, and distinguished for the abnormal development of a portion of the carpels, which forms in the centre of the fruit a protuberance similar to that which is seen in the Turk's-cap, or Turban, Gourds. This variety is middling early and moderately productive.

Yellow Pear-shaped Tomato (*T. Poire Jaune*).—This is simply a variety of the Pear-shaped Tomato with bright-yellow fruit. As in the case of the red-fruited form, there are numerous kinds of it, differing from one another in size and earliness.

STRAWBERRY TOMATO, SMALL MEXICAN TOMATO, or BARBADOES GOOSEBERRY.

Physalis pubescens, L.   Solanaceæ.

French, Alkékenge jaune doux.   *German*, Judenkirsche.   *Flemish*, Jodekers.   *Italian*, Alchechengi giallo.   *Spanish*, Alquequenje.   *Portuguese*, Alkekengi.

Strawberry Tomato (⅛ natural size).

Native of South America.—Perennial. —A plant with a very branching, angular stem, from about 2½ to over 3 ft. high. Leaves heart-shaped or oval, soft, hairy, and somewhat clammy; flowers solitary, small, yellowish, marked with a brown spot in the centre; calyx bladder-shaped, very large, enclosing one juicy orange-yellow fruit about the size of a cherry; seed small, lenticular, smooth, pale yellow. A gramme contains about 1000 seeds, and a litre of them weighs about 650 grammes. Their germinating power lasts for eight years. CULTURE.—In the south of France this plant grows very well in the open air, without requiring any particular attention, but in the climate of Paris it is advisable to sow it in a hot-bed, and treat the plants like Egg-plants or Tomatoes.

USES.—In the south of Europe the fruit is valued on account of its slightly acid taste. It is eaten raw.

Another species (*Physalis peruviana*, Hort.) is grown for the sake of its yellow berries, which are eaten raw or made into a preserve. It differs but little from *P. pubescens*. *P. Barbadensis*, Jacq., is also in cultivation.

The plant which was introduced within the last few years under the name of the Small Mexican Tomato (*Petite Tomate du Mexique*) is probably *Physalis edulis*, Sims. This species, which is an annual one and of rapid growth, ripens its fruit perfectly in the climate of Paris. It is rather to be considered a medicinal plant than one suitable for table use.

TUBEROUS GLYCINE.

Apios tuberosa, Mœnch ; *Glycine Apios*, L.   *Leguminosæ.*

Apios tubéreux.

Native of North America.—Perennial.—Roots spreading horizontally, and bearing tuberous enlargements about the size of a hen's egg ; stems hairy, twining, several yards in length ; leaves pinnate, consisting of six leaflets with an odd one, downy ; flowers of various shades of purple, and borne in dense clusters on axillary stalks. The seed does not ripen in France. CULTURE.—As this plant does not ripen its seeds in our climate, it is multiplied by division in March and April, or in the latter part of summer. The divisions are planted in good, light, well-drained soil, and from 3 to 5 ft. apart in every direction. The stems should be supported by poles or stakes, as those of the Yams are in China. The only attention required is to keep the ground free from weeds by an occasional hoeing. The tubers are not large enough to be gathered for use until the second or third year after planting. USES.—The tubers, which are sometimes as large as a man's fist, are starchy, and have an agreeable flavour when boiled like Potatoes, for which they have been recommended as a substitute. The plant, however, has the disadvantage of running very much at the root, and requiring stakes ; and besides, the tubers are rather slow in attaining their full growth.

TURNIP.

Brassica Napus, L.   *Cruciferæ.*

French, Navet. *German*, Herbst-Rübe. *Flemish* and *Dutch*, Raap.   *Danish*, Roe.
Italian, Navone. *Spanish* and *Portuguese*, Nabo.

Native country uncertain.—Biennial.—The Turnip has been cultivated from a very early period. There appears to be no doubt that it originated either in Europe or Western Asia, but the precise locality is unknown. The root is swollen and fleshy, variable in shape according to the variety, being cylindrical, conical, pear-shaped, spherical or flattened, and equally variable in colour, being white, yellow, red, gray, or black; the flesh is white or yellow, sometimes more or less sugary, and sometimes pungent and slightly acrid. Leaves oblong, usually lyrate, and divided to the midrib in the lower part, sometimes oblong entire, and always of a clear-green colour, and more or less rough to the touch; flower-stem smooth, branching; flowers yellow, in terminal spikes, and succeeded by long, slender, cylindrical, long-pointed siliques or seed-vessels, each of which contains from fifteen to twenty-five very small spherical seeds of a reddish-brown colour, and sometimes, but rarely, almost black. A gramme contains about 450 seeds, and a litre of them weighs about 670 grammes. Their germinating power lasts for five years. The varieties of Turnips are exceedingly numerous, and we must confine ourselves to the enumeration of the kinds which are most commonly cultivated.

CULTURE.—The Turnip is essentially an autumn-cropping plant, the main crop always coming in late in the season, and the time of sowing varying only a few days, according to the earliness of the different varieties. In the neighbourhood of Paris, the latest varieties are sown from the 25th of June to the 25th of July, and the earliest kinds from the 25th of July to the 25th of August. After this date, sowings may be made up to about the middle of September of very early kinds, from which a supply of half-grown roots may be obtained towards the end of the year, and even in spring, as Turnips when not fully grown will not be injured by being left in the open ground during the winter, if they are protected by a covering of dry leaves or straw. It is rather difficult to grow Turnips in spring, and the earliest and tenderest varieties are the only kinds that can be satisfactorily employed for that purpose; and even then it sometimes happens that the plants run to seed without forming roots fit for use. The seed may be sown in February in a cold frame, the only kinds employed for this purpose being the Early Flat varieties, the Round Croissy Turnip, and the Jersey Navet. After the 15th of March, the seed may be sown in the open ground, and by making successional sowings about once a month, a continuous supply may be obtained up to the coming in of the ordinary season's crop. Turnips are generally sown broadcast in beds, but the work of thinning out, hoeing, and all other operations connected with their culture is more easily done when they are sown in drills. The seedlings are hardly overground when they are liable to be attacked by their greatest enemy, the Turnip fly, from which it is most difficult to protect them, seed having sometimes to be sown twice or thrice over in consequence of the ravages of this insect. As soon as the young plants are well up, and have made a few leaves, thinning out should commence, and be continued at intervals until all the plants are finally placed a suitable distance apart. Plentiful watering is necessary, if the weather is hot and dry, as, in order to insure good quality in the roots, the plants must not be allowed to suffer any check in their growth. For table use, the roots are usually taken up before they have attained their full size, being more tender and more delicate in flavour when only half or three-quarters grown.

A good variety, or growing the best kinds, is not the whole secret of securing the best roots. This can only be done through good cultivation, and Turnips will repay attention as well as any other crop.

Poor, gravelly soil will never produce tender, sweet roots ; well-manured land seldom fails to grow good Turnips. It is, therefore, well to see that the soil has been properly prepared for them before sowing the seed. This applies to crops at all seasons. In spring the earliest should be sown on a favourable spot on a south border. The first time the soil is in good working order in March put the first seed in out-of-doors, and sowings may be made monthly from then until the end of August, putting different kinds in to follow one another according to their earliness.

Early in the season Turnips may form a first crop on the ground for the year; but later on, especially in the case of the winter ones, the seed may generally be sown on ground which has been cleared of Peas, Potatoes, or such like. In spring deep digging and plenty of manure suits them well, but in sowing after other crops, as suggested, manure is not often wanted and the soil need not be turned over; a hoeing and raking of the surface will suffice in most cases. Drills should be drawn not more than 2 inches deep, and 1 ft. apart is a good distance in spring, but 18 inches may be given to those that have to stand the winter. Turnip seed germinates freely; it is rarely bad, and therefore thin sowing should be the rule. The young plants soon appear above ground, and in favourable weather they grow so quickly that it is almost necessary to begin thinning as soon as the plants can be taken hold of, as crowding has an injurious effect on them at first. It is a good plan to thin them all twice. At first they should be thinned out to 6 inches apart, and the second time every other one should be removed, which will leave the plants for the crop standing at 1 ft. apart or thereabouts.

Snails are sometimes troublesome ; they eat off the young plants, but a slight dusting of lime or soot generally prevents them from doing much harm, and dressings of the kind assist greatly in keeping away the grub and insects that often disfigure the roots. The Turnip fly, too, does not like coming in contact with soot or lime, and altogether a slight dusting of one or the other, or both of these, may be given to the plants in a young state, whether they are much in want of it or not. At all times the surface of the soil between the rows should be kept open and free from weeds, and this is best done by using the Dutch hoe frequently. In hot, dry weather Turnips soon become bitter and stringy, and in this state they are far from good; but by a little forethought and attention no one need ever be obliged to use such, as by sowing small patches frequently a constant supply of delicate roots may be secured. When many of them become ready for use together, part of them may be taken up and stored in a cool shed. They will keep longer there than they would do in the ground, but Turnips taken up too soon lose part of their flavour; therefore they should always be left in growing quarters as long as possible. In winter some take up their Turnips and store them away like Beet or Carrots, but nothing is gained by doing that, and it should never be practised unless the weather is unusually severe. The Chirk Castle should never be stored, except for convenience, as it is rarely injured by frost, but in frosty or snowy weather it is sometimes difficult to get them out of the ground.

Turnips do not submit readily to forcing. Frames are the only places in which they can be treated properly. They must not be forced hard, as this causes them to run to leaf and flower without forming bulbs. The best way is to make up a very gentle hot-bed in February or March. Place a frame and some rich soil on the top, and sow the seed broadcast thinly. Give abundance of air as soon as the young plants can be seen, and never coddle

2 F

them up with coverings or maintain a very close atmosphere unless the weather really demands it. As the plants increase in size, thin them out to a few inches apart, and the bulbs may be used as soon as they are the size of cricket-balls. As an artificial manure for Turnips, nothing equals superphosphate. This may be dug into the ground before sowing, or it may be sprinkled thinly in the drills when opened for the reception of the seed.

The Soil most suitable for Turnip culture is a rich, friable, sandy loam, on which medium-sized roots of excellent quality may be produced without the aid of much manure; and the fresher the soil the better flavour the crop,—for which reason preference is always given to those grown on arable land after corn crops, as the kitchen-garden soil is frequently too rich in decayed vegetable matter, and has to support a much greater variety of tap-rooted plants, which extract the elements necessary for their growth from the soil. For this reason the main crop for winter use should be grown in a similar manner to main crops of Potatoes, outside the kitchen garden proper; and if fresh land be available every year, the results will be all the better. In light dry soils well-decomposed manure must necessarily be supplied; for if the young plants lack nourishment sufficient to insure a healthy growth, insect plagues invariably attack them in dry periods, and the crop will be hard and stringy. But perhaps the most difficult soils to deal with are stiff, cold, retentive ones, for without a good seed-bed successful results are well-nigh hopeless. Under such circumstances it is a good practice to draw deep drills the required distances, and fill them up with light rich soil, wood-ashes, bone-dust, or guano, in which to deposit the seed, whereby the young plant gets quickly into rough leaf, and grows out of the reach of insects. In dry soils Turnips are often, in hot seasons,

not only of inferior quality, but it is also difficult to get the seeds to germinate freely and regularly, and to induce the young plants to make a sufficiently rapid growth to escape the ravages of the fly.

CULTURE IN MARKET GARDENS.— The earliest sowing of Turnips is made in the end of January or early in February, in pits or frames, or on hot-beds without frames; and main sowings are made broadcast on a field about the end of February, or in March, to be succeeded by another sowing made in April. After the plants come up they are thinned, and the surface soil is at the same time loosened by means of small hoes. The largest roots are first drawn for market; thus the plants get thinned, and those that remain have more space for development. For early crops, when grown in brick pits, 2 or 3 ft. of rough fermenting material is cast into the pit and firmly trodden down, and on this is placed a few inches in thickness of garden soil, which is also made firm. The seeds are then sown broadcast, and afterwards the frame is kept close and moist until germination has taken place, when plenty of air is admitted on every favourable opportunity. If the seedlings come up too thickly, they are thinned out to 3 or 4 inches apart. Frame Turnips are never large; the aim is to grow them quickly to the size of a hen's egg, when they are tender and of good flavour, and to market them at once. The method of growing them in hot-beds without frames is to cast out trenches 18 inches deep, 6 ft. wide, and of any length, and firmly fill them with manure; over this a coating of soil is placed, and rolled or beaten solidly with the back of a spade; the seed is then sown, slightly covered, and finished off by rolling again; hoops made of hazel sticks are then fixed over the beds, so that they can be covered with mats, and in the event of hard frosty weather setting in, some strawy litter is added to the covering. If the weather is mild, the mats are let down every day so as to admit light to the young plants; and as soon as it can be done with safety, they are removed from over the beds and left erect around their sides in order to ward off winds. Sometimes the aid of either frames or hoops and mats is dispensed with, and the crop is grown on hot-beds like those just described, a little loose litter being merely strewn over the surface until the plants are established; in this way excellent Turnips are produced a week or two later than those which have been protected. Some growers use the space between the lines of frames for growing Turnips; and well it answers for that purpose, as, owing to the soil being below the general level, it keeps comparatively moist, and the belts of frames protect the plants considerably. The soil between Turnips is kept stirred with the hoe as frequently as possible, for no crop is more benefited by surface stirrings than this. Spring Turnips are generally got off the ground in time to permit of it being cropped with French Beans, summer Cabbage, Spinach, or Celery.

Uses.—The roots are eaten boiled, and served up in various ways. In spring the young shoots or "tops" may also be used, especially if grown in a dark place, when they furnish a very delicately flavoured vegetable, somewhat like the Sprouting Broccoli.

White Carrot-shaped Turnip (*Navet Long des Vertus*).—Root pure white, cylindrical, ending in a long point, pretty often curved or twisted, 6 to 8 inches long and 2 inches or less in diameter, projecting overground for nearly one-fourth of its length; flesh white, very tender, sugary; skin very smooth, and of a dull white colour, not only on the underground portion of the root, but also on the neck; leaves small, dark green, numerous, deeply cut, and forming a rather thick tuft. This variety grows very well in light, moist, deep soil, and is extensively cultivated in the fields about Paris for market supply.

Long White Vertus, or Jersey Navet, Turnip (¼ natural size).

White Carrot-shaped Turnip (⅓ natural size).

Long White Vertus, or **Jersey Navet, T.** (*Navet Long des Vertus Marteau*).—Root white, nearly cylindrical, but swollen at the lower end, which is quite obtuse or rounded, 5 or 6 inches long, and about 2 inches broad in the thickest part; flesh white, very tender, and sugary; leaves numerous, comparatively short, divided to the midrib in roundish lobes, and of a dark, shining-green colour. This is pre-eminently the kitchen-garden variety of Turnip, and is the kind which is most generally grown by the market gardeners of Paris, so that it is rare to find the Central Market without it at any season. In the open ground the root is formed in two months or two months and a half, and the variety is also one of the best for forcing. Like Radishes, the roots become hollow at the centre, if allowed to grow too large, and they are generally gathered for use when about two-thirds grown.

Long White Clairfontaine T. (*Navet de Clairfontaine*).—Root spindle-shaped, commencing to narrow immediately below the neck, straight, rather smooth, of a slightly grayish-white colour, 6 to 8 inches long, and from $1\frac{1}{5}$ to $1\frac{3}{5}$ inch in diameter at the neck, which projects about 1 inch overground; flesh white, rather close and firm, but tender; leaves long, half-erect, with roundish lobes, and of a rather dark green. A middling early variety, suitable for growing in ordinary soil, being hardier and requiring less attention than the two preceding varieties.

Freneuse T. (*Navet de Freneuse*).—Root entirely sunk in the ground, spindle-shaped, with a wrinkled skin of a grayish-white colour, and rather numerous rootlets,

Teltow Turnip
($\frac{1}{3}$ natural size).

Freneuse Turnip ($\frac{1}{3}$ natural size).

narrowing from the neck like a Salsafy root, 5 or 6 inches long, and $1\frac{1}{5}$ inch, or at most $1\frac{3}{5}$ inch, in diameter at the neck; flesh white, dry, sugary, and very firm; leaves small, short, very much divided, and of a dark-green colour, forming a rosette which lies flat upon the ground. This variety is grown in the vicinity of Paris in the fields, in somewhat poor or gravelly soils, in which it succeeds better than in stiff soil. When grown in stiff soil, the root is often misshapen. It is the most highly esteemed of the dry-fleshed Turnips.

The *Jargeau* and *Rougemont* Turnips (*N. de Jargeau* and *N. de Rougemont*), the latter of which is a great favourite in the neighbourhood of Pithiviers, are small dry-fleshed Turnips which exhibit no perceptible difference from the Freneuse variety.

Teltow T. (*Navet Petit de Berlin*).—Root entirely sunk in the ground, conical or pear-shaped, short and small, from $2\frac{2}{5}$ to $3\frac{1}{5}$ inches long, and $1\frac{2}{5}$ inch broad at the neck, and of a grayish-white colour; flesh very dry but not hard, sugary, and almost floury; leaves very small, with roundish lobes, not more than 5 or 6 inches long, drooping on the ground and withering when the root is fully formed. This is an early variety and succeeds very well in light sandy soil. The root, when cooked, has a peculiar flavour, completely differing from that of all other Turnips; it is milder and more sugary, and the flesh is almost floury, instead of being juicy and melting. The roots will keep all through the winter and even far into the following year, if taken up and stored in half-dry sand.

Long White Meaux T. (*Navet de Meaux*).—Root very long, cylindrical, but ending in a point, and very often twisted or curved, projecting 2 or 3 inches overground, 12 to 16 inches in length and

2 or 3 inches in diameter. All the underground portion is white; the overground part is sometimes cream coloured and sometimes tinged with pale green. Flesh white, close, half-dry, rather sugary; leaves medium sized, lyrate, numerous, erect or half-erect. This is a very productive variety, and is principally grown in its native district for the supply of the Central Market of Paris in the latter end of winter. In order to keep them up to that time, the market gardeners of Meaux cut off the "tops" of the plants soon after taking them up, and pile the roots in trenches, covering them over with sand. During the

winter, they bring them to market in bundles, and, as the roots have been deprived of their leaves, they are fastened together by a straw rope passed through them near the top.

Green Tankard T. (*Navet Gros Long d'Alsace*). —Root half-projecting from the ground, nearly cylindrical in that part, and regularly narrowed in the portion underground — which is white, the overground part being green— 12 to 14 inches long, and about 3 inches in diameter; flesh white, tender, and rather juicy; leaves large, half-erect, rather broad, and of a clear-green colour. This is a very productive variety, as the root attains a considerable size. It is more grown for feeding cattle than for table use; nevertheless, if pulled while young and tender, it is not to be despised as a table vegetable. When grown in the fields, it is sown in July, and yields almost as heavy crops as the large late kinds, such as the Norfolk Turnips and others which require to be sown in June.

Long White Meaux Turnip (⅓ natural size).   Green Tankard Turnip (⅓ natural size).

Long Red Tankard T. (*Navet Rose du Palatinat*).—This variety exhibits the greatest resemblance to the preceding one, but is distinguished from it by having the upper or overground part of the root of a somewhat violet-tinted red colour instead of green. It is also, on the whole, somewhat shorter and thicker than the Green Tankard variety, like which it is more grown for cattle-feeding purposes than for table use. The Red Tankard Turnip is extensively cultivated and highly esteemed all through Central Europe, from Poland to England, but it is only in France that the most regular forms of it, as regards shape and colour, are to be found. The forms grown elsewhere generally have the roots too short and top-shaped, and the overground part too pale coloured, or more of a pink or lilac hue than really red.

The Navet-rave de Bresse is only a late form of this variety with an elongated root.

Long Yellow T. (*Navet Jaune Long*).—Root entirely sunk in the ground, clean skinned, smooth, regular in shape, gradually narrowed from neck to point, and of a somewhat dull or wan yellow colour. It usually does not exceed 6 or 7 inches in length, and the diameter at the neck averages about 2 inches. The flesh is yellow throughout, fine in texture, rather firm, sugary, and agreeably flavoured. Leaves half-erect, rather divided, and a remarkably dark-green colour. This is a somewhat late variety, but an excellent one for table use, being of very good quality and keeping well.

The Parisians are certainly mistaken in considering the Yellow-fleshed Turnips inferior to the other kinds. They have an idea that the yellow colour in these vegetables is always accompanied by a strong and bitter flavour, which is far from being exactly true, as amongst the Yellow-fleshed Turnips there are varieties the flesh of which is very mellow and very delicately flavoured, quite as much so, in fact, as that of the White-fleshed kinds. The prejudice, however groundless it may be, nevertheless exists, and consequently

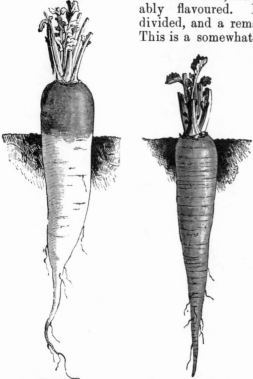

Long Red Tankard Turnip
(⅓ natural size).

Long Yellow Turnip
(⅓ natural size).

should be taken into account by those who cultivate vegetables for the markets.

Morigny Gray T. (*Navet Gris de Morigny*).—Root of a very long ovoid shape, projecting only about 1 inch overground, 6 or 7 inches long, and 2 inches broad in the thickest part, which occurs at about one-fourth or one-third of its length; skin rather smooth, iron gray or slate coloured; flesh white, rather tender, and sugary; leaves medium sized, half-erect, and of a clear-green colour. A rather early and good kitchen-garden variety. If sown rather late, the roots may often be kept in the ground through the winter, provided they are covered with straw or dried leaves.

Long Black T. (*Navet Noir Long*).—Root very long, spindle-shaped, clean skinned, almost entirely sunk in the ground, 6 to 8 inches long, and 2 inches or more in diameter at the neck; skin black, as dark coloured as that of the Winter Radish; flesh white or grayish-white; leaves rather stout, erect, and of a dark, shining-green colour. This is a rather early variety, and when sown not sooner than in August it keeps very well through the winter, like the preceding variety, if covered with straw or dried leaves. This method of preservation in winter is likewise generally applicable to all the varieties of Turnips which have the root deeply

Morigny Gray Turnip (⅓ natural size).   Long Black Turnip (⅓ natural size).   Croissy, or Des Vertus, Turnip (⅓ natural size).

sunk in the ground, and especially so to those kinds which grow with the neck of the root projecting a little above the surface and with the leaves erect rather than spreading. The roots thus protected can be taken up for use as they are required.

Croissy, or **Des Vertus, T.** (*Navet Rond des Vertus*).—Root sunk in the ground, round or slightly top-shaped, from 2⅖ to 3⅕ inches in diameter and depth, and with a tap-root of some length; skin white, smooth; flesh very white, tender, sugary, and very agreeably flavoured; leaves medium sized, erect, and of a clear-green colour. A very good early variety and a great favourite with the Parisian market gardeners. It is one of the best kinds for forcing.

Early Dutch Turnip (⅓ natural size).

Early Dutch T. (French, *Navet Turnep*; Dutch, *Witte Meirapen*).—Root somewhat top-shaped, slightly flattened, white, except on the part overground, which is usually tinged with green, nearly 5 inches in diameter in the widest part when well grown, and from $3\frac{1}{5}$ inches to $3\frac{3}{5}$ inches deep; neck broad; flesh white, tender, sugary, and softish; leaves stout and tall, erect, broad, and not much divided. Root rather late in attaining its full size. This variety is most generally grown for feeding cattle, and is seldom sent to table, although,

when taken young and tender, the roots are of good quality.

Limousin T. (*Navet du Limousin*).—Root roundish or slightly top-shaped when young or badly grown, very large, broad, and slightly flattened on the top when fully grown, when it not unfrequently measures 10 inches in its greatest diameter and at least 6 inches in depth; skin smooth, entirely white; flesh white, not very sugary; leaves very large and tall.

Limousin Turnip ($\frac{1}{5}$ natural size).

This variety is only grown in the fields. As it is a late kind, it is especially adapted for cool, moist climates, where it can be sown in June. It is the largest and most productive of the Turnips which are grown in France. Some other varieties, especially the White Norfolk, are rather like this Turnip in the appearance of the root and their habit of growth.

Strap-leaved White Globe T. (*Navet Blanc Globe à Feuille Entière*).—Root of regular spherical shape; skin very smooth and entirely white, except where it is marked by a few scars around the neck, indicating the positions of the earliest leaves; flesh white, firm, and close grained; leaves long, erect, entire, of a very long oval shape, toothed on the margin, and of a rather pale or light-green colour; neck very short and fine. One of the characteristics of this variety is the quickness with which the root swells and assumes the spherical shape. When fully grown it measures about 5 or 6 inches in diameter. This variety was recently raised in Anjou, and is especially suitable for field culture.

White Norfolk, or Cornish White, T. (*Navet de Norfolk Blanc*).— Root spherical or very slightly flattened at the top, pure white, 6 or 7 inches in diameter and about 5 inches deep when full grown; flesh white, tender, and somewhat watery; leaves very tall, erect or half-erect, with stout stalks or midribs. This is a very late variety and is exclusively grown in the fields. There is a sub-variety of it, the Green-top Norfolk Turnip (*N. de Norfolk à Collet Vert*), in which the overground part of the root is of a green colour, and another, the Red-top Norfolk Turnip (*N. de Norfolk à Collet Rouge*), in which the same part is of a reddish-violet colour. There is hardly any difference between these and the White variety in the size of the root

or in the manner of growing them. All these kinds should be sown
very early to attain their full size, and consequently they only succeed
well where the climate is moist and cool, or where the weather in
summer is not very dry. Nothing,
in fact, is more injurious to Turnips
than dry, hot weather, which causes
destructive insects to become more
active in their ravages, while the
growth of the plants is at the same
time, so to say, suspended by it.
While it lasts, they form no new
leaves, and those which they already
have are riddled into holes and
almost entirely destroyed by the
Turnip fly, to the great injury of the
growth of the roots.

Orange Jelly T. (*Navet Jaune
Boule d'Or.* English synonyms :
Golden Ball and Robertson's Golden
Stone Turnip).—Root perfectly spherical when not very much grown, but
slightly flattened when it has attained
its full size ; it is then generally 4
or 5 inches in diameter every way.
Skin very smooth and quite yellow ;
flesh yellow, softish, and fine flavoured,

White Norfolk, or Cornish White,
Turnip (⅓ natural size).

but slightly bitter ; leaves of medium height, rather broad, lyrate.
This variety is highly esteemed in Scotland and the north of
England.

Aberdeen T. (*Navet Jaune d'Aberdeen à Collet Vert.* English
synonyms: Green-topped Scotch and Early Yellow Field Turnip).—
Root spherical or slightly
flattened on the top, yellow
on the underground portion,
and green on the part overground, which is about one-
third of the length of the
root. When well grown the
root is about 6 inches in
diameter and about 5 inches
in length or depth. Flesh
pale yellow and rather firm ;
leaves tall, stout, half-erect,
smooth, and of a dark-green
colour.

Orange Jelly Turnip (⅓ natural size).

The variety known as the Border Imperial (*N. d'Aberdeen à Collet
Rouge*) is only a form of the present variety which has the neck of a
violet colour instead of green. Both kinds are exactly alike in their
habit of growth. They are good varieties for field culture, and are
considered by some persons in England to be hybrids between the true
Turnips and the Swedish Turnips or Rutabagas. This opinion we

believe to be an erroneous one, as from all the characteristics of their growth, and also from the indications furnished by their seed, the two Aberdeen varieties have every appearance of being true Turnips.

Early White T. (*Navet Blanc Plat Hâtif*).—Root exceedingly

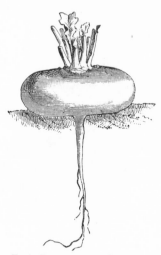

flat, like a broad disc in shape, pretty often sinuated and not regularly rounded in outline, 4 or 5 inches in its greatest diameter, and about 1½ inch in depth; flesh white, tender, not very sugary, and of good quality; leaves half-erect, lyrate, and divided at the base as far as the mid-rib. This is a very early variety, and is suitable both for forcing and for late sowing in the open air. Like all the flat varieties which we shall describe, this Turnip merely rests on the surface of the ground, into which it does not sink further than by sending down a slender perpendicular tap-root, which does not ramify until it reaches a certain depth.

Early Flat Red-top Garden T. (*Navet Rouge Plat Hâtif*).—The root of this va-riety is of the same size and shape as that of the preceding kind, but is distinguished from it by the violet-pink colour of the

Early White Turnip (⅓ natural size.)

overground part. It is grown and used in exactly the same way. In the east of France, under the name of *Navet à Collet Rose de Nancy*, a good form of this variety is cultivated, which almost resembles the Early Purple-top Munich Turnip.

White Strap-leaved American Stone T. (*Navet Blanc Plat Hâtif à Feuille Entière*).—This variety

is chiefly distinguished from the Early Flat White Turnip by having shorter leaves with an oblong entire blade, which is toothed on the margin, but not divided or lobed. The root also is slightly thicker and more rounded in outline. Along with the two preceding and the three following varieties, this is an excellent kind for forcing. As in the present instance, we shall often meet with similar varieties which only differ from each other in the leaves being divided in

White Strap-leaved American Stone Turnip (⅓ natural size).

the one kind and entire in the other. This difference by itself is of no importance, and is only noteworthy when combined with some special recommendation of earliness or good quality.

Red-top Strap-leaved American Stone T. (*Navet Rouge Plat Hâtif à Feuille Entière*).—A very flat variety, and of very regular shape, differing from the ordinary Flat Red-top Turnip in having entire leaves, not lobed at the base, and also by being at least four or five days earlier. The leaves are erect and stiff, and as they are also rather short, this is a very suitable variety for frame culture. It has also the good property of forming the roots freely, even when grown in spring, and of being slower to run to seed than most other Turnips. Yet, notwithstanding all these good qualities, it is possible that the following variety may, on account of its greater earliness, supersede it to some extent for forcing purposes. The present variety is also often sown in the open ground. It was raised in America.

Red-top Strap-leaved American Stone Turnip (⅕ natural size).

Milan Purple-top Strap-leaved T. (*Navet Rouge Très Hâtif de Milan à Châssis*). — This handsome variety is only a form of the preceding one, but is so distinct that it deserves a separate notice. The root is small or medium sized, very flat, quite smooth, pure white on the underground part, and of a lively violet-red colour on the upper part. The leaves, which are entire, rather erect, and very remarkably short, are few in comparison with the size of the root. It is one of the earliest varieties known, and is well adapted for forcing, even in spring.

Milan Purple-top Strap-leaved Turnip.

Early Purple-top Munich T. (*Navet Rouge Plat de Mai, de Munich*).—This variety has a root which resembles that of the ordinary entire-leaved Early Flat Red-top Turnip in shape and size, but differs from it in being of a darker colour on the overground portion, which is almost of a pure violet tint. The leaves are rather slight, lyrate, lobed, and comparatively small for the size of the root. The plant grows remarkably fast, and is, undoubtedly, the earliest of all Turnips, producing roots fit for use at least twelve or fifteen days sooner than the earliest entire-leaved varieties. It is the more suitable for forcing early as it

Early Purple-top Munich Turnip (⅕ natural size).

is best for table use when half-grown, or, at least, when very young; when fully grown, the roots have an unpleasantly strong and bitter flavour.

Early Flat Red-top Auvergne T. (*Rave d'Auvergne Hâtive*).—Root very flat on the top, about 2 inches deep, and often 6 or 7 inches across; skin very smooth, and of a rather pale violet-red colour on the whole of the overground portion of the root; flesh white, rather soft and watery; leaves tall, divided, broad, and numerous. This is a very productive variety, and succeeds best in granitic or schistose soils. It is more grown for feeding cattle than for table use.

Late Auvergne T. (*Rave d'Auvergne Tardive*).—Root two-thirds sunk

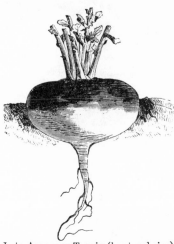

in the ground, top-shaped but tolerably flattened, 3 or 4 inches deep, and about 6 inches across; the overground portion is of a reddish-violet or rather dark-bronzy colour; leaves broad and stout, more tufty in growth and darker in colour than those of the Early variety. This variety is even more suitable for field culture than the preceding one, being seldom grown for table use outside of its native district. The central plateau of France, on account of its elevated position, possesses a climate very favourable to the cultivation of large-sized Turnips, and there we find the two largest kinds of Turnips that are grown in France, namely, the Auvergne and the Limousin varieties.

Late Auvergne Turnip (⅕ natural size).

The *Ayres* Turnip (*Rave d'Ayres*), which is grown in the departments of Tarn and Tarn-et-Garonne, appears to us to be identical with the Late Auvergne Turnip.

Yellow Dutch T. (French, *Navet Jaune de Hollande;* Dutch, *Hol-

landsche Gele Rapen*).—The root of this variety is flattened at the top, but still comparatively deep, so that it might be considered intermediate between the Round and the Flat varieties. It seldom exceeds 3 or 4 inches in its greatest diameter, while its depth or vertical measurement is between 2 and 3 inches. Skin of a uniform yellow colour on the underground portion of the root and of a clear green on the upper part; flesh yellow, tender, sugary; leaves medium sized, half-erect, and of a clear-green colour. This is a half-late kind and keeps well. It is one of the best kitchen-garden varieties.

Yellow, or Golden, Maltese T. (*Navet*

Yellow Dutch Turnip (⅕ natural size).

Jaune de Malte).—Root very much flattened at both ends, being about 2 inches deep, and 4 or 5 inches across in its widest part; skin and flesh pale yellow; neck green, very distinctly marked; leaves rather small and slight, divided, and of a dark-green colour. This is a good half-early variety, but the roots are sometimes rather strong flavoured. It is decidedly the flattest variety of all the Yellow-fleshed Turnips, amongst which it holds the same place that the Early White and Red Turnips occupy amongst the White-fleshed kinds.

Yellow Finland T. (*Navet Jaune de Finlande*).—Root perfectly flat and even concave underneath, so that the tap-root which descends into the ground appears to issue from the centre of a kind of depression or

Yellow, or Golden, Maltese Turnip
(⅓ natural size).

Yellow Finland Turnip
(⅓ natural size).

cavity; the upper part, on the contrary, is rather convex or conical in outline. The root is seldom of large size, being usually not more than 3 or 4 inches in diameter across, and 2 inches or less in depth. Skin very smooth, and of a fine golden-yellow colour, as is also the flesh; leaves very short and compact, not much divided, sometimes quite entire in the forms imported directly from Finland. This is an exceedingly hardy and rather early variety, and very suitable for sowing late in autumn. While the roots are young, the flesh is very fine and agreeably flavoured, but afterwards it becomes somewhat strong tasted and unpleasantly bitter.

Yellow Flat Purple-top Montmagny T. (*Navet Jaune de Montmagny*).—Root very handsome, flat, half-sunk in the ground, of a dark-yellow colour on the underground part and of a dark violet red on the portion overground, often 5 or 6 inches in diameter, and 3 inches or more deep; flesh yellow, rather firm, tender, and of very good quality; leaves medium sized, lyrate, of a dark-green colour, and generally spreading almost flat upon the ground. This very fine variety, which has been raised

Yellow Flat Purple-top Montmagny
Turnip (⅓ natural size).

recently, has already become highly valued and much sought after in the neighbourhood of Paris and in England. It is productive, half-early, and keeps well. The very striking contrast between the yellow and the red parts of the roots gives it a very peculiar and pleasing appearance, which, together with its earliness and the quite superior quality of the flesh, are powerful recommendations in its favour. It is one of the most agreeably flavoured of all the kitchen-garden varieties of Turnips, especially when taken young, before it has attained its full size.

Chirk Castle Black Stone T. (*Navet Noir Rond* ou *Plat*).—Root

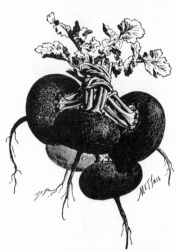

roundish, flattened, the diameter being nearly double the depth—usually 4 or 5 inches across and about 2 inches deep; skin of a uniform rather deep black or a very dark gray colour; flesh white, firm, close, half-dry, sugary, and very well flavoured; leaves lyrate, very slight, half-spreading, and of a deep-green colour. An early variety, of remarkably good quality, and bearing a striking resemblance to the Black Turnip Radish. The perceptible differences in shape which are often observed in this variety, depend chiefly upon the extent to which its growth has been developed. The root soon ceases to extend itself vertically, and then, in proportion as it swells horizontally, it either becomes more or less flat or else remains almost spherical.

Chirk Castle Black Stone Turnip
(⅓ natural size).

In addition to the foregoing varieties we may also mention the following:—

The White Stone, or Snowball, T., known also as the Early Stone and Six-weeks, is the variety generally grown for the supply of the London markets. It is a singular fact that, whilst white-fleshed Turnips are the only varieties grown for use in the south of England, in the north and in Scotland the yellow-fleshed are preferred.

Red-top American Stone, or Mousetail.—A very sweet early kind, and a good keeper.

Silverball.—A very early kind, with pure white flesh and handsome in shape.

Amber Globe T.—Root almost round or, more usually, top-shaped, pale yellow, with a green neck; leaves entire, long, and light coloured; flesh pale, sugary. An American variety, highly esteemed in the United States.

French Snowball T. (*Navet Boule de Neige*).—An early kind, with a globular or slightly flattened root of a pure-white colour. It differs from the White Dutch Turnip in having no green colouring around the neck.

Briollay T. (*Navet de Briollay*).—This variety, which was raised in Anjou, bears a tolerable resemblance to the White Tankard Turnip, but it is somewhat smaller, shorter, comparatively thicker, and grows more deeply sunk in the ground. It is also of better quality and more suitable for table use, being a true kitchen-garden Turnip and not a cattle-feeding variety, although it is often used for that purpose, as all other kinds of Turnips are when they have grown too large.

Early Chantenay T. (*N. de Chantenay Hâtif*).—This very much resembles the Round or Flat Black Turnip, like which it has the root tolerably flattened, but it is not so deeply coloured, being more gray than black.

Gray Luc T. (*Navet Gris de Luc*).—A small dry-fleshed Turnip, with a long root, tolerably like the Freneuse Turnip, but with the skin somewhat more wrinkled and grayish.

N. Gris Plat de Russie.—Root tolerably flattened, fully one-third broader than deep, with an iron-gray skin marked transversely with whitish lines. A hardy variety, but not superior to the Round Black Turnip.

Wolton's Hybrid T. (*N. Hybride de Wolton*). —Root almost perfectly spherical, sometimes slightly pear-shaped, entirely white on the part underground, and red on the upper part; flesh white, tender, and mild flavoured; leaves broad. Ripens half-early.

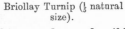

Briollay Turnip (⅓ natural size).

Yellow Scotch T. (*N. Jaune d'Écosse*).—An early variety, coming pretty near the Yellow Dutch Turnip, but somewhat paler in colour, and sometimes tinged with green at the neck. Root very clean skinned, almost entirely sunk in the ground; flesh pale yellow tender, and sugary.

Long Yellow Bortsfeld T. (*N. Jaune Long de Bortsfeld*).—This differs from the ordinary Long Yellow Turnip by being more slender in shape, by growing not so deeply sunk in the ground, and having the neck of a greenish colour. Its quality is good and it keeps well.

Large Yellow Globe T.—An American variety, coming very near the Yellow Dutch, but somewhat paler in colour and more spherical in shape.

Maltese T.—Root elongated, of a long ovoid shape, shorter and thicker than that of the Freneuse Turnip, which it resembles in its leaves and in the texture of the flesh of the root, which is very dry and firm. A good variety and still pretty largely grown in the vicinity of Paris.

Cruzy T. (*N. Rave de Cruzy*).—A very distinct variety. It is the only dry-fleshed Turnip which has a perfectly flat root. Skin of a somewhat grayish-white colour. The root is nearly twice as broad as deep, and is often irregular in shape.

Round Green-top Dry-fleshed T. (*N. Rond Sec à Collet Vert*).—Root globular, slightly flattened, rather resembling that of the *Des Vertus* or *Croissy* Round Turnip, but distinguished by the green tint of the neck and the flesh of the root being as firm and dry as that of the *Freneuse*

Round Green-top Dry-fleshed Turnip (⅓ natural size).

Turnip. The leaves are deeply lobed, half-spreading on the ground, and of a light-green colour. This is a half-early variety and keeps well.

Nancy Flat Purple-top T. (*N. Rouge de Nancy*).—A handsome form of the Early Flat Purple-top Turnip, remarkable for its earliness, the regularity of its shape, and the very deep colour of the upper part of the root. It hardly differs from the Munich Turnip, which even surpasses it in earliness.

Round White Sablons T. (*N. des Sablons*).—Root ovoid, one-third longer than broad, tolerably resembling that of the Croissy Round Turnip in every respect except its shape; flesh white, close, sugary, and half-dry.

Saulieu Gray T. (*N. de Saulieu*).—Root spindle-shaped, resembling that of a half-long pointed Carrot, four times as long as broad; skin gray, somewhat wrinkled; flesh firm, dry, sugary, and slightly yellowish in tint.

N. Scaribritsch.—Root flattened, clean skinned, and regular in shape, one-fourth broader than deep; neck fine, green coloured; the remainder of the root yellow; flesh yellowish white, tender, firm, and sugary; leaves very light coloured.

N. de Schaarbeck.—This variety is grown in the neighbourhood of Brussels, where it is highly esteemed. It is a flat white variety with a green neck, early and small sized, with flesh of fine texture and excellent quality.

Green-top Six-weeks T. (*N. de Six Semaines à Collet Vert*).—Root flattened, fully a third broader than deep, often growing to a considerable size, white on the underground part and green at the neck; flesh white, tender, sugary, and rather firm. Ripens early.

Petrosowoodsk's Purple T. (*N. Violet de Petrosowoodsk*).—A violet-coloured variety of the Finland Turnip, and similar in shape, having the same marked depression in the under part of the root around the tap-root. The leaves are sometimes lyrate and sometimes entire.

White Egg T.—Root ovoid, one-third longer than broad; skin very white and very smooth; flesh white, firm. This variety is highly thought of in the United States, where it is to be met with in large quantities in the markets.

Yellow Tankard T.—An English variety, with an elongated spindle-shaped root which is twice as long as broad, and of a pale-yellow colour, except at the neck, which projects slightly from the ground and is of a greenish colour. Flesh pale yellow, close grained, and of mild flavour. Ripens early.

UNICORN-PLANT.

Martynia, Lindl. *Sesamaceæ.*

French, Martynia. *German*, Gemsenhörner.

The plants of this genus are tall, stout, vigorous-growing annuals. Stem fleshy, $1\frac{1}{5}$ to $1\frac{3}{5}$ inch in diameter ; leaves large, heart-shaped, of a grayish-green colour, and somewhat hairy; flowers large, resembling those of a Catalpa in shape, and yellow or lilac, according to the species; fruit elongated, ovoid, curved, and terminating in a long hooked point, and enclosed in a soft green kind of shell which dries up when ripe, the fruit then becoming woody and of a blackish hue, and the extremity dividing into two long crooked horns, as it opens to allow the seed to escape; seed large, black, with an irregular rough or sha-greened surface. A gramme contains about 20 seeds, and a litre of them weighs about 290 grammes. Their germinating power lasts for one or two years. Cul-ture.—These plants require a moderate amount of heat, and it is advisable to sow the seed in a hot-bed and either allow the plants to complete their growth there or plant them out in good soil in a warm place. Uses.—The fruit, gathered while young and tender, is pickled in vinegar. It should be gathered when not more than half-grown, as, after that, it becomes too tough and leathery.

Unicorn-plant ($\frac{1}{8}$ natural size).

The Yellow-flowered species (*M. lutea*), figured in the accompanying illustration, is a native of Brazil, and is a plant of moderate size, somewhat trailing in habit, and yielding an abundance of small-sized fruits. It is the kind most grown for pickling in the United States.

M. proboscidea, Glox., a violet-flowered species, has fruit of larger size and with longer horns. It is a native of Louisiana.

AFRICAN VALERIAN.

Fedia Cornucopiæ, Gærtn. *Valerianaceæ.*

French, Valériane d'Alger. *German*, Algerischer Baldrian. *Flemish*, Speenkruid. *Dutch*, Speerkruid.

Native of Algeria.—Annual.—Stems erect, branching, smooth, 1 ft. to 16 inches high ; leaves almost all radical, oval oblong, entire, bluntly toothed, and of a rather dark, shining-green

African Valerian ($\frac{1}{3}$ natural size).

colour; flowers pink, in terminal clusters; seed yellow or grayish, oblong, thick, convex on one side, and marked on the other with a deep longitudinal furrow. A gramme contains about 250 seeds, and a litre of them weighs about 110 grammes. Their germinating power lasts for four years. The seed may be sown in the open ground, from April to August, in drills 10 to 12 inches apart. When thinned out and plentifully watered in hot weather, the plants quickly form rosettes of leaves, which are fit for use in about two months after sowing. The plant is somewhat sensitive to cold, and is not so suitable for sowing in autumn as the Corn-salad. The leaves are eaten as salad.

WATER CHESTNUT.

Trapa natans, L.　*Haloragaceæ.*

French, Macre.　*German*, Wasser-Nuss.　*Flemish* and *Dutch*, Waternoot.　*Spanish*, Nueis.

Native of S. Europe.—Annual.—An aquatic plant with a long stem which reaches to the surface of the water. Submerged leaves opposite; floating leaves alternate and arranged in a rosette at the top of the stem; blade of the leaf diamond-shaped, broader than long; flowers white, axillary; fruit large, of a dark-gray colour, bearing four

Water Chestnut (1/10 natural size).　　　　　　Fruit (natural size).

very stout spines arranged cross-wise, two of them being much longer than the others. A litre contains about 100 of these fruits, weighing about 500 grammes. Their germinating power does not last longer than one year, and to ensure even this they must be kept in water. The plant is not usually cultivated, the fruit being gathered where it grows wild. The kernel of the fruit, which is floury and of a very agreeable flavour, is eaten boiled.

WHITE QUINOA.

Chenopodium Quinoa, Willd.　*Chenopodiaceæ.*

French, Ansérine Quinoa blanc.　*German*, Peruanischer Reis-Spinat.

Native of Peru.—Annual.—Stem 4 to 6 ft. high; leaves arrow-shaped, divided into three not very deep lobes, smooth, glaucous, mealy, and of thin texture; flowers small, greenish, in compact corymbs; seed round and flat, small, white, numbering about 500 to the gramme, and weighing about 700 grammes to the litre. Their germinating power lasts for four years. Culture.—The plant is grown in the same way as Orache. The seed is sown in April, where the plants are to stand. The young plants should be thinned out 8 inches apart every way, and plentifully watered in hot weather, which is the only attention they require. The seed ripens in August or September. Uses.—The leaves are eaten like Spinach. In Peru the seeds are used in soups, cakes, and also for making a kind of beer. Before they are used for any of these purposes, they should be subjected to a preliminary boiling, in order to remove the acrid principle which they contain, and which, if allowed to remain, would render the flavour very unpleasant.

WOODRUFF.

Asperula odorata, L. *Rubiaceæ.*

French, Aspérule odorante. *German*, Waldmeister. *Dutch*, Leive vrouve-bedstroo.

Native of Europe.—Perennial.—This plant is chiefly found in woods or shady places. Stems weak, prostrate, bearing whorls of oval-lanceolate leaves which are finely toothed on the margin, and very rough to the touch, as are also the stems; flowers small, pure white, with four divisions, and growing together in a spreading corymb; seed almost spherical, gray, and bristling with a large number of very small recurved points. The whole plant exhales a very agreeable perfume, especially when dried. The Woodruff is seldom cultivated except as an ornamental plant. It is perfectly hardy, and grows well either in a bed or as an edging, if planted in good moist soil in a half-shady position. In the north of Europe the leaves are sometimes used to flavour drinks.

Woodruff ($\frac{1}{10}$ natural size; detached flowers, natural size).

WORMWOOD.

Artemisia Absinthium, L. *Compositæ.*

French, Absinthe. *German*, Wermuth. *Flemish*, Alsem. *Danish*, Malurt.
Italian, Assenzio. *Spanish*, Ajenjo.

Native of Europe.—Perennial.—This plant is often grown in gardens on account of its medicinal properties. Stems 3 to 5 ft. high, rough, and branching; leaves numerous, small, very much divided, and of a grayish colour, especially underneath; flowers greenish, very insignificant, borne in clusters at the ends of the branches; seed gray, very small, numbering about 11,500 to the gramme, and weighing about 650 grammes to the litre. Its germinating power lasts for four years on an average. Culture.—Wormwood may be multiplied either from seed or from cuttings or divisions of the roots. If planted in a somewhat sheltered position, the plants will be less likely to suffer in very severe winters. They require no other care, and will continue productive for ten years or longer. Uses.—The leaves are sometimes used for flavouring, but the plant is chiefly employed in the manufacture of various kinds of liqueurs.

YAM (CHINESE).

Dioscorea Batatas, Dcne. *Dioscoreaceæ.*

French, Igname de la Chine. *German*, Chinesische Yam. *Spanish*, Name, Igname.

Native of China.—Perennial.—The Yam was introduced into France in 1848, through the agency of M. de Montigny, the French Consul at Shanghai. It is a perfectly hardy plant, with annual twining stems,

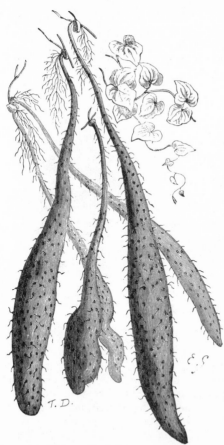

Chinese Yam (⅛ natural size).

which are smooth, of a green or violet colour, and grow from 6 to nearly 10 ft. long. Leaves opposite, heart-shaped, with a rather elongated point, of a dark-green colour, and exceedingly glossy or shining on the upper surface ; flowers diœcious, very small, white, growing in clusters from the axils of the leaves, and generally barren. Sometimes, instead of flowers, small tubers or bulblets are produced, from which the plants may be propagated. The stems trail along the ground, if they do not find some support on which they can climb. In climbing, they twine from right to left. From the neck of the root issue rhizomes of great length, which, as they descend into the ground, become swollen into somewhat of a club-shape. The flesh is slightly milky, and very floury when cooked. The rhizomes are furnished with numerous rootlets and almost imperceptible buds, from each of which a plant may be produced. They descend almost perpendicularly into the ground, attaining a length of from 2 to over 3 ft., their growth being most active in the latter end of autumn. Being perfectly hardy, they may be left in the ground during the winter, and will increase very much in size in the course of the second year, but their quality is not then so good as at the end of the first year.   The lifting of the rhizomes is a rather difficult and expensive operation, as they are rather brittle, and, in order to take them up whole, the ground must often be dug to the depth of a yard or more round each root.   This is probably the reason why the plant is so little cultivated in Europe, as otherwise it is very hardy and productive, and the rhizomes will compare favourably with Potatoes.   The flesh is white, light in texture, and very floury, is easily cooked, and has no disagreeably strong flavour.   Moreover, the rhizomes keep well and for a very long time.

CULTURE.—The Yam succeeds well in very good, moist, and sufficiently dug soil, and may be propagated by means of the axillary bulblets, or from rhizomes, either whole or cut into portions.   The method which generally produces the most certain and abundant results is to plant whole rhizomes, from 8 to 10 inches long and about as thick as one's finger.   It is advisable to furnish the plants with stakes or other supports to climb on, as the ground is then more easily hoed.   In very dry weather, watering is beneficial, as the Yam likes moisture and stops growing when it has not a sufficient supply of it. In November the time arrives for lifting the rhizomes, and if the soil is deep and rich enough, one may expect to meet with some which are thicker than the wrist towards the end and weigh over two pounds each.   Smaller ones also are usually found which are better for planting. Instead of planting them at once in the open ground, they may first be potted about the beginning of March, and planted out about the 15th of May.   The crop then comes in earlier, and is also heavier.

Many attempts have been made to raise a variety of Yam with shorter roots which would not penetrate so far into the ground.   These attempts cannot be said to have entirely failed; on the contrary, they have succeeded too well, as varieties have been raised with nearly round rhizomes, clustered around the neck of the plant, but of such feeble growth that the season's yield only represented three times the weight of the rhizomes which were planted.   A productive variety of Yam with short roots still remains to be discovered, and perhaps may be found amongst the numerous varieties lately imported from Japan, and which are now being experimented on in France.   The rhizomes are eaten like Potatoes, boiled, fried, and prepared in various ways.

A TABLE

Showing the Comparative Weight and Size of the Seeds of Kitchen-garden Plants, and also the Average and Extreme Periods of the Duration of their Germinating Power.

	Weight of a Litre * of Seeds.	Number of Seeds.	Duration of Germinating Power.	
			Average.	Extreme.
	Grammes.	In 1 gramme.*	Years.	Years.
Angelica	150	170	1 or 2	3
Anise	300	200	3	5
Artichoke	610	25	6	10*
Asparagus	800	50	5	8
		In 100 grammes.		
,, Bean	770	500 to 650	3	8
		In 1 gramme.		
Balm	550	2000	4	7
Basil	530	800	8	10*
,, Bush	500	900	8	10*
,, East Indian	580	1500	8	10*
		In 100 grammes.		
Beans	620 to 750	40 to 115	6	10*
,, Kidney	625 to 850	75 to 800	3	8
Beet, Leaf or Chard	250	60	6	10*
		In 1 gramme.		
Beet-root	250	50	6	10*
Borage	480	65	8	10*
Borecole	700	300	5	10
Burdock, Edible	630	80	5	6
Burnet, Salad. See Salad Burnet				
Broccoli	700	375	5	10
Cabbage	700	300	5	10
,, Chinese (Pak-choi) ...	700	300	5	7
,, ,, (Pe-tsai) ...	700	300	5	9
Caper	460	160	(?)	(?)
Capsicum	450	150	4	7
Caraway	420	350	3	4
Cardoon	630	·25	7	9
Carrot (with the spines) ...	240	700	4 or 5	10*

* The litre is nearly equal to 1¾ pint, imperial measure, and the gramme is equivalent to 15⅔ grains Troy. The asterisk in the last column denotes that the seeds had not all entirely lost their germinating power at the termination of the number of years indicated.

	Weight of a Litre of Seeds.	Number of Seeds.	Duration of Germinating Power.	
			Average.	Extreme.
	Grammes.	In 1 Gramme.	Years.	Years.
Carrot (without the spines) ...	360	950	4 or 5	10*
Caterpillars, Common (*Pods*)	200	3	6	10*
„ other varieties (*Pods*)	180	6	6	10*
Catmint	680	1200	5	6*
Cauliflower	700	375	5	10
Celery	480	2500	8	10*
Chervil	380	450	2 or 3	6
„ Sweet-scented	250	40	1	1
„ Turnip-rooted	540	450	1	1
Chickling-Vetch	750	4	5	(?)
Chicory	400	700	8	10*
		In 10 grammes.		
Chick-pea	780	30	3	8
		In 1 gramme.		
Cock's-comb Saintfoin (*Pods*)	110	9	5	7
Coriander	320	90	6	8
Corn-salad, Common	280	1000	5	10
„ Italian	280	1000	4	(?)
„ Large-seeded ...	240	600 to 700	5	10*
Cress, American	540	950	3	5
„ Common Garden ...	730	450	5	9
„ Meadow (or Cuckoo-flower)	580	1500	4	(?)
„ Parà	200	3400	5	7*
„ Water	580	4000	5	9*
Cucumber, Common	500	35	10	10*
„ Globe	500	100	6	(?)
„ Prickly-fruited Gherkin	550	130	6	7*
„ Snake	450	40	7 or 8	10*
Cumin	350	250	1	5
Dandelion	270	1200 to 1500	2	5
Dill	300	900	3	5
Egg-plant	500	250	6	10
Elecampane	440	530	5	6*
Endive	340	600	10	10*
Evening Primrose	375	600	3	5
Fennel, Common or Wild ...	450	310	4	7
„ (Finocchio)	300	200	4	5*
„ Sweet	235	125	4	7
Fennel-flower	550	220	3	(?)
Golden Thistle	125	200	3	7
Gombo or Okra	620	15 to 18	5	10*
Good King Henry	625	430	3	5
Gourds (vars. of *C. maxima*) ...	400	3	6	10*
„ („ *C. moschata*)	420	7	6	10*
„ („ *C. Pepo*) ...	425	6 to 8	6	10*
„ Bottle	360	8	6	10*
„ Custard Marrow ...	430	10	6	10*
„ Fancy	450	20	6	10*

	Weight of a Litre of Seeds.	Number of Seeds.	Duration of Germinating Power.	
			Average.	Extreme.
	Grammes.	In 1 gramme.	Years.	Years.
Gourds—Large Tours Pumpkin	250	3	4 or 5	9
Herb Patience	620	450	4	7
Hop	250	200	2	4
Horehound	680	1000	3	6
Hyssop	575	850	3	5
Ice-plant	760	5700	5	(?)
Jews' Mallow	660	450	5	10
Kohl-Rabi	700	300	5	10
Lavender	575	950	5	6
Leek	550	400	3	9
Lentils, Common, or Broad White	790	14	4	9
„ Small White	825	35	4	9
„ du Puy Green	850	40	4	9
Lettuce, Common	430	800	5	9
„ Perennial	260	800	3	5
Lovage	200	300	3	4
Maize, or Indian Corn	640	4 or 5	2	4
Malabar Nightshade	460	35	5	6
Mallow, Curled	530	300	5	8
Marigold, Pot	180	150	3	7
Marjoram, Sweet	550	4000	3	7
„ Winter	675	12,000	5	7
Meadow Cabbage	300	500	6	(?)
Melons	360	35	5	10*
„ Water	460	5 or 6	6	10*
Mugwort	600	8000	3	5
Mustard, Black or Brown ...	675	700	4	9
„ Chinese Cabbage-leaved	660	650	4	8
„ White, or Salad ...	750	200	4	10*
Nasturtium, Tall	340	7 or 8	5	5
„ Dwarf	600	15	5	8
Nightshade, Black	600	800	5	8
„ Malabar. See Malabar Nightshade				
Okra. See Gombo				
Onion	500	250	2	7
Orache	140	250	6	7
Parsnip	200	220	2	4
Parsley	500	350	3	9
Pea, Winged	800	15 to 18	5	10*
		In 10 grammes.		
Peas, Garden	700 to 800	20 to 55	3	8
„ Gray or Field	680 to 800	50 to 80	3	8
		In 1 gramme.		
Pea-nut	400	2 or 3	1	1
Plantain, Buck's-horn	740	4000	4	9
Purslane	610	2500	7	10
„ Winter	700	2200	5	7
Radish	700	120	5	10*

	Weight of a Litre of Seeds.	Number of Seeds.	Duration of Germinating Power.	
			Average.	Extreme.
	Grammes.	In 1 gramme.	Years.	Years.
Rampion	800	25,000	5	10*
Rhubarb	80 to 120	50	3	8
Rocket, Salad	750	550	4	9
„ Turkish	500	35 to 40	3	6
Rosemary	400	900	4	(?)
Rue	580	500	2	5
Sage, Common	550	250	3	7
„ Clary	650	200	3	(?)
Salad Burnet	280	150	3	9
„ Milk-vetch	210	6 or 7	3	8
Salsafy	230	100	2	8
Samphire	120	350	3	9
Savory, Summer	500	1500	3	7
„ Winter	430	2500	3	6
Scorzonera	260	90	2	7
„ French	220	1200	5	(?)
Scurvy-grass	600	1500 to 1800	4	7
Sea-kale	210	15 to 18	1	7
Skirret	400	600	10	10*
Snails (*Pods*)	150	4	5	9
Sorrel	650	1000	4	7
Soy Bean	725	7 or 8	2	6
Spinach, Prickly-seeded ...	375	90	5	7
„ Round-seeded	510	110	5	7
„ New Zealand	225	10 to 12	5	8
Strawberry	600	800 to 2500	3	6
„ Blite	800	5000	(?)	(?)
„ Tomato	650	1000	8	10*
Sweet Cicely	250	40	1	1
Tansy	300	7000	2	4
Tare, One-flowered	800	15 to 20	3	8*
Thyme	680	6000	3	7
Tomato	300	300 to 400	4	9
Turnip	670	450	5	10*
Unicorn-plant	290	20	1 or 2	(?)
Valerian, African	110	250	4	7
Wax Gourd	300	21	10	10*
Welsh Onion, Common	480	300	2 or 3	7
„ „ Early White ...	590	500	3	8
White Quinoa	700	500	4	5
Wormwood	650	11,500	4	6

INDEX.

Illustrations in Italics.